IFIP Advances in Information and Communication Technology 625

IFIP – The International Federation for Information Processing

IFIP was founded in 1960 under the auspices of UNESCO, following the first World Computer Congress held in Paris the previous year. A federation for societies working in information processing, IFIP's aim is two-fold: to support information processing in the countries of its members and to encourage technology transfer to developing nations. As its mission statement clearly states:

IFIP is the global non-profit federation of societies of ICT professionals that aims at achieving a worldwide professional and socially responsible development and application of information and communication technologies.

IFIP is a non-profit-making organization, run almost solely by 2500 volunteers. It operates through a number of technical committees and working groups, which organize events and publications. IFIP's events range from large international open conferences to working conferences and local seminars.

The flagship event is the IFIP World Computer Congress, at which both invited and contributed papers are presented. Contributed papers are rigorously refereed and the rejection rate is high.

As with the Congress, participation in the open conferences is open to all and papers may be invited or submitted. Again, submitted papers are stringently refereed.

The working conferences are structured differently. They are usually run by a working group and attendance is generally smaller and occasionally by invitation only. Their purpose is to create an atmosphere conducive to innovation and development. Refereeing is also rigorous and papers are subjected to extensive group discussion.

Publications arising from IFIP events vary. The papers presented at the IFIP World Computer Congress and at open conferences are published as conference proceedings, while the results of the working conferences are often published as collections of selected and edited papers.

IFIP distinguishes three types of institutional membership: Country Representative Members, Members at Large, and Associate Members. The type of organization that can apply for membership is a wide variety and includes national or international societies of individual computer scientists/ICT professionals, associations or federations of such societies, government institutions/government related organizations, national or international research institutes or consortia, universities, academies of sciences, companies, national or international associations or federations of companies.

More information about this series at http://www.springer.com/series/6102

Audun Jøsang · Lynn Futcher ·
Janne Hagen (Eds.)

ICT Systems Security and Privacy Protection

36th IFIP TC 11 International Conference, SEC 2021
Oslo, Norway, June 22–24, 2021
Proceedings

 Springer

Editors
Audun Jøsang (iD)
University of Oslo
Oslo, Norway

Lynn Futcher (iD)
Nelson Mandela University
Gqeberha, South Africa

Janne Hagen (iD)
University of Oslo
Oslo, Norway

ISSN 1868-4238   ISSN 1868-422X   (electronic)
IFIP Advances in Information and Communication Technology
ISBN 978-3-030-78122-4   ISBN 978-3-030-78120-0   (eBook)
https://doi.org/10.1007/978-3-030-78120-0

This Springer imprint is published by the registered company Springer Nature Switzerland AG
The registered company address is: Gewerbestrasse 11, 6330 Cham, Switzerland

Preface

We are proud to bring you this collection of papers selected for presentation at the 36th IFIP International Conference on ICT Systems Security and Privacy Protection, which was organised online from the University of Oslo during 22–24 June, 2021. The IFIP SEC conferences are the flagship events of the International Federation for Information Processing (IFIP) Technical Committee 11 on Information Security and Privacy Protection in Information Processing Systems. The proceedings of IFIP SEC 2021 contains 28 high-quality papers covering a wide range of research areas in the field of information security.

The papers submitted for review had author names, and hence were not anonymous for the reviewers. All reviewers had to indicate any conflict of interest with any particular paper, which then removed them from being eligible to review. The selection of papers was a highly challenging task: 112 received submissions were evaluated based on their significance, novelty, and technical quality. Each paper received at least three reviews, but most of them including all the accepted papers received four or more reviews by members of the Program Committee (PC). The PC members engaged in discussions over a three-week period, and the PC chairs held meetings electronically, to select the best papers. With 28 selected out of 112 submitted papers, the acceptance rate was 25%. The papers were authored by researchers from 16 different countries covering 4 continents.

We want to express our gratitude to all the contributors who helped to make IFIP SEC 2021 a success. There is a long list of people who volunteered their time and energy to put together the conference and who deserve acknowledgment. First of all, we want to thank all the authors of both the accepted and the rejected papers for trusting us by contributing their excellent work. We want to thank the members of the Program Committee and the sub-reviewers, who devoted significant hours of their time to evaluate all the submissions. We want to thank the Organizing Chair, Nils Gruschka, for the excellent job in setting up and running the technical platforms in order for the online conference to run smoothly. We also thank Steve Furnell, the Chair of IFIP TC 11, for assistance in planning the conference. Special thanks go to the keynote speaker, Ross Anderson from the University of Cambridge, UK, the recipient of the 2021 Kristian Beckman Award.

2021 marks the 60th anniversary of IFIP which was celebrated with a special panel of venerable IFIP representatives who have played important roles to ensure the continuing vitality of IFIP over the years. We would like to thank Louise Yngström, Bill Caelli, Yuko Murayama, Basie von Solms, and Leon Strous for their commitment to IFIP, and for taking part in the panel to share their memories from the past and to give us advice for the future of IFIP.

May 2021

Audun Jøsang
Lynn Futcher
Janne Hagen

About IFIP Technical Committee 11

IFIP TC 11 was originally established in 1983 and is formally titled *Security and Privacy Protection in Information Processing Systems*. TC 11 aims to increase the trustworthiness and general confidence in information processing and to act as a forum for security and privacy protection experts and others professionally active in the field. The organisation of the IFIP SEC conference represents a key element in supporting this, and is the flagship event within the annual calendar.

Alongside the SEC events, TC 11 has a wider breadth of activities and includes 14 Working Groups, covering a broad range of cybersecurity-oriented topic areas (and in some cases run jointly with other relevant Technical Committees). The current list is as follows:

- WG 11.1: Information Security Management
- WG 11.2: Pervasive Systems Security
- WG 11.3: Data and Application Security and Privacy
- WG 11.4: Network & Distributed Systems Security
- WG 11.5: IT Assurance and Audit
- WG 11.6: Identity Management
- WG 9.6/11.7: Information Technology Mis-Use and the Law
- WG 11.8: Information Security Education
- WG 11.9: Digital Forensics
- WG 11.10: Critical Infrastructure Protection
- WG 11.11: Trust Management
- WG 11.12: Human Aspects of Information Security and Assurance
- WG 8.11/11.13: Information Systems Security Research
- WG 11.14: Secure Engineering

All of the Working Groups are volunteer-based, and aim to advance the knowledge and practice within their respective topic areas. All have international memberships, typically spanning academic researchers, industry practitioners, and other relevant professionals. Many of the Working Groups also have their own individual conference and workshop events, offering further opportunities for sharing and promoting work in addition to the SEC conference.

For further details of these activities, and how to participate in the Working Groups, please see www.ifiptc11.org.

Organization

General Chairs and Program Committee Chairs

Audun Jøsang	University of Oslo, Norway
Lynn Futcher	Nelson Mandela University, South Africa
Janne Hagen	The Norwegian Water Resources and Energy Directorate, Norway

Organizing Chair

Nils Gruschka	University of Oslo, Norway

Program Committee

Rose-Mharie Åhlfeldt	University of Skövde, Sweden
Raja Naeem Akram	University of Aberdeen, UK
Magnus Almgren	Chalmers University of Technology, Sweden
Claudio Ardagna	Università degli Studi di Milano, Italy
Vijay Atluri	Rutgers University, USA
Man Ho Au	University of Hong Kong, China
Gergei Bana	Inria, France
Joao Paulo Barraca	Universidade de Aveiro, Portugal
Marcus Belder	DSTG, Australia
Karin Bernsmed	SINTEF, Norway
Tamás Bisztray	University of Oslo, Norway
Ravishankar Borgaonkar	SINTEF, Norway
Dagmar Brechlerova	EuroMISE Center, Czech Republic
Siri Bromander	mnemonic, Norway
Barbara Carminati	University of Insubria, Italy
Ricardo Chaves	IST/INESC-ID, Portugal
Robert Chetwyn	University of Oslo, Norway
Michal Choras	ITTI Ltd., India
K. P. Chow	University of Hong Kong, China
Nathan Clarke	University of Plymouth, UK
Miguel Correia	Universidade de Lisboa, Portugal
Jorge Cuellar	University of Passau, Germany
Nora Cuppens-Boulahia	Polytechnique Montréal, Canada
Paolo D'Arco	Università di Salerno, Italy
Ed Dawson	QUT, Australia
Sabrina De Capitani di Vimercati	Università degli Studi di Milano, Italy
Bart De Decker	Katholieke Universiteit Leuven, Belgium

Joeri de Ruiter	SIDN, Netherlands
Yvo Desmedt	University of Texas at Dallas, USA
Nicolás Emilio Díaz Ferreyra	University of Duisburg-Essen, Germany
Nicola Dragoni	DTU, Denmark
Isao Echizen	National Institute of Informatics, Japan
László Erdődi	University of Oslo, Norway
Olivier Festor	Inria, France
Simone Fischer-Hübner	Karlstad University, Sweden
Sara Foresti	Università degli Studi di Milano, Italy
Katrin Franke	NTNU, Norway
Steven Furnell	University of Nottingham, UK
Hélder Gomes	Universidade de Aveiro, Portugal
Rene Rydhof Hansen	Aalborg University, Denmark
Paul Haskell-Dowland	Edith Cowan University, Australia
Dominik Herrmann	University of Bamberg, Germany
Marko Hölbl	University of Maribor, Slovenia
Xinyi Huang Fujian	Normal University, China
Dieter Hutter	DFKI GmbH, Germany
Antonio Ken Iannillo	University of Luxembourg, Luxembourg
Pedro Inácio	Universidade da Beira Interior, Portugal
Martin Gilje Jaatun	SINTEF, Norway
Lech Janczewski	University of Auckland, New Zealand
Christian Damsgaard Jensen	DTU, Denmark
Jan Jürjens	Fraunhofer Institute, Germany
Georgios Kambourakis	University of the Aegean, Greece
Fredrik Karlsson	Örebro University, Sweden
Stefan Katzenbeisser	University of Passau, Germany
Dogan Kesdogan	Universität Regensburg, Germany
Dongseong Kim	University of Queensland, Australia
Kamil Kluczniak	Stanford University, USA
Andrea Kolberger	Anton Bruckner Private University, Austria
Zbigniew Kotulski	Warsaw University of Technology, Poland
Stephan Krenn	Austrian Institute of Technology, Austria
Lukasz Krzywiecki	Wroclaw University of Science and Technology, Poland
Tage Kulø	Norwegian Police ICT Services, Norway
Miroslaw Kutylowski	Wroclaw University of Science and Technology, Poland
Peeter Laud	Cybernetica, Estonia
Heejo Lee	Korea University, South Korea
Yingjiu Li	University of Oregon, USA
Maciej Liskiewicz	Universität zu Lübeck, Germany
Luigi Logrippo	Université du Québec, Canada
Javier Lopez	University of Malaga, Spain
Ijlal Loutfi	NTNU, Norway

Neeraj Suri   Lancaster University, UK
Kerry-Lynn Thomson   Nelson Mandela University, South Africa
Ding Wang   Peking University, China
Lingyu Wang   Concordia University, Canada
Morten Weea   University of Oslo, Norway
Edgar Weippl   University of Vienna, Austria
Tatjana Welzer   University of Maribor, Slovenia
Martin Wimmer   Siemens AG, Germany
Svetlana Yanushkevich   University of Calgary, Canada
Øyvind Ytrehus   University of Bergen, Norway
Vladimir Zadorozhny   University of Pittsburgh, USA
Filip Zagorski   Wroclaw University of Science and Technology,
                             Poland
Yuexin Zhang   Swinburne University of Technology, Australia
André Zúquete   Universidade de Aveiro, Portugal

Additional Reviewers

Marios Anagnostopoulos   Vasileios Kouliaridis
Filipe Apolinário   Chao Lin
Erjin Bao   Chang Liu
Nicola Bena   Louis Moreau
Filippo Berto   Wojciech Niewolski
Srini Bhagavan   Marcus Nohlberg
Niklas Bruns   Tomasz Nowak
Rohit Chadha   Ali Padyab
Anton Christensen   Sebastian Ramacher
Aveek Kumar Das   Musa Samaila
Edlira Dushku   Leonard Schild
Alberto Giaretta   Mariusz Sepczuk
Benoit Gonzalvo   Bernardo Sequeiros
Sandeep Gupta   Tiago Simões
Lejla Islami   Ricarda Weber
Prabhakaran Kasinathan   Colin Xiang
Yusuke Kawamoto

Contents

Application and System Security

Privacy

Network Security

Machine Learning for Security

Security Management

Digital Signatures

XML Signature Wrapping Still Considered Harmful: A Case Study on the Personal Health Record in Germany

Paul Höller[1]([✉]) [iD], Alexander Krumeich[1] [iD], and Luigi Lo Iacono[2] [iD]

[1] n-design GmbH Cologne, Cologne, Germany
{paul.hoeller,alexander.krumeich}@n-design.de
[2] H-BRS University of Applied Sciences, Sankt Augustin, Germany
luigi.lo_iacono@h-brs.de

Abstract. XML Signature Wrapping (XSW) has been a relevant threat to web services for 15 years until today. Using the Personal Health Record (PHR), which is currently under development in Germany, we investigate a current SOAP-based web services system as a case study. In doing so, we highlight several deficiencies in defending against XSW. Using this real-world contemporary example as motivation, we introduce a guideline for more secure XML signature processing that provides practitioners with easier access to the effective countermeasures identified in the current state of research.

Keywords: XML Signature · XML Signature Wrapping · SOAP · SAML · E-Health · Personal Health Record · PHR

1 Introduction

The eXtensible Markup Language (XML) [1] is a free open standard that defines a set of rules for specifying structured and portable document formats. Although being often criticized for its complexity [14], XML is used for hundreds of document formats including office-productivity tools, communication protocols, and industry data standards. The widespread use of XML is due in part to its versatility and rich set of tools and accompanying standards. With XML Security, e.g. it benefits from a powerful standard for the fine-grained protection of documents. However, since complexity and versatility are the natural enemies of security, it soon became clear that XML Encryption [2] and XML Signature [3] pose unique challenges when implementing security solutions.

XML Signature Wrapping (XSW) [22] is an example of vulnerabilities due to the complexity of generating and verifying digital signatures of XML documents. XSW allows an attacker to modify signed XML documents while maintaining a valid signature. XSW was the subject of intense research more than 15 years ago when it was first discovered [22]. At that time, many vulnerabilities and practical

© IFIP International Federation for Information Processing 2021
Published by Springer Nature Switzerland AG 2021
A. Jøsang et al. (Eds.): SEC 2021, IFIP AICT 625, pp. 3–18, 2021.
https://doi.org/10.1007/978-3-030-78120-0_1

attacks were found in real-world systems such as management and authentication interfaces of cloud services [11,20,28,29]. Since then, XSW-based vulnerabilities have been repeatedly reported in the wild to date, despite the scientific literature suggesting effective countermeasures [19,21]. One reason for this may be the many countermeasures proposed and discussed in the literature, only a few of which ultimately proved to be actually effective (see Sect. 2). Practitioners may be overwhelmed with having to read and understand the entire body of knowledge to develop robust XML signature creation and verification. To answer the question of whether XSW is still a prevalent vulnerability in practice, we studied a high-security system currently being implemented that uses XML and XML Security: the statutory Personal Health Record (PHR) [9, German only] in Germany. This PHR uses XML and XML security to manage medical data. Besides its high security demands, we chose this case study because the specifications are currently being implemented and the first PHR products are expected to enter the German market in mid-2021. Therefore, potentially discovered flaws and vulnerabilities may impact PHR implementations prior to release.

Contributions. We (a) give an overview on XSW attacks and countermeasures and extract the most effective ones. To study the applicability of these safeguards in practice, we (b) analyze the system specification of the PHR in Germany and (c) report XSW vulnerabilities that specification-compliant PHR implementations may contain. One vulnerability is a newly discovered XSW variant that has not previously been described in the literature. Based on the results, we (d) provide guidance to generate and verify signed XML documents, and (e) evaluate the guideline by adopting it back to the XSW-vulnerable PHR in Germany.

Our results show that XSW attacks are still very relevant in practical instances. Attackers might be able to bypass patient authentication in upcoming implementations of the PHR in Germany. Thus, they are able to obtain and manipulate health records of statutory health insurants in Germany. To prevent XSW attacks, we provide guidance for practitioners as coherent and actionable instructions.

2   Background: XML Signature Wrapping (XSW)

Although XML Signature is built on cryptographically secure signature schemes, it has significant shortcomings regarding its referencing mechanism. It enables the injection of malicious content at the very position where the recipient expects the true payload. The signature nevertheless remains valid for the originally signed element, which is moved to a different position within the same document (the actual *wrapping*) and thus remains accessible for the signature validation process via its reference. This was discovered by McIntosh and Austel, who introduced three attack variants [22].

Attack Variations. The three variants can be differentiated based on the contextual property of the signed element getting wrapped and violated. The *context* characterizes the position of an element regarding its sibling and parent elements. These context properties are not protected by the signature, which means that it cannot be verified, whether a signed element is placed at the originally intended position. This provides a target for manipulation. The *Simple Ancestry Context* describes the chain of ancestors of an element. When a signed element is moved away from its direct ancestor, e.g. while performing XSW, this context changes. The *Optional Element Context* represents that an element may not be required at a certain position. Therefore its absence cannot be recognized. Attacking such an element by wrapping it, aims at erasing it from the message instead of replacing it. The *Sibling Value Context* is not defined by the ancestor, but by the siblings of an element. So even if there was a way to protect the Simple Ancestry Context, a wrapping attack manipulating the sibling relationship can be performed. This context covers not only the direct siblings of the wrapped element itself, but also the siblings of ancestors. An example is shown in Fig. 1. Here, the signed element is `my:Data`, referenced by the signature. By introducing a second `soap:Body` subtree, the Simple Ancestry Context, described as `/soap:Envelope/soap:Body/my:Data`, is retained, but becomes ambiguous. An application will most likely process the unsigned message while the validity of the whole document is confirmed, due to the still-present signed element.

Countermeasures. Gajek et al. [5] identified the core problem that leads to XSW vulnerabilities. There is a semantic gap between business logic and signature verification components. As long as it is possible that different data is processed in these two steps, attacks on XML Signatures remain possible. As a fundamental mitigation, the authors suggest a different behavior for signature verification algorithms. Such a process should no longer return only a boolean value, representing the result of the validation. In addition (or instead), an *XPath* expression [26] specifying the precise location of the processed element should be returned. By using this reference in the follow-up it can be assured that the application operates on verified data.

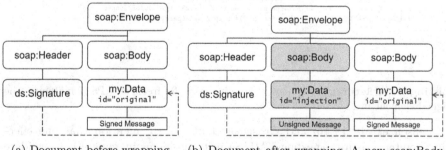

(a) Document before wrapping   (b) Document after wrapping. A new soap:Body is introduced, containing unsigned Data.

Fig. 1. XSW attacking the Sibling Value Context

In another publication, Gajek et al. propose the usage of *XPath* for an alternative signature referencing technique [4]. Usually, the `ds:Signature` element contains a URI, pointing to a special ID attribute of the signed element. Because this mechanism does not take into account the different element contexts presented earlier, it enables XSW. When using XPath instead, these contexts are encoded in the reference and therefore cannot be violated by a wrapping attempt. However, the ambiguity of the Sibling Value Context remains. Thus, the authors recommend the utilization of a *Predicate*, an additional XPath parameter, to specify exactly one of several homonymous siblings. For the example in Fig. 1 this would be `/soap:Envelope/soap:Body/my:Data[@id="original"]`, making only one single result possible (the ID has to be unique by the XML standard [25]). This style of an *absolute* XPath with predicates is defined as the FastXPath[1] subset by the authors.

However, using FastXPath makes new attacks possible. Jensen et al. [17] show that namespace prefix definitions can be excluded in a signature and thus be exploited by an attacker. This is the case when the FastXPath reference uses a namespace prefix, which is defined outside the signature element, so it will not be signed. In this situation, an attacker is able to redefine this prefix to an arbitrary namespace. This way, the result of the FastXPath can be altered. To completely rule out this possibility, it is suggested to make the FastXPath expression prefix-free. This is achieved by making use of an alternative XPath syntax, which allows stating `local-name()` and `namespace-uri()`. Applied to the example in Fig. 1 and inserted into a signature's reference element, this corresponds to the emphasized lines in Listing 1. A disadvantage of this method is the length and complexity of the resulting expression. It is very important to avoid even minor syntactical errors, which would lead to a wrong result and therefore a flawed signature.

```
1    <Reference URI="">
2      <DigestMethod Algorithm="http://www.w3.org/2001/04/xmlenc#sha256"/>
3      <DigestValue>avsLKDSsLWx+svKksvKSVD48lsv9vsd</DigestValue>
4      <Transforms>
5        <Transform Algorithm="http://www.w3.org/2002/06/xmldsig-filter2">
6          <XPath Filter="intersect">
7          /*[local-name()="Envelope" and namespace-uri()=http://www.w3.org/2003/05/soap-envelope]
8          /*[local-name()="Body" and namespace-uri()=http://www.w3.org/2003/05/soap-envelope]
9          /*[local-name()="Data" and namespace-uri()="http://namespace.org/2021/my"]
10         </XPath>
11        <Transform>
12      </Transforms>
13    </Reference>
```

Listing 1. A `Reference` element containing a prefix-free FastXPath matching the signed element in Fig. 1

Jensen et al. [15,16] and Gruschka et al. [12,13] mention that one effective countermeasure regarding XML Security problems in general is to validate XML schema definitions properly. A practical attack presented by Gruschka and Lo Iacono could have been defeated just by standardized schema validation [11].

---

[1] Because of the reduced functionality, *FastXPath* is also more performant.

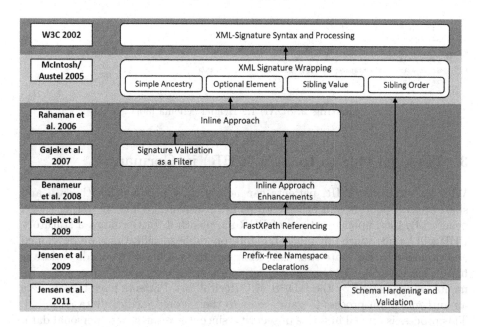

Fig. 2. Systematization of the body of knowledge on XSW attacks and countermeasures

Schema validation assures that an XML document complies to a well-defined structure and allowed contents. E.g. the *SOAP 1.2* schema, which comes with the official W3C standard, defines the `soap:Envelope` as an element containing zero to one `soap:Header` and exactly one `soap:Body`. Thus, a validation against this schema definition would also make the wrapping shown in Fig. 1 impossible. Nevertheless, Jensen et al. show that schema validation is not sufficient as a single countermeasure and can be heavily flawed due to the intended flexibility of XML documents [18]. The SOAP 1.2 definition of the `soap:Header` can serve as an example. As can be seen in Listing 2, it is defined by only one statement: `xs:any`. In combination with `namespace="##any"` and `minOccurs="0"` `maxOccurs="unbounded"`, this means, the SOAP Header can hold any element of unlimited amount from any namespace. The attribute `processContents="lax"` states that on the inserted elements themselves schema validation is only required if matching schema definitions are obtainable. Such an openness is necessary for a multi-purpose protocol like SOAP, but is not useful for security intentions. Because of this, Jensen et al. strongly recommend to harden the schema specifically for the application before relying on it for security improvements.

Summary. Figure 2 presents the body of knowledge presented in this section. It contains the most important publications and how they relate to each other. An arrow symbolizes an improvement over the preceding state of the art.

```
1    <xs:complexType name="Header">
2     <xs:sequence>
3      <xs:any namespace="##any" processContents="lax" minOccurs="0" maxOccurs="unbounded"/>
4     </xs:sequence>
5     <xs:anyAttribute namespace="##other" processContents="lax"/>
6    </xs:complexType>
```

Listing 2. SOAP 1.2 Header schema [30]

3   Personal Health Record (PHR) in Germany

With an electronic PHR, patients can access their personal health data and share it with doctors and other entities in healthcare. While the term is used generically, the implementations of PHR are plentiful. In Germany, a statutory PHR will be introduced by mid-2021. Interoperable specifications are developed and provided by the state-run institution gematik GmbH. Since medical data is highly sensitive, this system must meet very strict security and privacy requirements, as mandated by the GDPR (§9, Recital 35). Patients have to complete an authentication process to gain access to their stored medical data [7, p. 33]. This process is crucial in terms of security, since it gives access to personal data. Therefore, we analyzed this component in particular.

The PHR in Germany stores patients' health data in a central location. A multi-step login procedure must be passed before the PHR system grants access (see Fig. 3).

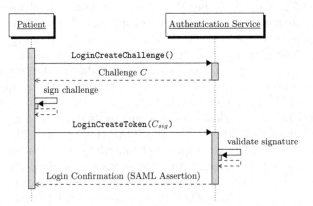

Fig. 3. Authentication protocol specified in the PHR in Germany for authenticating patients when accessing their medical records [6, p. 43]

The patient first asks the authentication service to create a login challenge. In response, the patient receives a nonce, which serves as a challenge. To prove their identity, the client signs this challenge. Since all protocol messages are SOAP messages, XML Signature and WS-Security are used for signing. The signed nonce is then transferred back with the patient's X.509 certificate to the authentication service (see Listing 3).

```
1   <soap:Envelope>
2    <soap:Header>
3     <wsse:Security>
4      <wsse:BinarySecurityToken wsu:Id="X509-7bd04a6a-...699f">
5       ...
6      </wsse:BinarySecurityToken>
7      <ds:Signature>
8       <ds:SignedInfo>
9        <ds:CanonicalizationMethod Algorithm=".../xml-exc-c14n#"/>
10       <ds:SignatureMethod Algorithm="...#sha256-rsa-MGF1"/>
11       <ds:Reference URI="#id-6c68f4bd-...4771">
12        <ds:Transforms>
13         <ds:Transform Algorithm=".../xml-exc-c14n#"/>
14        </ds:Transforms>
15        <ds:DigestMethod Algorithm=".../xmlenc#sha256"/>
16        <ds:DigestValue>/WjxNjONTXGfG...dI70=</ds:DigestValue>
17       </ds:Reference>
18      </ds:SignedInfo>
19      <ds:SignatureValue>...</ds:SignatureValue>
20      <ds:KeyInfo>
21       <wsse:SecurityTokenReference wsu:Id="STR-31aa259c-...7e1d">
22        <wsse:Reference URI="#X509-7bd04a6a-...699f"/>
23       </wsse:SecurityTokenReference>
24      </ds:KeyInfo>
25     </ds:Signature>
26    </wsse:Security>
27   </soap:Header>
28   <soap:Body wsu:Id="id-6c68f4bd-...4771">
29    <wst:Challenge>5vDFzMbgGgM7Os1hLOZwHebchHFMudpr</wst:Challenge>
30   </soap:Body>
31  </soap:Envelope>
```

Listing 3. Example `LoginCreateToken` request containing the challenge in the signed message `Body` [7]

To verify the signed challenge, the XML Signature (lines 7–25) of the `Body` (lines 28–30) must be checked using the `BinarySecurityToken` (lines 4–6) that includes the patient's X.509 certificate [7, p. 22]. The authentication service uses this certificate to generate the confirmation that the patient has authenticated successfully. A SAML assertion is issued in response. The signature generation and verification steps are the points where an XSW vulnerability may occur with severe consequences, in case attackers are able to gain access to patient records by spoofing the authentication with a successful XSW attack.

4 XSW Vulnerable PHR in Germany

The following analysis of the PHR's authentication component strictly complies with its specification [7]. Every product vendor must implement the software according to this specification. Thus, it has significant influence on the resulting systems. Especially in the field of XML Security any ambiguity in the service specification can create potential vulnerabilities (see Sect. 2). Below, we outline the shortcomings in the PHR specification that enable attack vectors.

4.1   Specification Weaknesses

The specification of the authentication component does not explicitly call for insecure technologies. It rather lacks concrete requirements that make an XSW attack less likely.

The specification requires to implement the SOAP extension Web Services Security (WS-Security) in the authentication component [7, p. 10]. This requires the use of XML Signature. This standard allows various implementations. While it is possible to apply the recommended *XPath referencing* [4], vendors more likely use the less secure, but more common *ID-based referencing*. That this is a de-facto industry standard can be assumed, because past work almost exclusively shows practical attacks regarding this mechanism. Since the specification does not specify the method to be used, we assume that the more insecure variant is used.

In fact, the specification states that *"all components verifying XML Signatures must at least apply FastXPath evaluation by Gajek et al. [4]"* [8, p. 23]. However, there seems to be a misunderstanding, as this FastXPath evaluation is not applicable to signature *verification*. The evaluation must rather be applied to the whole communication, which should have been specified at least for the requesting client. Thus, the referencing mechanism of the transmitted message remains unclear, rendering the intended *"FastXPath evaluation"* impossible. Beyond that, the specification does not advise to take care of the namespace prefix definitions, which can pose a threat to the FastXPath approach [17]. Although the specification defines prefixes in a binding way, a violation of this rule might occur and would be mitigated by Jensen et al.'s [17] prefix-free FastXPath variant.

Another XSW countermeasure, which proved effective, is schema validation (see Sect. 2). The specification requires this validation for the authentication service [7, p. 9]. But again, this requirement is very broad. It demands validation *"against the related schema files"* [7, p. 32]. However, it does not define which files are *"related"* to this operation. For example, in a general collection of important schema files issued by gematik [10], the SOAP 1.2 schema is not included. Ignoring this schema will lead to less secure implementations.

4.2   Attack Goals

In the protocol shown in Fig. 3 the request LoginCreateToken is the security-related step. In this message two elements can be attacked with XSW. One is the signed challenge, which serves as a server-sided timestamp. The authentication service only accepts messages containing a challenge previously generated by itself in response to the first request LoginCreateChallenge. This challenge element must be signed by the client. This serves as protection against replay attacks. However, attackers can circumvent this measure. They can come into possession of an old LoginCreateToken message, because one in an invalid state does not have to be kept secret. But by performing XSW on such a message, they can replace the expired challenge with a new one (the first communication step is not protected further) while keeping the signature intact.

The other object that can be manipulated is the patient's certificate, which is contained in every `LoginCreateToken` request. Because it is not signed, calling this attack *signature wrapping* is probably far-fetched. However, the foundational mechanics of the attack are the same as for the challenge, because the ID-based referencing is exploited.

The certificate plays two important roles in the communication. First, it contains the public key to perform the cryptographic signature validation. The certificate must be trusted in order for the validation to succeed. Second, the stored certificate owner information is used to assert the authentication, which is the goal of the whole login operation.

Now, when attackers can replace the message's certificate without invalidating the signature of the challenge, they can heavily influence the result. If they possess a certificate (not its private key) accepted by the service (regarding its root CA), they will receive an assertion issued for this certificate's owner. They can even place an arbitrary additional certificate in a way that the service still checks the validity of the original one but takes the information from the inserted one. The decisive factor is that the service might handle two separate certificates: One to validate the signature and one to extract an identity. Below, we provide a proof of concept based on the first case.

Explicitly attacking an embedded certificate has not been described by related work. This poses a novel threat for XML-based authentication systems.

4.3 Proof of Concept

To attack the authentication system, some preconditions have to be met. SOAP messages are usually transmitted via HTTPS. This is also the case in the gematik PHR [7, p. 9]. XSW is very unlikely to happen over a secured channel. At least a man-in-the-middle scenario can be excluded, because attackers must be able to read the messages in order to manipulate them. However, in large distributed systems there may still be intermediate systems like caches, load balancers, and firewalls that terminate a TLS connection. A compromise of such a component can be mitigated by message layer security. Attackers might also be able to get hold of a message in a different way, e.g. because it is stored somewhere unsafe. Additionally, the PHR services should follow a *defense in depth* approach. Thus, message security must be assured, even when TLS encryption is broken. In the following, we assume that an attacker possesses an unencrypted message of a user. Here, this would be the request `LoginCreateToken`.

We presented the Simple Ancestry and the Sibling Value contexts (see Sect. 2) and identified two attackable elements (see Sect. 4.2). When applying these two attack vectors on the critical message parts, four attacks are possible.

The **Simple Ancestry Attack** can be performed on the challenge (see Listing 4), and the certificate encoded in `BinarySecurityToken` (see Listing 5). This attack is feasible, since the signature will determine the signed body by its ID. We chose the element `Wrapper` in the example listing. This could be any suitable element type. The **Sibling Value Attack** is also feasible on challenge and certificate. For the challenge, a second body element needs to be introduced (see Listing 6). To attack the certificate, the containing element `Security` has to be doubled (see Listing 7). As an alternative, a second header element, which contains a second security element, can be introduced. A third variation would be having a second `BinarySecurityToken` in the same security element.

```
1   <Envelope>
2    <Header>
3     <Security>
4      <BinarySecurityToken>
5       ...
6      </BinarySecurityToken>
7       <Signature>...</Signature>
8     </Security>
9     <Wrapper>
10     <Body ID="signed-element-id">
11      <Challenge>
12       expired-signed
13      </Challenge>
14     </Body>
15    </Wrapper>
16    </Header>
17    <Body>
18     <Challenge>
19      fresh-unsigned
20     </Challenge>
21    </Body>
22   </Envelope>
```

Listing 4. Simple Ancestry Attack on challenge

```
1   <Envelope>
2    <Header>
3     <Security>
4      <BinarySecurityToken>
5       ...
6      </BinarySecurityToken>
7       <Signature>...</Signature>
8     </Security>
9    </Header>
10   <Body ID="signed-element-id">
11    <Challenge>
12     expired-signed
13    </Challenge>
14   </Body>
15   <Body>
16    <Challenge>
17     fresh-unsigned
18    </Challenge>
19   </Body>
20   </Envelope>
```

Listing 6. Sibling Value Attack on challenge

```
1   <Envelope>
2    <Header>
3     <Security>
4      <BinarySecurityToken>
5       _injected-cert-base64
6      </BinarySecurityToken>
7       <Signature>...</Signature>
8     </Security>
9     <Wrapper>
10     <BinarySecurityToken ID="cert-id">
11      _sign-certificate-base64
12     </BinarySecurityToken>
13    </Wrapper>
14    </Header>
15    <Body>
16     <Challenge>...</Challenge>
17    </Body>
18   </Envelope>
```

Listing 5. Simple Ancestry Attack on certificate

```
1   <Envelope>
2    <Header>
3     <Security>
4      <BinarySecurityToken ID="cert-id">
5       _sign-certificate-base64
6      </BinarySecurityToken>
7       <Signature>...</Signature>
8     </Security>
9     <Security>
10     <BinarySecurityToken>
11      _injected-cert-base64
12     </BinarySecurityToken>
13    </Security>
14    </Header>
15    <Body>
16     <Challenge>...</Challenge>
17    </Body>
18   </Envelope>
```

Listing 7. Sibling Value Attack on certificate

Viability and Potential Impact. It must be noted that these findings are purely theoretical at this stage. There are still some requirements to be met before this state of the specification manifests itself as a productive system. Among other things, the identified XSW flaws would have to actually be implemented and the code would have to withstand in-depth security audits. In addition, there are other security measures in the PHR architecture that could make successful XSW attacks difficult in practice. However, should the discovered XSW vulnerabilities be found in productive PHR systems in the future, as described, patient login would be de-facto insecure. An attacker would only need a patient's public-key certificate to gain unauthorized access to that same patient's health record.

Disclosure. We reported our discovered XSW flaws to the specification body of the PHR (gematik GmbH), the Federal Office for Information Security (BSI) and the Federal Ministry of Health. We also recommended changes to the signature generation and verification specifications as a mitigation that we derived from adopting our XML Signature guidelines.

5 Robust XML Signature Guidelines

Our observations show that industry and standardization still not consistently use the available research on XSW, its attack variants, and the proposed countermeasures. This is critical, since these have been known for more than fifteen years. This lack of knowledge transfer still has serious consequences, as can be seen by various CVEs[2] and as we have shown with the vulnerabilities we presented in the PHR in Germany. One reason for this could lie in the fact that the established scientific knowledge is not available as comprehensible and actionable instructions for developers explaining how to approach and implement signature creation and verification of XML documents. In fact, common sources for such material, such as OWASP, W3C, OASIS, and NIST, do not offer XSW guidance to date. To address this gap, we propose guidelines for XML Signature creation and verification, which avoid common errors leading to XSW vulnerabilities.

First of all, it is important to note that XSW vulnerabilities are not only caused by insufficient verification of the signed document, as many CVEs suggest by pointing to CWE-345 [23] or CWE-347 [24] as the root cause for the vulnerability. To mitigate the risks posed by XSW, both signature creation and signature verification must be considered. Therefore, we developed two guidelines that focus on both parts. These aim to provide standardization bodies, developers and auditors with straightforward access to the essential countermeasures.

---

[2] CVE-2020-5407, CVE-2020-5390, CVE-2020-13415, CVE-2018-18689, CVE-2017-10669, CVE-2017-1000452, CVE-2016-5697, CVE-2015-3932, CVE-2015-3931, CVE-2012-6426, CVE-2012-4418, CVE-2011-1411, CVE-2011-0730.

5.1   XML Signature Generation Guideline

From the systematization of XSW countermeasures (see Sect. 2), we derived
the ones that showed to be effective. Hence, these need to be considered when
designing the signature generation procedure.

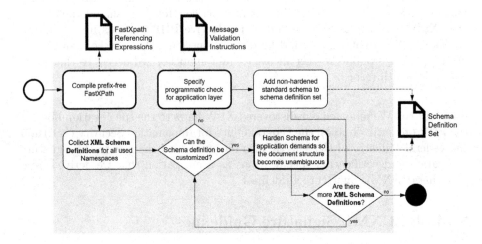

Fig. 4. Guideline to implement a XSW robust XML signature generation.

A key measure to mitigate XSW when generating a signature is to restrict the
signature referencing scheme to prefix-free FastXPath expressions (see Fig. 4).
The scheme can be defined as a constant string that points to the part of the
document to be signed and can be used repeatedly. If multiple documents parts
are to be signed, a corresponding number of expressions need to be specified
always using prefix-free FastXPath. If a different referencing scheme or expressions than those specified are used, signature creation should be aborted or its
implementation rejected during a review or audit, because this could indicate an
attack.

Hardening the underlying document schema definitions is an additional measure. This reduces and – in the best case – eliminates possible positions to which
signed elements can be relocated and wrapped within the document. To achieve
this, it is necessary to analyze all schema definitions and remove those definitions that allow for flexible and extensible document instances. As explained in
Sect. 2, such schema definitions should be replaced by hardened variants, i.e. an
xs:any type definition must be replaced with a concrete element type expected
in the application context.

Unfortunately, there might be some cases where a complete hardening is not
possible. This is the case when an exhaustive set of allowed elements cannot be
defined (e.g. in the SOAP header). XML Schema only allows to declare a list
of allowed elements (allowlist). A schema definition such as *"allow all elements*

except this one. . . " (denylist) is impossible. Such a definition would be necessary to prevent the attack vector shown in Listing 7. Instead, non-exhaustive allowlists will also deny some legal message parts. In these cases, when a certain schema cannot be hardened without losing standard conformance, a set of message validation instructions can be defined alternatively. These can be non-schema-based checks for certain element types and structures, which are performed by the application logic. This is different to real XML Schema validation, which takes place earlier in the message processing chain.

These steps in designing a XSW-robust signature generation procedure provide several technical specifications. These are the prefix-free FastXPath reference expressions, the hardened document schema definitions, and the set of message validation instructions with the latter two being optional. These artifacts are required as an input for designing and implementing the signature verification procedure (see Sect. 5.2). Note that the artifacts are not part of the message exchange.

5.2 XML Signature Verification Guideline

The XML Signature verification process builds on the artifacts developed during signature creation design (see Fig. 5). First, the signed XML document structure is validated against the hardened schema definitions and the set of message validation statements, where available. In addition, the `Signature` element must be checked for presence and schema conformance to mitigate known security vulnerabilities such as the absence of the same element. If one of these structural document checks results in an error, the signature verification process is aborted and the signed document is rejected.

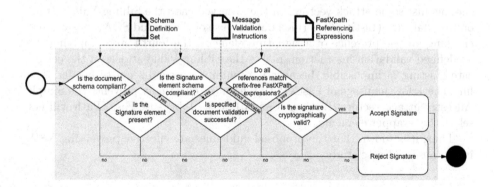

Fig. 5. Guideline for XML signature verification

The last validation step before the verification of the cryptographic signature refers to the references contained in the `Signature` element. These have to be prefix-free FastXPath expressions. Any other referencing scheme found results in rejection of the signed document. In case the expressions have been specified a-priori in the signature generation process, it is checked whether the references contained in the document match the specified ones. If this is the case, cryptographic signature verification of the validated document can be initiated based on the approved references. Only if all checks of the document structure, signature references and cryptographic signatures have been passed successfully, the signed XML document can be considered valid and released for further processing.

6   Case-Based Evaluation

As shown in Sect. 4, the PHR's user authentication has weaknesses regarding attacks on the Simple Ancestry, as well as on the Sibling Value Context of elements important for the process. The body of literature suggests that these are common XSW attack vectors. Therefore, we build on this case study to evaluate our proposed guideline.

Running through the design guideline, a set of schema definitions emerges, covering the SOAP 1.2 and WS-Security standards among others. Because of limitations of the XML Schema language, it is not possible to restrict the SOAP header without knowing an exhaustive list of required elements. Therefore, a message validation instruction must be developed, which is executed by the business logic and prevents the existence of *multiple* `ws:Security` header elements. Additionally, following the guideline results in prefix-free FastXPath references for both the `Challenge` and the `BinarySecurityToken` element, which must be used inside the message.

When performing signature verification, the previously generated resources are used. The schema validation (see Fig. 5) is already a successful countermeasure against some attack vectors. In the observed case, the Sibling Value attack on the challenge (Listing 6) is ruled out because of the second SOAP body. After checking for the presence of a signature element, the fourth step, applying the predefined validation instruction, makes the Sibling Value attack on the certificate (Listing 7) impossible, because it prohibits a second security header. The final check for the usage of FastXPath references eventually prevents the Simple Ancestry attack vectors (Listings 4 and 5), as well, because FastXPath will not select the wrapper elements.

Thus, it is shown that the proposed guidelines are effective preventing XSW in the observed case study.

7   Discussion and Limitations

Our guideline evaluation is limited to one case study. In future work, a more general evaluation should be done to prove its broad effectiveness. Moreover, it is not known, how target user groups would implement these recommendations. This requires further studies regarding the usability including developers, software architects and testers.

The relevance of XSW in modern IT landscapes can also not be proven by a single example. This might be an exceptional case. But, as the case study is focusing on a recent development with high demands towards security and privacy, it should not include known vulnerabilities. However, an additional quantitative study (e.g. crawling public XML Signature implementations on *GitHub*) could be useful to determine today's relevance of XSW.

One finding that deserves further research is the possibility of the wrapped certificate element. It should be investigated how common it is for SAML frameworks to use the information provided by the certificate as input data for the created assertion. If so, this novel attack vector could be a widespread problem in Single Sign-On and similar authentication technologies.

8   Conclusion and Outlook

Complexity and flexibility are the natural enemies of security. XML Signature Wrapping (XSW) is an exemplary vulnerability resulting from the complexity and flexibility of the XML signature standard. Although intensive scientific discussion has produced a number of effective countermeasures, XSW vulnerabilities continue to appear in practice to this day. Even in systems currently under development with high security requirements, such as the Personal Health Record (PHR) in Germany, we were able to discover potential XSW vulnerabilities that could have been avoided by considering the current state of research in the specification. A recent security analysis conducted by an independent research institute on behalf of gematik also noted in its report that the XML signature specification may contain vulnerabilities, without going into details [27]. gematik reacted immediately and extended some of the corresponding specification parts [8, p. 23]. However, these latest versions of their specifications are still vulnerable to XSW, as we discussed in Sect. 4. This emphasizes the need for more actionable and supportive guidance to empower practitioners to use XML Signature in a robust manner. We have made a contribution in this direction with the guidelines we have introduced in this paper. We intend to further refine our guidelines in participatory workshops with relevant user target groups and to recruit a relevant organization to adopt the guide for further dissemination.

Acknowledgement. We would like to thank our reviewers and Stephan Wiefling for their time and effort to give constructive feedback and thoughtful comments.

References

1. Bray, T., Paoli, J., Sperberg-McQueen, M., Maler, E., Yergeau, F.: Extensible Markup Language (XML) 1.0 (Fifth Edition). Recommendation, W3C, November 2008
2. Eastlake, D., Reagle, J., Hirsch, F., Roessler, T.: XML Encryption Syntax and Processing Version 1.1. Recommendation, W3C, April 2013
3. Eastlake, D., et al.: XML Signature Syntax and Processing Version 1.1. Recommendation, W3C, April 2013

4. Gajek, S., Jensen, M., Liao, L., Schwenk, J.: Analysis of signature wrapping attacks and countermeasures. In: ICWS 2019. IEEE, July 2009
5. Gajek, S., Liao, L., Schwenk, J.: Breaking and fixing the inline approach. In: SWS 2007. ACM (2007)
6. gematik GmbH: Systemspezifisches Konzept ePA (2019), revision 166371
7. gematik GmbH: Spezifikation Authentisierung des Versicherten ePA (2020), revision 244633
8. gematik GmbH: Spezifikation ePA-Aktensystem (2020), revision 245464
9. gematik GmbH: epa - elektronische patientenakte (2019). https://www.gematik. de/fileadmin/user_upload/gematik/files/Faktenblaetter/Faktenblatt_ePA_web.pdf
10. gematik GmbH: API Telematik, June 2020. https://fachportal.gematik.de/ downloadcenter/schemata-wsdl-und-andere-dateien
11. Gruschka, N., Lo Iacono, L.: Vulnerable cloud: SOAP message security validation revisited. In: ICWS 2009. IEEE (2009)
12. Gruschka, N., Luttenberger, N.: Protecting web services from DoS attacks by SOAP message validation. In: Fischer-Hübner, S., Rannenberg, K., Yngström, L., Lindskog, S. (eds.) SEC 2006. IIFIP, vol. 201, pp. 171–182. Springer, Boston, MA (2006). https://doi.org/10.1007/0-387-33406-8_15
13. Gruschka, N., Luttenberger, N., Herkenhöner, R.: Event-based soap message validation for WS-securitypolicy-enriched web services. In: SWWS 2016 (2006)
14. Hill, B.: Complexity as enemy of security (2007). https://www.w3.org/2007/ xmlsec/ws/papers/04-hill-isecpartners/
15. Jensen, M., Gruschka, N., Herkenhoner, R., Luttenberger, N.: Soa and web services: new technologies, new standards - new attacks. In: ECOWS 2007 (2007)
16. Jensen, M., Gruschka, N.: A survey of attacks in the web services world. In: Electronic Services: Concepts, Methodologies, Tools and Applications (2010)
17. Jensen, M., Liao, L., Schwenk, J.: The curse of namespaces in the domain of XML signature. In: SWS 2009. ACM (2009)
18. Jensen, M., Meyer, C., Somorovsky, J., Schwenk, J.: On the effectiveness of XML schema validation for countering XML signature wrapping attacks. In: IWSSC 2011 (2011)
19. Jensen, M., Schwenk, J., Bohli, J.M., Gruschka, N., Lo Iacono, L.: Security prospects through cloud computing by adopting multiple clouds. In: CLOUD 2011 (2011)
20. Jensen, M., Schwenk, J., Gruschka, N., Iacono, L.L.: On technical security issues in cloud computing. In: IEEE International Conference on Cloud Computing (2009)
21. Mainka, C., Jensen, M., Lo Iacono, L., Schwenk, J.: XSpRES - robust and effective XML signatures for web services. In: CLOSER 2012. SciTePress (2012)
22. McIntosh, M., Austel, P.: XML signature element wrapping attacks and countermeasures. In: SWS 2005. Association for Computing Machinery (2005)
23. MITRE: Cwe-345: Insufficient verification of data authenticity (2006)
24. MITRE: Cwe-347: Improper verification of cryptographic signature (2006)
25. OASIS: Web services security: Soap message security 1.1 (2004)
26. Robie, J., Dyck, M., Spiegel, J.: XML Path Language (XPath) 3.1. Recommendation, W3C, March 2017
27. Slany, D.W.: Sicherheitsanalyse zur Sicherheit der kritischen Komponenten der elektronischen Patientenakte nach §291a SGB V, March 2020
28. Somorovsky, J., Heiderich, M., Jensen, M., Schwenk, J., Gruschka, N., Lo Iacono, L.: All your clouds are belong to us. In: CCSW 2011 (2011)
29. Somorovsky, J., Mayer, A., Schwenk, J., Kampmann, M., Jensen, M.: On breaking SAML: be whoever you want to be. In: USENIX Security 2012, August 2012
30. W3C: SOAP 1.2-Schema (2007)

Trust Me If You Can: Trusted Transformation Between (JSON) Schemas to Support Global Authentication of Education Credentials

Stefan More[1]([envelope]) [ORCID], Peter Grassberger[1,2], Felix Hörandner[1] [ORCID],
Andreas Abraham[1] [ORCID], and Lukas Daniel Klausner[3] [ORCID]

[1] Graz University of Technology, Graz, Austria
{smore,fhoerandner,aabraham}@iaik.tugraz.at,
p.grassberger@student.tugraz.at
[2] lab10 collective, Graz, Austria
[3] St. Pölten University of Applied Sciences, St. Pölten, Austria
lukas.daniel.klausner@fhstp.ac.at

Abstract. Recruiters and institutions around the world struggle with the verification of diplomas issued in a diverse and global education setting. Firstly, it is a nontrivial problem to identify bogus institutions selling education credentials. While institutions are often accredited by qualified authorities on a regional level, there is no global authority fulfilling this task.Secondly, many different data schemas are used to encode education credentials, which represents a considerable challenge to automated processing. Consequently, significant manual effort is required to verify credentials.

In this paper, we tackle these challenges by introducing a decentralized and open system to automatically verify the legitimacy of issuers and interpret credentials in unknown schemas. We do so by enabling participants to publish transformation information, which enables verifiers to transform credentials into their preferred schema. Due to the lack of a global root of trust, we utilize a distributed ledger to build a decentralized web of trust, which verifiers can query to gather information on the trustworthiness of issuing institutions and to establish trust in transformation information. Going beyond diploma fraud, our system can be generalized to tackle the generalized problem for other domains lacking a root of trust and agreements on data schemas.

This work was supported by the European Union's Horizon 2020 Framework Programme for Research and Innovation under grant agreement № 871473 (KRAKEN) as well as the Josef Ressel Center for Blockchain Technologies and Security Management (JRC Blockchains). The authors would also like to thank TU Graz' Registrar's Office for insights into verification of (paper-based) diplomas.

Keywords: Blockchain · Distributed ledger · Web of trust · Trust management · Education credentials · Verification · Self-sovereign identity

1   Introduction

When applying for a job or a study program, applicants need to provide evidence of their past education achievements (e.g. graduation diplomas) so that the human resources department or institution is able to assess the applicants' qualifications and eligibility. Because applicants occasionally create fake education credentials or modify credentials of legitimate issuers [7], universities spend considerable effort to verify the authenticity of documents. Nowadays, education credentials can be represented as signed digital documents [18], e.g. as Verifiable Credentials in the Self-Sovereign Identity (SSI) context [41]. While digital signatures simplify the verification process, two challenges remain, which we tackle in this work – namely to evaluate a credential's issuer's legitimacy as well as to interpret the various data formats of credentials (cf. Sect. 4).

Challenge 1: Because education diplomas provide substantial value, a whole industry of fake universities (so-called diploma mills [5]) has arisen, which exist for the sole purpose of selling fake diplomas. Within the UK alone, 240 universities were identified as such fake universities according to the UK's Department of Education [40]. To avoid accepting such fake credentials, a verifier needs to spend considerable effort, money and resources to perform authorization of credential issuers, which is especially complex in a global setting with many different types of issuers alongside universities.

Challenge 2: Besides verifying an education credential's authenticity and legitimacy, a verifier also needs to be able to interpret the credential's content. Various data formats have been proposed for digital education credentials [10,41], but so far, no unified, widely accepted standards have emerged [10]. Therefore, verifiers have to spend additional resources to interpret the content of education credentials manually or with external help, which also hinders automated processing.

Contribution 1: *Verify Legitimacy of Diverse Credentials and Issuers.* In this paper, we use a distributed ledger (DL) to enable all involved institutions to publish trust information about credential issuers. This effectively forms a web of trust (WoT), a directed graph of trust statements published by institutions and based on previous manual evaluations (cf. Sect. 5). This web of trust further enables verifiers to define their own trust policies on how to automatically evaluate a (previously unknown) institution's legitimacy.

Contribution 2: *Verify Credentials Issued in Different Schemas.* Building on the above web of trust, we introduce a second graph in which involved parties can publish, discover and authenticate information to transform credentials between schemas (cf. Sect. 6). Given this information, verifiers are able to locally transform a credential from the issuer's schema into their preferred schema, possibly via several intermediate schemas. Combined with our web of trust, verifiers can interpret a credential's content and assess the trustworthiness of transformation information.

Since the tackled challenges are not limited to education credentials, but also apply in other contexts, we point out that our approach can also be applied in other domains where no globally trusted authority exists.

We demonstrate the feasibility of our framework with an **implementation**, which uses a Solidity smart contract on an Ethereum-based DL to manage the web of trust and the distributed file system IPFS to store the transformation information (cf. Sect. 7). We also evaluate and discuss several properties of our system (cf. Sect. 8).

2 Background

In this section, we introduce concepts relevant for our approach. A **Distributed Ledger (DL)** is a redundant data store on distributed nodes without central control. The nodes agree on a state by running a consensus protocol, and such nodes can be run by various parties, such as organizations or companies. DLs can be accessed through different access models, depending on who is allowed to participate in the network by joining it (public vs. private) or by who has read and write access to it (permissioned vs. permissionless). Many ledgers, such as Ethereum, support **Smart Contracts (SCs)**. SCs are code stored on the DL that is deterministically executed by the nodes performing the consensus protocol. Variables in the code are stored on the DL, as well, and can be read and modified using functions supplied by the contract. When a user sends a function call to a contract, the resulting state is only written to the ledger if all nodes agree on the result of the computation. In contrast to centralized and federated identity models [46], **Self-Sovereign Identity (SSI)** gives control over the identity solely to the user [32] without having a central trusted party. In this model, users create their own identity by using a **Decentralized Identifier (DID)** [35]. This DID can be registered on a DL and is used to resolve key material and other information needed to interact with its subject. In addition, it is used to link statements about the user to their identity. **Verifiable Credentials (VCs)** are used as a typical data format in SSI systems and are specified by the W3C [38]. While the schema of the envelope is defined by the W3C, the claims inside a VC are encoded according to a JSON schema [44] so that credentials are sufficiently flexible for various use cases. Obviously, this flexibility of the content's schema also represents a challenge for verifiers when facing content in an unknown schema. The **InterPlanetary File System (IPFS)** [34] is a distributed file system based on an open peer-to-peer network. Similar to a public DL, there is no central party controlling the system and everyone can join the network of nodes and retrieve data. As files on IPFS are content-addressed (i.e. a file is addressed based on a hash of its content), the files' integrity is ensured by design, which reduces the trust requirements towards the nodes. Hence, IPFS is an ideal data storage system for decentralized apps hosted on a DL.

3   Related Work

To authorize issuers of paper-based education credentials, there are only very fragmented and country- or even sector-specific accreditation lists by authorities on legitimate issuers, which moreover rarely include information for automated verification, such as public verification keys [14,23,33].

A number of projects [9–11] from public institutions and industry tackle the field of digital education credentials, with a strong focus on how to represent learning achievements. Some projects leave the assessment of the legitimacy of the credential's issuers to the verifier [24,29,41], while others propose centralized accreditation approaches [13,18–20], often limited to single countries or the EU and focusing merely on universities. In contrast, our approach is based on an open system, supporting the diverse needs of a global, growing and heterogeneous education world.

None of these projects are concerned with interoperability between different credential schemas. Although the W3C's VC standard [38] proposes a mechanism that would allow the transformation of a credential into another representation by its subject (using zero-knowledge proofs), we are not aware of any system that enables or supports the authenticated transformation of credentials between schemas directly by the verifier.

Research literature discusses further approaches for global identity and trust frameworks [27,28], with several publications focusing on DL technology: Alen et al. [4] introduce the concept of a decentralized public key infrastructure (DPKI). The concept proposes using a DL to map identifiers to key material, but does not define how to map entity identities to such identifiers. By suggesting central registrars, it effectively reuses the concept of a certificate authority. Trust over IP [12] combines DIDs, VCs and related technology and governance models into a stack compatible with our system. Alexopoulos et al. [3] discuss DL-based authentication and compare it to PKI and PGP's web of trust. Yakubov et al. [45] extend OpenPGP keys with the Ethereum address of their owner and provide a decentralized key server using smart contracts. Brunner et al. [8] provide a comparison of DL-based authentication frameworks, while Kuperberg [25] surveys blockchain-based identity management.

4   Architecture Overview

There are several *actors* in our system, also shown in Fig. 1:

Student. A natural person who earns credentials by studying and (eventually) graduating. The student is the data subject of a credential and thus needs a key pair and a corresponding DID registered on the ledger. Students may later act as applicants and present their credentials.

Credential Issuer. Any institution that issues education credentials, e.g. a university, school, online learning provider or other training institution. A credential issuer has a key pair and a corresponding DID registered on the ledger.

Trust Certifiers. All users who publish trust statements about the legitimacy (or illegitimacy) of issuers, the authenticity of transformation information, and their trust in other trust certifiers who publish trust statements. Credential issuers, verifiers and any other stakeholders can also act as trust certifiers – enabling an open system to support a diverse education landscape.

Verifier. An institution that accepts education credentials and wants to verify them, such as an employer or university. A verifier can also be a credential issuer (e.g. a university is usually both).

Creator. The actor that creates and publishes the smart contract of our system, which maintains a web of trust on the DL. It does not matter who publishes the contract, as the contract's code is public and everyone is able to verify its behavior.

The actors deal with **Credentials** in W3C VC format. The education data inside the VC envelope is encoded following a schema chosen by the credential issuer. While the schema is stated in the credential, its interpretation is not necessarily known to the verifier.

Entities in our system provide **Trust Statements**, statements on the trustworthiness and legitimacy of others to help verifiers in their assessment process.

Definition 1 (Trust Statement). *A trust statement is a tuple of the form* $\langle C, \mathsf{LL}, \mathsf{LC}, \mathsf{c}, \mathsf{u}, \sigma, \mathsf{t}, I \rangle$*, where C is the trust certifier, I is the credential issuer being certified,* $\mathsf{LL} \in [-1, 1]$ *is the level of legitimacy C asserts for I,* $\mathsf{LC} \in [-1, 1]$ *is the level of confidence C has in the statements published by I, c is the context of the certification (credential or transformation), u is the identifier of what I is trusted to issue (type of credential or transformation) and t is a timestamp. Additionally, σ is a cryptographic assurance (digital signature) of the certificate's integrity and authenticity. Depending on the system chosen, levels are allowed to be any real value in the interval, one of several discrete values, or even just in $\{-1, 0, 1\}$ (with 1 denoting the highest trust level).*

The **Web of Trust** is a collection of trust statements.

Definition 2 (Web of Trust). *A web of trust is a directed, edge-labeled multigraph $W = \langle V, E \rangle$, where the vertices V are entities (e.g. educational institutions) and the edges E represent trust statements, which are consequently labeled as stated in the definition above. For edge labels in a web of trust, the trust certifier–credential issuer parameters have to match the edge's vertices, i.e. for each edge e from v_1 to v_2, the corresponding label of e has to be of the form* $\langle v_1, \mathsf{LL}, \mathsf{LC}, \mathsf{c}, \mathsf{u}, \sigma, \mathsf{t}, v_2 \rangle$.

To facilitate interoperability between credential schemas, trust certifiers also issue **Transformation Information**.

Definition 3 (Transformation Information). *Transformation information is a set of (machine-readable) transformation rules that define how to transform a credential issued in one credential schema into another schema. Transformation Information is encoded in an implementation-specific format.*

Analogous to the web of trust, a **Transformation Information Graph** is a collection of transformation information.

Definition 4 (Transformation Information Graph). *A transformation information graph is a directed, edge-labeled multigraph $TIG = \langle V, E \rangle$, where the vertices V are URIs of credential schemas and each edge $e \in E$ from vertex X to vertex Y represents a transformation for transforming a credential of schema X into a credential of schema Y. An edge also contains the DID of the entity that published the transformation information and is signed by it.*

The WoT and the transformation information graph are maintained by a **Registry**, a data structure on the DL. The registry is managed by a smart contract (SC) which provides a single point of contact for trust certifiers and verifiers who want to access or append to either graph by calling the *get* or *add* function on the contract, respectively. In addition, the registry utilizes IPFS to store the transformation information. While the transformation information itself is stored on IPFS, the respective edge in the transformation graph contains the IPFS address of the information and information about its trust certifier. An example setup is shown in Fig. 3a.

A **Trust Policy** is defined by the verifier with rules on how to decide a credential issuer's legitimacy based on information obtained from the registry, i.e. trust statements and transformation information. Such a policy also defines suitable parameters for algorithms that find paths in the graphs and calculate legitimacy scores. Additionally, the trust policy contains the rules which are used to further check the credential's content, such as required study subjects or minimum grade point averages. The policy is defined locally by one or more domain experts. This approach allows verifiers to enforce their own rules and follow their locally relevant regulations.

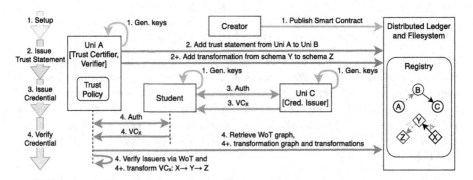

Fig. 1. Architecture and example dataflows of our system. University A, acting as trust certifier, adds an edge stating its trust about University B and publishes transformation information from schema Y to its schema Z. Later, University A, acting as verifier, verifies a credential issued by University C by additionally obtaining a previously registered edge from university B to C and a path from schema X to Y. They make sure that all transformation information is trusted by authenticating its issuer using the WoT.

5   Issuer Authorization

The first step needed to check a credential is to verify the legitimacy of the credential and its issuer using information published by other entities. This is also the basis for authenticated transformation of credentials between schemas, as described in the following Sect. 6.

Our approach can be split into four phases: (1) Initially, the registry and its smart contract are established on the DL. (2) The trust certifier identifies a credential issuer and publishes the certification information using the registry. (3) The credential issuer issues a credential to a student. (4) The student shows the credential to a verifier, who uses the information stored in the registry to verify the credential and the credential issuer's legitimacy. The main aspects of these phases are shown in Fig. 1 and discussed in the following paragraphs, while a formal description is given in Fig. 2.

(1) Setup: To set up the system, the creator publishes a smart contract on the $\overline{\text{DL}}$ which maintains the registry. This contract provides a single point to create or update (add) and retrieve (get) the lists of edges. Additionally, students, credential issuers and trust certifiers create their own key pairs and use them to establish their self-sovereign identities, i.e. derive and register DIDs. These DIDs with corresponding DID documents are registered on the DL to enable other parties to retrieve the respective public keys for signature verification processes.

(2) Issue Trust Statement: After having assessed a credential issuer's legitimacy (e.g. in a previously performed tedious manual process or using other channels), a trust certifier may share its decision with others by issuing a trust statement. Based on the previous assessment, the trust certifier chooses an appropriate level of legitimacy LL, which may also be a negative value if the trust certifier arrives at the conclusion that the credential issuer is an illegitimate institution. In addition, it adds the level of confidence in trust statements published by the credential issuer, represented by LC. The trust certifier publishes its assessment as a trust statement on the registry by setting the variables on the edge accordingly (cf. Sect. 4), using its private key to sign the edge, and publishes the signed edge by calling the smart contract through one of the DL's nodes. This creates a new edge in the registry's WoT graph pointing from the trust certifier to the prospective credential issuer. Optionally, the trust certifier may also issue transformation information or trust other entities to do so (cf. Sect. 6).

Revoke Trust Statement: As trust in other institutions changes and faulty entries occur, trust certifiers are able to add a new edge between the same vertices (but with a more recent timestamp) to the WoT, thereby altering the stated level of legitimacy or other attributes. Based on the timestamps, verifiers select edges at points in time based on the received credential and their trust policy.

(3) Issue Credential: After completing a course or graduating from a university, the student requests a VC for this accomplishment. Initially, the student proves their identity using their DID and private key. Then, the credential issuer loads the student's attributes from its student information system, encodes those

(1) <u>Setup</u>: **On any Creator:** Generate $(pk_a, sk_a) \leftarrow$ KeyGen(), create smart contract for WoT registry, publish smart contract at DL and announce its address $Addr_{SC}$ and code.

On all Students, Credential Issuers, and Trust Certifiers: Generate $(pk, sk) \leftarrow$ KeyGen(), create DID from pk and register pk at DL.

(2) <u>Issue Trust Statement</u>: **On Trust Certifier C:** Verify identity and legitimacy of issuer and obtain issuer's DID_{Iss} (out-of-band). Create the WoT edge e, which includes DID_C, DID_{Iss}, the level of legitimacy as issuer LL, the level of confidence as trust certifier LC, the context c (set to *credential*), the credential's type u and the current time t. Sign $\sigma_e \leftarrow$ SIG.Sign(e, sk_C), add the signature to the edge $e' = e \| \sigma_e$ and publish the signed edge e' via DL.Call($Addr_{SC}$, add_{WoT}, e').

On all DL nodes: Receive the trust certifier's request and add e' to the WoT graph's list of edges.

<u>Revoke Trust Statement</u>: as Phase (2) with different values for LL and LC.

(3) **Issue Credential:** **On Student S:** Request verifiable credential at university and send DID_S as well as proof of ownership of sk_S.

On Credential Issuer Iss: Verify student's identity and ownership of DID_S. Encode the student's attributes A_S using $schema_{Iss}$ into A'_S and generate credential cred, which includes the encoded attributes A'_S, student's DID_S and DID_{Iss}. Sign the credential $\sigma_{cred} \leftarrow$ SIG.Sign(cred, sk_{Iss}) and issue it to the student.

(4) <u>Verify Credential</u>: **On Student S:** Send DID_S, proof of ownership of sk_S and $cred'$ to the verifier.

On Verifier V: Load up-to-date WoT $\leftarrow$ DL.Call($Addr_{SC}$, get_{WoT}) and issuer's $pk_{Iss} \leftarrow$ DL.Resolve(DID_{Iss}), where DID_{Iss} from $cred'$. Verify that issuer was not revoked/expired, allowed to issue and that credential was really signed by that issuer by verifying SIG.Verify($cred'$, pk_{Iss}) = 1. Find paths from verifier to issuer relevant w. r. t. $cred'$ by paths $\leftarrow$ pathfinder(WoT, DID_V, DID_{Iss}, $c_{cred'}$, $u_{cred'}$). Authenticate edges in paths by verifying $\forall$path $\in$ paths, $\forall$edge e $\in$ path : SIG.Verify(e, pk_C) = 1, where DID_C from edge e and $pk_C \leftarrow$ DL.Resolve(DID_C). Compute overall legitimacy of issuer and verify using policy that calcscore(paths) $\geq policy_{minscore}$.

Fig. 2. Issuer authorization protocol.

attributes using a suitable JSON schema and places the encoded attributes into a VC. The credential issuer finally signs the VC and hands it to the requesting student for their own use. The issuing of credentials is independent of the registry and a DL may only be needed to retrieve the student's public key via its DID for authentication.

(4) **Verify Credential:** When a student presents a credential to a verifier (e.g. within an application process), the verifier needs to verify it according to its trust policy. The verifier first retrieves the registry's WoT graph by calling the smart contract's get_{WoT} function using a DL node. On this graph, the verifier performs the path-finding algorithm defined in its policy. The verifier also verifies the signature of each trust statement in the trust paths with public keys obtained from the DL. If there are multiple paths towards a credential issuer, the verifier's trust

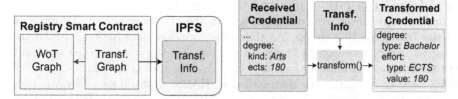

(a) Registry setup: Edges in the Transf. Graph are authenticated using the WoT.

(b) Transformation process using Transf. Info discovered using the Transf. Graph.

Fig. 3. Example transformation with information authenticated using the WoT.

policy may select which paths are relevant. This enables different verification scenarios, such as "Was the credential issuer trusted at the point in time the credential was issued?" and "Is the credential issuer trusted right now?". On the identified paths, the verifier computes an overall "legitimacy score" and compares this score with the policy's requirements. Next, the verifier verifies the credential's signature with the public key that has been registered in the DL for the credential issuer's DID, including a revocation check by consulting the respective revocation registry. The verifier concludes the process by checking the credential with regard to a set of rules stated in the trust policy, such as the precise field of study or certain grade requirements. Optionally, if the verifier does not support the schema of the received credential, the verifier may engage in a transformation process and transform the credential into a supported schema as described in Sect. 6.

6   Credential Transformation

The second step during checking of a credential is to check the content of the credential using a local policy. The transformation steps described in this section help verifiers who are not familiar with the issued credential's schema and, therefore, need support to interpret the credential correctly.

We extend two of the previously described phases to enable transformations between schemas: (2+) Trust Certifiers knowing how to interpret a credential's schema and transform it into another schema publish this transformation information to the DL's registry to help others. For example, a university having dealt with credentials in a foreign schema previously (as verifier) may publish its transformation information into a local schema (as trust certifier). To establish trust in this transformation information, we build upon the web of trust approach as established in phase (2) above. (4+) After verifying the student's credential, the verifier transforms the credential into a supported schema by querying the transformation graph for suitable transformation information, verifying its authenticity and its publisher's legitimacy using the WoT graph.

Figure 3a illustrates how the WoT is used to authenticate the transformation information, and a formal view on the extended phases is given in Fig. 4.

(2+) **Issue Transformation:** If a trust certifier has information about how to transform a credential from one schema to another, they can add this information to the transformation graph. As the transformation information may be too large, it is not stored on the ledger itself. Instead, the trust certifier publishes the transformation information on IPFS, which results in a content-dependent IPFS address (basically the information's SHA256 hash). This address is then added to the new edge and sent to the transformation graph by calling add_T.

Issue Trust Statement: Analogous to the assessment of a credential issuer's legitimacy, trust certifiers assess and share the legitimacy to publish transformation information and thereby state that they trust the other entity and its transformation information. This statement is published in the same way as in phase (2), with the context c set to *transformation*, and added to the WoT graph by calling add_{WoT}. The identifier u defines the respective schema.

(4+) **Transform:** After phase (4) has verified the credential as well as the credential issuer's legitimacy, the verifier retrieves transformation information from the registry by calling get_T and uses it to transform the credential into a schema known to the verifier's policy engine, as illustrated in Fig. 3b. Initially, the verifier loads the transformation graph and finds a path from the credential's schema to the known schema. In each step, while traversing the path, the verifier verifies the signature on the edge and assesses the legitimacy of the edge's publisher using the WoT graph. It is also possible to define a rule in the policy requiring the creator of a transformation to possess a minimum legitimacy level and discard all other transformations. The verifier then loads the transformation from IPFS and verifies its integrity by computing the hash value and comparing it with the (content-dependent) address value stored on the edge. Afterwards, the verifier executes the transformation on the credential. If multiple relevant paths with transformation information exist, it depends on the trust policy which one is used – or if all are used and a trust decision is made by a human actor. Finally, the verifier obtains a credential represented in a supported schema, which simplifies further checks according to the trust policy (or manually by humans).

Of course, transformations between schemas have limitations. For example, if a target schema requires values that are not available in the source schema, a direct transformation might not be possible. In that case, the verifier or its policy have to decide whether the presented credential is considered sufficient or whether in light of these missing values (which are e.g. simply mapped to defaults), is deemed insufficient for the assessment.

7   Prototype

This section describes the prototype implementation of our concept, which highlights the feasibility of our system.

Distributed Ledger (DL): We host our smart contract and its registry on an Ethereum-compliant DL. While the choice of permission model depends on the concrete use case, we used a public permissionless ledger for the proof-of-concept

(2+) **Issue Transformation: On Trust Certifier** C: Define transformation information $\mathsf{transf}_{X \to Y}$ from schema_X to schema_Y and publish it on IPFS on address $\mathsf{Addr_T}$. Create transformation edge e_T, which includes $\mathsf{DID_C}$, the URIs identifying the source schema schema_X and target schema schema_Y, the IPFS address of the transformation $\mathsf{Addr_T}$ and the current time t. Sign the edge $\sigma_{\mathsf{e_T}} \leftarrow \mathsf{SIG.Sign}(\mathsf{e}_T, \mathsf{sk_C})$ and send it to contract by calling $\mathsf{DL.Call}(\mathsf{Addr_{SC}}, \mathsf{add_T}, \mathsf{e}'_T)$. **On all DL nodes:** Add e'_T to the transformation graph's list of edges.
Issue Trust Statement: as Phase (2) with the certification's context c set to *transformation* and the identifier u to a URI identifying a credential schema.

(4+) **Transform: On Verifier** V: Load up-to-date transformation graph $\mathsf{transg} \leftarrow \mathsf{DL.Call}(\mathsf{Addr_{SC}}, \mathsf{get_T})$ and find paths from issuer's to verifier's schema by $\mathsf{paths_T} \leftarrow \mathsf{pathfinder}(\mathsf{transg}, \mathsf{schema_{Iss}}, \mathsf{schema_V})$. For each path in $\mathsf{paths_T}$ and each edge in path, authenticate edge by using WoT, extract transformation address $\mathsf{Addr_T}$, load transformation $\mathsf{transf} \leftarrow \mathsf{IPFS.Load}(\mathsf{Addr_T})$ and transform credential $\mathsf{cred}' \leftarrow \mathsf{transform}(\mathsf{transf}, \mathsf{cred})$ for the next iteration. Each time, verify that cred fulfills $\mathsf{policy_{rules}}$ or reject stating a reason. Accept cred for further human processing.

Fig. 4. Credential transformation protocol.

implementation, thus allowing participation without prior registration. While this is not a requirement, we host both graphs inside the same smart contract and thus on the same ledger. The registry was implemented as a smart contract using the Solidity smart contract language [16]. As an optional component, we operate a lightweight "listener" node inside the trust boundary of the verifier as an optional performance optimization to reduce the latency between the verifier's client and the DL node as well as to mitigate censorship attacks (cf. Sect. 8). This node receives and verifies all blocks of the ledger, but does not participate in the consensus protocol. Since the verifier is only concerned with the state of the registry's smart contract, all other transactions can be discarded, thus minimizing storage needs.

Distributed Storage Layer: As transformation information data is potentially too large to be stored directly on the DL, our implementation uses IPFS as the distributed storage layer due to its availability and maturity, although other distributed file systems could be used instead. Important properties are integrity protection of data and content-addressable file resolution.

Client Components: To add and retrieve edges from the registry, we implemented client components in JavaScript. All components use the Ethereum JSON RPC interface [15] to communicate with DL nodes. For the trust certifier, we use *web3.js* to create transactions and the *MetaMask* browser extension as the wallet to sign and send them to the DL. For the verifier, we implemented a client to retrieve and visualize the WoT graph and to compute paths in the graph, serving as the data source for the verification.

Transformation System: Transformation information is discovered using the registry's transformation graph and authenticated using the WoT graph, as explained in Sect. 6. The transformation information can be encoded by any means as long as the verifier is able to execute them. In our implementation, we used *jsonpath-object-transform* [26] and published corresponding templates encoded in JSON to IPFS. Other approaches to transform JSON between different schemas or to another representation (such as XML) include table-based transformations, more generic templating systems using JSONPath [22] and systems based on XML's XSLT (including its experimental variant JsonT [21]).

Trust Policy: The policy not only defines how to evaluate a credential's legitimacy, but also specifies a set of rules on whether the content of the credential is acceptable. For example, a university might want to restrict acceptable credentials to Bachelor's certificates during the application process for a Master's program. Our system does not hard-code such rules, but instead hands over all retrieved data to a policy system [2, 6, 30]. This policy system then executes a policy defined by domain experts, such as the university's registrar's office, providing them with a high-level way to define rules [31, 42, 43].

8   Discussion

This section discusses further aspects of our concept and prototype.

Local Trust: A tackled challenge is the authenticity and legitimacy of credentials that use unknown schemas. To avoid a signature becoming invalid due to transforming the credential, the verifier first verifies the signature of the original credential and only then converts the credential (based on trusted transformation information) locally. Both signature verification and credential transformation occur locally in the verifier's trust domain, and only trusted transformation information is used. Consequently, it is guaranteed that the transformed credential has the same meaning as the incoming signed one.

Revocation: Revocation of trust statements is an important feature in any trust management system [1]. In our proposed system, a trust certifier can revoke a trust statement at any time by issuing a new trust statement with a reduced legitimacy level – even with a negative value to explicitly declare mistrust in the credential issuer. Additionally, a credential issuer can revoke a credential after it has been issued, e.g. by publishing a corresponding statement to a revocation registry, which is checked by the verifier. Checks for both types of revocations need to be performed during credential verification by the verifier.

Smart Contract Security: Depending on the access model of the DL, many or even all entities can write data into the registry. Since all information published in the registry is signed by its publisher, this is not a problem for the authenticity of transformation information and trust statements. Nevertheless, an overfull registry could lead to performance issues during verification. To mitigate this issue, the smart contract serving the registry can be equipped with access control mechanisms. For example, it is possible to enforce that a credential issuer can only add edges which are outgoing from its own vertex. Preventing an attacker from adding invalid edges starting at the vertex of a legitimate entity keeps the path-finding algorithms from having to verify many invalid signatures to find the valid ones. Furthermore, it is possible to only allow adding edges to trust certifiers who are already part of the graph. While this keeps attackers away, it also hinders legitimate entities from joining the graph. Thus it depends on the concrete use case which mechanisms should be used.

Since a smart contract is code and code could contain bugs that malicious parties might be able to exploit [39], it is important to apply secure software development practices when adding access control mechanisms. This is even more important when considering that smart contracts cannot be changed after they have been deployed on a DL [36,37].

Operational Costs: To evaluate our concept, we deployed a smart contract that maintains a registry as described in Sect. 4, which manages the two graphs represented as a list of edges. The smart contract does not perform additional checks to verify the publisher, so a verifier needs to retrieve the full graphs and filter out any irrelevant or invalid edges. While a public DL enables an open system, all write operations on the ledger have a cost. In the Ethereum context, the cost of a contract call is measured in units called *gas* and depends on the required computational effort. Adding an edge to our registry costs about 78 000 gas, worth about US$ 10 in January 2021.[1] In contrast to write operations, read operations are free. As the majority of operations in our system are of the latter kind, the total costs are still relatively low.

Since costs of using a public ledger are hard to predict in advance, private or consortium ledgers represent alternatives. In such ledgers, members of a consortium operate all nodes of the ledger, removing the need for an incentive system like gas. This limits the expenses to the costs needed to host the nodes but restricts (write) access to consortium members.

Performance Evaluation: We evaluated graphs with up to 10 000 edges and measured the performance of different operations using an Ethereum-based DL. Adding a new edge to the graph is not a time-critical operation and only performed whenever a new trust statement is issued. The *add* call to our contract only took less than 1 s, while integration of the edge into the ledger depended on the ledger's block time (around 13 s for mainnet Ethereum [17]). Likewise, the retrieval of a graph with 10 000 edges from remote DL nodes (with *get*) took under one second. Performance is of even smaller concern if the verifier retrieves edges from a local "listener" node (cf. Sect. 7).

Sybil Attacks and Censorship: The existence of fake universities issuing (fake) credentials also makes the existence of fake trust certifiers issuing trust statements to (fake) universities plausible. However, since such fake trust certifiers are neither trusted by a verifier nor have a trust path from the verifier

---

[1] Computed by multiplying gas price (https://etherscan.io/chart/gasprice) and ether price (https://etherscan.io/chart/etherprice) on 22 January 2021.

to them, these (fake) trust statements have no influence on a credential's verification. Although the decentralized and distributed nature of DLs provides resistance against censorship and denial-of-service attacks [3], a node might still provide bogus information to a verifier, hence a verifier needs to establish a trust relationship with at least one node. One way of doing this is having the verifier operate its own node as discussed in Sect. 7. Another way is to ask multiple or even all nodes to attest a certain set of edges represents the full graph and that no edges were censored.

9   Conclusion

In this paper, we introduced a system that simplifies the time-consuming and costly task of verifying credentials and the legitimacy of the credentials' issuer. While we placed the focus on the education domain, our approach can be generalized to other domains facing the same problems. Our open and decentralized system introduces a web of trust maintained by a smart contract on a DL. We build upon this trust assessment framework for transformation information, as well. Participants of our system publish transformation information on IPFS and a trust statement therefor on the DL. If confronted with a credential in an unknown schema, verifiers look up a transformation chain on the DL, as well as trust paths within the WoT to assess the legitimacy of these transformation steps. As a result, verifiers are able to transform received credentials to a supported data schema and automatically check their content. Finally, our implementation demonstrates the feasibility of our concept while the extensive discussion highlights additional benefits, such as the verifier's control over their trust decisions and the ledger's resistance against censorship.

References

1. Abraham, A., More, S., Rabensteiner, C., Hörandner, F.: Revocable and offline-verifiable self-sovereign identities. In: TrustCom/BigDataSE 2020. IEEE (2020)
2. Alber, L., More, S., Mödersheim, S.A., Schlichtkrull, A.: Adapting the TPL trust policy language for a self-sovereign identity world. In: Open Identity Summit 2021. OID 2021, Gesellschaft für Informatik (2021, in press)
3. Alexopoulos, N., Daubert, J., Mühlhäuser, M., Habib, S.M.: Beyond the hype: on using blockchains in trust management for authentication. In: TrustCom/BigDataSE/ICESS 2017, pp. 546–553. IEEE (2017)
4. Allen, C., et al.: Decentralized public key infrastructure. White Paper, Rebooting the Web of Trust (2015)
5. Bear, J., Ezell, A.: Degree Mills: The Billion-Dollar Industry That Has Sold Over a Million Fake Diplomas. Prometheus Books (2012)
6. Becker, M.Y., Fournet, C., Gordon, A.D.: SecPAL: design and semantics of a decentralized authorization language. J. Comput. Secur. **18**(4), 619–665 (2010)
7. Børresen, L.J., Meier, E., Skjerven, S.A.: Detecting fake university degrees in a digital world. In: Corruption in Higher Education: Global Challenges and Responses, Global Perspectives on Higher Education, vol. 46, pp. 102–107. Brill | Sense (2020)

8. Brunner, C., Knirsch, F., Unterweger, A., Engel, D.: A comparison of blockchain-based PKI implementations. In: Proceedings of the 6th International Conference on Information Systems Security and Privacy, ICISSP 2020, pp. 333–340. SciTePress (2020)

9. Camilleri, A.F., Duffy, K.H., Otto, N.: Modeling Educational Verifiable Credentials. Draft community group report, W3C Verifiable Credentials for Education Task Force (2020). https://w3c-ccg.github.io/vc-ed-models. Accessed 22 Jan 2021

10. Camilleri, A.F., Tück, C.: Higher Education Interoperable Data Initiative (HEIDI). Living document (2020). https://heidirepo.github.io/HEIDI. Accessed 22 Jan 2021

11. Connecting Europe Facility: EBSI: Use Cases and Functional Documentation (2020). https://ec.europa.eu/cefdigital/wiki/display/CEFDIGITALEBSI/Use+Cases+and+Functional+Documentation. Accessed 22 Jan 2021

12. Davie, M., Gisolfi, D., Hardman, D., Jordan, J., O'Donnell, D., Reed, D.: The trust over IP stack. IEEE Commun. Stand. Mag. **3**(4), 46–51 (2019)

13. Digital Credentials Consortium: Building the Digital Credential Infrastructure for the Future (2020). https://digitalcredentials.mit.edu/wp-content/uploads/2020/02/white-paper-building-digital-credential-infrastructure-future.pdf. Accessed 22 Jan 2021

14. ETER: European Tertiary Education Register (2020). https://www.eter-project.com. Accessed 22 Jan 2021

15. Ethereum: Ethereum JSON RPC API (2020). https://eth.wiki/json-rpc/API. Accessed 22 Jan 2021

16. Ethereum: Solidity Documentation (2021). https://docs.soliditylang.org. Accessed 22 Jan 2021

17. Etherscan: Ethereum Blocktime (2021). https://etherscan.io/chart/blocktime. Accessed 22 Jan 2021

18. European Commission: Europass Digital Credentials Infrastructure (2020). https://ec.europa.eu/futurium/en/europass/europass-digital-credentials-infrastructure. Accessed 22 Jan 2021

19. FutureTrust Consortium: Global Trust Service List (2020). https://pilots.futuretrust.eu/gtsl. Accessed 22 Jan 2021

20. Gräther, W., Kolvenbach, S., Ruland, R., Schütte, J., Torres, C., Wendland, F.: Blockchain for education: lifelong learning passport. In: Proceedings of the 1st ERCIM Blockchain Workshop. European Society for Socially Embedded Technologies (2018)

21. Gössner, S.: Transforming JSON (2006). https://goessner.net/articles/jsont. Accessed 22 Jan 2021

22. Gössner, S.: JSONPath - XPath for JSON (2007). https://goessner.net/articles/JsonPath. Accessed 22 Jan 2021

23. HEDD: UK Higher Education Degree Datacheck (2020). https://hedd.ac.uk/about. Accessed 22 Jan 2021

24. IMS Global Learning Consortium: Open Badges v2.0. Technical report (2018). https://www.imsglobal.org/sites/default/files/Badges/OBv2p0Final/index.html

25. Kuperberg, M.: Blockchain-based identity management: a survey from the enterprise and ecosystem perspective. IEEE Trans. Eng. Manag. **67**(4), 1008–1027 (2020)

26. Lane, D., Vontas, C., Rückstieß, T., Poggi, D.: jsonpath-object-transform (2017). https://github.com/dvdln/jsonpath-object-transform. Accessed 22 Jan 2021

27. Lee, A.J., Yu, T.: Towards quantitative analysis of proofs of authorization: applications, framework, and techniques. In: Proceedings for the 23rd IEEE Computer Security Foundations Symposium, CSF 2010, pp. 139–153. IEEE (2010)

28. Li, N., Winsborough, W.H., Mitchell, J.C.: Distributed credential chain discovery in trust management. J. Comput. Secur. **11**(1), 35–86 (2003)
29. MIT Media Lab Learning Initiative and Hyland Credentials: Blockcerts - An Open Infrastructure for Academic Credentials on the Blockchain (2016). https://www.blockcerts.org. Accessed 22 Jan 2021
30. Mödersheim, S., Schlichtkrull, A., Wagner, G., More, S., Alber, L.: TPL: a trust policy language. In: Meng, W., Cofta, P., Jensen, C.D., Grandison, T. (eds.) IFIPTM 2019. IAICT, vol. 563, pp. 209–223. Springer, Cham (2019). https://doi.org/10.1007/978-3-030-33716-2_16
31. Mödersheim, S.A., Ni, B.: GTPL: A graphical trust policy language. In: Open Identity Summit 2019, OID 2019, pp. 107–118. Gesellschaft für Informatik (2019)
32. Mühle, A., Grüner, A., Gayvoronskaya, T., Meinel, C.: A survey on essential components of a self-sovereign identity. Comput. Sci. Rev. **30**, 80–86 (2018)
33. Office for Students: OfS Register (Spreadsheet) (2021). https://apis.officeforstudents.org.uk/OfsRegisterDownload/api/Register/. Accessed 22 Jan 2021
34. Protocol Labs: IPFS Documentation (2021). https://docs.ipfs.io. Accessed 22 Jan 2021
35. Reed, D., Sporny, M., Longley, D., Allen, C., Grant, R., Sabadello, M.: Decentralized Identifiers (DIDs) v1.0. W3C working draft, W3C (2021). https://www.w3.org/TR/2021/WD-did-core-20210128/
36. Rodler, M., Li, W., Karame, G.O., Davi, L.: Sereum: protecting existing smart contracts against re-entrancy attacks. In: Proceedings of the 26th Annual Network and Distributed System Security Symposium, NDSS 2019. Internet Society (2019)
37. Rodler, M., Li, W., Karame, G.O., Davi, L.: EVMPatch: timely and automated patching of ethereum smart contracts. In: 30th USENIX Security Symposium. USENIX Security 2021. USENIX Association (2021)
38. Sporny, M., Longley, D., Chadwick, D.: Verifiable Credentials Data Model 1.0. W3C recommendation, W3C (2019). https://www.w3.org/TR/2019/REC-vc-data-model-20191119/
39. Torres, C.F., Baden, M., Norvill, R., Pontiveros, B.B.F., Jonker, H., Mauw, S.: ÆGIS: shielding vulnerable smart contracts against attacks. In: Proceedings of the 15th ACM Asia Conference on Computer and Communications Security, ASIA CCS 2020, pp. 584–597. ACM (2020)
40. UK Department of Education: Higher Education Degree Datacheck (2020). https://hedd.ac.uk/about. Accessed 16 Oct 2020
41. W3C Verifiable Credentials for Education Task Force: vc-ed (2020). https://w3c-ccg.github.io/vc-ed. Accessed 22 Jan 2021
42. Weinhardt, S., Omolola, O.: Usability of policy authoring tools: a layered approach. In: Proceedings of the 5th International Conference on Information Systems Security and Privacy, ICISSP 2019, pp. 301–308. SciTePress (2019)
43. Weinhardt, S., St. Pierre, D.: Lessons learned – conducting a user experience evaluation of a trust policy authoring tool. In: Open Identity Summit 2019, OID 2019, pp. 185–190. Gesellschaft für Informatik (2019)
44. Wright, A., Andrews, H., Hutton, B.: JSON Schema Specification (2020). https://json-schema.org/specification.html. Accessed 22 Jan 2021

45. Yakubov, A., Shbair, W., State, R.: BlockPGP: a blockchain-based framework for PGP key servers. In: Proceedings of the 6th International Symposium on Computing and Networking Workshops, pp. 316–322. IEEE (2018)
46. Zwattendorfer, B., Zefferer, T., Stranacher, K.: An overview of cloud identity management-models. In: Proceedings of the 10th International Conference on Web Information Systems and Technologies, WEBIST 2014, vol. 2, pp. 82–92. SciTePress (2014)

SIUV: A Smart Car Identity Management and Usage Control System Based on Verifiable Credentials

Ali Hariri[1,2(✉)], Subhajit Bandopadhyay[1,3], Athanasios Rizos[1],
Theo Dimitrakos[1,4], Bruno Crispo[2], and Muttukrishnan Rajarajan[3]

[1] Munich Research Center, Huawei Technologies Duesseldorf GmbH,
Munich, Germany
{ali.hariri,subhajit.bandopadhyay,athanasios.rizos,
theo.dimitrakos}@huawei.com
[2] Department of Computer Science and Information Engineering,
University of Trento, Trento, Italy
{ali.hariri,bruno.crispo}@unitn.it
[3] Institute for Cyber Security, School of Mathematics,
Computer Science and Engineering, City, University of London, London, UK
{subhajit.bandopadhyay,r.muttukrishnan}@city.ac.uk
[4] School of Computing, University of Kent, Canterbury, UK

Abstract. The automotive industry is witnessing an accelerated growth in digital innovations that turn modern vehicles into digital systems. This makes the security of modern vehicles a crucial concern as they have evolved into cyber-physical and safety-critical systems. Therefore, stateful identity management and continuous access control have become a paramount requirement in smart vehicles. Indeed, several Identity and Access Management (IAM) frameworks have been proposed in the automotive field, but context awareness and continuity of control remain overlooked. To address these challenges, we present SIUV: a stateful smart-car IAM that is based on Usage Control (UCON) and Verifiable Credentials (VCs). SIUV uses Attribute Based Access Control (ABAC) policies to issue privileges to subjects (i.e. drivers or applications) according to their credentials and claims. The issued privileges are then used to decide whether to grant or deny access to in-car resources. Furthermore, the system continuously monitors subject claims, resource attributes and environmental conditions (e.g. location or time). Hence, if a change occurs, the system re-evaluates policies and updates or revokes issued privileges and usage decisions accordingly. We describe the architecture of SIUV, discuss the evaluation results, and define future directions.

Keywords: UCON · IAM · Automotive · Smart car · Verifiable Credentials · Principle of Least Privilege · ABAC · ALFA · XACML · Ed25519

© IFIP International Federation for Information Processing 2021
Published by Springer Nature Switzerland AG 2021
A. Jøsang et al. (Eds.): SEC 2021, IFIP AICT 625, pp. 36–50, 2021.
https://doi.org/10.1007/978-3-030-78120-0_3

1 Introduction

The exponential growth of the Internet of Vehicles (IoV) innovations, such as autonomous driving, driver assistance, vehicle connectivity, infotainment and shared mobility has recently gained a notable attention in the automotive industry. Such services and innovations are supported by the integration of smart sensors as well as the shift from electromechanical to interconnected software-based systems in modern vehicles [6, 9]. In addition, vehicular systems are transforming towards centralised architectures in order to support dynamic services and functionalities. Particularly, Service-Oriented Architectures (SOAs) are increasingly being adopted in automotive frameworks, due to their flexibility. SOAs provide a better abstraction and separation between hardware and software, and allow smoother changes and integration of services. However, the flexibility and dynamicity of SOAs comes at the expense of the simple security of the statically predefined functions of existing architectures. Although SOAs are being adopted in automotive architectures, typical SOA security measures are not completely sufficient due to the safety-critical nature of vehicles [23].

The security of modern vehicles has gained more focus in the research community and the automotive industry. For instance, Miller and Charlie [18] performed an attack that allowed them to gain access to critical physical systems such as steering and braking systems. As a result, few millions of cars had to be recalled from the market. Similarly, Dürrwang et al. [12] exploited a vulnerability that allows an unintended deployment or a prevention of deployment of airbags. More recently, Wouters et al. [26] uncovered a vulnerability that allowed them to clone a key fob of a Tesla Model S in less than two minutes. Researchers have also studied the state of the art of automotive security and defined open problems and challenges [3, 23]. Dynamic access control and identity management are among the critical challenges that need to be addressed, because vehicles are transforming into digital systems where applications are provided by third party providers. The behaviour of such applications is dynamic and cannot be known in advance, so they cannot be trusted unconditionally. Therefore, such applications must be continuously verified and their internal and external communications and access to resources must be controlled and monitored [3, 7, 23].

Several researchers have proposed vehicular access control frameworks to address the aforementioned challenges. For instance, Hamad et al. [13] introduced an authentication and authorisation framework, based on a trust management model, that blocks or allows communications initiated by in-car applications Kim et al. [16] developed a decentralised access control framework by integrating an Attribute Based Access Control (ABAC) module in AUTOSAR adaptive platform [2]. Rumez et al. [22] also introduced a distributed ABAC tailored for automotive architectures. Both [16] and [22] focused on protecting Electronic Control Unit (ECU) diagnostic interfaces from unauthorised access. Likewise, Ammar et al. [1] developed an end-to-end Role Based Access Control (RBAC) mechanism that regulates access to On-Board Diagnostics-II (OBD-II) ports.

In spite of the significant contributions of the aforementioned works, context awareness, continuity of control and dynamic identity management remain overlooked. These aspects are crucial because vehicles are real-time mobile systems whose environmental conditions change continuously as they move. Thus, access to vehicular resources must be continuously monitored and controlled to ensure correct, safe and secure usage as circumstances change. The Principle of Least Privilege (PoLP) is also another challenge that need to be addressed in order to mitigate insider threats and eliminate the risk of unintended or malicious use of unnecessary capabilities. Furthermore, identities and privileges of subjects (i.e. drivers, passengers and applications) need to be continuously managed, monitored and updated according to contextual changes. To address these challenges, we present Usage Control System Plus (UCS+): an optimised, efficient and modular implementation of the Usage Control (UCON) model tailored for embedded and safety-critical systems such as smart cars. More importantly, we introduce SIUV: a vehicular Identity and Access Management (IAM) system that supports dynamic and stateful identity management, context-aware and continuous usage control, as well as the PoLP. SIUV incorporates a centralised stateful and dynamic Security Token Service (STS) that manages, authenticates and verifies identities, and issues privileges in exchange using Verifiable Credentials (VCs). The STS exchanges external VCs that hold identity claims about subjects with internal VCs that enclose subject privileges and capabilities. The STS uses policy-based decision making to that defines how to exchange identity claims with privileges taking environmental conditions into account. It also uses continuous monitoring and policy re-evaluation in order to manage the life-cycle of privileges and adapt to changing situations. Following the trend of adopting SOAs in vehicles, we also propose an SOA-based vehicular IAM architecture that consists of the aforementioned STS in addition to distributed UCS+ instances that protect localised in-car resources. We only focus on protecting internal vehicular resources, but SIUV can be extended to control external communications. To sum up, the main contributions of this work are as follows:

- **Dynamic and continuous authorisation:** optimised, efficient and modular implementation of the UCON model (Sect. 3.1)
- **Context-aware STS:** policy-based STS that manages a continuous life-cycle of privileges and adapts to changing situations (Sect. 3.2)
- **SIUV:** SOA-based dynamic and context-aware IAM system (Sect. 3.3)

The rest of this paper is organised as follows: Sect. 2 presents the technical background, namely the UCON model, the used policy language, and VCs. We describe UCS+ as well as SIUV architecture and STS in Sect. 3. An example use case and the evaluation of the system are discussed in Sect. 4. Finally, we define future directions and draw conclusions in Sect. 5.

2   Background

This section outlines the theoretical and technical background of SIUV.

2.1 Access and Usage Control

ABAC [14] is one of several access control models used to protect digital resources. It provides more flexibility and finer-grained control than preceding models as it manages access rights based on attributes of subjects, resources and the environment. ABAC's evaluation semantics, architecture, administration and policy language are defined in a comprehensive standardised reference model known as the eXtensible Access Control Markup Language (XACML) [20]. Although ABAC is fine-grained and flexible, it does not support continuity of access and mutability of attributes during evaluation. For this reason, the UCON model was proposed by Park and Sandhu [21] as a generalisation that goes beyond ABAC and other models to support context awareness, mutability of attributes and continuity of control. UCON continuously monitors attribute values and re-evaluates policies when a change occurs in order to guarantee that access rights still hold whilst usage is still in progress. The model categorises decision predicates as "*pre*", "*ongoing*" and "*post*". "*pre*" predicates are evaluated when an access request is made in order to decide whether to grant or deny access; "*ongoing*" predicates are evaluated during the time span of access, and they decide whether to revoke or retain access; and "*post*" predicates are evaluated after the end/revocation of access. In addition, UCON introduces obligations and advice; such that obligations are actions that must be fulfilled, whereas advice refers to actions that are recommended. The novelties of UCON make it an excellent baseline for dynamic applications, such as IoV, where the context changes continuously and resource usage is long-lived.

2.2 Abbreviated Language for Authorisation (ALFA)

Abbreviated Language For Authorisation (ALFA) [19] is a pseudocode domain-specific policy language that maps directly to XACML without adding any new semantics. It is much less verbose than XACML and thus more human readable and shorter in size. We use ALFA as the baseline policy language of the IAM because its compact size allows faster parsing and evaluation, which is imperative in safety-critical applications like smart vehicles. In addition, a policy-based IAM allows a dynamic and codeless behaviour that adapts according to the context.

2.3 Verifiable Credentials (VCs)

Verifiable Credentials are digital identifiers that provide cryptographic proofs to support the validity and reliability of a claim. The W3C VC data model [25] specifies the roles of claims, credentials, presentations etc. to help conform to a common structure. We construct such claims as privileges, which authorise a subject to use specified car resources. If we consider a VC as a presentation graph, it could consist of different credentials which are linked to each other contextually and packaged together to give a unique presentation by the holder. Access to car resources requires appropriate authorisation and should be controlled through credentials and continuously monitored through policies and usage-checks. A VC is suited to store such credentials because it is cryptographically verifiable and tamper-resistant. The set of claims that a VC makes on behalf of the issuer or multiple issuers can refer to a common or multiple subjects too, thus making the case for multiple identity properties be used for a distinct purpose. The VC information flow allows an issuer to issue credentials to the holder. The credentials are stored in a wallet and the holder decides whether to present the information in the form of a credential or presentation to the verifier. Every credential or presentation includes a proof mechanism that helps the verifier to verify the authenticity of the VC with the Verifiable Data Registry (VDR). We adhere to the W3C VC model [25] that specifies that every VC must include a proof mechanism to support the verifiability of the credentials. We used Ed25519 [4], a twisted Edwards curve digital signature algorithm, based on elliptic curve cryptography. As of today, Ed25519 is the most popular instance of EdDSA and is based on the Edwards Curve25519. Although there are many variants of Ed25519-original [4] such as NIST [8], IETF [15] etc. that specifies some refined security properties, we use the Ed25519 instance by LibSodium [10], a widely popular cryptographic library. Brendel et al. [5] discusses the game-based definitions of the security properties of the Ed25519 signature scheme and provably defines Ed25519-LibSodium [10] to be more resilient against key substitution attacks as well as message bound security than other Ed25519 instances [4,8,15].

3   SIUV

In this section, we describe the STS in addition to the architecture of SIUV.

3.1   Usage Control System Plus (UCS+)

Lazouski et al. [17] introduced a Usage Control System (UCS) prototype that realises the UCON model. They used a policy language that extends XACML semantics with UCON novelties and defines an architecture to enforce UCON policies. The language adds an implicit temporal state that is captured by classifying policy rules as *"pre"*, *"ongoing"* and *"post"*. UCS enforces continuous usage control by adding an authorisation session, continuous monitoring of attributes and re-evaluation of relevant policies when a change occurs. However, sessions in UCS are limited to the duration of active authorisations only. This is not sufficient for applications, such as smart vehicles, that include continuous interactions before or after access (e.g. ensure safe release of resources). This was among the motivations for our team to introduce UCS+: an enhanced and optimised UCON framework that conserves a full ABAC baseline and supports auxiliary evaluators like trust/confidence level. UCS+ extends authorisation sessions to cover continuous interactions and monitoring before granting access, during authorisation and during revocation of access in order to support pre- and post-usage interactions such as multi-factor authentication, safe revocation, etc. (e.g. safely stop the vehicle before completely revoking access). UCS+ uses ALFA - instead of XACML - as the baseline policy language, which results in a considerable improvement in performance and efficiency due to ALFA's compactness. UCS+ leverages the publish/subscribe pattern to maximize concurrency between policy parsing and evaluation, and attribute retrieval. This maximizes performance and minimizes the need for high network speeds or high computational resources. UCS+ also improves the ability to upgrade or substitute component services and migrate to a distributed deployment where necessary. We presented, in [11], a variant of UCS+ that integrates a trust level evaluation engine and is tailored for zero-trust Internet of Things (IoT) networks. In this paper, we describe another variant that is optimised for efficient continuous authorisation in embedded systems including automotive units. Figure 1 illustrates the architecture of UCS+, which consists of 8 major components as follows: `Context Handler` (CH) is the core component that receives access requests and manages authorisation workflows. `Message Bus` supports communications between components using the Publish/Subscribe (Pub/-Sub) pattern. `Policy Enforcement Point` (PEP) is the interface of UCS+ and the component that protects resources. It creates access requests, invokes the CH and enforces decisions. `Policy Decision Point` (PDP) is the component that evaluates policies and makes access decisions. `Policy Administration Point` (PAP) stores and manages policies and is used by the PDP to retrieve applicable policies. `Policy Information Point` (PIP) defines where to find attributes and how to monitor them. `PIP Registry` manages PIPs and defines which PIPs are responsible for which attributes. `Session Manager` (SM) manages and keeps track of all ongoing sessions to support the continuity of control. `Attribute Table` (AT) is a cache of attribute values and other metadata. `Attribute Retriever` (AR) is an auxiliary component in charge of querying and updating attribute values. `Obligation Manager` (OM) handles and manages policy and rule obligations.

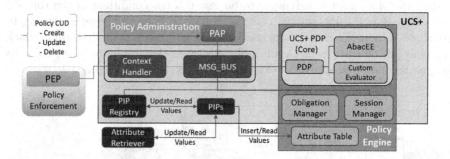

Fig. 1. UCS+ architecture

3.2   SIUV Security Token Service (STS)

In a typical STS, a particular set of privileges may be bound to specific attributes. Thus, all subjects that have these attributes will always have the same privileges regardless of the context. In addition, issued privileges do not change even if attributes change. This usually results in subjects being either overprivileged or underprivileged. To solve such issues, we introduce a stateful policy-based STS that exchanges external VCs about identity claims (identity VCs) with internal contextualised VCs that determine the privileges of the corresponding subject (privilege VCs). The STS model shares some common principles with UCS+, namely policy-based decision making, session-based continuous monitoring, as well as policy re-evaluation and revision. While UCS+ uses these concepts to manage authorisations, the STS uses them to improve the dynamicity as well as situation and change awareness throughout the life-cycle of identity claims and privileges. The STS employs policy-based decision making in order to dynamically exchange identity claims with privileges according to situation-aware policies. In addition, session-based continuous monitoring allows the STS to manage a continuous lifecylce of privileges starting from their issuance and lasting until their revocation or expiry. The privilege life-cycle may also last beyond revocation in order to support post-revocation interactions such as graceful revocation or safety actions. Finally, policy re-evaluation allows the STS to react to changes in identity claims or environmental conditions, which may result in privilege escalation, degradation or revocation. The architecture of the STS is shown in Fig. 2. The PEP receives identity VCs from the subject, verifies them using the Claims Verifier subcomponent, then sends a privileges request to the CH. The CH retrieves relevant policies from the PAP, collects required attributes from PIPs then invokes the SM to create a session and manage the life-cycle of the privileges to be issued. Thereupon, the CH invokes the PDP to evaluate the policies, then returns the evaluation decision to the Privileges Issuer subcomponent of PEP, which issues privilege VCs.

We use ALFA policies to determine how the STS issues privileges according to identity claims and environmental attributes. We particularly use rule obligations to determine the specific privileges that must be issued. Thus, each rule is used to define a set of privileges to be issued if the conditions of the rule are met. This allows a fine-grained control on how to issue privileges according to attribute values. We use the "permitUnlessDeny" combining algorithm, which combines all obligations from all applicable rules that evaluate into permit as long as no deny rule apply. An example policy is shown in Listing 1.1.

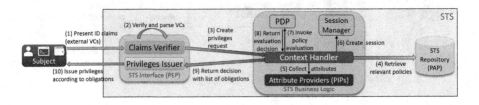

Fig. 2. SIUV STS architecture

3.3 SIUV Architecture

In this section, we present the architecture of SIUV as shown in Fig. 3. The STS runs on the general-purpose computer gateway, whereas UCS+ instances run on the ECUs that they protect. The VDR is a logical component and is implemented as a distributed hashtable. Since Smart-car Identity management and Usage control system based on Verifiable credentials (SIUV) is based on SOA, all communications use the Ethernet protocol. Moreover, AUTOSAR specifies the SOME/IP[1] protocol that supports TLS, thus communications between SIUV components are protected. Furthermore, additional features, such as end-to-end encryption[2], can be used to enhance the protection between components. We describe the components that support dynamic and stateful identity management, and context-aware and continuous usage control of localised in-car resources.

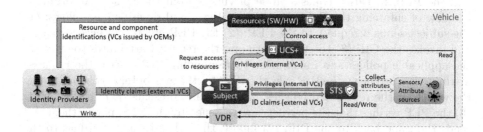

Fig. 3. SIUV architecture

Identity Providers (IdPs) are authorities that issue identity VCs about drivers, passengers, applications or in-car resources. An example of an issuer is the department of motor vehicles that issues driving licenses, or an Original Equipment Manufacturer (OEM) that asserts claims about an ECU.

A subject may be a driver, a passenger, an application or a resource that needs to access other resources, and is represented by a digital wallet that holds the subject's VCs. The digital wallet interacts with the issuers and the STS to present/obtain VCs, and with UCS+ instances to request access to resources.

The VDR is a distributed hashtable that holds revocation lists and issuers' public keys. The VDR may also be used to store other relevant information like metadata about proofs or schemas and structures of VCs.

The STS is the core component that provides dynamic identity and privilege management of subjects. It exchanges external identity VCs with internal privilege VCs. The combination of VCs and the STS protects against identity theft as privileges issued by the STS are cryptographically verifiable and cannot be manipulated. This also allows *unlinkability* and maximizes privacy of subjects because they do not need to share identity information with the OEMs of the vehicle's components. It runs on the centralized general-purpose gateway, which has enough computational power to support the functionalities of the STS as discussed in Sect. 4.2.

---

[1] https://www.autosar.org/fileadmin/user_upload/standards/foundation/1-0/
  AUTOSAR_PRS_SOMEIPProtocol.pdf.

[2] https://www.escrypt.com/en/news-events/autosar_security.

Localised UCS+ instances are used to protect resources such as domain controllers or ECUs. However, they do *not* control the low level behaviour of such components as this imposes a safety risk. Rather, they only control the usage of high level APIs, services and functions exposed by such components. Localised UCS+ instances make usage decisions according to resource and localised context attributes as well as privileges issued by the STS. Thus, the STS handles the global context of the whole vehicle, while localised UCS+ instances manage localised authorisation contexts of individual components. To enforce the PoLP, we modified the physical architecture of UCS+ by making the PEP act as the AR of the PIP. Therefore, the PIP invokes the PEP to collect the required privileges and the PEP, in turn, requests these privileges from the wallet. Accordingly, the flow of enforcing the PoLP is shown in Fig. 4 and described as follows: (1) the subject sends a request to the PEP; (2) the PEP creates an access request and invokes the CH; (3) the CH determines the required attributes to evaluate the applicable polices and invokes the corresponding PIPs; (4) if the required attribute is a privilege, the PIP asks the PEP for the attribute; (5) the PEP asks the wallet for the required privileges and the wallet presents them if they exist; (6) the PEP verifies that the privileges were issued by the STS, parses them and sends the value back to the PIP; (7) finally, the PIP returns the values to the CH, which invokes the PDP to evaluate the policy and make a decision.

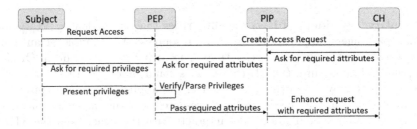

Fig. 4. Sequence diagram of enforcing the PoLP

3.4 Revocation of VCs

When an IdP revokes an external VC, such as a driving license, the IdP updates the revocation list in the VDR. The update then gets communicated to all participating entities through the VDR. If the STS is using the updated VC in an active session, then a policy re-evaluation will be triggered in that session. Based on the policy re-evaluation, the STS may revoke all internal VCs that were issued when the revoked external VC was still valid. When the STS revokes internal VCs, it also updates the VDR, thus the update gets communicated to all localised UCS+ instances. This triggers a re-evaluation in the UCS+ sessions that are using the revoked internal VC, and the corresponding access decisions will be updated according to the policy re-evaluation. We assume that OEMs define safety procedures in the policies they install on localised UCS+ instances so that revocation of access does not cause safety threats. For instance, OEMs may define policy obligations that safely stop the vehicle before completely revoking access or delay revocation of access until the vehicle stops.

4 Experimental Evaluation

In this section, we describe two use-cases and present the outcome of the experimental evaluation of SIUV.

4.1 Use Case

One possible use case of the proposed IAM system is travelling between the borders of two countries where driving rules are different. For instance, the minimum age to drive is 17 in Denmark and 18 in Sweden. Thus, we assume a 17-year-old driver with a valid driving license in Denmark. The driver presents the license and ID credentials to the STS in the car and the STS issues a "canDrive" privilege. This privilege is then used by localised UCS+ instances to grant access to the necessary components that allow the driver to drive the car. As soon as the car crosses the borders to Sweden, the location attribute is updated and the STS re-evaluates relevant policies. In this case, the STS finds that the "canDrive" privilege is not valid anymore, so it revokes it. This is demonstrated in the non-inclusive policies of Listing 1.1. The localised UCS+ instances receive the revocation update from the VDR, and revoke access to the protected components in a safely manner. However, policies of localised UCS+ instances may include obligations that can take safety-related actions upon the revocation of privileges as shown in Listing 1.2. This use case demonstrates that SIUV supports both centralised and distributed control. Centralised control is performed by the STS that monitors the global context and verifies credentials that are relevant to all resources. Distributed control is enforced by localised UCS+ instances that monitor local contexts relevant to the protected resources only. SIUV allows the car to monitor both global and local contexts and react accordingly. Alternative solutions that only support centralised control cannot react to changes that are only relevant to a particular resource. On the other hand, solutions that only support distributed control introduce a performance overhead because global context and attributes have to be monitored by all nodes.

A car rental service is also another relevant use-case of SIUV as car owners can restrict the use of their cars according to rental agreements. For instance, a car owner can restrict the mobility of their rented car to a specific city or specific area. Thus, if the driver goes beyond the restricted area, SIUV can warn the driver or perhaps engage the autopilot to safely stop the car as defined by policies. A car owner can also use SIUV to limit the maximum speed that can be reached by the driver who rents the car. Moreover, a car owner can define a specific time period during which the car can be used by the driver according to the rental agreement. Owners can also define policies that deny access to resources that are not needed by drivers who rent the car (e.g. diagnostic interfaces).

Listing 1.1. STS policies

```
policySet privileges {                                                          1
    apply permitUnlessDeny                                                      2
    policy driver {                                                             3
        target clause Attributes.isRegistered                                   4
        apply firstApplicable                                                   5
        rule driver_dk {                                                        6
            target clause Attributes.license.expiry > time.now()               7
                    and Attributes.license.issuer == ''borger.dk''             8
                    and Attributes.location == ''Denmark''                     9
            condition Attributes.age > 17 and Attributes.ucs.step == ''ongoing''  10
            permit                                                             11
            on permit {                                                        12
                obligation canDrive { command = ''issue_privileges''           13
                                     canDrive = true }                         14
        }}                                                                     15
        rule driver_dk_eu {                                                    16
            target clause Attributes.license.expiry > time.now()              17
                    and Attributes.license.issuer == ''borger.dk''            18
            condition Attributes.age > 18 and Attributes.ucs.step == ''ongoing''  19
            permit                                                            20
            on permit {                                                       21
                obligation canDrive { command = ''issue_privileges''          22
                                     canDrive = true }                        23
        }}                                                                    24
        rule revoke {                                                         25
            deny                                                              26
            on deny {                                                         27
                obligation canDrive { command = ''revoke_privileges''         28
                                     canDrive = false }                       29
    }}};                                                                      30
    policy wiperControl { ... };                                              31
    };                                                                        32
```

Listing 1.2. STS policies

```
policy engineControl {                                                        1
    apply firstApplicable                                                     2
    target clause Attributes.resourceId == ''engine''                         3
    rule drive {                                                              4
        target clause Attributes.api == ''engineAPI'' and Attributes.action == ''startEngine''  5
        condition Attributes.canDrive == true and Attributes.ucs.step == ''ongoing''  6
        permit                                                                7
    }                                                                         8
    rule revoke {                                                             9
        condition Attributes.ucs.step == ''post''                            10
        deny                                                                 11
        on deny {                                                            12
            obligation safeStop { command = ''autopilot''                    13
                                 action = ''safe_stop'' }                    14
    }}};                                                                     15
```

4.2   Test Cases

We implemented UCS+ and SIUV using C++ and evaluated them on a computer
running Ubuntu 20.04LTS Linux OS with Core i7-9850H CPU. Modern car-
ECU specifications, such as [24], include high-end processors and higher memory,
which closely compares to the computational resources we use in our simulation,
since UCS+ is highly optimised for similar systems as mentioned in Sect. 3.1.

We measured the time required to evaluate STS and UCS+ policies as well as the overhead cost of an increasing number of attributes. We also measured the time required to issue and verify VCs as well as the effect of the number of claims on the issuance and verification time. Finally, we evaluated the performance penalty of enforcing the PoLP especially with an increasing number of privileges. The results are shown in Fig. 5 and discussed in the following subsections.

Performance of Policy Evaluation in UCS+: For this evaluation, we ran five tests with an increasing number of attributes that need to be collected by PIPs. It is necessary to note that this usually depends on the PIPs and how they collect attribute values. For instance, if a PIP needs to retrieve an attribute value over the network, then the network delay would affect the policy evaluation time. However, UCS+ caches attributes in the AT, so only policy evaluations that need an uncached attribute value would be affected by such overhead. For this reason, we only measure the time required for policy evaluation when the attributes are already cached. We ran each test 1000 rounds and observed a standard deviation of 19.2 μs. Table 1 and Fig. 5 show the average time required for policy evaluation in each test. The results demonstrate that our implementation is lightweight, very efficient and highly optimised, which make it suitable for embedded and safety-critical systems like vehicles.

Performance Evaluation of Issuing and Verifying VCs: We ran five different test cases with an increasing number claims. In each case, we ran the test 1000 rounds and computed the average time and the standard deviation. The observed standard deviation was 13.8 μs and the results are shown in Table 2. The results show that the number of claims does not have a significant effect on the efficiency of issuing and verifying VCs. In addition, they show that the time required to issue or verify a typical VC is less than 0.5ms. This is because we used Ed25519 digital signatures, which are faster than any ECDSA or EdDSA instances in terms of signature generation and verification.

Performance Evaluation of the PoLP Enforcement: The implementation of the PoLP includes back and forth communication between the wallet and the PEP, and between the PEP and the PIP. Undoubtedly, this introduces a performance overhead especially because the PIP asks for privileges sequentially and synchronously. To measure this overhead, we conducted 4 test cases with an increasing number of privileges. The average time to enforce the PoLP was computed as well as the standard deviation after running each test case 1000 times. We noted a standard deviation of 44.7 μs. The results presented in Table 3 show that the overhead increases significantly and linearly as the number of required privileges increases. However, the number of privileges required for a specific action is not expected to be high, so such overhead can be tolerated. Nonetheless, we plan to explore more efficient approaches to enforce the PoLP.

Table 1. Average time to evaluate ALFA policies as the number of attributes increases

Number of attributes	1	3	5	10	20
Average time to evaluate a policy (in μs)	9	11	18	27	29

Table 2. Average time to issue and verify a VC as function of the number of claims

No. of claims → / Avg. time (μs) ↓	1	3	5	10	20
Issue a VC (μs)	86	97	105	136	196
Verify a VC (μs)	115	119	125	142	172

Table 3. Average time to enforce the PoLP as function of privilege number

No. of privileges → / Avg. time (μs) ↓	1	3	5	10
Enforce the PoLP	300	952	1554	3136

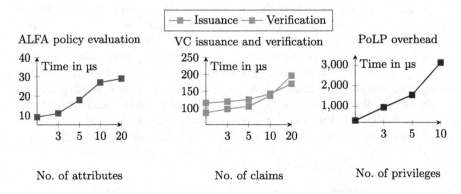

Fig. 5. Performance results of issuing and verifying VCs, and enforcing the PoLP

5   Conclusion and Future Work

We demonstrated the usage of VCs and UCON to support dynamic and stateful identity management and continuous usage control in smart vehicles. We specifically introduced a highly efficient implementation of the UCON model designated as UCS+. We also introduced a centralised STS that exchanges identity VCs with privilege VCs that determine what subjects are allowed to do inside the vehicle. We also proposed an SOA-based architecture for a vehicular IAM that uses a centralised STS for identity management and distributed UCS+ instances to protect resources. SIUV addresses the problem of dynamic identity management as well as statefull access control in smart vehicles whose contexts change continuously. The evaluation of the proposed system showed promising results and significant improvements over similar works.

Future directions should aim at providing anonymity or pseudonymity and maximizing privacy of the subject such that issuers or verifiers cannot identify the subject properties. Particularly, we plan to investigate the addition of a negotiation protocol between the wallet and other components in order to regulate the disclosure of credentials and privileges. In addition, we intend to explore selective disclosure and zero knowledge schemes as well as predicate proofs. This allows to minimise identity information sharing while still being able to create a fully functional ecosystem of multi-party credential exchange and identity verification. We also intend to use JSON-LD, to interpret and serialize linked data in JSON and be able to support signature sets, signature chaining etc.

References

1. Ammar, M., Janjua, H., Thangarajan, A., Crispo, B., Hughes, D.: Securing the onboard diagnostics port (OBD-II) in vehicles. In: 8th Embedded Security in Cars (ESCAR USA) (2020)
2. AUTOSAR: Explanation of Adaptive Platform Design, March 2019. https://www.autosar.org/fileadmin/user_upload/standards/adaptive/19-11/AUTOSAR_EXP_PlatformDesign.pdf
3. Bernardini, C., Asghar, M.R., Crispo, B.: Security and privacy in vehicular communications: challenges and opportunities. Veh. Commun. **10**, 13–28 (2017)
4. Bernstein, D.J., Duif, N., Lange, T., Schwabe, P., Yang, B.-Y.: High-speed high-security signatures. In: Preneel, B., Takagi, T. (eds.) CHES 2011. LNCS, vol. 6917, pp. 124–142. Springer, Heidelberg (2011). https://doi.org/10.1007/978-3-642-23951-9_9
5. Brendel, J., Cremers, C., Jackson, D., Zhao, M.: The provable security of ed25519: theory and practice. In: 2021 IEEE Symposium on Security and Privacy (SP), vol. 1, pp. 715–732 (2021). https://doi.org/10.1109/SP40001.2021.00042. ISSN: 2375-1207
6. Burkacky, O., Deichmann, J., Doll, G., Knochenhauer, C.: Rethinking car software and electronics architecture, February 2018. https://www.mckinsey.com/industries/automotive-and-assembly/our-insights/rethinking-car-software-and-electronics-architecture
7. Burkacky, O., Deichmann, J., Klein, B., Pototzky, K., Scherf, G.: Cybersecurity in automotive: mastering the challenge, June 2020. https://www.mckinsey.com/industries/automotive-and-assembly/our-insights/cybersecurity-in-automotive-mastering-the-challenge
8. Chen, L., Moody, D., Regenscheid, A., Randall, K.: Recommendations for discrete logarithm-based cryptography: elliptic curve domain parameters. Technical report, National Institute of Standards and Technology (2019)
9. Deichmann, J., Klein, B., Scherf, G., Rupert, S.: The race for cybersecurity: protecting the connected car in the era of new regulation, October 2019. https://mckinsey.com/industries/automotive-and-assembly/our-insights/the-race-for-cybersecurity-protecting-the-connected-car-in-the-era-of-new-regulation
10. Denis, F.: libsodium: a modern and easy-to-use crypto library (2017). https://libsodium.gitbook.io/doc/
11. Dimitrakos, T., et al.: Trust aware continuous authorization for zero trust in consumer internet of things. In: 2020 IEEE 19th International Conference on Trust, Security and Privacy in Computing and Communications (TrustCom), pp. 1801–1812 (2020). https://doi.org/10.1109/TrustCom50675.2020.00247
12. Dürrwang, J., Braun, J., Rumez, M., Kriesten, R.: Security evaluation of an airbag-ECU by reusing threat modeling artefacts. In: 2017 International Conference on Computational Science and Computational Intelligence (CSCI), pp. 37–43. IEEE (2017)
13. Hamad, M., Prevelakis, V.: Secure APIs for applications in microkernel-based systems. In: ICISSP, pp. 553–558 (2017)

14. Hu, V.C., et al.: Guide to attribute based access control (ABAC) definition and considerations (draft). NIST Special Publication 800(162) (2013)
15. Josefsson, S., Liusvaara, I.: RFC8032: Edwards-curve digital signature algorithm (EdDSA). Request for Comments, IETF (2017)
16. Kim, D.K., Song, E., Yu, H.: Introducing attribute-based access control to AUTOSAR. Technical report, SAE Technical Paper (2016)
17. Lazouski, A., Martinelli, F., Mori, P.: A prototype for enforcing usage control policies based on XACML. In: Fischer-Hübner, S., Katsikas, S., Quirchmayr, G. (eds.) TrustBus 2012. LNCS, vol. 7449, pp. 79–92. Springer, Heidelberg (2012). https://doi.org/10.1007/978-3-642-32287-7_7
18. Miller, C., Valasek, C.: Remote exploitation of an unaltered passenger vehicle. Black Hat USA 2015, p. 91 (2015)
19. OASIS: Abbreviated language for authorization Version 1.0 (2015). https://bit.ly/2UP6Jza
20. OASIS: eXtensible Access Control Markup Language (XACML) Version 3.0 Plus Errata 01 (2017). http://docs.oasis-open.org/xacml/3.0/xacml-3.0-core-spec-en.html
21. Park, J., Sandhu, R.: The UCONABC usage control model. ACM Trans. Inf. Syst. Secur. (TISSEC) **7**(1), 128–174 (2004)
22. Rumez, M., Duda, A., Gründer, P., Kriesten, R., Sax, E.: Integration of attribute-based access control into automotive architectures. In: 2019 IEEE Intelligent Vehicles Symposium (IV), pp. 1916–1922. IEEE (2019)
23. Rumez, M., Grimm, D., Kriesten, R., Sax, E.: An overview of automotive service-oriented architectures and implications for security countermeasures. IEEE Access **8**, 221852–221870 (2020)
24. Samsung: Automotive Processor Exynos Auto V9. https://www.samsung.com/semiconductor/minisite/exynos/products/automotiveprocessor/exynos-auto-v9/
25. Sporny, M., Longley, D., Chadwick, D.: Verifiable credentials data model 1.0. Technical report, W3C, November 2019. https://www.w3.org/TR/vc-data-model/
26. Wouters, L., Marin, E., Ashur, T., Gierlichs, B., Preneel, B.: Fast, furious and insecure: passive keyless entry and start systems in modern supercars. In: IACR Transactions on Cryptographic Hardware and Embedded Systems, pp. 66–85 (2019)

Vulnerability Management

A Performance Assessment of Free-to-Use Vulnerability Scanners - Revisited

Ricardo Araújo[1], António Pinto[2,4], and Pedro Pinto[3(✉)]

[1] Instituto Politécnico de Viana do Castelo, Viana do Castelo, Portugal
riaraujo@ipvc.pt
[2] CIICESI, ESTG, Politécnico do Porto, Porto, Portugal
apinto@inesctec.pt
[3] Instituto Politécnico de Viana do Castelo IPVC, ISMAI & INESC TEC,
Viana do Castelo and Porto, Portugal
pedropinto@estg.ipvc.pt
[4] CRACS & INESC TEC, Porto, Portugal

Abstract. Vulnerability scanning tools can help secure the computer networks of organisations. Triggered by the release of the Tsunami vulnerability scanner by Google, the authors analysed and compared the commonly used, free-to-use vulnerability scanners. The performance, accuracy and precision of these scanners are quite disparate and vary accordingly to the target systems. The computational, memory and network resources required be these scanners also differ. We present a recent and detailed comparison of such tools that are available for use by organisations with lower resources such as small and medium-sized enterprises.

Keywords: Vulnerability scanning · Comparison · Open source · Tsunami

1 Introduction

Hackers are launching more sophisticated attacks on every possible weakness of computer networks and systems [19]. Vulnerability scanning tools are automated tools that scan applications and networks, trying to identify security vulnerabilities, such as outdated or non-patched software. On the one hand, a systematic vulnerability scanning procedure tends to be more efficient in protecting an organisation [4], be it a manual or an automated test. On the other, a manual security testing requires more resources (human and financial), hampering its adoption in small and medium-sized enterprises (SMEs). As an alternative, open source or free-to-use automated vulnerability scanning tools may be used by organisations to better improve their cybersecurity resilience, even in the case of SMEs.

The detection efficiency of vulnerability scanning tools is heavily dependent on their vulnerability database. A large database will enable a more thorough detection. New vulnerabilities are discovered frequently, which means that these tools

© IFIP International Federation for Information Processing 2021
Published by Springer Nature Switzerland AG 2021
A. Jøsang et al. (Eds.): SEC 2021, IFIP AICT 625, pp. 53–65, 2021.
https://doi.org/10.1007/978-3-030-78120-0_4

are only efficient if they maintain a steady pace of updates to their vulnerability databases. One would expect that, if such a tool is developed by a large company or organisation, its vulnerability database would also be a large one, it would see frequent updates and would be a single tool that would be sufficient for SMEs. We assume that SMEs will have a small in-house support team with only a periodic availability to pursue vulnerability assessments.

More recently, the Tsunami[1] vulnerability scanner was made open source by Google and, despite being clearly marked as a non-official product, it triggered the assessment work described herein. In short, the authors focused on answering the following questions:

- Q1: What is the most efficient, free-to-use, vulnerability scanning tool currently available?
- Q2: How does Tsunami compare to similar tools currently available?
- Q3: Is Tsunami well suited to be used by SMEs?

This paper is organised in sections. Section 2 presents the related work, clarifying the differences from the work herein to theirs. Section 3 presents the technical features of the selected vulnerability scanners and the test-bed designed to compare and assess them. Section 4 compares the selected tools and presents results and our analysis. Finally, Sect. 5 concludes the work.

2 Related Work

There are research works that focus on comparing tools that evaluate a specific type of vulnerability, such as web application scanning tools. Examples being [3,8–10,13,15,16]. Others focus on one specific problem, such as SQL injection attacks [2].

In [20], the authors compare free and commercial off the shelf vulnerability scanning tools. Despite assessing a large set of such tools and considering both functionality and the possibility of correlating the outcomes of the tools with additional information. While valid research at the time, it is now mostly outdated. Some of the referenced tools are no longer available.

In [12], the authors also present a large quantitative comparison of vulnerability scanning tools. Their focus was on the direct output of the tools or, in other words, the number of vulnerabilities these tools identify. They focused on functionality and on accuracy. Our work differs by focusing on tools to be usable by SMEs. Moreover, newer tools were launched, not available at the time, some being open source and free-to-use tools. Additionally, they did not perform resource usage comparison. They conclude that some tools are better at detecting vulnerabilities of Windows systems, others at detecting vulnerabilities of Linux systems.

In a more recent work [14], the authors presented a performance-based comparison between two tools: Nessus and Retina. They selected these two because they considered them as the most used free vulnerability scanning tools. Of the

---

[1] https://github.com/google/tsunami-security-scanner.

two, Retina has now been discontinued by its developer, which issued a notification stating its end of life by December 31, 2019. We aim to perform a similar work to the one of Kushe but being a more up to date, more complete and more thorough one.

Similar work was presented in [5], where the authors opted for comparing a dedicated, hardware-based commercial tool against a open source, free-to-use, software-based tool. While they conclude that the commercial solution is faster at presenting results, they did not assess the efficiency in their findings. Moreover, it was a small comparison of just two tools.

In [11], the author questioned the performance of vulnerability scanning tools as a method to remedy the security issues these tools identify. He concludes that manual effort will always be needed to reach a complete accuracy. Moreover, the author concludes that the remediation guidelines outputted by the tools is very cumbersome to address.

In our work, we focused on the use of larger spectrum vulnerability scanning tools as these would require less time and resources to implement, while still being able to detect web application vulnerabilities. Moreover, the research works that compare vulnerability scanning tools have not been revisited recently.

3   Experimentation and Setup

A Vulnerability Scanner is a standalone application or program using a Graphical User Interface (GUI) or a Command Line Interface (CLI) with procedures to detect vulnerabilities and exploits in a given machine that is being analysed. These procedures and their effectiveness depends on multiple factors such as Operating System (OS), installed programs, existing services, their versions and configurations. Thus, the scanners rely on signatures of known vulnerabilities and exploits and either maintain them in a local database that maybe updated online or require a set of detection plugins or scripts that must be installed before scanning.

Given the research questions Q1 and Q2, the selected set of tools to analyse was narrowed to the following: OpenVAS [1], Nessus [18], Nexpose [17], and Tsunami [6]. Tsunami has been made available on GitHub in June of 2020. To answer all the three questions, a test-bed was designed and setup and the features of the selected scanners were compared.

3.1   Scanners Technical Features

Table 1 presents the selected vulnerability scanners and their main properties regarding their license, the availability of their source code, their mode of operation and the update process of their vulnerability lists. All selected vulnerability scanners are free-to-use. Nessus Essentials is free for personal use but limits scanning to 16 different IPs. Nexpose offers a 1 year trial, after which turns into a paid tool. Nexpose was included in the current analysis to detect if there is a significant difference between free-to-use and paid scanners. OpenVAS and Tsunami provide their versions as open source. OpenVAS, Nessus and Nexpose use a GUI while Tsunami operates in the CLI environment. Regarding the update process, OpenVAS, Nessus and Nexpose have a local database with the vulnerabilities signatures that are updated online, while Tsunami uses detection plugins.

Table 1. Selected vulnerability scanners

	License and source code			Operation		Vulnerabilities list update		
	Free to use	Trial period	Open source	GUI	CLI	Local DB	Online DB	Plugins or scripts
OpenVAS	x		x	x		x	x	
Nessus	(x)			x		x	x	
Nexpose	(x)	x		x		x	x	
Tsunami	x		x		x			x

The output of the selected vulnerability scanners is a PDF file with a non-standard organisation containing a set of potential vulnerabilities identified by a Common Vulnerabilities and Exposures (CVE) identification. The list of these vulnerabilities and their CVE ID is maintained publicly [7]. Each CVE record comprises the identification number, a description, and at least one public reference. These CVE records are sent to National Vulnerability Database (NVD) that extends their classification with additional information, severity scores and impact ratings. The severity scores are expressed by Common Vulnerability Scoring System (CVSS), an open framework used for communicating the characteristics and severity of vulnerabilities. The score is obtained by using three metric groups: Base, Temporal, and Environmental. The Base metrics produce a score ranging from 0 to 10, which can then be modified by the scoring of the Temporal and of the Environmental metrics.

3.2   Test-Bed Design and Setup

A test-bed was setup in order to test and evaluate all the vulnerability scanning tools identified in Sect. 3.1. The test-bed topology is depicted in Fig. 1 and comprises multiple virtual machines hosted on a laptop with an Intel core i7-4710HQ CPU @ 2.50 GHz processor, 12 GB of RAM, a 256 GB SSD, running the Windows 10 64bit OS. The use of virtualisation was selected in order to produce comparable results. The VirtualBox 6.1 was the adopted virtualisation solution. Five virtual machines were deployed, one to act as the scanner, and the remaining 4 to act as targets. Kali Linux was selected due to the simple installation process of the required tools for scanning. In order to minimise impacts of the installation of the tools, after the initial setup of the Kali Linux OS, a snapshot was taken and all tools were installed over that initial snapshot. This was made to maintain the same exact configuration on the system, prior to each tool installation. While the tests were executed, the target virtual hosts were disconnected from the Internet.

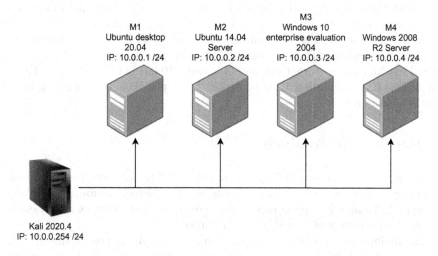

Fig. 1. Test-bed topology

The targets were selected in order to be as diverse as possible. Of the 4 virtual machines, two were Linux-based and two were Windows-based. Each set of two machines per platform were selected to represent a client version and a server version of each platform. Android targets were also considered at the beginning but, because the first tests showed that, due to strict firewall configurations, no result were reported by the selected tools, Android targets were dropped. Thus, the set of target virtual machines comprised:

– a Ubuntu Desktop 20.04 (as M1);
– a Ubuntu Server 14.04 (as M2);
– a Windows 10 Enterprise (as M3);
– a Windows 2008 R2 Server (as M4).

Of note is the fact that the M1 and M3 targets are standard installations of the respective OS, whereas M2 and M4 were deployed using metasploitable, version 3^2. The metasploitable virtual machines are ones that are specifically setup with older software in order to have a large number of security vulnerabilities. As our focus was also on assessing the detection capabilities of the scanning tools, the later virtual machines were considered as the most relevant to test. These were tested without modifications or configurations, aside from disabling the MySQL server of M2 and enabling ping replies on M4. MySQL was disabled because to the excessive time taken by the Tsunami password brute-forcing with

---

² https://github.com/rapid7/metasploitable3.

Ncrack. Ping was enabled to ease the use of scanning tools that first checked the targets liveliness with a ping request.

A bash script was developed in order to monitor and record the execution time (duration), RAM memory and CPU usage on the Kali virtual machine, in a systematic way. For the network usage monitoring, on the same Kali virtual machine, and whenever a vulnerability scan was started, the **tcpdump** command was executed with arguments to identify the packets sent by the Kali virtual machine to the target machine, i.e. using 10.0.0.154 as the source IP and 10.0.0.X as the destination IP, where the "X" is the IP address of each target presented in Fig. 1.

4   Results and Analysis

Using the topology shown in Fig. 1, four vulnerability scanning tasks were executed per each of the four target machines, and per each of the four vulnerability scanners. In total, 64 vulnerability scans were conducted. Average and standard deviation values were obtained per each scanner.

The preliminary results shown that Tsunami was the fastest, using the least resources. Upon further evaluation, we came to the conclusion that, currently, the Tsunami tool does not contain enough vulnerability detection plugins and because of this, it detects almost no vulnerabilities and requires low resources to do so. This reasoning motivated us to not include Tsunami in the figures of this section.

Figure 2 shows the average duration of the performed scan tasks. Here, one can observe that the standard targets (M1 and M3) are scanned fastest by all tools due to having the least vulnerabilities and the least services available through the network. On the other hand, M2 and M4, being metasploitable-based targets, took the most time to scan. Other observation that can be made is that, of the three shown, Nessus was the fastest one and OpenVAS was the slowest one. OpenVAS took almost 5 times more to scan M4 when compared to the other tools.

Figure 3 a) shows the average network usage in terms of the number of packets, per second, sent by the Kali machine to the target machines. All vulnerability scanning tools report more network usage when scanning the M2 target, which runs a metasploitable Ubuntu Server. This is expected as this target is the one with the most services available through the network. When comparing tools, OpenVAS is the tool that uses more network resources, followed by the Nessus tool.

Figure 3 b) shows the average CPU used by the Kali machine during execution of the different tools. The tool that uses most CPU is the OpenVAS. This was expected as this tool also used more network resources and took the most time to complete. Nonetheless, the overall CPU usage of all tools is very low, maxing below 3,5%. Worthy of note, and because of being so low average values, is the fact that this resulted was the one that has shown the greater standard deviation.

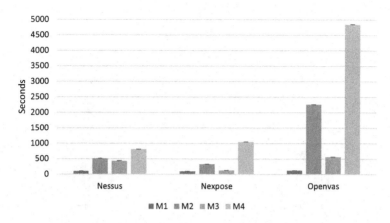

Fig. 2. Scan duration in seconds

Figure 3 c) shows the average memory used by the Kali machine during execution of the different tools. One conclusion that can be made is that all tools use a similar amount of memory independently of the scanned target. The tool that requires the most amount of memory is Nexpose, using almost four times the memory needed by the other two tools.

Table 2. Vulnerability identification results for M2

Vulnerability	CVSS	Nessus	Nexpose	OpenVAS
CVE-2010-1574	10 (v2)		FP	
CVE-2015-3306	10 (v2)	TP		TP
CVE-2015-5377	9.8			FP
CVE-2017-3167	9.8	FP	FP	
CVE-2017-3169	9.8		FP	
CVE-2017-7679	9.8		FP	
CVE-2018-1312	9.8		TP	
CVE-2018-5337	9.8			FP
CVE-2018-5341	9.8			FP
CVE-2019-12815	9.8		TP	
CVE-2017-9788	9.1		FP	
CVE-2016-5387	8.1		TP	
CVE-2017-15715	8.1		TP	

Tables 2 and 3 show the vulnerability identification results achieved by the different tools. In this tables, only vulnerabilities with an assigned CVE identification were considered. Vulnerabilities with an assigned CVE identification are published online and known by all vulnerability scanner tools, thus becoming a ground truth to which results of others tools can be compared. A list comprising all vulnerabilities reported by all tools, separated by target (M2 and M4), was

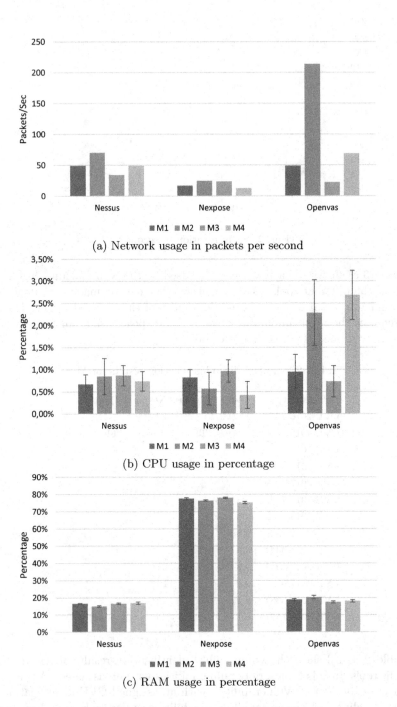

(a) Network usage in packets per second

(b) CPU usage in percentage

(c) RAM usage in percentage

Fig. 3. Network, CPU and RAM usage

compiled. The real presence of each vulnerability was then manually confirmed. In order to avoid such manual verification to become cumbersome, the full list of vulnerabilities was reduced to the ones that presented a score above 7.5, based on CVSS in version 3, plus the ones that presented a maximum score of 10, independently of the CVSS version.

Table 3. Vulnerability identification results for M4

Vulnerability	CVSS	Nessus	Nexpose	OpenVAS
CVE-2010-0219	10 (v2)			TP
CVE-2010-1574	10 (v2)		FP	
CVE-2012-2688	10 (v2)	TP		
CVE-2015-1635	10 (v2)		TP	TP
CVE-2017-7213	10 (v2)			TP
CVE-2015-5377	9.8			FP
CVE-2015-8249	9.8			TP
CVE-2017-11346	9.8			TP
CVE-2017-3167	9.8	FP	FP	
CVE-2017-3169	9.8	TP		
CVE-2017-7668	9.8	TP		
CVE-2017-7679	9.8	TP		
CVE-2018-5337	9.8			FP
CVE-2018-5338	9.8			TP
CVE-2018-5339	9.8			TP
CVE-2018-5341	9.8			FP
CVE-2020-10189	9.8	TP		
CVE-2017-5648	9.1			TP
CVE-2017-9788	9.1	TP		
CVE-2016-10012	7.8			TP

In order to better evaluate the vulnerability scanning tools, both accuracy and precision of the detected vulnerabilities was analysed. For this specific analysis, only M2 and M4 related results were considered. Reason being that these were the ones that had multiple identifiable vulnerabilities. The reader should recall that M1 and M3 are standard, recent and fully updated installations of Ubuntu and Windows 10, respectively.

Equations 1 and 2 were used to calculate accuracy and precision, respectively. These equations consider the number of True Positives (TP), False Positives (FP) and False Negatives (FN). TP being the number of vulnerabilities identified that are really present in the target. FP being the number of vulnerabilities identified that are not present in the target. FN being the number of vulnerabilities that are present in the target but not identified.

$$\text{Accuracy } (\%) = \frac{\text{TP}}{\text{TP} + \text{FP} + \text{FN}} (\times 100) \qquad (1)$$

$$\text{Precision } (\%) = \frac{\text{TP}}{\text{TP} + \text{FP}}(\times 100) \tag{2}$$

In a more straightforward way, with Eq. 1 we expect to evaluate if a tool is capable of detecting all available vulnerabilities within a target. i.e. its accuracy. With Eq. 2 we expect to evaluate if a tool only detects existing vulnerabilities and not false ones, i.e. its precision. The results shown in Fig. 4 resulted from calculating these equations from the data of the vulnerability identification results shown in Tables 2 and 3. From these results, the overall obtained accuracy is at most 50% for the case of the M4 scan with OpenVAS, this means that multiple vulnerabilities were not detected by all tools. In terms of accuracy we can see that OpenVAS and Nessus performed better for M4, a Windows machine, while Nexpose was more accurate for M2, a Ubuntu machine. In terms of precision, the overall better performing tools was OpenVAS with 100% accuracy for M2, and almost 80% for M4. The least precise tool was Nexpose, with 50% accuracy for both M2 and M4.

After evaluating the performance, resource usage, accuracy and precision of the selected vulnerability scanning tools, conclusions regarding the three questions listed in Sect. 1 can be drawn.

- Q1: What is the most efficient, free-to-use, vulnerability scanning tool currently available?

The correct answer to Q1 seems to be that there is no one tool that can be classified as the best at all evaluated criteria. For instance, while OpenVAS is the tool that uses more CPU and network resources and takes the most time, it is also the one that uses less memory and has a better overall precision. Nonetheless, in terms of accuracy it is better when scanning Windows-based targets, and not so good when scanning Linux-based targets. Nexpose, for instance, has an average precision of 50% for both Linux and Windows-based targets but, when analysing its accuracy, the results show very poor overall results.

- Q2: How does Tsunami compare to similar tools currently available?

In its present state, Tsunami cannot be considered as a candidate substitute to other tools such as Nessus, Nexpose or OpenVAS. The key reason being the currently lack of openly available detection plugins. Tsunami architecture is plugin oriented, where each plugin will detect the presence of a specific vulnerability. When the authors stated this work, the number of plugins available was almost nonexistent, meaning that Tsunami was unable to detect any vulnerability that were present in the targets. The author believe that, in the future, Tsunami may become a relevant candidate if its authors release a number of detection plugins comparable to the remaining tools.

- Q3: Is Tsunami well suited to be used by SME's?

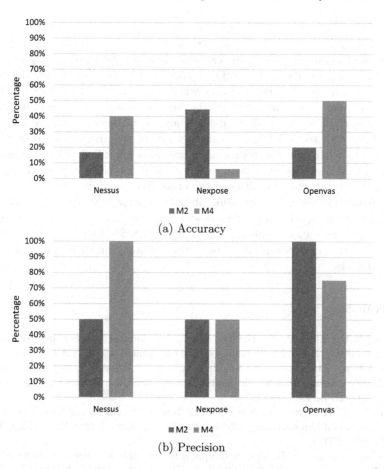

(a) Accuracy

(b) Precision

Fig. 4. Comparison of detection capabilities

The short answer to this question is no, at the moment it can not. Despite being open source and free-to-use, their current lack of detection plugins plus its mode of operation, makes it unsuitable for use in SMEs that do not have human resources capable of developing their own plugins for Tsunami. Moreover, the way the results are reported by Tsunami (JSON format) make it best suited for use in automatic assessments of a development pipeline in a product development life cycle.

5   Conclusions

Organisations may benefit from a systematic and periodic vulnerability assessment using free-to-use scanning tools. Using automated vulnerability scanning tools also reduces the required human, technical and financial resources when compared to manual penetration testing. With the release of Tsunami, yet another free-to-use vulnerability scanning tool, the authors decided to perform an updated evaluation of the existing similar tools. The evaluation considered both the performance of the tools, but also their accuracy and precision.

The obtained results show that OpenVAS was the tool that achieved the best overall precision and the best accuracy when scanning Windows-based systems. Nexpose was the tool that achieved the best accuracy when scanning Linux-based systems. In terms of CPU, memory and network usage, the results differ greatly from tool to tool but a common trait, of requiring more resources to scan systems with more vulnerabilities, was also identified. The authors also concluded that Tsunami, by having a very small detection capabilities, is still far from the detection capabilities of the other free-to-use tools.

The manual confirmation of vulnerabilities reported by all tools was focused on the critical ones, with a CVSS above 7.5. As future work, the authors will proceed with the manual confirmation of all vulnerabilities reported by all tools to have a better understanding of both the accuracy and the precision of the evaluated tools.

References

1. Aksu, M.U., Altuncu, E., Bicakci, K.: A first look at the usability of openvas vulnerability scanner. In: Workshop on Usable Security (USEC) 2019. NDSS (2019)
2. Ali, A.B.M., Abdullah, M.S., Shakhatreh, A.Y.I., Alostad, J.: SQL-injection vulnerability scanning tool for automatic creation of SQL-injection attacks. Procedia Comput. Sci. **3**, 453–458 (2011)
3. Amankwah, R., Chen, J., Kudjo, P.K., Towey, D.: An empirical comparison of commercial and open-source web vulnerability scanners. Softw. Pract. Exp. **50**(9), 1842–1857 (2020)
4. Austin, A., Williams, L.: One technique is not enough: a comparison of vulnerability discovery techniques. In: 2011 International Symposium on Empirical Software Engineering and Measurement, pp. 97–106. IEEE (2011)
5. Chimmanee, S., Veeraprasit, T., SriphREw, K., Hemanidhi, A.: A performance comparison of vulnerability detection between netclarity auditor and open source nessus. In: Proceeding of the 3rd European Conference of Communications (ECCOM 2012), pp. 280–285 (2012)
6. Cimpanu, C.: Google open sources Tsunami vulnerability scanner. ZDNet, July 2020. https://www.zdnet.com/article/google-open-sources-tsunami-vulnerability-scanner/
7. The MITRE Corporation: Common Vulnerabilities and Exposures (CVE). https://cve.mitre.org/. Accessed 10 Feb 2020
8. Daud, N.I., Bakar, K.A.A., Hasan, M.S.M.: A case study on web application vulnerability scanning tools. In: 2014 Science and Information Conference, pp. 595–600. IEEE (2014)
9. Doupé, A., Cova, M., Vigna, G.: Why Johnny can't Pentest: an analysis of black-box web vulnerability scanners. In: Kreibich, C., Jahnke, M. (eds.) DIMVA 2010. LNCS, vol. 6201, pp. 111–131. Springer, Heidelberg (2010). https://doi.org/10.1007/978-3-642-14215-4_7

10. Fonseca, J., Vieira, M., Madeira, H.: Testing and comparing web vulnerability scanning tools for SQL injection and XSS attacks. In: 13th Pacific Rim International Symposium on Dependable Computing (PRDC 2007), pp. 365–372. IEEE (2007)
11. Holm, H.: Performance of automated network vulnerability scanning at remediating security issues. Comput. Secur. **31**(2), 164–175 (2012)
12. Holm, H., Sommestad, T., Almroth, J., Persson, M.: A quantitative evaluation of vulnerability scanning. Inf. Manag. Comput. Secur. **19**(4), 231–247 (2011)
13. Kals, S., Kirda, E., Kruegel, C., Jovanovic, N.: Secubat: a web vulnerability scanner. In: Proceedings of the 15th International Conference on World Wide Web, pp. 247–256 (2006)
14. Kushe, R.: Comparative study of vulnerability scanning tools: Nessus vs Retina. Secur. Future **1**(2), 69–71 (2017)
15. Mburano, B., Si, W.: Evaluation of web vulnerability scanners based on owasp benchmark. In: 2018 26th International Conference on Systems Engineering (ICSEng), pp. 1–6. IEEE (2018)
16. Qianqian, W., Xiangjun, L.: Research and design on web application vulnerability scanning service. In: 2014 IEEE 5th International Conference on Software Engineering and Service Science, pp. 671–674. IEEE (2014)
17. Rapid7: Free Nexpose Community 1-Year Trial. https://www.rapid7.com/info/nexpose-community
18. Tenable: Nessus Vulnerability Assessment Tool. https://www.tenable.com/products/nessus. Accessed 10 Feb 2020
19. Wang, Y., Yang, J.: Ethical hacking and network defense: choose your best network vulnerability scanning tool. In: 2017 31st International Conference on Advanced Information Networking and Applications Workshops (WAINA), pp. 110–113 (2017)
20. Welberg, S.: Vulnerability management tools for cots software-a comparison. Hg. v. University of Twente (2008). https://research.utwente.nl/files/5101819/Vulnerability_management_tools_for_COTS_software_-_a_comparison_v2.1.pdf

QuickBCC: Quick and Scalable Binary Vulnerable Code Clone Detection

Hajin Jang[1], Kyeongseok Yang[1], Geonwoo Lee[1], Yoonjong Na[1],
Jeremy D. Seideman[2], Shoufu Luo[2], Heejo Lee[1(✉)], and Sven Dietrich[2(✉)]

[1] Korea University, Seoul, South Korea
{hajin_jang,ks8171235,2016320146,nooryyaa,heejo}@korea.ac.kr
[2] City University of New York, New York, USA
{jseideman,sluo2}@gradcenter.cuny.edu, spock@ieee.org

Abstract. Due to code reuse among software packages, vulnerabilities can propagate from one software package to another. Current code clone detection techniques are useful for preventing and managing such vulnerability propagation. When the source code for a software package is not available, such as when working with proprietary or custom software distributions, binary code clone detection can be used to examine software for flaws. However, existing binary code clone detectors have scalability issues, or are limited in their accurate detection of *vulnerable code clones*.

In this paper, we introduce QuickBCC, a scalable binary code clone detection framework designed for vulnerability scanning. The framework was built on the idea of extracting semantics from vulnerable binaries both before and after security patches, and comparing them to target binaries. In order to improve performance, we created a signature based on the changes between the pre- and post-patched binaries, and implemented a filtering process when comparing the signatures to the target binaries. In addition, we leverage the smallest semantic unit, a *strand*, to improve accuracy and robustness against compile environments. Quick-BCC is highly optimized, capable of preprocessing 5,439 target binaries within 111 min, and is able to match those binaries against 6 signatures in 23 s when running as a multi-threaded application. QuickBCC takes, on average, 3 ms to match one target binary. Comparing performance to other approaches, we found that it outperformed other approaches in terms of performance when detecting well known vulnerabilities with acceptable level of accuracy.

Keywords: Binary code clone · Static analysis · Security vulnerability · Patch signature

---

H. Jang, K. Yang, and G. Lee—Contributed equally to this work.

A. Jøsang et al. (Eds.): SEC 2021, IFIP AICT 625, pp. 66–82, 2021.
https://doi.org/10.1007/978-3-030-78120-0_5

1   Introduction

Vulnerability propagation, as a result of code reuse, often occurs during the software development life-cycle. One of the best methods to mitigate vulnerability propagation is through *code clone detection*. Tools that perform code clone detection accomplish this by searching for duplicated code fragments in a source code base [18]. When leveraged to find vulnerable code clones, these tools can assist in finding propagated vulnerabilities which originated in external software components. The latest source code clone detector has already been effectively used in practice [19].

Binary code-level vulnerable code clone detection is as important as source code-level vulnerable code clone detection, for three main reasons. First, many programs and firmware are only distributed as binaries, such as commercial operating systems and proprietary software. Second, a user often downloads and runs many open-source software (OSS) programs as a precompiled binary. Vulnerabilities can be added or removed while software distributors compile original source code using their compile options. Finally, a vulnerability can also propagate through *library linking*. Even if the source code of a program itself is free from vulnerabilities, one of its dependent libraries can introduce a vulnerability, regardless of how secure the program itself is.

However, existing binary code clone detectors have issues with scalability. Additionally, the environment in which the program was compiled can dramatically affect the structure of the binary, and it is one of the main obstacles of the binary code clone detection [24]. Some detectors focus on accuracy by relying on more precise, but slower techniques. While the satisfiability modulo theories (SMT) solver or symbolic execution with a theorem prover can cover up the change caused by the compile environment, they also slow down the overall process [13, 15].

Another issue is that many existing binary code clone detectors can compute the similarity of two target functions, but cannot efficiently distinguish between a vulnerable binary and a patched binary. For example, when there is a vulnerable function A and a patched function B, the fundamental structures of these two functions are the same. Therefore, a study that only performs code clone detection using a simple similarity metric tends to consider A and B to be similar.

For these reasons, we introduce QuickBCC, a scalable binary code clone detection framework for vulnerability scanning. We built QuickBCC to find vulnerable code clones while achieving fast performance with a high degree of accuracy. It operates by extracting semantics from binaries before and after a security patch and statically comparing them to target binaries, balancing performance and accuracy. In order to improve the performance, the signature was built from the changes between the pre- and post-patched binaries, and a filtering process was put in place before comparing it to the target binaries. For example, rather than comparing all parts of the target function with all parts of the signature function, comparing them with only the changed parts of the signature function (Fig. 1) can be done much faster. In addition, we improved accuracy and

(a) Target Binary   (b) Whole code as a signa-   (c) Partial code as a signa-
                          ture   ture

Fig. 1. Changed code comparison

robustness against compile environments by lifting binary code to an intermediate representation (IR) and extracting the smallest semantic unit, the *strand*
[9]. Because a strand provides the smallest data flow, it can respond to a variety
of environments.

We accelerated the overall detection process by selecting and extracting only
the core data flow (semantics that trigger the vulnerability) from a given vulnerability, and heavily optimizing the framework. We have seen that QuickBCC
took an average of only 3 ms to match a target binary. It can preprocess 5,439
target binaries within 111 min while matching them against 6 vulnerability signatures only takes 23 s when multi-threaded. QuickBCC proved its accuracy by
detecting one signature from multiple binaries. For example, QuickBCC detected
CVE-2019-1547 and CVE-2019-1563 from every vulnerable version of OpenSSL
binaries included in the target set. Even if the framework cannot overcome every
difference presented by different compile environments, its high performance can
be exploited to widen its coverage.

We summarize our contributions as follows:

- **Practical detection of binary code clones:** We present the QuickBCC
  framework, which is scalable and fast enough to be used as a practical vulnerability detection method.
- **Vulnerable code clone detection:** We propose a novel approach of distinguishing vulnerable code clones from ordinary binary code by introducing
  the ideas of a *removal mark* and an *addition mark*.

2   Related Works

2.1   Source Code Clone Detection

Source code clone detection aims to find code clones within the program source
code; Some detection methods can also be used to detect vulnerabilities present
in source code, by comparing program code to known vulnerable code.

For example, the authors of ReDeBug [17] implemented a system to find unpatched code in OS distribution. They used a tokenization technique to normalize source code, and enabled high-performance large-scale analysis of code. VUDDY [19] is a scalable vulnerable code clone detector with function-level granularity. The normalization techniques proposed in that research enabled faster large-scale analysis of code while detecting more types of code clones and reporting significantly low false positives. MVP [26] is also a scalable vulnerable code clone detector, operating slower than the other two approaches, but with higher precision and recall, by using the vulnerability signature of a function and its patch signature.

2.2 Binary Code Clone Detection

Binary code clone detection methods are capable of detecting binary code (i.e. machine code) clones or their corresponding assembly expression. For example, BinSequence [16] was designed to disassemble, normalize, and compare code fragments by creating fingerprints at the instruction level, the basic block level, and the structure level. Their approach works by building up signatures from paths in basic blocks. In contrast, our method works by looking at the sets of instructions in order to take into account differences in compile environments.

The *Esh* system [9] detects similar procedures based on the idea of *similarity by composition*, by which they break code up into smaller fragments called strands and measure similarity between strands of two binary functions. Inspired by *Esh*, our work follows the same idea, building up a function similarity metric from a strand similarity while keeping performance in mind by introducing a light-weight similarity metric with filtering methods.

XMATCH [14], which can be used in cross-platform bug search, lifts raw binary codes to IR, then extracts a conditional formula. Extracted formula is the semantic feature of raw binary code and used to matching similar binaries.

Another approach is to use Control Flow Graphs (CFG) to compare binaries. BinHunt [15] is useful for finding similar programs based on semantics, and can be useful in comparing CFGs. However, this method does not scale well with a large number of differences in the binaries. BinARM [25] compares binaries with fuzzy matching accelerated by extensive filtering with features and execution paths of binary program.

Some research tried to integrate techniques frequently used in machine learning into binary code clone detection. discovRE [13], designed to measure structural similarity of binaries using approximated subgraph isomorphism for bug search, was able to accelerate the overall comparison running time by filtering out irrelevant target functions using a kNN-based filter. Asm2Vec [11] improved robustness of binary search clone detection against compiler optimization and obfuscation, achieving its goal through learning vector representations of an assembly function. Gemini [27] used a deep neural network to generate embeddings of binary function and calculated similarity of binary functions as the distance between two embeddings. SAFE [21] provided architecture to calculate the binary similarity using embedding of fucntions on self-attentive neural network.

INNEREYE [30], and DEEPBINDIFF [12] leveraged NLP techniques to implement a robust and cross-architectural binary code clone detector. INNEREYE interpreted an instruction as a word and a basic block as a sentence to generate expressions of binary functions. DEEPBINDIFF extracted code semantics and control flows of a binary, and used a k-hop greedy matching algorithm to measure the difference between block embeddings. However, a learning-based approach requires extensive training time before detecting binary code clones. In contrast, QuickBCC can be run properly on ordinary desktop computer, without the powerful GPU or specialized hardware often required for efficient neural network computation.

The FIBER system [29] was designed to sit between source and binary code clone detection, by attempting to use as much source code information as possible to help generate a binary signature. Their system was designed to look for patch presence – whether a particular vulnerability has had a patch applied to mitigate it. While the FIBER system leverages source code and patch information to generate accurate signatures, our primary focus is on detecting binary code clones when source code is not available. SPAIN [28] also used patched binary and its corresponding vulnerable binary to extract the patch pattern and later search similar patches using the extracted patch pattern.

Hash-based approaches, such as MinHash [23], capture semantics from binary functions to create a signature, and then use the hashed signature for comparison. Our method uses a hash-based approach in order to define and easily compare our function representation. The general subject of binary signatures and fingerprints has been explored in a recent study [7], leading to research in authorship, code reuse, and binary semantics.

FirmUP [10] analyzes vulnerabilities by extracting strands from all functions of the vulnerable binary and comparing the two target binaries through the *Back-and-Forth Game algorithm*. This method has a large overhead in terms of size and speed; the entire binary of the target vulnerability is used, and all functions within are compared, so execution speed is very slow.

3   Approach

In Sect. 3, how QuickBCC compute the similarity of two binary function is explained. And overview and detail of QuickBCC's architecture is also covered in this section.

3.1   Similarity and Equivalence Metric

The goal of this work is to design a function-level binary code clone detector, $\mathcal{D}$, that detects **semantic clones** [8]. Two functions F, F' are semantic clones if they provide the same functionality, denoted as $F \equiv F'$.

The code clone detector $\mathcal{D}$ consists of two components: a scoring function $\mathcal{B} : \mathbb{F} \times \mathbb{F} \to [0, 1]$, which takes two functions F_x and F_y as its input and computes a similarity score, and a threshold value t, such that

$$F_x \equiv F_y \ \ if \ \ \mathcal{B}(F_x, F_y) \geq t \ , \ \ F_x \not\equiv F_y \ \ if \ \ \mathcal{B}(F_x, F_y) < t \tag{1}$$

In this work, we propose the scoring function $\mathcal{B}$ as a similarity measurement built on *n-gram similarity* [20] of *strands* [9]. First, a function F_x is decomposed into a set of strands, i.e. $F_x = \{s_1, s_2, \cdots\}$. Given a strand $s = i_1 i_2 i_3 \cdots i_k$ where i_k are instructions, we derive a n-gram set s' from s by extracting all n-grams of instructions. For example, if $n = 3$, we can build an n-gram set as:

$$s' = \{i_1 i_2 i_3, i_2 i_3 i_4, i_3 i_4 i_5 \cdots\} \tag{2}$$

In order to quantitatively determine the similarity, we used the Jaccard Index. The Jaccard index is a representative algorithm that obtains the similarity between two sets when the data does not have an order or quantity, is used. The *n-gram similarity* of two strands s_x and s_y is defined as the Jaccard Index of their corresponding n-gram sets, s'_x and s'_y respectively:

$$Sim(s_x, s_y) = \frac{|s'_x \cap s'_y|}{|s'_x \cup s'_y|} \tag{3}$$

If F_x, F_y have n, m strands (e.g. $\{s_{x_1}, s_{x_2}, \cdots, s_{x_n}\}$, $\{s_{y_1}, s_{y_2}, \cdots, s_{y_m}\}$) respectively, then we calculate the similarity score between the two functions as:

$$\mathcal{B} = Score(F_x, F_y) = \frac{1}{n} \sum_{i=1}^{n} \max_{j=[1,m]} (Sim(s_{x_i}, s_{y_j})) \tag{4}$$

To provide symmetry to the scoring function $\mathcal{B}$, $\mathcal{B}$ can be modified as:

$$\mathcal{B} = max(Score(F_x, F_y), Score(F_y, F_x)) \tag{5}$$

Therefore, using $\mathcal{B}$ can quantitatively evaluate the similarity between the two functions. QuickBCC uses $\mathcal{B}$ defined in Eq. (5).

Now we present an overview of QuickBCC's architecture in Fig. 2. QuickBCC consists of three main steps: (1) vulnerability preprocessing, (2) target binary preprocessing, and (3) matching. Each step makes use of one or more of its major components, the binary preprocessor, and the code clone detector.

3.2   Binary Preprocessor

Disassembler. The fingerprint generator uses radare2 [6] to retrieve basic blocks and disassembled functions from binary. The disassembler works by performing a control flow graph (CFG) analysis on each function. When the optional addition and removal marks (Sect. 3.3) are supplied, the preprocessor works only on functions and instructions indicated by the marks. We used diaphora [4], an open-source binary diffing tool running on IDA [3] to create vulnerability signatures (Sect. 3.3).

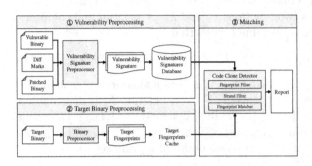

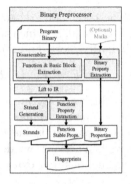

Fig. 2. Overview of the QuickBCC architecture

Fig. 3. Overview of the binary preprocessor

Lifting to IR. QuickBCC leverages on an *intermediate representation* (IR) rather than relying on specific instruction sets. First, the use of an IR allows us to write a much simpler strand generation algorithm, which contributes to the performance. Additionally, we can reuse one codebase and algorithm over multiple architectures. We chose VEX-IR [2,22] as the basis of our work. VEX-IR is capable of *static single assignment* (SSA), which lets us create strands with a relatively simple algorithm (Fig. 4).

```
 1 | t2 = LDle:I32(0x0007bc64)
 2 | PUT(a4) = t2
 3 | t3 = GET:I32(r13)
 4 | t5 = Add32(t3,0x00000014)
 5 | PUT(v1) = t5
 6 | PUT(ip) = 0x0007b620
 7 | t8 = LDle:I32(t2)
 8 | PUT(a1) = t5
 9 | t14 = Add32(t8,0x00000001)
10 | PUT(a3) = t14
11 | PUT(ip) = 0x0007b62c
12 | STle(t2) = t14
13 | PUT(lr) = 0x0007b634
NEXT: PUT(pc) = 0x00027648; Ijk_Call
```

```
         t66 = Add32(t65,0x00000064)
         <Def:[t66]> <Ref:[t65, 100]>

                  Opcode = 7685
       Operands (Def) = 1 temp var
       Operands (Ref) = 1 temp var, 1 imm value

  MD5("7685___R0_T1_M0____R0_T1_M0__I32/100")
```

Fig. 4. Example of VEX-IR basic block

Fig. 5. Example of the instruction abstraction

Strand Generation. Recall that a strand is a set of instructions in one basic block that is required to compute one variable. Therefore, one strand represents one independent data flow. The strand generator performs data-flow analysis by inspecting the define-reference dependencies among instructions within a basic block. Thanks to the SSA property of VEX-IR, we were able to deploy a simple algorithm to create strands, such as the one used in Esh [9]. We tweaked the characteristics of strands to improve accuracy and performance in two ways. First, one instruction can be included in only one strand to prevent duplication of instructions, which lowers overall accuracy by over-representing some instructions. Incidentally, the reduced number and size of strands helped the detector's

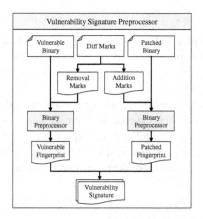

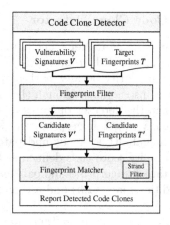

Fig. 6. Overview of the vulnerability signature preprocessor

Fig. 7. Overview of the code clone detector

performance. Second, a strand cannot span across multiple basic blocks. Splitting one long data flow improves performance by letting the code clone detector to be simplified.

After generating a strand, QuickBCC abstracts each instruction of the strand. This makes QuickBCC robust against changes to the compile environment, and enables fast comparison between two instructions. The change in the compile environment easily influences memory address offsets and registry allocation, so the instruction abstractor removes them. It leaves opcode and count of defined/referenced operands per operand type while keeping the values of immediates. Finally, each abstracted instruction is hashed with MD5. Figure 5 illustrates the process of instruction abstraction. We chose MD5 as a hash function because MD5 had enough collision resilience for this task while being faster than other cryptographic hash functions (Fig. 5).

3.3 Vulnerability Signature Generator

A vulnerability signature is an extended fingerprint, containing additional security patch information. The vulnerable signature preprocessor is built on the binary preprocessor. Figure 6 represents the overview of the vulnerability signature preprocessor. It takes a pair of vulnerable and patched binaries along with a set of diff marks extracted from the binary diffing tool in Sect. 3.2. *Diff marks* represent the changes between vulnerable binary and patched binary. It consists of removed instructions from the vulnerable binary (a *removal mark*) and added instructions from the patched binary (an *addition mark*), the combination of which make up the security patch. Each set of marks is given to the binary preprocessor to track relevant strands from the vulnerable and patched fingerprints. This process helps QuickBCC locate the vulnerable and patched code in the target binaries.

3.4   Code Clone Detector

Fingerprint Matcher. The matcher computes the similarity of two functions by making use of the n-gram similarity between two strands as a basis. We chose n-gram similarity because each n-gram captures correlations of a small range of adjacent instructions through the ordering within the n-gram.

When the detector operates in sub-function level granularity, the similarity between a target fingerprint and a signature fingerprint is defined based on the vulnerability score vs and patch score ps, as defined in Eq. (6), (7), (8). Vulnerability score vs is defined as the similarity between a removal mark (rm) and a target fingerprint, and patched score ps is defined as the similarity between an addition mark (am) and a target fingerprint.

$$F_x = \{rm_x, am_x\} \qquad F_y = \{rm_y, am_y\} \tag{6}$$

$$vs = Sim(rm_x, rm_y) \qquad ps = Sim(am_x, am_y) \tag{7}$$

$$Sim(F_x, F_y) = vs - a \cdot ps \tag{8}$$

ps tends to have a higher false-positive rate than vs, so the coefficient a was given to mitigate the side effect for the worst-case scenario. We chose $a = 0.2$ in the evaluation.

Fingerprint and Strand Filtering. When a user inputs a target binary, the matcher filters target fingerprints and vulnerability signatures, trimming out irrelevant ones. We define a *stable property* as a property of an entity within a binary that is minimally affected by a change of compile environments. We can find stable properties at each level of binary, such as a binary itself, a function, or a strand. Determining which properties are stable is crucial for the scalability of binary code clone detection. It allows us to reduce the search space we should test to find similar code fragments, improving the performance.

We leveraged stable properties as a filtering mechanism to find out if a target entity is irrelevant from a vulnerability signature. For example, the total count of external library function calls is not likely to change in different compile environments. Therefore, we depend on external call count to eliminate irrelevant target functions.

4   Evaluation

In Sect. 4, we show that QuickBCC can scan large volume of binaries with accuracy and high perfomance. Comparison with other approach is included later in this section.

4.1   Environmental Setup

Test Environment. We performed all evaluations on an Ubuntu 20.04 LTS machine equipped with an Intel Core i5-9400 6-core 6-thread CPU. We built the framework with the .NET Core 3.1.10 and Python 3.8.5 runtime. When the tools we compared required a Windows environment, we evaluated it with a Windows 10 v20H2 virtual machine guest running on the same machine. Later, the OS of the machine is changed to Arch Linux when we evaluated accuracy of QuickBCC. But changing the OS of the machine did not affect accuracy.

Target Binaries. We chose Debian Live amd64 GNOME ISO images from the past 3.5 years (versions 9.0.0–10.8.0) as the source of our binaries. We chose Debian because (1) Debian officially tracks vulnerability information of the packages in its security tracker [1], (2) which enabled us collecting signature binaries. We used it as a ground truth. We extracted binaries from the */bin, /sbin,* and */usr* directories of the *filesystem.squashfs* from the live image, excluding symlink files. Table 1 shows the statistics of the target binary set.

Table 1. Target binaries used in evaluation

debian-live-amd64-gnome (9.0.0–10.8.0)	
# Binary File	143,018
# Binary File Size (Total)	19.4 GB
# Binary File Size (Avg Per File)	143.2 KB
# Target Func (Total)	51,654,380
# Target Func (Avg Per File)	361.2
# Target Func After Filtering (Total)	3,228,042
# Target Func After Filtering (Avg Per File)	22.6

Table 2. Vulnerable binaries used in evaluation

OSS	CVE	Package	Vuln version	Patched version	Lang
OpenSSL	CVE-2018-0734	libssl1.1	1.1.0h-4	1.1.0j-1~deb9u1	C
	CVE-2019-1547	libssl1.1	1.1.0k-1~deb9u1	1.1.0l-1~deb9u1	
	CVE-2019-1563	libssl1.1	1.1.0k-1~deb9u1	1.1.0l-1~deb9u1	
WavPack	CVE-2018-19841	libwavpack	5.0.0-2+deb9u2	5.1.0.6	C
TagLib	CVE-2017-12678	libtag	1.11.1+dfsg.1-0.1	1.11.1+dfsg.1-0.3	C++
Binutils	CVE-2018-6543	binutils	2.30-2	2.30-3	C

Vulnerability Signatures. We collected real-world software for multimedia processing in popular use [5], especially pre-installed software (amd64) in the Debian distribution image. Table 2 shows the list of vulnerability signatures we collected.

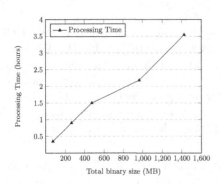

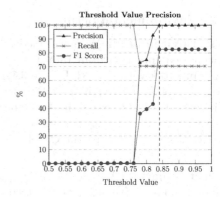

Fig. 8. Relation between total binary size and processing time

Fig. 9. Precision and Recall of each Threshold value

Threshold. We conducted an experiment to determine the threshold value. We checked the result by increasing the threshold value from 0.5 to 1 by 0.02. We used live images from Debian from the past two years, and tested with the 6 signatures mentioned in Table 2. Figure 9 shows that if we use a threshold value of 0.84 or higher, we can see a corresponding precision value of 1.0 and high value of F1 score.

4.2   Vulnerable Code Clone Detection

We first matched the 6 vulnerability signatures we generated with Debian 9.0.0 live image to evaluate its performance. And later we matched the 6 vulnerability signatures whole target binaries with 52.6 million target functions from 139,446 target binaries to evaluate its accuracy.

Table 3. Performance of QuickBCC in single-threaded environment

Preprocessing + Matching (1st run)		
Threads	1	6
Run Time	8 h 53 m 34 s	1 h 51 m 33 s
Preprocessing Time	8 h 53 m 19 s	1 h 51 m 10 s
Preprocessing Time (per file)	5692 ms	–
Matching Time	15 s	23 s
Matching Time (per file)	3 ms	–
Matching Time (per signature)	0.01 ms	–

Cache Loading + Matching (2nd+ run)		
Threads	1	6
Run Time	3 m 24 s	3 m 9 s
Cache Load Time	1 m 34 s	2 m 5 s
Cache Load Time (per file)	19 ms	–
Matching Time	1 m 50 s	1 m 4 s
Matching Time (per file)	3 ms	–
Matching Time (per signature)	0.01 ms	–

Performance. Table 3 shows the fast performance and high scalability of Quick-BCC. The framework required 111 min to scan 5,439 files (from Debian 9.0.0 only) in the first run with 6 threads, which involved preprocessing and matching. The framework caches preprocessed target functions to accelerate later runs. When it loaded the cached fingerprints, it completed the overall scanning in 4 min. The ability to scan 2.1 million functions from an entire Linux desktop distribution in a few minutes effectively demonstrates the high scalability of QuickBCC.

The filtering system of QuickBCC also played a significant role in improving scalability. The framework filtered out 94.9% of the target functions before the actual matching was performed. As a result, it took only 59 s to match 6 vulnerability signatures with all 5,439 binary files and 11 ms to scan each target binary with scalability (Fig. 8)

Table 4. Detected vulnerable code clones for each target OS

Target OS version	Detected signature	TP	FP	TN	FN
9.0.0	4	4	–	1	2
9.1.0	4	4	–	1	2
9.2.0	4	4	–	1	2
9.3.0	4	4	–	1	2
9.4.0	4	4	–	1	2
9.5.0	4	4	–	1	2
9.6.0	4	4	–	2	1
9.7.0	4	4	–	2	1
9.8.0	4	4	–	2	1
9.9.0	4	4	–	2	1
9.11.0	4	4	–	2	1
9.12.0	3	3	–	3	1
10.0.0	1	1	–	5	–
10.1.0	1	1	–	5	–
10.2.0	–	–	–	6	–
10.3.0	–	–	–	6	–
10.4.0	–	–	–	6	–
10.5.0	–	–	–	6	–
10.6.0	–	–	–	6	–
10.7.0	–	–	–	6	–
10.8.0	–	–	–	6	–

Accuracy. Table 4 show our matching results. QuickBCC detected 49 vulnerable code clones from 6 target binaries. Detected clones consist of 49 true-positives, 0 false-positive, 71 true-negatives, and 18 false-negatives. We tested the framework with a threshold t of 0.84 and a coefficient a of 0.2. An analysis of each case is shown below.

OpenSSL Vulnerabilities. We created the signatures of CVE-2019-1547 and CVE-2019-1563 from the OpenSSL 1.1.0k (vulnerable) and 1.1.0l (patched)

binaries. Three branches of OpenSSL, including the 1.1.0 and 1.0.2 branches, had these vulnerabilities. As a result, QuickBCC detected two vulnerable code clones for CVE-2019-1563 vulnerability. Debian 9 includes OpenSSL 1.1.0 (*libcrypto.so.1.1*) and 1.0.2 (*libcrypto.so.1.0.2*) binaries, and both of them were found to be vulnerable. Therefore, three vulnerable code clones were detected for the two signatures CVE-2019-1547 and CVE-2019-1563, all of which were true-positives.

In contrast, the CVE-2018-0734 signature created false-negatives that the code clone was not found from the OpenSSL binaries. We had looked through the impacted OpenSSL source file and discovered the target binary did contain source code older than the binary we used to create the vulnerability signature. Since the target binary did not have an exact code pattern QuickBCC was searching for, we saw the framework worked as intended.

WavPack Vulnerability. We found one true-positive vulnerability code clone of CVE-2018-19741 from a vulnerable libwavpack binary, while avoiding false-positives.

TagLib Vulnerability. Since the patch of CVE-2017-12678 is changing casting and the changed binary is tiny, we got false negatives from the low similarity score.

Binutils Vulnerability. No code clones were found from the CVE-2018-6543 signature. We had looked through the Binutils packages of the target and concluded that it is a true-negative. The version of the binary used to create a vulnerability signature was different from the target binaries.

4.3   Comparison

Table 5. Comparison with *Esh* about the time required to match one pair of strands

Signature	Target	Time (milliseconds)	
		Esh	QuickBCC
Heartbleed (GCC)	Heartbleed (GCC)	672	0.192
Heartbleed (Clang)	Heartbleed (Clang)	676	0.281
Shellshock (GCC)	Shellshock (GCC)	820	32.677
Shellshock (ICC)	Shellshock (ICC)	861	95.082
Average		$757 \cdot 10^5$	**32.08**

We compared QuickBCC with *Esh* [9], which is the most recent and similarly designed system. Esh provides its matcher source code, its binary dataset, and four sample strands. We evaluated Esh by matching a pair of sample strands and measuring the comparison time. We could only use the provided strands with Esh, as we did not have access to its preprocessor. For QuickBCC, we preprocessed target object files from the Esh dataset and matched all strands of the target function with the signature function, calculating the matching time per strand.

Table 5 shows the results we found comparing Esh and QuickBCC. We found QuickBCC was about 22 times faster than Esh on average, with acceptable levels of accuracy. Esh took about 850 ms to match a pair of strands from a Shellshock vulnerability, while QuickBCC took only about 60 ms. It means that Esh takes more than a day to scan a large amounts of binaries such as Debian live image. The comparison shows the performance advantage of the QuickBCC framework. We achieved this by a fast method of comparing semantics with n-gram similarity and using extensive filtering.

5   Discussion and Future Work

5.1   Robustness to Multiple Compile Environments

We proved QuickBCC worked well when we controlled the compile environments to make signatures in each evaluation, but some elements of the compile environment were hard to mitigate. For example, QuickBCC had an issue matching binaries from two different platforms. We propose to solve this problem by preparing a set of signatures per vulnerability, where each signature stands for one compile environment. It is a reasonable workaround based on what we have seen. First, running the matcher multiple times is not a significant burden, thanks to its filtering and high performance. Second, merging several similar signatures into one signature would significantly reduce the number of required signatures. Finally, the practical number of required vulnerability signatures is not very high, since most platforms use a limited number of compile environments.

For example, We can create minimal signatures per vulnerability that they can span signatures from almost all compiler options. In the case of CVE-2019-1563, a signature compiled with O3 can detect vulnerabilities in unpatched binary that compiled with O1, O2, O3, Og, and Ofast. The signature compiled with O0, though, could only detect unpatched binaries that compiled with O0. In this case, only 1/3 of the signature (O0, O3) could cover all optimization levels.

5.2   Better Vulnerability Signature Generation

Employing a better binary diffing method would improve QuickBCC's accuracy. Conventional binary diffing algorithms used in QuickBCC mark instructions moved by a patch or compile environment difference as deleted or added instructions. It can cause false-negatives on vulnerable code clone detection, so a user has to review and fix the diff results. It would be useful to create a binary diffing method specific to QuickBCC's vulnerability signature generator.

Next, automatically creating vulnerability signatures would be another milestone of this research. We experimented vulnerability signature auto-generation by exploiting binary debug symbols, but that method had limitations. Compiler optimization distorted the mapping between the source patch line and the binary instruction offset, reducing the accuracy of generated signatures. We expect that combining our effort with the conventional binary diffing method would be a breakthrough.

6   Conclusion

We presented QuickBCC, a scalable binary code clone detection framework for practical vulnerability scanning. We managed to extract and statically compare semantics, to achieve high performance and accuracy. We also leveraged the notion of strands and introduced a similarity metric for ordered sets to the world of binary code clones. We invented the removal mark and the addition mark to enable effective vulnerable code clone detection for binaries. QuickBCC demonstrated its fast performance with extensive filtering and code optimization, while it proved to be accurate enough to detect a vulnerable code clone from a similar yet different set of binaries.

Acknowledgement. We thank Seongbeom Park for his contribution on the signature generation. This work was supported by the Institute of Information & communications Technology Planning & Evaluation (IITP) grant funded by the Korea government (MSIT) (No. 2019-0-01697, Development of Automated Vulnerability Discovery Technologies for Blockchain Platform Security), the National Research Foundation (NRF), Korea, under project BK21 FOUR, and the Research Foundation City University of New York.

References

1. Debian Security Tracker (1997–2021). https://security-tracker.debian.org/tracker. Accessed 15 Apr 2021
2. VEX-IR (2004–2021). https://sourceware.org/git/?p=valgrind.git;f=VEX/pub/libvex_ir.h;a=blob_plain. Accessed 15 Apr 2021
3. IDA: About (2005–2021). https://www.hex-rays.com/products/ida/. Accessed 15 Apr 2021
4. Diaphora, the most advanced Free and Open Source program diffing tool (2015–2021). https://github.com/joxeankoret/diaphora. Accessed 15 Apr 2021
5. https://popcon.debian.org/
6. radare (2021). https://rada.re/n/radare2.html. Accessed 15 Apr 2021
7. Alrabaee, S.: Efficient, scalable, and accurate program fingerprinting in binary code. Ph.D. thesis, Concordia University (2018)
8. Bellon, S., Koschke, R., Antoniol, G., Krinke, J., Merlo, E.: Comparison and evaluation of clone detection tools. IEEE Trans. Software Eng. **33**(9), 577–591 (2007). https://doi.org/10.1109/TSE.2007.70725
9. David, Y., Partush, N., Yahav, E.: Statistical similarity of binaries. In: Proceedings of the 37th ACM SIGPLAN Conference on Programming Language Design and Implementation, PLDI 2016, pp. 266–280. ACM, New York (2016). https://doi.org/10.1145/2908080.2908126

10. David, Y., Partush, N., Yahav, E.: FirmUp: precise static detection of common vulnerabilities in firmware. In: ASPLOS 2018, pp. 392–404, May 2018. https://doi.org/10.1109/SP.2017.62
11. Ding, S.H., Fung, B.C., Charland, P.: Asm2vec: boosting static representation robustness for binary clone search against code obfuscation and compiler optimization. In: 2019 IEEE Symposium on Security and Privacy (SP), pp. 472–489. IEEE (2019)
12. Duan, Y., Li, X., Wang, J., Yin, H.: Deepbindiff: learning program-wide code representations for binary diffing. In: Proceedings of the Network and Distributed System Security Symposium (2020)
13. Eschweiler, S., Yakdan, K., Gerhards-Padilla, E.: discovRE: efficient cross-architecture identification of bugs in binary code. In: Proceedings of the 2016 Network and Distributed System Security (NDSS) Symposium (2016)
14. Feng, Q., Wang, M., Zhang, M., Zhou, R., Henderson, A., Yin, H.: Extracting conditional formulas for cross-platform bug search. In: Proceedings of the 2017 ACM on Asia Conference on Computer and Communications Security, pp. 346–359 (2017)
15. Gao, D., Reiter, M.K., Song, D.: BinHunt: automatically finding semantic differences in binary programs. In: Chen, L., Ryan, M.D., Wang, G. (eds.) ICICS 2008. LNCS, vol. 5308, pp. 238–255. Springer, Heidelberg (2008). https://doi.org/10.1007/978-3-540-88625-9_16
16. Huang, H., Youssef, A.M., Debbabi, M.: BinSequence: fast, accurate and scalable binary code reuse detection. In: Proceedings of the 2017 ACM on Asia Conference on Computer and Communications Security, pp. 155–166. ACM (2017)
17. Jang, J., Agrawal, A., Brumley, D.: ReDeBug: finding unpatched code clones in entire OS distributions. In: 2012 IEEE Symposium on Security and Privacy, pp. 48–62, May 2012. https://doi.org/10.1109/SP.2012.13
18. Kamiya, T., Kusumoto, S., Inoue, K.: CCFinder: a multilinguistic token-based code clone detection system for large scale source code. IEEE Trans. Software Eng. **28**(7), 654–670 (2002)
19. Kim, S., Woo, S., Lee, H., Oh, H.: VUDDY: a scalable approach for vulnerable code clone discovery. In: 2017 IEEE Symposium on Security and Privacy (SP), pp. 595–614, May 2017. https://doi.org/10.1109/SP.2017.62
20. Kondrak, G.: N-Gram similarity and distance. In: Consens, M., Navarro, G. (eds.) SPIRE 2005. LNCS, vol. 3772, pp. 115–126. Springer, Heidelberg (2005). https://doi.org/10.1007/11575832_13
21. Massarelli, L., Di Luna, G.A., Petroni, F., Baldoni, R., Querzoni, L.: SAFE: self-attentive function embeddings for binary similarity. In: Perdisci, R., Maurice, C., Giacinto, G., Almgren, M. (eds.) DIMVA 2019. LNCS, vol. 11543, pp. 309–329. Springer, Cham (2019). https://doi.org/10.1007/978-3-030-22038-9_15
22. Nethercote, N., Seward, J.: Valgrind: a framework for heavyweight dynamic binary instrumentation. SIGPLAN Not. **42**(6), 89–100 (2007). https://doi.org/10.1145/1273442.1250746
23. Pewny, J., Garmany, B., Gawlik, R., Rossow, C., Holz, T.: Cross-architecture bug search in binary executables. In: Proceedings of the 2015 IEEE Symposium on Security and Privacy, SP 2015, pp. 709–724. IEEE Computer Society, Washington, DC (2015). https://doi.org/10.1109/SP.2015.49
24. Rahimian, A., Shirani, P., Alrbaee, S., Wang, L., Debbabi, M.: Bincomp: a stratified approach to compiler provenance attribution. Digit. Investig. **14**, S146–S155 (2015)

25. Shirani, P., et al.: BINARM: scalable and efficient detection of vulnerabilities in firmware images of intelligent electronic devices. In: Giuffrida, C., Bardin, S., Blanc, G. (eds.) DIMVA 2018. LNCS, vol. 10885, pp. 114–138. Springer, Cham (2018). https://doi.org/10.1007/978-3-319-93411-2_6
26. Xiao, Y., et al.: {MVP}: detecting vulnerabilities using patch-enhanced vulnerability signatures. In: 29th USENIX Security Symposium (USENIX Security 2020), pp. 1165–1182 (2020)
27. Xu, X., Liu, C., Feng, Q., Yin, H., Song, L., Song, D.: Neural network-based graph embedding for cross-platform binary code similarity detection. In: Proceedings of the 2017 ACM SIGSAC Conference on Computer and Communications Security, pp. 363–376 (2017)
28. Xu, Z., Chen, B., Chandramohan, M., Liu, Y., Song, F.: Spain: security patch analysis for binaries towards understanding the pain and pills. In: 2017 IEEE/ACM 39th International Conference on Software Engineering (ICSE), pp. 462–472. IEEE (2017)
29. Zhang, H., Qian, Z.: Precise and accurate patch presence test for binaries. In: 27th USENIX Security Symposium (USENIX Security 2018), pp. 887–902 (2018)
30. Zuo, F., Li, X., Young, P., Luo, L., Zeng, Q., Zhang, Z.: Neural machine translation inspired binary code similarity comparison beyond function pairs. arXiv preprint arXiv:1808.04706 (2018)

Automatic Inference of Taint Sources to Discover Vulnerabilities in SOHO Router Firmware

Kai Cheng[1,2], Dongliang Fang[1,2], Chuan Qin[1,2], Huizhao Wang[1,2],
Yaowen Zheng[3], Nan Yu[2], and Limin Sun[2(✉)]

[1] School of Cyber Security, University of Chinese Academy of Sciences,
Beijing, China
[2] Beijing Key Laboratory of IoT Information Security Technology,
Institute of Information Engineering, Chinese Academy of Sciences,
Beijing, China
{chengkai,fangdongliang,qinchuan,wanghuizhao,yunan,sunlimin}@iie.ac.cn
[3] Nanyang Technological University, Singapore, Singapore
yaowen.zheng@ntu.edu.sg

Abstract. Cyberattacks against SOHO (small office and home office) routers have attracted much attention in recent years. Most of the vulnerabilities exploited by hackers occur in the web servers of router firmware. In vulnerabilities detection, static taint analysis can quickly cover all code without depending on the runtime environment compared to dynamic analysis (e.g., fuzzing). However, existing static analysis techniques suffer from a high false-negative rate due to the lack of resolution of indirect calls, making it challenging to track tainted data from a common source (e.g., *recv*) to a sink. In this work, we propose a new heuristic approach to address the challenge. Instead of resolving the indirect calls, we automatically infer taint sources through identifying functions with key-value features. We can bypass the indirect calls with the inferred taint sources and track the taint to detect vulnerabilities by static taint analysis. We implement a prototype system and evaluate it on 10 popular routers across 5 vendors. The proposed system discovered 245 vulnerabilities, including 41 1-day vulnerabilities and 204 vulnerabilities never exposed before. The experimental results show that our system can find more bugs compared to a state-of-the-art fuzzing tool.

1 Introduction

The *Internet of Things* (IoT) is one of the fastest emerging technologies in the last decade. According to the Statista research, by 2025, there will be more than 21.5 billion active IoT devices installed world-wide [16]. They are usually connected to the Internet through the small office and home office (SOHO) routers. Unfortunately, due to the lack of advanced defense mechanisms and the Internet-facing characteristic, SOHO routers have become hotbeds for remote exploitation [17]. For example, in 2019, Echobot, a new variant of Mirai, hit

© IFIP International Federation for Information Processing 2021
Published by Springer Nature Switzerland AG 2021
A. Jøsang et al. (Eds.): SEC 2021, IFIP AICT 625, pp. 83–99, 2021.
https://doi.org/10.1007/978-3-030-78120-0_6

the Internet [9]. This sophisticated attack exploited up to 71 vulnerabilities in various SOHO routers, leading to serious consequences, such as remote code execution and command injection.

Most SOHO routers implement a customized web server to manage and configure the functionality of the devices. One of the common web servers is the *HTTP* server, which provides network services through the HTTP protocol. These web servers directly receive requests from the network, which are attacker-controlled data, making them susceptible to vulnerabilities. There have been many works for discovering vulnerabilities in SOHO routers in recent years, including static analysis [6,13] and dynamic analysis [5,20–22]. Most of the vulnerabilities found in SOHO routers are related to the web server. In this paper, we also aims at discover vulnerabilities in the web server of the SOHO router.

In dynamic analysis, the mainstream approach is to discover vulnerabilities by greybox fuzzing on simulated firmware [21,22] or blackbox fuzzing on physical device [5,20]. However, both methods currently face the problem of traditional fuzzing itself, such as low code coverage, which can lead to a large number of false negatives. In static analysis, the related works [6,13] use static taint analysis to discover a class of vulnerabilities called the taint-style vulnerability, in which data are passed from an attacker-controlled source to a security-sensitive sink without sanitization [19]. Compared with dynamic analysis, static analysis tests the code without actually executing it on the runtime environment and thus is a more practical and economical option for testing router firmware. For example, static analysis can analyze the firmware of a large number of routers without the need for expensive real-world devices. Moreover, for some types of vulnerability detection, static analysis enables higher code coverage with a lower false negative. In this work, we focus on using static analysis to find taint-style vulnerabilities in SOHO router firmware.

Challenges in Discovering Taint-Style Vulnerability. By nature, the effectiveness of finding taint-style vulnerabilities heavily relies on a good data dependency analysis tool; indeed, to find a defect, the tool has to construct a path in which taint is propagated from an attacker-controlled source to a security-sensitive sink. However, in binary analysis, the presence of indirect calls makes it difficult for existing static taint analysis technique to track tainted data from a common source (e.g., *recv*) to a sink. As a result, lots of vulnerabilities were missed. Although existing work used heuristics to bypass indirect calls and found subsets of taint-style vulnerabilities, these heuristics are inefficient. For example, in DTaint [6], the author manually specified some vendor-customized functions (e.g., *find_var* and *websGetVar*) as taint sources. In KARONTE [13], the author used a preset list of network-encoding strings (e.g., "soap" or "HTTP") as the keywords to infer taint sources. However, the former requires manually find special functions by firmware reverse-engineering; the latter's heuristic approach is not comprehensive enough to infer taint source with unknown strings (e.g., "entrys" in Fig. 1).

Our Approach. To address these challenges, we propose a new heuristic app-roach to automatically infer taint sources instead of solving the indirect calls. Specifically, we observed a class of functions that obtain values by indexing key-words from user requests. These values are attacker-controlled. Therefore, these functions can be used as taint source for taint-style vulnerability detection. By inferring these taint sources, our taint analysis does not necessarily start from the common source (e.g., *recv*). Instead, it can start directly with the inferred taint sources. Throughout this paper, we refer to these functions as *key-value functions*. To identify key-value functions, we first summarize the features of such functions and find key-value functions through data-flow analysis. Second, some key-value functions obtain data locally rather than from the network, so we filter these functions to reduce false positives. Third, a taint source summary is generated and passed to static taint analysis engine for vulnerabilities detection. We implement a prototype system and evaluate it on 10 popular routers across 5 vendors. The proposed system discovered 245 vulnerabilities, including 41 1-day vulnerabilities and 204 vulnerabilities never exposed before.

Contributions. In summary, we make the following contributions in this paper:

- We proposed a new approach for inferring taint source automatically on the firmware of SOHO routers. With the inferred taint source, we achieved static taint analysis on binary to discover vulnerabilities.
- We implemented a system prototype and evaluated it on ten real-world firmware images, showing that our tool can successfully find key-value taint sources, resulting in the discovery of 245 vulnerabilities. Compared to a state-of-the-art fuzzing tool, our prototype can discover more vulnerabilities.

2   Background and Motivation

2.1   Typical Architecture of SOHO Router

In addition to providing its routing network services, the SOHO router typically utilizes a built-in web server for administration and configuration. Then, the user can connect to its management interface through a web browser and configure the various functionalities for the router, such as setting the wireless password, IP address, whitelists. Moreover, some router vendors provide mobile APPs to manage the devices [5]. The administration and configuration are usually based on standard protocols, such as HyperText Transfer Protocol (HTTP), and their typical implementation is composed of a frontend, a backend, and a database. The frontend provides an interface to guide the user in configuring the router, the backend processes user requests and parses the requests to perform corre-sponding functionalities, and the database stores the obtained configuration [20].

2.2   Key-Value Features

A typical user request sent to the SOHO router contains a URL and several different key-value pairs. When a request is received, the backend parses the

```
POST /goform/addressNat HTTP/1.1
Host: 192.168.1.1
Content-Length: 37
Content-Type: application/x-www-form-urlencoded
User-Agent: Mozilla/5.0
Cookie: password=12345

entrys=sync&mitInterface=aaa&page=bbb
```

```
1  void fromAddressNat(webs_t wp) {
2    char list[0x200], gotopage[0x100];
3    char *entry = websGetVar(wp,"entrys",0);
4    char *ifindex = websGetVar(wp,"mitInterface",0);
5    // bug1: CVE-2020-13390
6    sprintf(list, "%s;%s", entry, ifindex);
7    char *page = websGetVar(wp, "page", 0);
8    // bug2: CVE-2018-18708
9    sprintf(gotopage,"advance.asp?page=%s",page);
10 }
```

Fig. 1. A motivation example.

```
1  int KeyValue1(char *key,char *value,int length) {
2    // input = 'aaa=xxx&bbb=xxx&ccc=xxx'
3    while (strncmp(input++, key, len(key)) == 0) {
4      // get the index of a value
5      v_index = input + len(key);
6      for (j = 0;j < length && v_index[j] != '&';j++)
7        value[j] = character_conversion(v_index[j]);
8    }
9    return 0;
10 }
```

(a) key-value model one.

```
1  char* KeyValue2(char *key) {
2    // the parsed (key, value) is saved
3    // in a struct data.
4    while(data)
5      if (strcmp(data->key, key) == 0)
6        return data->value;
7      data = data->next; // get next (key,value)
8    }
9    return 0;
10 }
```

(b) key-value model two.

```
1  char* KeyValue3(char *key,char *value,int length) {
2    v_index = KeyValue2(key);
3    if (v_index != 0)
4      strncpy(value, v_index, length);
5    return 0;
6  }
```

```
1  char* KeyValue4(char *key) {
2    v_index = KeyValue2(key);
3    return v_index;
4  }
```

(c) key-value model three.

Fig. 2. The abstract C codes of three key-value function models.

request to obtains the key and corresponding value. Then the webserver configures the routers according to the obtained value. However, the program often lacks security checks for these values, resulting in many vulnerabilities, e.g., memory corruptions, command injections, cross-site scripting (XSS).

Motivating Example. We demonstrate this in the following example, based on a real-world firmware image. The left half of Fig. 1 shows a POST request and the right half of Fig. 1 shows the procedure of processing the request in the backend. This example corresponds to two known vulnerabilities, CVE-2018-18708 and CVE-2020-13390. The POST data contains three parameter-keys: "entrys", "mitInterface" and "page". While processing these parameter-keys in the backend, their values are read by function websGetVar through indexing the key (line 3, 4 and 8) and directly passed to sprintf without any sanitization. Therefore, when the length of string *entry* or the length of string *ifindex* is larger than 0x200, a stack-based buffer overflow could be triggered at line 6. Another stack-based buffer overflow could be provoked at line 10 when the length of string *page* is larger than 0x100.

Key-Value Function Model. In Fig. 1, function websGetVar matchs a key from the data struct *wp* and returns a value. Throughout this paper, we call the

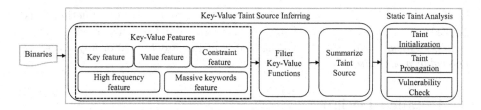

Fig. 3. Overview

function like `websGetVar` as a key-value function. Our goal is to automatically identify key-value functions and discover vulnerabilities by tracking the value through static taint analysis.

Different SOHO router vendors implement key-value functions in different manners. According to our observation, there are two main implementation methods of key-value functions: the value is indexed by the key and (a) saved by a pointer parameter or (b) saved by a return pointer. As shown in Fig. 2, the abstract C codes of these two implementation methods correspond to the function `KeyValue1` and `KeyValue2`. For the function `KeyValue1` in Fig. 2(a), the data *input* is the raw request posted by user. `KeyValue1` gets the address *v_index* of the corresponding value by finding the keyword *key* in *input* through calling a strcmp-like function (line 3–5). The raw value is then copied to the buffer pointed by the parameter *value* through a loop after examining some special characters (line 6–7). For the function `KeyValue2` in Fig. 2(b), the raw request has been split into (key, value) pairs and saved to a structure object *sd*. Then, `KeyValue2` indexes the keyword *key* by calling the strcmp-like function and returns a value *sd->value* (line 3–7).

There are some features in the two implementation of the key-value function. (1) *Key feature*: a parameter to key directly propagates to an argument of the strcmp-like function which is invoked in a loop; (2) *Value feature*: the pointer to value depends on one parameter (e.g., `KeyValue1`) or the return value (e.g., `KeyValue2`), and the data dependency graph contains a loop; (3) *Constraint feature*: key-value function may have a constant parameter that limits the value's length. However, this feature is optional and does not always exists in the implementation.

Besides, the behavior of calling key-value function to process requests has 2 additional features: (4) *High frequency feature*: the key-value function was called multiple times under different call-sites. (5) *Massive keywords feature*: different call-sites will refer to various constant keywords.

Except for the two implementation methods described above, some functions are wrappers for key-value functions. These functions also have key-value functionality, but they do not implement *key feature* and *value feature* themselves. As shown in Fig. 2(c), function `KeyValue3` calls a key-value function `KeyValue2` to get the value *v_index* and copies it to a memory block pointed by parameter *value* through calling a strcpy-like function. And function `KeyValue4` calls the key-value function `KeyValue2` to get the value *v_index* and returns it.

To better describe the following design, we refer to the functions like KeyValue1 as *key-value model one*, refer to the functions like KeyValue2 as *key-value model two*, and refer to the functions like KeyValue3 or KeyValue4 as *key-value model three*.

3   Detailed Design

In this section, we illustrate the detailed design of our system. As shown in Fig. 3, the proposed system is comprised of two major components. Its input is a binary with mainstream architectures (e.g., ARM, MIPS) used in embedded systems. To implement architecture-agnostic, it first converts the binary machine code into the intermediate representation (IR) [11]. Therefore, the proposed static binary analysis based on the VEX IR, which is a popular IR widely used in many program analysis tools, including Valgrind [11] and Angr [15]. To infer taint source, it first identifies the key-value features with static analysis. Then, it filters key-value functions by retrieving keywords from the local files extracted from the firmware image. Finally, it summarizes the taint source function and passes the summary information to the static taint analysis engine for vulnerabilities detection. To discover vulnerabilities, it first initializes data from the inferred taint source and tracks the taint through static taint analysis. Then, it detects taint-style vulnerabilities based on the constraints of the tainted data.

3.1   Key-Value Taint Source Inferring

This section describes how to infer the taint sources by identifying the key-value features with static analysis.

Identify Key-Value Function. As we mentioned in Sect. 2.2, a typical key-value function has some apparent features, as follows: *key feature*, *value feature*, *constraint feature*, *high frequency feature*, and *massive keywords feature*.

To find the above five features, our system first uses IDA Pro, the most powerful reverse-engineering tool in the market, to automatically identify functions in the target binary. Then, it selects the candidate functions through *high frequency feature* instead of analyzing all the functions, which can improve the analysis's efficiency. According to our experiments, key-value functions are typically called more than 100 times, which is the threshold for filtering. To identify the *massive keywords feature*, our system analyzes each candidate function's contexts at different call-sites to check whether it contains a pointer argument that points to a constant string. If not found or the number of constant string found does not exceed half the number of times the candidate function is called, our system removes the function from the candidate set. For *constraint feature*, our system also analyzes the function's contexts to summarize whether constant values are assigned to the same parameter at different call-sites. If found, the parameter is marked as a length constraint of the value. In the following, we illustrate how to identify *key feature* and *value feature* through data-flow analysis for the remaining candidate functions.

First, our system adopts the same approach proposed in [13] to identify strcmp-like functions automatically. Second, for a candidate function, our system generates a control flow graph (CFG) and traverses the CFG to find loops. If the CFG contains a loop and calls a strcmp-like function in the loop, our system backward traces the arguments of the strcmp-like function by following the conventional use-def chains. *Key feature* is identified if one of the strcmp-like function arguments depend on one parameter of the candidate function. Third, for *value feature* in model one, the bytes in value are moved through a loop from one buffer to another, where the address of another buffer is a pointer parameter of the candidate function. Our system forward traces all parameters of the candidate function and try to find a parameter, which is a pointer and is used to an address of a byte-store instruction(e.g., the register R4 in STRB R0, [R4,R5] in ARM). If found, our system backward traces the address of the byte-store instruction (e.g., the register R4 and R5) to generate a data dependency graph (DDG). *Value feature* is found if there is a loop in the DDG. As a result, the candidate function is recognized as the *key-value model one*. Otherwise, our system backward traces the return value of the candidate function to generate a DDG. If there is a loop in the DDG, the candidate function is recognized as the *key-value model two*.

If the candidate function is neither *key-value model one*, nor *key-value model two*, we determine whether it is *key-value model three*. To identify this model, our system analyzes all its callees. If there is a callee that meets the features of *key-value model two*, our system iteratively analyzes its callers and determine whether its caller is *key-value model three* by the following two conditions.

(1) The key-value function and its caller have the same argument *key* that points to a constant string.
(2) For the function like KeyValue3, the caller's return value depends on the key-value function's return value. For the function like KeyValue4, the value returned from the key-value function is copied to the memory block pointed to by the caller's pointer parameter. The copy is implemented by some library functions (e.g., strcpy, strncpy, memcpy, etc.).

Once founding a new key-value function, our system continues to analyze its callers according to the above two conditions until no other key-value function is found.

Filter Key-Value Functions and Generate Summary of Taint Sources. There are also some functions that show the features, but they are not handling key-value pair from network inputs (e.g., parsing local configuration files). The values read from local files are not controlled by an attacker. Therefore, these key-value functions should not be treated as taint sources. We introduced how to filter them in the following. First, our system collects all constant keywords at its calling contexts for each identified key-value function. Then, our system

extracts all the files in the firmware image and matches the content in texts
with regular expressions to look up strings like *key=value* or *key:value*. Lastly, if
most of the keywords of a key-value function (more than 80% of the number of
times the key-value function is called) are in the local file, this key-value function
is not considered as a taint source. Besides, our system filters which key-value
functions are called no more than 100 times.

For the identified taint sources, our system summarizes their parameters and
return values. The summary information includes the parameter or return value
that needs to be tainted, and the parameter represents the length constraint of
the value and parameter for keywords. This information is passed to the static
taint analysis engine for taint-style vulnerabilities detection.

3.2   Static Taint Analysis

The static taint analysis aims at find taint-style vulnerabilities by tracking the
tainted data from the taint sources identified above.

Table 1. The taint propagation rules in VEX IR

IR statements	Description	Taint rules
$t_i = GET(r_j)$	Assign a value from register r_j to Temp t_i	$r_j \mapsto t_i$
$PUT(r_j) = t_i$	Assign Temp t_i to register r_j	$t_i \mapsto r_j$
$t_i = t_j$	Assign Temp t_j to Temp t_i	$t_j \mapsto t_i$
$t_i = binop(t_n, t_m)$	Assign result of $t_n \Diamond_b t_m$ to Temp t_i	
	$\Diamond_b ::= +, -, *, /, \ll, \gg$	$t_n \mapsto t_i, t_m \mapsto t_i$
	$\Diamond_b ::= <, >, <=, >=, ==, ! =$	$t_n \rightsquigarrow t_i, t_m \rightsquigarrow t_i$
$t_i = ITE(t_j, t_n, t_m)$	If t_j is true, $t_i = t_n$, otherwise, $t_i = t_m$	$t_n \mapsto t_i, t_m \mapsto t_i$
$t_i = LDle(t_j)$	Assign value loaded from address t_j to t_i	$t_j \mapsto t_i, *t_j \mapsto t_i$
$STle(t_j) = t_i$	Store t_i to the memory at address t_j	$t_i \mapsto *t_j$

$t_n \mapsto t_i$ denotes that the taint propagate from t_n to t_i.
$t_n \rightsquigarrow t_i$ denotes that if t_n is taint, its constraint is t_i.

Taint Initialization and Propagation. Instead of starting from the entry
point (e.g., `main`) of a program, our system starts with the functions that invoke
the taint sources. It marks the argument register or returned register at each
call-site that invokes a taint source as taint with a unique id according to its
summary information. The unique id can distinguish tainted data that comes
from different call-sites and helps us associate the tainted data with various
keywords. Then, the tainted data is propagated forward along the def-use chains
through the analysis of VEX IR's statements and expressions. In the forward
taint analysis, Table 1 shows the taint propagation rules. Specially, when an IR
statement's operator is a comparison (e.g., *binop* is $CmpLE$) and the tainted
data is one of its operands, our system collects the constraint (e.g., $x < 8$ where

x is taint). Moreover, if the comparison operand is not a constant (e.g., $x < y$ where x is taint), our system backward tracks the operand y to find its value within the current function. If operand y is found to be assigned a constant, our system updates the corresponding constraint. Another consideration is the taint propagation rule between the memory accesses with load and store operations. As shown in Table 1, the load operation LDle corresponds to two rules $t_j \mapsto t_i$ and $*t_j \mapsto t_i$. The former denotes that a value t_i is read from a tainted address t_j, and the value t_i is marked as taint. In this case, the loaded value t_i may be an integer or a character. The latter denotes that the object to which pointer t_j points is tainted data, and the loaded object t_i is marked as taint. In this case, the tainted data previously stored in memory through the STle operation is loaded with the same address. For the taint propagation in memory accesses, our system only tracks the global address, stack address, and simple indirect memory access with the same register base and constant offset (e.g., $STle(r_0 + 0x20)$ and $LDle(r_0 + 0x20)$).

For the interprocedural taint analysis, we apply the method of generating taint summaries to improve the efficiency of taint analysis [12]. When a callee is encountered in the taint analysis, our system ignores the callee if its arguments are not tainted. Otherwise, our system follows the callee and generates a summary for the callee. The taint summary describes the tainted parameters of input and the new parameters or return values that are tainted after analyzing the callee. Therefore, when the same callee is encountered, if the tainted data being tracked is in the taint summary of the callee, our system uses the summary to quickly propagate the taint. Otherwise, it analyzes the callee again and update the taint summary.

For the library functions, our system also adopts the taint summaries to propagate taint. Their taint summaries are generated manually, and we just implement summaries for some common string-related library functions (e.g., strcpy, memcpy, strstr, strcmp, etc.). For example, when meeting the library function strcpy(*dest, *src), the taint propagates from parameter src to parameter dest. In taint analysis, library functions are not followed if they do not implement summaries.

Vulnerability Check. In our system, we mainly discover the stack-based buffer overflow and command injection vulnerabilities. When the taint reaches a string-copy sink, such as strcpy(*dest, *src), and the copy's memory block pointed to by destination dest is a stack address, our system first calculates the maximum size max_buffer of the destination buffer. Then, our system checks the constraints of the tainted data. If the constraints are empty, an alert is generated. If the constraints are not empty and contain a symbolic constraint, the sink is security and no alert is generated. such as len < x, where the symbol len is the length of the string pointed to by the tained pointer and the symbol x is a symbolic value. Otherwise, our system solves the constraints to obtain the minimum value of the string length `len`. If the minimum value is larger than the `max_buffer`, an alert is generated. For command injection, if the taint reaches a command-execution sink (e.g., `system` and `popen`) and the constraints of the taint are empty, an alert is generated.

4 Evaluation

4.1 Implementation

We have implemented a prototype on top of VEX IR using python. In particular, we first utilize the IDA Pro to identify functions and generate a control flow graph (CFG) for the target program. Then, we load the target binary and convert assembly code into VEX IR by Angr's API based on the generated CFG. Finally, based on the IR, we implemented the data-flow analysis to infer key-value functions and taint analysis to discover vulnerabilities.

4.2 Experiment Setup

In the experiment, we selected 10 router's firmware images from five different vendors. Table 2 shows the summary information of 10 firmware images. We utilize Binwalk [3] to unpack the firmware images and extract the web-server programs that handle requests. The architecture of these programs includes ARM32 and MIPS32, which are the mainstream architectures used in SOHO routers. All the experiments were conducted on a Ubuntu 18.04.4 LTS OS with a 64-bit 8-core Inter(R) Core(TM) i7-8550 CPU and 24 GB RAM.

Table 2. Information of SOHO routers and analyzed programs

ID	Vendor	Product	Version	Architecture	Program	Size (KB)
1	NETGEAR	Orbi RBR20	V2.6.1.36	ARM32	net-cgi	696
2	NETGEAR	WNDR4500v3	V1.0.0.50	MIPS32	net-cgi	694
3	NETGEAR	R8500	V1.0.2.116	ARM32	httpd	1,506
4	NETGEAR	R7800	V1.0.2.46	ARM32	net-cgi	581
5	Tenda	AC9V1.0	V15.03.05.19	ARM32	httpd	960
6	Tenda	AC9V3.0	V15.03.06.42_multi	MIPS32	httpd	2,039
7	Tenda	G3V3.0	V15.11.0.6	ARM32	httpd	1,676
8	Mercury	Mer450	MER1200GV1.0	MIPS32	nginx	759
9	D-Link	DAP-1860	v1.04B05	MIPS32	uhttpd	1,137
10	TP-Link	TL-WR940N	V6_200316	MIPS32	httpd	1,899

Table 3. The summary of identified key-value functions

ID	Program	No. All identified K-V	No. K-V af. Filtering	No. Called	No. KeyKey	Time (sec.)(sec.)	True taint source functions
1	net-cgi	5	2	1,072	988	34.1	0x39864, 0x19b1c
2	net-cgi	3	2	956	908	26.1	0x40e8dc, 0x42c6c8
3	httpd	5	1	1,307	1,275	38.5	0x190c0
4	net-cgi	3	2	713	692	23.3	0x10678, 0x27bf4
5	httpd	9	1	491	485	27.5	0x2b9d4
6	httpd	7	1	491	485	40.8	0x430468
7	httpd	10	1	613	547	25.7	0x1c634
8	nginx	0	0	0	0	22.4	None
9	uhttpd	2	2	598	585	24.0	0x417574, 0x4a19d0
10	httpd	11	1	1,134	1,103	55.2	0x526710
Total	-	55	13	7,375	7,068	317.6	13

4.3 Key-Value Taint Source Inferring

Table 3 shows the results of key-value functions that our system automatically recognizes. It identified a total of 55 functions with key-value feature in 317.6 s. After filtering, it obtained 13 key-value functions, all of which have been verified as the **true taint source** by binary reverse-engineering. The true taint source refers to the constant key and corresponding value obtained by the key-value function are from network requests. The 13 taint source functions were called a total of 7,375 times, and 7,068 constant keys were found at these call-sites. With the exception of firmware MER450 with ID 8, which did not find the key-value function, the other nine firmware images inferred 1 or 2 taint sources. We found that these taint sources can be divided into two categories. One is to

Table 4. The summary of the vulnerabilities that our system found

ID	Product	Alerts		True alerts		Vulnerabilities		Time (sec.)
		MEM	CMD	MEM	CMD	MEM	CMD	
1	Orbi RBR20	1	2	0	0	0	0	68.7
2	WNDR4500v3	65	5	41	4	31	4	51.8
3	R8500	57	10	37	5	31	5	83.2
4	R7800	68	12	36	2	30	2	65.9
5	AC9V1.0	76	15	67	7	30	5	71.6
6	AC9V3.0	85	11	78	3	35	3	78.5
7	G3V3.0	28	2	25	2	22	2	59.5
8	Mer450	0	0	0	0	0	0	-
9	DAP-1860	52	16	48	16	24	16	42.6
10	TL-WR940N	5	0	5	0	5	0	207.2
Total	-	510		376		245		729.0

Table 5. Known published vulnerabilities

Model	Vulnerabilit ID
Tenda AC9V1	CVE-2018-14492, CVE-2018-14559, CVE-2018-16333, CVE-2018-16334,
Tenda AC9V3	CVE-2018-18706, CVE-2018-18707, CVE-2018-18708, CVE-2018-18709,
	CVE-2018-18727, CVE-2018-18728, CVE-2018-18729, CVE-2018-18730,
	CVE-2018-18731, CVE-2018-18732, CVE-2020-10987, CVE-2020-13389,
	CVE-2020-13390, CVE-2020-13391, CVE-2020-13392, CVE-2020-13393, CVE-2020-13394

get key-value pairs from HTTP protocol-based requests and the other is to get key-value pairs from SOAP protocol-based requests. Firmware images with IDs 1, 2, 4, and 9 contain both types of taint sources, while taint sources in other firmware images fall into the first category.

4.4 Effectiveness of Vulnerability Detection

In the current prototype, we detect memory corruptions (MEM) and command injections (CMD). All the taint sources came from the key-value functions we inferred. Table 4 summarizes the results. For the 10 firmware images, our system reported 510 alerts in about 12 min, among which 376 were true positives (an accuracy of 73.7%). In this paper, we treat the vulnerabilities that meet anyone following the condition as duplicate vulnerability. 1) The tainted data that trigger the vulnerability is propagated from the same source, where the address of the call-site called the taint source is the same. 2) The tainted data from different sources trigger vulnerability at the same sink point. Therefore, we manually verified each true alert by reverse-engineering, removed the duplicate vulnerabilities and found 245 different vulnerabilities, including 208 memory corruptions and 37 command injections.

Vulnerability Verification. For the 245 different vulnerabilities, we verified them using dynamic analysis and static analysis. For dynamic analysis, we acquired three physical devices (NETGEAR R8500, NETGEAR R7800, and Tenda AC9V3) and successfully crafted PoEs for all the 106 vulnerabilities in the three devices, including 96 memory corruptions and 10 command injections. Since we do not have physical devices for the other 7 routers, we did not dynamically validate all vulnerabilities. For the remaining 139 vulnerabilities, we have verified them by binary reverse-engineering. The taint sources of all these vulnerabilities are the key-value function identified by our system. We manually analyzed each of the remaining vulnerabilities and found that the value that key-value function obtained from the request was propagated to the sink without any sanitization. Therefore, we believe that the remaining 139 vulnerabilities are true positives.

Further, to match the known vulnerabilities, we collected vulnerability information for the relevant devices from the Internet (e.g., exploit-db [2] and MITRE CVE [1]). As shown in Table 5, we found 21 CVE IDs with vulnerability details that match the vulnerabilities found by our system. All these IDs belong to

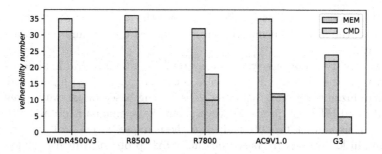

Fig. 4. Comparative evaluation: our system vs. SRFuzzer

Tenda AC9V1 and Tenda AC9V3, and the 21 IDs correspond to 41 different vulnerabilities. The reason is that an ID may correspond to multiple different vulnerabilities in the same device or different devices. For the remaining 204 vulnerabilities, no public disclosure information can be found. We have reported the 204 vulnerabilities to relevant vendors (responsible disclosure).

4.5 Comparison

Lastly, we conducted a comparison experiment with the state-of-the-art tool SRFuzzer [18]. SRFuzzer is the first whole-process fully-automatic framework for fuzzing web server of SOHO router. It obtains key-value pairs by capturing and parsing as many requests as possible and tests the device by mutating the values. In contrast, we search functions that process key-value in binary through static analysis and detect vulnerabilities by tracking values through taint analysis. Note that we only compare the ability to discover memory corruption and command injection.

SRFuzzer is not open-source, and 10 firmware images were analyzed according to the paper [18]. We selected 5 of the 10 firmware images for the comparison experiment. Figure 4 shows the results of the comparison. On the same 5 firmware images, SRFuzzer found 59 vulnerabilities, including 48 memory corruptions and 11 command injections. As a comparison, our system discovered 162 vulnerabilities, including 144 memory corruptions and 18 command injections. For these two types of vulnerabilities, our system detected more vulnerabilities than SRFuzzer in all five firmware images, except for the command injections in R7800.

For the other 5 firmware images, we did not find the corresponding firmware version of NETGEAR Orbi on the Internet, failed to unpack the firmware of NETGEAR Insight through Binwalk [3], and did not identify key-value functions after extracting the target programs from TP-Link TL-WVR900G, Mercury Mer450, and Asus RT-AC1200. In the 5 firmware images, SRFuzzer found a total of 28 command injections and 0 memory corruption, including 1 in firmware of NETGEAR Insight, 2 in firmware of Mercury Mer450, and the remaining 25 in firmware of TP-Link TL-WVR900G. However, all of the 27 command injections in Mer450 and TL-WVR900G are found in Lua script files, not binaries.

Vulnerability detection in script files is beyond the scope of our system. Overall, even within the same 10 firmware, our system was able to find more bugs than SRFuzzer.

There are two reasons why our system found more vulnerabilities than SRFuzzer on the test set. First, static analysis can achieve higher code coverage than fuzzing. Second, SRFuzzer does fuzzing based on key-values obtained from captured HTTP requests. However, some key-value pairs obtained through static analysis cannot be obtained from these requests. For example, requests that contain key-values are based on the SOAP protocol, which is widely used in router configuration. Another example is some hidden URLs that cannot be triggered by the SOHO router's management interface through a web browser.

5   Discussion

In this section, we discuss the limitations of our system and what improvements could be made in the future. During the experimental evaluation, we found that the backend program in firmware of some routers does not always follow the three patterns described in Sect. 2.2 to parse the user requests. Therefore, our system cannot automatically infer the taint source and initialize the tainted data, resulting in the system missing some potential vulnerabilities in these firmware.

According to our analysis, there are three main reasons. First, the backend CGI program gets value from the HTTP request by calling function `getenv` with a keyword. For example, in the firmware of NETGEAR R7800, the CGI program *net-cgi* obtains a string value by calling `getenv("HTTP_USER_AGENT")` in function `sub_4DCD8` and propagates the value to `strcpy` without checking the string length. This is a memory corruption vulnerability found by KARONTE [13] and will be missed by our system. Second, the backend program directly reads value from the HTTP request without using any keyword. Third, the backend program invokes the script file (e.g., Lua script in Mer450 and TL-WVR900G) to parse and process the HTTP request. For example, in the vulnerability CVE-2017-15614 found by SRFuzzer [18], the value of "outif" keyword is read and propagated to function `sys.fork_exec` in the pptp_client.lua file. In the first case, we can find the corresponding vulnerability by setting `getenv` as the taint source. In the latter two cases, we will analyze more firmware to find other patterns for inferring the taint source and try to analyze scripting languages to discover more potential vulnerabilities.

6   Related Work

Fuzzing on Embedded Devices. Many related works utilize fuzzing to discover vulnerabilities on physical device or on emulated firmware. Wang et al. [18] proposed a fuzzing framework RPFuzzer for detecting vulnerabilities in specific router protocols. To tackle the challenge of lacking in access to firmware images of some embedded devices, IoTFuzzer [5] detects memory corruption by performing black-box fuzzing on the real-world devices with the rich communication information in the companion mobile apps. Zhang et al. [20] proposed a fully-automatic fuzzing framework called SRFuzzer to discover variation vulnerabilities in web servers of SOHO routers. It utilized the key-value feature in the request and the configuration-read model in the communication to guide the mutation for fuzzing. However, the fuzzing based on physical devices is limited by the high expensive cost and is not suitable for large-scale devices analysis. Muench et al. [10] achieved effective memory corruption detection on embedded devices through partial and full firmware emulation. Zheng et al. [22] proposed a technique called "augmented process emulation" to enhance throughput and guarantee correct emulation of the given program by switching between user-mode emulation and full system emulation. To improve the efficiency of fuzzing, they also adopted static analysis to help generate useful inputs for fuzzing [21]. However, due to different peripherals and frequent I/O interactions, current emulation techniques do not guarantee successful emulation of various firmware.

Static Vulnerability Discovery. Most of the vulnerability discovery based on static analysis foucus on traditional PC programs [4,12] and source code [7,8,19]. Few techniques exist to detect vulnerabilities on embedded devices. Firmalice [14] was specifically developed to detect the authentication bypass vulnerability in binary firmware. DTaint [6] detected taint-style vulnerabilities in firmware through building intra- and inter-procedural data flow in a bottom-up manner with pointer alias analysis. KARONTE [13] first proposed to discover multi-binary vulnerabilities through modelling interaction between multiple binaries in the firmware. However, DTaint relies on the symbols of the function to manually specify specific taint source to detect associated vulnerabilities; KARONTE relies on network-encoding keywords to infer the taint source. For example, keyword strings associated with "HTTP". In contrast, our system is able to automatically infer taint source functions and obtain large amounts of tainted data to reduce false negatives.

7 Conclusion

In this work, we propose a new heuristic approach to discover vulnerabilities in the firmware images of SOHO routers whithout addressing indirect calls. Specially, we automatically infer taint sources through identifying functions with key-value features. With the inferred taint sources, we track the taint to detect vulnerabilities by static taint analysis. We implement a prototype system and evaluate it on 10 popular routers across 5 vendors. The proposed system discovered 245 vulnerabilities, including 41 1-day vulnerabilities and 204 vulnerabilities never exposed before. The experimental results show that our system can find more bugs compared to a state-of-the-art fuzzing tool.

Acknowledgement. This work was supported by the National Key R&D Program of China (Grant No. Y950201104), and Key Program of National Natural Science Foundation of China (Grant No. U1766215).

References

1. Common vulnerabilities and exposures. https://cve.mitre.org/
2. Exploit database of the website. https://www.exploit-db.com/
3. Firmware analysis tool. https://github.com/ReFirmLabs/binwalk
4. Balakrishnan, G., Gruian, R., Reps, T., Teitelbaum, T.: CodeSurfer/x86—a platform for analyzing x86 executables. In: Bodik, R. (ed.) CC 2005. LNCS, vol. 3443, pp. 250–254. Springer, Heidelberg (2005). https://doi.org/10.1007/978-3-540-31985-6_19
5. Chen, J., et al.: IoTFuzzer: discovering memory corruptions in IoT through app-based fuzzing. In: NDSS (2018)
6. Cheng, K., et al.: DTaint: detecting the taint-style vulnerability in embedded device firmware. In: DSN (2018)
7. Corteggiani, N., Camurati, G., Francillon, A.: Inception: system-wide security testing of real-world embedded systems software. In: USENIX Security (2018)
8. Davidson, D., Moench, B., Ristenpart, T., Jha, S.: {FIE} on firmware: finding vulnerabilities in embedded systems using symbolic execution. In: USENIX Security (2013)
9. Eli Kreminchuker, M.Z.: Echobot malware now up to 71 exploits, targeting scada (2019). https://www.f5.com/labs/articles/threat-intelligence/echobot-malware-now-up-to-71-exploits-targeting-scada
10. Muench, M., Stijohann, J., Kargl, F., Francillon, A., Balzarotti, D.: What you corrupt is not what you crash: challenges in fuzzing embedded devices. In: NDSS (2018)
11. Nethercote, N., Seward, J.: Valgrind: a framework for heavyweight dynamic binary instrumentation. ACM Sigplan Not. **42**(6), 89–100 (2007)
12. Rawat, S., Mounier, L., Potet, M.-L.: Static taint-analysis on binary executables (2011). http://web.cs.iastate.edu/~weile/cs513x/5.TaintAnalysis2.pdf
13. Redini, N., et al.: Karonte: detecting insecure multi-binary interactions in embedded firmware. In: SP (2020)
14. Shoshitaishvili, Y., Wang, R., Hauser, C., Kruegel, C., Vigna, G.: Firmalice-automatic detection of authentication bypass vulnerabilities in binary firmware. In: NDSS (2015)
15. Shoshitaishvili, Y., et al.: Sok:(state of) the art of war: offensive techniques in binary analysis. In: SP (2016)
16. Statista: Internet of things (IoT) (2020). https://www.statista.com/topics/2637/internet-of-things/
17. TrendMicro: Smart yet flawed: IoT device vulnerabilities explained (2020). https://www.trendmicro.com/vinfo/us/security/news/internet-of-things/smart-yet-flawed-iot-device-vulnerabilities-explained
18. Wang, Z., Zhang, Y., Liu, Q.: Rpfuzzer: a framework for discovering router protocols vulnerabilities based on fuzzing. KSII TIIS **7**(8), 1989–2009 (2013)
19. Yamaguchi, F., Maier, A., Gascon, H., Rieck, K.: Automatic inference of search patterns for taint-style vulnerabilities. In: SP (2015)
20. Zhang, Y., et al.: SrFuzzer: an automatic fuzzing framework for physical soho router devices to discover multi-type vulnerabilities. In: ACSAC (2019)

21. Zheng, Y., Song, Z., Sun, Y., Cheng, K., Zhu, H., Sun, L.: An efficient greybox fuzzing scheme for Linux-based IoT programs through binary static analysis. In: IPCCC (2019)
22. Zheng, Y., Davanian, A., Yin, H., Song, C., Zhu, H., Sun, L.: FIRM-AFL: high-throughput greybox fuzzing of IoT firmware via augmented process emulation. In: USENIX Security (2019)

Covert Channels and Cryptography

ESQABE: Predicting Encrypted Search Queries

Isaac Meers[1]([✉])(ID), Mariano Di Martino[1](ID), Peter Quax[2](ID),
and Wim Lamotte[1](ID)

[1] UHasselt - Hasselt University - tUL, Expertise Centre for Digital Media (EDM),
Wetenschapspark 2, 3590 Diepenbeek, Belgium
`isaac.meers@uhasselt.be`

[2] UHasselt - Hasselt University - tUL - Flanders Make, Expertise Center for Digital
Media (EDM), Wetenschapspark 2, 3590 Diepenbeek, Belgium

Abstract. All popular search engines implement HTTPS to protect the
privacy of their users. Unfortunately, HTTPS encryption only covers
Application layer headers and information will still leak through side-
channels and other protocols used in a conversation between browser
and server. This paper presents a novel eavesdropping approach called
ESQABE, which combines these sources of information in order to determine what a subject is querying a search engine for in a real-life situation.
To achieve this goal, packet length and timing information of the autocomplete functionality are used in combination with the home page contents of the search result links subsequently opened by the user. ESQABE
is evaluated by automated tests using realistic search queries and based
on real-life behavior. The technique is able to correctly predict the search
query in 33% of the cases which is a significant improvement when compared to related work. In 41% of the cases, the correct query was included
in the top 3 of most likely predictions. In most other cases no prediction could be made. To better protect the user, we contribute a browser
extension that effectively hides the search query for the eavesdropper.
The tool not only protects users but also visualizes what information is
leaking to an eavesdropper.

Keywords: Eavesdropping · Privacy · Network security

1 Introduction

Search queries are often exploited as a valuable source to predict user interests.
In contrast to simply opening a website for any reason, entering a search query in
an engine often implies an actual interest in a specific subject. This could include
highly personal (and thus, privacy-sensitive) information about users such as shopping interests, religious beliefs, political preferences, etc. Obtaining an anonymized
set of queries has already led to the identification of a real person [1].

To protect the privacy of users, internet traffic nowadays is mostly encrypted.
According to the Google Transparency Report[1], US users spent 97% of their time

---

[1] https://transparencyreport.google.com/https/overview.

© IFIP International Federation for Information Processing 2021
Published by Springer Nature Switzerland AG 2021
A. Jøsang et al. (Eds.): SEC 2021, IFIP AICT 625, pp. 103–117, 2021.
https://doi.org/10.1007/978-3-030-78120-0_7

in Chrome on HTTPS websites in 2020. The main advantage of applying encryption from a privacy perspective is the protection against eavesdropping or man-in-the-middle attacks. However, HTTPS is an application layer protocol and does not cover metadata of lower layer protocols, such as IP addresses on the network layer. The amount of unencrypted information per packet is limited, but eavesdroppers can combine it with other sources and use it to identify their subjects. When a user searches, a lot of traffic which leaks metadata is generated. First, the autocomplete functionality generates traffic to keep the list of suggestions up to date. Next, when the user submits his query, the list of search results which contains hyperlinks to relevant websites is loaded. And when the user visits these websites, the browser will establish new HTTPS connections to the relevant servers to download web pages. This results in a temporary increase in network traffic flowing between the user and the internet. In this work, this meta-information is used to identify search queries entered by users. But as noted in Sect. 3.6, not all search engines are vulnerable and especially privacy aware search engines do a better job at protecting their users by sending less information to their servers. Concretely, the following contributions are presented in this paper:

- A novel approach, ESQABE, to determine the contents of search queries entered by subjects using only information available to a passive eavesdropper (i.e., HTTPS encrypted traffic). ESQABE outperforms existing approaches as it is able to correctly predict the search query in over 32% of the cases where other approaches as KREEP [8] only reach 15% on top-50 accuracy.
- A browser extension that protects users against the eavesdroppers using ESQABE, but also educates which data still leaks to an eavesdropper.
- The source code of both ESQABE and the protection tool, as well as the dataset of traces used for evaluation, are made available at https://github.com/isaacme/ESQABE.

2   Related Work

Table 1. Comparison of related work with ESQABE

	KREEP (2019) [8]	Oh et al. (2017) [9]	Chen et al. (2010) [2]	ESQABE
Protocols	HTTPS	Tor	Wi-Fi WPA	HTTPS, DNS
Data needed	Language model and avg. typing speeds	Fingerprints for target keywords	None	None
Targeted keywords	In dictionary (>12k words)	300 targets	Unlimited	Unlimited
Information sources	Auto-complete requests	Fingerprinting TOR-traffic	Auto-complete responses	Auto-complete + subsequent requests

Other attempts that try to identify search queries sent by a user, operate on a different level compared to ESQABE. Table 1 shows a comparison of the major differences of ESQABE to the related works described in this section.

KREEP [8] – a passive eavesdropping approach – identifies the complete search query while only using the requests generated by the autocomplete functionality. They first extract the requests which are sent when a new character is typed into the search bar and use these to determine the total query length. Secondly, they tokenize these requests (separating spaces from other characters) to find the length of the different words in the query. Based on the inter arrival times between keystrokes, a neural network identifies words using a dictionary. The training set of this network was composed of keystrokes recorded from 83000 typists using QWERTY keyboards and typing English words. The predictions of the neural network are filtered based on the info of the tokenization algorithm. Finally, a language model is used to further reduce these predictions to a list of 50 hypothesis queries. For 15% of the tested search queries in [8], the generated list of 50 hypothesis queries included the actual query. This is clearly less effective than our approach, but the results cannot be compared directly as will be described in Sect. 4.

ESQABE builds further on the detection and tokenization algorithms of KREEP, these are discussed in detail in Sect. 3.2. In contrast to our approach, KREEP assumes the user is typing in English and using a QWERTY keyboard. It is also assumed that all words in the search query appear in the language model used by the eavesdropper. This limits the real-world effectiveness of KREEP, as users might search for brand names (typically limited in a dictionary) or in other languages, neither of which are included in the model. In ESQABE, we also investigate subsequent traffic (like site visits), but in KREEP solely the timings of keystrokes based on packet inter-arrival times are used.

In [9], website fingerprinting approaches are used to fingerprint individual queries or keywords. They take into account all traffic generated when searching, starting from the moment the user commences typing until 5 s after the results page is loaded. Instead of using HTTPS captures directly, the captures contained traffic as generated by the Tor browser. This attack identifies if the query contains one of the 300 predefined targeted keywords with a precision of 91% and a recall of 81%. Which specific keyword from the list was found could be determined with 48% accuracy. The use case of this approach differs from ours as [9] can be used to filter specific keywords in firewalls while ESQABE focuses more on query reconstruction without a limited predefined list.

An older attack [2] describes a method relying on the sizes of the responses for the autocomplete traffic. In contrast to our approach, this attack is described to work with Wi-Fi WPA encrypted packets and thus cannot use IP addresses to filter the autocomplete traffic. They determine the query incrementally by trying to add each character (a-z, ␣) and keeping the one with the response sizes closest to the captured response. This attack assumes that the eavesdropper who tries to guess the query gets the same suggestions as the target. But, this attack should be reevaluated as suggestions generated by search engines nowadays are tailored to the specific user resulting in different response sizes.

3 ESQABE: Encrypted Search Query Analysis by Eavesdropping

In this section we describe ESQABE, an approach that makes it possible for a passive eavesdropper to determine a user's search query from encrypted network traffic. The main idea of ESQABE is to combine the available metadata of the encrypted communication with information gathered from the unencrypted network traffic. This is subdivided in several steps of information retrieval:

1. The lengths of the words in the search query are derived from the autocomplete traffic. This information is used to generate a *pattern* of the query. This step is based on the detection and tokenization algorithms of KREEP.
2. A list of the search results opened by the user is composed. The sudden increase of bandwidth usage caused by opening a new website is used to detect when the user opened a result. Info from DNS queries and TLS Client Hello messages is used to identify which website the result linked to.
3. The home pages of these websites are visited and the words matching the patterns of the first step are extracted. For each word extracted, the amount of occurrences on the home pages is counted.
4. If a Wikipedia article was among the results the user opened, its fingerprint is used to reduce the list of potential queries.

Finally, a ranking of possible search queries is generated. The larger the amount of occurrences, the higher the word appears in the ranking.

3.1 Prerequisites

We assume the eavesdropper has the ability to capture encrypted network traffic traces from the client containing the entire search action (beginning when a user starts typing their query and ending when they stop opening results). These traces do not only contain the communication between the browser and the search engine server, but also other traffic generated by the computer (e.g., DNS traffic). This traffic can easily be captured by the owners of the internet gateways users connect with. Apart from home and company networks these also include those of hotels, airports, museums etc. On open Wi-Fi networks, not only the owners but also other users and even passersby can capture enough traffic. ISP's and regimes in less democratic countries are also positioned on the path between client and server. Users connected through a VPN hide the necessary data from most of the previous instances but make the data available to the VPN provider who they have to trust. The following realistic assumptions are made:

- All captured connections use HTTP/1.1 or HTTP/2. HTTP/3 and QUIC are out-of-scope of this paper. As Google Search on Google Chrome utilizes QUIC, a significant amount of queries is not directly susceptible to ESQABE. Nevertheless, a large number of queries is made using HTTP/1.1 and HTTP/2 (e.g., on networks blocking UDP, other browsers etc.).

- All websites visited by the user are encrypted through HTTPS. Extraction of information from HTTP traffic is straightforward as it is not encrypted. For this reason HTTP traffic is considered out-of-scope.
- It is assumed that for communication only TLS encryption is used. So IP, TCP and TLS headers are captured unencrypted.
- The user typed their complete search query without typographical mistakes or corrections. Some search engines correct minor mistakes after query submission. If the words of the correction are of the same length as the words in the erroneous query, then the effectiveness of ESQABE will not be decreased. According to [3], only 10–15% of queries entered contain errors.
- ESQABE is optimized for the extraction of search queries made using Google Search. Nonetheless, the techniques described can be used on other search engines as long as they provide an autocomplete functionality. This assumption is discussed in depth in Sect. 3.6.

3.2   Step 1: Extracting Search Query Length

Table 2. An overview of autocomplete requests on Google Search while entering *Hasselt University* as a query using HTTP/2. On the left, the details as visible in the browser are shown. On the right, the sizes of the packets as visible by an eavesdropper.

Actual request			Eavesdropper	
Query parameter	HTTP header (B)	Increment	Frame length (B)	Increment
...				
hassel	720	+1	206	+1
hasselt	721	+1	206	+0
hasselt%20	724	+3	208	+2
hasselt%20u	725	+1	209	+1
...				
hasselt%20university	735	+1	216	+1

The first step taken in ESQABE is extracting the traffic generated by the autocomplete functionality to determine the lengths of the different words in the search query. As search engines encrypt their application layer data with HTTPS, extraction methods need to be based on the information available in the non-encrypted headers of underlying protocols. The method used to achieve this is based on the detection and tokenization mechanisms from KREEP [8].

Detecting the packets is based on the fact that the only difference between all autocomplete requests is the query parameter. As shown in the example of Table 2, the size of the header always increments by one byte for each new character added. A space is encoded as %20 and thus uses 3 bytes. For websites using HPACK compression with HTTP/2, these increments are not as consistent. HPACK uses a static Huffman code to encode string literals in which most alphanumeric characters are represented in 5 to 7 bits (in contrary to 8 bits with HTTP/1.1). As string literals cannot end in the middle of a byte, padding is used to fill the gap. When the added character is encoded in less bits than the padding in the previous request, the new request will have the same size. Nevertheless, this pattern of packets with incrementing size is still distinguishable from other traffic when HPACK is used. The right side of Table 2 shows an example of what the eavesdropper sees when HPACK is used, note that due to the compression a space causes a 2 byte instead of a 3 byte increment.

The detection of KREEP often fails on longer traces we used. KREEP is not optimized for traces that include the visits of the search engine results afterwards. To overcome this issue, a maximum is set on the time between key presses. Especially in the case of Google Search, detection of anomalies due to a parameter called gs_mss is improved. Not much details about the parameter are known, but when it suddenly appears it contains the query as typed until that point and keeps the same value for all subsequent requests. The increment in size it causes can be calculated and equals the length of the encoded query until this point plus the length of &gs_mss= which is 8 characters. Apart from adaptations to the length detection algorithm, a filter was added to only include IP addresses from the search engine – based on a reverse DNS lookup (for example, Google hosts are all within the domain 1e100.net).

After the autocomplete requests are extracted, they are analyzed in the tokenization phase in order to determine the length of the different words in the query. The fact that a space is encoded as %20, which causes a 2 or 3 byte increment, makes it distinguishable from other (single-byte) characters for an eavesdropper. This way we can easily split the query into separate words. Note that not all search engines encode a space as %20; some use + which is encoded using a single byte. For this limited amount of search engines the tokenization approach cannot be used and as a consequence these search engines are not vulnerable to ESQABE. A comparison of the applicability of popular search engines is discussed in Sect. 3.6.

3.3   Step 2: Identifying Opened Search Results

Once a user has submitted a search query, a list of results is shown - including hyperlinks to the relevant web page. Opening a web page from this list implies that the user leaves the search engine and sets up (a) connection(s) to a new website. Although the IP address of the server of this website is visible to the eavesdropper, this does not imply that the specific website on that IP address can be determined. This is due to the very common use of name-based virtual hosting, where multiple sites are hosted on the same server. In this case, distinction between sites is made by its hostname in the host in the HTTP headers, which are encrypted by HTTPS and not visible to the eavesdropper. Nevertheless, even in such conditions, identification of the website is rather straightforward as its hostname is sent in different protocol layers as well. DNS and the TLS Server Name Indication extension (SNI) default to sending the hostname in plain text. In ESQABE, these hostnames are linked to connections by investigating the SNI extension if available. For all other cases, a dictionary is created by examining captured DNS responses. If for one IP address several hostnames are found, the last entry that happened before the TLS Client Hello of the connection is used. The cases in which encrypted DNS or TLS Encrypted Client Hello are used will be discussed in Sect. 5.

Extracting the hostnames from the complete network traffic trace provides the eavesdropper with preliminary insights into what the user has connected to. However, this list not only contains hostnames of websites the subject intentionally visited as a result of the search query, but also includes others as a consequence of background traffic or third party resources used by these websites (e.g. scripts, images and style sheets). For example, the response of `uhasselt.be` indicates to the browser that it needs to fetch a script from `cdn.jsdelivr.net`. The web browser of the subject can only start to open new connections for these resources after the response of `uhasselt.be` starts arriving. Thus, the browser will always connect to the website requested by the user first (in this example `uhasselt.be`) and fetch the extra resources afterwards. Opening a web page causes a significant amount of data to be transferred between the subject and the internet. An eavesdropper will see this sudden increase in bytes transferred from and to their subject and can use this to identify a web page visit.

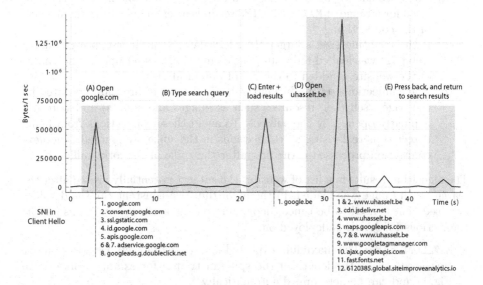

Fig. 1. Visualization of the amount of data when a user searches for Hasselt University and opens the university website. Below the graph, all SNI values for TLS Client Hello messages are shown (grouped by 2 s time frame).

The graph in Fig. 1 shows the characteristics of a page load visually. Phase A, C and D can all easily be detected due to the sudden change in data-rate. The amount of background traffic, that is being generated at the same time as the user is visiting a web page, is insignificant in comparison to the page load and does not affect the graph. Users executing other more network-heavy apps generate more traffic and make the extraction of the page load harder. These are often related to streaming services and games for which filters could be written based on known IP ranges or domain names. The bottom of the graph shows the new TLS connections set up by the subject during the capture of this trace.

With all this information, we propose the following strategy to obtain a realistic list of websites visited by the subject. The algorithm assumes a limited time frame in which the search took place. The timestamp of the last autocomplete packet (step 1) is the starting point of the algorithm.

1. The first step is to extract all new connections opened in the given time frame. As web pages are loaded using HTTPS, each connection to a new website is set up using a TLS handshake. These all start with a client sending a *Client Hello* message, which is used as an indicator for a new connection.
2. The *Server Name Indication* extension or dictionary as described in Sect. 3.3 is used to link each connection with the hostname of the visited website.
3. At the beginning of the time frame, the subject just landed on the page containing the search results. From here, ESQABE iterates chronologically over all new connections. For each connection the following is done:
   (a) The total size of the traffic between the subject and the internet is calculated for a range of MAX_LOAD_TIME seconds after the *Client Hello* message of the connection.
   (b) If the resulting size is larger than MIN_PAGE_SIZE, it is expected that a web page was loaded right after the connection was set up. The hostname of the website is added to the list of potential visits.
   (c) The connections set up during the load of the page are those initiated by the page itself (i.e., resources such as images and scripts) and were not explicitly opened by the subject. To avoid these connections from being detected as real visits, all connections in the spike are ignored. The next connection processed is the first after the spike in network traffic.

The algorithm results in a list of websites the subject potentially visited after the search results page was loaded. In the algorithm two constant threshold values are used. These need to be tuned, depending on the network conditions for the connections ESQABE is deployed on.

- MAX_LOAD_TIME: The maximum expected load time of a web page. In practice this needs to be the length of the spike in traffic (for example phase D in Fig. 1) and can be determined automatically.
- MIN_PAGE_SIZE: The minimum size of a web page. If this value is too small, system background traffic will be classified as website visit. But if this value is too large, legitimate website visits could be ignored.

3.4 Step 3: Visiting Home Pages of Websites

Combining both the information about the length of the different words in the search query, as well as the identity of the websites visited subsequently, we now try to deduce the complete search query. Websites mentioned in the search results are assumed to contain at least some information related to the search query, otherwise they would not have appeared in the search results. However, as explained earlier, we only know the hostname of the visited results and not the specific pages on that site. Fortunately, this does not imply that the home page cannot provide us with valuable information. We split this into several options:

- **The result links to the home page.** This is the most trivial case. When the subject opened a search result pointing to the home page of a website, this page will contain at least a part of the search query. Otherwise, it would not have appeared in the results. This happens when the user, for example, searches for a specific company, website, person or a keyword a company advertises on.
- **The result links to a Wikipedia article.** Wikipedia articles very often show up in the top search results. According to [6], a Wikipedia article appears in the first four results for 35% of their list of popular queries. For 73% of the queries of the dataset used in Sect. 4, the first page of search results contains a links to a Wikipedia article. As Wikipedia contains information about all sorts of topics, scraping its home page will not provide any useful information at all for ESQABE. Therefore, for Wikipedia pages, another approach is taken and described in Sect. 3.5.
- **The result links to another platform or webshop.** Platforms and webshops, like Booking.com, AirBnB, Steam and IMDB, provide a lot of items. On their home pages, they only feature a fraction of their assortment. This is however not implemented and left for future work, but we expect that depending on the platform, a similar approach to Wikipedia can be taken.
- **In all other cases,** the home page still provides a lot of relevant information about the topic. For example, company websites often feature several of their products on their home page, the home page of a television station lists the programs they broadcast and news websites feature their recent articles.

For each website in the list obtained in the previous section, the word(s) that match(es) the pattern of the search query are extracted. This is done by opening the home pages of the candidate websites with the Selenium WebDriver. To extract the word combinations, the following approach is taken for each website:

1. The home page of the website is fully loaded (until the `onload` event fires).
2. A small scroll movement is executed to trigger the loading of content below the fold, which due to lazy loading may not have been loaded otherwise.
3. All visible text is extracted from the `<body>` using the `innerText` property.
4. The strings of the title tag, image alt-tags, and selected page meta-tags (name, description, og:title, twitter:title, etc.) are extracted separately.
5. Once this extraction is finished, a regular expression generated from the word lengths of the search query is used to extract all matching strings.
6. The resulting sets of strings are combined in an associative array of counters with the string serving as key, ordered by decreasing number of appearances.

3.5   Step 4: Wikipedia

The home page of Wikipedia does not provide useful information for ESQABE. As there are millions of articles published on Wikipedia, it is impossible for an eavesdropper to determine which article was visited without additional information. However, if another result was opened besides the Wikipedia article, we can use the visit to Wikipedia to reduce the list of potential search queries by comparing web page fingerprints.

For each potential search query, the Wikipedia API is consulted to retrieve the corresponding article(s). Only the articles with the same title as the search query are selected. Sometimes a lookup will return a disambiguation page; in that case the 5 uppermost articles on this page are selected. If no relevant article can be found for a potential query, this query is ignored. Each selected article is visited in Google Chrome and Mozilla Firefox and separate network traffic traces are captured. These are provided (labeled) as the training set to a naive Bayes classifier as described by [7]. Note that these classifiers can also cause false positives. An existing implementation by Dyer et al. [5] is used in ESQABE. Eventually the capture of the Wikipedia traffic by the subject is tested against this classifier to determine which Wikipedia article was visited. The search query associated to this article is placed at the top of the list of potential search queries.

3.6   Vulnerable Search Engines

While we have mainly considered Google Search, other engines utilizing auto-complete functionality can be vulnerable to ESQABE as well. These engines all use HTTPS. The autocomplete requests vary subtly between search engines, as shown in Table 3. Some of them require small tweaks to ESQABE, especially during the phase of length detection, but the main concept remains unchanged.

Table 3. Comparison of applicability to multiple search engines

	Google	Baidu	Bing	Yahoo	Yandex	DuckDuckGo	Startpage.com
HTTP	HTTP/2	HTTP/1.1	HTTP/2	HTTP/2	HTTP/2	HTTP/2	HTTP/2
Space	%20	%20	%20	%20	+	+	+
Trigger	new character	new character	new character	new character	new character	new character 300 ms throttle	timeout
Special	gs_mss counter	counter	counter	/	/	/	random string
Applicable?	Yes	Yes	Yes	Yes	Only total length	No	No

Firstly, the absence of HTTP/2 (e.g., Baidu) in autocomplete traffic makes it easier to detect sequences as every new character causes a 1 byte increase. Secondly, some search engines encode their spaces as a + instead of a %20 in the autocomplete request, making a space indistinguishable from an alphanumeric character. However, while the length of the individual words in the query cannot be determined, their total length can still be utilized. Thirdly, DuckDuckGo throttles its autocomplete requests for 300 ms, dropping redundant requests occurring within this interval. As the amount of requests is used by the eavesdropper to determine the length of the query, DuckDuckGo is not vulnerable to our method. Fourthly, Startpage.com goes a step further and does only request new suggestions at the moment the subject stops typing. In addition, they even include a header containing a random length string which is changed at every request. Consequently, Startpage.com is also not vulnerable to ESQABE. In contrary to the other search engines, DuckDuckGo and Startpage.com are mainly focused on protecting the privacy of their users. Apart from not using their data for advertisement purposes, we also discovered that they are better in protecting their users from potential eavesdroppers.

4   Experimental Evaluation

4.1   Approach

To simulate realistic searching behavior, queries from real life datasets were used in our automated testing approach. Few datasets are available due to obvious privacy concerns [1], but agencies specialized in search engine optimization keep lists of the globally most popular queries[2]. We used an extraction of this list from May 2020 which is calculated using data from the last 6 months. To also include regional queries, the most popular terms from Google Trends[3] were added. As search results were opened automatically we filtered out keywords related to adult and illegal content to prevent security and legal risks. The list was generated during May 2020 and consists of 452 unique queries.

The tests were all automated through a script that uses the Selenium WebDriver. All tests were executed using version 76 of Firefox on a device running macOS 10.14. As the exploited characteristics originate in the web application itself or in user behavior, the browser should not have large impact on attack performance. At the beginning of every set of tests, a fresh Firefox profile was generated, clearing all browser caches. During each test, TShark was used to capture a network traffic trace, just like a possible eavesdropper would. Firefox was instructed to generate an SSLKEYLOGFILE for debugging purposes; this way the trace could be decrypted if necessary for further investigation. For all queries in the dataset, three captures were executed with respectively one, two and three results opened afterwards.

A real user visiting a website is mimicked by the following steps:

1. Open a fresh browser window and navigate to https://google.com.
2. After the page is fully loaded, click on the search box.
3. Mimic a user who is typing the query by entering one character at a time and leaving pauses of 0.3 s between two characters. Note that the inter key interval has no impact on the attack performance on search engines like Google Search, which do not implement throttling.

---

[2] https://www.mondovo.com/keywords/most-searched-words-on-google/.
[3] https://trends.google.com/.

4. When done with typing, press enter and wait for the results page to load.
5. Extract the hyperlinks of the search results from the results page, and pick the results that will be opened. To simulate a real visitor, the results chosen are based on the actual click through rates of search results on a certain position. As Google does not provide this data, they are based on the analysis of 5 million search query logs by an external company[4].
6. A selected page is opened, and after the page has been loaded, a small scroll movement is executed to simulate a user searching for information. After a delay of 3 s, the back button is pressed and the next page is opened. This step is repeated until all selected pages are visited.
7. After the visits, the browser tab is closed and the capture is finished.

4.2   Results

Table 4. Correctly identified query length

Type of trace	KREEP short[a]	KREEP long[b]	ESQABE long[b]
Correct total length	99.70%	19.13%	92.90%
Correct word length	74.89%	19.03%	87.97%

[a] Captured traffic traces end after query was completely typed. Measurements as described in [8].
[b] Traces generated as described in Sect. 4.1

Detecting the lengths of the different words of the search query is the first step of ESQABE. The results of this steps are shown in Table 4. We noticed that the original version of KREEP underperformed in our tests in comparison to the measurements in [8]. The traces used to evaluate KREEP stop immediately after the query was typed and do not include the load of the search results page. Our traces are longer as they also contained the visits to the search result links, which caused issues with the detection phase. These issues appeared because the approach taken to detect the autocomplete traffic was not restrictive enough. For example, requests made by the browser to load the search results page were often identified as autocomplete requests. In ESQABE we made improvements to KREEP to overcome these issues as described earlier in Sect. 3.2.

The next step is the detection of the visited search results. The goal of this step is to identify the domain name of the result which the user opened. In 78.80% of all search results opened by the subject, the domain name was identified correctly by the algorithm. The algorithm failed sometimes when the subject opened multiple results of the same domain as in these cases no new TLS handshake took place. In other cases the algorithm wrongly identified a domain which hosts assets as the search result opened by the user. And in some cases small results were ignored as they were categorized as background traffic.

---

[4] https://backlinko.com/google-ctr-stats.

Table 5. Accuracy of ESQABE for complete search query identification. The table shows the amount of test cases for which the correct query could be determined.

# of opened search results	Correct guess	Top-3 accuracy
1	27%	35%
2	35%	44%
3	36%	46%
1, 2 or 3	33%	41%

And finally, the total performance of ESQABE is evaluated and shown in Table 5. The more search results are visited by the subject, the more information is available to the eavesdropper and the more search queries are detected correctly. Succeeding in, or failing with this approach is highly dependant on the search queries and the websites visited afterwards, as already discussed in Sect. 3.4. Overall, ESQABE outperforms KREEP as it succeeded in predicting the specific query for 33% of our tests. In [8], KREEP returned 50 hypothesis queries for each test case and in up to only 15% of the cases this included the actual query. However, note, that the results cannot be compared directly as the testing strategies differ. KREEP was tested on pieces of sentences extracted from the Enron email corpus and English gigaword newswire corpus as for these key inter-arrival intervals are available. These extractions are valid English clauses, but do not reflect what a real user would enter in a search engine. We, on the other hand, need realistic queries to evaluate ESQABE. This means that the results of KREEP and ESQABE cannot be directly compared side by side; a dataset of keystrokes of realistic search queries would need to be available.

Note that ESQABE has its limits. It is mostly interesting for eavesdroppers who target a specific victim and follow them for a longer period of time to observe patters in the search behavior. Then, they can take into account the second and third guesses which are often correct as shown in Table 5. Also note, we simulated a user who is focused on one task. A user who extensively multi tasks and constantly switches between websites can load other pages while making a web search. This can currently not be detected and can mislead ESQABE. However, some search engines generate requests for logging when a user opens a result, it is left for further research if this can be used to differentiate traffic.

5   Defense Mechanisms

It is clear that HTTPS on its own is insufficient to protect users from eavesdroppers. The combination of limited pieces of – sometimes seemingly innocent – information, can enable an eavesdropper to find out a lot about their subjects. Luckily, when a piece of information is missing, ESQABE and similar methods become harder or even impossible to execute. Using minor defense mechanisms can yield a significant impact, even without limiting functionality for end users. We created a browser extension that implements multiple defense mechanisms.

The first set of defenses focuses on preventing the detection of query length. Some of these were already suggested in [8]. As described earlier, Startpage.com appears not to be vulnerable for our eavesdropping approach and is used as a source of inspiration as well. A first, non-intrusive, approach is the addition of padding to the autocomplete requests. Adding random padding – even a small amount – makes it impossible to tokenize the words of the search query. The differences between a space and a normal character disappear in the padding.

Padding does not protect against detection of total query length. Rather, it will make length guessing only harder as the pattern is less distinguishable. To effectively hide the length, the request length should be in range of other background traffic on the same TCP connection (e.g., traffic for analytics), which is impossible to guess for future requests. Combining random padding with throttling of the requests would effectively hide query length for the eavesdropper as ESQABE counts the autocomplete requests for its guess. When throttling is enabled in the extension, it intercepts the autocomplete requests and drops them during certain intervals. However, throttling will impact the user experience as the refresh rate of the suggestions is limited. The approach of DuckDuckGo is to wait at least 300ms between requests, which is less intrusive than Startpage.com which debounces for 500ms. Just as Startpage.com, our extension also provides an option to completely turn off autocompletion.

The second line of defense is to make it impossible to find the domain the subject connected to. Encrypting DNS and TLS Client Hello messages would be a good starting point, as extraction then needs to shift to other less straightforward approaches. New protocols as DNS-over-HTTPS and TLS Encrypted Client Hello (ECH) are created to solve these problems. Our browser extension guides the user in the processes to enable ECH and shows a warning when it is not enabled. However, these protocols do have their flaws as well. In [10], a fingerprinting attack is discussed which can be used to identify selected domains from DNS-over-HTTPS traffic. In [4], another approach is proposed based on extraction from reverse DNS and the Subject Alternative Name field present in HTTPS certificates. This technique does not need the generation of fingerprints in advance and achieved an accuracy of 50.5% when tested on all websites in the Tranco top 6000. Encrypted DNS and ECH make the detection harder but not impossible for the eavesdropper. Another option is using decoy traffic to mislead eavesdroppers. This approach involves additional network traffic which can delay the effective page load. In our extension it is possible to enable random visits to other Wikipedia articles in the background.

6   Conclusion

In this work we have shown that eavesdroppers can combine pieces of seemingly innocent leaked information in order to obtain more intelligence about their subjects. We have described ESQABE, a technique to derive the text string a user entered as a query in a web search engine from information available to an eavesdropper. The approach is, contrary to previous work, applicable in a real world scenario independent of the language and contents of the query. In our open world approach only a limited number of assumptions is made and with a correct answer in 33% of all test cases, we have shown the viability of our approach. There are surely opportunities to extend ESQABE in order to avoid certain limitations and increase its effectiveness. For example, the applicability of this approach on traffic traces containing QUIC traffic needs further investigation. However, as every key press generates a new autocomplete request, they still have the potential to be recognized by an eavesdropper. We also created a browser extension which implements basic defense mechanisms against ESQABE. Source code for both ESQABE and the browser extension is made available at https://github.com/isaacme/ESQABE, together with the captured datasets.

References

1. Barbaro, M., Zeller, T.J.: A face is exposed for AOL searcher no. 4417749. https://www.nytimes.com/2006/08/09/technology/09aol.html. Accessed 23 Nov 2020
2. Chen, S., Wang, R., Wang, X., Zhang, K.: Side-channel leaks in web applications: a reality today, a challenge tomorrow. In: 2010 IEEE Symposium on Security and Privacy, pp. 191–206 (2010). https://doi.org/10.1109/SP.2010.20
3. Cucerzan, S., Brill, E.: Spelling correction as an iterative process that exploits the collective knowledge of web users. In: Proceedings of EMNLP 2004. pp. 293–300 (July 2004), https://www.aclweb.org/anthology/W04-3238
4. Di Martino, M., Quax, P., Lamotte, W.: Knocking on IPs: identifying https websites for zero-rated traffic. Secur. Commun. Networks (2020). https://doi.org/10.1155/2020/7285786
5. Dyer, K.P., Coull, S.E., Ristenpart, T., Shrimpton, T.: Peek-a-boo, I still see you: why efficient traffic analysis countermeasures fail. In: 2012 IEEE Symposium on S&P, pp. 332–346. IEEE (2012). https://doi.org/10.1109/SP.2012.28
6. Lewandowski, D., Spree, U.: Ranking of wikipedia articles in search engines revisited: fair ranking for reasonable quality? J. Am. Soc. Inf. Sci. Technol. **62**(1), 117–132 (2011). https://doi.org/10.1002/asi.21423
7. Liberatore, M., Levine, B.N.: Inferring the source of encrypted http connections. In: Proceedings of the 13th ACM Conference on Computer and Communications Security, New York, pp. 255–263. CCS 2006. Association for Computing Machinery (2006). https://doi.org/10.1145/1180405.1180437
8. Monaco, J.V.: What are you searching for? a remote keylogging attack on search engine autocomplete. In: 28th {USENIX} Security Symposium ({USENIX} Security 19), pp. 959–976 (2019)
9. Oh, S.E., Li, S., Hopper, N.: Fingerprinting keywords in search queries over tor. Proc. Priv. Enhancing Technol. **4**, 251–270 (2017). https://doi.org/10.1515/popets-2017-0048
10. Siby, S., Marc, J., Diaz, C., Vallina-Rodriguez, N., Troncoso, C.: Encrypted DNS privacy? → a traffic analysis perspective. In: NDSS. Internet Society (2020). https://doi.org/10.14722/ndss.2020.24301

Reconnection-Based Covert Channels in Wireless Networks

Sebastian Zillien$^{(\boxtimes)}$ and Steffen Wendzel

Centre of Technology and Transfer, Worms University of Applied Sciences,
Worms, Germany
szillien@hs-worms.de

Abstract. In recent years, malware is increasingly applying means of hidden communication. The emergence of network-capable *stegomalware* applies such methods to communication networks. In this paper, we introduce and evaluate two covert channels that utilize reconnections to transmit hidden information in WiFi networks. We implement these covert channels in the 802.11 protocol by abusing the authentication mechanism of these networks. Furthermore, we propose detection methods and countermeasures for both covert channels. Our implementation and quickstart guide are available as open source code on GitHub to aid replicability (https://github.com/NIoSaT/WiFi_Reconnection_CovertChannel).

Keywords: Network covert channel · Wireless networks · Steganography · Information hiding · Network security

1 Introduction

Covert channels are secret and policy-breaking communication channels [14]. In networks, they are increasingly used by steganographic malware (*stegomalware*) to hide the exfiltration of stolen passwords or command and control (C&C) channels. On the other hand, covert channels can also be used to circumvent government censorship. However, the majority of reported covert channel cases are of illegitimate nature and used as part of stegomalware [2,8].

Several techniques to implement such network covert channels have been published so far. These techniques can be organized in a *hiding pattern*-based taxonomy [9,13]. Patterns fall into two broad categories, timing and storage channel patterns. Timing channel patterns transmit their hidden data by manipulating temporal attributes of network traffic, like inter-arrival times or the order of packets. Storage channel patterns transmit their hidden data by manipulating values of the network traffic, like source addresses or the size of packets.

The most recent pattern, PT15, uses artificial reconnections to transmit hidden data [10]. It was only analyzed for the MQTT protocol so far. Pattern PT15 falls into the category of timing channels. Many network types, including wireless networks, have some sort of connection mechanism that can be abused for this type of covert channel.

© IFIP International Federation for Information Processing 2021
Published by Springer Nature Switzerland AG 2021
A. Jøsang et al. (Eds.): SEC 2021, IFIP AICT 625, pp. 118–133, 2021.
https://doi.org/10.1007/978-3-030-78120-0_8

In this paper, we show that the artificial reconnections pattern can be used in the widely-deployed 802.11 WiFi networks. We provide two different implementations that exploit the connection establishment mechanism of 802.11 networks to realize a reconnection-based covert channel. When clients connect to a wireless network, they move through 3 states. Each state allows for different frames to be used by the client. A regular use of the network is only possible in state 3. Starting in state 1, a client moves to state 2 with a successful authentication, a deauthentication moves the client back to state 1. From state 2 they move up to state 3 by associating. A disassociation moves the client back to state 2. These steps all happen unencrypted so it is easy for an attacker to observe these steps or even inject spoofed frames to interfere with the connection process.[1] We use these properties to realize our covert channels by disconnecting selected clients in a certain order to transmit a secret message.

Since our covert channels are bound to a physical location, they are not ideal to control a botnet or trojan virus. Our main application scenario is the hidden exchange of data, such as encryption keys, in public places. A sender and (multiple) receiver(s) can exchange such data "over the air" without physically meeting or directly exchanging data between their devices.

The remainder of this paper is structured as follows. We first highlight fundamentals and related work in Sect. 2 and then present our concept in Sect. 3. We discuss the implementation of our two methods in Sect. 4 and 5. Afterwards, we evaluate their performance in terms of robustness and throughput. Next, we present and evaluate passive countermeasures (detection approaches) in Sect. 6, followed by active countermeasures (limitation of channel capacity) in Sect. 7. In Sect. 8, we compare our covert channel with two other publications' wireless covert channels. Section 9 concludes and provides an outlook on future work.

2   Fundamentals and Related Work

To transmit data using PT15, the sender forces clients to reconnect to a network or a server while the receiver monitors the network. The receiver then decodes the ordering of the reconnecting clients to retrieve the hidden data. Since the pattern PT15 is still new, there are no publications on it outside of the initial publication [10]. However, there are several related covert channels.

Kraetzer et al. implement and analyse two different covert channels in 802.11 networks [7]. A covert storage and a covert timing channel. For both covert channels, the covert sender is artificially duplicating frames. Therefore, both channels require other clients in the network that send legitimate data to provide the cover traffic. For the storage channel, the covert sender duplicates a foreign packet but modifies the duplicated packet to include the hidden data. For the

---

[1] A common attack on this process is the "deauthentication attack", a type of denial of service attack. An attacker continuously sends spoofed deauthentication frames which force a client back into state 1. This effectively disables network access for this client as long as the attacker keeps sending these frames.

timing channel, the covert sender waits until a certain client sends a packet and then the covert sender sends a duplicate of the original packet.

In [3], Classen et al. introduce four approaches for covert channels in wireless networks. The focus of their work is on the physical layer. They encode hidden data by modifying physical aspects of wireless frames, like frequency or phase shift.

HICCUPS (*Hidden Communication System for Corrupted Networks*) [11] was one of the earliest published covert channels for 802.11 networks. The approach functions similar to [7], by modifying header values of wireless packets. HIC-CUPS also offers a "corrupted frame mode", in which the covert sender embeds the hidden data in the payload part of the packet but sets an intentionally wrong CRC value. The covert receiver knows how to interpret the hidden data, while other clients will ignore the packet as malformed.

In [6], Holloway and Beyah propose a timing covert channel called *Covert DCF* for 802.11 networks that works by manipulating the random back-off time of the CSMA/CA mechanism. To send a secret symbol, the covert sender replaces the random back-off time with a chosen delay. The covert receiver observes the inter-arrival times of the frames and decodes the secret symbol.

In [15], Zhao describes a covert channel based on the 802.11e QoS standard. The channel manipulates 8 bits of the frame header in order to encode the hidden data, while using legitimate network frames as the carrier. Association frames are used to signal the beginning and the end of a message. Zhao also proposes a transmission mode where the entire message body of wireless frames is used for the hidden data to increase the bandwidth of the covert channel.

Recently, Guri showed how data can be exfiltrated from air-gapped systems over WiFi signals using the so-called *AIR-FI* covert channel. Therefore, signals in the 2.4 GHz WiFi frequency bands are generated through DDR SDRAM memory buses; these signals can be recognized by closely located receivers [5].

Additional publications deal with further aspects of network covert channels, see [13,14] (and references therein) for an overview of hiding techniques. For instance, Carrega et al. present methodological approaches to gather data for stegomalware detection as a joint effort of two EU projects [2] while Carrara and Adams discuss non-traditional out-of-band covert channels [1].

3   Concept and Implementation

Both of our covert channels share the same basic approach: Covert sender and covert receiver agree upon which WiFi clients they want to use for the cover channel. We call them $C_1, ..., C_n$. Covert sender and receiver now agree on an encoding schema. Each client C_i is associated with a secret symbol S_i. To send the symbol S_i the covert sender forces the client C_i to reconnect to the network. The covert receiver continuously monitors the network for reconnections. If the receiver recognizes a reconnection of client C_i, it interprets it as the symbol S_i. For instance, to send the secret message $S_1|S_2|S_3|S_1$, the covert sender would force reconnections from the clients in order of $C_1|C_2|C_3|C_1$. Figure 1 shows the setup and concept of our covert channels.

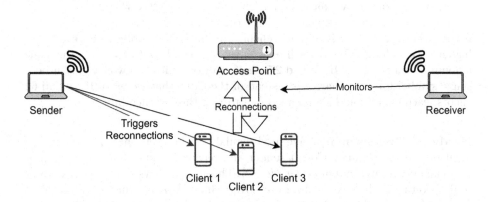

Fig. 1. Concept of the covert channel

Both of our covert channels are *indirect* covert channels. That means the covert sender does not directly communicate with the covert receiver by exchanging network packets. Instead, the covert sender manipulates a third party, called central element, and the covert receiver monitors the reactions of the third party to recognize the secret messages. In a direct covert channel, the covert sender directly sends data to the covert receiver. This makes it easier to find the covert sender and receiver once the covert channel is found.

The indirect approach provides two benefits to our covert channels:

1. *Anonymity:* Both, sender and receiver do not have to "join" (authenticate against) the WiFi network, they can work solely from the "outside". If the covert channel is detected, there is no evidence on who is the covert receiver. It is even possible to use the covert channel while the covert sender does not know who the covert receiver is. Only the covert sender interacts actively with the network but uses frames with a spoofed source address.
2. *Decoupling of Sender & Receiver:* Although our covert channel relies on wireless transmissions, covert sender and covert receiver never have to be in signal range of each other. The covert sender and covert receiver only need to be within range of the used clients $C_1, ..., C_n$. Therefore, our covert channel can almost double the range of a direct wireless communication between sender and receiver. The actual range of the covert channel is largely dependant on the RF environment, the signal power of the clients and the antenna gain of the receiver.

Proof of Concept Encoding. Our proof of concept implementation uses three clients C_1, C_2, C_3. We thus have three possible secret symbols S_1, S_2, S_3. Therefore, we implemented a ternary encoding with which we can encode 27 different characters (26 letters and space) with 3 digits. To encode a message the sender first converts the message to a list of numbers. Each number is then transformed to a 3 digit ternary code. Each code symbol $(0, 1, 2)$ corresponds to a certain client. As an example we have $26_{10} = 2 \times 3^2 + 2 \times 3^1 + 2 \times 3^0 = 222_3$.

This concept can be expanded with more clients. Only the capabilities of the network hardware limit how many clients can be used. More clients result in a higher covert channel bandwidth as we need less symbols to transmit the same amount of information. If we had 27 clients to work with, we would only need a single symbol for each character instead of the three that we used. If we had 64 clients, each client could signal a symbol from a Base64 encoding.

Hardware Requirements. We used regular "of the shelf" hardware to implement our covert channel. Covert sender and receiver require a wireless adapter that can operate in the *monitor mode* [12]. This mode allows the wireless adapter to do two things that we need for our covert channel: *1)* capture all frames that are sent in a network so that the device does not drop packets not intended for it. This allows the covert receiver to monitor all reconnections that occur within the network. *2)* inject spoofed frames into the network; the covert sender uses this feature to send the forged deauthentication/disassociation frames.

The specific models we used are ALFA AWUS036**NH** (receiver side), ALFA AWUS036**NHA** (sender side), ALFA AWUS036**ACM** Wireless USB Adapter (measurements and recordings), and ESP32 development boards as clients (these are often used in IoT devices).

4   Covert Channel Method 1

Our first method uses a deauthentication attack to force clients to reconnect to the network. This allows us to use any clients that are present in the network.

Scenario. This covert channel could be used to hide the process of exchanging encryption keys between two parties. Both parties would agree on a time and a public place, likely a café or an airport. They also need to agree on a list of clients they want to use beforehand. The two parties would arrive separately at the public place as to not raise suspicion. They exchange secret keys over the covert channel and leave separately.

4.1   Covert Sender

We implemented the sender side in form of a python script with the Scapy framework (https://scapy.net/). An important part of the performance of the covert channel is the correct timing of the clients' reconnections. If a client would be forced to reconnect before finishing the first reconnection, the transmission of the symbol would fail. Therefore we implemented an option --`wait` to add delays between reconnections. We also added the --`delay` option, which adds a delay after three reconnections, i.e. after each letter. This is used to spread the transmission over a longer time to be stealthier.

Another aspect that needs to be configured is the amount of deauthentication frames that the sender uses to force the reconnection of a client. We found that a single deauthentication frame would not always result in the reliable deauthentication of a client. We noticed that programs like the aircrack suite also use multiple deauthentication frames. Therefore, we also added an option to change the extend of the deauthentication burst.

The sender-side procedure is explained below:

a) The input string (secret message to be transferred) is converted to numbers in the range of 0 to 26. All characters that are not in the lower alpha set are mapped to 0, which is the number for the space character.
b) The numbers are then converted to a three-digit ternary code.
c) The symbols are all concatenated into a single list.
d) The sender iterates over the list and the symbols 0, 1 and 2 are mapped to the clients that are used in the covert channel.
e) Before each reconnection, the sender waits for the duration of the configured delay of the `--wait` option. After the transmission, the additional delay from the `--delay` option is performed.
f) For each symbol, the configured number of deauthentication frames are sent.
* Steps d), e) and f) are repeated for each symbol that is transmitted.

Our proof of concept sender works on a "best effort" principle. That means the covert sender does not know if a client actually performed a reconnection or if the covert receiver actually received the symbol.

4.2 Covert Receiver

We also implemented the covert receiver in the form of a python script that uses Scapy. Our receiver implementation only needs to know which client corresponds to which code symbol and does not need additional configuration parameters, as the receiver can work with any possible configuration of our sender side script.

Receiving Procedure. Our proof of concept receiver constantly monitors the network and decodes everything that is received using the following procedure:

a) Continuously monitor the network for reconnecting clients.
b) If a known client reconnects, append the corresponding symbol to the receiver list.
c) When the number of symbols in the receiver list is a multiple of three, decode the list to a string.
* Repeat steps a)–c) until interrupted.

4.3 Evaluation

We evaluated the performance of method 1 in two ways. We tested the reliability and the data throughput of the covert channel.

Reliability. We found three stages where a transmission error could occur. a) from the sender to the client, b) "inside" the client and c) from the client to the receiver. We performed all our tests on an isolated network, while other wireless networks were present. We used a home router (TP-Link WR703N) as access point and three ESP32 boards as clients.

a) The first problem are unreliable deauthentications. To get an overview on how the deauthentication attack performed with various burst sizes, we conducted three test runs. The results of this test are shown in Table 1. As shown, we achieved high success rates with 64 to 80 deauthentication frames. But we never reached a 100% success rate in all three tests. That means we can improve the reliability of step a) but we do not make it completely reliable.

Table 1. Results: deauthentication test

Number of deauthentication frames	Success rate		
	Test 1	Test 2	Test 3
1	0%	3%	2%
10	36%	32%	53%
64	98%	94%	97%
70	98%	93%	96%
80	100%	100%	97%
150	79%	89%	95%

b) The second problem are the reconnection times of different clients. As stated above, clients need a measurable amount of time to reconnect. And if a new reconnection is triggered too early, it will result in a transmission error. Therefore, we added an option for a delay after each reconnection to our code. We performed several tests to find out how different clients react to a deauthentication attack. To do this, we caused 20 deauthentications for each client and recorded the time it took them to reconnect. If a client took longer than 10 s to reconnect or did not reconnect at all, we recorded 10 s as reconnection time.

We found that an iPhone and an Amazon Fire Tablet performed poorly in this test; their reconnection times were slow and inconsistent between 5 and 10 s. The ESP32 boards were significantly faster, but even their reconnection times varied between 0.2 and 2 s. We can use the delay option of our sender to optimize the delay to improve the error source b). But we cannot completely eliminate the problem since the sender does not know if the client is actually done with the previous reconnection.

c) The last step of the transmission, from the client to the receiver, is outside of our control. The client performs a reconnection and exchanges information with the access point the receiver tries to listen to. But as this step is again wireless, there are several ways that the signals could get corrupted on their way to the receiver. 802.11 networks have multiple mechanisms that make wireless transmissions reliable, but these mechanisms work to make the transmission reliable for the actual participants and not for external listeners. So even if step a) and b) succeed, it is still possible for the transfer to get corrupted in step c).

Running Errors. One problem of our encoding scheme are "running errors". Since we use a three-digit code, all transmissions are aligned in groups of three. If the receiver now misses a single symbol, all following symbols are out of alignment by one step. The same happens when a single spurious symbol is received, all future symbols are then pushed back by one and are out of alignment. Figure 2 visualizes this problem.

Original	123 123 123 123 123 123 123
a)	123 123 123 122 312 312 312 3
b)	123 123 123 131 231 231 23

Fig. 2. Two transmission errors in ternary encoding

Summary. Given that even after above-mentioned optimizations are applied, we do not reach a reliability of 100% (but get close to it), it would be beneficial for the covert channel to implement some sort of error correction or acknowledgement mechanic for real world applications. A simple method would be to split a secret message into multiple smaller messages and stop and restart the transmission with a delay after each part.

Data Throughput. We tested the influence of several configuration parameters on the data throughput. To measure this, we transmitted the same message with different configuration parameters. As we expected, the burst size did not influence the data throughput in a significant way. The frame-sending process itself is fast and the biggest part of the duration comes from artificial delays we had to add. As expected, the two delay options (after each reconnection and after each three reconnections) scaled linearly. The higher the delays the worse the throughput.

We also tested the maximum data throughput that we could achieve. We optimized the settings for our network environment and clients to transmit *HelloWorld* in 20.143 s. That means we transmitted 30 tenary symbols in 20 s (0.5 letters/s).

To encode 27 different characters, we would need 5 binary digits. Therefore, *HelloWorld* would need 50 binary symbols (1 and 0). That means we would transmit 50 bits of information in roughly 20 s, which results in 2.5 *bits/s*.

With additional clients, we could not increase the symbol rate but each symbol could hold more information. If we had 27 clients, we would only need a single symbol for each letter of our message and with 64 clients we could transmit 6 bits worth of data with a single reconnection.

Therefore we could theoretically increase the throughput almost indefinitely, but handling hundreds of clients would be impractical and could result in problems with the access point.

5   Covert Channel Method 2

Our second method uses clients that can be controlled by the sender. Therefore, we no longer need to use a deauthentication attack, instead the clients reconnect themselves when triggered by the sender.

Scenario. This covert channel could be used as a form of number station to distribute new encryption keys to field agents. The sender is set up in a public place like a café with IoT equipment and repeatedly sends out secret data over the covert channel. The agent could then visit the café at a suitable time, receive the keys and leave again without having personal contract with anybody that could reveal their hidden identity. A dissident could also use this method to send illicit information to the press without risking prosecution from the government.

5.1   Covert Sender

The core idea of the sender is still the same as with method 1. The sender reconnects certain clients in a certain order to transmit the hidden data. The difference is that the sender can now directly control the clients and the clients can report their status back to the sender.

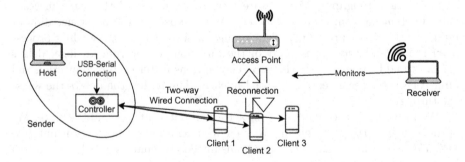

Fig. 3. Technical realization of method 2

Sender-Client Communication. We used a simple connection with two wires between the sender and each client, see Fig. 3. One for data from the sender to the client and one for data from the client to the sender. The client constantly reports its connection status to the sender. This is done via the voltage level of the *status wire*. A high voltage signals that the client is connected to the network and ready for a new reconnection. A low voltage means the client is currently not connected to the network and therefore not ready for a new reconnection. The sender uses the *command wire* to trigger a reconnection of the client. The command wire is normally on a low voltage level and to trigger a reconnection, the sender sends a pulse of high voltage over the command wire. The client detects the rising voltage edge and performs a reconnection.

Hardware Requirements. In addition to the hardware that we used for method 1, we also used the inputs and outputs of an Arduino microcontroller to implement the two-way communication between sender and clients.

Sending Process. The sending process for method 2 is similar to method 1. The main difference is that the sender does not use a guessed delay after each reconnection but instead uses the status information from the clients to time reconnections: First, the input string is converted to a list of clients (see Sect. 4.1 for details). Next, the sender waits until the particular client is ready for a reconnection. Then, the sender sends the reconnection signal to the client and waits for the client to finish the reconnection, before the sender moves on to the next symbol.

The two-way communication between sender and clients allows us to time the reconnections precisely without guessing the needed delays. We still added an additional delay after each symbol sent which can be used to spread the transmission over a longer time.

5.2   Covert Receiver

The receiver is the same one as for method 1, i.e. it monitors the network for reconnections, logs them and decodes the message.

5.3   Evaluation

Robustness. With method 2 we were able to significantly improve the reliability of our covert channel. The two-way communication between sender and client increased the reliability of steps a) and b) (see Sect. 4.3) to 100% in all our tests. The problem with step c) still exists and could not be solved with method 2. To improve step c) we would need some sort of error correction or acknowledgement mechanism.

Data Throughput. The status information from the clients allows us to use tighter timings on the reconnections, so we were able to significantly increase the maximum throughput of our covert channel. We were able to transmit 36 letters in under 21.3 s. With these numbers we send 1.698 letters per second or 5.1 symbols per second. With the same calculations from method 1, we transmit roughly 180 binary bits worth of information in 21.2 s or 8.5 bits/s. In comparison, method 2 is 3.4 times faster than method 1. As before, utilizing more clients would increase the throughput further (again not by increasing the symbol rate but by making each symbol carry more information).

6   Passive Countermeasures: Covert Channel Detection

To get a baseline for the detection of our covert channel, we created reference recordings in multiple network environments. A university building, a home network and our test network. For our detection, we focused on two types of frames: deauthentication and association request frames. Our reference recordings all had similar statistics. Table 2 shows the results of our tests conducted in the eduroam network in a university building. Recording 3 had the most "interesting" frames of all our recordings. The home and testbed recordings were all more similar to recording 1 and 2.

Table 2. Results of the eduroam Measurements

	Recording 1	Recording 2	Recording 3
Recording length	68 min	71 min	60 min
Frames recorded	268.086	575.577	629.203
Deauth. frames	1	0	24
Asso. req. frames	7	4	47

6.1   Detection of Covert Channel Method 1

To generate data for our detection, we performed recordings of transmissions of our covert channel. We used several different configurations – Table 3 presents some of these results. As shown, method 1 creates high numbers of deautentica-tion frames. This is due to the burst size that is required to achieve a reconnection of the client.

For our detection, we used a sliding window approach. That means that we did not look at the complete transmission at once, but instead analyzed it in smaller slices. This allows us to use the approach on a recording or with live traffic. Our detection works as described in Algorithm 1.

Table 3. Method 1: results of the covert channel measurements

	Test 1	Test 2	Test 3
Recording length	56 s	52 s	54 s
Frames recorded	9688	9123	9250
Deauth. frames	6762	6156	6272
Asso. req. frames	30	30	30

Algorithm 1: Detection Algorithm - Method 1

Read/Sniff frames for L seconds;
Loop
    $C :=$ Count of the deauthentication frames in the window;
    if $C >= T$ **then**
      | raise alarm;
    end
    Discard oldest n seconds of frames;
    Read/Sniff frames for n seconds;
EndLoop

6.2 Detection of Covert Channel Method 2

To detect our second covert channel, we recorded multiple transmissions with different configurations. Table 4 shows representative results of our tests. As can be seen, we no longer have deauthentication frames in our recordings – only disassociation and association frames, since the clients produce these frames when they reconnect. Therefore, we slightly modified our detection approach: the detection now considers the number of association requests to differentiate between legitimate and covert channel traffic.

Table 4. Method 2: Results of the Covert Channel Measurements

	Test 1	Test 2	Test 3
Recording length	21 s	2.3 min	18.4 min
Deauth. frames	0	0	0
Disas. frames	107	105	108
Asso. req. frames	108	107	108

6.3 Evaluation of Detection Methods

To evaluate our detection methods, we used 100 recordings of legitimate traffic and 30 recordings for each covert method (to achieve a 1:3 ratio as covert traffic is usually not as present as normal traffic and we wanted to show its detectability under harsh circumstances which would potentially lead to a higher number of false positives).

For method 1, we used delay values from 0 s to 2 s and for method 2 we used delay values from 0 s to 30 s. For both methods, we transmitted multiple different messages. However, as our detection method neither depends on the information *which* clients get disconnected nor their *order*, we do not discriminate between plaintext and randomized messages as they make no difference. Figure 4 shows the ROC curves of our detection approaches with sliding window-based detection threshold.

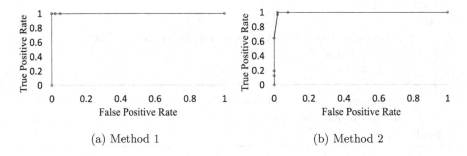

(a) Method 1   (b) Method 2

Fig. 4. ROC curves - detection of methods 1 and 2

As shown, we achieved a perfect detection for method 1 (AUC = 1.0, optimal with $T = 15$). This is due to the fact that we have to use deauthentication bursts with method 1. Thus, even a single reconnect produces more deauthentication frames than all legitimate recordings had in their entire length.

When we used high thresholds with method 2, we had false negatives, but with smaller thresholds we were able to reliably detect our recordings without adding too many false positives (AUC = 0.9994, optimal with $T = 15$). We can configure method 2 to be more stealthy, but then we would have to sacrifice large amounts of bandwidth, as legitimate traffic has largely different statistics compared with our covert channel.

7   Active Countermeasures: Covert Channel Limitation

We found multiple potential approaches to counter a deauthentication attack and therefore our first method. The most prominent one is the new WPA3 standard that secures the connection process of 802.11 networks. This new standard can, if no backwards compatibility to older standards is enabled, block our first method completely. But our second method would still work in WPA3 only networks.

Therefore, we propose another countermeasure that will also disrupt our second method. So-called spurious disruptions were used already years ago for local covert channels in order to limit their channel capacity [4]. We apply spurious disruptions by having the access point disconnecting randomly selected clients in randomized intervals. Each reconnection of a client that belongs to the covert channel results in a decoding error for the receiver. We tested this idea for both of our covert channels with good results. As described before in Sect. 4.3, our encoding is susceptible to spurious symbols. This countermeasure introduces many spurious symbols, as the receiver can not distinguish between a reconnection from the covert channel or a reconnection from the countermeasure. In our tests, we were able to successfully disrupt all messages that we sent, by reconnecting a client every 10 s. Depending on the timing, the first letters of a message were transmitted correctly, but no message was transmitted completely without disruption.

A countermeasure like this does also affect legitimate users of the network. We performed empirical tests to estimate the effects on other network users. To do this, we connected an iPhone and an Amazon Fire Tablet to our test network and used the devices to surf the internet and stream videos, while periodically disconnecting the devices from the network. We did not notice any problems from an end user standpoint. Videos kept playing and websites were loading at regular speeds. Other devices with other usage scenarios might experience recognizable problems.

The covert channel on the other hand could defend itself by adding error correction to the transmission. With added error correction, it is a matter of trading bandwidth for reliability. Since both covert channels do not provide a high bandwidth, they are vulnerable to such countermeasures.

8   Comparison with Other Covert Channels

In this section, we compare the performance of our covert channels with two other covert channels that exploit characteristics of wireless networks.

8.1   Kraetzer et al.: WLAN Steganography

In [7], Kraetzer et al. also analyzed their covert channels based on bandwidth, reliability and detectability. For their covert storage channel, which duplicates wireless packets and replaces the payload with the covert data, they calculated a theoretical bandwidth of 4 bytes per second in their chosen configuration. In practice, they were able to achieve 2.1 bytes per second, as the sending process was slowed down since the sender had to wait for appropriate packages to duplicate.

Their covert timing channel was not evaluated with a real-world test, but they gave a bandwidth of 0.2 bytes per second. This lower bandwidth was expected, as their timing channel only transmits a single bit per packet.

Our covert channel delivered 0.3125 bytes per second (method 1) and 1.06 bytes per second (method 2). Our tests were conducted with 3 clients. With additional clients, we could increase the throughput. With 64 clients we could theoretically achieve 1.1 bytes/s and 3.8 bytes/s.

As for the robustness, Kraetzer et al. also found that their covert channel was not 100% reliable. They encountered transmission errors in form of duplicated letters. They were not able to find the source of these errors, which matches our difficulties with unreliable wireless transmissions. The authors did not provide test results for the detection of their covert channels in form of a ROC curve or a confusion matrix. But they found their storage channel to be easily detectable, by comparing the payloads of retransmitted frames.

8.2   Zhao: Covert Channels in 802.11e Wireless Networks

The covert channel described in [15] manipulates bits of the frame header in order to encode the hidden data. The covert channel has a bandwidth of 8 bits per frame. The author did not provide any test results on the real-world bandwidth of the covert channel. But since 802.11 networks operate at high frame rates, a generally higher bandwidth seems reasonable.

The covert channel can use the acknowledgement functionality of 802.11 networks to increase the reliability of the covert channel.

Zhao's covert channel creates additional association frames, as in case of our covert channel. Zhao argues that frequent association and reassociations are more common in a QBSS (*QoS Basic Service Set*), which would make the covert channel harder to detect. But the author does not provide measurements to support this claim.

Other than the increase in association frames, the covert channel does not create abnormal traffic, which could provoke errors in regular network participants. The author did not propose a statistical detection approach.

9   Conclusion

We introduced the first WiFi-based realization of covert channels that exploit artificial reconnections. The indirect nature of our two covert channels provides them with two benefits: range and anonymity of the participants. This is amplified by the usage of wireless networks as they are, by nature, broadcast networks.

Both of our covert channels suffer from similar problems, as they both cannot guarantee that a signal actually reaches the receiver, which is a common problem with blindly operating network covert channel senders.

With the detection approaches that we developed, we were able to detect both of our covert channels with minimal and none errors, respectively. But our covert channels do not interfere with the network usage of regular users, so it is unlikely that an administrator will actively look for them. More crowded networks might show different statistics, that hinder detection.

In future work, we plan to investigate whether networks show drastically different reconnection behavior when there are more devices in the network, which could change the detection results. We also plan to add the error-correcting and -detecting functionality of our covert channels and to investigate additional detection methods.

Acknowledgements. The authors like to thank Laura Hartmann for providing her comments on this paper.

References

1. Carrara, B., Adams, C.: Out-of-band covert channels-a survey. ACM Comput. Surv. (CSUR) **49**(2), 1–36 (2016). https://doi.org/10.1145/2938370
2. Carrega, A., Caviglione, L., Repetto, M., Zuppelli, M.: Programmable data gathering for detecting stegomalware. In: 2020 6th IEEE Conference on Network Softwarization (NetSoft), pp. 422–429 (2020). https://doi.org/10.1109/NetSoft48620.2020.9165537
3. Classen, J., Schulz, M., Hollick, M.: Practical covert channels for WiFi systems. In: 2015 IEEE Conference on Communications and Network Security (CNS), pp. 209–217, September 2015. https://doi.org/10.1109/CNS.2015.7346830
4. Fadlalla, Y.: Approaches to Resolving Covert Storage Channels in Multilevel Secure Systems. Ph.D. thesis, University of New Brunswick (1996)
5. Guri, M.: AIR-FI: Generating covert Wi-Fi signals from air-gapped computers. arXiv/CS.CR (2020)
6. Holloway, R., Beyah, R.: Covert DCF: A DCF-based covert timing channel in 802.11 networks. In: 2011 IEEE Eighth International Conference on Mobile Ad-Hoc and Sensor Systems, pp. 570–579. IEEE (2011)
7. Krätzer, C., Dittmann, J., Lang, A., Kühne, T.: WLAN steganography: a first practical review. In: Proceedings of the 8th Workshop on Multimedia and Security. MM&Sec 2006, New York, NY, USA, pp. 17–22. Association for Computing Machiner (2006). https://doi.org/10.1145/1161366.1161371
8. Mazurczyk, W., Wendzel, S.: Information hiding: challenges for forensic experts. Commun. ACM **61**(1), 86–94 (2017). https://doi.org/10.1145/3158416
9. Mazurczyk, W., Wendzel, S., Cabaj, K.: Towards deriving insights into data hiding methods using pattern-based approach. In: Proceedings of the 13th International Conference on Availability, Reliability and Security. ARES 2018. ACM (2018). https://doi.org/10.1145/3230833.3233261
10. Mileva, A., Velinov, A., Hartmann, L., Wendzel, S., Mazurczyk, W.: Comprehensive analysis of MQTT 5.0 susceptibility to network covert channels. Comput. Secur. 104 (2021). https://doi.org/10.1016/j.cose.2021.102207
11. Szczypiorski, K.: HICCUPS: hidden communication system for corrupted networks. In: International Multi-Conference on Advanced Computer Systems, pp. 31–40 (2003)
12. The aircrack project: airmon-ng monitor mode (2019). https://www.aircrack-ng.org/doku.php?id=airmon-ng&s[]=monitor
13. Wendzel, S., Zander, S., Fechner, B., Herdin, C.: Pattern-based survey and categorization of network covert channel techniques. ACM Comput. Surv. **47**(3) (2015). https://doi.org/10.1145/2684195
14. Zander, S., Armitage, G., Branch, P.: Covert channels and countermeasures in computer network protocols. IEEE Commun. Mag. **45**(12), 136–142 (2007). https://doi.org/10.1109/MCOM.2007.4395378
15. Zhao, H.: Covert channels in 802.11e wireless networks. In: 2014 Wireless Telecommunications Symposium, pp. 1–5 (2014). https://doi.org/10.1109/WTS.2014.6834991

Minecraft Altered Skin Channel (MASC)

Sam Abrams, Brandon Keller$^{(\boxtimes)}$, Kenneth Nero, Gino Placella,
and Daryl Johnson

Rochester Institute of Technology, Rochester, NY 14623, USA
{sxa7263,bnk5096,kbn1798,gap6768,Daryl.Johnson}@rit.edu

Abstract. Governments across the world are increasingly pushing for encryption backdoors and other privacy breaking features. One possible method to maintain privacy in a post-encryption environment is to utilize covert channels as a means to hide traffic from monitoring authorities. Covert channels have often been used to hide unwanted or prohibited web traffic, however, the traffic need not be malicious for there to be a necessity for privacy.

In this paper we explore a novel covert channel named Minecraft Altered Skin Channel (MASC) that exploits the inherent inefficiencies within Minecraft skin images. Data is transferred by reflecting a modified skin image off of the publicly accessible Minecraft Skin servers. We utilize a custom steganographic algorithm and a public Application Programming Interface (API), which when combined, grant the ability to quickly and asynchronously send and receive encoded messages without any direct communication between the two or more participating parties. We demonstrate the effectiveness of the scheme by implementing an efficient sender-receiver proof of concept. Finally, we go on to empirically analyze the program's results and show the comparatively high bitrate of the channel.

Keywords: Covert channel · Security · Steganography · Minecraft

1 Introduction

Covert channels existed long before the internet. However, only since 1973 and the publication of [5] have covert channels become almost exclusively associated with digital networking. The Internet Corporation for Assigned Names and Numbers (ICANN) gives the example of a hidden pocket in a briefcase as a physical implementation of such a channel; by hiding something within another means of transport, a hidden, or covert, channel is created [6]. While the medium may have changed, the need to secretly transport data has remained. In [5], the author defined "covert channels" as methods of communication that are "not intended for information transfer at all". While this definition is by no means perfect, it does manage to encapsulate nearly all modern covert channels, including our Minecraft Altered Skin Channel, MASC.

© IFIP International Federation for Information Processing 2021
Published by Springer Nature Switzerland AG 2021
A. Jøsang et al. (Eds.): SEC 2021, IFIP AICT 625, pp. 134–145, 2021.
https://doi.org/10.1007/978-3-030-78120-0_9

Covert channels have historically been used for two purposes: hiding malicious communication and hiding legitimate traffic that requires secrecy. Malicious covert channel based communication is present in large amount of malware, taking advantage of hidden traffic to avoid detection by firewalls and other network inspection devices. Legitimate traffic does the same thing, but for a good reason. An example of legitimate traffic is a whistle blower in an authoritarian state that cannot have their communication detected without consequence. While both uses of covert channels exist, it is more common to see these channels used for malicious activity simply because of the volume of cybercrime and its need to avoid detection. Given this growing concern of cybercrime and increased investment into detecting these hidden transmissions, there is an ever-growing need for new covert channels across a variety of mediums that MASC seeks to fill.

The rest of this work is organized as follows, Sect. 2 provides background on game-based covert channels, Sect. 3 provides an overview of the proposed channel, Sect. 4 outlines the encoding and decoding process, Sect. 5 outlines the performance of the proposed channel, Sect. 6 outlines potential countermeasures that could be employed against the channel, and Sect. 7 provides conclusions and recommendations for future works.

2   Background

Game based covert channels are not a novel concept. There are many examples of behavioral and storage based channels implemented within video game protocols. Our initial work was strongly influenced by the Runescape channel developed by Kim *et al.* [3], a storage channel that took advantage of item placement within a player's inventory to communicate between two users. Using item placement is an obvious choice for Minecraft, a game that revolves around building and crafting, and so is not as exciting as we wanted. Additionally, using game server reliant systems severely limits throughput. Minecraft servers are limited to 20 Hz [2] refresh rate, making it incredibly difficult to pass more than a few bytes per second. For example, if we were to represent a certain item type within the game as a alphanumeric character, we could place or remove 20 blocks per second. That would limit the potential rate to 20 characters per second, or approximately 20B/s, too slow to effectively pass any data beyond a short text message. Being limited by server tick rate is a problem faced by many game based channels. Some channels increase bitrate by taking advantage of games with refresh rates as high 128 Hz, but even then the max bandwidth is relatively low. Our channel avoids the bottleneck of refresh rate by transcending the direct game servers. Instead, we communicate with the Minecraft Session servers, which store the avatar skins displayed in game.

Others have also sought to use games as a medium for covert channels. The Castle channel, proposed in [4], encodes data into player actions within RTS games. This platform relies on other players being in the same game at the same time. A limitation the asynchronous nature of our platform allows us to avoid. In another example, the proposed platform in [7] uses player movement within first person shooter games to transmit data to other players. This falls victim to the same limitation previously discussed as movement data will need carried from a source client, to the game server, and then to receiving client.

3 Minecraft Skin Channel

Minecraft is an open world survival sandbox game developed by Mojang and initially released in November 2011 [1]. Minecraft allows for an enormous amount of user customization, including the ability for users to create and modify the texture files that determine how the game looks. The feature we leverage for our covert channel is the ability of players to change their in-game avatar's texture file. These "skin" files are created in a specific format in order to give the avatar a different appearance in-game. The current format used by Minecraft has an 832 pixel "dead space" in the 64×64 pixel texture image that is not displayed in-game or processed in any way. By using this dead space and a custom steganography algorithm, we are able to encapsulate messages into skin files with our own pixel data, thereby introducing arbitrary data into an otherwise legitimate texture file. A sample file with this dead space highlighted is shown in Fig. 1.

Since our channel does not rely on an avatar being in game, we discovered that we can use Mojang's official Texture Servers to distribute our files without limitations. The server is simple to navigate. One player will upload a created texture under their username, which allows any player to download the same texture by referencing the username of the creator. We use this simple process to transfer the encoded skin file from the sender, through the server, into the hands of the receiver. The only time login credentials are required is for the initial upload of a texture. That means the receiver can remain totally anonymous, and even the sender can be semi-anonymous by creating an unassociated Minecraft account. This provides the users with a simple, efficient, and effectively anonymous process for sending and receiving data.

The channel operates using several command line arguments that the sender will specify. They will provide data to be encoded that is less than or equal to 4992 characters of a limited character set consisting of 39 characters, an original 'skin' file, and a seed to be used for lookup table generation. The sender's username, password, and email address are also required in order to communicate with the Mojang Texture Servers. The message will then be encoded and transferred into the 'dead' space of the provided 'skin' file. The results are uploaded to the Mojang Texture Servers and stored under the senders specified username.

In order to receive the data, the receiver needs the sender's Minecraft username and the lookup table seed. The 'skin' file is downloaded from the texture servers with two API calls. The first API call accesses the universally unique identifier based on the sender's username, then the second API call obtains the encoded texture link and downloads it. Once downloaded, the pixels held in the 'dead' space of the 'skin' file are enumerated and decoded. Once decoded, the skin file is discarded and the message is output to the command line. The process is very linear, requiring no decisions or verification, and is shown in Fig. 2.

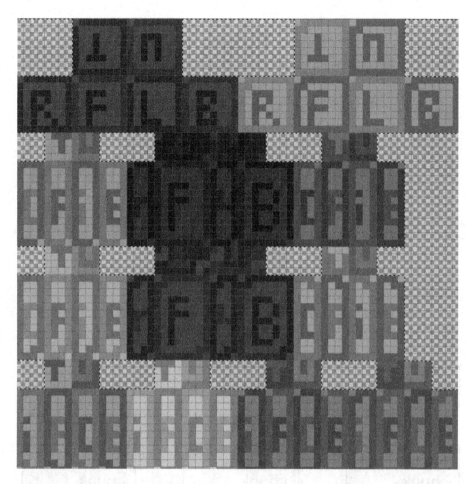

Fig. 1. A sample Minecraft skin file. The unused pixels are shown in grey/white checkerboard

4   Encoding and Decoding

Functionality of MASC is separated into two sections: the client and the back-end encoder/decoder. Our encoder uses an unrestricted form of steganography to embed six-character chunks of data into the allowed pixels. Typically, steganography must alter as few bits as possible in an image in order to maintain that image's integrity and appearance. MASC does not have this constraint. It can modify the selected pixels without fear of modifying the image's appearance as the modified pixels are not displayed at any time. Encoding works by using the pixel's color values to store a binary string, which in turn is simply a number that represents the alphanumeric string. Obtaining that number is the key to MASC's quick and space efficient operation. With that number, a custom pixel

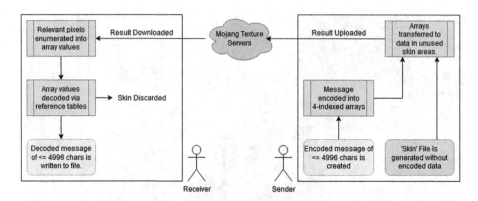

Fig. 2. A diagram exploring the communication architecture for sending and receiving messages utilizing a minecraft skin

can be created and then embedded into the base Minecraft skin image following the pixel location guidelines.

To calculate the number representing each six character string, five distinct steps must be taken. This process is shown in part in Fig. 3.

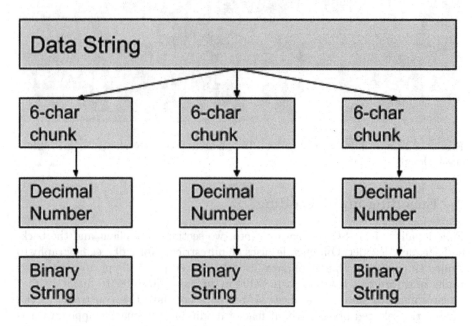

Fig. 3. A graphical representation of the pixel encoding process

4.1   Encoding

Data Processing. This step is a simple validation of the data to be encoded. MASC utilizes a limited character set of 39 characters, shown in Fig. 5 and Fig. 6, requiring that any unavailable characters be removed before encoding. Any of these characters found will be replaced with a space, and all lowercase letters are converted to uppercase. As there is a 4992 character limit, any data exceeding this limit is removed.

Original text: hello!my n*me is B&B
Replacement text: HELLO MY N ME IS B B

The Split. Once all unrecognized characters have been removed, the data string must be split into six character chunks to be encoded. If the number of characters is not divisible by six, spaces will be prepended to the data string. This allows for even data chunks while also allowing for easy detection and removal after the decoding process.

Original text: HELLO MY NAME IS BOB
Replacement text: [␣␣␣␣HE], [LLO MY], [NAME], [IS BOB]

Calculation. Each of these six-character chunks is then encoded one at a time. To begin the encoding process, each chunk is decomposed into its characters which are then operated on individually. Each of these characters is assigned a unique number from 0 to 38, determined by the lookup table, an example of which is found in Fig. 5. The lookup table is randomly generated during runtime from a seed provided by the user. Once the character's value is determined, it is multiplied by the number of permutations, including repetition, that are possible within the remaining space of the chunk. The parameters to determine this number of permutations are 39 characters in $5-i$ spaces where i is the index of the character in the six-character chunk. This multiplication by the number of permutations is essential for properly creating the unique identifier for a given six-character string. The full assignment and multiplication operation is repeated for each of the six characters, and all six values resulting from these operations are summed. This summed value becomes the numerical representation of the chunk. The general formula for an entire six-character chunk is found below.

$$\sum_{i=0}^{5} lookup(chunk[i]) * 39^{5-i}$$

Using the string "SAMUEL" as the original input, the calculation would be performed as follows. The reference table utilized for this specific example is in Fig. 5.

$$S = 6 * 90,224,199 = 541,345,194$$

where 90,224,199 is the number of permutations with n=39 & 5 items included.

$$A = 2 * 2,313,441 = 4,626,882$$

$$M = 14 * 59,319 = 830,466$$

$$U = 11 * 1,521 = 16,731$$

$$E = 0 * 39 = 0$$

$$L = 10 * 1 = 10$$

```
      541,345,194
        4,626,882
          830,466
           16,731
                0
 +               10
----------------
      546,819,283
```

Following the completion of all calculations, the final result is 546,819,283 as noted above.

Binary Conversion and Color Dictionary. The number representing the chunk is then converted into its binary form and padded with zeros as necessary to fit evenly into four eight bit sections. The eight bit sections are then placed into a dictionary representing a pixel's colors. The last item in Step 4 is to add one (shown as "+1") to the "A" value to ensure that the pixel is not completely transparent.

Input: 546,819,283
Binary: 00100000100101111100110011010011, where the leading zeros have been added for usability
Split: [00100000+1], [10010111], [11001100], [11010011]
Output: {A:00100001, R:10010111, G:11001100, B:11010011}

Embedding. After all the data has been encoded into a list of structures representing RGB values, the list is passed to an embedding function, which simply places each pixel into the image at the next slot available from the allowed pixels list. A simplified diagram of this process is shown in Fig. 4.

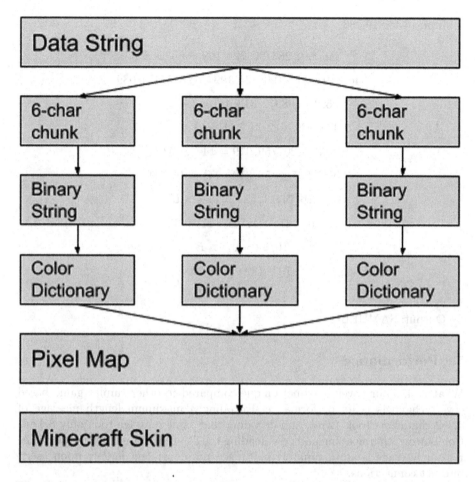

Fig. 4. A simplified representation of the encoding process. The Binary String refers to the binary representation of the permutation number.

4.2   Decoding

Decoding is a quick matter of reversing the encoding process. One section of the process is worth expanding upon, as the reversal of the forward process is slightly different than what may be intuitive. When converting from a large number back to a six character chunk, order of operations is from first character to last, rather than a true inverse of the encoding process. The reverse reference table utilized in this specific example is in Fig. 6. This table is a completely reversed table of the one generated for encoding. Every other operation is inverted as expected: multiplication becomes division and addition becomes subtraction. Comparing the example below to the example in the "Calculation" section shows how each operation is repeated in inverse.

Input: 546,819,283

$$546, 819, 283/90, 224, 199 = 6- > S$$
$$546, 819, 283 - (90, 224, 199 * 6) = 5, 474, 089$$
$$5, 474, 089/2, 313, 441 = 2- > A$$
$$5, 474, 089 - (2, 313, 441 * 2) = 847, 207$$
$$847, 207/59, 319 = 14- > M$$
$$847, 207 - (59, 319 * 14) = 16, 741$$
$$16, 741/1, 521 = 11- > U$$
$$16, 741 - (1, 521 * 11) = 10$$
$$10/39 = 0- > E$$
$$10 - (39 * 0) = 10$$
$$10/1 = 10- > L$$

Output: SAMUEL

5   Performance

What makes our covert channel unique compared to other similar game based covert channels is its performance. Encoding a maximum length message of 4,992 characters took 12 ms, and decoding that same message took only 8.4 ms. Combined with uploading and downloading the file, the overall transmission time for our message is approximately half a second, dependent largely upon users' internet connections.

Hahn *et al.* note that their channel, Castle, a covert channel implemented in real-time strategy games, "has about 100x more bandwidth than other proposed game-based covert channels" [4]. Castle is capable of 50–200 B/s, and with tuning can transmit up to 400 B/s. Our initial estimate for our channel was 166 B/s, with a 30 s transmission time. Since that estimate, we have completely revised our encoding, decoding, and transmission algorithm, resulting in a current bandwidth of 9,984 B/s, approximately 60 times more efficient than previously estimated. This estimate was calculated by measuring the time for encoding data, uploading the skin, downloading the skin, and decoding the file compared to the total amount of bytes worth of text that can be conveyed. Compared to the "52 s for the transfer of a short 10KB text news article" [4] using the proposed Castle covert channel, our final channel is incredibly fast, with an estimated transmission time of roughly 1.5 s for the same 10KB of data. More drastic is the comparison to the channel proposed in [7] which demonstrated transmission rates around 7–9 bits per second.

6 Countermeasures

MASC relies on the private infrastructure provided to the public by Mojang. At any time, Mojang could implement changes that would drastically impact the functionality of MASC. The single most effective change that could block MASC in its current implementation would be to trim the excess pixels stored in the avatar skin. Instead of having a 64×64 image, the skin could be trimmed to fit into a 32×64 image with no unused pixels. Doing so would prevent MASC from modifying the pixels without constraint as is allowed by the current format. Being required to match colors and opacity would severely limit the amount of bits we could modify in an image, and thus limit the bandwidth of the channel. Another route Mojang could take is to zero-out all unused pixels in images stored on their servers, which would accomplish the same thing as trimming without the need for change to existing skin formats.

7 Conclusion and Future Works

In this paper we have demonstrated a working covert channel taking advantage of an inefficiency discovered in Minecraft skins. Our novel character encoding scheme allows for very high bandwidth without making sacrifices to performance or compromising the underlying game's functionality. Future research into MASC could include implementing an in-game API to pull Minecraft skins from nearby players, making for a more typical network traffic sequence. Additionally, there is no method for sequential transfers of data; adding an acknowledgement function could allow for transferring more than the current limit of a single message. A final future option would be to add functionality for modifying the displayed pixels on a Minecraft skin. Doing so would be much less efficient due to needing to match the existing colors, but would allow for more data to be passed in one upload and for the noted counter measures to be rendered irrelevant.

Acknowledgments. The authors would like to thank Ryan Cervantes for his guidance and continued support throughout the research process.

Appendix

'E' 0	'T' 1	'A' 2
'O' 3	'I' 4	'N' 5
'S' 6	'R' 7	'H' 8
'D' 9	'L' 10	'U' 11
'C' 12	' ' 13	'M' 14
'F' 15	'Y' 16	'W' 17
'G' 18	'P' 19	'B' 20
'V' 21	'K' 22	'X' 23
'Q' 24	'J' 25	'Z' 26
'0' 27	'1' 28	'2' 29
'3' 30	'4' 31	'5' 32
'6' 33	'7' 34	'8' 35
'9' 36	'.' 37	',' 38

Fig. 5. The lookup table used for encoding in the provided example

0 'E'	1 'T'	2 'A'
3 'O'	4 'I'	5 'N'
6 'S'	7 'R'	8 'H'
9 'D'	10 'L'	11 'U'
12 'C'	13 ' '	14 'M'
15 'F'	16 'Y'	17 'W'
18 'G'	19 'P'	20 'B'
21 'V'	22 'K'	23 'X'
24 'Q'	25 'J'	26 'Z'
27 '0'	28 '1'	29 '2'
30 '3'	31 '4'	32 '5'
33 '6'	34 '7'	35 '8'
36 '9'	37 '.'	38 ','

Fig. 6. The reverse lookup table used for decoding in the provided example

References

1. Minecraft Wiki. https://minecraft.gamepedia.com/
2. Tick. https://minecraft.gamepedia.com/Tick
3. Dane, J., Kim, N.: Runescape Based Covert Channel (2017)
4. Hahn, B., Nithyanand, R., Gill, P., Johnson, R.: Games Without Frontiers: Investigating Video Games as a Covert Channel. arXiv:1503.05904 [cs], May 2015. http://arxiv.org/abs/1503.05904

5. Lampson, B.W.: A note on the confinement problem. Commun. ACM **16**(10), 613–615 (1973). https://doi.org/10.1145/362375.362389

6. Piscitello, D.: What Is an Internet Covert Channel? ICANN Blog, August 2016. https://www.icann.org/news/blog/what-is-an-internet-covert-channel

7. Zander, S., Armitage, G., Branch, P.: Covert channels in multiplayer first person shooter online games. In: 2008 33rd IEEE Conference on Local Computer Networks (LCN), Montreal, QB, Canada, pp. 215–222. IEEE, October 2008. https://doi.org/10.1109/LCN.2008.4664172, http://ieeexplore.ieee.org/document/4664172/

Lattice-Based Weak Curve Fault Attack on ECDSA

Weiqiong Cao[1,2], Hongsong Shi[1(✉)], Hua Chen[2], Wei Wei[1], and Jiazhe Chen[1]

[1] China Information Technology Security Evaluation Center, Building 1, yard 8,
Shangdi West Road, Haidian District, Beijing 100085, China
[2] Trusted Computing and Information Assurance Laboratory, Institute of Software,
Chinese Academy of Sciences, South Fourth Street 4#, ZhongGuanCun,
Beijing 100190, China

Abstract. ECDSA algorithm is usually used in ICT system to ensure the authenticity of communication. But the weaknesses in various implementations of ECDSA may make its security deviate from theoretical guarantee. This paper proposes a new lattice-based weak curve fault attack on ECDSA. Since the ECDLP is not required to be computationally practical on the whole group of $\langle G \rangle$ (G is the specified base point of ECDSA), our approach extends the existing attacks along this line. In detail, the proposed attack assumes a segment of consecutive bits of the curve parameter a in the Weierstrass equation of ECDSA can be disturbed randomly by fault injection and thus is changed into a'. An analysis about the density of smooth numbers demonstrates the faulty parameter a' can be used for our attack with high probability. Then we show a' can be recovered by a dedicated quadratic residue distinguisher. Some reduced information about the nonce used in ECDSA signature generation can be obtained by solving the instances of ECDLP on the new curve about a'. With the help of these information, we can construct a new model of lattice to recover the private key with the lattice basis reduction techniques. Further, we show the same strategy can defeat the nonce masking countermeasure if the random mask is not too long, and makes the commonly employed countermeasures ineffective. To our knowledge, the problem remains untraceable to the existing weak curve fault attacks. Thus the proposed approach can find more applications than the existing ones. This is demonstrated by the experimental analysis.

Keywords: ECDSA · Weak curve · Fault attack · Lattice attack

1 Introduction

1.1 Existing Work on Fault Attacks

Elliptic curve digital signature algorithm (ECDSA) has found its extensive use in practice. It is mainly used for data authentication in network communication protocols (e.g., TLS protocol), financial IC cards and various embedded

© IFIP International Federation for Information Processing 2021
Published by Springer Nature Switzerland AG 2021
A. Jøsang et al. (Eds.): SEC 2021, IFIP AICT 625, pp. 146–161, 2021.
https://doi.org/10.1007/978-3-030-78120-0_10

cryptographic devices. Over the last decades, side channel attack (SCA) and fault attack (FA) have been found to be exploitable on different implementations of ECDSA. As in the SCAs [1,3], obtaining useful side channel information is generally the initial step of various attacks. For example, in [11,20,21], an adversary, when collecting enough side channel information about the nonce or some intermediates, can construct specific instances of shortest vector problem (SVP) or closest vector problem (CVP) in lattice, and then employ the lattice basis reduction methods to recover the signature key.

In this paper, we are interested in fault attacks. The structure of FA is similar to SCA on ECDSA. Firstly, FA manages to obtain some valid bit-leaked information about the nonce in ECDSA, and then translates the obtained information into a lattice so as to recover the private key by lattice basis reduction algorithms. The difference of FA from SCA is that, the leakage information is actively induced by fault injection approaches, such as laser injection, electromagnetic injection or voltage glitch interference. The induced signal can perturb the execution flow of the signature generation, which makes some instructions skipped or intermediates faulty, and then makes the target produce faulty signatures. A dozen of fault attacks on ECDSA have been proposed since very early of this century. Here we only review those being related to lattice analysis.

In PKC 2005 [18], Nacache et al. introduced a lattice-based fault attack on DSA. In their approach, some least significant bits of nonce are set to be 0 by inducing voltage glitch, and then the private key in DSA is recovered by solving an instance of CVP in lattice. Schmidt et al. in FDTC 2009 [24] introduced a new differential fault model. If a point addition or doubling operation during the scalar multiplication (ECSM) in signature generation is skipped by fault injection, some bits of the nonce can be obtained by differential analysis. Nguyen et al. [22] summarized this kind of fault attacks and called them lattice-based fault attacks. Cao et al. in ICISC 2015 [4] also introduced a random fault model targeting the y-coordinate of intermediate point during the calculation of ECSM, which can tolerate more random faulty bits. In [14], Kim et al. showed that the fault on modulus p can also be applied to do FA on ECDSA. The attack assumes fault injection can flip every bit of the modulus p, and then obtain a weak curve on which solving elliptic curve discrete logarithm problem (ECDLP) is computationally practical. The solution reveals some leakage information about nonce k, by which two faulty signatures are enough for constructing a lattice to recover the private key. However, the approach requires a strong fault model that only one bit (or a few bits) of p is flipped and the faulty modulus p' is known to the adversary. Moreover, it requires all the prime factors p_i of p' and the orders n_i of subgroups $\mathbb{Z}/p_i^{e_i}$ (where $p' = \prod_{i=1}^{u} p_i^{e_i}$, $p_i < p_j$ for $1 \leq i < j \leq u$ and $e_i \in \mathbb{N}$) to be relatively small, such that the time complexity $O(\sqrt{n_u})$ of solving ECDLP in this case is practical. In addition, in order to mount lattice attack, the product $n'(= \prod_{i=1}^{u} n_i)$ of all the orders n_i should satisfy $n' \geq n^{1/2}$, that is, the bit length of n' should be greater than half of the key length of ECDSA, which restrains the applicability of the fault attack.

1.2   Our Approach

In this paper, we propose a lattice-based weak curve fault attack on ECDSA. Here an elliptic curve is defined as weak curve if ECDLP in a *subgroup* of the point group $\langle G \rangle$ is computationally solvable in practice, where G is the base point of ECDSA algorithm. (See Definition 3 for detail.) Note the definition does not require ECDLP in the whole group of $\langle G \rangle$ being computationally solvable, which is the main difference of our approach from the existing attacks.

In more detail, we consider a continuous segment of the curve parameter a can be randomly disturbed by fault injection. The faulty value of a, called a' hereafter, is not required to be known, but can be guessed by a specific quadratic residual distinguisher, see the Algorithm ALG-GUESS-PARA in Sect. 3.2. Then if the induced curve is weak such that the ECDLP in some subgroup of $\langle G \rangle$ can be solved practically, we can obtain enough reduced information about the nonce. Formally, the weakness is characterized by a factor d of the order n' of G in the weak curve. And the reduced information is expressed in the form of modulo d, see the Algorithm ALG-OBTAIN-NONCEINFO in Sect. 3.2. Then this type of information can be employed to construct a new model of lattice for key recovery (see Sect. 3.3). The dimension N of the lattice is tightly related to the module d. In short, the bigger d is, the smaller N would be.

In addition, for ECDSA with random scalar masking, the proposed approach is still practical without any additional masked bits leakage. For example, if $k' = k + \lambda n$, where k is the real scalar and λ is a 64-bit random number, the approach can succeed by selecting a bigger modulus d (see Sect. 3.4).

Our study on the density of smooth numbers shows the probability of existing some big prime factors in n' is much greater than that of all the prime factors of n' being small (see Sect. 3.5). It thus indicates the proposed approach can find more applications than the existing weak curve fault attacks. This is demonstrated by the experimental analysis in Sect. 4.

2   Preliminaries

In this paper, we consider the elliptic curves on prime field $\mathbb{F}_p$, where p is a prime. Generally, the Weierstrass equation of the elliptic curves on $\mathbb{F}_p$ is given by

$$E(a,b) : y^2 = x^3 + ax + b \bmod p,$$

where parameters $a, b \in \mathbb{F}_p$ satisfy $4a^3 + 27b^2 \neq 0$. The group of rational points on the elliptic curve $E(a, b)$ is defined by

$$\mathbf{G} = \{(x,y) | y^2 = x^3 + ax + b \bmod p, x, y \in \mathbb{F}_p\} \cup \{\mathcal{O}\},$$

where $\mathcal{O}$ is the infinite point. Let G be an element in $\mathbf{G}$ with order n (which is usually a prime), $\langle G \rangle$ be the additive subgroup of $\mathbf{G}$ generated by G (where $\mathcal{O}$ is the identity element of $\langle G \rangle$). For any $P = (x,y) \in \langle G \rangle$, its inverse element $-P \in \langle G \rangle$ is $(x, -y)$. For any integer $k \in \mathbb{Z}_n$, the calculation of $kG = G + G + \ldots + G$

(k times) is called ECSM in $E(a,b)$, and can be calculated using point doubling and addition operations [10].

Point Addition

If $P = (x_1, y_1) \in \langle G \rangle$, $Q = (x_2, y_2) \in \langle G \rangle$, and $P \neq \pm Q$, then $(x_3, y_3) = P + Q$ satisfies

$$\begin{aligned} x_3 &= \lambda^2 - x_2 - x_1 \\ y_3 &= \lambda(x_1 - x_3) - y_1 \end{aligned}, \text{ where } \lambda = \frac{y_2 - y_1}{x_2 - x_1}.$$

Point doubling

If $P = (x_1, y_1) \in \langle G \rangle$ and $P \neq -P$, then $(x_3, y_3) = 2P$ satisfies

$$\begin{aligned} x_3 &= \lambda^2 - 2x_1 \\ y_3 &= \lambda(x_1 - x_3) - y_1 \end{aligned}, \text{ where } \lambda = \frac{3x_1^2 + a}{2y_1}.$$

An important notice is that the parameter b is not involved in the calculation of point doubling and addition. The order of $E(a,b)$, denoted by $\#E(a,b)$ can be calculated using SEA algorithm [9].

2.1 ECDSA Digital Signature Algorithm

The ECDSA signature generation algorithm is described in Algorithm 1 with some less important details being abstracted away. The randomly generated nonce k is involved in the calculations of ECSM kG (step 3) and s (step 6), which are exactly the targets of our attacks.

Algorithm 1. Signature generation of ECDSA

Input: The definition of a specific elliptic curve $\mathrm{E}(a,b)$, a base point G of the curve with order n, private key $d_A \in \mathbb{Z}_n$, message m.

Output: Signature pair (r, s).

1: $e = H(m)$, where H is a cryptographic hash function;
2: Generate k randomly from $\mathbb{Z}_n$;
3: $Q(x_1, y_1) = kG$;
4: $r = x_1 \bmod n$;
5: **if** $r = 0$ **then** goto step 2;
6: $s = k^{-1}(e + d_A r) \bmod n$;
7: **if** $s = 0$ **then** goto step 2;
8: **return** (r, s)

2.2 Smoothness of Weak Curve Order

The following definitions are required to better describe our approach. For all of them, let n be the order of point G in $E(a,b)$.

Definition 1. *Denote the prime factorization of n by $n = \prod\limits_{i=1}^{u} q_i^{e_i}$, where $q_i \in \mathbb{N}$ is a prime factor of n, $e_i \in \mathbb{N}$ denotes the degree of q_i in the factorization and $q_i < q_j$ for $1 \leq i < j \leq u$. For $y \in \mathbb{N}$, if the biggest prime factor q_u meets $q_u \leq y$, then n is called y-smooth.*

Definition 2. *The elliptic curve discrete logarithm problem (ECDLP) in $E(a, b)$ is defined as: given $G \in \mathbf{G}$ with order n and an element $Q \in \langle G \rangle$, compute the value $k \in \mathbb{Z}_n$ such that $Q = kG$.*

To our knowledge, the best known generic algorithm [23, 28] in classical computer for solving ECDLP in arbitrary elliptic curves needs $O(\sqrt{q_u})$ group operations in computation. We call an ECDLP instance practically solvable if its solving complexity is not bigger than a predefined constant x. In this paper, we set PRAC_COMP= 2^{64} group operations by considering currently achievable computing power of classical computers, which can be redefined to adapt to the future development of computing technology.

Definition 3. *With respect to the group $\langle G \rangle$, we call n practically solvable smooth if the ECDLP on $\langle G \rangle$ is practically solvable; we call n partially solvable smooth if there exists a factor d of n such that the ECDLP on $\langle (n/d)G \rangle$ (with order d) is practically solvable; Finally, we call n practically unsolvable smooth if n does not belong to the above two cases.*

In this paper, $E(a, b)$ is defined as weak curve if the order n of the chosen base point G of $E(a, b)$ is partially solvable smooth or practically solvable smooth.

2.3   Existing Fault Attacks on Weak Curves

In this section, we introduce an existing fault attack on the weak curves with solvable smooth order [2, 14], which can also be used to the weak curves with partially solvable smooth order.

It is assumed that the y-coordinate of G is disturbed by a fault injection process, i.e., $G = (x_G, y_G)$ is changed into $G' = (x_G, y_{G'})$ with $y_G \neq y_{G'}$. Then with overwhelming probability, the faulty G' is not on the original curve $E(a, b)$ (the only exception being $y_G = -y_{G'}$). Note since parameter b is not involved in the calculation of scalar multiplication, G' can be viewed on a new curve $E(a, b')$, and then $Q' = kG'$ is calculated on the curve $E(a, b')$, where $b' = y_{Q'}^2 - x_{Q'}^3 - ax_{Q'} = y_{G'}^2 - x_G^3 - ax_G$.

Assume the induced curve has a solvable smooth order $n' = \prod_{i=1}^{u} q_i^{e_i}$ with respect to the group $\langle G' \rangle$. Then given Q', G' and n', the following approach can be used to compute the scalar k. Firstly, the reduced value $k \bmod q_i$ can be obtained by solving the ECDLP instance $\frac{n'}{q_i}Q' = k\frac{n'}{q_i}G'(i = 1, ..., u)$ with Pollard-rho algorithm [28]. Next, the reduced value $k_i = k \bmod q_i^{e_i} (i = 1, ..., u)$ can be obtained by Pohlig-Hellman algorithm [23]. Finally, the modulo-n' reduced value $t = k \bmod n'$ can be obtained by Chinese remainder theorem(CRT). Hence, $k = t + \varepsilon n'$, where $\varepsilon \in \{0, ..., \lfloor n/n' \rfloor\}$. Enumerate all the possible values of ε to calculate the corresponding k, when $Q = kG$, k is just the correct one that we are looking for.

The above approach shows that n' must be solvable smooth so as to solve the ECDLP instances on $\langle G' \rangle$ and $\lfloor n/n' \rfloor \leq$ PRAC_COMP. Otherwise, the approach cannot be applied in practice.

2.4   Lattice Basis Reduction

Lattice analysis is a key technique to our approach. We thus give some fundamental background about lattice attacks.

Let $B = \{b_1, \ldots, b_N\} \subseteq \mathbb{R}^m$ be a series of N linearly independent vectors. The lattice generated by B is defined as $\mathcal{L}(B) = \left\{ \sum_{i=1}^{N} x_i b_i : x_i \in \mathbb{Z} \right\}$, where B serves as a basis for the lattice $\mathcal{L}(B)$, and we call the integers N and m its rank and dimension respectively. If $m = N$, $\mathcal{L}$ is called a N-dimensional full rank lattice. The shortest vector problem (SVP) and closest vector problem (CVP) are two computational complexity problems crucial to lattice-based cryptography. We give them below.

Definition 4. *[17]*

(1) **Shortest Vector Problem***: Given a basis of a lattice $\mathcal{L}$, find a lattice vector $v \neq 0$ such that $\|v\| \leq \|u\|$ for any nonzero vector $u \in \mathcal{L}$.*
(2) **Closest Vector Problem***: Given a basis of a lattice $\mathcal{L}$ and a target vector $t \in \mathbb{R}^m$, find a lattice vector $v \in \mathcal{L}$ closest to the target t, which means $\mathrm{dist}(v, t) \leq \mathrm{dist}(u, t)$ for any vector $u \in \mathcal{L}$, where $\mathrm{dist}(\cdot, \cdot)$ denotes the Euclid norm of two points.*

For a N-dimensional approximate SVP, there exist some polynomial-time basis reduction algorithms which can output short lattice vectors when the approximate factor is large enough. Among those algorithms, LLL algorithm [15] is the most typical one, and BKZ-algorithm [6] has been the most practical algorithm for lattice basis reduction based on a series of optimizing technique [25, 26].

For random lattices with dimension N, Gaussian heuristic gives a probable estimation on the length of shortest lattice vector in the sense of average as in [19], from which Gaussian expected the shortest length of a N-dimensional lattice $\mathcal{L}$ could be defined to be

$$\sigma(\mathcal{L}) = \sqrt{\frac{N}{2\pi e}} \mathrm{vol}(\mathcal{L})^{1/N},$$

where vol denotes the volume or determinant of $\mathcal{L}$.

Generally, the actual shortest lattice vector is much easier to be found as the increment of the gap between the shortest length and the Gaussian heuristic. If it is significantly shorter than $\sigma(\mathcal{L})$, it can be located in polynomial time by using LLL and related algorithms. Heuristically, assuming the lattice $\mathcal{L}$ behaves like a random lattice, if there exists a lattice vector whose distance from the target is much shorter than $\sigma(\mathcal{L})$, this lattice vector is expected to be the closest vector to the target. Accordingly, this special CVP instance usually could be solved by Babai algorithm or embedding-based SVP.

3   Lattice-Based Weak Curve Attack

In this section, we present our lattice-based weak curve attack on ECDSA. The attack consists of two steps: 1) Obtain the reduced information of the nonce by weak curve fault attack; 2) Construct an instance of CVP by virtue of the reduced information, and resolve it to recover the private key.

3.1   Fault Model

The fault attacks we consider in this paper aim at modifying the curve parameter a by inducing fault to the corresponding physical storage cells (RAM, EEPROM or CPU register for example). Further, we mainly consider a type of random fault, in which a continuous l-bit segment of a is modified randomly by fault injection and the starting bit location of fault is also randomly picked. The fault can be permanent or transient. A permanent fault means the value corresponding to the parameter is definitely changed, and fixed on the faulty value. A transient fault means the parameter keeps the faulty value unless the original value is explicitly restored. The length l of faulty bits is usually valued from $\{1, 8, 16, 24, 32\}$ considering the byte-based cell structure of storage.

Assume, before running the signature generation (Algorithm 1), an adversary induces a permanent (or transient) fault to the parameter a of elliptic curve $E(a, b)$. Denote the modified parameter by a' and suppose it is different from a in a continuous l-bit segment. Therefore, the base point $G = (x_G, y_G)$ will be on a new curve $E(a', b') : y^2 = x^3 + a'x + b' \bmod p$, and $b' = y_G{}^2 - x_G{}^3 - a'x_G \bmod p$. Correspondingly, the ECSM $Q = kG$ of step 3 in Algorithm 1 will be actually computed on the new curve $E(a', b')$ (since parameter b is not involved in the calculation of ECSM). Let the new order of G on $E(a', b')$ be n'. Finally, the faulty signatures (r', s') are output to the adversary.

Note that our single fault model has the following limitations: 1) parameter a must be involved in the calculation of ECSM (except that a is sometimes substituted with $p - 3$ when $a = p - 3$ for the sake of resource optimization); 2) There is no point validation checking whether the input or output point is on the original elliptic curve during the calculation of ECSM. Otherwise, our attack will not work.

3.2   Proposed Fault Attack on Weak Curves

Suppose the signatures on the weak curve can be retrieved after the signature generation procedure. We will run the following two algorithms sequentially to obtain some reduced information about the nonce k. Then, in Sect. 3.3 we will use the obtained information to construct lattices and recover the private key.

Algorithm ALG-GUESS-PARA: Guess and Determine a' and $x_{Q'}$

Step 1-1. If assuming the fault injection step induced a randomly located and randomly valued continuous l-bit segment errors to a, then a' could be characterized by $a' = a \oplus \beta 2^\sigma$, where $\beta \in \mathbb{Z}_{2^l}$ is an unknown l-bit random integer, l_a is the bit length of a and σ is an unknown random integer in interval $[0, l_a - l]$. Let $\mathbf{T}$ be the set for storing all the possible values of a'. Hence, the initial number of the possible values for a' is $|\mathbf{T}| = (l_a - l + 1)2^l$.

Step 1-2. Run the signature generation procedure to obtain a faulty signature pair (r', s'). Then deduce the x-coordinate $x_{Q'} \bmod p$ of the faulty point Q' from r'. We separate two cases to consider the deduction.

- If $p < n$ then $x_{Q'} \bmod p = r' \bmod n$;
- If $p > n$, we have the deduction as follows. Note that $hn = \#E(a, b)$ (where $\#E(a, b)$ is the number of point and h is the cofactor on $E(a, b)$). By Hasse theorem [10], we have $p + 1 - 2\sqrt{p} \le hn \le p + 1 + 2\sqrt{p}$. Hence, $x_{Q'} \bmod p = r' + \lambda n < p$, and the integer λ is valued not greater than h (h is usually 1 or 2 in a standard curve) when $p > 2^6$, i.e., $x_{Q'}$ has at most $h + 1$ values depending on the concrete values of p and n.

Step 1-3. Sieve **T** to find valid a'. For each possible $a' \in \mathbf{T}$, calculate $b' = y_G^2 - x_G^3 - a' x_G \bmod p$, and for each value $x_{Q'}$ derived in step 2, compute

$$Y = x_{Q'}^3 + a' x_{Q'} + b' \bmod p.$$

If Y is a quadratic residue modulo p, keep a' in **T**. Otherwise, eliminate it from **T**.

Step 1-4. If $|\mathbf{T}|$ is greater than 1, go to **Step 1-2**; otherwise, regard the only value in **T** as the faulty parameter a'. Then run the SEA algorithm [9] to compute the order n' of G on $E(a', b')$, and factorize it using some algorithms in subexponential time (such as Pollard $p-1$ or number field sieve algorithms). Note when $n' \le 512$, the factorization step is practical which is enough to factorize n in current standard ECC. If the factorization result shows that n' is partially solvable smooth, we get a valid a'; otherwise repeat Algorithm ALG-GUESS-PARA to induce a new curve until getting a valid a' with partially solvable smooth n'. (Note we don't require n' to be *solvable smooth*.) The condition can be satisfied after a number of trials considering the density of smooth numbers (See Sect. 3.5 for detail). So in the following we assume there exists a factor d of n' such that d is practically solvable smooth with respect to $E(a', b')$ (see the definitions in Sect. 2.2). Finally, we end the algorithm.

The above "quadratic residue" distinguisher can eliminate about a half of the invalid values in each invocation. Hence, the total time complexity is about $O((l_a - l + 1)2^{l+1})$.

Algorithm ALG-OBTAIN-NONCEINFO: Obtain Reduced Value of Nonce k

Based the derived valid a' and the selected small factor d of n', run the following steps to collect as much as useful reduced information about the nonce.

Step 2-1. Run the signature generation procedure with different message to get a signature (r', s'), and based on the derived (a', b') compute possible values $\{x_{Q'}\}$ and Y as above. Since there is only one correct value for $x_{Q'}$, to remove the erroneous computed values, we discard the signature (r', s') if more than one Y derived from it are quadratic residue modulo p, and re-generate a new signature (r', s') until the condition is satisfied. When the correct $x_{Q'}$ on curve $E(a', b')$ is calculated, we could obtain two possible points $(x_{Q'}, \pm\sqrt{Y})$ of Q'.

Step 2-2. Without loss of generality, assume $Q'_1 = \left(x_{Q'}, \sqrt{Y}\right) = \mu G$ for $\mu \in \mathbb{Z}_n$.
Let $\ell = n'/d$, we can construct the instance of ECDLP

$$\ell Q'_1 = \mu(\ell G)$$

in the d-ordered subgroup $\langle \ell G \rangle$ and solve it to obtain $\mu \mod d$. Specifically,
if Q'_1 is the correct choice of Q', we have $k = \mu \mod d$; otherwise $-Q'_1$ is the
correct choice of Q', and we have $k = (d - \mu) \mod d$.

Step 2-3. Repeat the above two steps N times to obtain N groups of valid
signature result $\{r_i, s_i\}_{i=1}^N$ and N groups of reduced information about the
nonces $\{k_i\}_{i=1}^N$, where each reduced information is denoted by

$$k_i = c_i + \lambda_i d$$

for $i = 1, ..., N$, where $c_i = \begin{cases} \mu_i, \text{ for } y_{Q'} = \sqrt{Y} \\ d - \mu_i, \text{ for } y_{Q'} = -\sqrt{Y} \end{cases}$ and $0 < \lambda_i < n/d$.

In the above Algorithm ALG-OBTAIN-NONCEINFO, solving the ECDLP in
the d-ordered subgroup consumes the main computation time, and its time com-
plicity $O(\sqrt{q_{max}})$ (where q_{max} is the biggest prime factor of d) is less than
PRAC_COMP since d is selected to be practically solvable (see Sect. 2.3).
Hence, Algorithm ALG-OBTAIN-NONCEINFO is practically feasible.

3.3   Proposed Lattice-Based ECDSA Key Recovery Algorithm

We show how to use the signature result $\{r_i, s_i\}_{i=1}^N$ and the reduced information
about $\{k_i\}_{i=1}^N$ to construct a new model of lattice and then recover the private
key d_A.

For each $i \in \{1, ..., N\}$, we first assume the correct value of c_i is identified.
Substituting the corresponding k_i into s_i, we have

$$s_i(c_i + \lambda_i d) = e_i + r_i d_A, \tag{1}$$

where e_i is the hash value of message m_i and $0 < \lambda_i < n/d$. The identification
of correct value of c_i is discussed at the end of this subsection.

The equation (1) can be transformed as

$$\lambda_i = A_i d_A - (B_i - n/(2d)) \mod n, \tag{2}$$

where $A_i = s_i^{-1} d^{-1} r_i \mod n$ and $B_i = d^{-1}\left(c_i - s_i^{-1} e_i\right) \mod n + n/(2d)$. Since
$0 < \lambda_i < n/d$, there exists a $h_i \in \mathbb{Z}$ such that

$$|A_i d_A + h_i n - B_i| < n/(2d) \qquad (i = 1, ..., N). \tag{3}$$

We can construct a lattice $\mathcal{L}$ by the above inequalities (3), and the row vectors
$\{b_1, ..., b_{N+1}\}$ of the matrix

$$\mathbf{M} = \begin{bmatrix} n & 0 & 0 & \cdots & 0 \\ 0 & n & 0 & \cdots & 0 \\ \vdots & & \ddots & & \vdots \\ 0 & \cdots & 0 & n & 0 \\ A_1 & A_2 & \cdots & A_N & 1/(2d) \end{bmatrix}$$

construct a basis of $\mathcal{L}$.

Let the target vector $t = (B_1, \ldots, B_N, 0) \in \mathbb{R}^{N+1}$. There exists a lattice vector $v = xM = (h_1 n + A_1 d_A, \ldots, h_N n + A_N d_A, d_A/(2d))$ with the coordinate vector $x = (h_1, \ldots, h_N, d_A) \in \mathbb{Z}^{N+1}$. From inequalities (3), we have

$$\|v - t\| < \sqrt{N+1}\, n/(2d). \tag{4}$$

As introduced in [22], we also assume heuristically $\mathcal{L}$ behaves like a random lattice. According to Sect. 2.4, if $\|v - t\|$ is much less than $\sigma(\mathcal{L})\, (= \sqrt{\frac{N+1}{2\pi e}} \mathrm{vol}(\mathcal{L})^{\frac{1}{N+1}})$, we expect v to be the closest vector from t in $\mathcal{L}$, where $\mathrm{vol}(\mathcal{L}) = \det(M) = n^N/(2d)$ ($\det(M)$ is the determinant of M). Hence, it is required

$$\|v - t\| < \sqrt{N+1}\, n/(2d) \ll \sqrt{\frac{N+1}{2\pi e}} \left(n^N/(2d)\right)^{\frac{1}{N+1}}. \tag{5}$$

Let $f = \lceil \log n \rceil$ and $l_d = \lceil \log d \rceil$. If $N > \frac{f + \log \sqrt{2\pi e}}{l_d + 1 - \log \sqrt{2\pi e}}$ and $l_d > \log \sqrt{2\pi e} - 1$, heuristically the inequality (4) can be viewed as a special instance of CVP in lattice $\mathcal{L}$. Consequently, the vector v can be determined by solving the instance of CVP to reveal the private key d_A. If $d_A G$ is equal to the public key P_A, the attack is successful.

In addition, the inequality (3) is equivalent to

$$|A_i d_A + h_i n - B_i| < n/2^{l_d} (i = 1, \ldots, N), \tag{6}$$

which is a hidden number problem(HNP)[20,21]. By the same way, it can be transformed into a CVP to recover d_A.

It is assumed above that all the values of $\{c_i\}_{i=1}^N$ are correctly guessed before the lattice attack. The reality is that there are two solutions for each c_i after the Algorithm ALG-OBTAIN-NONCEINFO, and it is not sure which one is the correct. Hence, 2^N kinds of combinations about the possible c_i would be generated and only one combination is correct. Although it is computationally difficult to make it certain in general, from the above analysis, we know the required number N of faulty signatures for lattice attack depends on the size of factor d. Or in order to ensure the practicality of the lattice attack, d should not be too small. In fact, the larger d is, the smaller N would be. For example, d is generally recommended to satisfy $d \geq 2^8$ such that $N \approx 45$ for 256-bit ECDSA. So when N is not too big, it is still possible to enumerate all the possible c_i in practice. Specifically, the worse-case time complexity for the enumerating lattice attack in this case is $2^N T$, where T represents the time required for each running of the lattice attack.

3.4 Attack on ECDSA with Scalar Masking

Generally, scalar masking is one of the most common countermeasures for ECDSA to resist SCA. For example, nonce k_i during signature generation is masked as k_i' with a random number α_i, i.e., $k_i' = k_i + \alpha_i n (i = 1, \ldots, N)$. This countermeasure also could block the existing lattice attacks [11,20,21], since it is required to obtain all the bit leakage information of $\{\alpha_i\}_{i=1}^{N}$. By comparison, our attack is affected much less, specifically as follows.

With the masked nonce k_i', we have

$$Q = k_i'G \text{ and } s_i = k_i^{-1}(e_i + r_i d_A) = k_i'^{-1}(e_i + r_i d_A) \mod n.$$

Accordingly, the reduced information derived by weak curve fault attack meets $k_i' = c_i + \lambda_i d$, where l_{α_i} denotes the bit length of α_i and $\lambda_i < 2^{f+l_{\alpha_i}-l_d}$. Substitute k_i' into s_i and mount lattice attack. If $l_d > \log\sqrt{2\pi e} + l_{\alpha_i} - 1$ and $N > \frac{f+\log\sqrt{2\pi e}}{l_d-l_{\alpha_i}+1-\log\sqrt{2\pi e}}$, the private key d_A can be recovered by constructing an instance of CVP. There is no bit leakage of α_i required in our lattice attack except a bigger d. Moreover, the required d can be obtained with high proportion in experiments. For example, if $l_{\alpha_i} = 32$, the experimental success rate of fault injection is still up to 80% since l_d is recommended as 40 (see Sect. 4). Obviously, our lattice attack is more practical on ECDSA with scalar masking.

3.5   The Density of Smooth Numbers

When comparing with existing weak curve fault attacks in [2,7,14] (which require n' must be solvable smooth so as to solve ECDLP instances on $\langle G' \rangle$ and $\lfloor n/n' \rfloor \le$ PRAC_COMP), our attack puts weaker condition on the process of fault injection. Specifically, the order of the induced weak curve in the proposed method is only required to be partially solvable smooth in the proposed attack, which is weaker than the existing attacks. The following analysis on the smoothness of a random number demonstrates that the weaker condition improves the applicability of proposed attack significantly.

Let z be an integer with prime factorization $z = \prod_{i=1}^{u} p_i^{e_i}$. We say z is y-smooth if $\max_{1 \le i \le u}\{p_i\} \le y$, as mentioned in Sect. 2.2. We denote by $\psi(x,y)$ the number of integers $z \le x$ such that z is y-smooth. In [8], a result on the bound of $\psi(x,y)$ shows smooth numbers with suitable x, y are relatively common to meet. Specifically, let ϵ be an arbitrary positive constant, then for $x \ge 10$ and $y \ge (\ln x)^{1+\epsilon}$, we have

$$\psi(x,y)/x = e^{-(1+o(1))u\ln u} \qquad \text{as } x \to \infty,$$

where $u = \ln x/\ln y$ and e is the natural number. Note for a fixed x the density of smooth numbers (i.e., $\psi(x,y)/x$) is an increasing function with respect to the bound y of factors. For instance, we can roughly get $\psi(2^{256}, 2^{247})/2^{256} = 0.963$ and $\psi(2^{256}, 2^{128})/2^{256} = 0.25$ (where $o(1)$ is set to be 0 in the approximation). It means smooth (integer) numbers in the scope of $[1,x]$ with at least one large factor could be much more frequent than those with only smaller factors. Note the action of n' is not uniformly random, since the injected fault is only considered to impact very limited bits of the parameter a of the curve. However, as in [8], we make a heuristic assumption that the probability of sampling n' in this method is subject to the density given by $\psi(x,y)/x$. In this view, Fig. 1

shows the probability (Y-axis) of generating a point in 256-bit ECDSA curve with y-smooth order n'(X-axis). If considering practicality the 2^{128}-smooth n' (with probability 25% in Fig. 1) is required by existing weak curve attacks. Our attack extends the possibility of fault attacks on ECDSA with 256-bit private key. In more detail, considering the case that n' is 2^{247}-smooth (with probability 96.3%), though solving ECDLP in the case is currently unpractical, if collecting enough reduced information about the nonce with respect to a small factor d of n' (which is close to 2^9), our attack is still practical. This is supported by the experiments in Sect. 4.

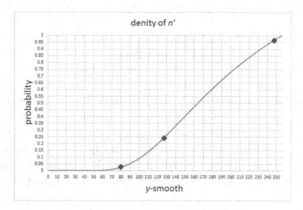

Fig. 1. The density for y-smooth n'

In conclusion, since with high probability the order n' has at least a big prime factor in factorization (determined by PRAC_COMP), the existing weak curve attacks (which require n' to be practically solvable smooth) may not be efficient in practice. In comparison, our attack can survive in this case with high probability, since we only need n' to be partially solvable smooth. The price is that our new constructed lattice model needs more faulty signatures (in number N), which is much greater than the one in [14]. But this is affordable in practice, since we can usually ask the target to generate enough faulty signatures once the fault has been induced, especially when it is permanent.

4   Experimental Analysis

In this section, we do the experiments to validate the applicability of the proposed attack. The emphasis is on checking Algorithm ALG-OBTAIN-NONCEINFO and the lattice-based key recovery algorithm. Therefore, the fault injection process is not conducted in experiments. For more information on engineering aspects of fault injection, we refer to the reference [13]. The experiments were conducted on a computer with 3.4 GHz 8-core CPU, 8G memory and

Windows7 OS. The order n' (derived by the faulty a') is calculated by SEA algorithm implemented in Miracl library [16], and the constructed CVP instances are solved by BKZ algorithm [6] implemented in NTL library [27] with block size 10.

Two types of 256-bit curves over prime field $\mathbb{F}_p$ are targeted in experiments, which are NIST P-256 [5] (hereafter called P-256) and the curve recommended in SM2 digital signature algorithm (hereafter called SM2-curve which still can be employed as the curve of ECDSA) [12] respectively. Then for each curve, two types of bit perturbation experiments are simulated, including the single-bit flipped fault and 16-bit random fault. The single-bit flipped fault is to flip a bit-by-bit. Then there are 256 cases in total. The 16-bit random fault is to randomly pick a starting bit location, characterized by a random integer $\sigma \in [0, 240]$, and then XOR the continuous 16-bit segment (identified by σ) of parameter a with a 16-bit random number $\beta \in \{0,1\}^{16}$, such that $a' = a \oplus (\beta 2^{\sigma})$. The experiments are also done for 256 times. As a whole, four types of different experiments are conducted, and each is done 256 times.

We then use the obtained a' to compute n' for each experiment. Figure 2 shows the proportion γ (Y-axis) of partially solvable smooth n' when its factors d satisfies $l_d \geq X$ (X-axis), and Fig. 3 shows the proportion γ (Y-axis) of the unsolvable smooth n' available for our attack when d satisfies $l_d \geq X$ (X-axis) in each type of experiment. (Note each experiment type includes 256 concrete experiments.) From Fig. 2, we can find that the proportion of partially solvable smooth orders accounts for 94.9% at least when $l_d \geq 8$, which is far greater than the proportion (35%) of solvable smooth orders required in the previous weak curve attacks. Moreover, as shown in Fig. 3, even under the case that n' is unsolvable smooth (accounting for about 65% proportion in each 256 experiments), there still are 92.5% unsolvable smooth n' available for our attack. Obviously, most of the weak curves derived from 256 fault simulations can be applied to our attack, which increases the success rate of fault injection sharply. In addition, from Figs. 2 and 3, no matter whether the curve is P-256 or SM2-curve, and the fault type is single-bit flipped fault or 16-bit random fault, all the proportions of the four types of experiments are roughly similar with the density mentioned in Sect. 3.1. Hence, our attack is effective for most of ECC signatures based on prime field.

Finally, based on a faulty a' in SM2-curve, select d with different bit length, and carry on the corresponding lattice attacks. As shown in Table 1, N is the number of signatures required to achieve 100% success rate of lattice attack, T is the required time of each lattice attack in seconds and O is the maximum time complexity of the attack including the enumerating of c_i (see Sect. 3.3). For example, when $l_d = 16$, the require time for each lattice attack is about 0.255 s, the required number N is 19 and hence the total maximum time require in the whole attack is about 0.255×2^{19} s. From Table 1, even under the worst case $l_d = 8$, the complexity of enumerating the correct c_i in lattice attack is computationally feasible since $2^{45} < $ PRAC_COMP. In addition, to speed up enumerating, the case $l_d \geq 16$ with time complexity $2^{19}T$ is generally selected in experiments, whose proportion of partially solvable smooth n' is also up to 92.6%

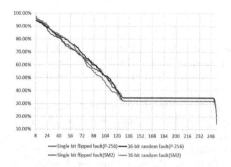

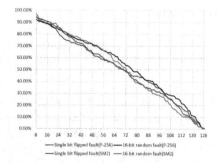

Fig. 2. The proportion γ of partially solvable smooth n' when $l_d > X$

Fig. 3. The proportion γ of unsolvable smooth n' available for our attack when $l_d > X$

at least (see Fig. 2). The results show that the success rate of fault injection is significantly high when ensuring the successful lattice attacks. To sum up, our attack is feasible and effective towards most of ECDSA-like algorithms based on Weierstrass equations of prime finite fields, and increases the success rate of fault injection dramatically.

Table 1. The number of faulty signatures and complexity for lattice attack

Items	$l_d = 8$	$l_d = 9$	$l_d = 16$	$l_d = 32$	$l_d = 64$
N	45	40	19	9	5
$T(s)$	≈ 5.788	≈ 3.675	≈ 0.255	≈ 0.021	≈ 0.005
O	$2^{45}T$	$2^{40}T$	$2^{19}T$	2^9T	2^5T

5 Conclusion

We propose a new lattice-based weak curve fault attack on ECDSA which combines the advantages of weak curve fault attack and lattice attack. The order n' of the weak curve generated by faulty a' is not required to be solvable smooth, and the reduced information of nonces is obtained by solving the ECDLP constructed in a small subgroup, by which a new model of lattice attack is constructed to recover the private key. The experiments showed the success rate of fault injection that there exists a solvable smooth factor d of n' satisfying $l_d \geq 8$ can be as high as 94.9%. In addition, for ECDSA with w-bit scalar masking, our attack still works with high success rate of fault injection by selecting an appropriate d satisfying $l_d - w > \log \sqrt{2\pi e} - 1$.

Acknowledgments. This work is supported by the National Key Research and Development Program of China (No. U1936209), the National Cryptography Development Fund of China (No. MMJJ20170214, MMJJ20170211) and the National Natural Science Foundation of China (No. 61802439).

References

1. Aranha, D.F., Novaes, F.R., Takahashi, A., Tibouchi, M., Yarom, Y.: Ladderleak: breaking ECDSA with less than one bit of nonce leakage. In: Proceedings of the 2020 ACM SIGSAC Conference on Computer and Communications Security, pp. 225–242 (2020)
2. Biehl, I., Meyer, B., Müller, V.: Differential fault attacks on elliptic curve cryptosystems. In: Bellare, M. (ed.) CRYPTO 2000. LNCS, vol. 1880, pp. 131–146. Springer, Heidelberg (2000). https://doi.org/10.1007/3-540-44598-6_8
3. Brumley, B.B., Tuveri, N.: Remote timing attacks are still practical. In: Atluri, V., Diaz, C. (eds.) ESORICS 2011. LNCS, vol. 6879, pp. 355–371. Springer, Heidelberg (2011). https://doi.org/10.1007/978-3-642-23822-2_20
4. Cao, W., et al.: Two lattice-based differential fault attacks against ECDSA with wNAF algorithm. In: Kwon, S., Yun, A. (eds.) ICISC 2015. LNCS, vol. 9558, pp. 297–313. Springer, Cham (2016). https://doi.org/10.1007/978-3-319-30840-1_19
5. Certicom Research. Recommended Elliptic Curve Domain Parameters Standards for Efficient Cryptography (SEC) 2 (2000). https://www.iso.org/standard/76382.html
6. Chen, Y., Nguyen, P.Q.: BKZ 2.0: better lattice security estimates. In: Lee, D.H., Wang, X. (eds.) ASIACRYPT 2011. LNCS, vol. 7073, pp. 1–20. Springer, Heidelberg (2011). https://doi.org/10.1007/978-3-642-25385-0_1
7. Ciet, M., Joye, M.: Elliptic curve cryptosystems in the presence of permanent and transient faults. Des. Codes Cryptogr. **36**(1), 33–43 (2005)
8. Coppersmith, D., Odlzyko, A.M., Schroeppel, R.: Discrete logarithms in GF(p). Algorithmica **1**(1–4), 1–15 (1986)
9. Elkies, N.D., et al.: Elliptic and modular curves over finite fields and related computational issues. AMS IP Stud. Adv. Math. **7**, 21–76 (1998)
10. Hankerson, D., Menezes, A.J., Vanstone, S.: Guide to Elliptic Curve Cryptography. Springer, New York (2006). https://doi.org/10.1007/b97644
11. Howgrave-Graham, N.A., Smart, N.P.: Lattice attacks on digital signature schemes. Des. Codes Cryptogr. **23**(3), 283–290 (2001)
12. International Standard ISO/IEC 14888–3:2006(E): IT Security techniques Digital signatures with appendix Part 3: Discrete logarithm based mechanisms (2018). https://www.iso.org/standard/76382.html
13. Karaklajić, D., Schmidt, J.-M., Verbauwhede, I.: Hardware designer's guide to fault attacks. IEEE Trans. Very Large Scale Integr. (VLSI) Syst. **21**(12), 2295–2306 (2013)
14. Kim, T., Tibouchi, M.: Bit-flip faults on elliptic curve base fields, revisited. In: Boureanu, I., Owesarski, P., Vaudenay, S. (eds.) ACNS 2014. LNCS, vol. 8479, pp. 163–180. Springer, Cham (2014). https://doi.org/10.1007/978-3-319-07536-5_11
15. Lenstra, A.K., Lenstra, H.W., Lovász, L.: Factoring polynomials with rational coefficients. Mathematische Annalen **261**(4), 515–534 (1982)
16. MIRACL Ltd.: Multiprecision Integer and Rational Arithmetic Cryptographic Library (2019). https://github.com/miracl/MIRACL
17. Micciancio, D., Goldwasse, S.: Complexity of Lattice Problems: A Cryptographic Perspective, vol. 671. Springer, New York (2002). https://doi.org/10.1007/978-1-4615-0897-7
18. Naccache, D., Nguyên, P.Q., Tunstall, M., Whelan, C.: Experimenting with faults, lattices and the DSA. In: Vaudenay, S. (ed.) PKC 2005. LNCS, vol. 3386, pp. 16–28. Springer, Heidelberg (2005). https://doi.org/10.1007/978-3-540-30580-4_3

19. Nguyen, P.Q.: Hermites constant and lattice algorithms. In: Nguyen, P., Vallée, B. (eds.) The LLL Algorithm. Information Security and Cryptography, pp. 19–69. Springer, Heidelberg (2010). https://doi.org/10.1007/978-3-642-02295-1_2

20. Nguyen, P.Q., Shparlinski, I.E.: The insecurity of the digital signature algorithm with partially known nonces. J. Cryptol. **15**(3), 151–176 (2002). https://doi.org/10.1007/s00145-002-0021-3

21. Nguyen, P.Q., Shparlinski, I.E.: The insecurity of the elliptic curve digital signature algorithm with partially known nonces. Designs Codes Cryptogr. **30**(2), 201–217 (2003). https://doi.org/10.1023/A:1025436905711

22. Nguyen, P.Q., Tibouchi, M.: Lattice-based fault attacks on signatures. In: Joye, M., Tunstall, M. (eds.) Fault Analysis in Cryptography, pp. 201–220. Springer, Heidelberg (2012). https://doi.org/10.1007/978-3-642-29656-7_12

23. Pohlig, S., Hellman, M.: An improved algorithm for computing logarithms over GF(p) and its cryptographic significance (Corresp.). IEEE Trans. Inf. Theory **24**(1), 106–110 (1978)

24. Schmidt, J., Medwed, M.: A fault attack on ECDSA. In: 2009 Workshop on Fault Diagnosis and Tolerance in Cryptography (FDTC), pp. 93–99. IEEE (2009)

25. Schnorr, C.-P., Euchner, M.: Lattice basis reduction: improved practical algorithms and solving subset sum problems. Math. Program. **66**(1–3), 181–199 (1994). https://doi.org/10.1007/BF01581144

26. Schnorr, C.P., Hörner, H.H.: Attacking the chor-rivest cryptosystem by improved lattice reduction. In: Guillou, L.C., Quisquater, J.-J. (eds.) EUROCRYPT 1995. LNCS, vol. 921, pp. 1–12. Springer, Heidelberg (1995). https://doi.org/10.1007/3-540-49264-X_1

27. Shoup, V.: Number Theory C++ Library (NTL) version 9.6.4 (2016). http://www.shoup.net/ntl/

28. Van Oorschot, P.C., Wiener, M.J.: Parallel collision search with cryptanalytic applications. J. Cryptol. **12**(1), 1–28 (1999)

Application and System Security

HyperSec: Visual Analytics
for Blockchain Security Monitoring

Benedikt Putz(✉) ⓘ, Fabian Böhm ⓘ, and Günther Pernul ⓘ

University of Regensburg, Regensburg, Germany
{benedikt.putz,fabian.boehm,guenther.pernul}@ur.de

Abstract. Today, permissioned blockchains are being adopted by large organizations for business critical operations. Consequently, they are subject to attacks by malicious actors. Researchers have discovered and enumerated a number of attacks that could threaten availability, integrity and confidentiality of blockchain data. However, currently it remains difficult to detect these attacks. We argue that security experts need appropriate visualizations to assist them in detecting attacks on blockchain networks. To achieve this, we develop HyperSec, a visual analytics monitoring tool that provides relevant information at a glance to detect ongoing attacks on Hyperledger Fabric. For evaluation, we connect the HyperSec prototype to a Hyperledger Fabric test network. The results show that common attacks on Fabric can be detected by a security expert using HyperSec's visualizations.

Keywords: Distributed ledger · Permissioned blockchain ·
Information security · Visual analytics · Security monitoring

1 Introduction

New use cases of distributed ledger technology (DLT) are proposed on a daily basis by academia and practice, leading to an increasing number of projects and solutions. Beyond that, blockchain applications are increasingly being used in real large-scale supply chain environments, such as the TradeLens [10] and DLFreight [20] platforms. At first glance, DLT seems to increase an application's security or even solve existing applications' security issues. However, the task of securing the DLT itself is often neglected in practice due to its complexity and the number of serious challenges connected to it.

The complexity of blockchain technology makes it particularly challenging to identify malicious activities [4]. In any blockchain network, there are several independent peers operated by independent organizations, where each organization only has a limited view of the network. Each node also has various data sources from its components, making it difficult to obtain an overview of the

---

B. Putz and F. Böhm—Contributed equally to this manuscript.

ⓒ IFIP International Federation for Information Processing 2021
Published by Springer Nature Switzerland AG 2021
A. Jøsang et al. (Eds.): SEC 2021, IFIP AICT 625, pp. 165–180, 2021.
https://doi.org/10.1007/978-3-030-78120-0_11

network's state [17]. Since blockchain is a networked database, it also requires monitoring both the host and the network, which results in a large volume and velocity of observable data.

Fully automated systems for live attack detection on blockchains do not yet exist. Even if respective technologies for blockchain security monitoring were available, human experts remain indispensable as their domain knowledge is crucial to identify and analyze intricate attack patterns [2]. Therefore, we need a way to make the heterogeneous data at hand available for domain experts. Visualizations offer a well-known path to achieve this goal. A visual representation can help a domain expert make sense of the displayed information and efficiently draw conclusions [12]. These observations lead to our work's research question:

RQ. *What are appropriate visualizations to assist security experts in detecting DLT threats?*

In this work, we make a two-fold contribution to this research question. We first characterize the domain problem: monitoring permissioned DLTs for attacks. This domain problem and derived general design requirements serve as the foundation for our visualization approach. The second part of our contribution is the task-centered design and prototypical implementation of *HyperSec*, a visual representation of security-relevant DLT information to support security experts' monitoring tasks.

The remainder of this work is structured as follows. Section 2 gives a brief overview of related academic work in the field of security visualizations in the blockchain domain. In Sect. 3, we flesh out the domain problem faced by security experts monitoring permissioned blockchain environments for immediate threats. Section 4 then introduces our visualization design and its prototypical implementation using open source technologies. Afterwards, we evaluate our visualization design by simulating attacks in Sect. 5. We discuss how an expert may proceed after an attack has been detected in Sect. 6. Finally, Sect. 7 concludes our work with a summary and possible future research directions.

2   Related Work

Recently, Tovanich et al. [23] carried out a systematic review to structure existing work on the visualization of blockchain data. Their research and previously conducted studies [19] identify several visualization approaches with a focus on criminal and malicious activity [8,13]. These surveys highlight that visualization tools for blockchains are on the rise. However, most of these existing visualization approaches for criminal or malicious activities in blockchains focus on historical analysis, i.e. detecting the events only after they have occured [23].

To effectively prevent attacks upfront, blockchain networks have to be actively monitored by blockchain security experts. Several studies discuss external and internal threats that could impair a blockchain network's functionality [9,18].

Zheng et al. propose a framework for monitoring the Ethereum blockchain's performance [24]. They introduce some respective metrics while using both node logs and Remote Procedure Calls (RPC) to gather data. Threat indicators to detect malicious activities in a blockchain network have recently been introduced by Putz et al. [17]. Based on this limited body of work from academia, blockchain metrics and threat indicators need to be made available to security experts for effective monitoring. Existing monitoring solutions like the dashboard by Bogner [3] focus only on transaction activity but do not consider other security-relevant data and metrics.

An approach pointing in this direction is the Hyperledger Explorer [21], the Hyperledger project's tool for monitoring Hyperledger blockchains. The Explorer connects to a local blockchain node and extracts data about blocks, transactions, peers, and more into a local PostgreSQL database. Additionally, a web application is available for inspecting blockchain data, including some basic visualizations of transaction data. However, these visualizations are not tailored to provide the necessary insights or indicators to detect threats. In addition, there is a Hyperledger Labs project integrating Fabric with ElasticSearch and Kibana, resulting in a Kibana dashboard able to display some transaction data [1]. Unfortunately, their visualizations are not very well suited to detecting blockchain threats in Hyperledger Fabric. In our experiments we found that the necessary integration and aggregation of additional data sources and custom visualizations are difficult to achieve in standard products like the Elastic stack.

Analyzing related work highlights an evident lack of dedicated and security-specific visualization approaches enabling security experts to monitor blockchain networks in real-time, while detecting common indicators of compromise or ongoing attacks on the network. Our work contributes a valuable solution approach to this issue.

3   Blockchain Security Monitoring

This Section addresses the first part of our contribution. Within our main contribution, we follow the user-centered and problem-driven Nested Blocks and Guidelines model (NBGM) for visualization designs [14,16]. This allows us to identify and address security experts' core problems and lay a foundation for a visualization design fitting their needs.

The first step of the NBGM is the definition of a domain problem. We characterize the problem at hand based on two primary sources of information. First, we consider reports from blockchain security professionals [11]. Second, we analyze literature on blockchain attacks to identify concerns for operators of a blockchain node [7,9,18]. We begin by outlining the overall blockchain security monitoring process in Sect. 3.1. The domain problem is then specified according to Miksch and Aigner's design triangle through more in-depth descriptions of specific users (Sect. 3.2), their tasks (Sect. 3.3), and data elements (Sect. 3.4) [15]. We address the second step of the NBGM (*Data/Operation Abstraction*) in

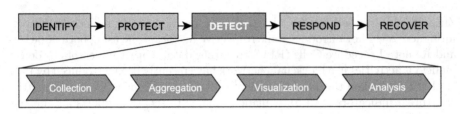

Fig. 1. Blockchain Security Monitoring process based on the NIST Cybersecurity Framework [5].

Sect. 3.5 by deriving general design requirements for a visualization approach to support blockchain security monitoring.

3.1 Blockchain Security Monitoring Process

Before we dive into users, tasks, and available data, we first need to understand the overall process underlying blockchain security monitoring. This subsection introduces our conceptual process based on the NIST Cybersecurity Framework for protecting critical infrastructures [5]. As shown in Fig. 1, the framework has five main functions: *Identify, Protect, Detect, Respond* and *Recover*. We apply these functions to a permissioned blockchain network. The *Identify* function serves to identify relevant assets and risks. This problem has been already addressed in prior work [17]. *Protect* involves a variety of protection measures applied to the system: identity management and access control, data security, secure configuration, and backups/log files, among others. These protection measures are usually part of the blockchain framework itself, with additional measures being applied at deployment time (such as secure configuration and appropriate backup procedures) [22]. The *Detect* function currently lacks appropriate visualization and analysis tools. It's the focus of this work and further developed in the following subsection. During the *Respond* phase, threats detected using our visualization approach are met with a response plan and appropriate mitigation actions. Finally, the *Recover* function provides appropriate tools to restore functionality after an attack has occurred. *Respond* and *Recover* are not specifically part of this work as attacks need to be identified before effective *Respond* and *Recover* can take place. Corresponding tools might be integrated into future work to permit swift threat response.

The *Detect* function can be subdivided into four smaller process steps. Relevant data needs to be collected (*Collection*) and aggregated to provide appropriate metrics if necessary (*Aggregation*). Data and metrics can then be visualized (*Visualization*) allowing domain experts to identify possible threats (*Analysis*). Please note that all steps beside *Analysis* can be performed automatically.

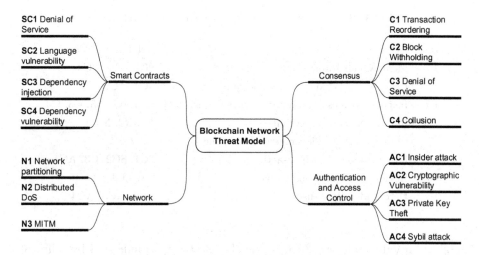

Fig. 2. Blockchain Networks Threat Model in attack tree notation.

3.2 Users

The intended users of visualization designs within the *Detect* function in the blockchain monitoring process are domain experts. These experts are responsible for analyzing blockchain data to identify malicious events within this function [11]. More specifically, we define the domain experts as security professionals knowledgeable in the cybersecurity domain. Therefore, we expect them to have the expertise to decide whether specific events or event series indicate an imminent threat to the blockchain. Within a permissioned blockchain, these security experts are responsible for monitoring the distributed network through the view of the local organization's blockchain node. Other organization's nodes could also be monitored, but data availability is likely limited due to access restrictions within the blockchain network.

3.3 Tasks

Visualizations or any other tool supporting the *Detect* function of the blockchain security monitoring process should be based on the tasks that the respective users need to carry out. Following the user characterization above, we derive the crucial tasks of the domain expert's work.

To illustrate the monitoring task's complexity, we show an overview of possible attacks in an attack tree notation in Fig. 2. The listed attacks are based on prior work [17,18] and related literature surveys [7,9]. For each leaf on the tree, there are various ways to successfully deploy the attack, which we did not include for conciseness. The attack tree focuses on the blockchain network and nodes. Therefore, it does not include application-specific attacks such as web

Table 1. Security expert tasks and related attacks (cf. Fig. 2).

Task	Description	Related attacks
T1	Identify vulnerable smart contracts	SC1, SC2, SC3
T2	Identify blockchain framework vulnerabilities	SC4, AC2
T3	Inspect log files of running services on demand	SC4, N1, N3, C3, C4
T4	Review networking activity	N1, N2, N3
T5	Compare transaction metrics over time	N2, C2
T6	Explore block and transaction history	SC1, SC2, C3, AC1
T7	Review configuration changes	C1, AC1
T8	Detect identity abuse	AC1, AC3, AC4

application vulnerabilities. Each of the shown attacks is indicated by different combinations of threat indicators [17]. Security experts need to identify threats based on these indicators as part of the *Analysis* process step. Visualizing the indicators provides the necessary overview to identify vulnerable components for in-depth analysis. Therefore, domain experts' overarching task is the *analysis of blockchain data to identify possible threats*, which is to be supported by visualizations. To allow domain experts to execute this work adequately, we have identified more specific tasks based on the attacks and corresponding threat indicators from prior work [17]. These tasks are shown in Table 1.

Each task comprises several sub-tasks that help accomplish the main task. To identify vulnerable smart contracts (*T1*), the expert may manually inspect smart contract code or scan smart contracts for vulnerabilities and inspect scan results. Identifying framework vulnerabilities (*T2*) can be accomplished by reading release notes for the framework and its dependencies. Since many anomalies can have multiple causes (i.e., low transaction throughput), log file inspection (*T3*) helps to identify the root cause of anomalies. To review networking activity (*T4*), the main indicators are the count of active connections to other peers, the activity level of those connections, and last seen times of offline peers. Transaction metrics (*T5*) include throughput, latency and unprocessed transactions. Block and transaction history monitoring (*T6*) implies watching the chain of blocks for inconsistencies such as changed blocks or missing transactions. Reviewing configuration changes (*T7*) includes both active and proposed changes to be able to intervene in case of manipulation attempts. Identity abuse (*T8*) is possible during all phases of an identity's lifecycle, so an expert must monitor issuance, usage in transactions, and revocation.

3.4   Data Elements

Blockchain Frameworks such as Ethereum and Hyperledger Fabric offer a number of data sources for monitoring. The most obvious data sources are blocks and associated transaction data [23]. These can be used to derive active users, smart contracts, and the general level of activity on the network (i.e., transaction throughput). Numerical data on network activity is also provided through metrics, which can be used to raise alerts for anomalous behavior. On a more technical level, each component of the blockchain node also provides log files. These files give detailed information about smart contract execution, consensus protocol violations, and other node internals. They can be helpful to determine the root cause of an anomaly.

3.5   Design Requirements

To wrap up this first part of our contribution, we derive the following general requirements for visualizations aiming to support the *Detect* function of the blockchain security monitoring process. The requirements are based on the above user, task, and data characterizations. Although we follow these requirements in the remainder of this work to design our prototype, they can serve as a general collection for respective visualization designs. We summarize the requirements under several main views that a Visual Analytics system supporting the domain experts' tasks should comprise:

R1 - General Security Information: A view should allow users to overview a series of general, security-relevant information from the monitored blockchain. Attention should be drawn to any changes on the blockchain's overall configuration (*T7*). Whenever new smart contracts are deployed to the blockchain, they should be checked (automatically or manually) for vulnerabilities. The results of these checks need to be made available for the analysts (*T1*). Additionally, newly discovered vulnerabilities within the applied blockchain framework should be shown to users within this general view (*T2*).

R2 - Network View: Another view should provide access to any data and metrics related to the peers and their network activities. This includes displaying available information about the peers themselves and the respective identities that interact with the blockchain on behalf of the peers (*T8*). This view should also provide visual access to any network-related metrics that assess the overall network's health (*T4*).

R3 - Transaction View: Domain experts need to access a view displaying information about the blocks and transactions being handled by the blockchain. This includes detailed information on the blocks and transactions themselves (*T6*) as well as a time-based view on transaction-related metrics allowing to identify any changes in typical structure and processing of transactions (*T5*).

R4 - Interactivity and Details: Any of the previously mentioned views (R1–R3) needs to be fully interactive to provide the best possible support for domain experts' tasks and enable exploratory analysis. Whenever suspicious actions or threat indicators are identified, experts also need access to further details and underlying log files (*T3*).

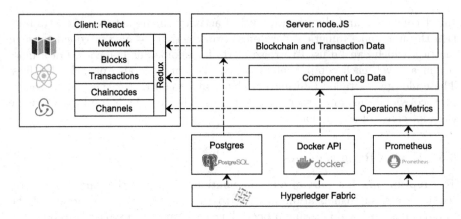

Fig. 3. Prototype architecture and data flows.

4   HyperSec: Hyperledger Security Monitoring Using Visual Analytics

We now introduce our prototype **HyperSec** (**Hyper**ledger **Sec**urity Explorer), a modified version of the open-source project Hyperledger Explorer based on the design requirements introduced in Sect. 3.5. The prototype is open-source and available online, along with a demo deployment[1]. Our modifications address the two remaining layers of the NBGM by designing our solution based on the domain problem and implementing it within a prototype.

4.1   Architecture and Technology

We choose Hyperledger Explorer as a starting point since it already provides a working synchronization architecture based on Hyperledger Fabric's block event subscription. We extend the existing architecture to allow for more comprehensive accessibility of relevant data and effective security monitoring. This results in the architecture displayed in Fig. 3. We keep the basic structure (data sources, server, and client) of the original architecture for interoperability and transparency reasons. However, in our previous study [17] we found that security-relevant information for Hyperledger Fabric must be retrieved from several data sources: the Hyperledger Fabric SDK, operations metrics, and the application logs available via Docker. Block data is already stored in Hyperledger Explorer's PostgreSQL database. We integrate additional metrics and log sources through server-side proxies to the respective Prometheus and Docker APIs. The React client accesses these through the API exposed by the Hyperledger Explorer server.

---

[1] https://github.com/sigma67/hypersec.

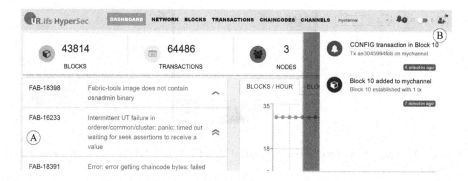

Fig. 4. *Dashboard* view: Security issues, alerts and general overview.

We implement the views defined in Sect. 3.5 by adapting existing views from the Hyperledger Explorer project. This allows us to retain the frontend structure while introducing new monitoring capabilities. Therefore, domain experts do not need to work with a completely new interface but rather get additional relevant information on the respective views. The updated views host a series of interactive visualizations based on the *visx*[2] visualization primitives for React. They all follow a similar structure: relevant data is retrieved from the client's *Redux* state handling, transformed for use in the visual display, mapped into visual primitives, and finally rendered [6].

4.2   Visual Representations and Interactions

We now go into more detail on our HyperSec prototype's visual representations addressing the requirements *R1–R3* and their interactivity (*R4*). As mentioned before, we integrate the visualizations into existing Hyperledger Explorer views to retain the familiar structure for domain experts. This Section is structured accordingly to the naming of the original Hyperledger Explorer views.

Views *Dashboard* and *Chaincodes*: To fulfill the Design Requirement *R1*, we adjust two views of the Hyperledger Explorer. First off, directly on the Explorer's landing page, called "Dashboard", we show a list of known Hyperledger Fabric issues of High/Highest importance from the Hyperledger JIRA[3] ordered by last updated (Fig. 4**A**). Any list item can be expanded to reveal additional information about the issue. Although there is no issue category directly reflecting security issues, this information is highly relevant for *T2 – Identify blockchain framework vulnerabilities*. Additionally, there is no other source for the respective information. In the side menu (Fig. 4**B**), an alert appears whenever the configuration of the monitored Hyperledger Fabric blockchain is changed (*T7*).

To allow domain experts to detect vulnerable chaincodes, we include available security scans in the respective "Chaincodes" view. Whenever a smart contract

---

[2] https://airbnb.io/visx/.

[3] https://jira.hyperledger.org.

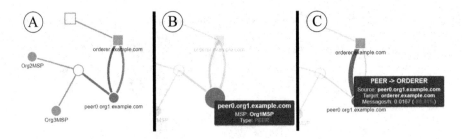

Fig. 5. *Network* view: Interactive visualization of network traffic between peers and orderers.

went through a security scan, analysts can directly check this scan's results in the HyperSec prototype (*T1*). We use the open-source static analysis tool revive-cc[4] to detect security vulnerabilities and store the scan result in the Hyperledger Explorer PostgreSQL database. To ensure the scans are up to date, we set up automated jobs to regularly generate security reports of deployed chaincodes.

View *Network*: The *Network* view targets design requirement *R2* intended for tasks *T4* and *T8*. The original Hyperledger Explorer shows a tabular list with basic information about the peers connected to the monitored Hyperledger Fabric network. In our HyperSec prototype, we extend this table with a force-directed node-link diagram to effectively visualize networking activity (Fig. 5**A**). The nodes' different shapes indicate different peer types within the network: Circles are used to display peers while rectangles represent orderers. Links between the glyphs are used to display known networking activities.

However, the unavailability of core information restricts this view's expressivity. While rich information about the peers can be easily retrieved from the Hyperledger Explorer, no data about the peers' network connections is provided. Therefore, HyperSec retrieves networking information directly from Hyperledger Fabric through the Prometheus API. By doing so, experts get at least some information about the peers' networking activity within the own Membership Service Provider (MSP). However, as the Hyperledger Fabric network is decentralized, it is not possible to get any information about other MSPs' networking activities. Because of this restriction, we introduce two empty nodes in the node-link diagram (uncolored nodes in Fig. 5**A**), which mark the border of the monitoring visibility regarding networking activities. Nodes within the owned MSP are colored; those within other MSPs are greyed out.

Links connecting the nodes in the graph represent known network connections. Again, outside the own MSP's borders, experts do not get much information. Therefore, we connect any foreign peer and orderer to the respective artificial node. The coloring of the links follows a continuous scale from −1 to 1. This scale measures the current deviation of the link's message traffic from the average, by comparing traffic in the last hour with traffic in the previous seven

---

[4] https://github.com/sivachokkapu/revive-cc.

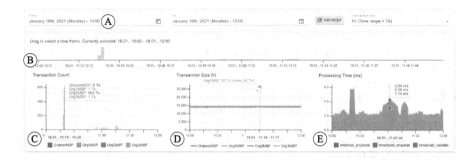

Fig. 6. *Transactions* view: Interactive visualizations for transaction count, size and processing time.

days. If this deviation is low, the link is colored in a green tone. A red link, in contrast, marks a high variation of message numbers.

The node-link diagram is fully interactive. Nodes are draggable to ensure that security analysts can adjust the layout to their own needs if necessary. Hovering over nodes (Fig. 5**B**) or links (Fig. 5**C**) highlights the hovered object and shows additional status information about it.

View *Transactions*: This view (*R3*) satisfies tasks *T5* and *T6*. Some modifications to the original simple table view ensure that the transactor identity and transaction size are visible. The primary adjustment we made to this view is introducing four visualizations (Fig. 6). To ensure a high performance of the visualizations even when dealing with several thousands of transactions, we implement an efficient data bucketing algorithm which allows easy and fast look up of relevant transaction data (see Algorithm 1).

We make small adjustments to the original timeframe selection (Fig. 6**A**). The selection defines the time range for which information about transactions should be displayed. On the right side of the timeframe selection, we added a dropdown menu to select the aggregation granularity (1 min, 1 h, 12 h, 24 h) for the visualizations. This helps security experts if they need to compare and contextualize available information.

The wide bar chart (Fig. 6**B**) always displays the entire selected date range. Each bar represents the number of transactions within a specific range of time specified through the aggregation granularity. This bar chart supports analysts in navigating the selected time range. A brushing interaction (horizontal dragging on the chart) selects an even smaller time range for detailed analysis. On interaction, the other visualizations (Fig. 6**C**, **D**, and **E**) and the transactions table are dynamically updated with data from this narrowed time range.

A stacked bar chart (Fig. 6**C**) visualizes the number of transactions per aggregation window. However, it does this only for the transactions selected through the brushing interaction on the visualization Fig. 6**B**. It shows the transaction count's composition based on which MSP contributed how many transactions. The scatterplot Fig. 6**D** shows the transaction size in bytes throughout the time

---

Algorithm 1: Transaction data bucketing

Input: Time Window from timestamp t_s to t_e with $t_s, t_e \in T$, $t_s < t_e$, and
$T \in \mathbb{R}$. Aggregation granularity $s_b \in \mathbb{R}$

Output: Map M^{tx} with transactions sorted into the respective time-based
bucket

1 **function** generateTxBuckets(t_s, t_e, s_b):
2     $L^{tx} \leftarrow getTransactionListForTimeWindow(t_s, t_e)$;
3     $M^{tx} \leftarrow$ new $Map()$;
4     $t_b \leftarrow t_s$;
5   **while** $t_b < t_e$ **do**
6        $i_b \leftarrow \lfloor t_b/s_b \rfloor$;
7        $b \leftarrow$ new $Bucket()$;   // Object for transactions and meta-data.
8        $M^{tx}_{i_b} \leftarrow b$;
9        $t_b \leftarrow t_b + s_b$;
10   **end while**
11   **foreach** $tx \in L^{tx}$;   // Find correct $Bucket$ and update with tx.
12   **do**
13        $i_{tx} \leftarrow \lfloor (t_{tx} - t_s)/s_b \rfloor$;
14        $M^{tx}_{i_{tx}} \leftarrow M^{tx}_{i_{tx}} \cup parse(tx)$
15   **end foreach**
16   **return** M^{tx};
17 **end**

---

range for each MSP. Each circle on the scatterplot represents the average size of transactions submitted by a specific MSP. This aggregation is performed to scale the chart for large numbers of transactions. During attacks, thousands of transactions can be submitted within just minutes, thus freezing the chart if each transaction were drawn individually. The stacked area chart Fig. 6**E** finally shows the development of three different metrics, which we identify as helpful to get an idea for the processing time in seconds that a transaction needs from proposal to validation. As information for processing times are not available distinctively per transaction but continuously per time unit, we choose to display this metrics with a continuous visualization technique.

The visualizations Fig. 6**C**, **D**, and **E** are again fully interactive. Hovering individual bars or hovering along the continuous sizes and times displays additional information as tooltips. Different metrics can also be toggled using the legend icons below the visual representations.

5   Evaluation

For our evaluation, we focus on three common attacks that cover the majority of the tasks outlined in Table 1: **SC2**, **N2**, and **AC1**. We simulate these attacks a Hyperledger Fabric test network, which the HyperSec prototype is connected to.

SC2 refers to a language vulnerability, i.e. a software bug that exposes chaincode to malicious exploits. A security expert may become aware of such an exploit by identifying vulnerable smart contracts (*T1*) and by inspecting transaction history (*T6*). For example, consider a read-after-write vulnerability detected by the chaincode scanner *revive-cc*. The security expert can inspect an automatically generated chaincode scan in the *Chaincodes* view. Intuitively, the experts check for past exploitations using the *Transactions* view. Thereto, the transactions table can be filtered using the chaincode name and applicable time frame. The filtered transactions can be inspected individually to find unusual read/write sets.

N2 refers to a distributed denial of service attack. If a peer or orderer is targeted by a traffic-based denial of service attack, its connection to other peers will be impaired as well. The *Network* view (Fig. 5C) shows high deviation in gossip communication traffic to the targeted peer during such an attack (*T4*). If the local peer is targeted, the metrics in the *Transaction* view (Fig. 6E) show increased transaction processing latency due to high peer load (*T5*). For attackers that can send transaction to the network, transaction-based DoS is more effective. Figure 6**C** and 6**D** show two such attempts using high transaction volume (**C**) and large transaction size (**D**). Figure 6**E** also shows spikes in processing latency during the time of attack (spikes 1 and 3 in that chart).

To investigate the source of the anomaly, experts can check the peer logs, which are available in the Network view (*T3*). They cross-reference any error messages with open issues in the Hyperledger JIRA, which are available in the Dashboard view (*T2*).

AC1 refers to an attack where an insider abuses valid credentials for malicious purposes. Consider an insider attempting to corrupt the blockchain network's configuration using a configuration transaction. Security experts are immediately notified about the configuration change in the notification sidebar (*T7*, see Fig. 4). Details of the attempted configuration change are available in the transaction history table (*T6*), where the full read-write set of the transaction is available by selecting the respective transaction.

6   Discussion

The evaluation has shown that the visualizations can assist a security expert in detecting ongoing attacks. If an attack is detected, the next steps in the Cybersecurity Framework (see Fig. 1) are *analysis*, *respond* and *recover* activities, which are discussed hereafter.

Analysis. Based on the present threat indicators the expert then proceeds with *analysis* of the root cause. The logs shown in HyperSec can be a starting point, but may only show symptomatic errors. In-depth analysis of application and network logs on the systems running blockchain components can yield further information. The expert must determine if it is a crash fault or a byzantine fault. At the same time, a communication channel should be available with other organizations of the consortium to determine if it is a more widespread problem. Guidelines and checklists can help structure this process.

Respond. Once the cause is identified, the expert contacts operations teams to request mitigation actions. Local or network configuration changes can mitigate crash faults and network/consensus threats (see Fig. 2). Compromised smart contracts may require an upgrade, or even a ledger rollback if the consequences were severe. Hyperledger Fabric supports ledger snapshots for this purpose [22]).

Recover. After mitigation of an attack, evidence collection is another subject of interest. System and Docker logs are the primary source of evidence, complemented by ledger transaction data stored in HyperSec's PostgreSQL database. However, the forensic analysis of attacks on Hyperledger Fabric is a topic in need of further research.

7   Conclusion

This work introduced the task-oriented design and prototypical implementation of HyperSec, a visual analytics security monitoring tool tailored for Hyperledger Fabric. Throughout the design of HyperSec, we followed the NBGM design methodology. The domain problem describes the activities of the blockchain security monitoring process to be supported by visualizations. Subsequently, we identified the involved users, their specific tasks, and the available data elements. These considerations culminated in design requirements that apply to any visualization system aiming to support blockchain security analysts. Our prototype HyperSec picks up on these design requirements. It extends the open-source architecture of Hyperledger Explorer with additional security-relevant data sources. The data is aggregated, processed and displayed in appropriate visualizations supporting blockchain security analysts to detect potential attacks.

Our prototype might not cover every possible subtask of the defined tasks of blockchain security analysts. This is in part due to limited availability of data provided by Hyperledger Fabric itself. We plan to update our prototype as additional data sources become available in the future, and are open to contributions from the community.

The security of the monitoring tool itself is also important, as it should not contribute additional attack vectors by leaking blockchain data. During our implementation we found some bugs and vulnerabilities within Hyperledger Explorer, which we subsequently fixed and contributed to the upstream project.

References

1. Baset, S., Prehoda, B.: Hyperledger Labs Blockchain Analyzer, March 2021. https://github.com/hyperledger-labs-archives/blockchain-analyzer. 30 May 2019
2. Ben-Asher, N., Gonzalez, C.: Effects of cyber security knowledge on attack detection. Comput. Hum. Behav. **48**, 51–61 (2015). https://doi.org/10.1016/j.chb.2015.01.039

3. Bogner, A.: Seeing is understanding: anomaly detection in blockchains with visualized features. In: Proceedings of the 2017 ACM International Joint Conference on Pervasive and Ubiquitous Computing, New York, NY, USA, pp. 5–8. ACM (2017). https://doi.org/10.1145/3123024.3123157

4. Boshmaf, Y., Al Jawaheri, H., Al Sabah, M.: BlockTag: design and applications of a tagging system for blockchain analysis. In: Dhillon, G., Karlsson, F., Hedström, K., Zúquete, A. (eds.) SEC 2019. IAICT, vol. 562, pp. 299–313. Springer, Cham (2019). https://doi.org/10.1007/978-3-030-22312-0_21

5. Calder, A.: NIST Cybersecurity Framework (2018). https://doi.org/10.2307/j.ctv4cbhfx

6. Chi, E.: A taxonomy of visualization techniques using the data state reference model. In: Proceedings of the IEEE Symposium on Information Visualization 2000, pp. 69–75. IEEE Computer Society (2000). https://doi.org/10.1109/INFVIS.2000.885092

7. Dabholkar, A., Saraswat, V.: Ripping the fabric: attacks and mitigations on hyperledger fabric. In: Shankar Sriram, V.S., Subramaniyaswamy, V., Sasikaladevi, N., Zhang, L., Batten, L., Li, G. (eds.) ATIS 2019. CCIS, vol. 1116, pp. 300–311. Springer, Singapore (2019). https://doi.org/10.1007/978-981-15-0871-4_24

8. Di Battista, G., Di Donato, V., Patrignani, M., Pizzonia, M., Roselli, V., Tamassia, R.: Bitconeview: visualization of flows in the bitcoin transaction graph. In: 2015 IEEE Symposium on Visualization for Cyber Security (VizSec), pp. 1–8. IEEE (2015). https://doi.org/10.1109/VIZSEC.2015.7312773

9. Homoliak, I., Venugopalan, S., Reijsbergen, D., Hum, Q., Schumi, R., Szalachowski, P.: The security reference architecture for blockchains: towards a standardized model for studying vulnerabilities, threats, and defenses. IEEE Commun. Surv. Tutor. (2020). https://doi.org/10.1109/COMST.2020.3033665

10. Jensen, T., Hedman, J., Henningsson, S.: How TradeLens delivers business value with blockchain technology. MIS Quart. Execut. (2019). https://doi.org/10.17705/2msqe.00018

11. Kacherginsky, P.: Attacking and Defending Blockchain Nodes. In: DEFCON 2020, p. 54 (2020)

12. Keim, D., Andrienko, G., Fekete, J.-D., Görg, C., Kohlhammer, J., Melançon, G.: Visual analytics: definition, process, and challenges. In: Kerren, A., Stasko, J.T., Fekete, J.-D., North, C. (eds.) Information Visualization. LNCS, vol. 4950, pp. 154–175. Springer, Heidelberg (2008). https://doi.org/10.1007/978-3-540-70956-5_7. iSSN: 03029743

13. McGinn, D., Birch, D., Akroyd, D., Molina-Solana, M., Guo, Y., Knottenbelt, W.J.: Visualizing dynamic bitcoin transaction patterns. Big Data 4(2), 109–119 (2016). https://doi.org/10.1089/big.2015.0056

14. Meyer, M., Sedlmair, M., Quinan, P.S., Munzner, T.: The nested blocks and guidelines model. Inf. Vis. 14(3), 234–249 (2015). https://doi.org/10.1177/1473871613510429

15. Miksch, S., Aigner, W.: A matter of time: applying a data-users-tasks design triangle to visual analytics of time-oriented data. Comput. Graph. 38, 286–290 (2014). https://doi.org/10.1016/j.cag.2013.11.002

16. Munzner, T.: A nested model for visualization design and validation. IEEE Trans. Visual Comput. Graphics 15(6), 921–928 (2009). https://doi.org/10.1109/TVCG.2009.111

17. Putz, B., Pernul, G.: Detecting blockchain security threats. In: 2020 IEEE International Conference on Blockchain (Blockchain), pp. 313–320. IEEE (2020). https://doi.org/10.1109/Blockchain50366.2020.00046

18. Putz, B., Pernul, G.: Trust factors and insider threats in permissioned distributed ledgers. In: Hameurlain, A., Wagner, R. (eds.) Transactions on Large-Scale Data- and Knowledge-Centered Systems XLII. LNCS, vol. 11860, pp. 25–50. Springer, Heidelberg (2019). https://doi.org/10.1007/978-3-662-60531-8_2

19. Sundara, T., Gaputra, I., Aulia, S.: Study on blockchain visualization. Int. J. Inform. Visual. **1**(3), 76–82 (2017). https://doi.org/10.30630/joiv.1.3.23

20. The Linux Foundation: DLTLabs Case Study - Hyperledger (2020). https://www.hyperledger.org/learn/publications/dltlabs-case-study

21. The Linux Foundation: Hyperledger Explorer (2020). https://www.hyperledger.org/use/explorer

22. The Linux Foundation: Hyperledger Fabric 2.3 Documentation (2020). https://hyperledger-fabric.readthedocs.io/en/release-2.3

23. Tovanich, N., Heulot, N., Fekete, J., Isenberg, P.: Visualization of blockchain data: a systematic review. IEEE Trans. Visual. Compute. Graphics 1 (2019). https://doi.org/10.1109/TVCG.2019.2963018

24. Zheng, P., Zheng, Z., Luo, X., Chen, X., Liu, X.: A detailed and real-time performance monitoring framework for blockchain systems. In: Proceedings - International Conference on Software Engineering (2018). https://doi.org/10.1145/3183519.3183546, iSSN: 02705257

100 Popular Open-Source Infosec Tools

Rauli Kaksonen$^{(\boxtimes)}$ (iD), Tommi Järvenpää, Jukka Pajukangas, Mihai Mahalean, and Juha Röning(iD)

University of Oulu, Oulu, Finland
{rauli.kaksonen,tommi.jarvenpaa,jukka.pajukangas,mihai.mahalean,
juha.roning}@oulu.fi
https://www.oulu.fi

Abstract. We examined the popularity of open-source tools used for information security analysis (infosec tools). This information would be useful, e.g. in security research, but it was not available. In our study, we created first a corpus of 423 tools from various sources. Then we collected source popularity metrics by Google search, tweets, GitHub stars, SecTools.org ranking, and cross-references between tools. We found a strong correlation between the metrics. We created an aggregate popularity metric from Google search, GitHub stars, and tool cross-reference source metrics using principal component analysis. The aggregate metric explains 70% of the variance in the source metrics. The three most popular tools are Metasploit, Nmap, and Wireshark. We estimated the impact of source metric errors and concluded that the aggregate metric gives an estimate of tool popularity, rather than an exact popularity rank. Furthermore, we divide the tools into overlapping categories by tool scope and type of activity. In the top 100, 51 tools are in the network scope, 27 in the host scope, 15 in the storage scope, 13 in the passwords scope, and 4 in the other tools scope.

Keywords: Information security · Infosec · Security analysis · Open-source tools · Popularity

1 Introduction

Open-source tools are widely used for information security tasks like penetration testing, incident response, and digital forensics. A survey among forensics experts found that 69% of the responders used open-source tools at least sometimes while only 5% had never used them [29]. In another survey, one key requirement for cyber-forensics research was the requirement for "backing for and improvement of open-source tools" [28]. The experience of the authors supports that open-source tools are widely used by the security community.

However, when we tried to find out which tools are popular, we could not find a lot of concrete information. Studies often refer to open-source tools to be used for a particular purpose [4,30,33]. However, usually the tools are chosen by the researchers or selected by limited surveys. This feels quite unsatisfactory.

© IFIP International Federation for Information Processing 2021
Published by Springer Nature Switzerland AG 2021
A. Jøsang et al. (Eds.): SEC 2021, IFIP AICT 625, pp. 181–195, 2021.
https://doi.org/10.1007/978-3-030-78120-0_12

Objective data on tool popularity would help e.g. to choose a set of representative tools for research, to examine the properties of the popular tools, and to find alternative tools for a task.

As the security community and open-source community operate in the Internet, representative information about the security tools and open-source software should be discoverable on-line. We were able to identify the following sources of open-source tools used for information security tasks (*infosec* tools):

- **SecTools.org** lists 125 Network Security Tools ranked based on suggestions by the community [20]. The site excludes tools they maintain themselves.
- **GitHub** is a code hosting site [9]. It is very popular and hosting more than 50% of the tools which data we collected for this study. GitHub allows users to give stars for the project they like.
- **Google code archive** contains the projects from the discontinued Google code hosting site [11]. Most projects are moved to other sites, many to GitHub.
- **Sourceforge** is an older open-source project hosting site [22]. Roughly 20% of the projects we collected have a project page there, but many indicate that they have moved elsewhere, usually to GitHub.
- **GitLab** is a challenger for GitHub [10], but just a handful of the security tools we collected are using it. There is a star-system similar to GitHub.
- **Infosec-specific distributions and images** are available with preinstalled infosec tools, e.g. Linux distributions ArchStrike [1], BlackArch [2], CAINE [3], Fedora Security Lab [6], Kali [13], Penroo [17], Remnux [19], and SIFT [21]. For Microsoft Windows there is e.g. Flare VM [7].

We outlined the following research questions for this study:

1. What sources contain quantitative data on the popularity of open-source infosec tools?
2. Do the sources agree on the popularity of tools?
3. How can the tools be divided into relevant categories by task they perform?
4. What are the most popular tools in general and per category?

The rest of this document is organized as follows. In Sect. 2, we present the proposed infosec tool popularity metrics and the tool categorization scheme. In Sect. 3, we present the results and estimate the reliability of the results. Finally, in Sect. 4 we discuss the results and conclude this study.

2 Methods

The purpose of this study is to identify the most popular open-source infosec tools. These tools are used for a variety of tasks: network scanning, traffic analysis, traffic generation, web security, disk and memory forensics, file analysis, host analysis, password cracking, etc. For this study, we ruled out software that provides security-related functionality continuously, e.g., VPNs, and firewalls, and tools intended mainly for software development. We adapted the definition "popular" from Merriam-Webster [14], and define a *popular infosec tool* being a frequently encountered tool, commonly considered for a task, or widely approved as a tool to use.

2.1   Collecting a Corpus of Tools

To measure the popularity of infosec tools, we first collected a corpus of tools by the following methods.

– List the tools in the infosec Linux distributions and the Flare VM
– Add open-source tools from SecTools.org [20]
– Add tools identified in prior work, such as in CinCan project [4]
– Add infosec tools the authors know about
– Later, check URLs in the downloaded pages for yet unlisted tools

To help excluding tools that are not security-related we filtered out tools that are present in Debian and Ubuntu, i.e. "normal" Linux distributions [5,23]. We stored the information of tools in a database. Each tool was given a unique name, which typically matches the package names used in the Linux distributions.

2.2   Google Tool Name Search

Popularity can be measured by web searches. Bagrow et al. found that the fame of scientists correlates with Google search counts [25]. Weiss measured open-source project success by counting web pages and project references [34]. Web searches have been used to find correlations between various terms and concepts [26], even using forensics terms [32].

A simple search using tool names would not produce good results for tool names like "Flare" or "Volatility", which have other more popular meanings. We need to adjust or filter out the meaningless search results. For this, we entered tool URLs, such as home and/or source code repository addresses, into our database. Next, we downloaded the first 100 returned pages by each tool name search and checked the pages for URLs that refer to infosec tools. This gives us information if the search returned relevant data. When checking for URLs we accept all sub-pages of the tool URL, e.g. URL https://nmap.org/download.html for https://nmap.org. We also ignored the schema difference of (http, https) and the domain name component www in the link assignment process.

Search hit counts follow an exponential distribution, which is normalized by taking the double logarithm of the search count. We calculate *name popularity* (P_n) for a tool as

$$P_n = \begin{cases} \log\log(\frac{S_t}{S_d}S), & \frac{S_t}{S_r} \geq 0.5 \ and \ \frac{S_r}{S_d} \geq 0.2 \\ \text{otherwise} & \text{undefined} \end{cases}, \tag{1}$$

where S is the total search hit count, S_d is the number of downloaded pages, S_r is the count of pages with references to any infosec tools URLs, and S_t is the count of pages with references to the tool which name was used in the search. The condition $\frac{S_r}{S_d} \geq 0.2$ filter out pages not relevant for infosec. The condition $\frac{S_t}{S_r} \geq 0.5$ filter out cases where the tool name matches some generic term in the infosec domain. Figure 1 shows name popularity value distribution.

We used the Google Custom Search engine API to search for the names [12]. According to its documentation, the Google Custom Search is intended to create search engines for websites, blogs, etc. However, it allowed us to make scripted searches for a small cost. When we compared the search counts returned by the API to the counts we get got from the normal Google search, we noticed that the API returned significantly smaller numbers of results. It appeared that this is expected when using a custom search engine [18]. Nonetheless, the results acquired by a single custom search engine should be comparable with each other.

2.3   Google Tool URL Search

As we defined the relevant URLs for tools, we can perform the popularity search using the URLs themselves. Google Custom Search API parameter `linkSite` allows us to do so [12].

Unfortunately, we noticed that many pages returned by the URL search did not refer to the URL and we did not consider the data trustworthy. In the end, we did not use the URL search counts.

2.4   Twitter Tool Name Search

When using Twitter hits as a measurement of tool popularity, we could not just use the tool name as the search term, as with the Google searches. Thus, we used the tool categories we define later, and the term "infosec", to narrow our search. A tweet query starts with a tool's name and the `AND` operator. Then follows the category names in braces separated by the `OR` operator. For example:

```
"nmap" AND ("infosec" OR "network scan" OR "traffic analysis" OR "packet injection" OR
"packet capture" OR "web security" OR "disk forensics" OR "file analysis" OR "host scan" OR
"memory forensics" OR "malware execution" OR "disassembly" OR "password cracking")
```

We then filtered away tweets where the search terms are found only in metainformation of the tweet. Next, we downloaded the five most recent tweets to see how many of them were related to the tool. We excluded the tool if less than two of the tweets were related. So, the tool *tweet popularity* is

$$P_t = \begin{cases} \log \log S_f, R'_5 \geq 2 \\ \text{otherwise undefined} \end{cases}, \tag{2}$$

where S_f is the number of filtered tweets, and R'_5 is the number of relevant tweets in the most recent five tweets. The data value distribution looks exponential, and as with name popularity, we take double logarithm of the search count. Figure 1 shows tweet popularity value distribution. The searches were performed by GetOldTweets3 library [8].

2.5   SecTools.org Ranking

The site SecTools.org provides page "Top 125 Network Security Tools" [20]. There are both commercial and open-source tools divided into various categories.

For this study, we use the rank of a tool in the Top 125 list as the *SecTools popularity*

$$P_s = -\text{SecTools.org rank}. \qquad (3)$$

We negate the rank for the first tool to have the highest popularity value. Figure 1 shows SecTools popularity value distribution.

2.6   GitHub Stars

Source code repository GitHub is hosting source code for many infosec tools [9]. The repository allows users to give starts to projects. For this study, we use the star count of a tool project as *GitHub popularity*

$$P_g = \log(\text{GitHub star count}). \qquad (4)$$

The star count distribution is exponential, and we use logarithm to get a normally distributed value, as shown in Fig. 1. Many tools have not initially been in GitHub and they have received stars only after the project moved to GitHub. So, a popular tool might have a low GitHub star count as it only recently moved to GitHub. To study this, we also collected the project creation dates from GitHub.

2.7   Tool Cross-references

None of the presented metrics give values for all tools. So, we constructed a new metric that would give a popularity value for most tools. Many Internet pages refer to multiple infosec tools. Some list tools which are used by the author, others provide a set of tools for a particular infosec task, some may compare tools, some intent to provide a comprehensive list of tools, etc. To tap this information, we took advantage of pages we downloaded for the tool name search to see how many cross-references there are between the tools.

Tool's *cross-reference popularity* (P_c) is calculated by adding up the number of downloaded pages concerning the tool t,

$$P_c = \log \sum_p \begin{cases} 1, & t \subseteq R_p \\ 0, & \text{otherwise} \end{cases}, \qquad (5)$$

where p stands for the downloaded pages and R_p is the set of tools referenced in the page. We take *log* of the value as the distribution visually looks exponential When the reference count was less than three, we treat the value as undefined. The resulting metric, shown in Fig. 1, is not normally distributed.

2.8   Aggregate Popularity Metric

When we examined the different popularity metrics, we noticed a strong correlation between them, but also that they do not completely agree on the popularity of the tools. This may be as the sources are indicating a different kind of popularity. We do not know the motives of people creating web pages, tweeting, or marking tools as their favorites. We may not have found all the relevant pages, and not all references come with URLs, but a tool may be mentioned using the name only.

We need to extract the common popularity, if any, from the source metrics. Principal component analysis (PCA) is a way to reduce dimensions from data in multiple dimensions [31]. PCA constructs new uncorrelated variables, where the first variable explains as much variation as possible in a single axis. The next variable explains the second largest chunk of variation, and so on. As the source variables in our case are popularity metrics, we expect the first axis to represent the underlying overall popularity. The amount of variation explained by the first axis tells how much the sources agree on the popularity.

We decided to exclude some source metrics from the aggregate popularity:

- URL popularity results were not reliable
- The tweet popularity calculation contains subjectively selected category names and manual filtering of the non-relevant tweets
- SecTools metric is only defined for 50 tools, with many high profile tools missing, so we do not think it is representative enough to be used.

We are left with three source popularities: name popularity P_n, Github popularity F_g, and cross-reference popularity P_c. For a tool to be included, we require at least two of the three values to be defined. For PCA we need to *impute* the missing value for the tools only having two source metric values. As the source metrics correlate strongly, we use linear regression to estimate the missing value using the two source metrics with value. Provided that the first principal component from PCA captures the majority of the variance, we can extract loadings L_n, L_g, and L_c for the source popularity metrics and calculate the aggregate popularity P for tools

$$P = L_n P'_n + L_g P'_g + L_c P'_c. \tag{6}$$

We mark the source metrics with ', as we need to normalize them to zero mean and unit variance.

2.9   Dividing Tools into Categories

We want to inspect tool popularity by tool categories. There exist several different categorizations for tools, e.g. by Ellison [27], Hogue [30], Kali Linux [13], *SecTools.Org* [20]. There is no consensus on how the tools should be categorized. We need a complete and relevant categorization, which is simple to assign for a large set of tools. With all this in mind, we defined our tool categories systematically along two dimensions: tool scope and tool activity type. Tool scopes are network, storage, host, passwords, and other. Active tool interacts with a live system, while passive only monitors the system or inspects artifacts.

A network tool actively sending and receiving data is categorized as a *packet injection* tool. A tool only listening, or receiving, data is categorized as a *packet capture* tool. When a tool scans a network, we categorize it as a *network scan* tool without repeating injection and capture categories. A tool that analyzes captured traffic is a *traffic analysis* tool. An important sub-category is *web security* tools that interact with Web servers or browsers. If the tool only interacts over HTTP, we do not add other categories.

Storage scoped tools work with file systems or with file-like data in databases, e-mails, etc. Tools working with file-like objects are categorized as *file analysis* tools and the ones working directly with file systems are categorized as *disk forensics* tools. We consider all these tools passive, as they work with data at rest.

Host scoped tools work with operating system or host machine. Tools which work with a live system are *host interactive* tools, while tools working with memory are *memory forensics* tool. Tools in the *malware execution* category are used to analyze and/or sandbox a running malware (or other kinds of software). *Disassembly* tools are intended to statically analyze or reverse-engineer software.

Many tools are intended to crack passwords or other authentication tokens. We divide these tools into *password on-line* and *password off-line* tools depending on activity type. Finally, the tools which do not conveniently fit any of the categories above, are categorized as *other*. Table 1 summarizes the presented categories.

Table 1. Categorization of security analysis tools

	Network	Storage	Host	Passwords
Passive	Traffic analysis	Disk forensics	Memory forensics	Password off-line
	Packet capture	File analysis	Disassembly	
Active	Network scan	*(always passive)*	Host interactive	Password on-line
	Packet injection		Malware	
	Web security		execution	

3 Results

The results were collected on November 2020. Our corpus included 423 different tools. Table 2 summarizes the source metrics by number of tools, type of value distribution (after taking the logarithms, when applied), and the top-3 tools by the metric. Figure 1 shows the value distribution histograms for the source metrics.

We correlated name popularity with the other metrics to see how well they agree or disagree with the popular tools, the results are plotted in Fig. 2. There is a significant correlation between the metrics. However, individual tool places are scattered, so the metrics do not agree on the ranking of each tool. Other metrics, except cross-reference, do not give ranking for tools that are low in the name popularity. The cross-reference metric provides popularity values for almost all tools which have name popularity. However, the correlation is somewhat weaker than by the other metrics. The values of cross-reference popularity concentrate around the median value, which means that small changes in those cross-reference values would mean large swings in the ranking of a tool.

Table 2. Source popularity metrics

Metric		Tools	Distribution	Top-3
Name	P_n	237	Normal	wireshark, nikto, nmap
Tweet	P_t	239	Unspecified	metasploit, wireshark, nmap
GitHub	P_g	232	Weak normal	jadx, ghidra, metasploit
SecTools	P_s	50	Linear	wireshark, metasploit, aircrack-ng
Cross-ref.	P_c	388	Unspecified	nmap, wireshark, metasploit

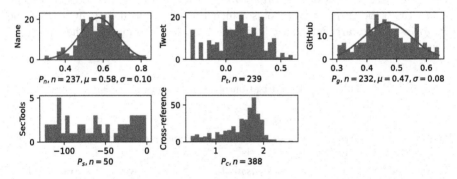

Fig. 1. Source metric value distribution histograms. Sample size is n. Mean (μ), standard deviation (σ), and ideal normal distribution graph is given for the metrics which follow normal distribution

3.1 Most Popular Tools

The aggregate popularity was created using principal component analysis of source metrics name popularity P_n, GitHub popularity P_g, and cross-reference popularity P_c. To calculate the most popular tools, we first imputed the missing source metric values for the tools which only had two values, using linear regression and the two values we know. Then we performed the analysis with values normalized to zero mean and unit variance. The aggregate popularity was calculated for 310 tools. The first component explains 70% of the variance, and

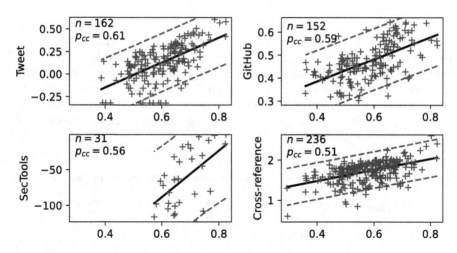

Fig. 2. Correlation of name popularity and other source metrics, n = sample size and p_{cc} = Pearson correlation coefficient. Dotted lines mark the 80% correlation band.

we use it as the aggregate popularity metric. We do not use the other two components, explaining 20% and 9% of the variance. Using the loadings from the first component, we can calculate the aggregate popularity for tools like this:

$$P = 0.6273P'_n + 0.5578P'_g + 0.5435P'_c \tag{7}$$

where P'_n, P'_g, and P'_c are normalized (zero mean and variance of one) popularity values of name, GitHub, and cross-reference. The loadings have the same sign and their values are close to each other, so the aggregate popularity is quite close to the average of the source popularities. Table 4 shows the resulting 100 most popular tools. The three most popular tools are Metasploit penetration testing framework [15], Nmap network scanner [16], and Wireshark traffic capture and analysis tool [24].

3.2 Reliability of the Results

Next we consider how reliable the average popularity metric is. For the Google search, it is uncertain how well the value matches the real page count as we lack visibility to the internals of the search system. The GitHub stars count is exact, but some tools have been longer than others in GitHub. In our analysis, there was only a small correlation between project age and the start count. The calculated cross-reference is not accurate if we have not found all relevant pages, or some references do not use the URLs we have collected.

We simulated the impact of errors by making changes to source metric values, recalculating the aggregate popularity, and noting the changes in the tool ranking due to the simulated errors. Table 3 shows the variation at ranks 3, 20, 50, and 100 for GitHub popularity error range $+100\%...-25\%$ and name popularity and cross-reference popularity error ranges $+100\%...-25\%$ and $+200\%...-50\%$. For example, when a tool around ranking 50 have name cross-correlation popularity error in range $+100\%...-25\%$, then the tool aggregate popularity ranking would vary by a maximum of ±30 positions.

Table 3. Ranking variation caused by source metric errors, by ranking

Rank	$P_g \, {}^{+100}_{-25}\%$	$P_n \, {}^{+100}_{-25}\%$	$P_n \, {}^{+200}_{-50}\%$	$P_c \, {}^{+100}_{-25}\%$	$P_c \, {}^{+200}_{-50}\%$
3	±1	±1	±1	±2	±2
20	±9	±6	±9	±13	±30
50	±20	±16	±21	±30	±37
100	±27	±22	±32	±39	±66

We should also consider the impact of imputing source metric values for those tools which only had two source values available. Within the set of 310 tools with aggregate popularity, the nick popularity value was imputed for 74 tools, the github popularity for 84 tools, and 152 tools had all three source metrics. Cross reference popularity was available for all included tools.

3.3 Most Popular Tools per Category

We then divided the top 100 tools into the categories we had defined. Table 5 then presents the tools in each of the categories. The superscript after each tool is the popularity rank of the tool. There is substantial overlap in the categories, as many tools are in several different categories. If we calculate the tool counts per scopes from Table 1 we get that 51 tools are in the network categories, 27 tools in host categories, 15 tools in storage categories, 13 tools in passwords categories, and four in the other category.

3.4 Availability of the Result Data

Tool data, including tool URLs, and raw popularity data is available in the Internet at https://gitlab.com/CinCan/infosec-tools.

Table 4. Top 100 tools

Tool	Name	GitHub	Cross	Tool	Name	GitHub	Cross
Metasploit	4	3	3	arachni	53	53	81
nmap	3	32	1	etherape	60	–	26
wireshark	1	52	2	dsniff	62	–	30
nikto	2	38	14	sleuthkit	56	70	31
mitmproxy	19	4	9	hping	25	111	33
mimikatz	20	11	6	ubertooth	42	84	41
sqlmap	8	5	64	capstone	–	34	151
hashcat	15	15	15	linenum	–	45	129
ghidra	17	2	95	social-engineer-toolkit	90	23	180
radare2	31	8	17	sslyze	98	59	39
tcpdump	6	79	5	rkhunter	51	–	85
apktool	10	12	99	dirbuster	57	–	74
powersploit	55	20	4	patator	69	58	115
ophcrack	21	–	7	rainbowcrack	80	–	37
socat	7	–	43	extundelete	67	–	68
smali	11	30	55	dnsrecon	91	82	22
masscan	39	7	61	pdfcrack	87	–	42
bloodhound	–	29	10	steghide	66	–	88
wpscan	26	28	19	sqlninja	97	–	25
dex2jar	30	17	45	oletools	100	81	28
aircrack-ng	12	64	8	bytecode-viewer	123	9	230
dnspy	34	6	140	volatility	–	43	212
john	–	40	12	dcfldd	88	–	60
ntop	9	46	103	bdf	–	56	166
jadx	48	1	191	skipfish	43	158	16
lynis	33	19	102	ngrep	46	150	27
p0f	16	–	50	kismet	–	124	13
nishang	63	33	11	weevely	47	63	235
cyberchef	49	13	91	tcpick	102	–	40
ilspy	35	10	190	wafw00f	54	61	228
impacket	73	24	23	ncrack	74	131	24
whatweb	41	54	29	fping	40	136	78
ddrescue	29	–	35	iodine	–	47	217
beef	–	27	72	netsniff-ng	94	109	21
zaproxy	70	18	79	dc3dd	93	–	73
crackmapexec	71	41	20	invoke-obfuscation	139	67	34
wifite	28	55	56	safecopy	99	–	71
clamav	5	87	138	winhex	23	–	270
cuckoo	–	37	62	sslscan	79	88	148
binwalk	38	21	174	rarcrack	114	–	46
theharvester	50	35	76	mtr	–	75	156
wfuzz	64	49	32	httpry	116	–	49
jd-gui	32	14	234	slowhttptest	104	101	63
chkrootkit	37	–	36	tcpreplay	68	128	110
responder	–	50	47	inetsim	118	–	52
ratproxy	45	–	18	exiftool	24	–	281
gobuster	44	44	108	angryip	105	62	204
w3af	36	48	125	oledump	111	–	84
androguard	82	51	44	testdisk	18	162	219
scapy	22	25	261	ssdeep	13	188	196

Table 5. Top 100 tools by categories, tool[ranks] by superscript

Category				
Network scan	metasploit[1] nmap[2] sqlmap[7] powersploit[13] masscan[17]	bloodhound[18] whatweb[32] crackmapexec[36] wifite[37] theharvester[41]	gobuster[47] arachni[51] hping[55] dnsrecon[66] skipfish[75]	kismet[77] fping[82] sslscan[89] mtr[91] angryip[97]
Traffic analysis	wireshark[3] tcpdump[11]	ntop[24] p0f[27]	scapy[50] dsniff[53]	netsniff-ng[84]
Packet capture	wireshark[3] tcpdump[11] aircrack-ng[21] ntop[24]	p0f[27] scapy[50] etherape[52] dsniff[53]	hping[55] ubertooth[56] ngrep[76] kismet[77]	tcpick[79] netsniff-ng[84] httpry[92]
Packet injection	metasploit[1] mitmproxy[5] sqlmap[7] socat[15]	aircrack-ng[21] impacket[31] crackmapexec[36] wfuzz[42]	responder[45] scapy[50] hping[55] ubertooth[56]	iodine[83] netsniff-ng[84] slowhttptest[93] tcpreplay[94]
Web security	nikto[4] mitmproxy[5] wpscan[19] whatweb[32]	beef[34] zaproxy[35] wfuzz[42] ratproxy[46]	w3af[48] arachni[51] sslyze[60] dirbuster[62]	sqlninja[69] skipfish[75] wafw00f[80]
Disk forensics	ddrescue[33] sleuthkit[54]	extundelete[65] dcfldd[73]	dc3dd[85] safecopy[87]	testdisk[99]
File analysis	radare2[10] clamav[38]	pdfcrack[67] oletools[70]	winhex[88] exiftool[96]	oledump[98] ssdeep[100]
Host interactive	metasploit[1] mimikatz[6] powersploit[13]	bloodhound[18] lynis[26] nishang[28]	chkrootkit[44] linenum[58] rkhunter[61]	bdf[74] weevely[78]
Memory forensics	volatility[72]			
Malware execution	radare2[10]	cuckoo[39]	inetsim[95]	
Disassembly	ghidra[9] radare2[10] apktool[12] smali[16]	dex2jar[20] dnspy[22] jadx[25] ilspy[30]	binwalk[40] jd-gui[43] androguard[49] capstone[57]	bytecode-viewer[71]
Password on-line	sqlmap[7] ophcrack[14]	aircrack-ng[21] crackmapexec[36]	wifite[37] dsniff[53]	patator[63] ncrack[81]
Password off-line	hashcat[8] john[23]	rainbowcrack[64] pdfcrack[67]	rarcrack[90]	
Other	cyberchef[29]	social-engineer-toolkit[59]	steghide[68]	invoke-obfuscation[86]

4 Discussion

In this study, we examined the popularity of open-source infosec tools. We did not find earlier studies on the subject. Objective data on tool popularity is required e.g. to use representative tools in research, to examine the properties of the popular tools, and to find alternative tools for a task.

We identified potential sources to extract tool popularity data: Google name search, Twitter search, GitHub stars, SecTools.org ranking, and tool cross-references. We noted a clear correlation between the different metrics. There is an underlying overall popularity, which is reflected on all of the metrics. However, the consensus does not go to the individual tool level, there is a lot of variation on the rank of a tool between the metrics. We used principal component analysis to extract the aggregate popularity from three source metrics: Google name search, GitHub stars, and tool cross-references. A tool had to have two out from the three source metrics to be included to the aggregate metric. We imputed values for missing GitHub star counts and Google name search counts. For these tools, the resulting aggregate metric is only based on two source metrics. Especially when we lack GitHub star count, we are quite dependent on Google search results as even the cross-reference count is calculated from the pages originally returned by Google.

The common popularity component explained 70% of the variance in the metrics. We then ranked the top 100 tools by the aggregate metric. The three top ranking tools are Metasploit, Nmap, and Wireshark. Generally, the top 100 tools contains roughly the tools we expected to be high on the list and many tools which we were not familiar with.

We estimated the reliability of the aggregate metric and concluded that errors in the source metrics in the range of −50%...+100% change the ranking of the tools around ranking 50 by a maximum by ±30 positions, less in higher rankings and if source errors are smaller. So, one should not take a tool rank as an exact number, but rather as an estimate of the popularity of the tool. We may have caused errors by missing a popular tool or failing to collect an relevant URL. We tried to avoid missing tools by collecting the corpus from many sources. Further, we have reviewed the URL lists by multiple people and also checked popular URLs in the downloaded pages.

To present the popularity by tool categories, we divided the tools by their scope and type of activity. Roughly half of the tools, 51 tools, are in the network scope and all top 5 tools are network tools. All network categories, network scan, traffic analysis, packet capture, packet injection, and web security, are popular. The large number of versatile network tools highlight the interest to the network security. Some of the packet and traffic tools may also be used for non-security development and administration.

In the storage scope, there are 15 tools equally split between disk and file tools. The scope is less popular than the network tools. There are 27 tools in the host scope, the disassembly tools being the most popular. Host interactive contains tools for all major operating systems, Windows being the most popular. Memory forensics and malware execution are a lot less popular categories, which may indicate that these tasks are less practised. In the password scope there are 13 tools, several tools in both on-line and off-line categories. There are just four tools in the other tools category.

Several popular tools are tool suites or frameworks, e.g. Metasploit and Radare 2, and they are in many categories. We assign just one popularity metric for a tool, so a tool popular in many categories may be in reality popular in only some of them. It was also quite challenging to categorize so many tools and sometimes it was not easy to determine the correct categories to the tools by reading the tool documentation only.

4.1 Future Work

This study provides information on which open-source tools, and tool categories, are popular in the infosec. The data can be used to direct future research to the relevant tools and tool categories.

One could study the properties of the popular tools and tool categories, e.g. the used programming language, tool age, number of active developers, etc. Further, it could be useful to map tools into infosec tasks to get insight into tasks and the tools used in them. The tool categorization could be refined to better capture the types of tools available. It would also be critical to detect if there are popular tools that have some risks associated with them, like lack of maintenance or use of outdated technology.

The reliability of the tool rankings could be improved by adding more sources of data, e.g. by scraping more web pages or scraping academic publications. It would be important to lessen the uncertainty by the use of the Google search engine. This is highlighted by the fact that after this study we have observed changes in the behavior of the Google Custom Search engine. It appears to return fewer pages compared to the results collected in November 2020. This does not seem to impact the relative rankings of the tools, but clearly, it would be highly beneficial to have more sources for the data.

Acknowlegements. This work is done in the CinCan project funded by CEF programme (2016-FI-IA-0095) and in the SECREDAS project funded by Horizon 2020 programme (grant agreement nr. 783119) and by Business Finland.

References

1. ArchStrike linux. https://archstrike.org/. Accessed 14 Apr 2021
2. BlackArch linux. https://blackarch.org/. Accessed 14 Apr 2021
3. CAINE linux. https://www.caine-live.net/. Accessed 14 Apr 2021
4. CinCan project. https://cincan.io/. Accessed 14 Apr 2021
5. Debian linux. https://www.debian.org/. Accessed 14 Apr 2021
6. Fedora Security Lab. https://labs.fedoraproject.org/en/security/. Accessed 14 Apr 2021
7. FLARE VM image. https://github.com/fireeye/flare-vm. Accessed 14 Apr 2021
8. GetOldTweets3. https://pypi.org/project/GetOldTweets3/. Accessed 14 Apr 2021
9. GitHub home page. https://github.com. Accessed 14 Apr 2021
10. GitLab home page. https://gitlab.com/. Accessed 14 Apr 2021
11. Google Code Archive. https://code.google.com/archive/. Accessed 14 Apr 2021
12. Google Custom Search. https://developers.google.com/custom-search. Accessed 14 Apr 2021
13. Kali linux. https://www.kali.org/. Accessed 14 Apr 2021
14. Merriam-Webster. https://www.merriam-webster.com/. Accessed 14 Apr 2021
15. Metasploit. https://www.metasploit.com/. Accessed 14 Apr 2021
16. Nmap. https://nmap.org/. Accessed 14 Apr 2021
17. Pentoo linux. https://www.pentoo.ch/. Accessed 14 Apr 2021
18. Programmable search engine help: Custom Search vs Google.com. https://support.google.com/programmable-search/answer/70392. Accessed 14 Apr 2021

19. REMnux linux. https://remnux.org/. Accessed 14 Apr 2021
20. SecTools.Org. https://sectools.org/. Accessed 14 Apr 2021
21. SIFT workstation linux. https://digital-forensics.sans.org/community/downloads. Accessed 14 Apr 2021
22. Sourceforge home page. https://sourceforge.net/. Accessed 14 Apr 2021
23. Ubuntu linux. https://ubuntu.com/. Accessed 14 Apr 2021
24. WireShark. https://www.wireshark.org/. Accessed 14 Apr 2021
25. Bagrow, J., Rozenfeld, H., Bollt, E., ben Avraham, D.: How famous is a scientist? - famous to those who know us. EPL (Europhysics Letters) 67 (2004)
26. Cilibrasi, R.L., Vitanyi, P.M.B.: The google similarity distance. IEEE Trans. Knowl. Data Eng. **19**(3), 370–383 (2007)
27. Ellison, D., Ikuesan, R.A., Venter, H.S.: Ontology for reactive techniques in digital forensics. In: 2019 IEEE Conference on Application, Information and Network Security (AINS), pp. 83–88 (2019)
28. Harichandran, V.S., Breitinger, F., Baggili, I., Marrington, A.: A cyber forensics needs analysis survey: revisiting the domain's needs a decade later. Comput. Secur. **57**, 1–13 (2016)
29. Hibshi, H., Vidas, T., Cranor, L.: Usability of forensics tools: a user study. In: 2011 Sixth International Conference on IT Security Incident Management and IT Forensics, pp. 81–91 (2011)
30. Hoque, N., Bhuyan, M.H., Baishya, R., Bhattacharyya, D., Kalita, J.: Network attacks: taxonomy, tools and systems. J. Netw. Comput. Appl. **40**, 307–324 (2014)
31. Jolliffe, I., Cadima, J.: Principal component analysis: a review and recent developments. Philos. Trans. R. Soc. A Math. Phys. Eng. Sci. **374**, 20150202 (2016)
32. Karie, N.M., Venter, H.S.: Measuring semantic similarity between digital forensics terminologies using web search engines. In: 2012 Information Security for South Africa, pp. 1–9 (2012)
33. Mandal, N., Jadhav, S.: A survey on network security tools for open source. In: 2016 IEEE International Conference on Current Trends in Advanced Computing (ICCTAC), pp. 1–6 (2016)
34. Weiss, D.: Measuring success of open source projects using web search engines. In: Scotto, M., Succi, G. (eds.) Proceedings of The First International Conference on Open Source Systems (OSS 2005), Genova, Italy, pp. 93–99 (2005)

RootAsRole: Towards a Secure Alternative to sudo/su Commands for Home Users and SME Administrators

Ahmad Samer Wazan[1,2(✉)], David W. Chadwick[3], Remi Venant[4],
Romain Laborde[2], and Abdelmalek Benzekri[2]

[1] Zayed University, Dubai, UAE
`ahmad.wazan@zu.ac.ae`
[2] Paul Sabatier University, Toulouse, France
[3] Kent University, Canterbury, UK
[4] LeMans University, Le Mans, France

Abstract. The typical way to run an administrative task on Linux is to execute it in the context of a super user. This breaks the principle of least privilege on access control. Other solutions, such as SELinux and AppArmor, are available but complex to use. In this paper, a new Linux module, named RootAsRole, is proposed to allow users to fine-grained control the privileges they grant to Linux commands as capabilities. It adopts a role-based access control (RBAC) [14], in which administrators can define a set of roles and the capabilities that are assigned to them. Administrators can then define the rules controlling what roles users or groups can assign to themselves. Each time a Linux user wants to execute a program that necessitates one or more capabilities, (s)he should assign the role to him/herself that contains the needed capabilities, providing there is a rule that allows it. A pilot implementation on Linux systems is illustrated in detail.

Keywords: sudo/su commands · Linux capabilities · Privilege escalation · Access control

1 Introduction

Administering an OS includes many tasks such as managing the OS users, file system, security policy, processes, system clock etc. Historically, Linux administration was based on the existence of one powerful user, called super user or root, whose id value is 0. The initial administration model was very simple because any user can manage any resource on the system as long as the effective user ID ($euid$) of the process run by the user is equal to zero. Indeed, every process on Linux systems has four types of group and user IDs, the most important ones are: Real ID ($ruid$, $rgid$) and Effective ID ($euid$, $egid$). Typically, real ID is used to show to which user or group the process belongs whilst Effective ID is used to determine the permissions granted to a process. According to the

© IFIP International Federation for Information Processing 2021
Published by Springer Nature Switzerland AG 2021
A. Jøsang et al. (Eds.): SEC 2021, IFIP AICT 625, pp. 196–209, 2021.
https://doi.org/10.1007/978-3-030-78120-0_13

initial administration model, any process whose *euid* or *egid* is 0 can achieve all the administrative tasks on Linux. This type of process is referred to as a privileged process [7]. Consequently, any regular user who wants to achieve an administrative task on Linux must change his *euid* or *egid* to 0.

This models creates a problem because all programs executed in the context of the super user can in fact lead to a privilege escalation attack when the executed program has an exploitable vulnerability or when the executed program has some arguments that allow malicious users to execute arbitrary commands on the system. For example, recently a vulnerability has been discovered in sudo program (setuid bit set) that allows any non privileged user to become root [11]. Another example, an administrator who adds to the *sudo* configuration file the possibility for a user test to run the command find could give the user test root access to the whole system, if he was not aware of the existence of the exec argument in the find command. This argument allows the test user to execute arbitrary commands on the system (see Fig. 1). In addition, the simple administration model can also cause disastrous problems on the system when users commit some fatal error such as "*rm -rf /*" which allows the user to remove the whole files system (see Fig. 2).

```
[awazan@dane: $ sudo find /home -exec sh -c 'whoami' \;
root
```

Fig. 1. Privilege escalation with Find command.

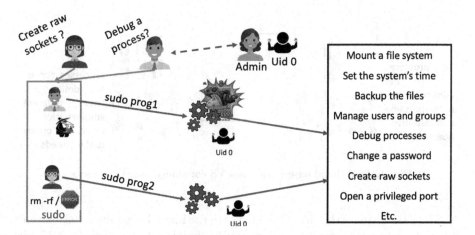

Fig. 2. sudo command.

As a consequence, a POSIX draft (POSIX draft 1003.1e) has been proposed in order to create special permissions called Linux capabilities[1]. Although the POSIX draft has been withdrawn, it has been integrated into the kernel of Linux since 1998. We use the term administrative privileges to refer to Linux capabilities. The power of the super user is divided into a list of sub-powers that can be distributed separately to processes by giving them only the administrative privileges they need [1] (see Fig. 3).

For different reasons Linux capabilities have not been widely used. The first problem comes from the use of extended attributes to store the capabilities of executable files (problem 1). Secondly, system administrators don't have a tool that allows them to distribute capabilities to Linux users in a fine-grained manner (problem 2). Fine-grained privilege distribution should give an administrator the ability to decide: (1) which capabilities to give to which users or groups, (2) with which programs and (3) on which resources users can use the granted privileges. Finally, Linux doesn't provide a tool that permits Linux users to know the capabilities that a program needs in order to run successfully (problem 3). Linux kernels come with an emulation mode that allows any process whose $euid$ is 0 to have the full list of Linux capabilities, emulating in this way the original administration model. As a consequence, the majority of Linux users still use su and $sudo$ commands to run privileged programs that obtain the full list of capabilities from the kernel because their $euid$ is equal to 0.

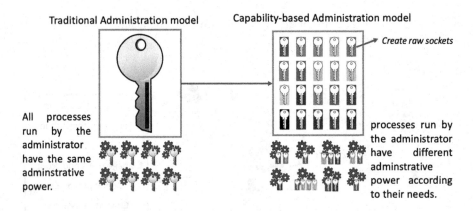

Fig. 3. Traditional based processes VS capability based processes.

Thus, the changes that have been made to the Linux kernel since 1998 haven't helped to concretely provide a more secure administrative model. In 2015, the kernel of Linux was modified in order to address the technical problems related to the storing of capabilities in the extended attributes of executable files (i.e.

---

[1] The capability term here should not be confused with the capability term used in access control literature that refers to a token given by the kernel to a process to access an object (e.g. file descriptor).

problem 1). In addition, this new feature added to the kernel makes it possible to extend the capability module by adding on the top of it a policy management tool that can be configured by the administrators of Linux system.

The objective of this paper is to allow administrator to restrict the use of Linux capabilities in their systems by resolving the problem 2, without necessarily having to extend their kernels with complex Linux security modules (LSM) such as SELinux and AppArmor. This can be especially suitable for home users and for SME administrators. Concretely, we are providing a module called RootAsRole that gives system administrators the possibility of finely controlling the distribution of administrative privileges to Linux users. We have implemented a role-based approach where each role maps to a set of capabilities that can be granted to users or groups of users. Linux users use our *sr* command to assume these roles and execute their privileged applications.

The paper is organised as follows. Section 2 describes Linux capabilities and shows what limited tools are available to distribute them to Linux programs. In Sect. 3, we review related work, whilst Sect. 4 introduces the RootAsRole module and shows its advantages by presenting one motivating scenario. In Sect. 5 we conclude with the limitations of our proposal and our future work.

2 Linux Capabilities

Starting with Kernel 2.2, Linux divides the traditional power of the superuser into smaller distinct units called capabilities [8]. There are currently 38 capabilities implemented in the kernel of Linux. In this system, the notion of a privileged process changes to represent any process that has one or more of the 38 capabilities in its credentials, and is no longer a process whose *euid* or *egid* is equal to zero. Root user is now considered as any other regular user. However, Linux still provides an emulation mode that allows any process whose *euid* or *egid* is equal to zero to automatically have the full list of available capabilities in its credentials and thereby become a privileged process.

All Linux capabilities start with the keyword cap, and each one of them allows a different set of administrative tasks. For example, any process that has the capability cap_net_admin can modify the network interface configuration, administer the IP firewall, and modify the routing tables as well as many other network related activities. The capability cap_dac_override allows the process to bypass file and directory permissions. Similarly cap_mac_override allows the Mandatory Access control rules to be overridden. A complete explanation of the Linux capabilities can be found in the Linux man [8].

The file /proc/[PID]/status lists the current values of the five sets for the process with the given PID. For any root process, the values of Permitted, Effective and Bounding capability sets are totally filled, whilst the Inheritable and Ambient sets are totally empty (Fig. 4). Since the reserved storage size for each capability set is 64 bits, and Linux has only defined 38 capabilities, this explains why the top 26 bits of each set are empty.

```
CapInh:   0000000000000000
CapPrm:   0000003fffffffff
CapEff:   0000003fffffffff
CapBnd:   0000003fffffffff
CapAmb:   0000000000000000
```

Fig. 4. Values of a shell run by root (cat /proc/$$/status).

Effective contains the set of capabilities that are currently used by the process. textitcap_capable() reads this set in order to verify whether a process is allowed to achieve a privileged task or not. Permitted contains the set of capabilities that a process can use, which is a superset of the Effective set. A process can drop a capability from its Effective and Permitted sets. Dropping a capability from the Effective set means that the process wants to temporarily disable the concerned capability, but removing a capability from the Permitted set means that the process permanently loses the capability. The Inheritable set is used by a process that wants to grant some capabilities to another process that results from an exec() call to its binary file. If a process has the cap_setpcap capability in its Permitted, this gives it the possibility to add additional capabilities to its Inheritable set. cap_bset is the capability bounding set of a process. This set is used to limit the capabilities that it may pass on to a new process obtained from an exec() call to its executable file. Without this set, attackers, who succeed in modifying the extended attributes of an executable file, could run processes that have the full set of root privileges. The cap_bset set is also considered to be a superset of the Inheritable set. The Ambient set is a relatively new addition to the Linux Kernel, which has been added to resolve the problems arising from the use of extended attributes to store the capabilities of executable files (see later).

Executable files only have the ability to store three sets of capabilities: Inheritable, Permitted and Effective. These sets are used to grant privileges to the process resulting from an exec() call of the binary file, by masking them against the capability sets of the calling process as described in the next section.

Linux stores the file capabilities in the extended attributes (xattrs) of binary files. This has been the cause of several different problems that has limited the use of the Linux capability model. In particular:

– some basic Linux commands don't use the extended attributes correctly. For example, the *mv* command preserves the extended attributes by default. However, the administrator doesn't get a warning message when moving files onto a file system that doesn't support the extended attributes, so they are lost. On the other hand, the cp command doesn't copy the extended attributes by default; the administrator must add the option – preserve=xattr. Other issues have been reported about archiving and backup tools that don't properly take care of the extended attributes [2];

– executing privileged scripts in a secure way is not possible. Linux administrators have to inject the root privileges into the interpreter program binary and not into the scripts. In this way, all scripts run by the interpreter will gain the privileges of their interpreter whereas the administrator may wish to give different privileges to different scripts;

– the xattrs are often lost when Linux packages are updated. This is a huge problem when the number of binaries containing capabilities is relatively big, or when a program calling a system binary is suddenly halted;

– the Linux kernel doesn't take into account the configuration of the LD_PRELOAD variable when capabilities are stored in binaries. LD_PRELOAD is an environment variable that contains the list of user-specified libraries that are dynamically loaded before all other shared libraries [3]. Typically, this feature can be used to intercept the standard system calls such as malloc(), open(), close(), etc.

Regarding the Linux capability model, we believe it has some limitations. As pointed out by Michael kerrisk [6] Linux doesn't have a central authority that determines how capabilities should be linked to the kernel features. We believe that this issue constitutes a significant obstacle, but this problem doesn't affect only RootAsRole but all other LSM modules. Further research is needed to handle this issue because kernel developers define the access controls on kernel resources in an ad-hoc manner [12].

3   Related Works

Some existing Linux security modules can be used to restrict the distribution of Linux capabilities to programs, such as SELinux, AppArmor and Grsecurity. However, these modules allow not only the capabilities' distribution to Linux programs to be managed, but also mandatory access control (MAC) rules to be defined. SELinux implements a label based access control (LBAC) model [13] and uses the extended attributes to store label values. As a consequence, SELinux suffers from the same problems that we mentioned earlier with regards to the extended attributes. In addition, SELinux is very hard to manage even by experienced administrators due to the difficulties with regards to the management of the LBAC system and the MAC policy. Thus, SELinux is not suitable for home users nor for SME administrators.

AppArmor presents an interesting approach because it uses pathname enforcement instead of labels. The syntax for writing AppArmor profiles is much easier than SELinux. AppArmor also provides a tool that automatically generates profiles for programs. The user runs the automation tool and his program at the same time and the tool then asks for the user/Administrator to approve the addition of each generated rule to the profile. Unfortunately, this learning mode fails very often to create automated profiles [9]. Grsecurity adopts like AppArmor a pathname enforcement approach. Grsecurity implements Role

Based Access Control (RBAC) model [10] that allows an administrator to determine for each program the authorized users and their associated roles as well as the access permissions on the resources that programs can access. It allows also to determine the list of Linux capabilities that any programs have the authorization to take. However, Grsecurity is not only a LSM module, it is presented as an extensive security enhancements to the Linux kernel because it proposes a set of protection measures against a set of well known security threats.

Theoretically, Linux home users and administrators can use these modules to prevent the privilege escalation problem. However, it is known that the MAC system is disabled on the majority of Linux systems. When activated, the default policy is only applied to the most high risk applications (such as network applications) while the other applications are left unconstrained. Thus, these MAC modules are useless to prevent the root privilege escalation problem because any unconstrained process that is run by *sudo/su* can easily deactivate any of these MAC modules or even remove them. In addition, many home and SME administrators may not need to extend their kernels with complex LSM modules but they may wish to restrict the distribution of Linux privileges without having to modify their kernels. Today, there is no solution to this type of users' need. As a consequence, most Linux users continue to use the *sudo/su* command to manage their own Linux systems because of the complexity of the MAC modules. Our objective is to provide a more usable module where the MAC rules are not needed or where they are only applied partially on the Linux system. This is the case for most home users and SME administrators.

4   RootAsRole Module

The pam_cap module is the only module that can be used by administrators to define how capabilities can be distributed to Linux users for systems where MAC rules are not implemented. This module has three major problems: the use of extended attributes to store the capabilities, no fine-grained distribution of capabilities to Linux users and no tool that can help Linux users to figure out the capabilities requested by a program.

In order to solve these problems, we have created the RootAsRole module. Roles are defined by an administrator in a central configuration file, and each role is assigned a set of capabilities. RootAsRole allows Linux users to use the *sr* command to assign roles to themselves. The *sr* command provides options that allow users to know what roles are currently assigned to themselves and what capabilities are assigned to each role.

An administrator defines the rules that allow the fine-grained distribution of capabilities to users and groups, without needing to inject the capabilities into the extended attributes of binary files. Administrators define the roles and the rules that allow users or groups to assign the roles to themselves. Each time a Linux user wants to execute a program that necessitates one or more capabilities, (s)he should assign the role to him/herself that contains the needed capabilities, providing there is a rule that allows it (Fig. 5).

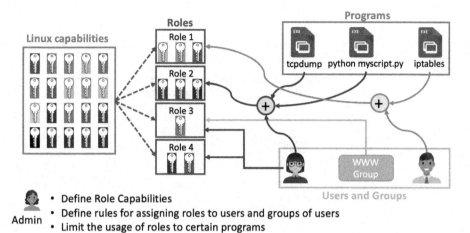

Fig. 5. Role definition in RootAsRole module.

The RootAsRole module comes with a configuration file called capability-role.xml that is stored in /etc/security. This file allows an administrator to define each role along with its list of capabilities, as well as the lists of users, groups and programs that can be assigned this role. In addition, users and groups can be constrained as to when the role can be assigned. For example, the following configuration file defines a role (role1) that has two capabilities (cap_net_raw and cap_net_admin). Users *guillaume* and *remi* can be assigned this role as can be the users of group *adm*. However, *remi* can only be assigned this role when he is executing the *tcpdump* command. The other users are not constrained and can be assigned this role with any program; they get a privileged shell inside which they can run any program (that only needs the user's assigned capabilities) (Fig. 6).

This configuration file limits the use of xattrs. It is read into a central database that allows administrators to keep track of the assigned roles and the programs that users can use with these roles.

When the administrator lists a program under a user, the user can only run this program with the capabilities. In some cases, a conflict may exist between the programs defined at the user level and those defined at the group level. For example, an administrator may restrict a user to execute only one program, but at the same time he authorises the user's group to execute any program. In these situations, we consider the configuration at the user level overrides the configuration at the group level i.e. the specific rule overrides the generic rule. In the example above, the configuration shows that *remi* can only run the *tcpdump* program, but if *remi* was a member of the *adm* group, which can run any program, this would not apply to *remi*. The RootAsRole module is released here [5] under GPL-3.0 License.

```
1  <configuration xmlns="http://mycapconf.xml">
2      <roles>
3          <role><!-- a role with 2 users, whose 1 has command restrictions -->
4              <name>role1</name>
5              <capabilities>
6                  <capability>cap_net_raw</capability>
7                  <capability>cap_net_admin</capability>
8              </capabilities>
9              <users>
10                 <user>
11                     <name>guillaume</name>
12                 </user>
13                 <user>
14                     <name>remi</name>
15                     <commands>
16                         <command>
17                             <program>/usr/sbin/tcpdump</program>
18                             <args>
19                                 <arg>-i eth0</arg>
20                             </args>
21                         </command>
22                     </commands>
23                 </user>
24             </users>
25             <groups>
26                 <group>
27                     <name>adm</name>
28                 </group>
29             </groups>
30         </role>
31 </configuration>
32
```

Fig. 6. Example Definition of a role in the configuration file.

5   Motivation Scenario

We will demonstrate the use of our RootAsRole module through one scenario. This scenario shows the advantage of our module with regards the existing tools that are used today to run administrative tasks. *Scenario* A user contacts his administrator to ask for a privilege that allows him to run a HTTP server that he developed using Python. His script needs the privilege cap_net_bind_service to bind the server socket to port 80. Without our module, the administrator has two options: (1) Use the *setcap* command to assign the capability to the Permitted set of the Python interpreter or (2) use the *pam_cap* module to assign the cap_net_bind_service to the user and then inject this capability into the Inheritable and Effective sets of the Python interpreter. Both solutions pose security risks. In the case of option (1) the Python interpreter can be used by any other user who will automatically gain the cap_net_bind_service privilege. In the case of option (2), all other python scripts run by the user will have the same privilege. It is not possible to run other Python scripts without giving them the privilege cap_net_bind_service. *Implementation* To demonstrate the implementation of this scenario, we selected the following python script, server.py, which can be used to run a HTTP server [4]. When executing the server.py script without any privileges, we get the *'permission denied'* error message (Fig. 7).

```
samer@samer-VirtualBox:-$ python3 server.py -p 80
Traceback (most recent call last):
  File "server.py", line 8, in <module>
    with socketserver.TCPServer(("", PORT), Handler) as httpd:
  File "/usr/lib/python3.7/socketserver.py", line 452, in __init__
    self.server_bind()
  File "/usr/lib/python3.7/socketserver.py", line 466, in server_bind
    self.socket.bind(self.server_address)
PermissionError: [Errno 13] Permission denied
```

Fig. 7. Run the Python HTTP server by a normal user.

The script requires the capability cap_net_bind_service to bind the server to port 80. When an administrator runs the script using the *sudo* command (*sudo python server.py -p 80*), the Python process is given the full set of privileges, because as indicated earlier, any process whose *euid* or *egid* is equal to zero automatically gets the full set of privileges (i.e. emulating mode). Figure 8 shows that process 5402 has the full set of Permitted, Effective and Bounding capabilities as these values correspond to the first 38 bits being set to 1.

```
samer@samer-VirtualBox:-$ cat /proc/5402/status
Name:      python3
SigQ:      0/15580
SigPnd:    0000000000000000
ShdPnd:    0000000000000000
SigBlk:    0000000000000000
SigIgn:    0000000001001000
SigCgt:    0000000180000002
CapInh:    0000000000000000  Inheritable
CapPrm:    0000003fffffffff  Permitted
CapEff:    0000003fffffffff  Effective
CapBnd:    0000003fffffffff  Bounding
CapAmb:    0000000000000000  Ambient
```

Fig. 8. Values of the capability sets for a process.

When an administrator uses the *setcap* command to assign the cap_net_bind_service capability to the python interpreter (Fig. 9) he creates a security risk because now all other users of the system will be able to run Python scripts with the same privilege.

```
samer@samer-VirtualBox:~$ sudo setcap cap_net_bind_service+ep /usr/bin/python3.7
samer@samer-VirtualBox:~$ python3 server.py -p 80
serving at port 80
```

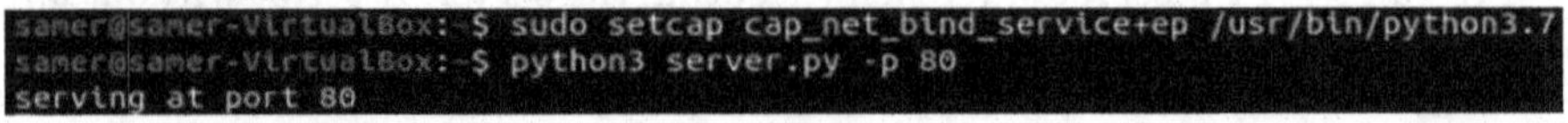

Fig. 9. Setting the Permitted and Effective capabilities for the Python2.7 interpreter.

The administrator can alternatively use the *pam_cap* module by first setting the cap_net_bind_service in the /etc/security/capability.conf file (*pam_cap*'s configuration file), and then using *setcap* command as in Fig. 10.

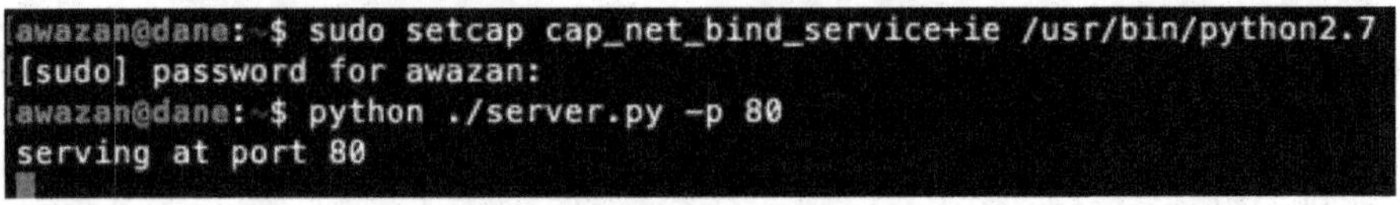

```
awazan@dane:~$ sudo setcap cap_net_bind_service+ie /usr/bin/python2.7
[sudo] password for awazan:
awazan@dane:~$ python ./server.py -p 80
serving at port 80
```

Fig. 10. Setting the Inheritable and Effective capabilities for the Python2.7 interpreter.

This solution raises another potential security risk because now any python script run by the same user will obtain the same privilege.

Our solution avoids these security risks. Suppose that the capabilityRole.xml contains the configuration shown in Fig. 11.

In this case, the user *awazan* can assign himself the role *role1* by using the *sr* command whenever he wants to run his HTTP server python script (server.py) – see Fig. 12.

As shown in Fig. 13, the user *awazan* cannot run another script with the same privilege. Generally, administrators may not want to limit the use of capabilities to certain scripts or programs, as this would create a lot of work for them. However, in some cases administrators may need this option especially when they don't completely trust all their users.

```
<role name="role1">
  <capabilities>
    <capability>cap_net_bind_service</capability>
  </capabilities>
  <users>
    <user name="root"/>
    <user name="awazan">
      <commands>
        <command>python /usr/local/Users/awazan/server.py</command>
      </commands>
    </user>
  </users>
  <groups>
    <group name="adm"/>
    <group name="office"/>
    <group name="secretary">
      <commands>
        <command>/usr/bin/printer</command>
        <command>/usr/bin/other</command>
      </commands>
    </group>
  </groups>
</role>
```

Fig. 11. Defining role1 for running the Python HTTP server.

```
awazan@dane: $ sr -r role1 -c "python /usr/local/Users/awazan/server.py"
Authentication of awazan...
Password:
Privileged bash launched with the following capabilities : cap_net_bind_service.
serving at port 80
```

Fig. 12. User awazan assigns the role role1 to execute the Python HTTP server.

```
awazan@dane: $ sr -r role1 -c "python /usr/local/Users/awazan/anotherprivilegedscript.py -p 80"
Authentication of awazan...
Password:
This role and command cannot be used with your user or your groups: Permission denied
```

Fig. 13. user awazan unable to run another Python script.

6   Discussion, Limitations and Conclusions

Our module RootAsRole provides new functionality to the Linux community by providing them with a module that allows Linux privileges to be given to users through the assignment of roles. Our module also allows home users and/or SMEs administrators to constrain the use of these privileges to certain programs (e.g., the Apache service or *tcpdump*). In addition, RootAsRole allows administrators to assign roles to sets of users through the group concept. Our *sr* commands is more secure than sudo/su commands because it comes only with two capabilities which are cap_setpcap and cap_setfcap, while sudo/su commands need the full list of Linux administrative privileges.

However we need to conduct a user study to analyze the usability issues of our module. We need to test the usability regarding the configuration of RootAsRole and the invocation of roles by users. But before conducting such study, we need to add more tools. Firstly, we are currently finalizing the implementation of a tool called *capable* that will allow an administrator to know the set of privileges requested by a program. In addition, we would like to implement a tool that allows system administrators to easily edit our central configuration file e.g. to add roles to the configuration file along with the list of privileges, users, groups and authorized programs. Secondly, we would like to add a GUI for setting the configuration policy. Thirdly, we will work on defining default policies for different distributions of Linux. Specifically, we will check the list of distributed tools and provide a pre-configured policy for these tools.

Finally, we would like to extend our module to handle more complex scenarios. For example, giving administrators the possibility to limit the use of privileges not only in terms of programs and resources but also in terms of additional contextual information such as time and location. We would also like to introduce additional RBAC features such as role hierarchies and separation of duties [10].

Acknowledgement. This work was partially supported by the European Union's Horizon 2020 research and innovation program from the project CyberSec4Europe [grant agreement number 830929].

References

1. Hallyn, S.E., Morgan, A.G.: Linux capabilities: making them work. In: The Linux Symposium, Ottawa, ON, Canada (2008). https://www.kernel.org/doc/ols/2008/ols2008v1-pages-163-172.pdf
2. Extended attributes: the good, the not so good, the bad (2014). https://www.lesbonscomptes.com/pages/extattrs.html. Accessed 28 Mar 2021
3. Linux manual page:ld.so, ld-linux.so - dynamic linker/loader. http://man7.org/linux/man-pages/man8/ld.so.8.html. Accessed 28 Mar 2021
4. Example code of Python http Server. https://docs.python.org/2/library/simplehttpserver.html. Accessed 28 Mar 2021
5. Code source of RootAsRole module. https://github.com/SamerW/RootAsRole. Accessed 28 Mar 2021
6. Kerrisk, M.: CAP_SYS_ADMIN: the new root (2012). https://lwn.net/Articles/486306/. Accessed 28 Mar 2021
7. Kerrisk, M.: The Linux Programming interface, ISBN 159327291X, No Strarch Press, October 1 2010
8. Linux capabilities man page. http://man7.org/linux/man-pages/man7/capabilities.7.html. Accessed 28 Mar 2021

9. Getting started with AppArmor. https://www.slideshare.net/pirafrank/getting-started-with-apparmor. Accessed 28 Mar 2021
10. Sandhu, R.S., Coyne, E.J., Feinstein, H.L., Youman, C.E.: Role-based access control models. Computer **29**, 38–47 (1996). https://doi.org/10.1109/2.485845
11. sudo vulnerability CVE-2019-14287. https://medium.com/@isharaabeythissa/cve-2019-14287-sudo-will-hit-your-root-4df17e6a089b. Accessed 28 Mar 2021
12. Zhang, T., Shen, W., Lee, D., Jung, C., Azab, A.M., Wang, R.: Pex: a permission check analysis framework for Linux kernel. In: 2019, Proceedings of the 28th USENIX Conference on Security Symposium, pp. 1205–1220 (2019)
13. Wang, Q., Chen, D., Zhang, N., Qin, Z., Qin, Z.: LACS: a lightweight label-based access control scheme in IoT-based 5G caching context. IEEE Access **5**, 4018–4027 (2017). https://doi.org/10.1109/ACCESS.2017.2678510
14. Sohr, K., Drouineaud, M., Ahn, G., Gogolla, M.: Analyzing and managing role-based access control policies. IEEE Trans. Knowl. Data Eng. **20**(7), 924–939 (2008). https://doi.org/10.1109/TKDE.2008.28

Privacy

Accept All: The Landscape of Cookie Banners in Greece and the UK

Georgios Kampanos[(✉)] and Siamak F. Shahandashti[(✉)]

University of York, York, UK
siamak.shahandashti@york.ac.uk

Abstract. Cookie banners are devices implemented by websites to allow users to manage their privacy settings with respect to the use of cookies. They are part of a user's daily web browsing experience since legislation in Europe requires websites to show such notices. In this paper, we carry out a large-scale study of more than 17,000 websites including more than 7,500 cookie banners in Greece and the UK to determine compliance and tracking transparency levels. Our analysis shows that although more than 60% of websites store third-party cookies in both countries, only less than 50% show a cookie notice and hence a substantial proportion do not comply with the law even at the very basic level. We find only a small proportion of the surveyed websites providing a direct opt-out option, with an overwhelming majority either nudging users towards privacy-intrusive choices or making cookie rejection much harder than consent. Our results differ significantly in some cases from previous smaller-scale studies and hence underline the importance of large-scale studies for a better understanding of the big picture in cookie practices.

Keywords: Cookie banners · Privacy options · Web measurement · Dark patterns · GDPR · Data protection act · User tracking

1 Introduction

Websites implement cookie banners to allow users to either consent to or reject third-party cookie tracking and manage their privacy settings. After tighter legislation came into force, namely EU's General Data Protection Regulation (GDPR) and UK's Data Protection Act 2018 (DPA), more and more websites have adopted such notices, making cookie banners a part of users' everyday life.

In theory, cookie banners (a.k.a. cookie notices) exist to empower users by informing them about tracking activity and allowing them to opt out if they wish to. However, real-world implementations of cookie banners appear to be a nuisance more than anything else [9]. Many websites design their notices to make opting out extremely hard, or remove the option completely as previous studies found [13]. Furthermore, pre-selected options that nudge users towards privacy-intrusive choices are rife and significantly impact user behaviour [14]. Both EU and UK regulators have clearly identified such practices non-compliant with the

© IFIP International Federation for Information Processing 2021
Published by Springer Nature Switzerland AG 2021
A. Jøsang et al. (Eds.): SEC 2021, IFIP AICT 625, pp. 213–227, 2021.
https://doi.org/10.1007/978-3-030-78120-0_14

GDPR and the DPA, including consent not being explicit and cookie rejection not being as easy as acceptance (See e.g. the EU's 2002 ePrivacy Directive [7], the 2020 European Data Protection Board guidelines [6], and discussions by Nouwens et al. [13]). Yet, even if users manage to navigate around the maze of options and select their privacy settings, their choices are more likely to be ignored entirely as a study of Consent Management Providers (CMPs) deployed in European websites observed [11]. Worryingly, we have seen such "dark patterns" employed by big-tech, such as Facebook [12].

The insight we have about the cookie banner landscapes and how they have changed as a result of legislation is mainly based on the analyses carried out on samples of high-traffic websites. Although such studies provide valuable information on how popular websites implement cookie banners, a natural question to ask is how well such observations generalise if a more comprehensive sample including lower-traffic websites is analysed. In this work, we aim to take a step towards investigating this question in the UK and Greece web landscapes.

We set out to establish the types of cookie banners with which users have to interact on a daily basis. Moreover, we will explore the distribution and availability of choices provided to users through cookie banner implementations. Using purpose-built software and with the aid of OpenWPM [4], we collected, categorised and analysed more than 7,500 cookie banners from more than 17,000 websites across Greece and the UK. We discuss our findings which interestingly in some cases substantially differ with previous results in the literature. Our results therefore is a step towards developing a more clear and comprehensive understanding of the cookie banner landscape in the two countries.

We consider Greece and the UK because of our familiarity with the respective languages and our hope that the comparison between the two provides interesting insight. On the one hand, websites in both countries adhere to very similar data protection laws. On the other hand however, the two countries vastly differ in their population size and their citizens' use of internet services [5].

2 Related Work

Studies in this area have mainly focused on the prevalence of cookie banners, the type of privacy options they offer, and whether they comply with the law.

In 2018, The Norwegian Consumer Council reviewed whether user interfaces of cookie notices and privacy settings provided by Google, Facebook and Microsoft Windows 10 discourage users from making privacy-aware choices [12]. They found that all three companies offer default settings that are considered privacy intrusive, and that the cookie notices contain misleading wording while privacy-friendly options require multiple steps to find. They noted that Google and Facebook "threaten users with loss of functionality or deletion of the user account" unless they agree to those privacy-intrusive settings.

A number of studies in this area focus on providing a big picture across the world or Europe. Habib et al. conducted a 150-website analysis in 2018–19 and found that privacy options are frequent within their sample with 89% websites with targeted advertising offering a way to opt-out [8]. However, they observed that, when visited from the US, only 28 out of 150 websites they considered displayed a cookie banner with only 5 of them offering a means to opt out. Degeling et al.'s study of 6,759 websites across the EU found adoption of cookie banners across the EU go up from 46.1% before the GDPR to 62.1% afterwards [2]. Utz et al. carried a manual inspection of 1,000 popular websites in the EU and observed that 27.8% provide no options, 68.0% allow confirmation only, while only 3.2% give a binary accept/reject choice [14]. Another study of top 100 websites in each EU country by van Eijk et al. found 52% of UK and 29% of Greek websites implementing a cookie banner [3].

Two recent studies have looked at whether cookie banners provided by Content Management Platforms (CMPs) adhere to EU regulations. In a study published in 2019, Matte, Bielova and Santos surveyed 1,427 European websites from which they found that 141 websites registered an affirmative consent before the user had performed any actions and 38 websites offered no "opt-out" option at all [11]. The authors observed that at least 50% of the websites in their dataset had pre-selected privacy options and at least 27 websites did not respect the user's choice even though they declined to be tracked by cookies. In a study published in 2020 considering 680 websites, Nouwens et al. found that 32% of them assumed "implicit consent" (agreeing without having any other option) [13], which make those websites not-compliant with GDPR. They also found that only 13% of websites had a "reject all" button which almost always required additional clicks to be seen by a user.

Taking a closer look at the sample sizes of the studies that focus on providing a big picture, we have Habib et al.'s study of 150 websites worldwide (50 from each group of high, middle, and low popularity) [8], Degeling et al.'s sample of 6,759 websites including 463 UK and 443 Greek ones [2], Utz et al.'s 1,000 randomly chosen from 500 top-ranking in each EU country [14], and van Eijk et al.'s sample of top 100 in each EU country [3]. Similarly for the studies that limit their attention to websites with CMP-provided banners, these include Nouwens et al.'s study of 680 such websites in the UK [13] and Matte, Bielova, and Santos's investigation of 1,426 websites including 149 .uk and 53 .gr websites [11]. Although such studies provide valuable insight, none goes beyond 700 websites in the two countries we consider. This is understandable due to the complexity of automating such studies and that the goal of the said studies was to focus on a global view or on CMPs, and not on the comprehensive landscape in specific countries. This opens a natural question whether similar trends can be seen if the scale of the sample sizes considered are increased. Indeed, it is not clear whether characteristics observed in high-traffic websites remain similar if low-traffic ones are considered. To answer this question, we focused on two specific countries: the UK and Greece, but scaled up the sample size nearly ten-fold by automating our scraping and analysis, allowing us to expand our research to more than 14,000 UK and 3,000 Greek websites.

While we developed purpose-built software, this study relied heavily upon existing software. We extended OpenWPM, an open-source web privacy measurement tool developed by Englehardt and Narayanan in 2016 to scrape and collect data [4]. OpenWPM allows researchers to detect and measure the use of third-party cookies (TPs), cookie synchronisation, as well as fingerprinting techniques. We modified OpenWPM to be able to recognise and store the website's cookie banner if one exists.

3   Research Questions, Methodology, and Implementation

In light of the results of the previous works, we aim to investigate the following research questions through a large-scale study of Greek and UK domains:

RQ1: What is the prevalence of cookie banners across the board when less popular websites in Greece and the UK are also considered?

RQ2: How does the distribution of options offered in cookie banners look like and what proportion of websites provide a direct cookie rejection option?

RQ3: What proportion of websites employ implicit consent?

RQ4: What proportion of cookie banners allows their users to manage their privacy settings and control which vendors track them?

RQ5: How do the countries compare in terms of the privacy options offered by cookie banners?

Our data collection included three steps. We first built a comprehensive set of functioning websites to analyse and extract their cookie banners. Then we crawled the identified websites and collected relevant data such as the source code of the cookie notices and screenshots of the webpages. Finally, we sanitised and structured the collected data into a data structure that facilitates analysis. In the following, we explain these steps in more detail. The code developed for this study and referred to throughout the paper is publicly available at the following repository: https://github.com/kampanosg/i-like-cookies.

3.1   Building the Target List

The first step is to identify websites to be analysed in this study. Using the Tranco top sites ranking [10], popular websites for the two countries were identified based on their Top Level Domains (TLDs): .uk and .gr. We decided to augment the TLD-based lists with other curated country-specific lists since many websites do not use the TLD of their country of origin, e.g., British Airways uses .com.

Ethical Considerations. Not all websites allow crawling and many explicitly state that they only allow "personal use" of their services and content to their visitors. To respect such restrictions imposed by the websites, we developed two parsers to identify and exclude such websites from our automated crawl:

1. A Robots Exclusion Standard parser (`step1b_checker_robots.py`) that verifies whether websites allow crawling by reading their `robots.txt` file;
2. A Terms of Service (ToS) parser (`step1c_checker_tos.py`) that makes best effort to find exclusionary terms, e.g. "for personal use only", to comply with the ToS of each website.

Table 1. The developed cookie banner options categories.

Category	Description
Affirmative	Options that prompt users to accept the use of cookies, e.g. "accept", "agree", "allow", and "OK"
Negative	Options that allow users to opt-out from cookie tracking, e.g. "decline", "reject", "disagree", and "no"
Informational	Options that take users to informational pages, e.g. "Privacy Policy", "learn/see more", and "see/show details"
Managerial	Options that allow users to opt in/out of specific trackers, e.g. "manage", "settings", and "vendors/partners"

3.2   Collecting Cookie Banners

The second step is to effectively identify and collect the cookie banners on the compiled set of websites. We achieve this by taking advantage of the "I don't care about cookies" (IDCAC) list (www.i-dont-care-about-cookies.eu), which provides an extensive selection of standard CSS selectors that cookie banners use. We parse these selectors and add them to a database. Furthermore, during testing, we identified and added 64 additional selectors to IDCAC.

After setting up the cookie selectors database, OpenWPM uses it to identify the cookie banners within the visited websites. We extended OpenWPM to detect cookie banners within a given website. For each website, we check whether it contains a CSS selector from the cached IDCAC list, using Selenium (www. selenium.dev), which allows for searching the HTML code of the website. When OpenWPM identifies a cookie banner, we perform additional analysis to make sure it is not a false positive, briefly by first ensuring that Selenium returned a valid HTML of a reasonable length, and then verifying that the returned HTML contains the terms "cookie" or "cookies".

When OpenWPM successfully identifies a cookie banner, it is stored in a database for further analysis. Combining the cached cookie selectors and Selenium's efficient Document Object Model (DOM) search enables the cookie banner extension to be efficient and robust.

3.3   Classifying and Normalising the Data

To our knowledge, no standard exists for cookie banners, and therefore, every website has a different implementation for their notices. Thus, the HTML code and the options they provide can be drastically different from website to website. Such complexity can make the data analysis difficult. Thus, before performing any research on the data, we transformed them into a consistent data structure.

First, we sanitised the collected data to identify and then classify the privacy options within the collected cookie banners. We identified four privacy option categories: *Affirmative, Negative, Informational* and *Managerial* as defined in Table 1. We developed these four categories by manually inspecting a random

Fig. 1. Three examples of cookie banners with different privacy options. Top: Affirmative and Informational, Middle: Affirmative, Managerial, and Informational, Bottom: Affirmative, Negative, and Managerial.

```
<div class="..." aria-hidden="true" data-contents="...">
  <div class="container">
    <p class="...">By visiting x.gr you agree to the use of cookies.</p>
    <a href="#" class="...">Agree</a>
  </div>
</div>
```

```
{
  "has_accept_btn": 1,
  "accept-btn_cta": "Accept",
  "privacy_text": "By visiting x.gr you agree to the use of cookies.",
  ...
}
```

Fig. 2. A cookie banner before (top) and after (bottom) normalisation

sample of the collected data during testing, further informed by our own experience with cookie banners in the wild. Using these categories allows us to classify the cookie banners by the types of options they provide and hence better understand user choices. Examples of cookie banners providing different combinations of these options can be seen in Fig. 1.

Manual inspection of the privacy options was necessary to account for local nuances. For example, although the noun $\alpha\pi o\delta o\chi\eta$ (lit. acceptance) was the most popular Affirmative call to action, a large number of banners used the verb $\delta\epsilon\chi o\mu\alpha\iota$ (I accept) indicating the same. We developed a comprehensive list of such variations and wrote a Python script (step3a_parse_cookie_banners.py) to categorise cookie banners.

After we categorised the privacy options, we transformed the collected data into a consistent data structure that allows for efficient querying. More specifically, we converted the arbitrary HTML form of the collected cookie notices into JSON to facilitate both manual and automated analyses. Figure 2 depicts an example banner before and after categorisation and normalisation.

Table 2. Breakdown of the number of websites per country that are included (by source) and excluded (by reason)

	Greece	UK	Combined
Included from Tranco	3,446	18,768	22,214
Included from country-specific lists	40	634	674
Excluded due to unavailability	−125	−305	−430
Excluded due to `robots.txt`	−204	−3,687	−3,891
Excluded due to Terms of service	−70	−760	−830
Total studied	**3,087**	**14,650**	**17,737**

4   Data and Results

In this section we specify the dataset and discuss our findings.

4.1   The Collected Dataset

Websites. The Tranco list contains a total of 1 M websites. From there, 3,446 are .gr websites and 18,768 are .uk ones. The additional country-specific lists provided an additional 674 websites: 40 additional Greek websites from TopGR (https://topgr.gr) and 634 additional UK websites from Kadaza (www.kadaza. co.uk) and Finder (www.finder.com/uk). Furthermore, we removed 125 Greek and 305 UK websites from the dataset as they were not accessible. In total, the initial dataset contained 3,361 Greek and 19,097 UK available websites.

We checked each website to determine whether they allow crawlers. The Robots Exclusion Standard parser yielded 3,157 Greek (93%), and 15,410 UK (69%) websites that allowed crawling. Then the Terms of Service parser determined that 3,087 Greek (91%) and 14,650 UK (65%) websites permitted our study to crawl them. Table 2, summarises the breakdown of our dataset.

OpenWPM. Successfully crawling websites for their cookie banners was possible by extending OpenWPM. In addition to cookie banners, OpenWPM also collected more than 15 M data points in Greece and the UK. This included information about the HTTP Requests and Responses (3.9 M), scripts that a website loads (7.6 M), and cookies stored in a user's web browser (2.3 M).

Viking. Collecting cookie banners for thousands of websites is a highly computing-intensive task, requiring over 24 h for a complete crawl in Greece for example, even with parallel crawlers. To overcome this limitation we utilised University of York's Viking cluster[1], a high-performance computing cluster with 173 nodes, 42 TB of memory, and 7024 Intel cores. While only using a fraction of Viking's resources (128 GB of memory and 32 cores) the crawl was completed in 8 h for Greece and just over 36 h for the UK.

---

[1] See www.york.ac.uk/it-services/research-computing/viking-cluster.

Table 3. Comparison of measured cookie banner prevalence rates. Sample sizes are approximates. Ranges indicate two methods of measurement.

Study	Year	Sample size		Prevalence	
	Conducted	UK	GR	UK	GR
Degeling et al. [2]	2018	500	500	67–82%	60–69%
van Eijk et al. [3]	2019	100	100	52%	29%
This work	2020	14,000	3,000	44%	48%

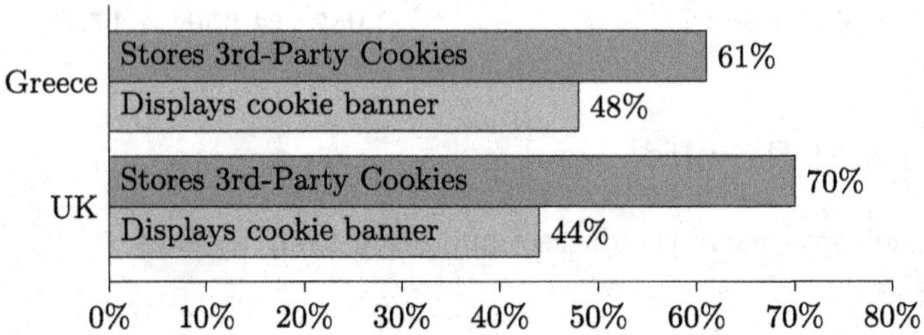

Fig. 3. Websites that store 3rd-party cookies and display a cookie banner.

4.2 Findings

RQ1: Prevalence Depends on Sample Size. Our findings show that almost half of the websites we surveyed display a cookie banner. More specifically, around 48% of Greek and 44% of the UK websites included a cookie notice.

When comparing our results with previous works of Degeling et al. [2] and van Eijk et al. [3], an interesting pattern emerges. As shown in Table 3, although both van Eijk et al.'s and our data collection were conducted after that of Degeling et al., we report lower prevalence than that of the earlier study. This is at odds with the reasonable expectation that the prevalence of cookie banners does not decrease substantially over time. What can explain this discrepancy is the sample size factor. Our results demonstrate that the observed prevalence depends on the size of the sample. That is, although the observed rates might rise initially as samples are expanded from the top hundred to a few hundred websites in each country, further expansion to a few thousands results in a decrease in observed prevalence rates. Hence, our results show that studies with smaller sample sizes might not provide an accurate representation of the big picture.

Using the additional data collected by OpenWPM, we found that 61% of Greek and 70% of UK websites store at least one third-party cookie on their user's browser. This suggests that around 13% of Greek and 26% UK websites have yet to comply with the GDPR or DPA, respectively, as shown in Fig. 3.

RQ2: Direct Opt-Outs are Rare. The distribution of the number of options cookie banners in our dataset provide is depicted in Fig. 4. As the figure shows, the most prevalent number of options in both countries is two. The mean number of options is 2.1 for Greece and 1.8 for the UK. The median number of options is 2 for both countries. This is in agreement with van Eijk et al.'s finding that the median number of choices in the top 100 popular websites that have a cookie banner in both countries was two [3].

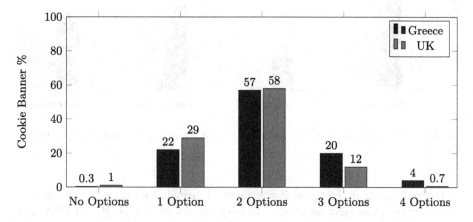

Fig. 4. Distributions of number of cookie banner options in Greece and the UK.

Worryingly, we can see in Fig. 4 that a considerable proportion of cookie banners provide either no option or only one option to the user. This prompts us to look into the distribution of the four categories of privacy options in the cookie banners. The results are depicted in Fig. 5. As the figure shows, although Affirmative options are quite ubiquitous in cookie banners in both countries (Greece: 95%, UK: 88%), Negative options are quite rare (Greece: 20%, UK: 6%). In the upcoming sections we will look further into the exact combinations of options provided by the websites to be able to draw further conclusions.

RQ3: Most Cookie Banners Nudge Towards Privacy-Intrusive Choices.

Considering all the ways the four categories of options that we have discussed may appear in a cookie banner results in 16 possible combinations. We depict the distributions of all these 16 option combinations in both countries in Table 4. The combinations are coded with abbreviations in the table, e.g. A-M- stands for the combinations in which at least an Affirmative choice is present, Negative absent, Managerial present, and Informational absent.

As Table 4 shows, by far the most prevalent combination is that of Affirmative and Managerial options (i.e. A-M-), with other combinations including an Affirmative option but excluding a Negative option (i.e. A-MI, A--I, and A---) following in terms of prevalence in both countries. This shows that at least 75% of cookie banners in Greece and 82% in the UK explicitly nudge their users towards accepting cookies.

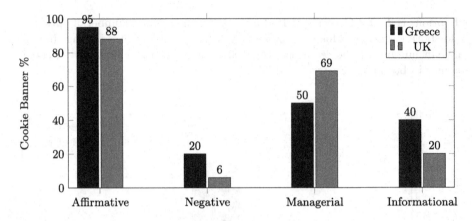

Fig. 5. The proportion of cookie banners in Greece and the UK providing each type of option.

Going beyond nudging, as Nouwens et al. argue [13], implicit consent and reject not being as easy as accept are both violations of GDPR and DPA. Let us now consider the 16 combinations against these two criteria.

For explicit consent, one requires at least an Affirmative or a Managerial option to be present so that the user can register their consent explicitly through one of these options. Hence, all combinations without any of these two options (i.e. -N-I, -N--, ---I, and ----) represent cookie banners that are violating this criterion. Hence, our results show that at least 16 Greek and 129 UK websites are non-compliant with GDPR and DPA since they do not provide the means for their users to register their explicit consent to the use of cookies. These constitute around 1% of Greek and 2% of UK websites with cookie banners.

The proportions of websites not providing an explicit consent option discussed above are large under-estimations since consent is not necessarily explicit in other combinations. More specifically, in our Affirmative category, apart from terms such as "accept" and "I agree" that clearly indicate consent, there are many other terms with less clear meaning such as "close", "continue", and "dismiss". These less clear terms roughly constitute around one sixth of all of the observed Affirmative options. We do not believe that such terms are sufficient to indicate explicit consent and hence estimate the level of non-compliance in terms of explicit consent to be around 15%.

The situation is much worse if the relative ease of Affirmative and Negative options are considered. Any combination with an Affirmative choice but without a Negative one (i.e. A-MI, A-M-, A--I, and A---) clearly does not provide a negative option as easily accessible as an Affirmative one. Furthermore, any cookie banner that only includes an Informative option or no option (i.e. ---I and ----) is defaulting on acceptance of cookies if the user navigates away from the cookie banner to interact with the website, hence not providing any means for the user to register their lack of consent. Therefore, all of these combinations do

Table 4. Distribution of the 16 combinations of Privacy Options in Greece and the UK, highlighting those that directly violate the GDPR and the Data Protection Act 2018. A: Affirmative, N: Negative, M: Managerial, I: Informational.

Combination	GR	UK	Consent explicit	Accept as easy as Reject
ANMI	4%	1%		
ANM-	5%	3%		
AN-I	10%	<1%		
AN--	2%	1%		
A-MI	5%	8%		No
A-M-	32%	47%		No
A--I	21%	8%		No
A---	17%	19%		No
-NMI	<1%	0%		
-NM-	<1%	<1%		
-N-I	0%	0%	No	
-N--	0%	0%	No	
--MI	<1%	1%		
--M-	4%	9%		
---I	1%	1%	No	No
----	<1%	1%	No	No

not satisfy the criterion either. This means that overall, our results demonstrate that at least 76% of Greek and 84% of UK cookie banners violate the GDPR and DPA in that they do not provide their users with a Negative option as easily accessible as an Affirmative one.

Degeling et al. [2] report their observations of a several types of cookie banners of top 500 websites in Greece and the UK. Three of their categories can be roughly comparable to collections of combinations we report. Cookie banners with "no options" in their work roughly correspond to combinations with neither an Affirmative nor a Negative option (i.e. --?? where ? is a wildcard). They report around 20% and 40% for this category (estimated from [2, Figure 5(a)]) compared to our 5% and 12% respectively for Greece and the UK. Cookie banners with "confirmation only" in their work roughly correspond to combinations with an Affirmative but not a Negative option (i.e. A-??). They report around 65% and 35% for this category (estimated) compared to our 75% and 82%. Cookie banners with a "binary" choice in their work roughly correspond to combinations with both an Affirmative and a Negative option (i.e. AN??). They report around 4% and 5% for this category (estimated) compared to our 20% and 5%. These comparisons show that observed practices may substantially vary between observations of smaller and larger sample sizes.

Limiting their attention to cookie banners provided by the 5 most popular CMPs in the UK, Nouwens et al. found around 75% violating the "reject as easy as accept" criterion [13]. Our analysis gives the rate of at least 84% for the violation of this criterion showing that the situation is much worse when a larger set of websites are considered.

In addition to privacy options, cookie banners usually contain a concise textual description as well. The text's primary function is to inform users why cookies are used and how they may affect them. This text is usually considerably shorter compared to the full Privacy Policy of the website. Examples of such texts can be seen in Fig. 1. The average length of cookie banner texts in Greek websites was 66 words, slightly longer than the UK average of 52 words.

Employing the term frequency–inverse document frequency (TF-IDF) formula to identify the most prominent terms in the cookie banner text corpus, we found that the most prominent terms in Greece and the UK are quite similar and dominated by terms with an apparent positive connotation such as "best"/"better"/"καλύτερη", "ensure", and "experience"/"εμπειρία". In fact, none of the top 50 prominent terms in either country (available from the repository) appear to have a negative connotation, whereas terms with a positive connotation such as "improve"/"βελτιώσει" and "enhance" constitute a considerable proportion of the list of terms.

To get a more comprehensive view of the connotations relayed by cookie banner texts in the UK, we performed an automated sentiment analysis of the words used in all UK banner texts using NRCLex [1]. The analysis found that a generally positive emotional affect was present in around 80% of the banner texts, whereas a generally negative affect was present in only around 14%. Besides, an overwhelming majority (of more than 9 in 10) of the texts with a negative affect also had a positive effect present as well. Looking at more specific emotional affects, trust and joy are among the most prevalent, present in around 66% and 46% of the texts, respectively. The prevalence of general and specific emotional affects is shown in Fig. 6.

The automated term prominence and sentiment analyses above suggest that websites tend to give a one-sided description of cookie usage, namely that it enhances browsing experience, conveniently leaving out that cookies can be used for tracking. This is in line with previous manual analyses of smaller samples, e.g. that of Utz et al. [14], that found similar biases in cookie banner texts.

RQ4: Managing Trackers is More Prevalent Than Opting Out. We aimed to determine whether websites allow their visitors to manage their privacy settings from the cookie notice. Our results show that Managerial options in cookie banners are significantly more prevalent compared to the Negative ones (See Fig. 5). More specifically, 59% of Greek and 69% of UK cookie banners offer a Managerial option compared to 20% and 6%, respectively, with a Negative one. Hence, users in both countries are several times more likely to be given an option to manage their cookies than an option to decline them.

RQ5: Users in Both Countries Lack Real Choice, But Practices Vary. The results discussed in the previous sections show that Greek and UK users

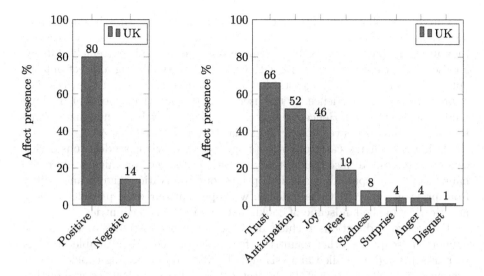

Fig. 6. Distributions of the emotional affects in the UK cookie banner text corpus

face a largely similar landscape in terms of the prevalence of cookie banners, widespread deployment of third-party cookies, and rampant use of nudging and lack of consent to cookies being much harder to register than consent. However, there are some notable differences between the two countries. With respect to using third-party cookies but not showing a cookie banner at all, the proportion of websites that are non-compliant with regulations in the UK is almost double that in Greece. Besides, cookie banner in Greece tend to provide slightly higher number of options.

Looking at the option types, affirmative options are prevalent in both, but negative options are much scarcer in the UK. From the other two types, managerial options are more prevalent in the UK and informational ones more in Greece. Looking at the option combinations, most have similar prevalence with three exceptions: although AN-I can be found in around 10% of banners in Greece, it is very rare in UK; similarly, A--I has a much higher share in Greece (21%) than in the UK (8%); on the other hand, A-M- is found in almost half of the cookie banners in the UK, but only in about a third in Greece.

5   Conclusion

We set out to conduct the most comprehensive study of cookie banners in the UK and Greece to date in the hope that a more thorough understanding of the cookie banner landscape in the two countries is beneficial for a rage of stakeholders including users, privacy-enhancing technology developers, and policymakers. By extending OpenWPM to detect and store cookie banners, over 17,000 websites were crawled and more than 7,000 cookie banners were collected.

Our results show that although around half of the websites in our dataset display a cookie notice, a substantial proportion do not show one even though they use third-party cookies. Furthermore, websites make it extremely difficult for users to opt-out from tracking with only a minority offering a direct opt-out option. Our analysis also suggests that websites present cookies as devices that improve browsing experience for the user while the negative aspects of tracking tend to be downplayed. Hence, we find clear evidence of websites nudging visitors towards privacy-intrusive choices and violating regulations.

Although in many cases our results agree with previous studies considering smaller samples, we also found that in some cases, e.g. prevalence of cookie banners and those providing specific options, our observations significantly differ from previous reported values. Hence, we hope that our work provides a more holistic view of the landscape of cookie banners in the two countries.

Future work directions include more comprehensive studies of the cookie banner landscape for other countries (for which our code is available and can be reused), a more detailed analysis and classification of varying cookie banner practices in specific subsets of the dataset, e.g., in different industries, and further analyses of the cookie banner text corpus.

References

1. Bailey, M.M.: NRCLex (2019). GitHub Repository. https://github.com/metalcorebear/NRCLex
2. Degeling, M., Utz, C., Lentzsch, C., Hosseini, H., Schaub, F., Holz, T.: We value your privacy ... now take some cookies: measuring the GDPR's impact on web privacy. In: NDSS. The Internet Society (2019)
3. van Eijk, R., Asghari, H., Winter, P., Narayanan, A.: The impact of user location on cookie notices (inside and outside of the European union). In: Workshop on Technology and Consumer Protection (ConPro 2019) (2019)
4. Englehardt, S., Narayanan, A.: Online tracking: A 1-million-site measurement and analysis. In: Proceedings of ACM CCS 2016 (2016)
5. European Commission: Digital Economy and Society Index (DESI) Report 2020: Use of internet services (2020)
6. European Data Protection Board: Guidelines 05/2020 on consent under Regulation 2016/679. Version 1.1 (2020)
7. European Union: Directive 2002/58/EC of the European Parliament and of the Council. Official Journal of the European Communities: L 201/37 (2002)
8. Habib, H., et al.: An empirical analysis of data deletion and opt-out choices on 150 websites. In: Symposium on Usable Privacy and Security (SOUPS) (2019)
9. Kulyk, O., Hilt, A., Gerber, N., Volkamer, M.: This website uses cookies: users' perceptions and reactions to the cookie disclaimer. In: European Workshop on Usable Security (EuroUSEC) (2018)
10. Le Pochat, V., Van Goethem, T., Tajalizadehkhoob, S., Korczyński, M., Joosen, W.: Tranco: a research-oriented top sites ranking hardened against manipulation. In: Network and Distributed System Security Symposium. NDSS (2019)
11. Matte, C., Bielova, N., Santos, C.: Do cookie banners respect my choice?: measuring legal compliance of banners from IAB Europe's transparency and consent framework. In: IEEE Symposium on Security & Privacy, pp. 791–809. IEEE (2020)

12. Norwegian Consumer Council: Deceived by design, how tech companies use dark patterns to discourage us from exercising our rights to privacy. Norwegian Consumer Council Report (2018)
13. Nouwens, M., Liccardi, I., Veale, M., Karger, D., Kagal, L.: Dark patterns after the GDPR: scraping consent pop-ups and demonstrating their influence. In: CHI Conference on Human Factors in Computing Systems, pp. 1–13 (2020)
14. Utz, C., Degeling, M., Fahl, S., Schaub, F., Holz, T.: (Un)informed consent: studying GDPR consent notices in the field. In: ACM SIGSAC Conference on Computer and Communications Security, pp. 973–990 (2019)

The AppChk Crowd-Sourcing Platform: Which Third Parties are iOS Apps Talking To?

Oleg Geier[✉] and Dominik Herrmann

University of Bamberg, Bamberg, Germany
{oleg.geier,dominik.herrmann}@uni-bamberg.de

Abstract. In this paper we present a platform which is usable by novice users without domain knowledge of experts. The platform consisting of an iOS app to monitor network traffic and a website to evaluate the results. Monitoring takes place on-device; no external server is required. Users can record and share network activity, compare evaluation results, and create rankings on apps and app-groups. The results are used to detect new trackers, point out misconduct in privacy practices, or automate comparisons on app-attributes like price, region, and category. To demonstrate potential use cases, we compare 75 apps before and after the iOS 14 release and show that we can detect trends in app-specific behavior change over time, for example, by privacy changes in the OS. Our results indicate a slight decrease in tracking but also an increase in contacted domains. We identify seven new trackers which are not present in current tracking lists such as *EasyList*. The games category is particularly prone to tracking (53% of the traffic) and contacts on average 36.2 domains with 59.3 requests per minute.

Keywords: Privacy · Transparency · Citizen science

1 Introduction

Modern smartphone apps communicate with several services at runtime, for instance, for debugging and tracking as well as displaying advertisements [7,13]. So far, there are no easily accessible means that allow users to analyze the communication behavior of apps. This lack of transparency makes informational self-determination hard to achieve. A user study on information asymmetries between app providers and users comes to the conclusion that *strengthening user's control* (36%) and *increasing transparency* (16%) are two of the top three requested measures [3].

While privacy research on desktop devices is well established [12,14,15,18] and has resulted in a number of transparency enhancing tools, there is a lack of tools for privacy research on smartphone apps, in particular for the iOS ecosystem. Existing tools are hard to set up or require a working Jailbreak to run;

© IFIP International Federation for Information Processing 2021
Published by Springer Nature Switzerland AG 2021
A. Jøsang et al. (Eds.): SEC 2021, IFIP AICT 625, pp. 228–241, 2021.
https://doi.org/10.1007/978-3-030-78120-0_15

only experts can use these solutions. Further, the results of one-off studies are outdated a few months after publication and often apply to the considered set of apps only. Many of these publications are not easily reproducible because they require a special experimental setup. Common setups require tethering the device to a computer, *jailbreaking* or *rooting* the device, routing the network traffic through a proxy, or patching the kernel to intercept system calls. Setting up the environment requires expert knowledge and time, which limits the target audience and the number of tested apps. Additionally, chances are lower that the study will be replicated whenever a new OS or app update is available.

We propose the *AppChk* platform to ease the evaluation for both, privacy experts and the general public. Our aim is to offer an easily accessible platform one can use without prior knowledge, which is future-proof, and keeps security and privacy measures intact. With *AppChk* we want to establish an on-going citizen science project to raise awareness for privacy practices in iOS apps; and create incentives for app providers to reduce third-party tracking. *AppChk* consists of two components, an iOS app[1] and a website (https://appchk.de). The app records application-specific network traffic; the website displays the results visually. *AppChk* allows its users to uncover known trackers as well as other high-frequented domains that are not considered a tracker yet. *AppChk* demands minimal user trust by following a privacy-by-design approach: The app uses an *on-device* VPN tunnel, i.e., traffic is not routed over our servers, and the app considers the headers of DNS queries only. No logging activity leaves the device unless the user opts in and chooses to upload a traffic recording to the *AppChk* website.

2   Related Work

Previous studies found that many third-party Android libraries collect Personally Identifiable Information (PII) and share it with advertising companies [7,13]. These libraries often require more permissions than the application would need, to gain access to PII data like IMEI, IMSI, location, and sensor-data – in some cases even users' email addresses, email subjects, and IP addresses [13].

Claesson et al. [2] find that apps become increasingly consumed by the advertising business. Grindr, a gay dating platform which performs particularly bad, shares data with 53 domains, 36 of which are related to advertising. At least seven contacted domains receive the user's gender, age, IP address, GPS location, and a unique device identifier; in four cases even a unique user id.

The detection of these threats is researched extensively on Android [2,4,8, 13,16]. However, there are only a few studies on iOS. This is in part due to the more restricted environment and the closed source nature of the OS [9–11]. Kurtz et al. have developed the testing platform SNOOP-IT for a dynamic analysis of iOS applications [10]. The analysis requires a jailbroken device and traces all system calls via `objc_msgSend` messages. Whenever a dynamic library is loaded, an API hook injects a tracing module to record all privacy-related API

---

[1] https://github.com/ubapsi/appchk-app.

calls at runtime. The authors extended their approach later with an automated testing capability (DiOS [11]). DiOS allowed them to scale up the study and test 1136 apps. Their implementation is based on Apple's UI Automation framework to simulate finger taps and perform screen navigation. Depending on the desired level of detail, their setup allows to test up to 500 apps daily. In their experiment almost half of all tested apps use tracking and advertising libraries.

Our setup is closely related to the one proposed by Amrein [1]. The SpySpy app monitors network traffic directly on the phone. Although the author states that SSL interception is an unwanted security risk, he does not abandon it completely. He argues that SSL interception is necessary to fully evaluate privacy risks. The proposed solution operates in two phases, an app screening and a network monitoring phase. The first phase uses a MitM server to intercept HTTPS connections to detect privacy violations. The second phase uses an on-device proxy to monitor network traffic. The proxy uses the results of the first phase to warn users about specific apps if necessary. Users can see the app-analysis results directly in the app.

Maass et al. propose *PrivacyScore* [15], a platform for website analysis and comparison. Their work goes beyond pure tracking analysis and evaluates websites based on security measures and recommended privacy practices. One of the core features are comparison lists. Websites from the same peer group are ranked according to the scoring on privacy and security features. The ranking creates an incentive for website operators to improve by reducing tracking [14]. Further, the authors provide a tool for data protection authorities and activists to verify the claims made by providers. With *AppChk* we aim to provide a similar service for iOS apps.

Apart from research, there are also tools used in practice; εxodus [4] and TrackerControl [8]. Both projects consider Android apps only. TrackerControl exposes tracking and allows its users to block tracking selectively. TrackerControl uses an on-device network proxy for monitoring. εxodus displays tracker usage, it is intended as an app index or app catalog. Their database is based on static analysis and contains 84855 applications and 340 trackers (as of February 2021).

3   Our Approach

We use an on-device *NEPacketTunnelProvider* proxy to capture all network traffic of the device. To the user this is presented as a VPN service. The advantage of an on-device proxy is that potentially sensitive data like browsing history and user-specific domains are not sent off to another party during analysis. Using on-device avoids pitfalls such as misconfigured VPN servers, which may leak IPv6 traffic or allows DNS hijacking [17]. Finally, on-device proxies do not have any impact on the speed of data transmission (no additional latency, no throughput limit). The device connects directly to the requested target.

The *AppChk* app only considers the domain names of outgoing connections. We do not look inside the traffic and hence do not depend on breaking TLS encryption. This ensures future reproducibility as it does not require a working Jailbreak or special setup. The *AppChk* app displays all network requests in realtime (cf. Fig. 1 left).

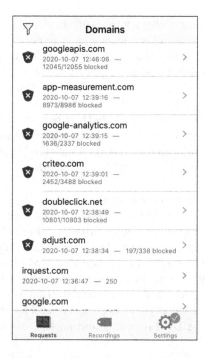

Fig. 1. Realtime domain requests (left), Co-occurrence analysis (right)

3.1 Design Goals

Our primary goal is to provide a platform that can easily be set up and be used by everyone, including novice users. *AppChk* should keep existing **privacy and security** measures intact. Therefore, we can not rely on a Jailbreak (new OS versions will close previous vulnerabilities), TLS interception (privacy invasion and data integrity), or an external proxy server (disclosing browsing history, requiring trust in the service provider). To be **future-proof**, our app works with TLS enabled and uses only documented APIs, which allows us to release the app on Apple's AppStore. Making *AppChk* **available** in the AppStore lowers the bar to participate in research. App evaluation becomes a continuous process and latest releases of frequently used applications get evaluated more quickly. We provide the *AppChk* app including its source code for public interest to keep the service active and up-to-date. *AppChk* app and website are designed with **ease of use** in mind. The app's design is unobtrusive yet helpful and the website aids novice users to judge whether a particular app uses tracking. With enough user-contributed reports, the website will foster **comparability** between apps, which might incentivize app vendors to enter into a competition for more privacy-friendly apps in their respective category (cf. [14]).

Privacy by Design. A recent Washington Post article by Geoffrey Fowler analyzed the newly introduced privacy labels for apps [5]. Fowler used *Privacy Pro*, a MitM VPN app by the company *Disconnect*. Contrary to *AppChk*, *Privacy Pro* routes the traffic over an external VPN server. This does not only require trust in the provider but may also put privacy at risk. The design of *AppChk* is not subject to this limitation. Users can download and use *AppChk* without prior explanation by an expert and will immediately see what network connections the device establishes. Users can further record the network activity within a short time interval of a few minutes and, if explicitly chosen, share their recordings on the *AppChk* website. As a user's recordings may include domain names deemed sensitive, the *AppChk* app displays what information has been collected. Users can review and delete individual domain names to sanitize the upload.

Data Minimization. *AppChk* does not collect more information than strictly necessary. Logged timestamps are only precise to *full seconds*. Further, the *AppChk* app minimizes the recorded data before it leaves the device. Absolute time information is replaced with relative time offsets based on a start date, which has a precision of *calendar weeks* only. Moreover, users can configure the *AppChk* app to automatically delete logs after a specified amount of time. This reduces the risk of inferring too much personal information from historical data that is kept on the device. Further, *AppChk* minimizes third party dependencies. The only used dependency is NEKit which is used for DNS resolving and packet transfer.

Transparency and User Control. The *AppChk* app allows its users to contribute app recordings. As recordings may include sensitive pieces of information, we have to handle them diligently. The *AppChk* app explains what data is shared and how it is used. Users are not obliged to contribute recordings, nor are they nudged to do so. We also give users the choice to exclude individual requests, on a subdomain level, from their contributions. As an additional defense-in-depth measure, we remove unique domains on the server side if a user sends them mistakingly. This filtering happens automatically by cross-correlation between different recordings of the same app. Domains that appear only in a single recording are removed. Users can also configure *AppChk* to ignore or block specific domains (DomFilter). If a domain is *ignored*, it will not be logged by the *AppChk* app. If a domain is *blocked*, *AppChk* will disconnect all network connections to that domain. Thus, *AppChk* can be used as an on-device content blocker. The filters give users greater control over their data; namely, what data is persisted and what data is shared with other parties. Lastly, the *AppChk* app offers users the option to export their recordings for independent analysis. *AppChk* exports the database as is, with everything ever recorded (and not deleted). Using data exports, users can use the app without ever sharing information with us.

3.2   App Recordings

AppChk can not differentiate between traffic from one application and another due to technical limitations of iOS. Instead, app recordings capture the domain names of all outgoing network requests during a particular time frame. A single recording may include requests from multiple apps and system background processes. Therefore, we urge users to quit all running applications before starting a new recording. App recordings temporarily disable any user set DomFilters. This might violate a user's decision to control how their data is processed. However, we made this decision for comparability reasons, to have an unaltered view of "what happened." Filters are mainly used to block third-party tracking – which is exactly what we want to detect with *AppChk*. Users are notified of the deactivation of filters when a recording is started.

3.3 Continuous Monitoring

Apart from using *AppChk* for on-the-spot app recordings, users can keep the app running in the background as an always-on network monitor (and tracking blocker). As long as *AppChk*'s on-device VPN service is active, *AppChk* will log network requests in the background, independently of recordings.

Co-occurence Analysis. One problem of looking at network requests alone is the sheer quantity of requests; some apps issue up to 445.7 requests per minute (cf. Sect. 4). This would overwhelm users if they would have to analyze each request separately. Therefore, we provide an in-app context analysis mechanism that relies on the time correlation of requests. This *co-occurrence analysis* feature helps users to attribute seemingly unrelated requests over a longer period of time. The analysis can also uncover new tracking domains, as many tracking requests happen in close proximity to one another.

Given a domain name X, we look for all domain names $Y_{1..n}$ which frequently appear simultaneously. Users can choose between different time windows of up to 30 s. With a time window of 0, the correlation function will consider requests which happened precisely at the same time (exact to the second). If the window size is greater than 0, results are sorted by close temporal proximity; requests that occur closer to the request(s) of the selected domain are preferred.

Co-occurences are displayed in a ranked list, which relies on the weighted score $(\overline{\Delta t}^2 + \frac{T}{2} + 1)/N$, where $\overline{\Delta t}$ is the mean temporal distance to the selected request entry, T the window size in seconds, and N the number of requests found within the time window. Δt can be at most T for window sizes greater than zero and is always 0 for a 0-s window. The ranking score strikes a balance between favoring domains with many requests and favoring domains with very close proximity. $\overline{\Delta t}^2$ prefers temporally closer results, while $\frac{1}{N}$ prefers results with higher occurrence counts. The weighting factor $\frac{T}{2}$ favors temporally nearby entries if the window size is small. We add $+1$ for numerical stability, otherwise a window size of zero will nullify the numerator.

Figure 1 (right) shows the co-occurrences of the domain app.adjust.com for a time window of $T = 5$ s. The domain gum.criteo.com is ranked second, even though the domain's requests are temporally closer to the requested domain (0.79 s vs. 1.14 s on average). The top-ranked domain has over twice as many intersections (405 vs. 181). The orange-colored bar indicates strong correlation, e.g., for the fifth rank, more requests balance the higher time divergence.

4 Evaluation

In this chapter, we look at some exemplary use cases for *AppChk*. In particular, we show what kind of information we can extract from the collected data. We conclude this chapter with an evaluation of 75 apps, including a comparison *before* and *after* the release of iOS 14, which was announced to introduce changes to acceptable data uses. We start by introducing the two datasets used for these analyses.

Dataset D1. In one of our evaluation use cases, we compare regional differences between app developers. For that we consider three geographic regions: Americas, Europe, and Other. We randomly sample 25 apps per region as follows. First, we obtain monthly top charts of July, August, and September 2020 for 11 countries from the app analytics provider *App Annie*.[2] We consider the Top 20 free apps for each list and month, yielding 660 apps. Second, we filter this list by removing all duplicates. We also remove apps that are not available in Germany and apps that have no company location attached. From the remaining 138 apps we sample 25 apps per region.

Each of the 75 apps is analyzed separately as explained in the following. First, a tester (one of the authors of this paper) quits all running applications and waits five seconds for background processes to finish. Then, the tester launches an app and uses it extensively to cover as much of the functionality as possible. Afterward, the tester quits the app and stops the recording. Whenever an app requires a user login, the recording only includes data up to the login screen. If present, register, login, and help buttons are tapped in any case.

Our D1 dataset holds 75 apps, 1093 recordings, 1062 unique domains, and 102 316 individual requests. 45.0% of all requests and 26.5% of all domains are tracking-related. Each app was recorded seven times before and seven times after the iOS 14 release. All iOS 13 recordings were recorded in the week before the release (Sept 12 to Sept 15). All iOS 14 recordings were recorded between Sept 28 and Oct 24.

Dataset D2. The second dataset includes all apps from D1, plus an additional 64 apps that not one of the testers but other users (unknown to us) submitted to the *AppChk* website. Most of the additional apps were tested only a single time (+76 recordings), limiting the validity of the results. We can use these recordings, however, to detect additional tracking domains.

4.1 Use Case: Tracker Detection

To detect previously unknown trackers, we can cross-correlate data of different apps and find domains that appear exceptionally often. Even with our limited dataset of 139 apps in dataset D2, we detect seven domains related to tracking that are not present in the commonly used tracking lists EasyList,

---

[2] AU, CA, CN, DE, ES, FR, GB, IT, JP, RU, UK, and US.

EasyPrivacy list, Peter Lowe's Ad and tracking server list, and εxodus ETIP list. We found `app-measurement.com` (in 77 apps), `ocsp.sectigo.com` (16), `inner-active.mobi` (10), `in.appcenter.ms` (7), `track.atom-data.io` (7), `liftoff.io` (7), and `taobao.com` (5). Further, we found that 7 out of 15 subdomains of `unity3d.com` (found in 17 apps) are not marked as trackers even though they should be. Some of these trackers seem to be exclusively designed for specific mobile operating systems. One of the most-used trackers, `app-measurement.com`, is not present in the εxodus tracker list. Thus, findings obtained with *AppChk* can be used to supplement existing lists of trackers.

Table 1. Tracker usage in apps and total network requests (in percent).

Domain	*AppChk*		Kurtz et al. [11]	
	Apps	Requests	Apps	Requests
apple.com	84.17	4.92	6.76	1.51
app-measurement.com	55.40	2.77		
crashlytics.com	48.92	0.56	5.68	0.58
facebook.com	46.76	2.67	13.96	3.47
doubleclick.net	33.09	1.02		
appsflyer.com	23.74	1.87		
adjust.com	22.30	5.47		
googleadservices.com	9.35	0.13	3.33	1.36
amazonaws.com	5.76	0.14	3.60	1.30
ioam.de	5.04	0.05	5.59	1.60
tapjoyads.com	4.32	0.12	5.86	1.99
flurry.com	2.16	0.06	23.15	5.41
chartboost.com	0.72	0.05	3.33	0.84
admob.com	0.72	<0.01	11.44	1.44

Table 1 compares the results of our study to the trackers found by Kurtz et al. [11]. 22.3% of the apps in D2 contact `adjust.com` at least once. Considering all apps, about 5.47% of the network requests in D2 are routed to `adjust.com`. We observe that the tracker landscape has changed drastically since 2014. Previously dominant trackers such as `flurry.com` and `admob.com` have a smaller market share than before. Other trackers have grown rapidly and taken their place. In contrast to our dataset, the dataset by Kurtz et al. did directly attribute the network traffic to a specific application. In our case, we also detect requests that originate from other apps or system services. That could explain why our study detects so much more domain calls to `apple.com`.

4.2   Use Case: Comparing Apps and App Groups

App Comparison. Maas et al. show that, at least for websites, adding a comparison of different providers on privacy and security practices creates a competition

Table 2. Regional differences; each with 25 apps and 219 recordings (min—avg—max).

Region	Total Req.	Req./min	Domains	Subdomains	Tracker
America	9198	3—32—75	4—10—21	4—20—60	0—29—64 %
Europe	37735	1—75—446	1—38—184	1—65—302	0—44—92 %
Other	13806	0—52—169	1—13—29	0—27—92	0—34—75 %

between these providers [14]. This competition sets incentives to reduce third party tracking. *AppChk* follows suit by allowing direct comparisons between apps: Users are able to compare two similar apps and decide which of the two respects their privacy better.

Consider the following example. *Viber* is an instant messaging app, which was hyped a few years ago as a secure and privacy-friendly alternative to Skype and WhatsApp. Their website states: "Our mission is to protect your privacy so that you never have to think twice about what you can or can't share when you're using Viber." Figure 2 shows the evaluation results for the Viber app as displayed on the *AppChk* website. Users can see, at a glance, whether an app uses tracking at all and to what extent. Further, users can see how many domains are contacted and what proportion of requests are known trackers (red color). In this example, the app connects to 12 different domains, eight of which are known trackers (`crashlytics.com`, `app-measurement.com`, `mopub.com`, `googlesyndication.com`, `doubleclick.net`, `appboy.com`, `mixpanel.com`, and `adjust.com`). 66% of all network requests go to tracking providers.

App Comparison Lists. On the *AppChk* website, users also have the ability to compare lists of apps with each other. For that, we tabulate key metrics for each app, e.g., the number of tracking domains, the percentage of tracking domains, and the number of requests per minute. The results are presented in a configurable and sortable table.

Group Comparison Lists. Comparison groups are similar to app comparison lists but compare groups of apps against each other, such as *free* versus *paid* applications. Han et al. [6] find that paying for an app does not guarantee an app to be free of trackers. Most paid apps even reuse the same tracking libraries and permissions as the free version. With *AppChk*, we can set up a continuous evaluation process. For now, groups can only be configured in the backend of the website, but we plan to allow users to do that on their own as well.

Our dataset D2 does not include any paid applications yet. We can, however, consider regional differences (cf. Table 2). Our classification depends on the location of the companies' headquarters. *Europe* is doing significantly worse than the other two regions, if comparing the amount and frequency of contacted domains. European apps contact, on average, three to four times as many domains as apps from other regions; simultaneously, the proportion of tracking domains increases by 10%.

Viber Messenger: Chats & Calls
Bundle-id: com.viber

App Categories: **Social Networking, Utilities**
Last Update: **2020-10-24, 23:14 UTC**

Number of recordings:
`14`
Rank: **20**, best: 18, worst: 14

Average recording time:
`00:00:43`
Rank: **45**, best: 00:04:24, worst: 00:00:23

Cumulative recording time:
`00:10:08`
Rank: **48**, best: 01:07:56, worst: 00:05:20

Average number of requests:
`20.4` (28.1/min)
Rank: **32**, best: 0/min, worst: 325.6/min

Total number of requests:
`448` (44.2/min)
Rank: **36**, best: 3/min, worst: 379.5/min

Number of domains:
`13`
Rank: **45**, best: 0, worst: 193

Number of subdomains:
`16`
Rank: **32**, best: 0, worst: 306

Tracker percentage:
`67.7%`
Rank: **67**, best: 0%, worst: 90.2%

Potential Trackers (9):

app-measurement.com (5) app.adjust.com (3) googleads.g.doubleclick.net (2) pubads.g.doubleclick.net (2) api.mixpanel.com
firebase-settings.crashlytics.com pagead2.googlesyndication.com venetia.iad.appboy.com ads.mopub.com

Domains (13):

viber.com (7) apple.com (6) app-measurement.com (5) adjust.com (3) doubleclick.net (3) appboy.com crashlytics.com googleapis.com
googlesyndication.com icloud.com mixpanel.com rakuten.com mopub.com

Subdomains (16):

app-measurement.com (5) app.adjust.com (3) content.cdn.viber.com (2) googleads.g.doubleclick.net (2) pubads.g.doubleclick.net (2)
abtest.api.viber.com account.viber.com api.mixpanel.com firebase-settings.crashlytics.com firebaselogging-pa.googleapis.com market.viber.com
p57-buy.itunes.apple.com pagead2.googlesyndication.com venetia.iad.appboy.com ads.mopub.com s-bid.rmp.rakuten.com

Fig. 2. App results overview with potential trackers highlighted in red.

This result, however, is biased by the skewed distribution of app categories over regions. The number of games is much higher in the group *Europe* (eight games whereas the other regions only have four games each). If we compare by category (cf. Table 3), we see that the *Games* category is one of the worst in terms of tracking. Additionally, the four worst apps overall are in the *Europe* region. All four apps (three games, one weather app) connect to at least 138 different domains each.

4.3   Comparison: iOS 13 vs. iOS 14

Our last evaluation example is a comparison study on differences between major iOS versions. The evaluation is performed on Dataset D1. This study intends to evaluate Apple's newly introduced "App tracking controls and transparency"

Table 3. App categories (in avg or avg—max). An app can have up to three categories.

Category	Req./app	Req./min	Domains	Tracker
Books (2)	52.8	49.3—57.2	15.0—16	33—50 %
Business (10)	23.1	27.3—60.0	9.2—18	**44**—75 %
Education (8)	24.3	19.5—54.5	8.6—14	27—60 %
Entertain. (23)	49.0	32.3—108.5	12.5—46	37—**92** %
Finance (10)	47.2	47.3—88.4	10.8—25	35—67 %
Food & Drink (5)	38.3	38.5—60.7	14.2—21	**44**—65 %
Games (24)	**164.7**	**59.3—417.3**	**36.2—184**	53—81 %
Health & Fit. (14)	22.8	29.9—147.7	7.9—19	19—66 %
Lifestyle (25)	49.2	55.1—168.8	13.6—46	34—68 %
Medical (11)	39.3	18.9—42.9	9.0—20	18—55 %
Music (7)	53.6	40.0—59.4	12.4—26	42—**92** %
Navigation (8)	35.7	38.4—108.8	8.4—21	27—54 %
News (7)	67.2	31.6—48.4	18.9—73	42—67 %
Photo & Vid. (10)	25.9	27.9—53.4	8.7—18	30—55 %
Productivity (18)	40.5	36.0—95.0	10.6—34	23—53 %
Reference (5)	34.1	24.8—41.4	8.8—14	19—50 %
Shopping (12)	59.4	54.9—156.3	13.0—25	**45**—65 %
Social Netw. (19)	24.6	32.0—168.8	7.9—28	27—75 %
Sports (3)	42.8	53.9—82.5	15.7—23	30—66 %
Travel (9)	**69.9**	**84.5—445.7**	**24.6—138**	34—60 %
Utilities (17)	23.8	31.9—71.5	9.9—34	30—66 %
Weather (2)	**171.8**	**229.7—445.7**	**70.0—138**	22—44 %

Table 4. Comparison between iOS 13 and iOS 14 (in total, or avg—max).

OS	Rec. Req.	Req./min	Domains	Subdomains	Tracker
iOS 13	549 51714	53.6—459.2	19.9—193	37.3—314	35.6—90.8 %
iOS 14	543 50581	51.2—302.6	20.1—206	38.9—351	34.0—89.2 %

feature. Our assumption is that the introduction of that feature incentivized developers to make changes to their apps' tracking functionalities. We hypothesize that these changes will reduce the number of connections to tracking domains.

Our results, which show only negligible differences, do not support this assumption. Table 4 suggests that iOS 14 recordings did contact slightly more unique domains – on average, an additional 0.2 domains (+1.0%) and 1.6 subdomains (+4.3%). Meanwhile, the tracker percentage dropped by 1.6%. We took a closer look at individual apps and chose four high-credibility commercial apps, and three tracking-intensive games (cf. Table 5). These results demonstrate that there is no clear trend towards less tracking. Some apps seem to use more tracking on iOS 14 than on iOS 13. With the exception of Google Chrome, big companies seem to have reduced tracking. We expect to see a more drastic change once the announced privacy features are in effect.

Table 5. App comparison between major iOS versions (iOS 13 ± difference in iOS 14).

App	Req./min	Domains	Subdomains	Tracker
IKEA	$18.3 - 4.9$	$6 + 0$	$11 + 1$	$35.4 - 8.3\,\%$
McDonalds - Non-US	$59.3 + 3.2$	$21 - 4$	$35 - 9$	$44.4 - 14.4\,\%$
Microsoft Teams	$47.5 - 25.7$	$10 - 3$	$22 - 10$	$13.1 - 2.0\,\%$
Cube Surfer!	$415.5 - 199.1$	$193 - 38$	$314 - 43$	$45.8 + 7.1\,\%$
Spiral Roll	$150.8 + 151.8$	$170 + 36$	$272 + 79$	$48.0 - 0.3\,\%$
Stack Colors!	$117.4 + 158.4$	$175 + 10$	$282 + 38$	$48.0 + 0.8\,\%$
Google Chrome	$25.8 + 25.5$	$8 + 33$	$17 + 67$	$12.1 + 35.4\,\%$

We added Google Chrome to highlight a potential caveat when conducting user studies with *AppChk*. Chrome is a browser that displays user-content. Most of what a user does in Chrome should not be assigned to the application itself but the requested website. Everything a user does during a recording, will influence the evaluation results. Even though user-content centered apps, such as Google Chrome, are more prone to error to a user's actions, other apps may experience similar traits. For example, network request can be triggered by many different environmental factors, such as daytime, location, WiFi connection, or individual system preferences. This shortcoming can be mitigated with more recordings as these would filter out outliers.

5   Discussion

Meaningful recordings depend on a high coverage. In our case studies, the recordings span 69 s (D2: 141 s) on average. In cases where an app presents a login screen, the average recording time drops to 30 s. Previous studies tested apps for 4 min [12] (normal usage) or 5 min [11] (random execution), i.e., which suggests that we should instruct app testers to use apps for longer periods of time. On the other hand, Kurtz et al. found that 77.7% of apps communicate within the first 30 s after launch [11].

AppChk can not detect whether communication with a third party resulted in an actual privacy violations (personal data being exposed). This kind of analysis requires in-depth inspection with specialized tools such as a MitM proxy (https://mitmproxy.org). The limitation to focus on uncovering connection attempts is a conscious design choice balancing the utility of the recordings and the privacy of the users.

Further, the *AppChk* app can not detect or prevent deliberately hidden or malicious information sharing. For example, data can be exfiltrated by hiding the request in an innocuous first-party domain requests. Resolving the destination of CNAME records is currently not supported but will be added in future work.

AppChk can not determine the origin of a network request. A system process or background app may interfere and inject wrong domains into the recording. Long-term recordings, which are not discussed in this paper, allow users to capture background activity. Background recordings could be used to reduce attribution errors by establishing ground truth for device-specific anomalies.

Tracker detection is currently done manually but could be automated to provide an always up-to-date tracking providers list. Further research is needed to compare the results of *AppChk* (iOS) to the tracking list of εxodus (Android).

We have shown that *AppChk* can be used to compare regional differences. Other interesting comparisons such as free vs. paid apps, correlation between app ratings and privacy, or changes in tracking after the introduction of privacy features can be introduced in the future. Further, we consider to integrate temporal analyses to detect trends, for instance, to find apps that improved recently. Uncovering such trends could help users choose one of multiple related apps.

6   Conclusion

AppChk is an easy-to-use tool to improve the transparency of iOS applications. Our platform allows users and privacy advocates to analyze mobile network traffic on the device (*AppChk* app) and share the results with our evaluation website (*appchk.de*). The *AppChk* app does not rely on deep packet inspection, TLS interception, a Jailbreak, or external servers, and it uses only well-documented APIs to be future-proof for upcoming iOS updates. This allows users to conduct a study immediately after a major OS update.

The *AppChk* website is built on the premise to provide comparable results. The website allows users to rank and compare apps and trackers.

AppChk can be used for app-group comparisons, highlighting systematic deficits, such as in the gaming category. The games considered in our study contact on average 36.2 domains with 53% of the traffic being directed to tracking domains. Moreover, during the course of our experiments we identified seven new trackers which are not present in current tracking lists such as *EasyList*.

AppChk fosters the idea that research can be an ongoing citizen science project, with enthusiastic people who are willing to contribute recordings on a regular basis. More people can test more applications in less time and keep the data up to date which results in better privacy for everyone. The results aid users in making an informed decision about whether an app respects their privacy and leads to public visibility and increased transparency. Ultimately, the improved transparency may create a competition between app vendors and incentivize them to reduce tracking.

Acknowledgements. This work received grant support from the German Federal Ministry of Education and Research (BMBF) within the project InviDas (16SV8538).

References

1. Amrein, S.: Does your phone spy on you? Master's thesis, ETH Zurich (2016)
2. Claesson, A., Bjørstad, T.E.: Out of control - a review of data sharing by popular mobile apps. Technical report, Norwegian Consumer Council (2020)

3. Döbelt, S., Halama, J., Fritsch, S., Nguyen, M.-H., Bocklisch, F.: Clearing the hurdles: how to design privacy nudges for mobile application users. In: Moallem, A. (ed.) HCII 2020. LNCS, vol. 12210, pp. 326–353. Springer, Cham (2020). https://doi.org/10.1007/978-3-030-50309-3_22

4. Exodus Privacy: εxodus (2017). https://exodus-privacy.eu.org/

5. Fowler, G.A.: I checked Apple's new privacy 'nutrition labels'. Many were false (2021). https://www.washingtonpost.com/technology/2021/01/29/apple-privacy-nutrition-label/

6. Han, C., et al.: The Price is (Not) Right: Comparing Privacy in Free and Paid Apps. PoPETs, pp. 222–242 (2020)

7. He, Y., Yang, X., Hu, B., Wang, W.: Dynamic privacy leakage analysis of Android third-party libraries. JISA, 259–270 (2019)

8. Kollnig, K.: TrackerControl (2019).https://github.com/OxfordHCC/tracker-control-android

9. Kurtz, A., Gascon, H., Becker, T., Rieck, K., Freiling, F.: Fingerprinting Mobile Devices Using Personalized Configurations. In: PoPETs, pp. 4–19 (2016)

10. Kurtz, A., Troßbach, M., Freiling, F.: SNOOP-IT: Dynamische Analyse und Manipulation von Apple iOS Apps. Sicherheit 2014 (2014)

11. Kurtz, A., Weinlein, A., Settgast, C., Freiling, F.: DiOS: Dynamic Privacy Analysis of iOS Applications. Technical report CS-2014-03, FAU Erlangen-Nürnberg (2014)

12. Leung, C., Ren, J., Choffnes, D., Wilson, C.: Should you use the app for that? Comparing the privacy implications of app- and web-based online services. In: Proceedings of the 2016 IMC, pp. 365–372 (2016)

13. Liu, X., Liu, J., Zhu, S., Wang, W., Zhang, X.: Privacy risk analysis and mitigation of analytics libraries in the android ecosystem. IEEE Trans. Mob. Comput. 1184–1199 (2019)

14. Maass, M., Walter, N., Herrmann, D., Hollick, M.: On the difficulties of incentivizing online privacy through transparency: a qualitative survey of the German health insurance market. In: International Conference on Wirtschaftsinformatik (2019)

15. Maass, M., Wichmann, P., Pridöhl, H., Herrmann, D.: PrivacyScore: improving privacy and security via crowd-sourced benchmarks of websites. In: Schweighofer, E., Leitold, H., Mitrakas, A., Rannenberg, K. (eds.) APF 2017. LNCS, vol. 10518, pp. 178–191. Springer, Cham (2017). https://doi.org/10.1007/978-3-319-67280-9_10

16. Papadopoulos, E.P., Diamantaris, M., Papadopoulos, P., Petsas, T., Ioannidis, S., Markatos, E.P.: The long-standing privacy debate: mobile websites vs mobile apps. In: Proceedings of the 26th International Conference on World Wide Web, pp. 153–162 (2017)

17. Perta, V.C., Barbera, M.V., Tyson, G., Haddadi, H., Mei, A.: A glance through the VPN looking glass: IPv6 leakage and DNS hijacking in commercial VPN clients. In: PoPETs, pp. 77–91 (2015)

18. Yang, Z., Yue, C.: A comparative measurement study of web tracking on mobile and desktop environments. In: PoPETs, pp. 24–44 (2020)

Compiling Personal Data and Subject Categories from App Data Models

Christian Burkert[(⊠)], Maximilian Blochberger, and Hannes Federrath

University of Hamburg, Hamburg, Germany
{burkert,blochberger,federrath}@informatik.uni-hamburg.de

Abstract. Maintaining documentation about personal data processing is mandated by GDPR. When it comes to application software and its operation, this obligation can become challenging. Operators often do not know enough about app internals to be comprehensive in their documentation or follow changes enough to be up-to-date. We therefore propose a semi-automatic process to compile documentation from the source of truth: the app data model. Our approach uses data model entity relations to determine identifiability of data subjects. We guide app experts to add the semantic knowledge that is necessary to determine subject categories and to subsequently compile a condensed listing of personal data. We provide evidence for the real-world applicability of our proposal by evaluating the data models of five common web apps.

Keywords: Data protection · Personal data identification · Data model

1 Introduction

GDPR requires operators of application software to create and maintain documentation about their processing of Personal Data (PD)[1], as stated in Article 30. Documenting such processing activities includes 'a description of the categories of data subjects and of the categories of personal data' (Article 30 (1)(e)). This requires the compilation of categorical descriptions for PD and semantic subject roles that are sufficiently detailed to, amongst others, allow regulatory authorities to assess the proportionality of data processing. However, to keep such documentation complete, correct, and up-to-date, requires great care and ongoing observation of changes to the software. Without automation, this will likely result in errors or deviation from the app as the source of truth. We therefore propose *Schemalyser*, a semi-automatic process to derive PD and subject categories from app data models. The underlying data models in the form of entities, attributes of entities and relations between entities can be extracted from various sources like source code [5] or database (DB) schemes [1] created by the app. Thereby, we are not reliant on the usage of relational DB. Schemalyser assumes

---

[1] We do not use the abbreviation PII to avoid confusion with non-GDPR definitions.

© IFIP International Federation for Information Processing 2021
Published by Springer Nature Switzerland AG 2021
A. Jøsang et al. (Eds.): SEC 2021, IFIP AICT 625, pp. 242–255, 2021.
https://doi.org/10.1007/978-3-030-78120-0_16

that data subjects, i. e., the identifiable natural persons, are themselves represented as one or more entities in the data model, which is usually the case for (collaborative) web apps and many other client-server software. To determine which data is personal and thus needs to be included in the compliance documentation, we can therefore utilise entity relations and the information whether data is connected to a data subject entity and how. This is in accordance with Article 4(1) GDPR, which defines that, what makes personal data personal, i. e., relatable to a natural person, is less a property of the data itself but more of its semantic context and the identifiability within.

By analysing five real-world app data models, we observed a high degree of interconnectivity among entities: Entities representing data subject are directly connected with 40 to 70% of all entities and over 80% are indirectly reachable. In other words, data subjects are identifiable for almost all application data. As a result, the documentation for PD of an app would comprise hundreds or thousands of attributes, thus loosing its informative purpose. Moreover, a user's name is indistinguishable in terms of identifiability from the number of likes the user has received for a chat posting, which raises the question of prioritized presentation. To the best of our knowledge, we are the first to tackle this *ubiquitous identifiability* problem by introducing differentiated identifiability classes and provide a process to compile condensed PD listings per subject category.

Our main contributions are: *a)* we describe the problem of ubiquitous identifiability in data models, *b)* we propose a semi-automatic expert process to derive PD and subject categories directly from the source of truth, and *c)* we provide evidence for the complexity of real-world data models and practical applicability.

The remainder of this paper is structured as follows: We first present related work in Sect. 2 before we introduce the Schemalyser approach in Sect. 3. Section 4 evaluates our proposal. Finally, we discuss the integration in development workflows in Sect. 5 and conclude in Sect. 6.

2 Related Work

As far as we are aware, we are the first to propose a process to semi-automatically compile Article 30-related compliance documentation from app data models. Martin and Kung [7] envision a data model-driven process to inventory personal data but do not name any existing approaches. Fakas et al. [4] propose a similar mechanism but to semi-automatically create responses to subject access requests, whereby data entries are identified by a human keyword search. Then, starting from matching instance, the operator iteratively browses neighbouring relations, and selects entities and attributes for the response. In contrast to Schemalyser, they do not consider identifiability classes, relation-defined roles or compiling categories. Furthermore, Schemalyser analyses abstract data models and derives information about instances that can potentially exist.

A similar approach, is used in [6] to generate Record of Processing Activitiess (RPAs) from formal Enterprise Architecture models and derive data recipients based on relations between business processes. However, individual business processes and their categories of PD and subjects are documented through expert interviews and out of scope in terms of composition. Regarding RPA best practices especially concerning the categories of PD and subjects, a recent analysis of RPA templates in [8] did not include categorisation aspects into their semantic model. Bercic and George [2] discuss identifiability in DBs from a legal pre-GDPR view and also conclude that all data that is linkable to a subject within a DB should be considered PD.

3   Schemalyser Approach

Our approach builds on a graph representation of the data model where the vertexes represent the data model entities and the edges represent directed 1:N relations between entities, i. e., foreign key (FK) relations. Since there can be multiple FK relations between the same two entities, the result is a multigraph. We call this graph a *scheme*: A scheme S is defined as a multigraph $S = (E, R)$ with a set of entities E and FK relations $R \subseteq E \times E \times \mathbb{N}$, where $(e_1, e_2, i) \in R$ denotes the i-th FK from entity e_1 to entity e_2. Note that entity attributes are left out for simplicity at this stage. For legibility, we will use the notation $(e_1, e_2) \in R$ to express that there exists an $i \in \mathbb{N}$ such that $(e_1, e_2, i) \in R$.

Based on this graph representation, our approach takes four partially automated steps to derive a condensed listing of PD per subject category, which are described in detail in the following.

3.1   Seed Identification

To determine what data within the scheme is potential PD, we first need to identify one or more *seed* entities: A seed $s \in E$ is an entity in the data model that represents a data subject or a role (e. g., user, reporter) and is modelled as a dedicated entity. A scheme can contain multiple seeds. Correctly and completely identifying all seeds requires domain knowledge about the app data model. However, we find that seeds typically stand out as central entities within the data model (cf. Sect. 4.1). Thus, to speed up their identification, we propose to rank the entities according to their degree centrality.

3.2   Identifiability Markup

Given the seeds as representations of data subjects in the data model, the second step now determines for the remaining entities a notion of identifiability with respect to each seed. In other words: does the data model associate a given entity with one or more of the seeds and if so how.

The naive approach would be to ignore the direction of relations and calculate the reachability graph of each seed s in an undirected scheme. We call this the partition $P_s \subseteq E$, which is defined recursively from base $\{s\}$ as:

$$P_s = \{s\} \cup \{e_2 \in E \mid \exists e_1 \in P_s \colon (e_1, e_2) \in R \vee (e_2, e_1) \in R\}$$

However, this simplistic approach neglects the cardinalities implied by the directionality of the relations, i.e., the direction implies whether an entity is related to exactly one instance of another entity or an arbitrary number of such instances. This distinction determines whether a relation to a seed allows to single out an individual data subject or a potential multitude of data subjects. Following this distinction, we subsequently formalise the direction semantic and introduce classes of identifiability.

Relation Direction Semantics. We distinguish two semantic sub-relations between a pair of entities depending on the direction of the FK relation: *extending* and *providing*:

1. *Extending* $e_1 \rightarrow e_2$ (n-to-1): Each instance of e_1 extends the context of exactly one instance of e_2 and is unambiguously associated with that instance.
2. *Providing* $e_1 \leftarrow e_2$ (1-to-n): An instance of e_1 can provide non-exclusive context to an arbitrary number of instances of e_2.

(a) Dedicated: n instances of entity e are related to a single instance of $e_\mathcal{D} \in \mathcal{D}_s$.   **(b)** Shared 'Original': An instance of e provides context for n instances of $e_\mathcal{D} \in \mathcal{D}_s$.

(c) Shared 'Extended': Entity e further extends or provides to shared entity $e_\mathcal{S} \in \mathcal{S}_s$.   **(d)** Shared 'Merged': Entity e is shared by extending s via multiple $e_{\mathcal{D}1}, e_{\mathcal{D}2}, \dots \in \mathcal{D}_s$.

Fig. 1. Identifiability classes for a seed from the perspective of other entities.

Identifiability Classes. Based on these relation semantics, we identified three class of identifiability of a seed s regarding another entity. The classes are not necessarily exclusive and are recursively defined as subsets of E as follows:

1. *Dedicated*: An entity is dedicated to a seed if it has a direct, extending FK path to the seed (see Fig. 1a):

$$\mathcal{D}_s = \{s\} \cup \{e \in E \mid \exists e_\mathcal{D} \in \mathcal{D}_s : (e, e_\mathcal{D}) \in R\}$$

   Example: A user (seed) has multiple addresses, e.g., invoice and delivery.
2. *Shared*: An entity has one or more indirect paths to the seed by providing for a dedicated entity (*original share*), by extending or providing for another

shared entity (*extended share*), or by extending dedicated entities through two or more distinct FK paths (*merged share*), see also Figs. 1b to 1d:

$$\mathcal{S}_s = \mathcal{S}_s^{Orig} \cup \mathcal{S}_s^{Ext} \cup \mathcal{S}_s^{Merged}$$

$$\mathcal{S}_s^{Orig} = \{e \in E \mid \exists e_\mathcal{D} \in \mathcal{D}_s : (e_\mathcal{D}, e) \in R$$
$$\wedge (e_\mathcal{D} = s \vee \exists e_{\mathcal{D}'} \in \mathcal{D}_s, e_{\mathcal{D}'} \neq e : (e_\mathcal{D}, e_{\mathcal{D}'}) \in R)\}$$

$$\mathcal{S}_s^{Ext} = \{e \in E \mid \exists e_\mathcal{S} \in \mathcal{S}_s : ((e, e_\mathcal{S}) \in R \vee (e_\mathcal{S}, e) \in R)$$
$$\wedge (\exists e_\mathcal{D} \in \mathcal{D}_s, e_\mathcal{D} \neq e : (e_\mathcal{D}, e_\mathcal{S}) \in R$$
$$\vee \exists e_{\mathcal{S}'} \in \mathcal{S}_s, e_{\mathcal{S}'} \neq e : ((e_{\mathcal{S}'}, e_\mathcal{S}) \in R \vee (e_\mathcal{S}, e_{\mathcal{S}'}) \in R))\}$$

$$\mathcal{S}_s^{Merged} = \{e \in E \mid \exists e_{\mathcal{D}1}, e_{\mathcal{D}2} \in \mathcal{D}_s : \{(e, e_{\mathcal{D}1}), (e, e_{\mathcal{D}2})\} \subseteq R\}$$

In $\mathcal{S}_s^{Orig}$ and $\mathcal{S}_s^{Ext}$ constraints are necessary to avoid that a *shared* classification propagates backwards to entities that caused it. In Fig. 1b, for instance, $e_\mathcal{D}$ does not receive the extended shared membership from e, because $e_\mathcal{D}$ is the sole origin of e's shared membership. Also note that the merged share classification is assigned after all entities have been otherwise classified and the dedicated, shared original and shared extended sets are stable. It does not cause further extended shares.

Example: Multiple users are participants in a chat room. Information about the chat room is attributable to all participants without being able to single out one participant.

3. *Unrelated:* There is no relation between the seed and the other entity:

$$\mathcal{U}_s = E \setminus P_s$$

Example: Global configuration of the application.

Based on these three identifiability classes, we can distinguish whether an attribute, according to the entity it belongs to, solely concerns an individual data subject (dedicated), potentially relates to a set of data subjects (shared), or can most likely be excluded from consideration as PD (unrelated).

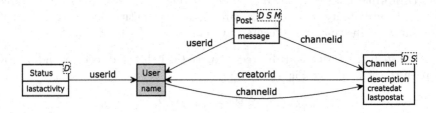

Fig. 2. Simple chat app data model with identifiability classes (D)edicated, (S)hared, and shared (M)erged assigned to each data model entity.

Example. To illustrate the classification, Fig. 2 shows the resulting identifiability classes for a data model of a simple chat app. In this example, the User entity is the seed. The other entities all have at least one dedicated path to User and therefore receive the D label. The relation between User and Channel through channelid is providing, hence Channel receives the original shared label S, which is then carried over as extending shared to Post. And finally, as Post has two dedicated paths, one direct and one via Channel, it receives the merged shared label M which implies S, because each dedicated path might associate a different user to Post that way, all of which then share Post's attributes.

3.3   Role Determination

During this step, a domain expert with knowledge about the data model is guided to determine roles of a user that are reflected in the data model. These roles eventually build the basis for categorising data subjects and grouping PD. We regard a role as a semantic distinction of a user's relation to the system that is characterised by the user engaging with the system in an optional manner. By being optional, it differentiates itself from a general engagement with the system, i.e., the default user role. For instance, a user chooses to report an issue by which they take the role of an issue reporter. In the data model, roles can be modelled in different ways, e.g., by having dedicated role entities or explicit FK attributes for a role. We find that roles are typically defined by the entities and attributes directly surrounding the seed, i.e., the first hops on a path between the seed and other entities. We call those *first-hop relations*. However, not every first-hop relation necessarily constitutes a role, because it might lack a defining characteristic like the optionality of the engagement. This is a semantic distinction that cannot generally be inferred solely based on the scheme. Therefore, during this step of determining roles, a domain expert has to classify, which first-hop relations define a role. For this classification process, we propose the following classes:

- *Integral*: The relation adds data for users in general that is integral and unconditional to the overall system functionality.
- *Role*: The relation describes an optional user engagement with the system that defines their capabilities and perception by the system and other users.
- *Conditional*: The relation provides details related to the usage of an optional feature which, other than a role, does not define their perception because it is less functionally significant or visible.

The distinction between roles and conditionals is gradual. Relations like the uploader of a file attachment to a post could be regarded as both a uploader role or a conditional usage of the feature to attach files to a post. We argue that, in this example, uploader should be considered a conditional because it is less significant and visible than the poster role which coincides with uploading a file. As roles will later form subject categories that should be meaningful to non-experts, they should be defined sparingly.

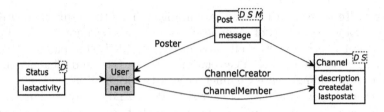

Fig. 3. Minimal chat app data model with three determined roles.

Revisiting the chat app example in Fig. 3, we deemed three out of the four first-hop relations as role-defining. The fourth relation between Status and User is obligatory for each user and thus integral.

3.4 Decisive Role Selection

During this step, a domain expert selects for each attribute of every entity with a dedicated and/or shared classification, which of the previously determined roles are decisive for this attribute. We consider a role as *decisive* for an attribute if the attribute's value is derived from a property or action of a member of that role. Potential candidates for decisive roles are all roles whose defining relation lies on a path from the respective entity to the seed. Note, that as we are only considering simple paths, i.e., paths where each node is at most visited once, there is always only one first-hop relation and thus only one role-defining relation on each path. We call the candidates that are deemed as non-decisive *subjected roles*. Subjected roles might be equally identifiable than the decisive role of an attribute. The distinction rather allows to prioritise and filter attributes as will be shown in the final step. For instance, a channel creator is subjected by messages of posts in their channel but does not decide them. In the following, we describe the substeps of enumerating paths and selecting candidates as well as lower-complexity alternatives for large data models.

Path Enumeration. To determine the candidates for decisive roles for a given seed and entity, we first have to find all paths between that seed and entity. However, we cannot simply list all simple paths between these nodes, because the paths have to account for the relation direction semantics described in Sect. 3.2 and the resulting propagation of identifiability classes. We denote the paths through which entities received their dedicated or shared classification as dedicated and shared paths, respectively.

As the propagation of the dedicated class follows only extending edges that are directed towards the seed, dedicated paths are strictly directed walks in the graph. Hence, dedicated paths are simple paths in a directed scheme graph with inverted directions. Regarding shared paths, we have to consider graph walks with mixed directions. However, as defined in Sect. 3.2, a shared path contains at least one providing relation and allows no back-propagation. Shared paths

Table 1. Enumeration of dedicated and shared paths for the chat app example.

Entity	$\mathcal{D}$ Paths	$\mathcal{S}$ Paths
Status	$\{U \leftarrow S\}$	$\{\}$
Post	$\{U \leftarrow P, U \leftarrow C \leftarrow P\}$	$\{U \rightarrow C \leftarrow P\}$
Channel	$\{U \leftarrow C\}$	$\{U \rightarrow C, U \leftarrow P \rightarrow C\}$

are therefore a subset of paths in an undirected graph. To illustrate this, Table 1 enumerates the dedicated and shared paths of the chat app from Fig. 4. Note that in this example, ignoring the constraints for shared paths would for instance incorrectly add the shared paths $U \leftarrow P$ and $U \leftarrow C \leftarrow P$ for entity Post, which would lead to a enlarged and misleading PD listing for the roles Poster and Channel Creator in the final step.

Candidate Selection. Candidates for a given entity are all roles whose defining relation lies on of the previously enumerated dedicated or shared paths. For large data models, the number of candidates might still be quite high. To speed up the manual selection process by the domain expert, we propose to present the candidates in descending order according to the following selection likelihood heuristic:

1. dedicated-only roles before mixed before shared-only roles, then
2. roles with shortest paths first, then
3. roles with lowest number of paths first.

We argue that dedicated-only roles are more likely decisive than mixed and shared-only roles because an identifiable individual is more likely the originator of an action or actively involved than a set of individuals. Regarding the influence of path length, we argue that shorter paths imply a more direct logical connection. The third ordering rule presumes that a higher number of paths using the same first-hop relation decreases the semantic specificity and is thus more likely to be a modelling artefact than semantically significant.

In completing this step, the domain expert selects one or more decisive roles for each attribute. Figure 4 shows the decisive role selection for the attributes of the chat app example. The Poster role is selected as decisive for the message of a post. The attributes of Channel have each a different decisive role. This selection is modelled after the Mattermost chat app, where the ability to set and change the description of a channel is given to every member of that channel.

Complexity and Path Enumeration Alternative. Listing all paths between the seed and the other entities has a $O(|E|!)$ computational and spacial complexity. For large and highly interconnected data models, it might therefore be practically infeasible to use the path enumeration approach, as we will show in Sect. 4. For those cases, it might be a sufficient compromise to determine candidates by checking for reachability via each role-defining relation instead. To do

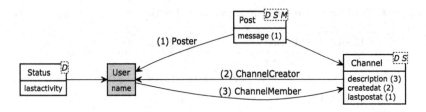

Fig. 4. Minimal chat app data model with decisive roles selected.

so, we check for each role-defining relation which entities are still reachable from the seed if all but this first-hop relation were removed. Given that the complexity of a reachability check between a single pair of entities is $O(|E| + |R|)$, the complexity for checking the reachability of a seed and all other entities via each role-defining relation is therefore $O(r|E|(|E| + |R|))$, where r is the number of role-defining relations. In the worst case of a fully meshed graph where $r = |E|$ and $O(|R|) = O(|E|^2)$ the complexity becomes quadratic. Despite reachability checking being a more efficient alternatives for large inputs, we recommend the path enumeration where possible, because being able to inspect a path can provide valuable context information to the domain expert.

3.5   Condensed PD Listing

For this final step, we propose a condensed per-role listing of PD to maintain readability and focus on those attributes that have a higher significance for a given role. To achieve this condensed listing, we use the dedicated/shared distinction and the decisive role selections to determine if an attribute should be listed as PD for a given role in detail or if it can be aggregated into a *grouping term*. To list PD for a given role, we list an attribute explicitly if the role is decisive for that attribute. If not, the attribute is represented by a grouping term. As a result, we have four sets of PD for each role that decrease in identifiability and significance:

1. *Dedicated decisive*: The attribute is significantly determined by a member of this role and the member can be singled out.
2. *Dedicated non-decisive*: The attribute is associated with an identifiable member of this role without being determined by them.
3. *Shared decisive*: The attribute is significantly determined by a member of this role but *no* member can be singled out.
4. *Shared non-decisive*: The attribute is not determined by this role and *no* member can be singled out.

The grouping terms used in the non-decisive sets can represent a subset of attributes of an entity, an entity as a whole, or multiple semantically related entities. A display name of an entity, i.e., a name dedicated for presentation to users, could for instance be used as an automatically derived term. In cases where such derived grouping terms might be too incomprehensible for the general public, a domain expert should assign fitting grouping terms manually. If the media supports hypertext, grouping terms should be expandable to the individual attributes summarised by them.

To illustrate the condensed listing, we again use the data model and roles from the chat app as shown in Fig. 4. The resulting PD listing is shown in Table 2. Entity names are used as grouping terms.

Table 2. Condensed PD listing for the chat app. Cursive entries are group terms.

Role	1. $\mathcal{D}$ decisive	2. $\mathcal{D}$ non-dec	3. $\mathcal{S}$ decisive	4. $\mathcal{S}$ non-dec
User	status lastactivity	–	–	–
Poster	message lastactivity	–	–	*Channel data*
Channel Creator	createdat	*Channel data Post data*	–	–
Channel Member	–	–	description	*Channel data Post data*

4 Evaluation

In this section, we evaluate the practicality of our proposal in terms of number and difficulty of necessary interaction, the complexity, as well as the degree of condensation achieved in the PD listing. To also gain an insight into costs for real-world apps, we used five common web apps (see Table 4) and analysed their data models. Lacking the necessary domain expertise for the software architecture of all those apps, we were only able to evaluate the manual steps for the Mattermost app, which we have extensively studied before [3].

4.1 Interaction Cost and Complexity

In this section, we assess the number of manual actions and the number of alternatives a domain expert has to choose from during each process step. An overview of the costs and complexities is provided in Table 3.

Seed Identification. This requires one manual step to select all seeds from a list of all entities. However, we find that seeds typically exhibit a high degree centrality and rank in the top two entities with the highest degree centrality in the tested apps, ranging from 41 to 69%. Therefore, the expert does not need to inspect all entities at this point. Calculating the degree centrality over the graph adds a $O(|E|^2)$ complexity. Note that in the following, we will assume that the number of seeds in a data model does not grow with the number of entities. Instead, we argue that the number of seeds depends on modelling styles and is typically in the low single digits. Our evaluation examples support this assumption having each only a single seed.

Table 3. Overview of the cost and complexity of our proposal.

Step	#Actions	#Decisions	Worst Case Complexity
1. Seed Identification	1	$O(1)$	$O(|E|^2)$
2. Identifiability Markup	–	–	$O(|E|^2(|E| + |R|)\deg_{\max})$
3. Role Determination	$O(|E|)$	3	–
4. Decisive Role Sel	$O(|E|)$	$O(|E|)$	$O(|E|!)/O(|E|^4)$
5. PD Listing	$O(|E|)$	1	$O(|E|^2)$

Identifiability Markup. Assigning identifiability classes is a fully automatic process. Our proof-of-concept implementation uses a breadth-first (BFS) approach to propagate the classes through the scheme graph. It repeats until the classes are stable, i.e., until it has gathered for each entity and identifiability class, all neighbouring entities that propagate that label to that entity. Note, that gathering all propagation origins is necessary to avoid back propagation (cf. Sect. 3.2). During a single BFS traversal we process each entity's neighbours, which leads to a complexity of $O((|E| + |R|)\deg_{\max})$ complexity, where $\deg_{\max}$ is the maximum node degree. To reach stability, a theoretical worst case of $|E|^2$ repeats would be necessary if every entity receives its classes from every other entity but with only a single new propagation per iteration. However, this is a very conservative estimation, since an increase in connectivity would also speed up propagation. In practice, reaching stability took 4 to 5 iterations for our test apps. In total, this step has at worst a $O(|E|^2(|E|+|R|)\deg_{\max})$ complexity.

Role Determination. During this step, all first-hop relations of every seed have to be inspected and categorised. In the worst case, if all seeds have disjoint first-hop relations and are fully connected, this takes $n_s|E|$ steps, where n_s is the number of seeds. During each step, one of three classes has to be selected. As an insight into real-world first-hop relation counts, Table 4 lists the degree $\deg(s)$ for each app's seed. We find that, as discussed in the seed identification step before, that seeds are typically highly connected with degrees roughly around half of $|E|$.

Decisive Role Assignment. Regarding interaction cast, the domain expert selects decisive roles for every attribute of every entity in a seed partition. For each attribute, all roles that lie on a path to that entity need to be considered. In the worst case of a fully connected graph, this requires $O(|E|)$ steps and $O(|E|)$ decisions each. Computationally, the selection of decisive role candidates requires either a path enumeration or reachability checks, which, as discussed at the end of Sect. 3.4, result in factorial or quadratic cost, respectively.

The selection of decisive roles can be partly automated if an entity has only a single role candidate. Integral-only cases can be auto-assigned to a generic user role, as can be conditional-only cases with additional info about the condition. Otherwise the domain expert has to manually select from the list of candidates. Table 5 provides the number of single-candidate and integral-only entities as well as the average number of candidates available for the non-automatable entities.

Table 4. Evaluation of automatic steps for sample data models.

Application	Full Scheme			Partition P_s				Ident. Cls.				Paths	
	$|E|$	$|R|$	$D[\%]$	$|P_s|$	$|R_s|$	$D[\%]$	$\deg(s)$	$|\mathcal{D}|$	$|\mathcal{S}|$	$|\mathcal{D} \cap \mathcal{S}|$	Ded.	Shared
Bugzilla 5.0	76	102	1.7895	61	100	2.7322	35	46	47	32	175	105908
Gitlab 12.7.5 CE	308	671	0.7096	289	669	0.8038	128	269	282	262	2997	>1M
Mattermost 5.18	40	54	3.4615	32	54	5.4435	27	28	23	19	41	1439
Taiga 5.5.7	68	116	2.5461	61	114	3.1148	29	54	56	49	238	103943
Zulip 3.2	77	116	1.9822	66	116	2.7040	46	45	54	33	54	226690

Table 5. Decisive role selection cost indicators for two practical examples.

Application	$|P_s|$	$|R_s|$	$\deg(s)$	Roles	Integral	Single Cand.	Avg. Cand.
Chat App Example	4	5	4	3	1	0	3
Mattermost	32	54	27	13	10	5	9

PD Listing. If grouping terms cannot be automatically derived from already available display names or descriptions, an expert has to manually assign $|E|$ terms if entities are not aggregated. Besides the grouping term assignment, the list construction is automatic. The construction inspects every entity and adds their attributes or grouping terms to the four sets of every role. With a worst case of $|E|$ roles this leads to a $O(|E|^2)$ complexity.

4.2 Degree of Condensation

The degree of condensation depends of cause on the composition of the data model. Our approach condenses attributes for which a role is not decisive. Consequently, the degree of condensation is inversely proportionate to the ratio of decisive roles to role candidates. Hence, if every role is decisive for every connected attribute, the condensation would be minimal. Applying this worst case to the chat example from Table 2, the attributes of Channel and Post would be listed for each of the three roles resulting into 14 attributes and zero grouping terms instead of the original 6 and 5. The condensation by the grouping terms depends on their defined scope, in this example an entity. Larger grouping scopes naturally result into fewer grouping terms per subject category.

5 Integration into Development Workflows

We argue that the best way to keep PD compliance documentation up-to-date and in sync with the app as its source of truth is to integrate Schemalyser into the development workflow. Thereby, vendors could offer PD listings like in Table 2 in a machine readable form as templates for customers' compliance documentation. In the following, we describe, how, by using code annotations, necessary domain knowledge could be added to further increase automation, and how Schemalyser can be used to monitoring changes to the data model.

Annotation. Our approach relies on expert knowledge about the app architecture, mainly to determine and select decisive roles. Ideally, this information is noted by experts in a machine-readable way, e. g., in the form of code annotations, such that tools like ours can utilise it. Listing 1.1 shows how such an annotation might look like for the Channel class of the running example in Python. The `roledef` annotation defines a (FK) attribute as a new role. The `role` annotation assigns such a defined role as decisive role for the given attribute.

Listing 1.1. Exemplary code annotion for roles and assigned decisive roles.

```
class Channel:
    creator_id: int      # roledef: ChannelCreator, default
    created_at: int
    description: str      # role: ChannelMember
    lastpost_at: int      # role: Poster
```

Compliance Monitoring. As a way to review or monitor compliance during development, Schemalyser could be integrated into testing: While tests are setting up a DB, a scheme could be dumped, pushed to the Schemalyser service, where it is compared to dumps of previous test runs and changes are flagged for review to ensure that additions of PD or identifying relations are intentional and compliant. Such change detection reapplies previous classifications to the new scheme whereupon new first-hop relations or role candidates trigger a review.

6 Conclusion

We have proposed a novel semi-automatic process to compile PD and subject categories, and condensed PD listings on the basis of app data models and entity relations. By analysing real-world app data models, we have pointed out the need for this condensed listing of PD to counter the effects of ubiquitous identifiability in data models, where over 80% of entities are attributable to data subjects. We argue that correctly assigning PD to subject categories requires a degree of architectural knowledge that is likely exclusive to the software vendor. We encourage vendors to add annotations about subject roles to their source code and follow our decisive role approach to make their knowledge accessible to customers in a machine readable way and allow a further automation of compiling comprehensive and up-to-date compliance documentation.

Acknowledgements. The work is supported by the German Federal Ministry of Education and Research (BMBF) as part of the project Employee Privacy in Development and Operations (EMPRI-DEVOPS) under grant 16KIS0922K.

References

1. Andersson, M.: Extracting an entity relationship schema from a relational database through reverse engineering. In: Loucopoulos, P. (ed.) ER 1994. LNCS, vol. 881, pp. 403–419. Springer, Heidelberg (1994). https://doi.org/10.1007/3-540-58786-1_93
2. Bercic, B., George, C.: Identifying personal data using relational database design principles. Int. J. Law Inf. Technol. **17**(3), 233–251 (2009)
3. Burkert, C., Federrath, H.: Towards minimising timestamp usage in application software. In: Pérez-Solà, C., Navarro-Arribas, G., Biryukov, A., Garcia-Alfaro, J. (eds.) DPM/CBT -2019. LNCS, vol. 11737, pp. 138–155. Springer, Cham (2019). https://doi.org/10.1007/978-3-030-31500-9_9
4. Fakas, G.J., Cawley, B., Cai, Z.: Automated generation of personal data reports from relational databases. J. Info. Know. Mgmt. **10**(02), 193–208 (2011)
5. Greiner, S., Buchmann, T., Westfechtel, B.: Bidirectional transformations with QVT-R: a case study in round-trip engineering UML class models and java source code. In: Hammoudi, S. (ed.) MODELSWARD 2016 - Proceedings of the 4th International Conference on Model-Driven Engineering and Software Development, Rome, Italy, 19–21 February 2016, pp. 15–27. SciTePress (2016)
6. Huth, D., Tanakol, A., Matthes, F.: Using enterprise architecture models for creating the record of processing activities (Art. 30 GDPR). In: 2019 IEEE 23rd International Enterprise Distributed Object Computing Conference (EDOC), pp. 98–104. IEEE, Paris (2019)
7. Martin, Y.-S., Kung, A.: Methods and tools for gdpr compliance through privacy and data protection engineering. In: 2018 IEEE European Symposium on Security and Privacy Workshops (EuroS&PW), pp. 108–111. IEEE, London (2018)
8. Ryan, P., Pandit, H.J., Brennan, R.: A common semantic model of the GDPR register of processing activities. In: Serena, V., Harasta, J., Kremen, P. (eds.) Legal Knowledge and Information Systems - JURIX 2020: The Thirty-Third Annual Conference, Brno, Czech Republic, 9–11 December 2020. Frontiers in Artificial Intelligence and Applications, pp. 251–254. IOS Press (2020)

Privacy Concerns Go Hand in Hand with Lack of Knowledge: The Case of the German Corona-Warn-App

Sebastian Pape[1(✉)] [iD], David Harborth[1] [iD], and Jacob Leon Kröger[2] [iD]

[1] Chair of Mobile Business and Multilateral Security, Goethe University,
Frankfurt, Germany
{sebastian.pape,david.harborth}@m-chair.de
[2] Weizenbaum Institute, TU Berlin, Berlin, Germany
kroeger@tu-berlin.de

Abstract. The German Corona-Warn-App (CWA) is one of the most controversial tools to mitigate the Corona virus spread with roughly 25 million users. In this study, we investigate individuals' knowledge about the CWA and associated privacy concerns alongside different demographic factors. For that purpose, we conducted a study with 1752 participants in Germany to investigate knowledge and privacy concerns of users and non-users of the German CWA. We investigate the relationship between knowledge and privacy concerns and analyze the demographic effects on both.

Our results indicate that knowledge about the CWA significantly reduces the privacy concerns about it. Non surprisingly, users have far lower privacy concerns than non-users, but they also have more knowledge about the app. We also find a positive significant effect of education and income and a small negative effect of age on the participants' knowledge. Furthermore, we find a significant negative effect of income and education on the privacy concerns. Our study has important implications for political decision-makers aiming at increasing adoption rates for helpful technologies to mitigate the severe effects of the pandemic. Most relevant here is to acknowledge the results regarding education, knowledge, privacy concerns and CWA use and devise effective strategies to reach certain groups in the society which are currently not using the CWA.

Keywords: Corona-Warn-App · Privacy concerns · Privacy literacy · Privacy awareness · Knowledge

1 Introduction

With the global pandemic caused by the severe acute respiratory syndrome coronavirus 2 (SARS-CoV-2), digital proximity tracing systems to identify people who have been in contact with an infected person became a hot topic. There have been many discussions on different implementations and their architecture [7], i.e. if the approach is centralised or decentralised. This discussion on the architecture and possible effects of it was mostly among experts and the academic

© IFIP International Federation for Information Processing 2021
Published by Springer Nature Switzerland AG 2021
A. Jøsang et al. (Eds.): SEC 2021, IFIP AICT 625, pp. 256–269, 2021.
https://doi.org/10.1007/978-3-030-78120-0_17

world has already done extensive investigations of users' privacy concerns (cf. Sect. 2). However, the role of users' actual knowledge about the app has hardly been studied. For that purpose, we investigate user knowledge and privacy concerns about the Corona-Warn-App (CWA), the digital proximity tracing app in Germany, based on an online survey with 1752 participants.

While the effect of privacy literacy on privacy concerns is not obvious in general [13], this case should be different. In contrast to systems like the one in China, the CWA was build with privacy in mind: It is based on the DP-3T protocol which ensures data minimisation, prevents abuse of data and the tracking of users [6]. Thus, we hypothesize:

H: *Knowledge about the Corona-Warn-App reduces privacy concerns.*

Beyond investigating the relation between knowledge and privacy concerns, we are also interested in demographic effects on both of them, i.e. CWA users and non-users, age, gender, income, education and experience with smartphones.

Section 2 lists related work, Sect. 3 describes the methodology and Sect. 4 the results of our survey. We discuss the results in Sect. 5 and conclude in Sect. 6.

2   Related Work

Various large surveys have been conducted to explore individuals' privacy concerns about contact tracing apps during the COVID-19 pandemic – for example, in the US [1,15,18,20,21,26,27,33], in the UK [1,2,17,19], in Ireland [23], in Australia [30], in France [1], in Germany [1,3,18], in Italy [1], in Switzerland [3], and in China [18], including cross-national surveys [1,3,18]. A review of 11 recent studies is provided in [22]. One of the few qualitative studies on the topic employs focus group design with 22 participants from the UK [32].

While the majority of participants typically supports tracking technologies for the purpose of containing the pandemic [1,19,22], previous studies show that privacy concerns (besides technical problems, general mistrust of technology and lack of perceived personal benefit) remain a major hurdle to user acceptance – many studies even identify privacy concerns as *the* main barrier to the widespread use of contact tracing apps [2,3,23,26,30,32]. Simko et al. [27] conducted a longitudinal study over seven months and found that privacy perceptions towards such apps remain relatively stable over time.

Specifically, people were found to worry about corporate surveillance [23], government surveillance [1,18,22,23], identification through mobility patterns [3], leakage of data to third parties or hackers [1,22,27,32], centralised data storage [33], exposure of social interactions [3], secondary data use [3,20,27], the risk of discrimination [22,32], and continuing surveillance after the pandemic [23]. However, survey results have revealed widespread knowledge gaps and misconceptions surrounding the data collected by contract tracing apps [27,32].

To increase the acceptance of co-location tracking, previous studies recommend a clear reasoning about the trustworthiness of the respective service provider [19], assurances of data protection [15, 19, 23], sunset clauses (i.e., statements that data storage is time-limited) [19], and – where relevant – transparency about data sharing and usage [26, 27]. Privacy concerns can further be alleviated by users' trust in certain publicly-funded institutions, such as the British National Health Service (NHS) [17].

3   Methodology

In this section, we briefly cover the development of the questionnaire, the data collection and the demographics of our sample.

3.1   Questionnaire

We adapted the construct for privacy concerns (PC) from Gu et al. [10] and applied it to the Corona-Warn-App. We calculated polychloric correlation between the five items of the construct and used this matrix to conduct the factor analysis. Polychloric correlations are usually used for categorial variables (as for PC which are measured on a seven-point Likert scale) [16]. The loadings are well above 0.8 with an explained variance of 87.4% and a Cronbachs Alpha of 0.96. This indicates that the five items represent privacy concerns about the CWA adequately.

To measure the knowledge of the participants about the CWA, we developed questions based on material provided by the official CWA FAQ [5], the Federal Government in Germany [4] and the Robert Koch Institute [24]. The questions covered how location data are processed, the functionality of the app, the voluntariness of installation and how a positive COVID-19 test result would be registered. The full questionnaire is listed in the appendix.

3.2   Data Collection and Demographics

We conducted the study with a certified panel provider in Germany (certified following the ISO 20252 norm). The survey was programmed with the survey software LimeSurvey (version 2.72.6) [25] and hosted on a university server. We sampled the participants in a way to achieve a representative sample for Germany. For that purpose, we set quotas to end up with approximately 50% females and 50% males in the sample as well as a distribution of age following the EUROSTAT2018 census [8]. Furthermore, we set a quota to end up with half of the sample using the CWA and the other half not using it.

Our resulting sample consists of 1752 participants. Following EUROSTAT 2018, participants are representative for Germany with respect to age and gender. The same diversity can be observed for income and education (see Table 1). 896 participants use the CWA (51.14%) and 856 do not (48.86%). 1299 use Android (74.14%), 436 use iOS (24.89%) and 17 stated to use smartphones with another mobile operating system (0.97%) such as Windows 10 Mobile.

Since we deliberately divided the sample into two approximately equal groups (CWA users and non-users), we need to check for statistically significant

Table 1. Participants' characteristics for age, gender, income and education

Demographics	N	%	Demographics	N	%
Age			**Gender**		
18-29 years	371	21.17%	Female	894	51.03%
30-39 years	316	18.04%	Males	853	48.69%
40-49 years	329	18.78%	Diverse	4	0.23%
50-59 years	431	24.60%	Prefer not to say	1	0.06%
60 years and older	305	17.41%			
Net income			**Education**		
500€- 1000€	160	9.13%	1 No degree	8	0.46%
1000€- 2000€	402	22.95%	2 Secondary school	187	10.67%
2000€- 3000€	404	23.06%	3 Secondary school$^+$	574	32.76%
3000€- 4000€	314	17.92%	4 A levels	430	24.54%
More than 4000€	292	16.67%	5 Bachelor's degree	240	13.70%
Prefer not to say	180	10.27%	6 Master's degree	285	16.27%
			7 Doctorate	28	1.60%

$^+$5 GCSEs at grade C and above

differences in the demographics between the groups. This is required in order to rule out confounding influences of these variables on our results. We conducted a Shapiro-Wilk test for normality for all variables and the variables are all not normally distributed. Thus, we conducted Wilcoxon rank-sum tests to analyse whether there are significant differences between CWA users and non-users for these variables. Age and gender show no statistically significant differences since we deliberately sampled our participants with equal distributions with respect to age and gender. There are statistically significant differences between users and non-users of the CWA for the remaining demographics. The income is statistically significantly higher for the users compared to the non-users. However, the median is the same which is why we argue that the absolute difference is not having a sub-stantial confounding effect on our later analysis. The same argumentation holds for education with a median of 4 for users and 3.5 for non-users, smartphone experi-ence in years with a mean 8.77 for users and 8.35 for non-users as well as experience in years with the respective smartphone operating systems (mean 7.85 for users and 7.46 for non-users). The used smartphone operating systems by participants in both groups is roughly similar with significantly more Android users in both groups (about three times more Android users compared to iOS). This distribu-tion of operating systems is representative for Germany [28]. Thus, all differences between groups are – although statistically significant – negligible for our conse-quent analysis since the absolute differences are relatively small.

4   Results

We focus on the investigation of participants' knowledge about the CWA and their privacy concerns. Figure 1a shows the number of correct answers for each

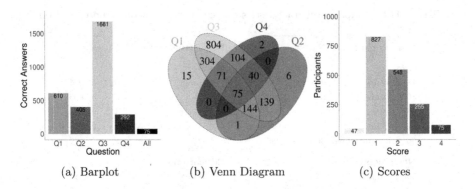

(a) Barplot   (b) Venn Diagram   (c) Scores

Fig. 1. Distribution of correct answers to the knowledge questions

question. Almost all participants were aware that the installation of the app is voluntary (Q3). Only 75 participants were able to answer all four questions correctly. The distribution of correct answers is shown by the Venn diagram in Fig. 1b. It also shows that only 804 participants were able to answer Q3 correctly. For our further analysis, we build a score for each participant by simply counting the correct number of answers (cf. Fig. 1c).

4.1 Analysis of Knowledge and Its Relation to Demographics

We investigate the different demographics based on their group properties: i) Binary groups: users and non-users of the CWA, females and males (GDR), and Android and iOS users (OS) ii) Categorical groups: age, income and education iii) Experience: years of experience with smartphones or the mobile operating system are more like continuous variables than categories, although the self-reporting of users required us to gather them in a discrete manner as number of years.

Binary Groups. We first tested the distributions of scores and the scores of the respective subgroups with Shapiro-Wilk [9, p. 182 ff.] tests for normal distribution. Neither of the (sub)sets is normally distributed ($p < 10^{-15}$). We tested the distributions of scores for homogeneity of variance with Levene's test [9, p. 186 ff.] which shows significant different variances for CWA users and non-users and different genders while there is no significant difference in the variance of different mobile operation system (MOS) users. Table 2 lists the different means for the relevant subgroups. With a Wilcoxon Rank Sum test [9, p. 660 ff.] we found that scores from CWA users and non-users differ significantly (cf. Fig. 2a). The effect sizes (r) for different genders and different MOS users were weaker and less significant.

In summary, we consider the differences in the scores of CWA users and non-users as relevant while the differences in the scores of females and males as well as Android and iOS users are existing but negligible.

Table 2. Score for binary groups, Levene's test and Wilcoxon Rank Sum

Variable	Means				Levene's test	Wilcoxon Rank Sum	
CWA	non-users:	1.38	users:	2.02	$F(1,1750) = 33.45^{***}$	$W = 234994^{***}$	$r = -0.36$
GDR	females:	1.66	males:	1.70	$F(1,1745) = 6.86^{**}$	$W = 365109^{+}$	$r = -0.04$
OS	Android:	1.68	iOS:	1.80	$F(1,1733) = 2.69$	$W = 263020^{*}$	$r = -0.06$

Significance codes: *** < 0.001 ** < 0.01 * < 0.05 $^{+}$ < 0.1

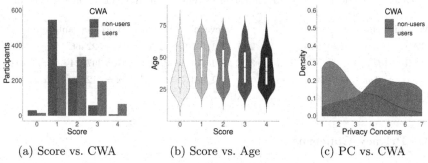

(a) Score vs. CWA   (b) Score vs. Age   (c) PC vs. CWA

Fig. 2. Distribution of scores and privacy concerns

Categorical Groups. For age, education and income, we used Jonckheere Terpstra (JT) tests [9, p. 684 f.] to identify a trend between the different (ordered) groups. Table 3 lists the means of the different groups. With increasing age, the score decreases which was confirmed with very high significance (cf. Fig. 2b). For income, we omitted the group of participants who did not reveal their income (180 part., mean 1.594). For the remaining groups, we see the lowest income group as an outlier and starting from the second lowest group, we see a rise of the score with increasing income. The JT test still reveals a significant rise of score with raising income, which gets highly significant if the lowest income groups is also excluded ($p < 10^{-6}$). As one can expect from the means regarding different groups of education, with higher education, the score increases significantly. Unfortunately, the JT test does not allow the calculation of effect sizes.

In summary, we find that the score depends on all three demographics, although we had an outlier for low incomes.

Experience. Since the years of experience with smartphones or the mobile operation system were not really a categorical variable, we used Spearman's rank correlations [9, p.223 ff.], but could not find a significant relation between score and years of experience with smartphones ($\rho = 0.03$, p-value < 0.19) or the mobile operating system ($\rho = -0.01$, p-value < 0.64). Additionally to the low significance, the correlation coefficient (ρ) is in both relations very close to zero which suggests no significant effect.

Table 3. Score for categorical groups and Jonckheere Terpstra test (JT)

Variable	Means	JT
Age	*18–29:* 1.797 *30–39:* 1.743 *40–49:* 1.739 *50–59:* 1.694 *60–99:* 1.534	572754 ↓***
Income	*.5k-1k:* 1.781 *1k-2k:* 1.614 *2k-3k:* 1.688 *3k-4k:* 1.748 *>4k:* 1.836	465749 ↑*
Educat	*1:* 1.13 *2:* 1.35 *3:* 1.57 *4:* 1.85 *5:* 1.83 *6:* 1.88 *7:* 1.96	682572 ↑***

Significance codes: *** < 0.001 ** < 0.01 * < 0.05 + < 0.1

Table 4. Concerns for binary groups, Levene's test and Wilcoxon Rank Sum

Variable	Means				Levene's test	Wilcoxon rank sum	
CWA	*non-users:*	4.64	*users:*	2.57	$F(1,1750) = 11.5$***	$W = 622466$***	$r = -0.54$
GDR	*females:*	3.64	*males:*	3.52	$F(1,1745) = 3.82$+	$W = 397724$	$r = -0.04$
OS	*Android:*	3.66	*iOS:*	3.31	$F(1,1733) = 1.28$	$W = 312620$**	$r = -0.08$

Significance codes: *** < 0.001 ** < 0.01 * < 0.05 + < 0.1

4.2 Privacy Concerns

In this subsection, we use the same structure for investigating differences between different groups for privacy concerns than in the section before.

Binary Groups. Again, we first tested the distributions of privacy concerns and the privacy concerns of the respective subgroups with Shapiro-Wilk tests for normal distribution. Neither of the (sub)sets is normally distributed ($p < 10^{-15}$). We tested the distributions for homogeneity of variance with Levene's test which shows significant different variances for the privacy concerns of CWA users and non-users but no significant differences in the variances for the privacy concerns of different genders or different mobile operation system (MOS) users. Table 4 lists the different means for the relevant subgroups. With a Wilcoxon Rank Sum test we find that privacy concerns from CWA users and non-users differ significantly (cf. Fig. 2c). The effect sizes (r) for different genders and different MOS users are weaker and less significant.

In summary, we consider the differences in the scores of CWA users and non-users as relevant while the differences in the scores of females and males as well as Android and iOS users are existing but negligible.

Categorical Groups. We used Jonckheere Terpstra (JT) tests to identify a trend between privacy concerns and age, education and income. Table 3 lists the means of the different groups. When looking at the means of age, there is no clear trend visible and the JT test does only find a low significance of the trend. For increasing income and education, the means are decreasing. The JT test confirms this trend with very high significance. For income, we again omitted the group of participants who did not want to reveal their income (180 participants, mean 3.976). Their mean is higher than those of all other groups which suits the idea that they did not want to reveal their income.

Table 5. Concerns for categorical groups and Jonckheere Terpstra Test (JT)Concerns for categorical groups and Jonckheere Terpstra Test (JT)

Variable	Means							JT
Age	*18–29:* 3.583	*30–39:* 3.730	*40–49:* 3.551	*50–59:* 3.619	*60–99:* 3.392			594366 ↓$^{+}$
Income	*.5k-1k:* 3.478	*1k-2k:* 3.772	*2k-3k:* 3.710	*3k-4k:* 3.487	*>4k:* 3.046			523662 ↓***
Educat	*1:* 4.60	*2:* 4.06	*3:* 3.82	*4:* 3.43	*5:* 3.42	*6:* 3.21	*7:* 2.68	520337 ↓***

Significance codes: *** < 0.001 ** < 0.01 * < 0.05 $^{+}$ < 0.1

In summary, we find that privacy concerns are related to income and education but hardly related to the different age groups (Table 5).

Experience. Similarly to the previous section, we used Spearman's rank correlations, but could not find a significant relation between privacy concerns and years of experience with smartphones ($\rho = -0.01$, p-value < 0.54) or the mobile operating system ($\rho = 0.02$, p-value < 0.49). Additionally to the low significance, the correlation coefficient (ρ) is in both relations very close to zero.

4.3 Relationship of Knowledge and Concerns

We tested for the correlation between knowledge (score) and concerns with Spearman's rank correlation rho and found a fairly large correlation coefficient ($\rho = -0.485$) with high significance ($p < 10^{-15}$). The correlation coefficient implies that participants with higher score, i.e. 3 and 4, had significantly less privacy concerns than the participants with lower scores as depicted in Fig. 3a.

We also investigated the relationship between score and privacy concerns for CWA non-users (cf. Fig. 3b) and users (cf. Fig. 3c) separately. As already discussed in the previous subsection, privacy concerns are significantly lower for CWA users compared with non-users. However, Fig. 3 also shows that the relation seems to be stronger for CWA users. We confirmed this finding with Spearman's rank correlation rho, calculated for both of the two subgroups. The correlation coefficient ρ for CWA non-users ($\rho = -0.279$) is smaller than those for users ($\rho = -0.422$), both coefficients derived with high significance ($p < 10^{-15}$).

In summary, a higher knowledge (score in the quiz) correlates fairly well with less concerns regarding the use of the CWA, but the observed effect is stronger for users than for non-users.

5 Discussion

While many previous studies in this field do not consider the influence of participant demographics (e.g., [2,21,23,26,29,30]), our analysis reveals various significant relationships between CWA-related knowledge, privacy concerns and demographic attributes, such as gender, age and income. In this section, we will discuss our findings regarding user knowledge, user concerns, and the relationship between knowledge, concerns and CWA usage, followed by a reflection upon this study's limitations.

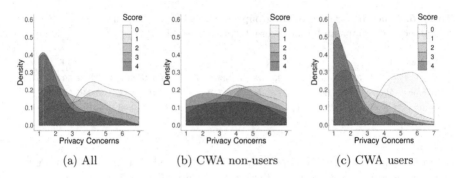

(a) All   (b) CWA non-users   (c) CWA users

Fig. 3. Density of concerns for different scores

5.1 Knowledge

We found CWA-related knowledge to be positively associated with participant income and level of education, and negatively associated with age. The outlier for low incomes could be explained by a prevalence of students within this group. No meaningful relation was found between knowledge and gender, MOS, and smartphone experience. These are novel findings as the related studies referenced in Sect. 2 did not examine such relationships between CWA-related knowledge and individual demographic characteristics. Looking at the broader literature on user knowledge and awareness, it should be noted that findings from existing research are often inconclusive about the demographic determinants of digital fluency [31]. As user knowledge plays an important role in CWA acceptance (cf. Sect. 5.3), further research into the influence of underlying socio-demographic factors is needed.

5.2 Concerns

Our results suggest that user privacy concerns are inversely associated with income and education. No meaningful relation was found for MOS, gender, age, and smartphone experience. While there are related studies that support our findings regarding gender [15,17,18,27], income [20,33], MOS [27] and education [18,20,33], we also discovered contradictory findings in the literature for gender [19,20,33] and age [1,2,17]. Zhang et al. [33], for instance, found that female respondents are less supportive of COVID-related surveillance policies, and - in contrast to the lack of correlation in our findings - several studies found that CWA-related privacy concerns are inversely associated with age [1,2,17]. Thus, the overall picture here is also inconclusive, suggesting the need for further research. Judging from previous work, the inconsistencies mentioned above could be caused by differences in response behavior between political camps [19,21] and geographical regions [18,27]. Our results are representative of the population of Germany, a typical WEIRD society (Western, Educated, Industrialized, Rich, Democratic), and cannot not be generalized to other world regions.

5.3 Knowledge vs. Concerns vs. CWA

In our sample, CWA usage was positively associated with user knowledge. Knowledge, in turn, was inversely associated with privacy concerns. These findings are in line with previous studies that identified privacy concerns as a major obstacle to the widespread adoption of contract tracing apps [2,3,23,26,30,32] and with research-based calls for transparency and user education as means of improving acceptance rates [19,26,27].

5.4 Limitations

Our study has the following limitations. First, our results are not generalizable to users of other contact tracing apps in other countries such as South Korea due to the technical architecture of the apps and cultural differences. Second, quantitative studies as ours are based on self-reports of the participants which can be biased due to misunderstandings of questionnaire items or wrong answers. Reasons for wrong answers of participants include, among others, the social desirability bias or a certain mood of the participants during the participation of the survey. Third, the translation of the constructs into German, which were originally developed in English, could be a source of error. This source of error cannot be ruled out when conducting studies in countries with other languages than the one of the original constructs.

6 Conclusion and Future Work

We showed a significant relationship between knowledge about the Corona-Warn-App (CWA) and related privacy concerns. We also found significant effects of education and income on knowledge (positive) and on privacy concerns (negative). Gender, preference for Android or iOS, and experience with smartphones or the mobile operating system did neither have significant effects on the knowledge nor on the privacy concerns.

Non surprisingly, users have far lower privacy concerns than non-users, but they also have more knowledge about the app. It is up to future work to establish the causality: Are CWA users more knowing and have less privacy concerns because they use and know the app? Or do knowing users have less privacy concerns and therefore tend to more likely use the app? In particular, in the context of privacy enhancing technologies, trust in the software or the provider has shown to have a significant impact on the users decision to use a certain technology [11,12,14]. Thus, In future work we also aim to consider the users' perceived benefits of the app and the user's trust into the health system (cf. [17]).

Our results – although assuming no causality – still have important implications for political decision-makers. Media and misinformation can influence people's concerns about the use of the CWA. With the CWA being developed with a high standard of privacy-preserving principles, one would expect to find a clear negative correlation (as we found) between knowledge and privacy concerns about the CWA. Thus, clear information campaigns are needed to avoid confusion among citizens regarding measures such as the CWA. There was a prolonged and polyphonic debate about the CWA prior to introducing it in Germany. This could be one of the reasons for our findings regarding the quiz.

Furthermore, the positive correlation of education and knowledge across users and non-users points towards the importance of educating individuals about technology from a young age on in order to enable them to make informed decisions. The importance of these two implications is strengthened in times of severe societal stress as we experience it now during the COVID-19 pandemic. Thus, it is even more important to conduct research as ours and consider the respective implications in order to create a more resilient society.

Acknowledgements. This work was supported by the Goethe-Corona-Fonds from Goethe University Frankfurt and the European Union's Horizon 2020 research and innovation program under grant agreement830929 (CyberSecurity4Europe).

A   Survey Questionnaire

Demographics
We asked for the following demographics, answer options are listed in brackets:

- Age[y]
- Gender (female, male, divers)[n]
- Education (no degree, secondary school, secondary school (>5 GCSE), A levels, bachelor, master, doctorate)
- Household income (in €: 0.5k-1k, 1k-2k, 2k-3k, 3k-4k, $>$4k)[n]
- Corona-Warn-App user (yes/no)
- mobile OS (Android, iOS, other)
- Experience with Smartphones[y]
- Experience in the mobile OS[y]

[n]prefer not to say option   [y] in years

Privacy Concerns (PC) Related to the Corona-Warn-App
The following items are measured with a seven-point Likert scale, ranging from "strongly disagree" to "strongly agree".

1. I think the Corona-Warn-App over-collects my personal information.
2. I worry that the Corona-Warn-App leaks my personal information to third-parties.
3. I am concerned that the Corona-Warn-App violates my privacy.
4. I am concerned that the Corona-Warn-App misuses my personal information.
5. I think that the Corona-Warn-App collects my location data.

Knowledge About the Corona-Warn-App
Please mark the correct statements (multiple answers possible).

1. The Corona-Warn-App ...
- collects location data and shares it with local health departments.
+ does not collect location data.
- collects location data and shares it with the Robert Koch Institute.

- collects location data and shares it with the Corona-Warn-App operators.
2. The Corona-Warn-App ...
+ records risk encounters in"public spaces.
- is a substitute for the official reporting channels required by the Infection Protection Act.
+ alerts users to encounters with positive-tested persons within the past 14 days.
- warns the user of positive-tested persons in the vicinity.
3. The installation of the Corona-Warn-App ...
+ is voluntary.
- is required by law for all persons who own an appropriate smartphone.
- is required by law for workers who cannot work in a home office.
- is required by law for persons with regular contact with more than 10 people.
4. The registration of a positive SARS-CoV-2 test result in the app is ...
+ done by the user via QR code or TeleTAN.
- transmitted automatically by the test laboratory.
- automatically transmitted to the Corona-Warn-App server.
+ only transmitted to the Corona-Warn-App server after the user gave consent.

References

1. Altmann, S., et al.: Acceptability of app-based contact tracing for COVID-19: cross-country survey evidence (2020)
2. Bachtiger, P., Adamson, A., Quint, J.K., Peters, N.S.: Belief of having had unconfirmed COVID-19 infection reduces willingness to participate in app-based contact tracing. NPJ Digit. Med. **3**(1), 1–7 (2020)
3. Bonner, M., Naous, D., Legner, C., Wagner, J.: The (lacking) user adoption of COVID-19 contact tracing apps-insights from Switzerland and Germany. In: Proceedings of the 15th Pre-ICIS Workshop on Information Security and Privacy, vol. 1 (2020)
4. Bundesregierung: Corona-warn-app: Frequently asked questions (2021). https://www.bundesregierung.de/breg-de/themen/corona-warn-app/corona-warn-app-englisch/corona-warn-app-faq-1758636. Accessed 10 Feb 2021
5. Corona-Warn-App Open Source Project: Frequently asked questions about the corona-warn-app (2021). https://www.coronawarn.app/en/faq/. Accessed 10 Feb 2021
6. DP-3T Project: Decentralized privacy-preserving proximity tracing (2020). https://github.com/DP-3T/documents/blob/master/DP3T%20White%20Paper.pdf. Accessed 10 Feb 2021
7. DP-3T Project: Privacy and security risk evaluation of digital proximity tracing systems (2020). https://github.com/DP-3T/documents/blob/master/Security%20analysis/Privacy%20and%20Security%20Attacks%20on%20Digital%20Proximity%20Tracing%20Systems.pdf. Accessed 10 Feb 2021
8. EUROSTAT: EUROSTAT 2018 (2021). https://ec.europa.eu/eurostat/de/home. Accessed 10 Feb 2021
9. Field, A., Miles, J., Field, Z.: Discovering Statistics Using R. Sage Publications, Thousand Oaks (2012)

10. Gu, J., Xu, Y.C., Xu, H., Zhang, C., Ling, H.: Privacy concerns for mobile app download: an elaboration likelihood model perspective. Decis. Support Syst. **94**, 19–28 (2017)
11. Harborth, D., Pape, S.: Examining technology use factors of privacy-enhancing technologies: the role of perceived anonymity and trust. In: 24th Americas Conference on Information Systems, AMCIS 2018, New Orleans, LA, USA, 16–18 August 2018. Association for Information Systems (2018)
12. Harborth, D., Pape, S.: How privacy concerns and trust and risk beliefs influence users' intentions to use privacy-enhancing technologies - the case of tor. In: 52nd Hawaii International Conference on System Sciences (HICSS) 2019, pp. 4851–4860 (2019)
13. Harborth, D., Pape, S.: How privacy concerns, trust and risk beliefs and privacy literacy influence users' intentions to use privacy-enhancing technologies - the case of tor. ACM SIGMIS Database: DATABASE Adv. Inf. Syst. **51**(1), 51–69 (2020)
14. Harborth, D., Pape, S., Rannenberg, K.: Explaining the technology use behavior of privacy-enhancing technologies: the case of tor and jondonym. Proc. Privacy Enhancing Technol. (PoPETs) **2020**(2), 111–128 (2020)
15. Hassandoust, F., Akhlaghpour, S., Johnston, A.C.: Individuals' privacy concerns and adoption of contact tracing mobile applications in a pandemic: a situational privacy calculus perspective. J. Am. Med. Inform. Assoc. **28**(3), 463–471 (2020)
16. Holgado-Tello, F.P., Chacón-Moscoso, S., Barbero-García, I., Vila-Abad, E.: Polychoric versus Pearson correlations in exploratory and confirmatory factor analysis of ordinal variables. Qual. Quant. **44**(1), 153–166 (2010)
17. Horvath, L., Banducci, S., James, O.: Citizens' attitudes to contact tracing apps. J. Exp. Political Sci. 1–13 (2020)
18. Kostka, G., Habich-Sobiegalla, S.: In times of crisis: public perceptions towards COVID-19 contact tracing apps in China, Germany and the US. Technical report, Social Science Research Network, Rochester, NY (2020)
19. Lewandowsky, S., et al.: Public acceptance of privacy-encroaching policies to address the COVID-19 pandemic in the united kingdom. PLoS ONE **16**(1), e0245740 (2021)
20. Li, T., et al.: What makes people install a COVID-19 contact-tracing app? Understanding the influence of app design and individual difference on contact-tracing app adoption intention. arXiv preprint arXiv:2012.12415 (2020)
21. Li, T., Faklaris, C., King, J., Agarwal, Y., Dabbish, L., Hong, J.I., et al.: Decentralized is not risk-free: understanding public perceptions of privacy-utility trade-offs in COVID-19 contact-tracing apps. arXiv preprint arXiv:2005.11957 (2020)
22. Megnin-Viggars, O., Carter, P., Melendez-Torres, G., Weston, D., Rubin, G.J.: Facilitators and barriers to engagement with contact tracing during infectious disease outbreaks: a rapid review of the evidence. PLoS ONE **15**(10), e0241473 (2020)
23. O'Callaghan, M.E., et al.: A national survey of attitudes to COVID-19 digital contact tracing in the Republic of Ireland. Irish J. Med. Sci. 1–25 (2020)
24. Robert Koch Institut: Infektionsketten digital unterbrechen mit der corona-warn-app (2021). https://www.rki.de/DE/Content/InfAZ/N/Neuartiges_Coronavirus/WarnApp/Warn_App.html, only in German. Accessed 10 Feb 2021
25. Schmitz, C.: LimeSurvey Project Team (2015). http://www.limesurvey.org. Accessed 10 Feb 2021
26. Sharma, T., Bashir, M., et al.: Eight months into the COVID-19 pandemic - do users expect less privacy? University of Illinois preprint (2020). http://hdl.handle.net/2142/109113. Accessed 10 Feb 2021

27. Simko, L., Chang, J.L., Jiang, M., Calo, R., Roesner, F., Kohno, T.: COVID-19 contact tracing and privacy: a longitudinal study of public opinion. arXiv preprint arXiv:2012.01553 (2020)
28. Statista: Marktanteile der führenden mobilen Betriebssysteme an der Internetnutzung mit Mobiltelefonen in Deutschland von Januar 2009 bis September 2020 (2020). https://de.statista.com/statistik/daten/studie/184332/umfrage/marktanteil-der-mobilen-betriebssysteme-in-deutschland-seit-2009/. Accessed 10 Feb 2021
29. Sun, R., Wang, W., Xue, M., Tyson, G., Camtepe, S., Ranasinghe, D.: An empirical assessment of global COVID-19 contact tracing applications. arXiv preprint arXiv:2006.10933 (2020)
30. Thomas, R., Michaleff, Z., Greenwood, H., Abukmail, E., Glasziou, P.: More than privacy: Australians' concerns and misconceptions about the covidsafe app: a short report. medRxiv (2020)
31. Wang, Q.E., Myers, M.D., Sundaram, D.: Digital natives and digital immigrants. Bus. Inf. Syst. Eng. 5(6), 409–419 (2013)
32. Williams, S.N., Armitage, C.J., Tampe, T., Dienes, K.: Public attitudes towards COVID-19 contact tracing apps: a UK-based focus group study. Health Expect. 24(2), 377–385 (2020)
33. Zhang, B., Kreps, S., McMurry, N., McCain, R.M.: Americans' perceptions of privacy and surveillance in the COVID-19 pandemic. PLoS ONE 15(12), e0242652 (2020)

Perceived Privacy Problems Within Digital Contact Tracing: A Study Among Swedish Citizens

Ali Padyab[ID] and Joakim Kävrestad[(✉)][ID]

University of Skövde, Skövde, Sweden
{ali.padyab,joakim.kavrestad}@his.se

Abstract. Several governments employed digital contact tracing using smartphone apps to combat the COVID-19 pandemic in 2020. Research shows that privacy concerns hinder the adoption of such apps, while privacy problems which emerged by using them are empirically unknown. This study aims to uncover the dimensions of privacy problems available in digital contact tracing through a survey from 453 citizens in Sweden. Our results show that respondents found privacy problems regarding surveillance, identification, aggregation, secondary use, disclosure, and stigma highly relevant in contact tracing apps. Among demographic factors, younger respondents were generally more concerned about privacy risks than older respondents. This study extends previous literature by revealing privacy problems arising from contact tracing apps.

Keywords: Digital contact tracing · Privacy · Surveillance · Identification · Aggregation · Secondary use · Disclosure · Stigma

1 Introduction

Digital contact tracing has been utilized by many governments throughout the globe as a strategy to slow down the quick spread of COVID-19. Several novel software applications (Apps) have been developed in many countries to combat the pandemic. The purpose of contact tracing apps is to use information and communication technologies to automate the process of identifying and notifying contacts of an infected person, and to map the route of disease transmission spread.

Compared to its manual process, digital contact tracing demands less labor and hastens to keep up with the current COVID-19 outbreak [7,11]. Many studies have explored contact tracing apps in the light of their adoption [32], design [3], technical features [29], effectiveness [6], legal [13], facilitators and barriers [19]. However, digitization of the process has raised an important concern about individual's privacy [7]. In a national survey of attitudes to COVID-19 digital contact tracing in the Republic of Ireland, citizens raised concerns regarding privacy and data security [21]. Similar results surfaced in surveys conducted in

Supported by VINNOVA.

the Netherlands, France, Germany, Italy, the United Kingdom, and the United States where citizens mentioned privacy as a strong reason not to use the contact tracing mobile applications [5,15]. Therefore, understanding the nuances of an individual's privacy concerns toward contact tracing apps is a central consideration needed to maintain public trust [7].

To this end, research on privacy aspects of contact tracing apps is limited to the perspectives of researchers and their opinions, whilst empirical studies emanating from citizens' privacy concerns are absent in digital contact tracing. Hence, more research is needed to uncover the dimensions of privacy risks available in digital contact tracing [6,21]. Therefore, the current study aims to address the following research questions: 1) How citizens perceive potential privacy problems related to digital contact tracing? and 2) How do various demographic factors affect perceived privacy problems by the citizens? To investigate the relationship between contact tracing apps and privacy concerns, we conducted a survey with 453 respondents in Sweden. The results showed that there is a meaningful relationship between perceived privacy problems and use of contact tracing apps. Moreover, the results will have implications to the development of effective privacy-protective mechanisms and policies that stem from citizen's privacy concerns.

The rest of this article is structured as follows: we first review the privacy problems emerged from the digital contact tracing within the COVID-19 pandemic era in Sect. 2 followed by the methodology employed in Sect. 3. In Sect. 4, we present the results and finally, we conclude the paper with indicating future direction of research in Sect. 5.

2 Background

Privacy according to Goodwin (1991) [12] is considered as an elastic and vague concept with a wide variety of definitions. Within these varied definitions of privacy, Solove (2006) [26] has attempted to focus on privacy harms or problems rather than creating a shared meaning. His taxonomy of privacy embodies sixteen different privacy violations for contemporary times [26]. For the purpose of the present study, privacy violations most relevant to contact tracing were considered for various reasons, among others, so that our study wouldn't be too extensive to report about in a conference paper. Yet, future research which includes more elements from Solove's taxonomy would be of great importance and interest. Below, we discuss the potential privacy violations from the taxonomy that we deemed most problematic in a typical contact tracing app:

2.1 Surveillance

Surveillance refers to "watching, listening to, or recording of an individual's activities" [26]. In digital contact tracing, surveillance is related to keeping track of app users, the contacts of an infected person, and their activities. Even if the person is not infected, the contacts and encounters are recorded, giving rise to more detailed surveillance on a person's movement, identity, mental health, social behavior, and associations (e.g., [23]).

2.2 Identification

According to Solove (2006) [26], "Identification is linking information to particular individuals". Depending on its implementation, contact tracing apps collect various information related to users (and contacts) such as personal information, device identifiers, and locations coordinates. Aggregation and performing data analytics on data extracted from various databases (e.g. health authorities and smart cities) makes it possible to make the identity of the users and their contacts known [9]. Research shows that both centralized and de-centralized systems suffer from the risk that people could be deanonymized [31].

2.3 Aggregation

"Aggregation involves the combination of various pieces of data about a person" [26]. Observation from countries such as China and South Korea shows that digital contact tracing apps were not sufficient to trace contacts, but more technologies were combined to even invade to private zones of individuals. Data from CCTVs and GSM/Cell towers/WiFi location were collected to be used through face recognition to co-traveler techniques to create more detailed movement patterns of individuals [22]. Early research indicates the accumulation of other potential types data such as data from social media platforms, credit card transactions, travel booking data, and other surveillance data points [24].

2.4 Secondary Use

Secondary use refers to "the use of data for purposes unrelated to the purposes for which the data was initially collected without the data subject's consent" [26]. In the context of contact tracing apps, secondary use could cause harm if a data holder shares and/or conducts additional processes to extract information about users, the pandemic (or not related to the pandemic) beyond their awareness. Here, the role of AI and Big data analytics is highlighted for various purposes such as de-identification of location histories, movement patterns, psychological behavior, and many more. Needless to say, it is possible to infer information about the user's whereabouts and track their location via fixed-location sensors, rouge devices, or QR-codes (e.g. NZ COVID Tracer app [33]).

2.5 Disclosure

"Disclosure involves the revelation of truthful information about a person that impacts the way others judge her character" [26]. Disclosure occurs in different ways within digital contact tracing. Spread of information about an infected person and his or her location to other contacts and government bodies is a reported privacy issue during the COVID-19 pandemic [34]. Another privacy violation occurs when an individual's contacts are disclosed, which may be considered private or controversial. For example, during the COVID-19 outbreak in a LGBTQ district in Seoul concerns were voiced in the gay community in the case of those who had not disclosed their sexuality to employers or family [10].

2.6 Stigma

In Solove's taxonomy, distortion "involves the spreading of information that affects the way society views a person ... distortion differs from disclosure, however, because with distortion, the information revealed is false and misleading" [26]. Stigma is a type of privacy harm emanated because of distortion. Studies from contact tracing for tuberculosis shows that a consequence of the identification of close contacts of infected cases is social stigma [2]. In contact tracing of COVID-19 infection many cases have been reported to "out" patients, false identifications, witch-hunts and abuse towards those who spread the virus with nicknames such as "super propagator", "super contaminator" or "super spreader" [10,17,27].

2.7 Perceived Privacy Problems and Digital Contact Tracing Apps

In the context of mobile apps, privacy violation is undesirable. Bansal et al. (2010) found in their study of E-Health records that individual's concern for information privacy has direct influence on attitude to "opt-in" and share personal health information [1]. Contact tracing apps are not exempted from mobile apps and various studies have pointed towards the privacy concerns of citizens in using such apps despite their perceived benefits [5,15,21]. It is reasonable to assume from the above arguments that those who are positive towards using an application for contact tracing will be less concerned with privacy issues relating to the application.

3   Methodology

This paper seeks to evaluate how Swedes perceive potential privacy issues related to contact tracing applications, and how various demographic factors affect this perception. A web-based survey was deemed a suitable approach for exploring this notion and we aimed to gather responses from at least 400 respondents. The survey began with a description of contact tracing apps which was followed by two question sections. The first section contained demographic questions and the second section contained one Likert scale with five statements for each of the six included dimensions of privacy concern. Likert scales were used because of their frequent prior use in research whenmeasuring perceptions and opinions of a population [16]. All questions were followed by a free-text field where the respondents could elaborate on their responses. The statements and questions in the survey will be outlined in the result section. Prior to distribution, the survey was subjected to pilot testing during which it was distributed to a small population and 35 answers were collected. Two peers, one with a background in information security and one with a background in statistics, were asked to review the survey in depth.

To generate a probability sample, a stratified sampling approach was used [14]. The population, Swedes, was divided into subgroups based on gender, age, and geographical region. Equal proportions of each subgroup were recruited to the survey using simple random sampling [25]. The practical sampling was performed by the survey provider Webropol, using their web panel. As such, the range of possible participants was restricted to members of their panel. Using a web panel has been suggested to provide a higher level of data reliability than surveys administered over telephones since it reduces the researcher bias [8].

The survey data was analyzed using the software SPSS[1]. As described by Joshi et al. (2015) [16], Likert scales assume that all statements in the scale measure the same underlying concept. Thus, Cronbachs Alpha was used to measure the internal consistency of each scale [28]. Cronbachs Alpha returns a value between 0 and 1 and a value over 0.65 is typically considered appropriate for studies with human participants, and was adopted as the threshold of acceptance for this study [30]. Next, the answers in each scale were transformed to an index value reflecting the composite score for each scale, allowing for parametric analysis [16]. Finally, answer groups were constructed based on the demographic questions and independent sample T-tests used to identify statistically significant differences between groups. The conventional significance level of 95% was used and T-test is considered to be robust regardless of distribution form given the relatively large sample in this study [20]. However, Mann-Whitney U-test was also used as a means of triangulation to increase the validity of the results [18]. When a statistically significant difference was identified, Pearson's correlation coefficient was computed to further analyze how the demographic affected the privacy concern. Pearson's correlation coefficient is a value between -1 and 1 and describes the linear correlation between two variables. -1 or 1 show perfect correlations while correlations under 0.3 or -0.3 are considered weak [4].

4   Results

After pilot testing, the survey was sent out to 2020 possible respondents and it was open for one week. 453 respondents answered the survey leading to an answer rate of 22%. The respondents were first asked five demographic questions. The questions (translated from Swedish) and proportions of respondents for each option is reflected in Table 1.

Following the demographic questions, the participants were provided with the following text (translated from Swedish) describing the concept of contact tracing applications:

---

[1] https://www.ibm.com/analytics/spss-statistics-software.

Table 1. Demographic properties of the sample

Question	Answer	Proportion
As what gender do you identify?	Male	51.7%
	Female	41.8%
	Other/Prefer not to say	0.2%
What is your highest level of education?	Elementary school	3.1%
	High-school	33.1%
	Higher education, 3 years or less	24.1%
	Higher education, more than 3 years	38%
	Doctoral education	1.8%
How old are you?	18–27	12.6%
	28–37	20.5%
	38–47	19.2%
	48–57	19.6%
	58–67	20.5%
	Above 67	11.3%
What is your main occupation?	Student	10.2%
	Working full time	54.3%
	Working part time	6.4%
	Retired	18.3%
	Business owner	4.6%
	Unemployed	3.5%
	Other/Prefer not to say	2.6%
What is the best description of where you live?	City, more than 250 000 inhabitants	29.4%
	City, more than 100 000 inhabitants	15.9%
	Town, more than 50 000 inhabitants	13.7%
	Town, more than 10 000 inhabitants	17.4%
	Community, more than 5000 inhabitants	7.7%
	Community, more than 1000 inhabitants	4.4%
	Smaller community/countryside	11.5%

This survey is about how you perceive integrity in relation to contact tracing applications. This type of apps can effectively support infection tracing and could have been used during the corona pandemic. The purpose of such an application is to keep track of persons that come in contact with each other in a way that could result in a spread of infection. To do this, the application needs to know where you are and sense who you are in contact with. It will also need to know if you are infected or not.

For this survey, we want you to imagine such an app and rate how well you agree with a number of statements. 1 means that you do not agree at all, and 5 means that you fully agree. Assume that the information in the application is shared between you and the healthcare system, unless stated otherwise.

Six themes will be described to you and we want you to respond to five statements for each theme.

The first of the six analyzed themes was *Surveillance* and the statements in this theme intended to evaluate respondents' concerns with privacy issues relating to it. The respondents were asked to rate how well they agreed with the statements on a 5-pointed scale (1 = Do not agree at all and 5 = Fully agree). One statement was reversed, meaning that fully agree signified a low level of concern. The answers to the reversed statements were flipped, and Cronbachs Alpha was used to measure the internal consistency of the scale, resulting in an alpha value of 0.807. Then, the mean answers to all statements were summarized and divided by 5 to compute an index value for the theme. Note that the analysis process was identical for all six themes but will not be described in detail for themes two to six to conserve space.

Table 2 displays, the statements and data generated during the analysis.

Table 2. Results in the theme surveillance

Statement	Mean	Index	95% CI
Surveillance is never good	3.17	3.18	3.09–3.26
This kind of monitoring is worth it, considering the benefits	3.19		
I worry that my data will be used to monitor what I do. For instance my mental health and social behavior	3.34		
I believe that the collected data will be used by governments for other purposes than infection tracing	3.13		
I believe that my activity will be tracked even if I am not infected	3.45		

The second theme was *Identification* and the Alpha for the scale was 0.754. Table 3 displays the results of the theme. Note that statements one and two were reversed in the creation of the index.

Table 3. Results in the theme Identification

Statement	Mean	Index	95% CI
It is good if such an application can help me identify infected persons I've have been in contact with	3.24	3.33	3.25–3.41
It is good if such an application can notify persons I've been in contact with while I've been infected	3.30		
Such an application should never spread my identity, even if it means that I cannot be identified to others as infected	3.67		
Such an application should only tell where an infected person has been, not the person's identity	3.63		
I think the collected data should be anonymous	3.90		

The third theme was *Aggregation* and the Alpha for the scale was 0.752. Table 4 displays the results of the theme. Note that statements one, four and five were reversed in the creation of the index.

Table 4. Results in the theme aggregation

Statement	Mean	Index	95% CI
It is okay for governmental bodies to combine information about me if it limits the spread of infection	3.19	3.33	3.25–3.41
I care about how governmental bodies share information about me	4.03		
I worry that data from a contact tracing app could be aggregated with data from other sources (e.g. social media)	3.47		
I want data from such an application to be combined with data from other sources to provide me with general health information	2.22		
It is okay if data from different sources are combined for research	3.45		

The fourth theme was *Secondary use* and the Alpha for the scale was 0.848. Table 5 displays the results of the theme.

The fifth theme was *Disclosure* and the Alpha for the scale was 0.788. Table 6 displays the results for the fifth theme. Note that statement five was reversed in the creation of the index.

The sixth theme was *Stigma* and the Alpha for the scale was 0.762. Table 7 displays the results for the theme. Note that statements two and five were reversed in the creation of the index.

The final question asked the respondents to answer "yes" or "no" to whether they would use a contact tracing application. 34.44% (156) respondents answered "yes" and 65.56% (297) answered "no".

Table 5. Results in the theme secondary use

Statement	Mean	Index	95% CI
I worry that the collected information will be used by others outside the healthcare system	3.92	3.97	3.88–4.05
I worry that AI can be used to extract information not related to a pandemic	3.84		
I worry that, for instance, banks and insurance companies can use the information to decide my fee or interest rates	3.51		
I worry that data about my contacts can be sold or handed to companies	3.97		
Information in such an application should only be used for its intended purpose	4.59		

Table 6. Results in the theme Disclosure

Statement	Mean	Index	95% CI
I worry that if I get infected, that information will be spread to other than my contacts	3.08	3.57	3.48–3.65
I worry that information about my location can be freely available for anyone	3.86		
I worry that information about my contacts will be available to healthcare providers	3.05		
I worry that information about my contacts will become available to others than healthcare providers	3.89		
Information collected by the application should be made freely available to government bodies	2.03		

Table 7. Results in the theme Stigma

Statement	Mean	Index	95% CI
I would worry about being branded as "Corona-infected" if I used such an application	2.32	2.73	2.65–2.82
I want others to know if one of my family members is infected by corona	2.50		
I would worry that my friends would dissociate themselves from me if they found out from such an application that I was infected	2.10		
I would worry that my employer and my colleagues would discriminate me if they found out that I was infected from such an application	2.53		
An application that can tell who is infected would make my social life easier	2.79		

Following the univariate analysis, sub-groups were created within the sample to identify demographic differences relating to privacy concerns in the six themes. Independent sample T-test was used as the primary means of hypothesis testing and Mann-Whitney U-test was used for validation purposes. The hypothesis tested for each demographic was expressed as follows:

Demographic X will affect how privacy problems in theme Y is perceived by the respondents

The corresponding null hypothesis was that no such difference could be observed. The remainder of this chapter will account for the groups created and hypotheses tested, statistics will only be provided in cases where the hypothesis is supported, for the purpose of saving space.

The first demographic was gender and the sample was divided based on the genders Male and Female, the option "Other/Prefer not to say" option was only selected by a single respondent and was subsequently disregarded in this analysis. Statistically significant differences between the gender groups could not be identified for any theme, and the null hypothesis is accepted for the demographic gender.

Next, level of education was analyzed. Two group sets were created for this purpose. First, we tested for differences between respondents with or without a degree from higher education and then we tested for differences between respondents with a doctoral degree or more than three years of higher education and the rest. No statistically significant differences could be identified, and the null hypothesis is accepted for the demographic education level.

Next, the impact of age was analyzed. Respondents aged 48 or more (n = 216) were placed in one group and the rest (n = 237) in the other group. Statistically significant differences were identified for four of the themes as seen in Table 8.

Table 8. Analysis of how age affects privacy concerns (Results are significant when p < 0.05). All reported correlations are significant at the 95% level.

Theme	Group	Mean	T-test(p)	Mann-Whitney(p)	Corr coef.
Surveillance	≤ 47	3.30	0.002	0.001	−0.161
	≥ 48	3.03			
Identification	≤ 47	3.50	0.000	0.000	−0.233
	≥ 48	3.15			
Aggregation	≤ 47	3.41	0.032	0.033	−0.110
	≥ 48	3.24			
Stigma	≤ 47	2.82	0.047	0.026	−0.105
	≥ 48	2.64			

As seen in Table 8, the results of the analysis suggest that younger respondents are more concerned about privacy aspects than older respondents. However, the correlation coefficients suggest that the relationship between the variables is weak. As such, the analysis concludes that age does affect how concerned a person is with privacy aspects relating to Surveillance, Identification, Aggregation and Stigma. However, the correlation coefficient suggests that the power of the relationship is low.

The next demographic to be analyzed was main occupation. To generate evenly sized groups, respondents who reported working full time were placed in one group and all others in the other group. No significant differences could be identified and the null hypothesis is accepted for the demographic occupation.

Next, the impact of place of living was analyzed and grouping variables created in three ways:

- Group 1: Respondents living in cities with more than 250 000 inhabitants, group 2: the rest
- Group 1: Respondents living in cities with more than 100 000 inhabitants, group 2: the rest
- Group 1: Respondents living in towns with more than 50 000 inhabitants, group 2: the rest

No significant differences could be observed and the null hypothesis is accepted for the demographic "place of living".

The final aspect to be analyzed was if the respondents' answers differed based on their willingness to use an application for contact tracing. The hypothesis in this case being that *Respondents who are positive towards using an application for contact tracing will be less concerned with privacy issues relating to the application.* The results of this analysis is presented in Table 9. Note that no correlation coefficient was computed since the willingness to use variable is dichotomous.

Table 9. Analysis of whether respondents who are positive towards using an application for contact tracing will be less concerned with privacy issues relating to the application (Results are significant when $p < 0.05$).

Theme	Group	Mean	T-test(p)	Mann-Whitney(p)
Surveillance	Yes	2.68	0.000	0.000
	No	3.44		
Identification	Yes	2.90	0.000	0.000
	No	3.56		
Aggregation	Yes	2.87	0.000	0.000
	No	3.57		
Secondary use	Yes	3.61	0.000	0.000
	No	4.15		
Disclosure	Yes	3.13	0.000	0.000
	No	3.80		
Stigma	Yes	2.23	0.000	0.000
	No	3.00		

5 Discussion and Conclusion

The aim of this study was to research: 1) How citizens perceive potential privacy problems related to digital contact tracing? and 2) How various demographic factors affect perceived privacy problems by the citizens?

A survey-based method was used to answer those questions and a stratified sampling approach was used to acquire a probability sample representative for the Swedish population. Indexes were created based on the survey data and reflected the respondents' level of concern about privacy risks related to six aspects of privacy derived from [26]: Surveillance, Identification, Aggregation, Secondary use, Disclosure, and Stigma.

In response to the first research question, the results reflect that the respondents are somewhat concerned about privacy risks in all themes. However, while the results for most themes are just above 3, which signifies a neutral standpoint, it is notable that the concerns for secondary use of data is close to 4, suggesting that the respondents are highly concerned about their data being used for other purposes that contact tracing. This is emphasized by looking at the mean values for individual statements, where statements relating to unpurposeful use of the data is generating a higher level of concern than other statements. The second notable conclusion in relation to the first RQ is that the respondents are generally less concerned about stigma coming from the use of the application.

In response to the second RQ, the impact of several demographic factors was evaluated but the only demographic factor that had any impact on the results was age. Younger respondents were generally more concerned about privacy risks than older respondents. However, even this effect was small suggesting that the results are general across Swedish population. A previous study showed that age is an important predictor of the acceptance of COVID-19 mobile applications [15]. Our results suggests that privacy could play a mediating role between age and contact tracing app use is and therefore interesting for future research to investigate. The respondents were asked to state if they would install and use an application for contact tracing and 34% responded that they would. It should be noted that this question was asked last and the result should be interpreted in the light of the possibility that the survey itself affects the respondents, positively or negatively. Using the responses to this question as a grouping variable revealed that respondents willing to install the application were significantly less concerned with privacy issues compared to those not willing to install the application. This was true for all the included themes, suggesting that privacy concern is an important factor when it comes to deciding to use an application or not. This further suggests that minimizing privacy issues and concerns in an important factor in successful deployment of a contact tracing application that needs to be used by the general public. That recommendation is a practical contribution of this study.

This study contributes with insight about how Swedish users perceive privacy risks with contact tracing applications. The results of the current study is in agreement with previous research indicating that privacy protection is critical if the contact tracing app is to be adopted [5,15,21]. This study extends previous literature in revealing privacy problems that arise from contact tracing apps, making this one the first in its domain. Nevertheless, a limitation of the study is that it was conducted with Swedish individuals only and the degree to which the results can be generalized outside of this population is unknown and should be further studied in future research, especially given that privacy concerns are know to be perceived differently in different nations. A second limitation is that this study is focused on six of the privacy dimensions presented by [26]. Future work could be expanded to cover more dimensions.

References

1. Bansal, G., Gefen, D.: The impact of personal dispositions on information sensitivity: privacy concern and trust in disclosing health information online. Decis. Support Syst. **49**(2), 138–150 (2010)
2. Cox, V., et al.: Critical changes to services for TB patients during the COVID-19 pandemic. Int. J. Tuberc. Lung Dis. **24**(5), 542–544 (2020)
3. Abeler, J., Bäcker, M., Buermeyer, U., Zillessen, H.: COVID-19 contact tracing and data protection can go together. JMIR Mhealth Uhealth **8**(4), e19359 (2020)
4. Akoglu, H.: User's guide to correlation coefficients. Turkish J. Emerg. Med. **18**(3), 91–93 (2018)
5. Altmann, S., et al.: Acceptability of app-based contact tracing for COVID-19: cross-country survey study. JMIR Mhealth Uhealth **8**(8), e19857 (2020)
6. Anglemyer, A., et al.: Digital contact tracing technologies in epidemics: a rapid review. Cochrane Database Syst. Rev. (8) (2020)
7. Bengio, Y., et al.: The need for privacy with public digital contact tracing during the COVID-19 pandemic. Lancet Digit. Health **2**(7), 342–344 (2020)
8. Braunsberger, K., Wybenga, H., Gates, R.: A comparison of reliability between telephone and web-based surveys. J. Bus. Res. **60**(7), 758–764 (2007)
9. Cyphers, B., Gebhart, G.: Apple and Google's COVID-19 exposure notification API: questions and answers (2020)
10. Döring, N.: How is the COVID-19 pandemic affecting our sexualities? An overview of the current media narratives and research hypotheses. Arch. Sex. Behav. **49**(8), 2765–2778 (2020)
11. Ferretti, L., et al.: Quantifying SARS-CoV-2 transmission suggests epidemic control with digital contact tracing. Science **368**(6491), eabb6936 (2020)
12. Goodwin, C.: Privacy: recognition of a consumer right. J. Public Policy Mark. **10**(1), 149–166 (1991)
13. Guinchard, A.: Our digital footprint under COVID-19: should we fear the UK digital contact tracing app? Int. Rev. Law Comput. Technol. **35**, 1–14 (2020)
14. Henry, G.T.: Practical Sampling, vol. 21. Sage, Thousand Oaks (1990)
15. Jansen-Kosterink, S.M., Hurmuz, M., den Ouden, M., van Velsen, L.: Predictors to use mobile apps for monitoring COVID-19 symptoms and contact tracing: a survey among Dutch citizens (2020)
16. Joshi, A., Kale, S., Chandel, S., Pal, D.K.: Likert scale: explored and explained. Curr. J. Appl. Sci. Technol. 396–403 (2015)
17. Lanese, N.: 'superspreader' in south korea infects nearly 40 people with coronavirus. https://www.livescience.com/coronavirus-superspreader-south-korea-church.html
18. Lincoln, Y.S., Guba, E.G.: Naturalistic Inquiry, vol. 75. Sage, Thousand Oaks (1985)

19. Megnin-Viggars, O., Carter, P., Melendez-Torres, G., Weston, D., Rubin, G.J.: Facilitators and barriers to engagement with contact tracing during infectious disease outbreaks: a rapid review of the evidence. PLoS ONE **15**(10), e0241473 (2020)
20. Norman, G.: Likert scales, levels of measurement and the "laws" of statistics. Adv. Health Sci. Educ. **15**(5), 625–632 (2010)
21. O'Callaghan, M.E., et al.: A national survey of attitudes to COVID-19 digital contact tracing in the republic of Ireland. Irish J. Med. Sci. (1971-) 1–25 (2020)
22. Park, O., et al.: Contact transmission of COVID-19 in South Korea: novel investigation techniques for tracing contacts. Osong Public Health Res. Perspect. **11**(1), 60–63 (2020)
23. Park, S., Choi, G.J., Ko, H.: Information technology-based tracing strategy in response to COVID-19 in South Korea-privacy controversies. JAMA **323**(21), 2129–2130 (2020)
24. Riemer, K., Ciriello, R., Peter, S., Schlagwein, D.: Digital contact-tracing adoption in the COVID-19 pandemic: it governance for collective action at the societal level. Eur. J. Inf. Syst. **29**, 1–15 (2020)
25. Scheaffer, R.L., Mendenhall III, W., Ott, R.L., Gerow, K.G.: Elementary Survey Sampling. Cengage Learning (2011)
26. Solove, D.J.: A taxonomy of privacy. U. Pa. L. Rev. **154**, 477 (2005)
27. Sotgiu, G., Dobler, C.C.: Social stigma in the time of coronavirus disease 2019. Eur. Respir. J. **56**(2), 2002461 (2020)
28. Tavakol, M., Dennick, R.: Making sense of Cronbach's alpha. Int. J. Med. Educ. **2**, 53 (2011)
29. Trivedi, A., Vasisht, D.: Digital contact tracing: technologies, shortcomings, and the path forward. SIGCOMM Comput. Commun. Rev. **50**(4), 75–81 (2020)
30. Vaske, J.J., Beaman, J., Sponarski, C.C.: Rethinking internal consistency in Cronbach's alpha. Leis. Sci. **39**(2), 163–173 (2017)
31. Vaudenay, S.: Centralized or decentralized? the contact tracing dilemma. Cryptology ePrint Archive, Report 2020/531 (2020). https://eprint.iacr.org/2020/531
32. Walrave, M., Waeterloos, C., Ponnet, K.: Adoption of a contact tracing app for containing COVID-19: A health belief model approach. JMIR Public Health Surveill. **6**(3), e20572 (2020)
33. Yang, F., Heemsbergen, L., Fordyce, R.: Comparative analysis of china's health code, Australia's COVIDSafe and New Zealand's COVID tracer surveillance apps: a new corona of public health governmentality? Media Int. Aust. **178**, 1–16 (2020)
34. Zastrow, M.: South Korea is reporting intimate details of COVID-19 cases: has it helped? Nature (2020)

Network Security

Secure and Scalable IoT: An IoT Network Platform Based on Network Overlay and MAC Security

Junwon Lee$^{(\boxtimes)}$ ⓘ and Heejo Lee

Korea University, Anam-dong, Seongbuk-gu, Seoul 136-713, South Korea
{junimirang,heejo}@korea.ac.kr

Abstract. IoT, which is closely connected with our daily life, shows high growth in the automotive, healthcare, and retail fields. IoT security threats can cause severe problems in our lives. However, the security of the IoT network is insufficient to cope with security threats. Therefore, an attacker can use man-in-the-middle-attacks (MITM), DNS manipulation, and route tampering for eavesdropping, privacy breach, service outages and delay, power consumption, and system manipulation. Currently, VPN and data encryption is applied to protect the IoT network from these security threats. However, due to the limited resources of IoT device, the TCP/IP-based VPN and encryption are also limited. Although a lightweight IoT communication protocol such as LoWPAN is used, TCP/IP-based VPN such as IPsec, OpenVPN, and Wireguard require bandwidth, CPU/memory, and electric power at the level of general endpoint devices.

In this paper, we propose a secure and scalable IoT (SSI) network platform that can prevent security threats while minimizing use of computing resources of an IoT device. SSI, which has a lower load than TCP/IP-based VPN, is a layer 2 VPN and supply data link frame encryption. L2TP and VXLAN are provided for a scalable layer 2 VPN, and the MACsec algorithm encrypts layer 2 frames. SSI shows 30% network speed improvement and 31.6% CPU usage reduction compared to IoT network applied OpenVPN.

Keywords: IoT platform · Network overlay · Network separation · VXLAN · L2TP · MACsec

1 Introduction

There are many types of IoT devices, including sensors, mobile devices, medical devices, wearable devices, home appliances, automotive and industrial devices. Gartner predicts that 1.9×10^9 IoT devices will be used for manufacturing and natural resources industries by 2028. Moreover, the IoT growth is very high in the automotive, healthcare, and retail fields [11]. IoT devices are required

© IFIP International Federation for Information Processing 2021
Published by Springer Nature Switzerland AG 2021
A. Jøsang et al. (Eds.): SEC 2021, IFIP AICT 625, pp. 287–301, 2021.
https://doi.org/10.1007/978-3-030-78120-0_19

to connect to humans, other devices, and systems without environmental constraints through an IoT network. IoT architecture has evolved from a closed and centralized network to a distributed cloud over the Internet. In the future, hyper-connectivity and Internet of Everything (IoE) [4], in which human, process, data, and things are interconnected, are expected to become the forms of IoT.

As IoT is widely expanded and closely connected to human life, IoT security threats will have an even more significant impact on privacy, health, reliability, and productivity. Considering these threats, we should approach IoT security with a different paradigm from endpoint security centered on end-user devices. OWASP has updated the IoT Top 10 threats for developers, manufactures, enterprises, and consumers. 5 IoT threats out of 10 threats (*"insecure network services"*, *"insecure ecosystem interfaces"*, *"insufficient privacy protection"*, *"insecure data transfer and storage"*, and *"lack of device management"*) are closely related to network security. In other words, we can effectively prevent many security threats by applying the secure IoT network platform [18].

In the former studies [8, 13, 20], we can find security threats related to the IoT network. Farris et al. describe the security threats (e.g., eavesdropping, denial of service, spoofing, MITM, routing attack, cloud service manipulation, privilege escalation, etc.) that can occur on IoT networks [8]. Minhaj et al. represent the end-to-end security and establishment/resumption of session in the network level security issues. In the IoT environment, which provides the same network to various devices, security threats can be propagated to other nearby devices due to the security hole of one device. Therefore, end-to-end protection for a device is essential [13]. Ryoo et al. reported that a security threat might arise when a home IoT device uses an insecure communication channel to interoperate with other devices. Also, it has shown that a user's conversation and video recordings may be revealed through weak communication channels, which may violate users' privacy [20]. In order to effectively respond to IoT security threats in various IoT devices, the IoT network platform that provides end-to-end encryption and network separation is required.

However, since the computing resources of the various devices are different, there are limitations in applying the same technology as the existing security architecture [12]. In the various studies, IoT network architectures have been proposed to minimize IoT security threats while minimizing the load of IoT devices for security functions. Farris et al. explained the necessity of traffic isolation and logical network separation in response to security threats [8]. Linda et al. described a network architecture using SD-VPN to improve the scalability and security of IoT [21]. Kumar et al. proposed an IoT model that securely exchanges messages between trusted publishers and subscribers using a many-to-many end-to-end encryption protocol [14]. McCormack et al. described an SDN-based IoT security gateway architecture using a micro-hypervisor that can easily provide new security functionality to respond to emerging threats [16]. Jason presented a WireGuard VPN that outperformed the throughput and response speed of IPsec and OpenVPN by applying a minimized key distribution process and stream cipher algorithm [7]. However, the former VPN models did not provide many-to-many and end-to-end encryption and a scalable network separation simultaneously. Moreover, since IPsec, OpenVPN, and WireGuard are TCP/IP-based VPNs, they inherit the TCP/IP properties that require network buffers and sockets. Therefore, when a TCP/IP-based VPN is applied to IoT, the bandwidth, processing power, battery power, and memory of IoT device are additionally affected [3].

In this paper, we propose an IoT-specific network security platform to protect IoT devices against network threats while also reducing the load on such devices, which typically have limited bandwith and computing resources. First, we analyze IoT-related vulnerabilities and attacks with the STRIDE model and describe the requirements for the secure network platform. Second, we design a secure and scalable IoT network platform taking into account the characteristics of IoT devices such as location limitation, device growth, and the limited computing resource. SSI provides a scalable VPN and many-to-many and end-to-end encryption in the layer 2 network. Below, we describe a novel approach different from the previous IoT network platforms.

- **An IoT network platform using L2TP and Virtual Extensible LAN (VXLAN) provides 16 million separated networks without any distance limitation.**
- **Many-to-many and end-to-end encryption using the MACsec algorithm does not require a session-specific key exchange procedure. Thus it will reduce the IoT bandwidth, CPU/memory usage.**
- **An IoT network platform with encryption and network separation can replace the security function of IoT protocol and minimize the resource consumption of IoT devices.**

In the experiment environment of SSI platform using Raspberry Pi 3B+ and AWS EC2, SSI improved network performance by 30% and reduced CPU usage by 31.6% compared to the OpenVPN network in which IPsec was applied.

2   Related Work

2.1   L2TP (Layer 2 Tunneling Protocol)

L2TP is a tunneling protocol to support layer 2 virtual private network. However, since the L2TP protocol alone does not provide encryption, it is often implemented with IPsec to provide confidentiality, authentication, and integrity. The endpoints of an L2TP tunnel are the LAC (L2TP Access Concentrator) and the LNS (L2TP Network Server) [15]. When L2TP is applied to the IoT network, a number of unspecified IoT devices perform the LAC role, and the CN receiving a tunnel link performs the LNS. Since the network applying MACsec must support unicast, broadcast, and multicast, SSI uses the L2TPv3 protocol that supports these communications [1].

2.2   MACsec (802.1AE, MAC Security)

MACsec is the layer 2 security protocol that provides authenticity and integrity for data-link layer frames. MACsec increases transmission efficiency by minimizing the header size compared to IPsec. This is very useful in the layer 2 IoT network, which provides low bandwidth, such as Long Range (LoRa) Wide Area Network (WAN). MACsec is a very useful protocol for high-speed connectivity as it can implement physical port-based encryption and decryption [6]. Moreover, the MACsec security mechanism does not affect the upper layer, so there is no need to modify the user application. However, in order to apply MACsec, the layer 2 network capable of unicast, broadcast, and multicast must be provided.

2.3   VXLAN (Virtual Extensible LAN)

In order to accommodate various protocols and services and to guarantee user mobility, layer 2 network virtualization is appropriate, and technologies such as VXLAN, Stateless Transport Tunneling (STT), Network Virtualization Using Generic Routing Encapsulation (NVGRE), and Locator/Identifier Separation Protocol (LISP). Among them, VXLAN is supported by most vendors and is being used to provide an overlay network in the cloud-scale datacenter, and its application range is expanding to the software defined wan (SD-WAN). VXLAN provides layer 2 network services like VLAN, but it has higher network scalability and availability than VLANs. VXLAN provides the layer 2 overlay network service over the layer 3 transport network. VTEP (VXLAN Tunnel Endpoint) provides 16 million unique VNIs (VXLAN IDs). It enables users to acquire sufficient virtualized network resources on a single underlay network.

3   Problem Analysis

3.1   Security Threats on the IoT Network

Security threats are various depending on the kinds of IoT networks and devices. Examples of security threats include speed delays for high-speed wireless networks such as 5th generation mobile network, Denial-of-service-attack (DoS) attacks for application servers located in the cloud, power consumption for low-power IoT devices and small mobility, eavesdropping for home IoT, and replay attacks for IoT servers and devices.

The IoT network as shown in Fig. 1, is exposed to various security threats [16]. According to the management entity of Internet, the Internet used in IoT networks can be classified into the public Internet and the trusted Internet. The public Internet is a network that allows anyone to access, and it contains risks that can include careless management and threats by attackers. On the contrary, the trusted Internet is relatively safe compared to the public Internet because it controls user access and allows access only to authorized users. However, it is expensive and inefficient to build a whole trusted network to prevent unauthorized access. Therefore, we should review countermeasures to supplement the vulnerability of IoT devices on the public Internet. We can find that the configuration of the local gateway is sometimes poorly managed in the home IoT environment [22]. In that case, it can cause DNS manipulation, traffic detour, and DoS due to unauthorized access by an attacker. In addition, if the network between the IoT device and the IoT server is very far, some sections of the public internet can be delayed and threatened by an attacker's route tampering and sniffing. Moreover, if the IoT server does not strongly authenticate the IoT device, rogue devices can connect to the IoT service.

Although the IoT attacks on the public Internet are different, security threats can be minimized by preventing the exposure of the communication from the IoT device to the server and encrypting traffic.

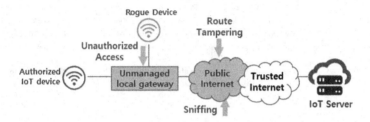

Fig. 1. IoT security threats in the network structure: Attackers can threaten IoT services at any location of a gateway, routing path, in addition to IoT devices.

3.2   Limitations of IoT Application Protocol

There are two popular IoT protocols: MQTT and CoAP are lightweight application protocols that can be used in IoT devices with limited resources. First, MQTT provides a machine-to-machine (M2M) network connection based on a TCP/IP network. MQTT consists of a broker that relays messages from a machine and a publisher that creates messages. MQTT shows a network diagram of the hub and spoke. It is used in low-bandwidth or low-reliability networks to ensure the reliability and data delivery with the minimum resource of device. Second, CoAP supports M2M applications using unicast and multicast without a broker based in the UDP network. CoAP with a point-to-point network architecture provides an asymmetric message exchange method [10].

Because MQTT and CoAP are application protocols for message delivery, they do not provide encryption by themselves. Therefore, MQTT and CoAP run on SSL/TLS and DTLS for encrypted data transmission. However, since the SSL/TLS and DTLS method requires key exchange for each session, an IoT device that attempts many-to-many encryption requires many key exchange procedures to attempt communication with all devices. Given the end-to-end encryption that requires no additional key exchange and an IoT network platform that only authorized devices can access, IoT applications such as MQTT and CoAP do not need to enforce SSL/TLS for secure data transmission.

Table 1. IoT Security Threat Analysis Using STRIDE Model

※ C&C*: Command and control server is controlled by an attacker

STRIDE	Vulnerabilities	Security Threats	Countermeasures
S (Spoofing)	Opened network	Unauthorized Access	Authentication
	Untrusted network		Data Encryption
	Insecure Transfer		
T (Tampering)	Opened network	Route Detour/Tampering	DATA Encryption
	Untrusted network	Broadcast false information	Network Separation
		Replay attack	Route Management
R (Repudiation)	Opened network	Misuse, Malfunction	Authentication
	Insecure Transfer		Data Encryption
I (Information Disclosure)	Opened network	Unauthorized Access	Authentication
	Insecure Transfer	Eavesdropping	Data Encryption
	Insecure Application	Privacy breach	Network Separation
D (Denial of Service)	Opened network	Service Outages/Delay	Network Separation
	Low Power supply	Power Consumption	Route Management
E (Elevation of Privilege)	Opened network	Misuse, Malfunction	Authentication
	Insecure ACL	System Manipulation	Network Separation
	Insecure Software	C&C* Connection	
	Hardcoded Password		

3.3 Security Threat Modeling Using STRIDE

STRIDE modeling helps to find all possible IoT security threats by analyzing the environment as a category of STRIDE security threats. Table 1 shows IoT vulnerabilities, security threats, and countermeasures by STRIDE classification [19]. Most vulnerabilities are caused by the IoT network exposed to the Internet. In order to provide the countermeasures, Authentication, Data Encryption, and Network Separation can be applied. In the countermeasures, the IoT network must provide authentication so that the only approved IoT devices can access the network. Second, Data encryption should work even on low-spec IoT devices using small computing resources. Third, route management should provide the trusted network in a wide area to block unauthorized users from intervening in the transmission route. Finally, in the network separation, the network access between each other services must be completely blocked even in the same transport route in order to guarantee various services. In addition, data encryption and network separation should be reviewed as a network platform to support various network protocols to ensure various communication.

4 Secure and Scalable IoT (SSI) Model

4.1 Overview

VPN and encrypted communication are required to prevent security threats in the IoT environment, but TCP/IP-based VPN and encryption is not suitable due to the limited resources of IoT device [3]. We designed SSI that overcomes the limitations of TCP/IP-based VPN and encryption using layer 2 overlay network and MAC security. SSI provides authentication, data encryption, route management, and network separation.

SSI provides configuration information to access Communication Node (CN) during the first authentication, and it provides the network separation information and encryption key information during the second authentication. MACsec, the end-to-end encryption algorithm that uses low CPU resources and supports various network protocols, has been applied for the data encryption. Route management is accomplished by connecting the IoT device to the nearest trusted Internet CN. Finally, the layer 2 overlay network based on L2TP and VXLAN is provided for the network separation. In the SSI diagram of Fig. 2, the IoT device is connected to the IoT server through CN. A single overlay network is provided between the IoT device and CN, and multi overlay networks are provided between CNs. Both single overlay networks and multi overlay networks provide the layer 2 network.

In the following subsections, we describe the MACsec and L2TP, and VXLAN as overlay network protocols. Next, we will look at the detailed elements of the SSI platform and the entire operation process, including authentication.

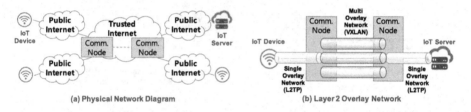

(a) Physical Network Diagram   (b) Layer 2 Overlay Network

Fig. 2. Overview Diagram of SSI: CN is built on the trusted Internet such as AWS, Azure, and GCP. CN bridges the L2TP tunnel to the VXLAN tunnel.

4.2   L2TP and VXLAN Based Overlay Network

The overlay network of SSI provides network separation and layer 2 network without limiting the distance between IoT devices and servers. The network segment (between IoT device and CN) that is connected to various IoT endpoints and does not require network separation is configured as a single overlay network using the L2TP protocol. However, the communication node, which is the connection hub of SSI, provides a sufficient number of overlay networks using VXLAN to relay many separated networks. Figure 2(b) shows that the communication node (CN) bridges the L2TP tunnel and the VXLAN tunnel.

For example, if IoT devices are assigned the same VNID (VXLAN ID) from each CN, they are connected to the same VXLAN tunnel and belong to a single broadcast domain. In other words, the IoT device and IoT server assigned the same VNID can be connected to the same broadcast domain regardless of their location.

4.3 End-to-End Encryption Using MACsec

Data may be exposed outside the transmission path in the overlay network of SSI where encryption is not applied. Even if L2TP/IPsec is applied, encryption is not applied to the multiple tunnels communicating with VXLAN. In this case, encryption for VXLAN should be added.

We applied the MACsec protocol to improve the security vulnerability of the overlay network using L2TP and VXLAN. In the network to which MACsec is applied, only the hosts that have been authenticated are subject to MAC-sec Key Agreement (MKA). If a host connected to the VTEP has not been authenticated by the authentication server, the MKA protocol does not proceed normally, so SAK (Secure Association Key) transmission will be blocked. In Fig. 3, a connectivity association key (CAK) is delivered to the approved CN via 802.1X authentication server, and CN shares CAK only for the supplicant who has completed authentication. Even though a rogue VTEP establishes a normal VTEP and VXLAN tunnel, IoT devices belonging to the Rogue VTEP cannot join MACsec communication because CAK is not provided.

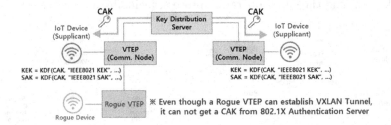

Fig. 3. CAK Delivery using 802.1X authentication server: IoT devices that do not complete 802.1X authentication cannot get a CAK for MACsec encryption.

MACsec uses the AES-GCM algorithm, and the symmetric key (SAK) used in the encryption algorithm is periodically generated in the host. SAK is encrypted using a key encrypting key (KEK) that is shared between hosts. AES-GCM algorithm is widely used for the data encryption required fast processing cause of supporting the parallel encryption method [17]. KEK, which encrypts SAK as a symmetric key continuously generated by the host, minimizes computing resources in contrast to the asymmetric key algorithm. Therefore, MACsec is considered a suitable encryption protocol for an IoT device.

In Eq. 1, the context is obtained from the bitwise operation of KS-nonce generated from a key server (KS), 32bit-value provided by member identifier (MI), and counter number maintained by KS. In Eq. 2, 3, key derivation function (KDF) generates SAK and KEK using a pseudorandom function [5,6].

$$Context = KS\text{-}nonce | MI\text{-}value\,list | Key\text{-}number \qquad (1)$$

$$SAK = KDF(CAK, \text{``}IEEE8021\,SAK\text{''}, Context, SAK\,length) \qquad (2)$$

$$KEK = KDF(CAK, \text{``}IEEE8021\,KEK\text{''}, Keyid, length) \qquad (3)$$

4.4   Network Architecture

SSI consists of a communication node (CN) that mediates different types of overlay networks, a CN controller that controls these CNs, and an authentication server that provides authentication and authorization. The L2TP authentication server provides the initial authentication and minimum information for configuring the L2TP tunnel, and the 802.1X authentication server provides VNID for relay to the VXLAN tunnel and CAK for MACsec encryption. CN bridges the L2TP tunnel to which the IoT device is connected to the VXLAN by referring to the VNID. After authentication and authorization of an IoT device and tunnel bridging of the CN, the IoT device uses CAK to apply MACsec encryption to end-to-end communication. Figure 4 shows the architecture where each element is connected and the logical network separation. Because the global IaaS such as AWS, Azure, and GCP has a dedicated Internet backbone for the stable and secure service when interworking between global regions, we use AWS IaaS for the trusted Internet. Besides, if you use IaaS compute nodes, you can quickly and build a communication node on the trusted Internet at low cost, and you can conveniently expand the scale.

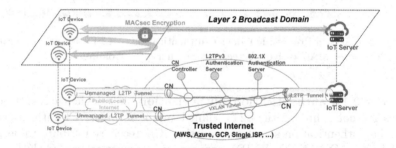

Fig. 4. SSI Platform using Global IaaS: The SSI platform built using the global IaaS provides the same layer 2 network and MACsec encryption to IoT devices and IoT servers (or another IoT devices).

Figure 5 explains the data transaction between SSI components divided by each step.

Step 1: IoT device authentication - After the permission of the L2TP authentication server, IoT devices receive session information to connect to the IoT network platform.

Step 2: L2TP tunnel with communication node (CN) - IoT devices (or local gateways) establish a tunnel with the nearest CN using L2TP session information.

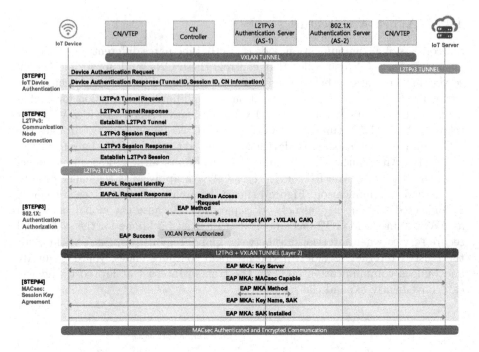

Fig. 5. SSI Platform Process: IoT device authentication → L2TP tunneling → 802.1X authentication → MACsec Key Agreement → Encrypted Communication

Step 3: 802.1X authentication/authorization - IoT devices access the communication node through the L2TP tunnel and perform 802.1X authentication. After the authentication server's permission, CN receives attribute value pairs (AVPs) (e.g., VXLAN ID (VNID), connectivity association key (CAK)).

✳ *Through the process up to this point, the IoT device can communicate with other devices in the same layer 2 network. However, for MACsec communication, the process of synchronizing the secure association key (SAK) must be finally performed.*

Step 4: MACsec session key agreement - The symmetric key is shared within the same VXLAN domain using the EAP protocol and is used for MACsec encryption.

In the surveys about IoT security [2,8,9], authentication, access control, network separation (or secure routing), encryption, detection, and SDN are represented as security aspects of IoT network. In Table 2, SSI supports all security aspects except detection. Detection can be easily applied without affecting the response time by mirroring traffic through CN.

Table 2. Security function comparison with previous IoT platforms

Function	SSI	Linda et al. (2018) [21]	Kumar et al. (2019) [14]	McCormack et al. (2020)[16]
Layer 2 Communication	Yes	No	No	No
Net Separation	Yes	Yes	No	No
Authentication	Yes	No	Yes	No
Access Control	Yes	Yes	No	Yes
Enc.(End-to-End)	Yes	No	Yes	No
Enc.(Many-to-Many)	Yes	No	Yes	No
Encryption(Datalink)	Yes	No	No	No
SDN	Yes	Yes	No	Yes
Detection	No	No	No	Yes

5   Evaluation

The experiment environment is configured to measure the response time, CPU usage, and speed delay due to the application of an encryption algorithm. We use a Raspberry Pi 3B+ as an IoT device and AWS EC2 as an IoT server to build the experiment environment. Amazon AWS is used for the trusted Internet to examine the effect of speed improvement. The average response time between EC2s, located in Seoul, South Korea, and Ohio, US, shows 180 to 190 ms. We compared the Network performance and CPU usage of SSI with IPsec (Strongswan) and OpenVPN.

Network performance is measured in the six VPN test cases depending on whether the overlay network and the encryption. To verify the performance of encryption, we use OpenVPN, IPsec, and MACsec protocols. We do not include the WireGuard, because it does not support the AES algorithm. MACsec and IPsec use the AES-GCM cipher algorithm. However, the AES-GCM algorithm of OpenVPN cannot be applied with a pre-shared key similar to the key exchange of SSI, so the AES-CBC algorithm is applied. IPsec of Strongswan and OpenVPN are evaluated to be very stable and fast in the layer 3 VPN. Table 3 shows the classification of 6 test environments. First, case 2 is a typical VPN using OpenVPN. Next, Case 3 shows the test case to evaluate the performance of overlay network using L2TP and VXLAN. Lastly, cases 4, 5, and 6 are the comparison of each VPN performance.

ICMP Response Time, File Download time, and Packet loss ratio are adopted as performance measurement items. First, while packets of 1508 bytes are transmitted from the IoT device to the IoT server 1000 times, we measured the ICMP response time to measure the Round Trip Time and the packet loss ratio. In Table 4, the overlay network has a similar response time compared to the public network, but it shows stable network performance without any packet loss. Next, download speed is measured. The download speed of each case is the average speed of downloading 10 files with different file sizes from 10 MB to 100 MB.

Table 3. Evaluation Case: Case type was chosen to compare the effects of the overlay network (1-3, 2-4) and VPN protocol (4-5-6).
＊ *Since OpenVPN does not support AES-GCM in PSK mode, AES-128-CBC is used*

Case	VPN Type	Network	Cipher Algorithm
1	None	No Overlay	None
2	OpenVPN	No Overlay	AES-128-CBC
3	SSI (No Encrypted)	L2TP + VXLAN	None
4	OpenVPN	L2TP + VXLAN	AES-128-CBC
5	IPsec	L2TP + VXLAN	AES-128-GCM
6	SSI (Encrypted)	L2TP + VXLAN	AES-128-GCM

Table 4. Network performance Comparison: The cases of 1–3 and 2–4 show that overlay network can improve the network performance. Moreover, the cases of 4-5-6 show that SSI's VPN is better than IPsec and OpenVPN.

Case	ICMP Response Time (ms)			Packet Loss (%)	Download Speed (MB/sec)
	Min	Avg	Max		
1	185	187	197	0.1	1.89 (0.0%)
2	212	213	254	0.8	1.48 (−21.7%)
3	191	193	215	0	2.07 (+9.5%)
4	210	211	228	0.3	1.92 (+1.6%)
5	194	198	383	0	1.63 (−13.8%)
6	192	193	205	0	1.94 (+2.6%)

We have confirmed that the performance is improved by applying the overlay network in the evaluation results. The MACsec algorithm has a lower CPU usage rate than IPsec. In the comparison of networks without data encryption in Table 4, the download speed of overlay network is improved by 10% compared to the public Internet, and no packet loss occurred. The download time of the SSI is improved by 31% compared to the public Internet applying OpenVPN. In addition, we compared the number of packets and data size transmitted when SSI, IPsec, and OpenVPN are applied on the overlay network. In transmitting a 10 MByte file, we have confirmed that MACsec transmitted 11.2 MB with 11,968 packets, IPsec transmitted 11.9 MB with 11,815 packets, and OpenVPN transmitted 12.0 MB with 19,842 packets. When comparing the total data transmission size and the number of packets, MACsec of SSI has worth considering communication efficiency.

We can confirm that the MACsec algorithm is more suitable for IoT than IPsec and OpenVPN in terms of CPU usage. Figure 6 graph shows the CPU usage while an IoT device (Raspberry Pi 3B+) downloads a 100 MB file. In the

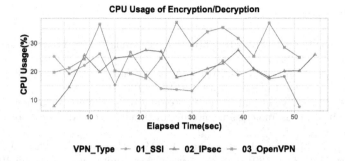

Fig. 6. CPU Usage for Data Transfer: (SSI: Avg 18.8%, IPsec: Avg 21.4%, OpenVPN: Avg 27.5%)

encrypted communication, the file download time of SSI and OpenVPN is the same at 51 s, and IPsec takes 56 s. During the download time, the average CPU usage of OpenVPN is 27.5%, IPsec is 21.4%, and SSI is the lowest at 18.8%. When considering that most IoT devices provide low power and low computing resources, MACsec applied to SSI is considered to be a very suitable cipher algorithm for IoT.

6   Conclusion

We expect that SSI effectively blocks MITM, route tampering, and privacy breaches occurring in the open IoT network by using an overlay network and many-to-many and end-to-end encryption. In addition, the MACsec encryption algorithm is effective for IoT devices due to low CPU usage, and the layer 2 overlay network helps to use various communication protocols. The experiment environment installed from the IoT device located in Seoul, South Korea to the IoT server located in Ohio, US, has verified that the network speed has improved by 30% and the CPU usage rate of the IoT device has decreased by 31.6%.

Since CNs are installed on the trusted public cloud, they are convenient to control and scale compared to a local network environment. Various NFVs of SDN and middleboxes requiring high availability can be applied to the SSI's CN. In other words, SSI is more efficient in providing flexible computing resources than installing a security gateway on the local edge network close to IoT devices.

We expect that SSI can provide a VPN network environment to collaborate with offices from outside. In further research, we plan to conduct research to develop a secure and scalable VPN for the business collaboration between telecommuting users through the improvement of SSI.

References

1. L2VPN (L2TPv3) (2020). https://www.yamaha.com/products/en/network/techdocs/vpn/l2tpv3/
2. Alaba, F.A., Othman, M., Hashem, I.A.T., Alotaibi, F.: Internet of things security: a survey. J. Netw. Comput. Appl. **88**, 10–28 (2017)
3. Bello, O., Zeadally, S., Badra, M.: Network layer inter-operation of device-to-device communication technologies in internet of things (IoT). Ad Hoc Netw. **57**, 52–62 (2017)
4. Bradley, J., Loucks, J., Noronha, A., Macaulay, J., Buckalew, L.: Internet of everything (IoE) (2013). https://www.ciosummits.com/IoE_-_Top_10_Insights_from_Cisco_s_IoE_Value_Index_Survey.pdf
5. Chen, L.: Nist special publication 800–108. Recommendation for Key Derivation Using Pseudorandom Functions (Revised) (2009). http://csrc.nist.gov/publications/nistpubs/800-108/sp800-108.pdf
6. Craig Hill, S.O.: Introduction to WAN MACsec (2018). https://www.ciscolive.com/c/dam/r/ciscolive/us/docs/2018/pdf/BRKRST-2309.pdf
7. Donenfeld, J.A.: WireGuard: next generation kernel network tunnel. In: NDSS (2017)
8. Farris, I., Taleb, T., Khettab, Y., Song, J.: A survey on emerging SDN and NFV security mechanisms for IoT systems. IEEE Commun. Surv. Tutorials **21**(1), 812–837 (2018)
9. Hassan, W.H., et al.: Current research on internet of things (IoT) security: a survey. Comput. Netw. **148**, 283–294 (2019)
10. Hei, I., Špeh, I., Šarabok, A.: IoT network protocols comparison for the purpose of IoT constrained networks. In: 2017 40th International Convention on Information and Communication Technology, Electronics and Microelectronics (MIPRO), pp. 501–505. IEEE (2017)
11. Hippold, S.: Gartner 2020 hype cycle for supply chain strategy shows internet of things is two to five years away from transformational impact (2021). https://www.gartner.com/en/newsroom
12. Hwang, Y.H.: IoT security & privacy: threats and challenges. In: Proceedings of the 1st ACM Workshop on IoT Privacy, Trust, and Security, pp. 1–1 (2015)
13. Khan, M.A., Salah, K.: IoT security: review, blockchain solutions, and open challenges. Futur. Gener. Comput. Syst. **82**, 395–411 (2018)
14. Kumar, S., Hu, Y., Andersen, M.P., Popa, R.A., Culler, D.E.: {JEDI}: Many-to-Many End-to-End encryption and key delegation for IoT. In: 28th {USENIX} Security Symposium ({USENIX} Security 19), pp. 1519–1536 (2019)
15. Lau, J., Townsley, M., Goyret, I.: Layer two tunneling protocol-version 3 (l2tpv3). RFC **3931** (2005)
16. McCormack, M., et al.: Towards an architecture for trusted edge iot security gateways. In: 3rd {USENIX} Workshop on Hot Topics in Edge Computing (HotEdge 20) (2020)
17. McGrew, D., Viega, J.: The Galois/Counter mode of operation (GCM). submission to NIST Modes of Operation Process 20, 10 (2004)
18. OWASP IoT Security Team: OWASP IOT Top 10 2018 (2020). https://owasp.org/www-pdf-archive/OWASP-IoT-Top-10-2018-final.pdf
19. Shahan, R., Phil Meadows, B.L.: IoT security architecture (2018). https://docs.microsoft.com/en-us/azure/iot-fundamentals/iot-security-architecture

20. Ryoo, J., Kim, S., Cho, J., Kim, H., Tjoa, S., Derobertis, C.: IoE security threats and you. In: 2017 International Conference on Software Security and Assurance (ICSSA), pp. 13–19. IEEE (2017)
21. Shif, L., Wang, F., Lung, C.H.: Improvement of security and scalability for IoT network using SD-VPN. In: NOMS 2018–2018 IEEE/IFIP Network Operations and Management Symposium, pp. 1–5. IEEE (2018)
22. Simpson, A.K., Roesner, F., Kohno, T.: Securing vulnerable home IoT devices with an in-hub security manager. In: 2017 IEEE International Conference on Pervasive Computing and Communications Workshops (PerCom Workshops), pp. 551–556. IEEE (2017)

Enriching DNS Flows with Host-Based Events to Bypass Future Protocol Encryption

Stanislav Špaček[1,2]([⊠]), Daniel Tovarňák[2], and Pavel Čeleda[2]

[1] Faculty of Informatics, Masaryk University, Brno, Czech Republic
[2] Institute of Computer Science, Masaryk University, Brno, Czech Republic
spaceks@ics.muni.cz

Abstract. Monitoring of host-based events and network flows are the two most common techniques for collecting and analyzing cybersecurity data. However, events and flows are either monitored separately or correlated as alerts in higher aggregated forms. The event-flow correlation on the monitoring level would match related events and flows together and enabled observing both data in near real-time. This approach allows substituting application-level flow information that will not be available due to encryption, which is being employed in a number of communication protocols. In this paper, we performed the event-flow correlation of the DNS protocol. We developed a general model that describes the relation between events and flows to enable an accurate time-based correlation where parameter-based correlation is not feasible. Based on the model, we designed three event-flow correlation methods based on common parameters and times of occurrence. We evaluated the correlation methods using a recent and public dataset, both with and without the extended flow information, to simulate DNS flow encryption. The results of the method combining parameter-based and time-based matching show that matching related DNS events to flows is possible and substitutes the data that might soon be lost in encryption.

Keywords: HIDS · NIDS · Event-flow correlation · DNS · Encrypted network traffic

1 Introduction

Monitoring of network flows using a Network Intrusion Detection System (NIDS) is a well-described and widely used technique of data analysis for cybersecurity. Over time it has evolved to use targeted Deep Packet Inspection (DPI) to extend the flow information with data from the application layer protocols. However, the recent shift to information privacy moved most of the formerly available data behind end-to-end encryption. If a network flow is encrypted, the enrichment by DPI is severely hampered, and the output of the monitoring is not as

A. Jøsang et al. (Eds.): SEC 2021, IFIP AICT 625, pp. 302–316, 2021.
https://doi.org/10.1007/978-3-030-78120-0_20

information-rich as in the past. As a result, NIDS threat detection and security analysis of the encrypted network flows requires new approaches to support cyber-security operations.

On the other hand, monitoring of host-based data by a Host-based Intrusion Detection System (HIDS) is another well-known technique to collect and analyze data in the form of events. The event monitoring provides information about the events taking place directly on the end-point devices. However, the dependency on the end-point devices is the drawback of this method. If attackers take control over the device, they may modify, remove, or otherwise tamper with the events. The flow monitoring may have its own dedicated infrastructure and is more robust to tampering attempts.

Using both NIDS and HIDS simultaneously, an occurrence may be observed from two different vantage points providing different information [3]. We high-light three main benefits of this approach:

- Providing cybersecurity operators with the correlated data through an appro-priate presentation layer will help them quickly identify all data related to a specific occurrence. That will improve their situational awareness and thus speed up the cybersecurity incident response process.
- Any tampering with one monitoring source can be detected by correlation with the other source. Detection of tampering attempts may assist in defense against stealthy persistent attackers.
- The approach allows enriching encrypted flows with host-based data transpar-ently for tools deployed on higher layers. Thus an existing anomaly detection or analysis infrastructure may be used to process encrypted traffic.

To examine the possibilities of correlating related events and flows, this paper aims to answer the following research questions. The first question is, *how reli-ably can the related DNS events and flows be matched?* The second question is, *what otherwise unavailable monitoring data can the event-flow matching provide when the DNS flow is encrypted?* To answer the first question, we developed a model that describes the relation between events and flows. Based on this model, we designed three matching algorithms using common parameters and times of occurrence. Then we evaluated the algorithms on a recent dataset collected dur-ing a complex cyberdefense exercise [11]. To answer the second question, we ran the matching algorithms on a dataset including simulated encrypted DNS flows.

Our results show that while parameter-based event-flow matching performs very well with DPI-enriched DNS flows, performance with basic DNS flows is lacking. The time-based matching, although generally less accurate, is not affected by DPI enrichment and thus performs better on basic or encrypted flows. A matching method combining these two approaches produced the most accurate results on both encrypted and unencrypted flows. We provide algo-rithms used in this research as open-source software to ensure repeatability and verifiability of our results [15].

The rest of the paper is structured as follows. Section 2 sets the context of this paper by presenting the related work. Section 3 introduces the flow and event capture model, that demonstrates the relation between events and flows. Section 4 specifies the event-flow matching methods tested in this paper.

Section 5 describes the actions performed on the public dataset to preprocess it before measurements. Section 6 discusses the results of the matching methods when run on the dataset. Section 7 summarizes lessons learned. Section 8 concludes the paper with answers to the posed research questions.

2   Related Work

There are three categories of related work. First, we discuss works that researched information leakage of the encrypted DNS network traffic, as these methods could be used to directly access the extended flow features of encrypted DNS flows. Second, we describe works that already focused on the event-flow correlation in the past. Finally, we mention the Collaborative Intrusion Detection Systems that combine aggregated alerts from both NIDS and HIDS.

Currently, there are two widely used approaches to encrypting DNS traffic – the DNS over TLS and the DNS over HTTPS protocols. None of these protocols allows the DPI enrichment of DNS flows, leaving only the basic flow features available. Subsequently, the performance of the extended flow-based NIDS is limited [13]. Possible weaknesses of the DNS encryption to flow analysis and website fingerprinting were researched in several prior works [7,9]. Their results show that extended flow feature extraction, e.g., the queried domain name, is generally possible. However, Bushart et al. mentioned techniques that may make this approach more difficult or even unfeasible in the future [2]. The main disadvantage of this approach is taking the role of an attacker against the monitored traffic. If host-based monitoring of the DNS resolver is an option, the extended flow features may be supplemented from server logs. However, a direct link connecting a network flow to events that it caused needs to be identified first.

The direct correlation of network and host-based data had been explored in the past. Dreger et al. provided a framework for enriching network monitoring with host-based context and noted the advantage of overcoming encryption [4]. More recently, Haas et al. proposed the Zeek-osquery platform for correlating network flows with the originating processes and users [5]. Henderson et al. proposed a time-based correlation algorithm and confirmed that this approach is viable by testing it with real network data [6]. They also discussed the limitations of the event-flow correlation. However, they investigated the correlation solely from the malicious event standpoint and did not consider network flow features aside from its start time, end time, and source. Furthermore, previous works considered the captured times of all correlated occurrences as synchronized and accurate, which is usually not the case when correlating data from devices across the network, as described by Brilingaite et al. [1].

Collaborative Intrusion Detection Systems (CIDS) comprise of several cooperating NIDS and HIDS that collect, share, and aggregate monitoring data for complex analysis of the state of the network. Taxonomy of the CIDS had been provided in a survey by Vasilomanolakis et al. [12]. However, the CIDS usually correlate events of higher, already aggregated forms, e.g. attack signature alerts, and are closely specialized in a particular area [10,14]. To our knowledge, no direct link between a network flow and events that it caused had been proposed yet.

3   Event and Flow Capture Model

This section introduces the event and flow capture model that demonstrates the relation between events and flows captured at different vantage points in the network [3]. Specifically, we define the relations between the times of occurrence of events and flows to allow designing time-based event-flow matching algorithms. Such an algorithm could be based on the start of the flow, end of the flow, and time of occurrence of an event. An event and a flow would be considered related if the event's time of occurrence fell into the interval between the flow start and the flow end. However, the environment where the events and flows are observed is too complex for this simple method to work.

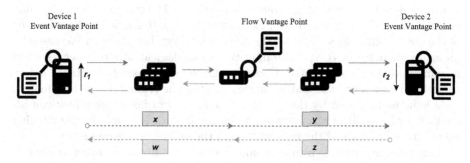

Fig. 1. The general event and flow capture model demonstrates the differences between the time of event occurrence and the time when the associated flow was observed; w, x, y, z are data transfer time intervals of various lengths; r is a time interval needed by a device to process a request and compose a response.

Time is a critical parameter when examining relations between data collected from different sources. However, when the data sources are physically separate, determining the time of occurrence becomes a problem, as time synchronization, network transfer times, and various delays need to be accounted for [1]. We have created a model representing the environment where events and flows are acquired. Furthermore, we have identified several obstacles that stand in the way of simple event-flow matching. The general event and flow capture model is depicted in Fig. 1.

The model shows a simple network of two devices communicating over a link consisting of an arbitrary number of hops. Events are generated and monitored on both the communicating devices, and a flow monitoring probe is installed on one of the hops. It is apparent from the model that simple time-based matching is not sufficient, as events and flows are captured at different places and at different times. The issues arising from this can be demonstrated in the sequence of actions during the start (Table 1) of the communication.

Table 1 represents the sequence of event and flow capture during communication start. The communication starts at time t_0 and a correspodign event on the initiating device (Device 1) is created. However, the flow is captured later,

Table 1. Event and flow capture sequence at the start of communication.

Step	Time	Action	Observed data
1	t_0	Request sent	Device 1 event
2	$t_0 + x$	In-flow created	Flow start
3	$t_0 + x + y$	Request received	Device 2 event
4	t_1	Response sent	Device 2 event
5	$t_1 + z$	Out-flow created	Flow start
6	$t_1 + z + w$	Response received	Device 1 event

when it enters the flow vantage point at time $t_0 + x$. The event on the responding device (Device 2) is captured even later, at $t_0 + x + y$. It is evident that the time of the flow capture does not mark the start of the flow, but the start increased by an arbitrary network travel time interval. An analogical situation occurs when a communication is terminated. Consequently, an event may be captured before the related flow is created and, analogically, after the related flow is terminated. This issue is mitigated by the use of biflow instead of flow. The biflow considers flows of both directions as parts of one communication and allows matching events from the start of the request flow to the end of the response flow.

Guaranteeing time synchronization between all the monitoring devices is another issue. The NTP protocol is still widely used to provide time synchronization as it can achieve millisecond precision with minimal drift. This precision proved to be sufficient for matching DNS request flows and events in a dataset encompassing circa 200 devices used in this paper. However, in larger environments and with chattier protocols, even a millisecond precision might not be enough to establish a relation between corresponding events and flows.

4   Event and Flow Matching Methods

The event and flow capture model shows that simple time-based event-flow matching does not guarantee good matching accuracy. The event-flow matching methods introduced in this chapter are optimized to pair the DNS request events and flows specifically. The general principle of these methods can be applied to other communication protocols. However, as network communication protocols are too diverse, it is improbable that a single event-flow matching method will work for every protocol.

4.1   Parameter-Based Matching Method

Matching based on common parameters present both in the logged event and in the captured flow is a natural approach to event-flow matching. Both the DNS request flows and the DNS request events contain four common parameters in total. The parameters are the *destination IP address, source IP address, source port*, and queried domain name (*qname*). This 4-tuple of parameters is usually sufficient to pair a DNS request event with a related flow. The matching algorithm is described by Algorithm 1.

The common 4-tuple provides a clear relationship between an event and a flow, but it does not always identify an event-flow pair uniquely. A DNS client may reuse a *source port* in any future request, even in a request for the same *qname* as in the past. This results in cross-pairing, where two or more flows share two or more events that cannot be possibly related when considering their times of occurrence. The cross-pairing is especially pronounced with DNS servers queried only for a limited domain pool. The issue is mitigated if a time-window for pairing is specified, and the events that fall outside of the window are not paired. In our dataset, a time window of five minutes proved to be sufficient to suppress most of the cross-pairs.

Algorithm 1: Parameter-Based Matching

---

    for each *flow* ∈ *flows* **do**
        for each *event* ∈ *events* **do**
            if *flow.dst_ip* = *event.server_ip* & *flow.src_ip* = *event.client_ip* &
            flow.src_port = *event.client_port* & *flow.qname* = *event.qname* **then**
               match *flow* with *event*
            end if
        end for
    end for

The main drawback of the parameter-based matching method is its reliance on a parameter that might not be available. The *qname* is a part of the extended flow information, and it needs to be extracted from the DNS packets by DPI on the flow monitoring probe. If the data cannot be extracted, the *qname* will be unavailable. In our dataset, nearly a fifth of the DNS flows was missing the extended flow information. Any such flows and their related events cannot be paired by this matching method.

The case of the missing *qname* is a sample of the issues caused to network flow monitoring by encrypted communication used on a large scale. If a flow is encrypted, its packets cannot be examined and parsed by DPI for extended flow information. The amount of information available in such a network flow is limited. In these cases, a successful pairing of a flow with its related event(s) provides information on the purpose of the communication that is no more accessible by just flow monitoring.

If the *qname* is missing, the method falls back to pairing based on the three remaining parameters. However, they are not enough to provide a reliable pairing (Sect. 6). A different and more accurate approach is needed, and a suitable candidate might be refined from this method by extending the use of the time-window specified earlier to filter out cross-pairings.

4.2   Time-Based Matching Method

The time-based matching method copes with the missing *qname* parameter and consequently hampered matching accuracy by introducing a comparison of times of capture for both the events and flows. The idea behind it is simple; if the three remaining common parameters match and the event's time of occurrence falls within the time interval defined by the start and the end of the flow, the event and the flow are considered related. However, such a simple time-based matching method does not consider the time differences, as demonstrated by the event and flow capture model, and needs to be modified.

To compensate for the different vantage points, random packet travel times, and drift in time synchronization between devices, defining a toleration time-window is necessary. This time window has two components – *event earliness* and *event lateness*. The *event earliness* is defined as a time value, indicating how much earlier may an event occur before the start of the request flow to be still considered related to that flow. Analogically, the *event lateness* is defined as a time value, indicating how much later may an event occur after the end of the request flow to be still considered related. The algorithm of time-based matching is described by Algorithm 2.

Algorithm 2: Time-Based Matching

---
    for each *flow* ∈ *flows* **do**
      for each *event* ∈ *events* **do**
        if *flow.dst_ip* = *event.server_ip* & *flow.src_ip* = *event.client_ip* &
        flow.src_port = *event.client_port* &
        flow.start − *event_earliness* ≤ *event.start* &
        flow.end + *event_lateness* ≥ *event.start* **then**
          match *flow* with *event*
      end if
      end for
    end for

The exact values of the *event earliness* and *event lateness* depend on the specific features of the network and devices that generate the data to be paired. They are affected mainly by the packet travel time between the flow vantage point and the DNS server, the time it takes the DNS server to respond to a query, and by the difference in local time of the flow vantage point and the DNS server. The smaller these differences are, the lower may be the *event earliness* and *event lateness*, and the more accurate will be the matching results. With the increasing time-window, the probability of pairing unrelated events and flows also increases. As a result, this matching method needs to be balanced between pairing unrelated events and flows (false positive) or missing a related pair (false negative).

4.3 Combined Matching Method

The combined matching method utilizes both the parameter-based and time-based matching approaches to compensate for their weaknesses. When pairing flows with valid extended flow information, including the *qname*, it uses the parameter-based matching. If it encounters an encrypted flow or a flow with missing or corrupted extended flow information, it falls back to the time-based matching. This way, it maintains the highest possible pairing accuracy for flows with all known parameters while retaining the ability to pair flows with partially known parameters.

The usability for both encrypted and unencrypted network flows and good matching accuracy makes this matching method a suitable candidate for real network traffic. Its performance has been tested, and the results show that it is indeed the preferred pairing method to match related DNS events and flows.

5 DNS Communication Dataset

The dataset used for evaluation in this paper is the Cyber Czech 2018 dataset [11]. It contains both the network flows and event logs, and all the devices in the dataset are time-synchronized with millisecond precision. The data in the dataset was captured during a cybersecurity exercise and generated by the actions of real users.

The initial dataset contained a total of 94 834 DNS biflows and 153 286 DNS events. This amount of DNS data is not final, however. We filtered out obvious white-noise data, as would do any current NIDS or HIDS. Most notably, we filtered out events that were not a DNS request, request events related to flows that circumvented the monitoring probe, and DNS flows to external DNS resolvers. In summary, any data where it was certain that it could not possibly have its either event or flow counterpart in the dataset and thus a correlation attempt would be futile. The filtering algorithm is described in detail in our open-source software [15].

Table 2. The DNS request datasets used for measurements.

	Events	Extended biflows	Biflows
All-information	65 682	54 819	0
Reduced-information	65 682	27 410	27 409

The resulting smaller DNS request dataset, containing events and flows that can be paired with high probability, is labeled the *all-information dataset*. To examine how the event and flow matching methods perform on basic (non-extended) DNS flows, we created one more dataset. The *reduced-information dataset* contains the same events and flows as the *all-information dataset*. However, half of the flows have been deprived of the extended flow information and reduced only to the basic flow features as if they were encrypted. The final contents of both datasets are summed up in Table 2.

6   DNS Event-Flow Matching

The performance of the matching methods on both datasets may be inspected in Tables 3 and 4. The measured metrics are *accuracy, precision, recall*, and *F1-score*. These metrics describe the performance even on a class-imbalanced data set with a high prevalence of true negatives (non-matches), which will be the usual input of the matching methods [8]. We provide supplementary materials; the code and both the filtered datasets used in this research, along with the necessary documentation to verify our results [15].

The metrics are affected by the properties of the dataset. Specifically, by the low number of unpaired events and flows, and by short server response times relatively to longer pauses between separate DNS queries. The achieved *precision, recall*, and subsequently *F1-score* values would be lower if the dataset filtering had been more lenient. Moreover, the *accuracy* metrics specifically was affected by the high number of true negatives in the dataset. The count of true negatives reached over 3.6 billions, a value several orders of magnitude higher than the 51 740 true positive pairs.

Due to the strict dataset filtering and therefore little room for error, the results are often very close. However, with the high volume of processed data, even a small difference in a metric might mean a much lower number of false positives or false negatives for the better performing method.

Table 3. Event-flow matching methods' results on the all-information dataset

	Param-based	Param-based (no qname)	Time-based (200 ms)	Combined (200 ms)
Acc	1,000000	0,999998	0,999998	1,000000
Pre	1,000000	0,888118	1,000000	1,000000
Rec	1,000000	1,000000	0,999826	1,000000
F1	1,000000	0,940744	0,999913	1,000000

Table 4. Event-flow matching methods' results on the reduced-information dataset

	Param-based	Param-based (no qname)	Time-based (200 ms)	Combined (200 ms)
Acc	0,999992	0,999998	0,999998	0,999999
Pre	1,000000	0,888118	1,000000	1,000000
Rec	0,500000	1,000000	0,999826	0,999903
F1	0,666667	0,940744	0,999913	0,999951

6.1   Parameter-Based Matching Method

The parameter-based matching method produces the best results when run on a dataset with valid extended flow information – known *destination IP address, source IP address, source port,* and *qname*. Because it considers all the parameters common to a DNS request event and flow, it can create a list of event-flow pairs that are related without a doubt. This method had been run on the *all-information dataset*, where it identified 51 740 pairs. This list of pairs is used throughout this paper as a ground truth. The results can be found under the key *Param-Based* in Tables 3 and 4.

Out of the 51 740 pairs, only ten pairs were cross-paired. The cross-pairing is caused by a client reusing a port to query the same server for the same domain in an interval so short that it cannot be distinguished which event is related to which flow. The matching was unique for the remaining pairs, so a flow was paired with only a single event and vice versa. This is caused by DNS requests' specific format, where one flow usually corresponds with one request for a single domain.

While the parameter-based matching method achieved the most accurate results on the *all-information dataset*, it was unable to create a pair if any of the parameters had been missing. Consequently, this method was able to create only 50 % of the pairs when run on the *reduced-information dataset*, producing the worst results of all tested methods. This drawback makes this method unsuitable for use in real traffic, where the collected information might be incomplete.

To lower the reliance on the *qname*, the parameter-based matching method had been modified to match by the three remaining parameters. Then it had been run again on both the datasets and the results can be found under the key *Param-Based (no qname)* in Tables 3 and 4. The *precision* is its weak spot, producing a high number of false positives. This is a serious drawback, as low *precision* may clutter the result with false positives so that important information may get overlooked. On the other hand, it is not influenced by flow encryption.

The parameter-based event-flow matching produces accurate results if complete monitoring information is provided. However, this is rarely the case in real traffic. When the monitoring provides information incomplete due to an overload, error, or encryption, the matching results are not satisfactory.

Table 5. The Jitter of events from flow start and flow end on the all-information dataset

Percentile	1	5	25	50	75	95	99
Event earliness (ms)	0	0	1	2	3	5	8
Event lateness (ms)	0	0	1	2	3	5	8

6.2 Time-Based Matching Method

Time-based event-flow matching is based on matching the *destination IP address*, *source IP address*, and *source port* similarly as the parameter-based matching method. It increases its matching accuracy by matching only those entities that occurred in a specific time-window. This method had been run on both the *all-information dataset* and the *reduced-information dataset*, where it produced the same results.

The first step in evaluating this matching method was the estimation of the size of the time-window. For all the related events and flows in the list of the confirmed event-flow pairs, we measured the jitter of the event time of occurrence from the flow start and from the flow end separately, to enumerate the *event lateness* and *event earliness*. As the DNS flow mostly consists of a single packet, the flow start and flow end times are equal; consequently, the *event lateness* and the *event earliness* are the same. The results may be observed in Table 5. Our results show that only 5 % of the related events happen at the same time as the DNS flow is captured. The possible reasons for this behavior are described in Sect. 3. On the other hand, most of the events are observed with at most 8 ms jitter from their related flows.

The 8 ms lower bound on the *event lateness* and the *event earliness* show the approximate size of the time-window to encompass most of the related events. However, it does not encompass all the events, and the larger the window is, the more probable it is that unrelated events and flows will be matched. The method had been run with different time-window settings on the *all-information dataset*, so the optimal size of the time-window could be found. The method's performance on these matching runs may be observed in Figs. 2 and 3.

Figure 2 depicts the performance for small time-window sizes. The *accuracy* is close to one, as it is influenced by the vast amount of true negatives. *Precision* is precisely one, as there are no false positives for small time-windows. As the time-window expands, the number of false negatives decreases, and thus the *recall* and *F1-score* rise fast until they reach the 99 percentile (8 ms). The resolution of the graph then must be increased, as the changes for large time-windows are more subtle. Figure 3 shows that the first false positives appear at the 300 ms mark as the *precision* drops. The *F1-score* also drops, as the increase of false positives (*precision* falling) is not sufficiently compensated by the increase of true positives (*recall* rising). Consequently, for time-windows larger than 200 ms, the performance of time-based matching on this dataset falls steadily.

The time-based matching method with 200 ms time-window performed better on both datasets than the parameter-based (no qname) method. It missed a few related pairs, producing false negatives, but the *precision* reached one with no false positive pairs matched. Rated by the *F1-score*, this method came second-best on the *reduced-information dataset*, proving decent performance on incomplete monitoring data.

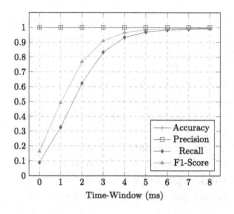

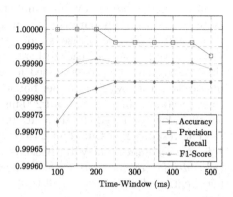

Fig. 2. Time-Based matching performance with small-sized time-window.

Fig. 3. Time-Based matching performance with large-sized time-window.

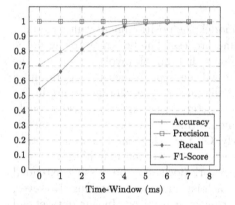

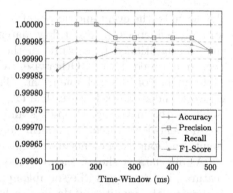

Fig. 4. Combined matching performance with small-sized time-window.

Fig. 5. Combined matching performance with large-sized time-window.

6.3   Combined Matching Method

The combined matching method uses the parameter-based matching where extended flow information is available and falls back to the time-based matching where it is not. The method had been run on both the *all-information dataset* and the *reduced-information dataset*. As the method used parameter-based matching on the the *all-information dataset*, it produced a list of event-flow pairs identical to the ground truth. The results on the *reduced-information dataset* are further explored.

Similarly to the time-based matching method, the combined method's performance with differently sized time-windows was examined on the small and large time-windows (Figs. 4 and 5, respectively). The method behaves similarly as the time-based matching, but with a few advantages. The *recall* starts at a much higher value for the small windows, even with no toleration time-window

(0 ms). This is caused by the number of flows the method had been able to match based on their parameters only, not even considering the time-window. As a result, the *F1-score* rise is more gradual even for small time-windows. The *precision* and *F1-score* reached higher values for the large-sized windows than time-based matching, as it missed fewer related pairs. The measured *F1-score* implies that the lower and upper bound for the time-window are the same as for time-based matching, 8 ms, and 200 ms, respectively. Consequently, the optimal time-window remained the same at 200 ms.

The results of this method on the *all-information dataset* and the *reduced-information dataset* may be observed in Tables 3 and 4. The results on the *reduced-information dataset* make this method a promising candidate for matching events and flows in the real traffic, where monitoring errors and encrypted flows are common.

7   Lessons Learned

As shown by the event and flow capture model, the positioning of vantage points strongly influences the event-flow matching process. The flow monitoring probe must be positioned to capture all the flows that might invoke events on the event-monitored devices. Otherwise, there will be gaps in measured data and a high number of unmatchable events. The distance of the vantage points in the network and network features like latency, jitter, and congestion, also strongly influence the matching. Drop-outs and monitoring errors make the parameter-based event-flow matching perform poorly. On the other hand, distant vantage points and long latency negatively influence the time-based matching.

As our dataset shows, the observed network flows may be missing extended features. In these cases, the suitable approach is time-based matching. However, it requires the monitoring devices to be time-synchronized. In our dataset, all devices had been synchronized by the NTP with millisecond precision. This precision proved sufficient for a network with around 200 devices. With larger networks and higher levels of DNS activity, a microsecond precision might be needed.

8   Conclusion

According to the results of our experiment described in Sect. 6, the most suitable matching method for real network traffic is the method that combines parameter-based and time-based matching. It has the most accurate matching performance on the traffic with valid extended flow information. When supplied with data missing this parameter, e.g., the encrypted flows, it falls back to time-based matching. The time-based matching needs to be optimized to the network's specifics and does not perform as good as the parameter-based matching. However, the ability to match network flows without extended flow information makes it a suitable candidate for matching encrypted flows.

We were able to identify the queried domain name (*qname*) parameter in case of a successful match when the event-flow matching methods were run on the encrypted DNS flows. This parameter is otherwise encrypted and unavailable to flow monitoring, so the event-flow matching may enrich flow monitoring with new data. With the rising amount of encrypted network traffic, event-flow matching might be the method to join the encrypted network flows with unencrypted information stored in event logs.

Acknowledgment. This research was supported by the CONCORDIA project that has received funding from the European Union's Horizon 2020 research and innovation programme under the grant agreement No 830927.

References

1. Brilingaitė, A., Bukauskas, L., Kutka, E.: Time-line alignment of cyber incidents in heterogeneous environments. In: ECCWS 2018 17th European Conference on Cyber Warfare and Security, p. 57. Academic Conferences and Publishing Ltd. (2018)
2. Bushart, J., Rossow, C.: Padding ain't enough: assessing the privacy guarantees of encrypted DNS. In: 10th USENIX Workshop on Free and Open Communications on the Internet ({FOCI} 20) (2020)
3. Collins, M., Collins, M.S.: Network Security Through Data Analysis: Building Situational Awareness. O'Reilly Media, Inc., Newton (2014)
4. Dreger, H., Kreibich, C., Paxson, V., Sommer, R.: Enhancing the accuracy of network-based intrusion detection with host-based context. In: Julisch, K., Kruegel, C. (eds.) DIMVA 2005. LNCS, vol. 3548, pp. 206–221. Springer, Heidelberg (2005). https://doi.org/10.1007/11506881_13
5. Haas, S., Sommer, R., Fischer, M.: Zeek-osquery: Host-network correlation for advanced monitoring and intrusion detection. arXiv preprint arXiv:2002.04547 (2020)
6. Henderson, S., Nicholls, B., Ehmann, B.: Time-based correlation of malicious events and their connections. https://resources.sei.cmu.edu/asset_files/Presentation/2019_017_001_539987.pdf. Accessed 15 Sept 2020
7. Houser, R., Li, Z., Cotton, C., Wang, H.: An investigation on information leakage of DNS over TLS. In: Proceedings of the 15th International Conference on Emerging Networking Experiments And Technologies, pp. 123–137 (2019)
8. Luque, A., Carrasco, A., Martín, A., de las Heras, A.: The impact of class imbalance in classification performance metrics based on the binary confusion matrix. Pattern Recogn. **91**, 216–231 (2019)
9. Siby, S., Juarez, M., Diaz, C., Vallina-Rodriguez, N., Troncoso, C.: Encrypted DNS - privacy? A traffic analysis perspective. arXiv preprint arXiv:1906.09682 (2019)
10. Teng, S., Wu, N., Zhu, H., Teng, L., Zhang, W.: SVM-DT-based adaptive and collaborative intrusion detection. IEEE/CAA J. Autom. Sin. **5**(1), 108–118 (2017)
11. Tovarňák, D., Špaček, S., Vykopal, J.: Traffic and log data captured during a cyber defense exercise. Data Brief **31**, 105784 (2020)
12. Vasilomanolakis, E., Karuppayah, S., Mühlhäuser, M., Fischer, M.: Taxonomy and survey of collaborative intrusion detection. ACM Comput. Surv. (CSUR) **47**(4), 1–33 (2015)

13. Velan, P., Čermák, M., Čeleda, P., Drašar, M.: A survey of methods for encrypted traffic classification and analysis. Int. J. Netw. Manage. **25**(5), 355–374 (2015)
14. Zhang, T., Zhu, Q.: Distributed privacy-preserving collaborative intrusion detection systems for VANETs. IEEE Trans. Sign. Inf. Process. Netw. **4**(1), 148–161 (2018)
15. Špaček, S.: Enriching DNS flows with host-based events to bypass future protocol encryption - scripts for data processing. Zenodo (2020). https://doi.org/10.5281/zenodo.4064934

Advanced Cowrie Configuration to Increase Honeypot Deceptiveness

Warren Z. Cabral[1,2] (ID), Craig Valli[1,2(✉)] (ID), Leslie F. Sikos[1,2(✉)] (ID),
and Samuel G. Wakeling[2(✉)] (ID)

[1] Cyber Security Co-operative Research Centre, Perth, WA, Australia
[2] Security Research Institute, Edith Cowan University, Perth, WA, Australia
`{c.valli,l.sikos,s.wakeling}@ecu.edu.au`

Abstract. Cowrie is a medium-interaction SSH, and Telnet honeypot used to record brute force attacks and SSH requests. Cowrie utilizes a Python codebase, which is maintained and publicly available on GitHub. Since its source code is publicly released, not only security specialists but cybercriminals can also analyze it. Nonetheless, cybersecurity specialists deploy most honeypots with default configurations. This outcome is because modern computer systems and infrastructures do not provide a standard framework for optimal deployment of these honeypots based on the various configuration options available to produce a non-default configuration. This option would allow them to act as effective deceptive systems. Honeypot deployments with default configuration settings are easier to detect because cybercriminals have known scripts and tools such as NMAP and Shodan for identifying them. This research aims to develop a framework that enables for the customized configuration of the Cowrie honeypot, thereby enhancing its functionality to achieve a high degree of deceptiveness and realism when presented to the Internet. A comparison between the default and configured deployments is further conducted to prove the modified deployments' effectiveness.

Keywords: Cybersecurity · Honeypots · Deception · Cowrie · SSH

1 Introduction

Honeypots are viable tools for network monitoring; to detect, record and analyze attacks in a network. Cybersecurity specialists and academic researchers use a collection of honeypots, i.e., honeynets – to monitor cyberattacks across networks and the entire cyberspace [1, 2]. They reveal an attackers IP, location, commands entered and can also be used to study targeted vulnerabilities and capture malware binaries. This research focuses on the Cowrie honeypot. *Cowrie*[1] interacts with cybercriminals within a simulated SSH environment. Simulation is a biology-inspired deceptive process through which the honeypot provides a service that functions like the actually expected system. For example, being an SSH honeypot, Cowrie simulates an SSH server's behaviour and

---

[1] https://github.com/cowrie/cowrie.

© IFIP International Federation for Information Processing 2021
Published by Springer Nature Switzerland AG 2021
A. Jøsang et al. (Eds.): SEC 2021, IFIP AICT 625, pp. 317–331, 2021.
https://doi.org/10.1007/978-3-030-78120-0_21

usually a Linux operating system (It can also be configured to simulate a Windows environment exposing SSH to a PowerShell session), thereby allowing cybercriminals to log into the system. Still, every command is only imitated and logged but not actually executed [3]. Hence, cybercriminals can easily detect the difference between a simulated session (honeypot environment) and a legitimate OS session [4]. High-interaction honeypots are challenging to identify because they provide the entire operating system to the cybercriminal rather than a simulated environment [5], and they typically are expensive to operate. Because of high operational costs, many honeypot operators rely on low-interaction or medium-interaction open-source honeypots to simulate vulnerable network services such as SSH, ICMP, and SCADA services. This is because they are not only cost-effective but are easily deployable and maintainable. However, the usage of this method of simulation also entails a number of operational weaknesses; poor deceptive capability and use of default deployments due to an absence of a standard deployment architecture and lack of knowledge on how to deploy honeypots securely and completely. Cybercriminals rely on numerous tools and strategies to detect honeypots these are:

i. *The mental mindset:* "Honeypot detection lies in a cybercriminal's ability to detect and find out about the deceptive nature of the honeypot". Tsikerdekis [6] wrote this, implying that a honeypot's detection lies in what a cybercriminal thinks about how a honeypot typically functions and interacts. This means a cybercriminal may believe that they are attacking a honeypot when it is the real system, or they think they are attacking the existing network but are instead interacting with a honeypot. Therefore, at times honeypot detection depends on the cybercriminal's thinking. For example, the honeypot environment may not be configured correctly; there may be a lack or absence of security mechanisms securing the honeypot. Therefore, the cybercriminal may realize the target is too easy and hence it is a possible trap. Another example is if a honeypot has a balance in functionality, accessibility, and interaction, the cybercriminal may engage with it thinking it is an actual system.

ii. *Default configurations:* As previously mentioned, honeypot deployments with default configuration settings are easier to detect and must be configured before deployment. According to Vetterl [7], the main cause for convenient and easy honeypot detection is that honeypot operators deploy honeypots with default configurations. Their research aimed specifically at Kippo and Cowrie honeypots. It was discovered that 72% of honeypots were deployed with default values. To confirm their hypothesis, the `uname-a` command was executed on the detected honeypots. The command returned the string `Linux [hostname] 3.2.0-4-amd64#1 SMP Debian 3.2.68-1+deb7u1 x8664 GNU/Linux\r\n` [8], which is indeed a default value for the Cowrie honeypot instance. Other features that determine honeypot configurations are default hostnames, banners, lack of functionality, insufficient input commands, and standard outputs.

iii. *NMAP*[2]: is a network mapping tool used for detecting and identifying open ports and services [9]. Default instances of Cowrie reveal port 2222 operating on a default

---

[2] https://nmap.org.

Cowrie SSH string. NMAP can also detect honeypots deployed within virtual environments. For example, static MAC addresses for the Cowrie honeypot deployed within a virtual machine [3].

iv. *Shodan*[3]: a scanning service developed by Matherly [10] used to "crawl" the Internet. When analyzing a device, Shodan queries the device's banners, IP address, protocols, port number, hostname, Internet Service Provider host and Geolocational IP information. It can also scan an entire IPv4 Internet address space and therefore is a solid indicator of what can be detected by third parties conducting reconnaissance scanning. Shodan then relates the scanned information into a freely searchable, longitudinally stored database. This database is indexed and searchable by numerous filters such as the ones mentioned above or a city, country, dates, or a device's operating system [6].

v. *Automated scripts*: some cybercriminals have automated scripts developed that can be executed to detect honeypots based on type, settings, and other default values. For example, the python script `cowrie_detect.py`[4] scans the network by collecting hostnames, ports, default arguments and accurately displays if the monitored machine is operating a Cowrie instance. This detection can be mitigated by modifying the default configuration files of the honeypot.

Over 19,208 open-source honeypots were detected using simple tools and signatures. The honeypots were concentrated across 637 autonomous systems, including research, enterprise, cloud and hosting networks [2]. This outcome is because these systems received no configuration before deployment and because cybercriminals are already aware of their default configurations [3, 7]. This research aims to mitigate this problem by modifying these configurations by studying the Cowrie honeypot's different artefacts and changing them to increase the honeypot's overall deceptiveness. This study further intends to educate security specialists and researchers on the differences between default and configured honeypot instances, i.e., centred on their deceptive ability and interaction with cybercriminals, it is critical to configure honeypots before deployment.

2   Research Process

This section describes the process in which this study was conducted. The research process (RP) comprises three main phases; sample selection, conduct experiments and observation.

2.1   RP-1: Sample Selection

The RP-1 phase consists of two steps (see Fig. 1):

i. *RP-1.1:* Acquire the latest stable version of the Cowrie honeypot using the `git-clone` command, i.e., Cowrie v2.1.0. After downloading the honeypot files, verify their cryptographic hash to ensure that they were copied with all dependencies and no file corruption.

---

[3] https://www.shodan.io/.

[4] https://github.com/boscutti939/Cowrie_Detect.

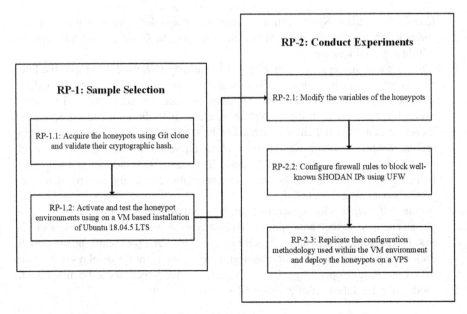

Fig. 1. Sample selection and conduct experiments research phases.

ii. *RP-1.2:* Activate and test the honeypot environments using virtual machine (VM) based installation of Ubuntu 18.04.5 LTS. A VM environment helps with frequent configurations during the testing phases and provides rollbacks to recover from erroneous designs via snapshots. These configurations can later be replicated (using an automated deployment script) for a configured honeypot deployment on a VPS, as discussed in RP-2.3.

2.2 RP-2: Conduct Experiments

The RP-2 phase comprises of three steps as described (see Fig. 1):

i. *RP-2.1:* As seen earlier for Cowrie [3], there is a default configuration file; `cowrie.cfg` can be analyzed and modified using a text editor. Similarly, Cowrie has numerous other files such as `ifconfig.py` (for changing the default MAC address and other base utilities), `userdb.txt` (for managing Cowrie's access credentials) and `honeyfs` files (for managing user groups, CPU information and others). These modifications can be achieved by manually inputting additional scripts, altering variables, enabling (uncommenting), or disabling (commenting) features within the application, or using automated scripts to generate a random set of values for deployment. In this scenario, the `obscurer.py`[5] script was used to automatically configure the Cowrie honeypot artefacts, as shown in Table 1. This script specifically targets the `honeyfs` file system of the Cowrie honeypot – the fake filesystem whose contents mimic an existing design. The script uniquely modifies the artefacts of the honeypot

---

[5] https://github.com/boscutti939/obscurer.

Table 1. Configurations employed by the `obscurer.py` script towards Cowrie artefacts.

Function name	Usage	File location
`ifconfig_py()`	Creates and modifies the address resolution protocol (ARP) table. Also, it rewrites the `ifconfig` command in Cowrie to show legitimate MAC addresses	`/src/cowrie/commands/ifconfig.py`
`version_uname()`	Alters the OS version username in `honeyfs` to a different OS version username	`/honeyfs/proc/version`
`meminfo_py()`	Alters the memory information using a random base value	`/honeyfs/proc/meminfo.py`
`mounts()`	Alters the name of a few mounted drives for the Cowrie instance	`/honeyfs/proc/mounts`
`cpuinfo()`	Edits information about the CPU model, clock speed, flags, and cache size for the Cowrie instance	`/honeyfs/proc/cpuinfo`
`group()`	Deletes the default user and group "phil" and adds some random usernames and groups pulled from the script	`/honeyfs/etc/group6`
`passwd()`	Deletes the default user "phil" and adds some random users pulled from the script	`/honeyfs/etc/passwd`
`shadow()`	Deletes the default user "phil" and adds some random users while generating salted hashed passwords for the users	`/honeyfs/etc/shadow`
`cowrie_cfg()`	Configures the Cowrie `cowrie.cfg` configuration file (the duplicate copy of the original Cowrie `cowrie.cfg.dist` file) to change the hostname, OS version name, SSH version, IP address, and other variables	`/etc/cowrie.cfg`
`hosts(cowrie_install_dir)`	Replaces the default/common host "nas3" with another hostname	`/honeyfs/etc/hosts`
`hostname_py(cowrie_install_dir)`	Changes the hostname file to a different hostname (name of the honeypot or server)	`/honeyfs/etc/hostname.py`
`issue(cowrie_install_dir)`	Changes the OS issue from the issue file in the `honeyfs` to a different OS issue	`/honeyfs/etc/issue`
`userdb(cowrie_install_dir)`	Creates and modifies the `userdb.txt` file and replaces whatever is in it with its unique users and passwords	`/etc/userdb.txt`
`fs_pickle(cowrie_install_dir)`	Executes the `createfs` command within the Cowrie repository to recreate the honeypot filesystem (This function is executed last by the `obscurer.py` script)	`/share/cowrie/fs.pickle`

each time it is executed. Furthermore, to reduce the Cowrie honeypot's identification probability, a custom introductory banner was created, and the interactive session timeout increased from 180 to 600 s. Additionally, the `txtcmds` file was configured to display fake outputs for commands such as `ip a`, which otherwise returned empty strings for default Cowrie versions.

ii. *RP-2.2:* Cybercriminals use scanning services such as Shodan and Censys for identifying whether they are connecting to legitimate servers or services. According to Chen, Lian [6], security specialists can create an IP blacklist as a predominant solution to block or inhibit scanners. Numerous open sources publish and update the various scanners' IP list. These IP addresses can be added to a firewall's blocklist for preventing automated scanning services up to a certain extent. However, it is essential to remember that an IP list encompassing a complete list of all the automated scanners cannot be established. A list of the well-known automated scanners and their subnets were identified. The developed blacklist was created by referring to GitHub, SANS Institute and Reddit, and the active honeypots themselves. To increase the honeypots deceptive potential against such scanners, the IP addresses were blocked by using the `ufw` firewall.

iii. *RP-2.3:* Once the configurations are complete, the next step of experimentation phase is to check if there is any increase in the honeypots' deceptive potential. This validation was achieved by replicating the actions seen in RP-2.1 and RP-2.2 by deploying three honeypots; one with default configurations and two using an automated Cowrie deployment script created by using the author's designs, to monitor and validate the deceptive effect of the default deployments versus those of the automatic deployment. These deployments were administered on a monthly cycle, as seen in Table 2.

Table 2. Cowrie deployment cycle.

Honeypot	Deployment type	Deployment period	Credentials
Cowrie A	Default	1st November 2020–29th November 2020	Default credentials
Cowrie B	Configured	30th November 2020–28th December 2020	Username: tech Password: enable
Cowrie C	Configured	29th December 2020–26th January 2021	Username: root Password: nproc

2.3 RP-3: Observation

The default honeypots were observed against the configured deployments to study the distinction between the initial and the modified deceptiveness displayed by the honeypots. The following variables can analyze this distinction:

i. *Emulated service activity (SI):* The number of times there was activity with an emulated service.
ii. *IP connections (IP):* the total sum of distinctive machines that attempted to gain access to the Cowrie honeypot.
iii. *Connection to deceptive ports (CDP):* the number of times a cybercriminal connected to deceptive TCP/UDP ports.
iv. *Brute force count (BF):* the highest number of times the same attacker tried to connect to the honeypot instance.

The correlations between these variables were established employing statistical tables in the results section of this research. These values are collected by Cowrie's log files and stored within their respective directories. Splunk was used to visualize the information and study cybercriminal behavior in the configured environment versus the default environment. In cases of a slight increase in the deceptive ability of the honeypots, RP-2 was conducted repeatedly until a satisfied deception capability was achieved (such as creating supplementary firewall rules). Additional arrangements to test the increase of the deceptive potential was achieved by scanning Cowrie with NMAP 7.80, Shodan and the `cowrie_detect.py` script using a Kali Linux (version) instance.

3 Results and Analysis

In this section, the results of each honeypot are shown and analyzed. These results include the NMAP and Shodan scans, log data collected from Splunk and the output from the `cowrie_detect.py` script. Please note that some data must be hidden due to security purposes, but conclusions can still be drawn.

3.1 NMAP Scan Analysis

NMAP scans were conducted using the command:

```
nmap -sV -Pn -p- [IP_address]
```

Table 3. NMAP scan output for Cowrie A.

Port	State	Service	Version
22/tcp	Open	SSH	OpenSSH (7.6p1 Ubuntu-4ubuntu0.3)
2222/tcp	Open	SSH	OpenSSH (6.0p1 Debian 4+deb7u2)

Where sV is used for service detection, Pn is used to suppress pings during scans to detect whether a host is up, and p is used to specify a port range. In this case, -p- scans all ports between 1–65535. The NMAP scan results are shown in Table 3 (for Cowrie A) and Table 4 (for Cowrie B and Cowrie C).

Table 4. NMAP scan output for Cowrie B.

Port	State	Service	Version
22/tcp	Open	SSH	`OpenSSH (7.6p1 Ubuntu-4ubuntu0.3)`
53/tcp	Closed	Domain	N/A
80/tcp	Closed	HTTP	N/A
47808/tcp	Closed	BACnet	N/A
10000/tcp	Closed	Sent-sensor-mgmt	N/A

The NMAP scan for Cowrie A revealed that the honeypot was listening on SSH port 22 operating on `OpenSSH (7.6p1 Ubuntu-4ubuntu0.3)` and port 2222 using `OpenSSH (6.0p1 Debian 4+deb7u2)`. A majority of default Cowrie instances operate on two SSH ports; port 2222 is the default port for the Cowrie honeypot and OpenSSH (6.0p1 Debian 4+deb7u2) standard SSH string as seen in the `cowrie.cfg` config file. These comparisons are solid indicators for a cybercriminal to notice that the machine they are trying to compromise might be a honeypot.

In contrast, Cowrie B and Cowrie C's results displayed that the honeypots allowed incoming connections on a single port, i.e., SSH port 22 using `OpenSSH (7.6p1 Ubuntu-4ubuntu0.3)`. It further detected four closed ports, as seen in Table 4, which is not the case for standard deployments. Furthermore, Cowrie B and Cowrie C did not produce any suspicious honeypot indicators such as standard operating ports, default SSH string versions and static MAC addresses. Therefore, having no default values of being a honeypot instance. The Splunk Log Analysis can prove this increased deceptiveness from NMAP scans (see Sect. 3.3), where Cowrie B and Cowrie C had a more significant percentage of SI, IP, CDP, and BF as equated to Cowrie A.

3.2 Shodan Scan Analysis

The Shodan scans revealed the same information about the honeypot instances as described in the NMAP scan. It showed that Cowrie A was listening on two open ports, port 22 and port 2222, while Cowrie B and Cowrie C were listening on port 22. It also displayed the default SSH algorithms used by Cowrie A (see `cowrie.cfg`) instead of those used by the other two honeypot instances (see Table 5). The default SSH strings are indicators for a cybercriminal to detect a Cowrie instance in conjunction with the discovered open ports. This indicator is not the case for Cowrie B and Cowrie C because they use configured SSH algorithms on port 22.

Table 5. SSH algorithms used by the Cowrie honeypot instances.

SSH algorithm	Cowrie A	Cowrie B & Cowrie C

KEX algorithms	`curve25519-sha256,`
	`curve25519-sha256@libssh.org,`
	`ecdh-sha2-nistp256,`
	`ecdh-sha2-nistp384,`
	`ecdh-sha2-nistp521,`
	`diffie-hellman-group-exchange-sha256,`
	`diffie-hellman-group-exchange-sha1,`
	`diffie-hellman-group14-sha1`
		`curve25519-sha256,`
		`curve25519-sha256@libssh.org,`
		`ecdh-sha2-nistp256,`
		`ecdh-sha2-nistp384,`
		`ecdh-sha2-nistp521,`
		`diffie-hellman-group-exchange-sha256,`
		`diffie-hellman-group16-sha512,`
		`diffie-hellman-group18-sha512,`
		`diffie-hellman-group14-sha256,`
		`diffie-hellman-group14-sha1`

Server host key algorithms	`ssh-rsa,`
	`ssh-dss`
		`ssh-rsa,`
		`rsa-sha2-512,`
		`rsa-sha2-256,`
		`ecdsa-sha2-nistp256,`
		`ssh-ed25519,`

Encryption Algorithms	`aes128-ctr,`
	`aes192-ctr,`
	`aes256-ctr,`
	`aes256-cbc,`
	`aes192-cbc,`
	`aes128-cbc,`
	`3des-cbc,`
	`blowfish-cbc,`
	`cast128-cbc`
		`chacha20-poly1305@openssh.com,`
		`aes128-ctr,`
		`aes192-ctr,`
		`aes256-ctr,`
		`aes128-gcm@openssh.com,`
		`aes256-gcm@openssh.com`

MAC algorithms	`hmac-sha2-512`
	`hmac-sha2-384`
	`hmac-sha2-56`
	`hmac-sha1`
	`hmac-md5`
		`umac-64-etm@openssh.com,`
		`umac-128-etm@openssh.com,`
		`hmac-sha2-256-etm@openssh.com,`
		`hmac-sha2-512-etm@openssh.com,`
		`hmac-sha1-etm@openssh.com,`
		`umac-64@openssh.com,`
		`umac-128@openssh.com,`
		`hmac-sha2-256,`
		`hmac-sha2-512,`
		`hmac-sha1`

Compression algorithms	`zlib@openssh.com`
	`zlib`
	`none`
		`None,`
		`zlib@openssh.com`

3.3 Splunk Analysis

Splunk was used to visualize data collected from the Cowrie logs. This information has been aggregated into three datasets based on a:

i. *24-h deployment*: As seen in Table 6, Cowrie A detected 998 instances of service emulation activity. Cowrie B did not detect any emulation activity cases because not even a single attacker gained access to the honeypot instance even after recording 4,601 brute force attempts from a single IP. The honeypot had emulation inactivity even after 7 and 28 days of being deployed. In contrast, Cowrie C attained 9,921 SI's, an 894.08% increase than Cowrie A. It also detected 243 distinct IP connections, a 38.85% and a 5.65% enhancement compared to Cowrie A and Cowrie B honeypots. Cowrie A established connections on port 2222 receiving 1,198 requests in terms of CDP, whereas Cowrie B connected to port 22 and port 443, receiving 10,549 and 3.922 probes, respectively. Cowrie C allowed connections on 16 deceptive ports. On

Table 6. Information collected from the Cowrie honeypots for a 24-h deployment.

Honeypot	SI	IP	CDP		BF
			Port	Count	
Cowrie A	998	175	2222	1,198	3,976
Cowrie B	0	230	22	10,549	4,601
			443	3,922	
Cowrie C	9,921	243	443	31,039	18,650
			22	18,598	
			80	12,391	
			993	6,040	
			25000	1,148	
			25	1,043	
			5555	412	
			143	287	
			465	224	
			587	133	
			995	46	
			2525	23	
			43	10	
			26	10	
			4013	2	
			2002	2	

its SSH port, it received 18,598 searches, a 1452.42% and 76.30% increase compared to the other honeypots. It also recorded the highest number of BF occurrences, 18,650 attempts.

ii. *7-day deployment*: In Table 7, the statistics show that the configured honeypots had many cybercriminals connected to deceptive ports. Cowrie A recorded 7,210 connections, Cowrie B had 79,492, and Cowrie C recorded 481,204 connections. Cowrie B verified a 1002.52% increase and, Cowrie C logged a 6,574.12% augmentation in terms of CDP compared to Cowrie A. The configured honeypots also showed superior deceptiveness in terms of SI (excluding Cowrie B), IP, and BF compared to Cowrie A.

iii. *28-day deployment*: Table 8 shows similar results to Table 6 and i.e., the configured honeypots had better deceptive indicators in terms of SI, IP, CDP, and BF. Cowrie A displayed 51,644 instances of emulation activity, received connections from 4,972 distinct IP addresses , allowed 49,340 connections to its SSH port and recorded

Table 7. Information collected from the Cowrie honeypots for a 7-day deployment.

Honeypot	SI	IP	CDP		BF
			Port	Count	
Cowrie A	10,347	1,198	2222	7,210	15,992
Cowrie B	0	1,589	22	55,722	18,541
			443	23,770	
Cowrie C	61,823	1,675	443	169,499	56,081
			22	129,893	
			80	85,451	
			993	72,946	
			25000	6,645	
			25	6,583	
			465	2,690	
			5555	2,663	
			143	2,306	
			587	1,574	
			995	470	
			3724	144	
			2525	123	
			26	90	
			43	70	
			110	40	
			8000	12	
			4013	2	
			2002	2	
			27018	1	

67,508 brute force attacks. On the other hand, Cowrie B detected a 100% decrease in SI activity, a 64.94% increase in IP connections, allowed 356.21% more deceptive connections compared to Cowrie A on the SSH port, and finally, a 16.02% rise in brute force attempts. Similarly, Cowrie C detected a 400.22% increase in emulation activity, a 134.37% rise in the number of different IP connections, connections to 21 deceptive ports and a 255.22% surge in the number of brute force attempts originating from a particular IP with 239,802 recorded attempts.

Table 8. Information collected from the Cowrie honeypots for a 28-day deployment.

Honeypot	SI	IP	CDP		BF
			Port	Count	
Cowrie A	51,644	4,972	2222	49,340	67,508
Cowrie B	0	8,201	22	225,096	78,328
			443	108,084	
Cowrie C	258,332	11,653	22	642,732	239,802
			443	588,977	
			80	334,188	
			993	268,812	
			25000	32,680	
			25	31,221	
			465	13,985	
			5555	12,370	
			143	12,321	
			587	8,249	
			995	2,463	
			3724	932	
			2525	346	
			26	231	
			43	190	
			110	120	
			8000	54	
			4013	13	
			2002	8	
			32400	8	
			27018	6	

3.4 Cowrie_detect.py Detection Analysis

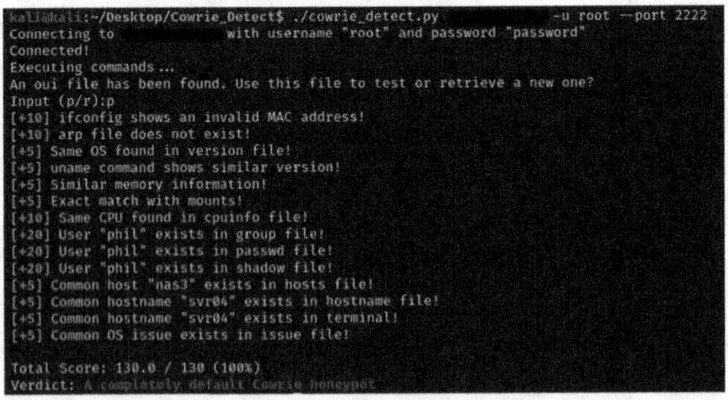

Fig. 2. `cowrie_detect.py` scan on Cowrie A

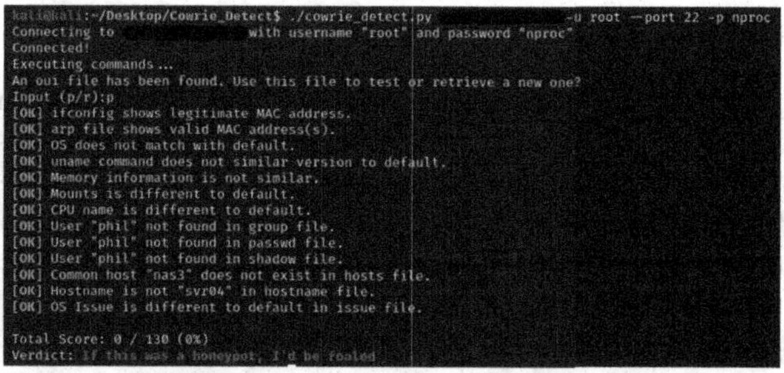

Fig. 3. `cowrie_detect.py` scan on Cowrie B and Cowrie C

Figure 2 shows that the automated script, `cowrie_detect.py,` detected Cowrie A as a default honeypot instance with a 100% certainty. The script's leading indicators to distinguish the default Cowrie instance were the existence of the standard user "`phil`" in the group, password and shadow files, and the presence of a static/invalid MAC address and the absence of an ARP file. Secondary detection indicators are the occurrences of an unconfigured `cowrie.cfg` file; default memory and CPU information and a pre-existing OS version used by the Cowrie host and the standard hosts "nas3" and "svr04". In comparison, Fig. 3 displays the output of the `cowrie_detect.py` when executed against Cowrie B and Cowrie C. The script could not find any default users, a static MAC address, default CPU data, standard memory information or default configured hostnames. Therefore, it can be verified that the revised versions of Cowrie are 100% more deceptive than the standard versions when scanned using the `cowrie_detect.py` script.

3.5 Miscellaneous Observations

According to the command line results, the most entered commands included `uname-s -v -n -r`, `cat /proc/cpuinfo| grep name | wc-1` and`cat /proc/cpuinfo| grep name | head -n 1 | awk'(print $4,$5,$6,$7,$8,$9;)'`. For the uname command, Cowrie A returns the default string, and for the cpuinfo commands, it produced the output: `Intel(R) Core (TM) 2 Duo E8200@` while the modified versions generated: `Intel(R) Core (TM) I7-2960XMCPU @ 2.70GHz`. These results show that the command fails on all default versions of the Cowrie instance. It is a powerful indicator for a cybercriminal to exit the environment upon connecting to the honeypot server immediately. Therefore, it was detected that 81% of attackers exited the honeypot session after executing the uname command in Cowrie A and 87% of attackers exited the interactive shell after entering the cpuinfo command – thus, verifying that on average, IP addresses stayed for 112.36 s when connected to Cowrie A. However, commands entered in the configured instances produced a legitimate string with unique information about the shell and CPU, unlike Cowrie A. Finally, Cowrie C showed that attackers executed 65% more commands and stayed within the interactive shell an average of 537.82 s after using the uname command before exiting the environment.

4 Conclusion

The results of the honeypot deployments show the effectiveness of having configured deployments over the default counterparts. Configured Cowrie honeypots provided an improvement in the information collected from cybercriminals, such as an increase in distinct IP connections, the types of commands being executed, files downloaded and VirusTotal submissions. These instances also displayed the number of brute force attempts and the top username and password combinations used. Cowrie B did not detect any SI activity because attackers could not access its interactive shell due to a more robust username/password combination. The most common login credentials in Cowrie A and Cowrie B's case were recorded to be "root" and "nproc". Therefore, Cowrie C was configured with this weaker username/password combination, although the automated script uniquely modified its other artefacts. In future, the obscurer script will be further modified, or a new script will be forked to include modifications to Cowrie's txtcmds and fs.pickle artefacts to provide a higher simulation in terms of command outputs. The script will also be configured to have several unique new users, hostnames, groups, file shares, hard drive sizes, mounts, CPU and RAM information, OS versions, IP addresses, MAC addresses and SSH versions. Further testings and analysis will also be carried out to show that the script does not configure the honeypot in some deterministic manner which scanning tools can soon automate.

Acknowledgements. The work has been supported by the Cyber Security Research Centre, whose activities are partially funded by the Australian Government's Cooperative Research Centres program.

References

1. Cabral, W.Z., Valli, C., Sikos, L.F., Wakeling, S.G.: Analysis of Conpot and its BACnet features for cyber-deception. In: Proceedings of the 19th International Conference on Security & Management. Springer (2020)
2. Morishita, S., et al.: Detect me if you… oh wait. An internet-wide view of self-revealing honeypots. In: 2019 IFIP/IEEE Symposium on Integrated Network and Service Management (IM), pp. 134–143. IEEE (2019)
3. Cabral, W.Z., Valli, C., Sikos, L.F., Wakeling, S.G.: Review and analysis of Cowrie artefacts and their potential to be used deceptively. In: Proceedings of the 6th Annual Conference on Computational Science and Computational Intelligence, pp. 166–171. IEEE (2019). https://doi.org/10.1109/CSCI49370.2019.00035
4. Zhang, F., Zhou, S., Qin, Z., Liu, J.: Honeypot: a supplemented active defense system for network security. In: Proceeding of the 4th International Conference on Parallel and Distributed Computing, Applications and Technologies, pp. 231–235. IEEE (2003). https://doi.org/10.1109/PDCAT.2003.1236295
5. Nicomette, V., Kaâniche, M., Alata, E., Herrb, M.: Set-up and deployment of a high-interaction honeypot: experiment and lessons learned. J. Comput. Virol. 7, 143–157 (2010). https://doi.org/10.1007/s11416-010-0144-2
6. Chen, Y., Lian, X., Yu, D., Lv, S., Hao, S., Ma, Y.: Exploring Shodan from the perspective of industrial control systems. IEEE Access 8, 75359–75369 (2020). https://doi.org/10.1109/ACCESS.2020.2988691

7. Vetterl, A., Clayton, R., Walden, I.: Counting outdated honeypots: legal and useful. In: 2019 IEEE Security and Privacy Workshops (SPW), pp. 224–229. IEEE (2019). https://doi.org/10.1109/SPW.2019.00049
8. Oosterhof, M.: Cowrie SSH and Telnet Honeypot: GitHub (2020). https://github.com/cowrie/cowrie
9. Lyon, G.F.: Nmap - network mapper (2021). https://nmap.org/
10. Matherly, J.: Shodan (2021). https://www.shodan.io/

Less is Often More: Header Whitelisting as Semantic Gap Mitigation in HTTP-Based Software Systems

Andre Büttner[1]([✉])[iD], Hoai Viet Nguyen[2][iD], Nils Gruschka[1][iD], and Luigi Lo Iacono[2][iD]

[1] University of Oslo, Gaustadalléen 23B, 0373 Oslo, Norway
{andrbut,nilsgrus}@ifi.uio.no
[2] Hochschule Bonn-Rhein-Sieg, Grantham-Allee 20, 53757 Sankt Augustin, Germany
luigi.lo_iacono@h-brs.de

Abstract. The web is the most wide-spread digital system in the world and is used for many crucial applications. This makes web application security extremely important and, although there are already many security measures, new vulnerabilities are constantly being discovered. One reason for some of the recent discoveries lies in the presence of intermediate systems—e.g. caches, message routers, and load balancers—on the way between a client and a web application server. The implementations of such intermediaries may interpret HTTP messages differently, which leads to a semantically different understanding of the same message. This so-called semantic gap can cause weaknesses in the entire HTTP message processing chain.

In this paper we introduce the header whitelisting (HWL) approach to address the semantic gap in HTTP message processing pipelines. The basic idea is to normalize and reduce an HTTP request header to the minimum required fields using a whitelist before processing it in an intermediary or on the server, and then restore the original request for the next hop. Our results show that HWL can avoid misinterpretations of HTTP messages in the different components and thus prevent many attacks rooted in a semantic gap including request smuggling, cache poisoning, and authentication bypass.

Keywords: HTTP · Web · Intermediaries · Semantic gap · Security · Header whitelisting

1 Introduction

When the web was created more than 30 years ago, no one had imagined that it would evolve into a global system used by billions of people for nearly every aspect of their daily lives. Due to the ever-growing number of users, web servers need to be offloaded to meet performance and scalability requirements. This is often realized by intermediate systems such as caches, which store static resources, or load balancers, which distribute requests across different server instances [10].

© IFIP International Federation for Information Processing 2021
Published by Springer Nature Switzerland AG 2021
A. Jøsang et al. (Eds.): SEC 2021, IFIP AICT 625, pp. 332–347, 2021.
https://doi.org/10.1007/978-3-030-78120-0_22

However, these various HTTP-based entities involved in the message processing pipeline can also induce problems. Web applications often suffer from differences in the processing of HTTP messages. It can lead to serious security vulnerabilities if the processing elements in the processing chain interpret the same message differently [4,31]. In this context, the HTTP header fields take on an important role, as they are essential for interpreting an HTTP message. Unfortunately, in practice they are not handled consistently by HTTP implementations, which can lead to, e.g., different perceptions of the syntactic validity or caching behavior of an HTTP message. Moreover, an HTTP header can include standardized and non-standardized header fields; both are permitted by the HTTP standard [12]. However, non-standardized header fields are ignored by some components, while having a decisive role for others, especially when it comes to access privileges. If the components are not complementing each other well, unintentional behavior can occur, which can consequently be abused by a malicious user.

The underlying problem of different processing and interpretation of HTTP messages by different processing units within a processing pipeline is called "semantic gap" [4,31]. Although this issue has been known for a long time, new types of semantic gap attacks are continuously being discovered [2]. Also, current security mechanisms like WAFs can only partly mitigate this threat (see Sect. 4). Therefore, attackers nowadays have a good chance to exploit a semantic gap for malicious purposes.

This paper presents a novel protection means that specifically addresses the semantic gap problem. Our analysis of known semantic gap vulnerabilities shows that most of them result from inconsistent processing of HTTP request header fields. We therefore suggest normalizing and filtering request header fields before they are processed by HTTP components. By passing only those header fields that are required by a particular intermediary and that can be reliably processed, attacks involving broken, malformed, or non-standardized header fields can be prevented. This can be used to defend against not only known attacks but also potential zero-day exploits, as is already being done for malware [28,35]. We provide the following main contributions:

1. The semantic gap in HTTP message processing is defined, known attacks that exploit the semantic gap are analyzed, and they are categorized according to their causes.
2. The concept of header whitelisting (HWL) is introduced as a measure to mitigate the semantic gap. A prototype implementation is presented and evaluated, showing effective protection against known attacks.

The remainder of this paper is structured as follows: Sect. 2 details the semantic gap in the context of HTTP-based software systems. Further foundations in terms of real-world attacks are presented in Sect. 3 followed by Sect. 4, which reviews the related work of proposed measures against these attacks. In Sect. 5 the HWL approach is introduced and its prototype implementation is described. In Sect. 6, we experimentally evaluate the effectiveness of HWL with respect to semantic gap attack evasion. The paper closes with a discussion in Sect. 7 and a conclusion with an outlook on future work in Sect. 8.

2   Semantic Gaps in HTTP Message Processing

Even though the HTTP protocol is specified in RFC standards, HTTP-based software systems tend to suffer from semantic differences when processing HTTP messages, which is summarized by the term *semantic gap*. Within the scope of this work, the semantic gap is defined as *inconsistent processing of HTTP messages inside a pipeline between the actual application logic and the intermediaries*. Such a behaviour can have serious consequences, as will be discussed in more detail in Sect. 3.

We identified three main causes of inconsistent HTTP message processing. The first one is ambiguous wording within the HTTP standard. It is generally forbidden, e.g., to include more than one header field with identical field name in HTTP messages. However, the HTTP standard leaves room for *well-known exceptions*. This ambiguity leads to widely varying HTTP implementations. Some may reject a request with duplicate header fields. Others will accept such requests and consider either the first or the last one and either ignore or remove the other instance. Furthermore, no limit is defined for the length of the header fields [12]. Both aspects can lead to a wide range of vulnerabilities, such as Request Smuggling or HTTP Header Oversize.

Another cause of inconsistent HTTP message processing is improper HTTP implementations. This is especially relevant for parsing the HTTP header. There are implementations that allow invalid syntax and ignore the affected header fields. Others clean up requests from invalid header fields, which in turn can affect subsequent HTTP-processing components. And yet other implementations completely reject requests with invalid syntax. If an intermediary and a server handle invalid meta characters in HTTP header fields differently, this can be exploited, e.g., to cause a denial-of-service.

A final major cause for a semantic gap is different HTTP versions used by the components involved or different specifications for the same version. For the widely used HTTP/1.1, e.g., there exists the outdated RFC 2616 [11] and the current RFC 7230 [12]. This results in implementations that conform to the outdated version, while others conform to the latest standard. Developers and server providers are certainly aware of this fact. Nonetheless, it is possible that there is still software in use that refers to the deprecated specification. This can be critical since RFC 2616 does, e.g., not explicitly forbid trailing whitespaces in header field names, while RFC 7230 requires the HTTP message to be rejected in this case. Accordingly, this can lead to HTTP Desync attacks. Another example is the line folding option that allows to span a header field value over multiple lines. This is supported in RFC 2616, but is deprecated in RFC 7230. It was demonstrated that this can be exploited for Request Smuggling. Additionally, there are also discrepancies between different HTTP versions. It has been shown, e.g., that a client can cause various types of denial-of-service attacks in cases where an intermediary supports HTTP/2 while the web server uses HTTP/1.1 [15]. This is due to header compression in HTTP/2, which is not supported in HTTP/1.1. In this case, a client sends header fields to the intermediary via HTTP/2 compression. Since these header fields are transmitted to the web server via HTTP/1.1, they must be decompressed and can be significantly larger. Therefore, there is an increased server load, which can lead to other connections being blocked.

In summary, there are many causes of semantic gaps in an HTTP message processing pipeline. These cannot be solved right away or easily, as it would require harmonizing all HTTP implementations to one single unambiguous specification. This is unrealistic considering how many HTTP-based software components are available and in use in the wild. As we will emphasize in the subsequent Sect. 3, effective means are nonetheless urgently required for web application developers and providers to cope with the security threats and risks stemming from semantic gaps rooted vulnerabilities.

3   Attacks Rooted in a Semantic Gap

In recent years, the semantic gap has been the root for many serious threats in web-based layered software systems that consist of various intermediaries. In this section, we provide an overview of semantic gap vulnerabilities in HTTP message processing as defined in Sect. 2. Attacks based on semantic gaps in other application layers, such as processing multiple cookies [3], are out of scope.

The *Response Splitting* attack [23] was one of the first vulnerabilities to exploit a semantic gap to perform web cache poisoning. Here, an attacker takes advantage of a parsing issue that occurs when carriage return (CR) and line feed (LF) characters are not sanitized or escaped properly. If a web server then reflects a value of the request in the response, an attacker can exploit both issues by sending a request with CR and LF characters in conjunction with a malicious response hidden in a header field value. The reflected malicious input forces the returned response to be interpreted as two responses. The second response, which is completely under the attacker's control, is then stored by the cache, effectively poisoning it with the attacker's malicious payload.

The *Request Smuggling* attack [27] exploits a semantic gap in parsing more than one `Content-Length` header fields—although forbidden according to RFC 7230 [12]—to smuggle a hidden request through an intermediary. With this technique, a malicious client can provoke a web cache poisoning if two intermediaries (one of these a cache) pick different `Content-Length` header fields and therefore read different amounts of the payload. The ambiguous interpretation of `Content-Length` header fields can also be applied to hide malicious requests from security intermediaries such as WAFs, Intrusion Detection Systems (IDS) or access control mechanisms. In a rather new variant of Request Smuggling, called *HTTP Desync* attack [22] similar effects can be achieved using the `Transfer-Encoding` or non-standardized headers like `X-Forwarded-Host`.

The *Host of Trouble* (HoT) attack [4] is another attack that aims to poison web caches or bypass security policies, e.g. in a WAF. Unlike Request Smuggling, this attack uses duplicate `Host` header fields. Although the presence of more than one `Host` header field is not compliant with RFC 7230, Chen et al. [4] uncovered many real-world HTTP implementations that ignore this requirement.

The *Cache-Poisoned Denial of Service* (CPDoS) attack [31] exploits semantic gaps to deny access to web resources by poisoning the cache with error pages. The three CPDoS attack variants *HTTP Header Oversize* (HHO), *HTTP Meta Character* (HMC), and *HTTP Method Override* (HMO) were introduced that exploit the mismatch between header size limits, meta character handling, and the method override header respectively. The authors showed in empirical studies that millions of web sites were vulnerable to CPDoS. Nathan Davison presented another variant of CPDoS by using the Hop-by-Hop header mechanism [7].

The *Web Cache Deception* (WCD) attack [14] aims to disclose sensitive information with the help of a cache. This can be achieved in cases where caches decide whether to store responses based on the URL and consider URLs with suffixes such as `.css` or `.png` as static. The attacker appends such suffixes to URLs of resources containing confidential information, which is then stored in the cache. In a 2020 analysis of the Alexa Top 5K, Mirheidari et al. found 340 web sites vulnerable to WCD attacks [30].

In addition to the attacks mentioned above, new attacks that exploit a semantic gap are published very frequently, e.g. [2]. Also, we found that some of the reported vulnerabilities can be exploited in different ways. For example, the `X-Original-URL` and `X-Rewrite-URL` header fields can be used for CPDoS attacks or the Hop-by-Hop mechanism can be used to cause Request Smuggling.

Table 1. List of attacks that exploit a semantic gap in the processing of HTTP messages inside a pipeline between the actual application logic and intermediate systems

Attack		Semantic gap	Embedment
Response splitting		Meta character handling	URL
Request smuggling		Content-Length, Transfer-Encoding, X-Forwarded-Host, X-Host, X-Forwarded-Server, X-Forwarded-Scheme, X-Original-URL, X-Rewrite-URL, Meta character handling	Header
Host-of-trouble		Host header	Header
CPDoS	HHO	Header size limit	Header
	HMC	Meta character handling	Header
	HMO	Method overriding headers, e.g. X-HTTP-Method-Override, X-HTTP-Method, X-Method-Override	Header
	Others	X-Original-URL, X-Rewrite-URL	Header
Hop-by-Hop		Connection header	Header
WCD		URL parsing	URL

This overview of attacks based on a semantic gap emphasizes their high relevance, especially when considering the flourishing number of attack variants. Their impact on real applications highlights the urgent need for efficient mitigation. As we already pointed out in Sect. 2, there is no easy way to eliminate the root cause of semantic gaps. However, as the summary view of Table 1 shows, in many cases the processing of the HTTP header is the starting point for the attacks. This suggests that a broad range of semantic gap based attacks can be mitigated by treating the HTTP header in some suitable manner. Before elaborating this observation further, we will first review the literature on proposed countermeasures to identify possible approaches to mitigate such vulnerabilities.

4   Related Work

Most of the literature about the attacks discussed in Sect. 3 also suggests mitigation measures. WCD attacks may be prevented if HTTP responses contain proper caching directives. A further proposed measure is to put static files into a separate directory and configure the web server or cache to only allow caching of the contents of this directory. In general, invalid URL paths should be handled with an error response [14]. CPDoS attacks can be avoided by configuring a cache in a way that HTTP responses with certain error status codes are not stored. Additionally, the `no-store` directive in error responses by the server application could prevent the cache from storing them [31]. A more stricter HTTP parsing could help to mitigate Request Smuggling [27]. To this end, e.g., a proof-of-concept implementation exists that hooks into a server's socket functions, monitors HTTP messages, and closes the connection if HTTP violations are detected [24]. This approach in particular enforces valid formatting of header fields and adds special treatment to the `Content-Length` and `Transfer-Encoding` headers. While this helps to mitigate a broad range of Request Smuggling attacks and other attacks based on invalid meta characters, cache poisoning, Hop-by-Hop and Host-of-Trouble vulnerabilities are not prevented. Also, the usage of HTTP/2 mitigates Request Smuggling issues due to the use of binary frames and streams [22]. Hop-by-Hop vulnerabilities are prevented by this as well, since the `Connection` header field is not used in HTTP/2. However, this does not solve vulnerabilities based on non-standardized header fields or HoT. Response Splitting can be avoided by validating input from the client, especially in query parameters, and by removing special characters from a string before including it in a response header value [23]. To prevent `Host` header field attacks, Chen et al. recommend to ensure compliance with RFC 7230 [4]. According to them, the attack is the result of incorrect implementations. They refer to the latest HTTP/1.1 specification which should, in contrast to RFC 2616, define more clearly how to deal with ambiguities of the host. For mitigating access control vulnerabilities, access restrictions should be defined through the web application and for each resource separately [29].

Web application firewalls (WAFs) are intermediaries that intend to prevent many different types of attacks against web applications. They can be operated in different ways, such as a (transparent) reverse proxy [19], a network bridge [21], embedded in the web application [9] or as a cloud service [20]. Different measures can be included in a WAF, for example input validation, protocol enforcement, authorization or cookie signatures [6,8,16]. There are whitelist, blacklist or hybrid models that can be applied to define rules for HTTP traffic [5]. Several WAFs provide default configurations that include mitigations against many attacks including the OWASP Top Ten [32]. This gives WAF users a basic level of protection and certainly prevents several types of attacks. Nevertheless, it does not provide absolute protection. Basically WAFs are also intermediaries that can be subject to semantic differences. There are reports about bypassing WAF rules, for instance by using Request Smuggling techniques [25] or non-standardized header fields [1]. Consequently, WAFs are also affected by the semantic gap. Another problem is the restrained use due to the complexity and required effort of configuring and updating WAF configurations [33].

In summary, the measures proposed in the literature are very fragmented and only apply to a specific type of attack. Hence, a comprehensive protection against semantic gap attacks is hard to achieve and requires to careful adopt all of the discussed countermeasures specifically tailored for each environment. As such, this is very error-prone and cannot always be implemented consistently for the complete processing chain. Mirheidari et al. take this line and suggest that there should be a different view of web application security [30]. They recommend not to focus on individual HTTP components but to have a holistic view of the entire system. We encourage this perspective as well and assume that the semantic gap is an important factor for the security of web applications regarding all HTTP components involved. We present such a more holistic approach to mitigating semantic gap attacks in the following section.

5   Header Whitelisting

As we noted in Sect. 3, almost all known semantic gap attacks have their roots in HTTP header parsing ambiguities (see Table 1). This suggests that many of the attacks can be thwarted by a strictly standard compliant message parsing. Since a comprehensive consistent implementation is a practically hopeless endeavor given the large number of different HTTP components that exist in practice, other approaches are required to counter the attacks. By introducing the so-called *header whitelisting* (HWL) we suggest that a specialized security intermediate normalizes the header using the HTTP standard as a baseline and reduces it to the minimum header fields required for processing by a particular component in the processing pipeline. In this paper we focus on attacks that are based on malicious request header fields. Therefore our approach is only applied to the request header.

Whitelisting is used for some time for various types of security mechanisms [34]. Network firewalls use whitelists to filter network traffic [17], for example. Spam filters use domain name server whitelists (DNSWL) that provide a list of trusted mail servers and IP addresses [26]. Header Whitelisting, as we introduce it in this paper, means that a request is transformed to consist only of required—and preferably standardized—header field names with expected header field values. When HWL is applied in front of an HTTP-processing entity, this entity will only receive HTTP requests whose headers are reduced to the fields it knows and minimally needs. As a result, requests containing malformed header entries are rejected or the affected entries are removed by HWL before

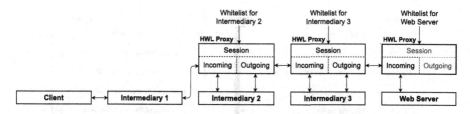

Fig. 1. Basic architecture of an HWL equipped HTTP-based software system. Intermediate systems and/or the web server are wrapped by HWL proxies tailoring the upstream HTTP message as individually required by each HWL-protected component.

they reach actual processing nodes. In addition, reducing the amount of header entries to the minimum necessary ensures that unknown or hidden functionality cannot be exploited. This is especially important if e.g. web frameworks are used in the application, as these contain a large number of functions and standard behaviors that are often neither known nor needed, but can potentially be used for attacks.

5.1   Architecture

Since every component that processes HTTP requests may process header fields differently, the idea is to isolate single components separately from invalid and needless header fields. This can be achieved by applying HWL to some or all of the components in the message processing pipeline, each with an individual whitelist (see Fig. 1). An HWL Proxy is introduced that can be wrapped around intermediaries and/or the application logic running on the server, enforcing an individual whitelist for each wrapped component. It consists of three core modules. The *Incoming* module receives the requests and applies header whitelisting. This means, it checks whether the HTTP header fields match with the configured whitelist and consequently removes all header fields that are not listed. The resulting request containing only whitelisted header fields is then forwarded to the protected component. The *Outgoing* module receives back the processed request from the protected component and restores the original request respecting modifications that are possibly done by the component. This request is then forwarded to the next HTTP component in the chain. Note that in case the HWL Proxy is deployed in front of a web application server, the Outgoing module is not required, because the server is the last instance that receives an HTTP request and therefore does not forward it further. The *Session* module handles the linking between a request in the Incoming module to the corresponding request in the Outgoing module and temporarily stores the removed header fields.

Our approach requires to modify a request before it enters and before it leaves a HWL-protected component. A request received by the HWL Proxy will be normalized and customized according to the underlying whitelist. After the request has been processed by the component, the HWL Proxy restores the original request and sends it to the next hop on the path. This can not be

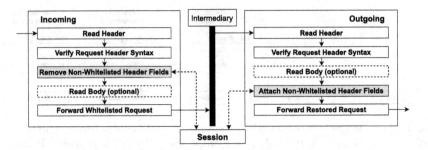

Fig. 2. HWL Proxy implementation showing the different processing steps for HTTP requests. Essential steps for the header whitelisting are highlighted in grey.

realized with a common proxy architecture, as common proxies only process a request or response once. Hence, to implement a proof-of-concept common proxies including most of the WAFs could not be used as starting point. We therefore implemented the HWL Proxy as a separate application. By this, it can be deployed as an extension to existing intermediaries and server applications.

5.2   Implementation

The HWL Proxy is implemented in Go and is available as open source[1]. Note that its standard http library was not used because it is subject to vulnerabilities as well [2]. Figure 2 shows an overview of the implementation.

Whitelist Specification. The whitelist for the HWL Proxy is defined as an array of item objects, specified in a JSON format. In a real-world scenario, this whitelist would be created by the operators of the intermediaries or web server, who are conscious about which header fields are required. The whitelist items contain a string parameter key which represents the header field name. In addition, each whitelist item can contain an optional second string parameter val. This can be used to specify an allowed header field value or range of values with a regular expression. If this parameter is not specified, any value allowed by the HTTP specification is accepted. An example whitelist that only accepts Host, Connection and Content-Length header fields may be specified as follows:

```
[
    {"key": "host"},
    {"key": "connection", "val": "(close|keep-alive)"},
    {"key": "content-length", "val": "\\d+"}
]
```

---

[1] https://github.com/digital-security-lab/hwl-proxy.

HTTP Request Processing. The header of a received HTTP request is read in and then parsed and verified according to the RFC 7230. Specifically, the syntax of the request line, the following header fields, and the end of the header section is validated. If a violation of the standard is found, the HWL Proxy sends a 400 Bad Request error response back to the client and closes the connection. This might occur, e.g., if the header contains invalid meta characters or if the header section is not terminated properly with a blank line. Otherwise, the whitelist is applied to the request header. The Incoming module iterates through all header fields and appends the current one to the list of whitelisted header fields, if it matches one of the specified items contained in the whitelist. Otherwise, it is added to the list of non-whitelisted header fields. Note that whitelisted header fields that appear multiple times in the original request but did not cause an error during request validation are also included multiple times in the list of whitelisted header fields. As mentioned in Sect. 2, RFC 7230 generally prohibits the use of duplicate header fields, thus the HWL Proxy takes care of this requirement. However, since exceptions are allowed an operator can explicitly specify expected duplicates in the whitelist configuration.

The header fields that are not whitelisted are kept in a temporary session so that the Outgoing module can access them later to reconstruct the original request. After the header whitelisting has been applied, the body of the HTTP request is processed (if any). If the whitelisted header fields contain a valid Transfer-Encoding: chunked or Content-Length header field, the body is read in accordingly. In case both of these header fields are present, the Content-Length header field is removed to avoid HTTP Desync attacks. If none of these header fields is present, no body is expected. As for the header parsing, in case any violation is detected, the HWL Proxy sends a 400 Bad Request error response directly to the client and closes the connection. Finally, the normalized and whitelisted HTTP request is delivered to the wrapped component.

The reception and verification of the HTTP header in the Outgoing module are identical to the according steps in the Incoming module. This applies also to the body. However, since the body parsing depends on the occurrence of certain header fields such as Content-Length and Transfer-Encoding, the body is received before attaching the non-whitelisted header fields to ensure the body always maintains the same size and encoding. After processing the body the non-whitelisted header field names are each compared with the header field names of the request received from the intermediary. A non-whitelisted header field is not appended to the request when the same header field was set by the intermediary. This is done to prevent duplicates that may occur in case the intermediary appended a header field that was already included in the original request received by the client.

The final step of this module is to forward the request containing the request line, the whitelisted header fields including the modifications made by the intermediary and the non-whitelisted header fields with the mentioned exceptions.

Table 2. List of the developed and analyzed test cases including the attacks and the software that were used within the test environment (`<SP>`: whitespace character).

ID	Attack type	Causing header	Intermediary	Web server
TC1	Request Smuggling	`Content-Length`	ATS 7.1.2	NodeJS 4.1.2
TC2	Request Smuggling	`Transfer-Encoding + <SP>`	ATS 7.1.2	NodeJS 4.1.2
TC3	Request Smuggling	`X-Rewrite-Url`	NGINX 1.1.15	Symfony 3.4.0
TC4	CPDoS	`X-Original-Url`	Varnish 6.3.1	Symfony 3.4.0
TC5	CPDoS	`X-HTTP-Method-Override`	Varnish 6.3.1	Play 1.5.0
TC6	Hop-by-Hop	`Connection`	Varnish 3.0.0	NodeJS 4.1.2
TC7	HoT	`Host`	ATS 7.1.2	Rails 5.2.0

Table 3. Test results for all seven test cases with all possible test setups (○: HWL disabled, ●: HWL enabled, ⊕: attack prevented ⊖: attack succeeded)

Intermediary	Server	TC1	TC2	TC3	TC4	TC5	TC6	TC7
○	○	⊖	⊖	⊖	⊖	⊖	⊖	⊖
○	●	⊕	⊕	⊕	⊕	⊕	⊖	⊕
●	○	⊕	⊕	⊖	⊖	⊖	⊕	⊖
●	●	⊕	⊕	⊕	⊕	⊕	⊕	⊕

HTTP Response Processing. As discussed and argued in the beginning of this section, HWL is applied to HTTP requests only. Therefore, the Incoming and Outgoing modules forward the unmodified response to previous HTTP component in the processing chain.

6   Evaluation

To evaluate our HWL approach, we recreated the attacks presented in Sect. 3 caused by irregularities in header fields in a lab environment, deployed our solution, and evaluated the effect of header whitelisting. The test environment consists of a web server, one intermediary and a client. This was implemented using three virtual server instances running Ubuntu 16.04 LTS. Different proxies and server application software were installed and configured in accordance with the original attack description. In total we created seven different test cases representing different attack constellations (see Table 2). Attacks that are not covered here are discussed in Sect. 7.

For each test case, an attack vector was created that causes a malicious behavior. Furthermore, it was defined what response would be expected and what response represents an unintentional behavior. Intermediary and web server software were selected that are vulnerable to the respective attack type.

As shown in Table 3, the seven test cases were executed and analyzed in four different setups with and without header whitelisting deployed at the intermediate and server to illustrate the effect of HWL on the attack. Every test case is defined by a certain request or sequence of requests. A simple command line application was developed as the client. It sends sequences of HTTP requests specified in text files and stores requests and received responses into result files for subsequent analysis. The requests sent were logged to ensure that the test was executed correctly, while the logged responses were used to distinguish between legitimate requests and successful or averted attacks.

Table 3 also shows the results of all combinations from the seven test cases and the four setups. The first setup (HWL Proxy deployed but not enabled) illustrates that all attacks were successfully replicated in our lab and that the HWL Proxy does not interfere with communication when disabled. The other three setups include at least one component—i.e., either the intermediary, the server or both—with header whitelisting enabled. The attacks in all seven test cases except from TC6 were prevented when HWL was applied at least on the web server. When HWL was applied on the intermediary only, the attacks in TC1, TC2 and TC6 were prevented. When HWL was applied to both intermediary and web server, all seven attacks were prevented successfully.

Through this experimental evaluation, we can show that the proposed HWL approach is an effective countermeasure against all seven attacks considered in the test cases. These tested attacks span all known attacks that can be traced back to irregularities in the header. Thus, HWL can be considered as the first approach that mitigates a broad variety of semantic gap attacks including Request Smuggling, Host-of-Trouble, and CPDoS. Although this is no guarantee that unknown attacks will also be prevented, the test results show that previously unknown request header attacks can be thwarted by HWL's request header normalization and minimization when the server and all intermediaries are wrapped by an HWL Proxy.

7 Discussion

As the evaluation shows, HWL is a promising new approach to closing most of the publicly known – and possibly some not yet known – semantic gaps in an HTTP message processing chain. These strengths, limitations, and other considerations are discussed below.

Strengths. The main objective of the proposed approach has been achieved. All attacks considered were successfully prevented by whitelisting and normalizing request header fields. Even if whitelisting was only applied to either the intermediary or the web server, some attacks could still be prevented. The best protection is achieved when HWL is applied to both the intermediaries and the server.

Another advantage of the HWL Proxy comes from its architecture, as it can be wrapped around arbitrary HTTP components. This eliminates ambiguities when parsing HTTP messages without having to change every single implementation.

HWL also potentially helps to prevent unknown attacks related to a semantic gap. The risk that new vulnerabilities based on semantic gaps can be successfully exploited is mitigated by HWL by transforming the HTTP request header to a minimal and standards-compliant equivalent before processing by potentially vulnerable HTTP components.

Limitations. An obvious limitation of the proposed HWL is its restriction to attacks that target request header fields. The semantic gap, however, can occur in all parts of HTTP messages. Web Cache Deception, e.g., occurs when the query string of a URL is manipulated. Also, Response Splitting is rather caused by query parameters than by request header fields. However, most of the known semantic gaps relate to request header fields (see Table 1) and for these HWL provides a first coherent protection mechanism.

The evaluation presented in Sect. 6 omits those attacks that are not related to the HTTP header, as preventing them is not the scope of this paper (see Sect. 3). Furthermore, only those CPDoS attacks were included that are due to certain non-standardized header fields. The HMC CPDoS variant is covered by test case TC2, which includes an invalid space character to achieve Request Smuggling. The HHO CPDoS variant was excluded, because it cannot be prevented by the HWL Proxy implementation described in Sect. 5. This would require the consideration of the header size, which may be included to the whitelist specification in future work.

Today CDN services are commonly used intermediaries for improving the performance of web applications. However, they were not included in the test cases for evaluation. The main reason is that the attacks considered, such as Request Smuggling, could not be recreated with the available services, as they have already applied patches against such attack vectors. Nevertheless, vulnerable CDNs will behave similar to the caches in our test environment and therefore should benefit from the use of HWL likewise.

Vulnerabilities. The introduced HWL Proxy is a novel component that may contain vulnerabilities in itself. Parsing errors may occur, e.g., which provide an additional attack surface for semantic gaps. This can be avoided by considering language-theoretic security approaches, which aim to make input validation more secure and advise against *ad hoc* methods [13]. When this is reliably applied to the HWL Proxy, robust message parsing is propagated to the components that the HWL Proxy protects.

In addition, an implementation of the HWL Proxy may be vulnerable to denial-of-service (DoS) attacks, especially if requests with many non-whitelisted header fields must be processed frequently. Depending on the implementation, this can lead to a heavy load on the HWL Proxy. Our current HWL Proxy prototype implementation does not restrict header field processing and is therefore potentially vulnerable to DoS attacks.

Whitelist Specification. The whitelist is a determining factor in the effectiveness of HWL. An incorrect whitelist configuration can lead to false-positives and thus to malfunction of the processing pipeline and the entire application. Furthermore, a cache may not work properly in case relevant header fields are not included in the whitelist. However, we assume that the risk here is lower compared to WAFs that are typically more complex [33]. A further measure to avoid false-positives can be to monitor the traffic in the testing phase when deploying the HWL Proxy in order to detect too restrictive policies.

There are concepts for WAFs to create rules autonomously during the test phase of applications [33,36]. This could be transferred to the header whitelisting as well. The HWL Proxy may learn which header fields are actually used and automatically create an appropriate whitelist.

Similar to WAFs, a default configuration for the whitelist proxy should be provided. For instance, a default whitelist could be created that contains all header fields from the IANA Message Header registry [18]. These are standardized in RFC documents and should therefore not be critical in most cases while providing a broad compatibility.

Deployment. In future work, it could be considered to standardize the whitelist approach. It may even be added to existing HTTP libraries. The only requirement to ensure its effectiveness is that the header whitelisting is applied before any header is processed.

Another option is to provide the HWL Proxy as Software-as-a-Service in a cloud. As this is already common for WAFs operated by e.g. CloudFront, Cloudflare or Akamai, this can be realized similarly for the header whitelisting. This requires only an appropriate routing and the possibility for a customer to configure the whitelist.

8   Conclusion and Outlook

In this paper, we presented and categorized attacks on Web applications that exploit the semantic gap of HTTP interpretation. Based on the observation that many of these attacks are based on malicious HTTP request headers, we introduced the concept of Header Whitelisting. The idea of this approach is to filter all but a predefined set of HTTP headers before HTTP intermediaries and HTTP servers. The evaluation of the prototype implementation showed that all tested attacks could be prevented successfully.

In the future, it is conceivable to standardize such a mechanism and to include it to actual HTTP-based software systems. In addition, the performance of this approach should be thoroughly investigated to identify implementation strategies with the least performance impact. Finally, advanced features like automatic whitelist generation, access control lists or processing of response headers shall be considered.

References

1. Bijjou, K.: Web application firewall bypassing - how to defeat the blue team (2015). https://owasp.org/www-pdf-archive/OWASP_Stammtisch_Frankfurt_-_Web_Application_Firewall_Bypassing_-_how_to_defeat_the_blue_team_-_2015.10.29.pdf
2. BitK: I found another way to do HTTP smuggling. https://twitter.com/BitK_/status/1351587043814604805
3. Calzavara, S., Rabitti, A., Bugliesi, M.: Sub-session hijacking on the web: root causes and prevention. J. Comput. Secur. **27**(2), 233–257 (2019)
4. Chen, J., Jiang, J., Duan, H., Weaver, N., Wan, T., Paxson, V.: Host of troubles: multiple host ambiguities in http implementations. In: 23th ACM SIGSAC Conference on Computer and Communications Security (CCS) (2016)
5. Clincy, V., Shahriar, H.: Web application firewall: network security models and configuration. In: IEEE 42nd Annual Computer Software and Applications Conference (COMPSAC) (2018)
6. Consortium, W.A.S., et al.: Web application firewall evaluation criteria, version 1.0 (2006)
7. Davison, N.: Abusing http hop-by-hop request headers (2019). https://nathandavison.com/blog/abusing-http-hop-by-hop-request-headers
8. Dermann, M., et al.: Best practices: use of web application firewalls. Technical report, The Open Web Application Security Project (2008)
9. Desmet, L., Piessens, F., Joosen, W., Verbaeten, P.: Bridging the gap between web application firewalls and web applications. In: 4th ACM Workshop on Formal methods in Security (2006)
10. Dikaiakos, M.D.: Intermediary infrastructures for the World Wide Web. Comput. Netw. **45**(4), 421–447 (2004)
11. Fielding, R., et al.: Hypertext Transfer Protocol - HTTP/1.1. RFC 2616, IETF (1999). https://tools.ietf.org/html/rfc2616
12. Fielding, R., Reschke, J.: Hypertext Transfer Protocol (HTTP/1.1): Message Syntax and Routing. RFC 7230, IETF (2014). https://tools.ietf.org/html/rfc7230
13. Ganty, P., Köpf, B., Valero, P.: A language-theoretic view on network protocols. In: D'Souza, D., Narayan Kumar, K. (eds.) ATVA 2017. LNCS, vol. 10482, pp. 363–379. Springer, Cham (2017). https://doi.org/10.1007/978-3-319-68167-2_24
14. Gil, O.: WEB CACHE DECEPTION ATTACK. In: Blackhat USA (2017). https://blogs.akamai.com/2017/03/on-web-cache-deception-attacks.html
15. Guo, R., et al.: CDN judo: breaking the CDN DoS protection with itself. In: Network and Distributed System Security Symposium (NDSS) (2020)
16. Hacker, A.J.: Importance of Web Application Firewall Technology for Protecting Web-based Resources. ICSA Labs an Independent Verizon Business, p. 7 (2008)
17. Hubbard, S., Sager, J.: Firewalling the net. BT Technol. J. **15**(2), 94–106 (1997)
18. IANA functions: Message headers (2020). https://www.iana.org/assignments/message-headers/message-headers.xhtml
19. Imperva: Transparent reverse proxy (2020). https://docs.imperva.com/bundle/v14.1-administration-guide/page/7200.htm
20. Jeremy, D., Hils, A., Kaur, R., Watts, J.: Critical capabilities for cloud web application firewall services (2020). https://www.gartner.com/doc/reprints?id=1-1XO56V9N&ct=191022
21. Keromytis, A.D., Wright, J.L.: Transparent network security policy enforcement. In: USENIX Annual Technical Conference, FREENIX Track, pp. 215–226 (2000)

22. Kettle, J.: Http desync attacks: Request smuggling reborn (2019). https:// portswigger.net/research/http-desync-attacks-request-smuggling-reborn
23. Klein, A.: Divide and conquer - http response splitting, web cache poisoning attacks, and related topics (2004). https://dl.packetstormsecurity.net/papers/ general/whitepaper_httpresponse.pdf
24. Klein, A.: Http request smuggling in 2020 - new variants, new defenses and new challenges (2020). https://i.blackhat.com/USA-20/Wednesday/us-20-Klein-HTTP-Request-Smuggling-In-2020-New-Variants-New-Defenses-And-New-Challenges-wp.pdf
25. Kogi, E., Kerman, D.: HTTP desync attacks in the wild and how to defend against them (2019). https://www.imperva.com/blog/http-desync-attacks-and-defence-methods/
26. Levine, J.R.: DNS Blacklists and Whitelists. RFC 5782 (2010). https://doi.org/ 10.17487/RFC5782. https://rfc-editor.org/rfc/rfc5782.txt
27. Linhart, C., Klein, A., Heled, R., Steve, O.: Http request smuggling (2005). https:// www.cgisecurity.com/lib/HTTP-Request-Smuggling.pdf
28. Lo, J.: Whitelisting for Cyber Security: What It Means for Consumers. Public Interest Advocacy Centre (2011)
29. Ltd., P.: Access control vulnerabilities and privilege escalation (2020). https:// portswigger.net/web-security/access-control
30. Mirheidari, S.A., Arshad, S., Onarlioglu, K., Crispo, B., Kirda, E., Robertson, W.: Cached and confused: web cache deception in the wild. In: 29th USENIX Security Symposium (USENIX Security) (2020)
31. Nguyen, H.V., Lo Iacono, L., Federrath, H.: Your cache has fallen: cache-poisoned denial-of-service attack. In: 26th ACM Conference on Computer and Communications Security (CCS) (2019)
32. OWASP Foundation: OWASP top ten web application security risks (2020). https://owasp.org/www-project-top-ten/
33. Pałka, D., Zachara, M.: Learning web application firewall - benefits and caveats. In: Tjoa, A.M., Quirchmayr, G., You, I., Xu, L. (eds.) CD-ARES 2011. LNCS, vol. 6908, pp. 295–308. Springer, Heidelberg (2011). https://doi.org/10.1007/978-3-642-23300-5_23
34. Saltzer, J.H., Schroeder, M.D.: The protection of information in computer systems. Proc. IEEE **63**(9), 1278–1308 (1975)
35. Shahzad, A., Hussain, M., Khan, M.N.A.: Protecting from zero-day malware attacks. Middle East J. Sci. Res. **17**(4), 455–464 (2013)
36. Torrano-Gimenez, C., Perez-Villegas, A., Alvarez, G.: A Self-learning anomaly-based web application firewall. In: Herrero, A., Gastaldo, P., Zunino, R., Corchado, E. Computational Intelligence in Security for Information Systems, pp. 85–92. Advances in Intelligent and Soft Computing, Springer, Heidelberg (2009). https://doi.org/10.1007/978-3-642-04091-7_11

Machine Learning for Security

TAR: Generalized Forensic Framework to Detect Deepfakes Using Weakly Supervised Learning

Sangyup Lee, Shahroz Tariq, Junyaup Kim, and Simon S. Woo[✉]

Sungkyunkwan University, Suwon, South Korea
{sangyup.lee,shahroz,yaup21c,swoo}@g.skku.edu

Abstract. Deepfakes have become a critical social problem, and detecting them is of utmost importance. Also, deepfake generation methods are advancing, and it is becoming harder to detect. While many deepfake detection models can detect different types of deepfakes separately, they perform poorly on generalizing the detection performance over multiple types of deepfake. This motivates us to develop a generalized model to detect different types of deepfakes. Therefore, in this work, we introduce a practical digital forensic tool to detect different types of deepfakes simultaneously and propose Transfer learning-based Autoencoder with Residuals (TAR). The ultimate goal of our work is to develop a unified model to detect various types of deepfake videos with high accuracy, with only a small number of training samples that can work well in real-world settings. We develop an autoencoder-based detection model with Residual blocks and sequentially perform transfer learning to detect different types of deepfakes simultaneously. Our approach achieves a much higher generalized detection performance than the state-of-the-art methods on the FaceForensics++ dataset. In addition, we evaluate our model on 200 real-world Deepfake-in-the-Wild (DW) videos of 50 celebrities available on the Internet and achieve 89.49% zero-shot accuracy, which is significantly higher than the best baseline model (gaining 10.77%), demonstrating and validating the practicability of our approach.

Keywords: Digital forensics · Domain adaptation · Few-shot learning · Weakly-supervised learning · Deepfake detection

1 Introduction

Deepfakes generated by deep learning approaches such as Generative Adversarial Networks (GANs) and Variational Autoencoders (VAEs) have sparked initial amusement and surprise in the field. However, the excitement has soon faded away and worries arose due to potential misuse of these technologies. Such concerns have become real, and deepfakes are now popularly used to generate fake videos, especially pornography, containing celebrities' faces [6, 14, 25]. In particular, these types of deepfakes are causing severe damage in the US, UK, and South Korea with

© IFIP International Federation for Information Processing 2021
Published by Springer Nature Switzerland AG 2021
A. Jøsang et al. (Eds.): SEC 2021, IFIP AICT 625, pp. 351–366, 2021.
https://doi.org/10.1007/978-3-030-78120-0_23

41% of the victims being American and British actresses, and 25% being female K-pop stars [7]. These images and videos are starting to become widespread on the Internet and are rapidly propagating through social medias [6,9]. Therefore, deepfakes-generated videos raise not only significant social issues, but also ethical and privacy concerns. A recent report [18] shows that nearly 96% of deepfake videos are porn with over 134 million views. However, despite the urgency of the problem, concrete media forensic tools for an effective detection of different types of deepfakes are still absent. Recently, several research methods have been proposed to detect GAN-generated images [16,26,27] and deepfake videos [3,11,20,25,28,29]. FaceForensic++ [22] offers fake video datasets. Most of the detection methods generally perform well only in detecting fake images generated in the same domain (i.e., training and testing data are created with the same method), but not in detecting those generated in a different domain (i.e., test deepfakes are generated with different methods). So if new deepfake generation methods are developed, can the existing detection methods effectively detect the new deepfakes? How can we detect new fake videos? Is there a systematic and more generalizable approach to detect new types of deepfakes? The main focus of our work is to develop a generalized detection model, which not only performs well in detecting fake videos generated in one source domain, but also in detecting fake videos created in other domains with high accuracy.

To achieve this, we propose a Transfer learning-based Autoencoder with Residuals (TAR) to improve the detection performance of different types of deepfakes. We also introduce a latent space Facilitator module with shortcut residual connections in the network to learn deep features of deepfakes effectively and apply transfer learning between different domains. Our few-shot sequential transfer learning procedure utilizes only a few data samples (only 50 frames, which is around 2 s of a video) to detect deepfake videos in different domains (e.g., transfer learning to Face2Face with FaceSwap trained model). Our contributions are summarized as follows:

- We propose a Transfer learning-based Autoencoder with Residuals (TAR) to improve the detection performance of three different types of deepfakes, achieving over 99% accuracy and outperforming other baseline models.
- We sequentially apply transfer learning from one dataset to another to detect deepfake videos generated from different methods and achieve an average detection accuracy of 98.01% with a single model for all deepfake domains, demonstrating superior generalizability over the state-of-the-art approaches.
- Further, we evaluate and compare our approach using 200 real-world Deepfake-in-the-Wild videos collected from the Internet, and achieve 89.49% detection accuracy, which is significantly higher than the best baseline models.

2   Related Work

Rössler et al. [22] originally developed FaceForensics++, with 5,000 videos (1,000 Real and 4,000 Fake) using four different deepfake generation methods to

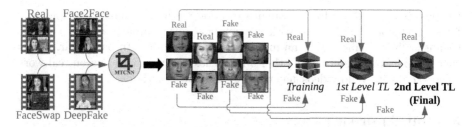

Fig. 1. Overview of our approach. Our proposed method learns features of deepfakes via Autoencoder with Residual blocks. Then, our multi-level transfer learning is sequentially performed with a small amount of training set in new target domains and the final model is created to effectively detect various types of deepfakes, including unseen or new deepfakes.

benchmark deepfakes detection performance. Facebook also released Deep Fake Detection Challenge (DFDC) dataset [8] with 5,250 videos (1,131 Real and 4,119 Fake), while Google released 3,363 videos (363 Real and 3,000 Fake) as part of the FaceForensics++ dataset [22]. For the detection of such deepfakes, deep learning-based methods in a supervised setting have shown high detection accuracy. Many Convolutional Neural Network (CNN)-based methods rely on content suppression using high-pass filters, either as a first layer [21] or using some handcrafted [4] and learned features [1]. Also, image splice or visual artifacts detection methods [13, 17, 23] try to exploit the inconsistency arising from splicing near the boundaries of manipulated sections in the image. Zhou *et al.* [31] built upon the idea of a high-pass filter method and attached a CNN-based model to capture both high-level and low-level details of the image. Tariq *et al.* [26, 27] proposed ShallowNet, an efficient CNN-based network to detect GAN-generated images with high accuracy even at a resolution as low as 64×64. Rössler *et al.* [22] significantly improved the performance on compressed images, which is essential for detecting deepfakes on social networking sites such as Facebook, Twitter, and WhatsApp. However, in the case of detecting new unseen deepfake generation methods, most approaches have failed to achieve high performance.

To address this challenge, we explore few-shot transfer learning through our TAR model. Since there will be new deepfake generation methods in the future, it would not be always feasible to collect and generate a large amount of new deepfake samples. To cope with this challenge, transfer learning (TL) with few-shot is the key to detect deepfakes generated through different methods (domains), that is, what has been learned in one domain (e.g., FaceSwap (FS)) can be exploited to improve generalization in another domain (e.g., Face2Face (F2F)). In this example sequence, we assume that Face2Face surfaced as a new deepfake method, with only a few videos to train. This approach enables the model to adapt to the new type of deepfake quickly. Nguyen *et al.* [19] implemented fine-tuning with 140 videos to the pretrained model to detect unseen deepfake generation method. However, it is hard to construct a dataset including 140 videos for the newly emerging deepfake generation method in a realistic scenario. Also, Cozzolino *et al.* [5] have explored the possibility of generalizing a single detection method to detect multiple deep-fake target domains. In this work, we compare our approach against Forensic-sTransfer [5] to demonstrate an improved generalizability. In particular, we further compare our results with other approaches and test with unseen real-world Deepfake-in-the-Wild videos generated by unknown methods.

3   Our Approach

Our Transfer learning-based Autoencoder with Residuals (TAR) model comprises a residual-based autoencoder with a latent space Facilitator module and transfers knowledge to learn deep features from different deepfake videos. The high-level overview of our approach is presented in Fig. 1. We train our initial model on one source domain dataset, such as DeepFakes [10] and apply transfer learning to the developed model using a small amount (few-shot learning) of data from another domain (e.g., FaceSwap [15]) to effectively learn features from both domains. Similarly, we perform additional transfer learning with a small amount of data in other domains (e.g., Face2Face [30]). After a sequence of transfer learning processes, we obtain our final model, as shown in Fig. 1, which can better detect deepfake videos generated by different methods (domains).

3.1   Base Network Architecture

We design our base network structure, as shown in Fig. 2, and develop an autoencoder architecture consisting of Residual blocks with a Facilitator module to explicitly force and divide the latent space between real and fake embedding. By comparing the activations in real and fake latent spaces, we can differentiate between real and fake images.

In addition, our proposed use of Residual blocks and Leaky ReLU is necessary to overcome the instabilities/weakness of prior approaches [5,26,27], such as "zero activations" (i.e., when both real and fake parts have no activation), while performing transfer learning experiments. We also discuss their limitations which motivate us to develop our TAR model in the Ablation Study section. In particular, the TAR architecture is deeper, more stable, and is readily extendable with more shortcut connections to better capture deep features for different types of deepfake detection, compared to other approaches. In our model, the encoder maps an image $\mathbf{x}$ to the latent space vector $\mathbf{H}$ and the decoder maps $\mathbf{H}$ to the reconstructed image $\mathbf{x}'$ as follows: $\mathbf{H} = \sigma(\mathbf{W}\mathbf{x}+\mathbf{b})$ and $\mathbf{x}' = \sigma'(\mathbf{W}'\mathbf{H}+\mathbf{b}')$, where $\mathbf{W}$ and $\mathbf{W}'$ are the weight matrices, $\mathbf{b}$ and $\mathbf{b}'$ are the bias vectors, and σ and σ' are the element-wise activation functions for the input images and the reconstructed images, respectively. Further, we divide the latent space $\mathbf{H}$ into two parts as follows: $\mathbf{H} = \{\mathbf{H_1},\mathbf{H_2}\}$, where we define the elements of the tensor $\mathbf{H_1}$ for real images and those of $\mathbf{H_2}$ for fake images at coordinates (i, j, k) by $(\mathbf{H_1})_{i,j,k}$ and $(\mathbf{H_2})_{i,j,k'}$. The dimension of each of the tensors $(\mathbf{H_1})_{i,j,k}$ and $(\mathbf{H_2})_{i,j,k'}$ is $M \times M \times N$, and the dimension of $(\mathbf{H})_{i,j,k}$ is $M \times M \times 2N$, where $1 \leq i \leq M$, $1 \leq j \leq M$, $1 \leq k \leq N$, and $N+1 \leq k' \leq 2N$ (e.g., $M = 15$ and $N = 64$ are used in our work).

Facilitator Module. For input image $\mathbf{x}_m$, the encoder generates the latent space output as follows: $Encoder(\mathbf{x}_m) = \mathbf{H}_m = \{\mathbf{H}_{m,1}, \mathbf{H}_{m,2}\}$. In order to separate real and fake latent features, we implemented a Facilitator module shown in Fig. 2, which forces the activations to be zeros for the opposite class and keeps the corresponding class. The activated $(\mathbf{H_m})_{i,j,k}$ by the Facilitator is defined as follows:

$$(H_m)_{i,j,k} = \begin{cases} (H_{m,1})_{i,j,k} & \text{if } k \leq N, c = 1 \text{ (real)} \\ (H_{m,2})_{i,j,k} & \text{if } k > N, c = 2 \text{ (fake)} , \\ 0 & \text{otherwise} \end{cases} \tag{1}$$

where c is the class, $(\mathbf{H_m}) \in \mathbb{R}^{M \times M \times N}$ and $1 \leq i \leq M, 1 \leq j \leq M$, and $1 \leq k \leq 2N$.

Loss Functions. We define two loss functions, L_{Activ} for the real and fake activations, and L_{Recon} for the reconstruction. We combine these two loss functions with Residual blocks with skip connections to improve the performance:

$$L = \lambda L_{Recon} + L_{Activ}. \tag{2}$$

First, we define the per-class activation of the latent space $A_{m,c}$ to be the L^1 norm of $A_{m,c}/K_c$, where K_c is the number of features of $H_{m,c}$ and $c \in \{1, 2\}$. For the activation of an input $\mathbf{x}_m$ with a given label $l_m \in \{1, 2\}$ and a latent feature tensor $H_{m,c}$, L_{Activ} and L_{Recon} are defined as follows:

$$L_{Activ} = \sum_m |A_{m,2} - l_m + 1| + \sum_m |A_{m,1} + l_m - 2|, \tag{3}$$

and we use L^1–norm for reconstruction loss (L_{Recon}),

$$L_{Recon} = \frac{\sum_m ||x_m - x_{m'}||_1}{N}. \tag{4}$$

For an efficient embedding of L_{Activ}, we set λ as 0.1 as determined empirically, thereby focusing more on embedding real and fake features through the encoder.

Classification and Leaky ReLU. In testing phase, if $A_{m,2} > A_{m,1}$, we consider the input $\mathbf{x}_m$ as fake. Otherwise, we classify it as real. However, for some small input images, we have empirically observed that $A_{m,1} = A_{m,2} = 0$ (zero activations). In this case, we cannot calculate the loss function or further perform classification. In order to prevent such situation, we use the Leaky ReLU function at the end of the last Convolution layer of the encoder and employ skip connections (see Fig. 2), where the Leaky ReLU function with a small slope allows effectively calculating the loss and classifying very small input images.

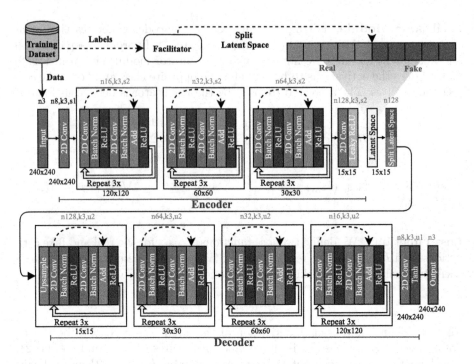

Fig. 2. Our TAR model architecture. Depending on the label of the input, real or fake, different latent space representations are enforced by the Facilitator module.

Residual Block with Shortcut Connections. We implement Residual blocks with shortcut connections inside our autoencoder architecture, which can effectively learn deep features of images and keep the feature information through the network. As shown in Fig. 2, we add three Residual blocks in the encoder and four Residual blocks in the decoder. Each Residual block repeats three times and each block consists of a Convolutional (Conv) layer, a Batch Normalization (BN) layer, and a ReLU, which is followed by another Conv layer and BN layer. Next, we add the input to the Addition layer to build the skip connection and pass it through the final ReLU (see Fig. 2). After applying Residual blocks, the number of Conv layers increases to 45, which can lead to vanishing gradient problems. However, as mentioned by He et al. [12], we can easily optimize a deeper network by adding the residuals or skip connections to the model structure.

Encoder. The input images have a resolution of $240 \times 240 \times 3$ (see Fig. 2). We use three Residual blocks ($120 \times 120 \times 16$, $60 \times 60 \times 32$, and $30 \times 30 \times 64$) in the encoder as shown in Fig. 2, where each Residual block repeats three times. The 2D Conv inside each Residual block, downsamples the input with a stride of 2 at the first loop (240×240 to 120×120, 120×120 to 60×60, etc.). After all the Residual blocks, we define one 3×3 Conv layer followed by a Leaky ReLU with a small slope value of 10^{-7} to avoid the zero activation problem described earlier. At the end of the encoder, we chose $M = 15$ and $2N = 128$, to build a latent feature tensor ($\mathbf{H}$) with a size of $15 \times 15 \times 128$. Therefore, the first 64 features ($\mathbf{H_1}$) are used to capture real images, and the other 64 features ($\mathbf{H_2}$), to represent fake images (see Fig. 2). During training, for each input $\mathbf{x}_m$, the selection block is chosen by the Facilitator module according to the class label $l_m \in \{1, 2\}$ to set zero values for non-activated class and activate only for the input class in Eq. 1.

Decoder. We configured the decoder using Residual blocks such as the encoder in reverse order as shown in Fig. 2. The difference from the encoder is that all Conv layers inside the decoder's Residual blocks have a stride of 1 since we are not reducing the size. To recover the original input image size, we scale up the input size by 2, using a 2×2 nearest neighbors upsampling layer before the first Residual block. The kernel size of the Conv layer is set to be the same as that of the encoder network. In the last layer, a single 3×3 Conv layer is used with tanh as the activation function.

3.2 Multi-level Sequential Transfer Learning

Since our goal is to develop an architecture that can detect deepfakes generated by different methods, we perform multi-level sequential transfer learning, as shown in Fig. 1. First, we train each model with respect to a specific generation method (domain) one at a time. For transfer learning, we performed few-shot learning from source domain s to target domain t. We call it first-level transfer learning, denoted by $s \rightarrow t$, where $s \neq t$, and $s, t \in \{FS, F2F, DF\}$. After this, we also conduct additional transfer learning toward a second target domain u using the previous transfer learned model; we call it second-level transfer learning, which we denote it by $(s \rightarrow t) \rightarrow u$, where $s \neq t \neq u$, and $s, t, u \in \{FS, F2F, DF\}$. The $\rightarrow$ arrow denotes the domain transfer sequence, where we only use 50 fake frames (2 s of a video) from the target domain to perform sequential few-shot transfer learning.

The main objective of our work is to develop a deployable, unified deepfake detection framework. If a new deepfake generation method is surfaced, the amount of data for training the model will be limited. We overcome this scenario with our multi-level sequential few-shot transfer learning approach. The first and second-level transfer learning simulates this scenario where each level represents the situation when a new deepfake generation method is present. We only re-train on few frames from a new type of deepfake video and update the model, preserving all the previous detection capacity.

4   Experiments

We evaluated our method on a popular benchmark dataset to measure the performance of a *single model* detecting various types of deepfakes simultaneously.

Table 1. Dataset summary for different experiments.

Category	Total Videos	Extracted Frames	D1: Base Dataset (Real:Fake)	D2: TL Dataset (Real:Fake)	D3: Test Dataset (Real:Fake)
Pristine (Real)	1,000	16,050	–	–	–
DeepFake (DF)	1,000	16,050	15,000:15,000	50:50	500:500
FaceSwap (FS)	1,000	16,050	15,000:15,000	50:50	500:500
Face2Face (F2F)	1,000	16,050	15,000:15,000	50:50	500:500
Deepfake-in-the-Wild (DW)	200	8,164	–	–	8,164:8,164

4.1 Dataset

FaceForensics++ Dataset. We utilized three different types of deepfake videos from Rössler et al. [22]. For each type, we extracted a total number of 16,050 frames from the videos. The details of the dataset are provided in Table 1.

Deepfake-in-the-Wild (DW) Dataset. To validate the effectiveness and practicability of the detectors, we used 200 freely accessible Deepfake-in-the-Wild (DW) videos of 50 celebrities from the Internet. From the 200 DW videos, we extracted a total number of 8,164 frames.

Dataset Settings. For training and testing, we divided the above-mentioned datasets into three categories (**D1–D3**) with no overlap to accurately characterize the performance.

- **D1: Base dataset.** The purpose of this dataset is to test the performance of a model for one source domain on which the model is originally trained. We also measure the zero-shot performance for the dataset on which the model is not trained. To evaluate the performance, we use 500 real and 500 fake images from the extracted frames as the test set, hence a total of three pairs of datasets, DF, FW, and F2F, as shown in Table 1. For simplicity, we refer these dataset pair with the fake class dataset name. For example, the Pristine and DeepFake dataset pair is referred to as DeepFake (DF).
- **D2: Transfer (few-shot) learning dataset.** We used the samples of 50 (2 s of a video) real and fake frames each. For evaluation, we used the test set from D3 (500 real and 500 fake frames) to check the model's performance.
- **D3: DW dataset.** We used this dataset only for testing the generalizability of our final model, as this dataset contains unseen videos generated with unknown deepfake generation methods. Therefore, this dataset can be served to assess realistic performance of the detection methods.

4.2 Evaluation Settings

Baseline Models. We compared our method against ShallowNet [27], Xception [2], and ForensicTransfer [5].

Table 2. Accuracy of base (green) and zero-shot performance accuracy (gray).

Methods	Base Dataset: DF (%)			Base Dataset: FS (%)			Base Dataset: F2F (%)		
	DF	*FS*	*F2F*	*FS*	*DF*	*F2F*	*F2F*	*DF*	*FS*
ShallowNet	63.0	48.0	53.0	58.0	44.0	46.0	57.0	51.0	50.0
Xception	99.6	50.0	50.3	92.0	50.1	51.5	99.3	71.4	50.4
FT	**99.8**	50.0	70.4	94.3	47.1	53.7	99.3	99.0	**73.5**
TAR(*Ours*)	**99.8**	50.1	**75.3**	**99.3**	50.8	70.5	**99.5**	99.7	52.2

Machine Configurations. We used Intel i9-9900k CPU 3.60 GHz with 64.0 GB RAM and NVIDIA GeForce Titan RTX. We tried our best to implement the baseline methods to their original description.

Training and Multi-level Sequential Transfer Learning Details. We trained each model with respect to one specific generation method at a time. For transfer learning, we performed few-shot learning from source domain (DF or FS or F2F) to target domain (FS or F2F, or DF) as the first-level transfer learning and denote it as $s \rightarrow t$, where $s \neq t$, and $s, t \in \{FS, F2F, DF\}$. We also conducted transfer learning toward a second target domain using the previous transfer learned model as the second-level transfer learning. We denote second-level transfer learning as $(s \rightarrow t) \rightarrow u$, where $s \neq t \neq u$, and $s, t, u \in \{FS, F2F, DF\}$.

5 Results

The detection performances of different methods are presented in Tables 2, 3 and 4, where the highest accuracy values are in bold face. The last 'Avg. Gain' column in Table 3 and 4 reports the average accuracy gain from the best baseline model of each method in detecting all deepfake domain datasets.

5.1 Base Dataset Performance (D1)

We compared our approach with three baseline models using D1 as shown in Table 2. First, after training with three source domains, our TAR model achieves higher accuracies of 99.80%, 99.30%, and 99.50% in detecting DF, FS and F2F, respectively, compared to ShallowNet (63.00%, 58.00%, and 57.00%), Xception (99.60%, 92.00%, and 99.30%) and ForensicTransfer (FT) (99.80%, 94.30%, and 99.30%). Generally, Xception and FT also performed well on base datasets, while ShallowNet performed poorly.

5.2 Zero-Shot Performance (D1)

Next, we also evaluated the base dataset-trained model with other domain datasets (i.e., testing the DF-trained model on F2F) for zero-shot performance

Table 3. Accuracy of first-level TL (blue) from base dataset (green).

Transfer Seq.	Test Data	Models			Avg. Gain
		Xce	FT	TAR	
DF → FS	DF	67.2	90.1	**91.6**	−2.0
	FS	54.0	89.9	**93.3**	
	F2F	62.6	90.9	80.1	
DF → F2F	DF	95.8	85.0	**98.9**	8.8
	F2F	69.7	81.6	**93.1**	
	FS	53.5	45.3	53.5	
FS → DF	FS	**92.0**	48.2	69.0	17.5
	DF	45.8	79.8	**98.5**	
	F2F	68.0	67.4	90.8	
FS → F2F	FS	**99.0**	56.6	84.6	16.0
	F2F	57.7	55.1	**84.7**	
	DF	49.8	56.5	85.3	
F2F → DF	F2F	95.4	98.7	**99.2**	1.7
	DF	92.6	99.0	**99.5**	
	FS	68.7	60.9	64.9	
F2F → FS	F2F	87.6	95.8	**97.7**	3.3
	FS	76.2	92.7	**97.4**	
	DF	87.2	94.4	97.8	

Table 4. Accuracy of second-level TL (blue) from first-level (green).

Transfer Seq.	Test Data	Models			Avg. Gain
		Xce	FT	TAR	
(DF→FS) →F2F	DF	88.2	64.3	**91.9**	17.1
	FS	55.1	50.0	**85.0**	
	F2F	71.7	62.3	**89.4**	
(DF→F2F) →FS	DF	75.4	90.0	**97.8**	6.5
	F2F	55.0	89.4	**94.9**	
	FS	67.5	89.8	**95.9**	
(FS→DF) →F2F	FS	48.8	66.5	**90.2**	18.1
	DF	**97.0**	47.3	84.9	
	F2F	62.7	57.8	**87.8**	
(FS→F2F) →DF	FS	48.4	77.5	**96.8**	22.7
	F2F	**96.4**	48.6	85.2	
	DF	64.7	59.9	**95.5**	
(F2F→DF) →FS	F2F	76.2	94.0	**98.5**	4.2
	DF	76.2	93.6	**97.4**	
	FS	86.9	93.9	**98.3**	
(F2F→FS) →DF	F2F	92.7	**97.4**	97.3	8.4
	FS	66.6	70.7	**96.7**	
	DF	95.9	**97.8**	97.1	

comparison. The FT model achieved 73.50% accuracy, which is 21.30% higher than that of TAR for F2F-trained model tested on FS. However, in all other zero-shot testing cases, our TAR model outperformed all other approaches for all datasets as shown in Table 2. Overall, our approach performed better than the-state-of-the-art methods in the same source domain, as well as different domains (zero-shot) except for one case.

5.3   Transfer Learning Performance (D2)

As shown in the last column of Table 3, for the first-level transfer learning, we observed that our TAR model gained average accuracy over the best performing baseline (Xception or FT) on all sequences ($s \rightarrow t$) except for only one case (DF→FS) in which FT achieved 90.30% average performance. By comparing Table 2 and 3, we observed that after transfer learning to a target domain, the accuracy of the target domain increases, but the base class accuracy decreases for all methods. For example, when we trained all three models on the DF base dataset, all methods had a test accuracy of over 99%, and a zero-shot accuracy of around 50% on the FS dataset (see Table 2). Now, when we performed transfer learning from this source domain (DF) to target domain (FS), the accuracy of FT increases from 50.00% to 89.90%, and TAR increases from 50.10% to 93.30%. However, the source domain accuracy, which was 99.80% for both FT and TAR, decreases to 90.10% and 91.60% respectively (see Table 2 and 3). For Xception, the drop was even worse, with a 99.60% to 67.20% drop on the source domain, while gaining only 6% on target domain. Compared to FT and TAR, Xception shows limited learning capacity during few-shot sequential transfer learning.

As shown in Table 4, after the second-level transfer learning, our approach achieves a higher performance over every sequence $((s \rightarrow t) \rightarrow u)$ compared to Xception and FT. The best performing sequence for both TAR and FT has "F2F→DF" as the source domain and FS as target domain, while Xception's best sequence is "F2F→FS" as the source and DF as the target. We can write the resultant domain transfer sequence as "(F2F→DF)→FS" for TAR and FT, and "(F2F→FS)→DF" for Xception. The best performing FT model "(F2F→DF)→FS" achieved an average accuracy of 93.83% on all three datasets, while the best performing TAR model "(F2F→DF)→FS" achieved 98.01% gaining 4.2% (see Table 4). However, Xception was not able to produce a similar generalization performance as FT or TAR, achieving an average accuracy of 85.01%. Although there are 4 cases out of 18 in which the performances of Xception and FT are better than that of TAR, the overall performance of TAR is better. Therefore, our approach generalizes much better and yields above 97% detection accuracy across all three datasets and shows significantly improved performance compared to zero-shot learning, as shown in Table 2. Furthermore, FT's original work [5] conducted experiments on multiple domains only on one case, whereas our research dealt with more complex cases to explore correlations between deepfake domains and to develop more generalized models.

Table 5. Zero-shot performance on Deepfake-in-the-Wild (DW) dataset. The → arrow denotes the domain transfer sequence.

Methods	Domain Transfer Sequence (Best Performer)	Original Acc. (%)	Contrast (C) Acc. (%)	Brightness (B) Acc. (%)	C + B Acc. (%)
Xception	F2F→FS→DF	50.23	58.11	66.92	78.72
FT	F2F→DF→FS	47.05	46.37	47.60	48.04
TAR (*Ours*)	F2F→DF→FS	**67.87**	**69.02**	**77.06**	**89.49**

5.4   Unseen DW Dataset Performance (D3)

It is critical to test the models against real-world deepfake data in addition to benchmark datasets. Therefore, we used 200 Deepfake-in-the-Wild (DW) videos to evaluate the models in real-world scenarios. The model zero-shot detection accuracy on this dataset is shown in Table 5, where we used the best performing multi-level transfer learning sequence, "(F2F→DF)→FS", for both FT and TAR models and "(F2F→FS)→DF" for Xception. As shown in the third column of Table 5, the accuracy of the second best performer from Table 4, FT, was only 47.05%. While TAR achieves an accuracy of 67.87% and 50.23% for Xception, which is higher than that of FT, it is much lower than the results for the previous datasets.

Through our evaluation, this low performance strongly indicated that deep-fakes in the wild were generated using more diverse, different, and complex methods than DF, F2F, and FS. Possibly, they could have leveraged additional post-processing methods to improve the quality of deepfakes. For example, we first noticed that the lighting in the DW dataset tends to be darker than that in the benchmark dataset. Hence, we first tried to balance the brightness and contrast of the DW videos [24] by increasing both the darkness and contrast by 30% to better match the lighting conditions with the benchmark datasets. As shown in Table 5, increasing only the contrast yielded a slight accuracy improvement from 67.87% to 69.02% for the TAR model and 50.23% to 58.11% for Xception, but FT model has a drop in accuracy from 47.05% to 46.37%. After adjusting the brightness of the DW frames, our TAR model achieved a 77.06% accuracy, which is almost 10% higher than in the previous case. After applying both contrast and brightness changes together, Xception yields 78.72% accuracy, while our approach achieves 89.49%, which is much higher. On the other hand, the best performing baseline FT was not significantly improved, only achieving 48.04% accuracy at best. Therefore, our approach adapting to new domains with multi-level transfer learning clearly outperforms other methods on unseen real-world dataset, demonstrating the effectiveness of TAR against real-world deepfakes.

We plan to train our model with both brightness and contrast adjustments using data augmentation in the future. In this way, we can improve the performance of detecting DW or other new types of deepfakes without any inference-stage adjustments.

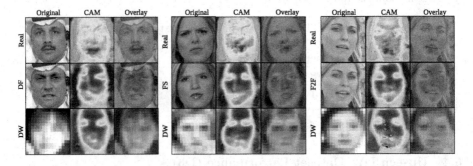

Fig. 3. A side-by-side comparison of 1) real vs. fake frames, 2) Class Activation Map (CAM) outputs, and 3) overlaid images of original input and CAM, using three different examples from each base dataset (DF, F2F, and FS). We also present sample images from the DW dataset in the same order, where we do not have an original real input image. The DW face images are intentionally blurred to hide the identity.

6 Analysis and Discussion

6.1 Classification Activation Map (CAM)

To observe the fake frame activations of our model, we utilized CAM to generate the implicit attention of CNNs on an image. We used the best performing second-level transfer learned TAR model, "(F2F→DF)→FS", to show the activations from the decoder. In Fig. 3, we present a side-by-side comparison of 1) original real versus fake images, 2) CAM outputs, and 3) overlaid images of original images and CAM, using three different examples from each dataset (DF, F2F, and FS). We also present sample images from the DW dataset in the same order, where we do not have an original real input image. The DW face images are intentionally blurred to hide the identity. Figure 3 clearly shows that our model produces much intense fake activation around the face than real images; the activated part is focused on the nose, the forehead, the cheek, etc. Since our model is a multi-level transfer-learned across DF, F2F, and FS, we did not observe any particular activation patterns for a specific model, and our approach detects all deepfake types effectively in a similar way.

6.2 Ablation Study

We conducted an ablation study to check the impact of Leaky ReLU and residual connections in our model and summarized our finding. First, we removed the residual addition from our Residual blocks and replaced Leaky ReLU with ReLU. Our model started to show several zero activations in the last layer of the encoder for both real and fake images during training. We observed that this phenomenon occurred more frequently on small images. Further research is needed to find the exact causes of this phenomenon. Next, we replaced the ReLU function with a Leaky ReLU and re-ran the same experiment. This time, there were much less zero activations, because the Leaky ReLU allows small negative values, instead of zeros. To completely eliminate this zero activation issue, we added back the residual addition inside Residual blocks. As a result, we did not observe any zero activation cases during training anymore, even with small, upscaled images. This ablation experiment supports our motivation to use Residual blocks and Leaky ReLU function for our TAR model.

6.3 Discussion

Recently, deepfake porn videos have surged, with the vast majority featuring female celebrities' face photos to develop sexually explicit videos without the celebrities' knowledge or consent. These videos, rapidly spreading throughout the Internet, cause serious issues as they harass innocent people in the cyberspace. Because of the urgency of the problem and the absence of effective tools to detect these videos, we have undertaken this research to investigate real-world deepfake videos, in order to construct the Deepfake-in-the-Wild (DW) video dataset. We obtained freely available videos from the Internet, and all researchers in this study were informed about the detailed research protocol. We also consulted with the Institutional Review Board (IRB) in our institution, and received confirmation saying that approval was not required, since the videos are already available on the Internet. Moreover, we cropped the face regions and deleted the rest of the images, and further discarded the original videos.

To preserve and protect the privacy of the celebrities, we blurred their faces in this work. Also, we do not plan on distributing any explicit content and leak celebrities' private information.

6.4 Deployment

To address the urgency of this matter, we have developed an online testing website since Dec. 2019[1], where people can upload images to check deepfakes using our model. We developed the interface such that it provides the probability of the image being fake and demonstrated that TAR can be practically deployed and used to circumvent the deployed real-world deepfakes.

7 Conclusion

Malicious applications of deepfakes, such as deepfake porn videos, are becoming increasingly prevalent these days. In this work, we propose TAR to improve the generalized performance of multi-domain deepfake detection and test it on unseen real-world deepfake videos to evaluate its practicability. A facilitator module splits our TAR model's latent space into real and fake latent spaces, enabling the encoder to focus more on learning the latent space representation, which results in a more accurate real and fake classification. Our multi-level sequential transfer learning-based autoencoder with Residual blocks significantly outperforms other state-of-the-art methods in detecting multi-domain deepfakes from the FF++ dataset. Furthermore, TAR achieves 89.49% accuracy in detecting 200 real-world Deepfake-in-the-Wild videos of 50 celebrities, which is significantly higher than the state-of-the-art methods. Our results suggest that sequential learning-based models are an interesting venue to explore for analyzing and detecting fake and manipulated media in real-world settings and other analogous vision tasks that require domain adaptation. The code of our work is available on GitHub[2].

Acknowledgments. This work was partly supported by Institute of Information & communications Technology Planning & Evaluation (IITP) grant funded by the Korea government (MSIT) (No.2019-0-00421, AI Graduate School Support Program (Sungkyunkwan University)), (No. 2019-0-01343, Regional strategic industry convergence security core talent training business) and the Basic Science Research Program through National Research Foundation of Korea (NRF) grant funded by Korea government MSIT (No. 2020R1C1C1006004). Additionally, this research was partly supported

---

[1] http://deepfakedetect.org.

[2] https://github.com/Clench/TAR_resAE.

by IITP grant funded by the Korea government MSIT (No. 2021-0-00017, Original Technology Development of Artificial Intelligence Industry) and was partly supported by the Korea government MSIT, under the High-Potential Individuals Global Training Program (2019-0-01579) supervised by the IITP.

References

1. Bayar, B., Stamm, M.C.: A deep learning approach to universal image manipulation detection using a new convolutional layer. In: Proceedings of the 4th ACM Workshop on Information Hiding and Multimedia Security, pp. 5–10. ACM (2016)
2. Chollet, F.: Xception: deep learning with depthwise separable convolutions. In: Proceedings of the IEEE Conference on Computer Vision and Pattern Recognition, pp. 1251–1258 (2017)
3. Ciftci, U.A., Demir, I., Yin, L.: Fakecatcher: Detection of synthetic portrait videos using biological signals. IEEE Trans. Pattern Anal. Mach. Intell. (2020)
4. Cozzolino, D., Poggi, G., Verdoliva, L.: Recasting residual-based local descriptors as convolutional neural networks: an application to image forgery detection. In: Proceedings of the 5th ACM Workshop on Information Hiding and Multimedia Security, pp. 159–164. ACM (2017)
5. Cozzolino, D., Thies, J., Rössler, A., Riess, C., Nießner, M., Verdoliva, L.: Forensictransfer: weakly-supervised domain adaptation for forgery detection. arXiv preprint arXiv:1812.02510 (2018)
6. Croft, A.: From porn to scams, deepfakes are becoming a big racket-and that's unnerving business leaders and lawmakers (2019). https://fortune.com/2019/10/07/porn-to-scams-deepfakes-big-racket-unnerving-business-leaders-and-lawmakers. Accessed 8 Jan 2021
7. Dickson, E.: Deepfake Porn Is Still a Threat, Particularly for K-Pop Stars (2019). https://www.rollingstone.com/culture/culture-news/deepfakes-nonconsensual-porn-study-kpop-895605. Accessed 8 Jan 2021
8. Dolhansky, B., Howes, R., Pflaum, B., Baram, N., Ferrer, C.C.: The deepfake detection challenge (DFDC) preview dataset. arXiv preprint arXiv:1910.08854 (2019)
9. Edwards, C.: Making deepfake porn could soon be as 'easy as using Instagram filters', according to expert (2019). https://www.thesun.co.uk/tech/9800017/deepfake-porn-soon-easy. Accessed 8 Jan 2021
10. FaceSwap Devs: Deepfakes faceswap - github repository (2021). https://github.com/deepfakes/faceswap. Accessed 8 Jan 2021
11. Güera, D., Delp, E.J.: Deepfake video detection using recurrent neural networks. In: 2018 15th IEEE International Conference on Advanced Video and Signal Based Surveillance (AVSS), pp. 1–6. IEEE (2018)
12. He, K., Zhang, X., Ren, S., Sun, J.: Deep residual learning for image recognition. In: Proceedings of the IEEE Conference on Computer Vision and Pattern Recognition, pp. 770–778 (2016)
13. Huh, M., Liu, A., Owens, A., Efros, A.A.: Fighting fake news: image splice detection via learned self-consistency. In: Ferrari, V., Hebert, M., Sminchisescu, C., Weiss, Y. (eds.) ECCV 2018. LNCS, vol. 11215, pp. 106–124. Springer, Cham (2018). https://doi.org/10.1007/978-3-030-01252-6_7
14. Kan, M.: Most AI-Generated Deepfake Videos Online Are Porn (2019). https://www.pcmag.com/news/most-ai-generated-deepfake-videos-online-are-porn. Accessed 8 Jan 2021

15. Kowalski, M.: Faceswap - github repository (2021). https://github.com/ MarekKowalski/FaceSwap. Accessed 8 Jan 2021

16. Lee, S., Tariq, S., Shin, Y., Woo, S.S.: Detecting handcrafted facial image manipulations and GAN-generated facial images using Shallow-FakeFaceNet. Appl. Soft Comput. **105** (2021). https://doi.org/10.1016/j.asoc.2021.107256

17. Matern, F., Riess, C., Stamminger, M.: Exploiting visual artifacts to expose deepfakes and face manipulations. In: 2019 IEEE Winter Applications of Computer Vision Workshops (WACVW), pp. 83–92. IEEE (2019)

18. Mehta, I.: A new study says nearly 96% of deepfake videos are porn (2019). https:// tnw.to/OXuTG. Accessed 8 Jan 2021

19. Nguyen, H.H., Fang, F., Yamagishi, J., Echizen, I.: Multi-task learning for detecting and segmenting manipulated facial images and videos. In: 2019 IEEE 10th International Conference on Biometrics Theory, Applications and Systems (BTAS), pp. 1–8. IEEE (2019)

20. Nguyen, H.H., Yamagishi, J., Echizen, I.: Capsule-forensics: using capsule networks to detect forged images and videos. In: ICASSP 2019–2019 IEEE International Conference on Acoustics, Speech and Signal Processing (ICASSP), pp. 2307–2311. IEEE (2019)

21. Rao, Y., Ni, J.: A deep learning approach to detection of splicing and copy-move forgeries in images. In: 2016 IEEE International Workshop on Information Forensics and Security (WIFS), pp. 1–6. IEEE (2016)

22. Rössler, A., Cozzolino, D., Verdoliva, L., Riess, C., Thies, J., Nießner, M.: Faceforensics++: learning to detect manipulated facial images. In: ICCV 2019 (2019)

23. Salloum, R., Ren, Y., Kuo, C.C.J.: Image splicing localization using a multi-task fully convolutional network (MFCN). J. Vis. Commun. Image Represent. **51**, 201–209 (2018)

24. Shorten, C., Khoshgoftaar, T.M.: A survey on image data augmentation for deep learning. J. Big Data **6**(1), 60 (2019). https://doi.org/10.1186/s40537-019-0197-0

25. Tariq, S., Jeon, S., Woo, S.S.: Am i a real or fake celebrity? Measuring commercial face recognition web APIs under deepfake impersonation attack (2021)

26. Tariq, S., Lee, S., Kim, H., Shin, Y., Woo, S.S.: Detecting both machine and human created fake face images in the wild. In: Proceedings of the 2nd International Workshop on Multimedia Privacy and Security, pp. 81–87. ACM (2018)

27. Tariq, S., Lee, S., Kim, H., Shin, Y., Woo, S.S.: Gan is a friend or foe?: A framework to detect various fake face images. In: Proceedings of the 34th ACM/SIGAPP Symposium on Applied Computing, pp. 1296–1303. ACM (2019)

28. Tariq, S., Lee, S., Woo, S.S.: A convolutional LSTM based residual network for deepfake video detection (2020)

29. Tariq, S., Lee, S., Woo, S.S.: One detector to rule them all: Towards a general deepfake attack detection framework. In: Proceedings of The Web Conference 2021 (2021). https://doi.org/10.1145/3442381.3449809

30. Thies, J., Zollhofer, M., Stamminger, M., Theobalt, C., Nießner, M.: Face2Face: real-time face capture and reenactment of RGB videos. In: Proceedings of the IEEE Conference on Computer Vision and Pattern Recognition, pp. 2387–2395 (2016)

31. Zhou, P., Han, X., Morariu, V.I., Davis, L.S.: Learning rich features for image manipulation detection. In: Proceedings of the IEEE Conference on Computer Vision and Pattern Recognition, pp. 1053–1061 (2018)

Anomaly Detection for Insider Threats: An Objective Comparison of Machine Learning Models and Ensembles

Filip Wieslaw Bartoszewski[1(✉)], Mike Just[1], Michael A. Lones[1], and Oleksii Mandrychenko[2]

[1] MACS Department, Heriot-Watt University, Edinburgh, Scotland
fwb2@hw.ac.uk
[2] Fortinet UK Ltd., Edinburgh, Scotland

Abstract. Insider threat detection is challenging due to the wide variety of possible attacks and the limited availability of real threat data for testing. Most previous anomaly detection studies have relied on synthetic threat data, such as the CERT insider threat dataset. However, several previous studies have used models that arguably introduce bias, such as the selective use of metrics, and reusing the same dataset with the prior knowledge of the answer labels. In this paper, we create and test a host of models following some guidelines of good conduct to produce what we believe to be a more objective comparison of these models. Our results indicate that majority voting ensembles are a simple and cost-effective way of boosting the quality of results from individual machine learning models, both on the CERT data and on a version augmented with additional attacks. We include a comparison of models with their hyperparameters optimized for different target metrics.

Keywords: Anomaly detection · Insider threat · Machine learning · Ensembles

1 Introduction

An insider threat is a computer security issue involving attacks from inside the defensive perimeter of organisations. According to the Ponemon Institute, the average remediation cost of an insider credential threat was $871,686, with the average annual cost per company rising by 31% over the last two years [7]. While insider threats are an important security issue, there are challenges with studying them, including the lack of real world data. Companies are rarely willing to share information about attacks or behavioral logs for various reasons, including data privacy. As a result, researchers use synthetic datasets to train and test machine learning models. The CERT dataset [5] is the primary dataset for studying insider

Supported by The Datalab, https://www.thedatalab.com/.

A. Jøsang et al. (Eds.): SEC 2021, IFIP AICT 625, pp. 367–381, 2021.
https://doi.org/10.1007/978-3-030-78120-0_24

threats, though it may lack the variety required for extending our understanding of insider threats since each release contains only a handful of scenarios.

Furthermore, recent research on anomaly detection (including insider threat detection) has highlighted some apparent bias in several studies [4]. Practices contributing to this bias include selectively choosing metrics to present results, and designing models that are explicitly informed by the answer labels from the data. While there are examples of good practice, such as studies that use independent teams to create the attack data and detection models [14, 20], little research has taken an objective view of modeling insider threat attacks.

Our aim is to present an objective analysis and comparison of a variety of machine learning models and ensembles (combinations of models with a voting function) for detecting insider threats. Our work with ensembles focuses on heterogenous approaches, which combine different types of machine learning models. We compare several machine learning models for anomaly detection, including different versions with parameter choices optimized for separate quality metrics. We also compare the un-optimized and out-of-the box classifiers with their optimized counterparts, showing how optimizing models within an ensemble changes classifications. We present results of the models developed both on the CERT 4.2 release (*original dataset*) and four different attack scenarios that we recreated and inserted into test data (*augmented dataset*). To avoid bias, we do this *after* creating our models. We believe that our work contrasts the common practice in insider threat literature, where, in our opinion, models have been over-fitted by design and chosen after analysing the answer files.

2   Background

Researchers seem to agree that modeling insider threats is a complicated task [2, 5, 11, 12], leading many to instead model normal behavior and then detect outliers that could represent malicious activity. There are numerous examples of different types of anomaly detection for identifying insider threats, e.g., Hidden Markov Models (HMM), Naive Bayes, and Random Forest [3, 10–12, 14].

Researchers studying insider threat detection use several machine learning models that most frequently use either sequences of activities or feature vectors for their input. Those who represent the data as sequences of activities commonly use algorithms based on HMM, first introduced for detecting insider threats by Rashid et al. [14], who created sequences from week-long fragments of the CERT dataset. Other examples include Dahmane and Foucher [3], who prepared sequences for their HMM model with a clustering algorithm, and Lo et al. [12] who compared the performance of an HMM model against various distance measurement methods comparing sequence data. Yuan et al. [18] fed sequences of data into a Long Short-Term Memory (LSTM) neural network to receive a fixed size matrix and used a convolutional neural network for anomaly detection.

A different approach to represent input for machine learning models is to use feature vectors or their derivatives. Here, the input becomes a set of vectors that represent features, such as number of times an event repeats, day of the week, event type etc. Haidar and Gaber [6] split the types of features into frequency, time-based, and nominal. They used these with One-Class Support Vector Machine (OCSVM) and Isolation Forest (IF) algorithms for ensemble-based anomaly detection. Other work with feature vectors includes Le et al.'s work on Self-Organising Maps (SOM) [9]. In the same paper, they used HMMs and decision trees to analyze the problem using both supervised and unsupervised models, using both sequences and feature vectors. They concluded that the unique characteristics of every model warrant further study. Legg et al.'s [11] work with user modeling involved comparing daily behavior for each user. The models formed tree-like structures with hierarchy reflecting how often an action was performed. Some authors, who wanted to capture more information from the data than simple activity counts, tried creating synthetic features that enumerate possible actions. Tuor et al. [16] created a 414-element feature vector, which was then used to create a feature matrix containing behaviors of all the users in the CERT dataset. It was subsequently used as input for Deep Neural Network (DNN) models, including a DNN and an LSTM-Recurrent Neural Network (RNN) combination, similar to Yuan et al.'s model [18].

Previous work on ensembles was done by Parveen et al. [13] and Haidar et al. [6]. In both cases, the ensembles were homogenous, created out of the same types of model, with each trained and tested on different folds of the dataset. Parveen et al. used ensembles made out of either one- or two-class SVM models and combined them to create an ensemble with a smaller false positive rate. Haidar et al.'s ensembles aggregated votes of OCSVM or IF models with oversampling techniques in order to flag non-malicious anomalies. Knowledge of those non-malicious anomalies was used while retraining the model, further decreasing false positive rates.

While anomaly detection seems to be the most feasible way of detecting insider threat, some researchers have created models of insider attacks. Agrafiotis et al. [1] analyzed numerous cases of insider attacks and tried to pinpoint common denominators linking the attack scenarios, ultimately creating several attack archetypes. Ruttenberg et al. [15] used such attack archetypes in an architecture similar to a Bayesian network (BN). Indicators and detectors assessed the probability of user behaviors being a part of a known archetype. The authors highlighted ease of transferability of the system between clients, but warned there was a "conceptual gap" where the indicators and detectors could not capture the concept of less common attacks. They also mentioned using optimization methods to improve the model's performance. While lacking a more detailed description of the optimization process, their chosen single metric, utility, improved almost twice in comparison to the original model's.

2.1 Critique of Previous Work

Previous research into anomaly detection of insider threat has often suffered from three key shortcomings. Firstly, results are often presented with a limited selection of metrics. Emmott et al. [4] highlighted such biased results where AUC (Area Under the ROC Curve) was used as the main, and sometimes only metric (e.g., [19]), or renaming existing metrics (e.g., referring to the commonly accepted metric, *recall*, as a *true detection rate* [8]). Emmott et al. considered anomaly detection across different fields, with insider threat detection being given as an example of a high point difficulty problem—meaning that anomalies might be very similar to baseline behavior. Secondly, models are often created with prior knowledge of answers in the dataset. Recent research [14,20] provides a nice counterexample to this practice whereby models were tested on attack data developed by a team separate to the one responsible for creating the detection models. Thirdly, results are not consistently presented alongside the limitations of the approach.

We posit that these pitfalls can be easily addressed by following the guidelines of good conduct [4]. Firstly, multiple metrics should be used to describe outcomes of the model. Secondly, models should ideally be created without prior knowledge of answers in the dataset. Finally, informing the readers about any shortcomings of the experiment design is vital, e.g., Lo et al. [12] highlight that their model was only tested for users known to contain attacks in their behavior.

3   Methodology

In this section we describe our dataset and feature extraction (Sect. 3.1), our machine learning models and their optimization (Sect. 3.2) as well as our ensemble creation (Sect. 3.3), our approach to adding attack examples to create an augmented dataset (Sect. 3.4) and our reporting metrics (Sect. 3.5).

3.1   Original Dataset and Feature Extraction

The CERT dataset [5] is a synthetic dataset that was created as part of a project at Carnegie Mellon University to answer a specific problem in the insider threat field: the difficulty of obtaining data. The dataset was created using several interdependent systems to create log behaviors of a virtual organisation. The attacks in the CERT data were developed manually after consultations with counter-intelligence experts and included during the dataset creation. The authors highlighted that despite their efforts to introduce inconsistencies, the data was still cleaner than real-world equivalents.

There are several releases of the CERT dataset, varying in number of attacks, users, length, how advanced the text generation methods were, and others. We decided to use the release 4.2 (which we refer to as the *original dataset*), with 501 days of activity logs and 1000 users—70 of whom performed attacks of 3 possible scenarios. The attacks could be events either occurring during a single day, or contain actions scattered over two months of user's activity. While there are newer releases of the CERT data available, r4.2 is often chosen due to the number of anomalies it contains. For example, at the time or writing, the newest dataset, r6.2, contains only 5 attacks (we recreate the scenarios introduced in r6.2 as our additional attack insertions for our *augmented dataset*—see Sect. 3.4). We believe that using this release will allow us, and other academics, to more easily compare results.

The CERT dataset (r4.2) contains behavior data for 1000 users over a period of a year and a half. We separated data into parts containing actions of single users. Each part consisted of samples representing a 24-hour day of a user's actions. We refer to samples and days of behavior interchangeably. A *sample* is a sequence of actions, sorted by the timestamps in the CERT dataset. We enumerated and encoded actions as numbers in a sequence. The sequence was changed into a fixed length feature vector containing counts of every action performed, for models requiring other type of input. The possible actions were: logging in, logging off, connecting a removable drive, disconnecting a removable drive, email events, file manipulation events, http access events (including browsing, downloading and uploading) and a parsing error event accounting for any unknown actions or dirty data. The first 21 days of every user's activity were used as the training set, with the rest of the data being the test set. We confirmed that no attacks occurred in those 21 days. This number was chosen as the average number of working days in a month.

3.2   Models and Their Optimization

We used several anomaly detection models (from the scikit-learn Python package [17]) for our analysis: Local Outlier Factor (LOF), One-Class Support Vector Machine (OCSVM/SVM), and Isolation Forest (IF). HMM models were implemented using the hmmlearn package. We chose LOF for its explainability and simplicity, SVM for its sensitivity to outliers, and HMM for its ability do identify sequences of events. The inclusion of the IF model was inspired by its use by Emmott et al. [4], since they recommended it as a "go-to model" that scaled up better than other solutions. Every model generated a label for every single sample it encounters: 1 for normal behavior and -1 for an anomaly.

Local Outlier Factor models calculate the local density of each sample based on the distance to its neighbors. Comparing those densities for each sample lets the model decide which cases are inliers (normal behavior) and which are outliers (anomalies, therefore suspected attacks).

One-Class Support Vector Machine models approximate a hyperplane that separates samples belonging to different classes during the training. During the classification step the labels are assigned based on which side of the plane the samples lie. The one-class variant can be used for anomaly detection, with the hyperplane encapsulating the inliers.

Hidden Markov Models assume that samples are created by a Markov process containing a number of hidden states. Every new part of the sample sequence corresponds to a change of the hidden state.

Isolation Forest models recursively partition the data, assuming that anomalies are easier to separate from the set than inliers. The model iteratively selects a feature, chooses a random value between minimum and maximum of that feature, and separates the data based on this value. The idea behind it is that, with samples representing common behavior forming a cluster, one needs more partitions to reach them than anomalies.

Table 1. Model suffixes

Suffix	Optimization
no suffix	Default
_acc	Accuracy
_auc	Area under the ROC curve
_rec	Recall
_f1	Fscore, (just SVM model)

Table 2. Ensembles

Name	Models used
ensFirst	HMM_tt, LOF, SVM
ensBest	LOF_auc, LOF_rec, SVM
ensWorst	HMM_wb, SVM_acc, SVM_rec
ensSec	LOF, SVM, IF
ensSecAuc	IF_auc, LOF_auc, SVM_f1
ensSecAcc	IF_acc, LOF_acc, SVM_acc
ensSecRec	IF_rec, LOF_rec, SCM_rec
ensThird	HMM_tt, HMM_wb, IF, LOF, SVM
ensAll	HMM_tt, HMM_wb, IF, IF_acc, IF_auc, LOF_acc, LOF_auc, LOF_rec, SVM, SVM_acc, SVM_rec

Motivated by the observation that previous research on insider threat detection has rarely used optimization, we decided to compare the results of our models when optimized for different performance metrics. To optimize our models we used gridsearchCV from scikit-learn library [17]: a method that exhaustively searches through given sets of model parameters to find the best combination for a chosen metric, e.g., accuracy. We optimized the LOF, SVM and IF models for accuracy, AUC and recall. Due to implementation issues with the library for the out-of-the-box AUC optimizer for SVM, optimizing the SVM model for AUC was unsuccessful—hence, we used F1 score. Two pairs of models, despite being optimized for different metrics had the same sets of parameters: Accuracy and F1 score for the SVM models, and Accuracy and Recall for the Isolation Forest models. We speculate that this was caused by a declared parameter space becoming too small when running the optimizer. When describing models or ensembles used in our work we use the optimized metric as a suffix to identify which version is used (see Table 1). All models were optimized on the original dataset.

The HMM models could not be optimized using the gridsearchCV methods due to not being implemented in the sciki-learn library. Rather, our code used the hmmlearn library, which was not compatible with the gridsearchCV optimizer method. To address this, we created two different versions of the HMM model, HMM_tt and HMM_wb which had different anomaly thresholds. HMM_tt calculates the threshold based only on the training samples, while HMM_wb uses both training and test data.

3.3   Ensembles

Ensembles are classifiers that aggregate results of other classifiers. They can be used to reduce the bias or variance of the models to create a new model more powerful than the sum of its parts. We decided to build on the work of Parveen et al. [13] and Haidar and Gaber [6] and created several ensembles that group different types of models instead of just one (with separate instances learning on different folds of the training set).

We aimed to create an ensemble that was computationally effective and worked in a way that was intuitive and transparent for the user. In this study we used *majority voting*, since this was the easiest to interpret scheme for combining the outputs of individual models. The ensemble added up the classifications of the models. The majority decided a final verdict. We decided to create ensembles with only odd number of models that could vote. This was done to avoid a tied vote between the models. Some of the ensembles utilized optimized versions of models (see Sect. 3.2). For the full list of the created ensembles and what models were used, see Table 2.

ensFirst The first trial ensemble we designed, with the goal of quickly putting together models with diverse ways of learning from data.

ensBest and ensWorst Those two ensembles were built after we ran experiments for single models described in Sect. 4.1. We wanted to create ensembles out of the three best and worst models respectively.

ensSec We wanted to create an ensemble with every single model in it controlling for versions optimized for a different metric. We created four versions of this ensemble, one default with unoptimized models, and three with models optimized for accuracy, AUC and recall.

ensThird This ensemble was created to utilize all unoptimized types of machine learning models we present in this study in one ensemble: LOF, SVM, IF and HMM.

ensAll This ensemble was created to test if an ensemble that aggregated results of a larger number of models performed better, including several versions of the same model types optimized for different metrics.

3.4 Creating an Augmented Dataset

In order to test our models on new attacks not present in the original CERT dataset release, we developed a flexible generation and insertion pipeline to produce an *augmented dataset*. Firstly, we randomly selected a set of 28 benign users from the original (r4.2) dataset. We chose 28 users since we created 28 combinations of attack scenarios and anomaly frequency (described below).

Secondly, we set the number of insertions to be present in the data, which corresponded to the desired anomaly frequency rate—in our case between 1 and 7 attacks per user. The insertions were a sequence of events that represented the attack in the data. We read the benign user data and randomly chose a number of days, corresponding to the anomaly frequency, as the desired days of attacks.

Thirdly, we selected a scenario to generate and insert into the data. We selected three attack scenarios to recreate from a different release of the CERT dataset (Scenarios 1, 4 and 5 from r6.2), keeping their original numbering, as well as creating our own, Scenario 6. Note that we had already created our models prior to becoming aware of the details of the r6.2 dataset, thereby providing some independence, and reducing bias, in our model creation. Scenario 1 involves a person copying sensitive files on a pen drive and uploading them to Wikileaks. Scenario 4 is a person sending confidential files to their private email. Scenario 5 is a person browsing through restricted files and uploading them to Dropbox. Scenario 6 is a person copying confidential files onto a pen drive. Our generation function created sequences representing the scenario and inserted them into a chosen sample. Every attack was generated separately, adding noise to the attack (e.g., different times of attack or number of sensitive files stolen), even within actions of the same user. We kept track of which samples were altered to create ground truth labels for the anomaly detection models. At this stage the data was ready for the model to be trained and tested. The augmented dataset consists of actions of only 28 malicious users. Each of the four scenarios has between one and seven days inserted with attack actions. We reused CERT data to create it.

3.5 Result Metrics

We wanted to ensure that our results were easy to compare and recreate, especially for researchers interested in generating their own synthetic data insertions. With this in mind, we chose to use the area under the ROC curve (AUC), Accuracy and Recall. AUC is a number describing the area under the plot of true positive rate against the false positive rate, with 1 characterising a perfect model and 0.5 being analogous to a random choice. AUC is the most commonly reported metric in anomaly-based insider threat detection. Accuracy (Acc) was chosen as a metric affected by anomaly threshold of the model and not calculated solely based on the internal scoring function like AUC, and recall (Rec) as a measure of how many attacks were detected, without information about false positives.

Our choice of reporting additional metrics was inspired by existing guidelines laid out by Emmott et al. [4]. In particular, we wanted to be transparent on the documented results of our models even if they did not perform well.

4 Results

Every model has a separate instance for every user from the data. We will refer to these instances as user models. The results presented in Tables 3 and 4 show the means calculated from the results of all the user models in the corresponding dataset. The tables contain results from both default and optimized models and have the models sorted from top to bottom based on their AUC.

4.1 Evaluation of Models on Original Data

Default SVM has the best AUC and recall, though it also has the second worst accuracy (with SVM_acc scoring lower). The LOF models have the most consistent scores across the non-ensemble models. EnsFirst has the highest average of all the metrics in comparison to the other models and ensembles. IF and HMM models have comparable results, with mediocre AUC between 0.651 and 0.629, but high accuracy, comparable to LOF models and ensembles.

4.2 Evaluation of Models on Augmented Data

Since we designed the models with knowledge of the original dataset, to follow one of the guidelines laid out in Sect. 2.1, we evaluated the models on the

Table 3. Model and ensemble results for original dataset, ordered by AUC

Classifier	AUC	Recall	Accuracy
SVM	0.956	0.992	0.238
LOF_rec	0.937	0.784	0.962
LOF_auc	0.935	0.785	0.961
ensFirst	0.916	0.882	0.919
ensAll	0.913	0.512	0.956
ensThird	0.901	0.639	0.945
ensBest	0.895	0.785	0.961
ensSec_acc	0.859	0.633	0.928
ensSec	0.857	0.848	0.899
LOF	0.843	0.810	0.927
LOF_acc	0.839	0.871	0.926
ensSec_auc	0.836	0.570	0.950
ensSec_rec	0.826	0.105	0.969
IF	0.651	0.225	0.928
IF_auc	0.640	0.082	0.969
IF_acc/rec	0.639	0.038	0.987
HMM_wb	0.629	0.034	0.979
HMM_tt	0.629	0.626	0.962
ensWorst	0.480	0.109	0.880
SVM_acc/f1	0.391	0.708	0.216
SVM_rec	0.148	0.103	0.830

Table 4. Model and ensemble results for augmented dataset, ordered by AUC

Classifier	AUC	Recall	Accuracy
ensFirst	0.966	1.000	0.909
LOF_auc	0.959	0.814	0.947
LOF_rec	0.958	0.814	0.947
SVM	0.955	1.000	0.265
ensThird	0.944	0.699	0.937
ensAll	0.943	0.585	0.942
LOF_acc	0.925	0.854	0.919
ensBest	0.912	0.814	0.947
LOF	0.863	0.693	0.917
ensSec	0.862	0.731	0.889
ensSec_acc	0.826	0.582	0.915
ensSec_auc	0.813	0.582	0.936
ensSec_rec	0.810	0.019	0.953
HMM_wb	0.767	0.112	0.904
HMM_tt	0.767	0.959	0.963
IF_auc	0.596	0.025	0.958
IF_acc/rec	0.590	0.008	0.971
IF	0.579	0.076	0.917
ensWorst	0.412	0.019	0.840
SVM_acc/f1	0.368	0.714	0.174
SVM_rec	0.052	0.025	0.843

augmented dataset, whose creation is described in Sect. 3.4. In contrast to the earlier experiment (see Sect. 4.1), this dataset was much smaller (28 users instead of 1000) and contained only malicious users. Results of the experiment on this data can be found in Table 4. The model with the best AUC is ensFirst, and LOF_auc is the best non-ensemble. EnsFirst is tied with SVM for the best recall, but the latter still has poor accuracy. SVM_acc still has the worst accuracy of all the models. LOF models still have the best, most consistent scores out of non-ensemble models.

4.3 Comparison Between Default and Optimized Implementations

For results of optimized and default models, see Tables 3 and 4. The comparison of the ROC curves for each model family are shown in Fig. 1. Since both HMM models have the same values for the scoring function, their ROC curves are overlapping. The internal scoring function of ensembles was the vote count, meaning that their ROC curve could have only two or three points of inflection, depending on the number of models that contributed to the ensemble, so we

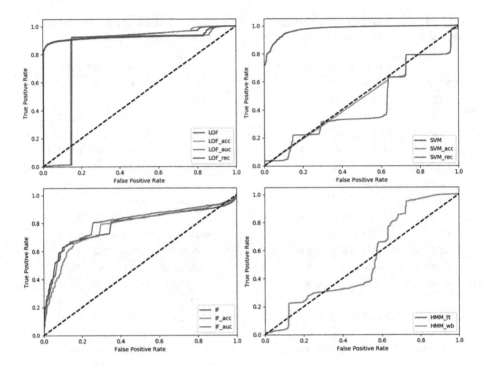

Fig. 1. Comparison of ROC curves of models tested on original CERT data

decided not to show them. The ROC curves for models run on the augmented dataset were sufficiently similar to those for the original dataset that we have also not included those curves.

5 Discussion of Results

The model with the best results on the original dataset demonstrates the importance of reporting multiple metrics. For example, the default implementation of the SVM model showed high AUC = 0.956 and Recall = 0.992 and simultaneously one of the lowest accuracy scores, Acc = 0.238, compared to the other models. This suggests that the SVM can be an overly sensitive classifier and we do not recommend using it to solve high point difficulty anomaly detection problems. The other versions of the SVM model were found to have similarly low results as both SVM models had the lowest AUC. SVM_acc had the lowest accuracy, and SVM_rec even produced a result of Rec = 0.103, with only 3 other models displaying lower recall: IF_acc/rec, IF_auc and HMM_wb.

The ensemble models were among the highest scoring considering all the metrics, excluding the ensWorst ensemble, which was made specifically using the three models with the lowest AUC in the original experiment. The best performing, ensFirst, consisting of default versions of LOF, SVM and HMM_tt models, was also our first experiment in aggregating results from single models. We believe that using such ensembles could be an easy and cost-effective way of boosting detection rates of insider attacks. Implementing a voting system has a negligible cost in comparison to training and using singular models. Depending on what sort of models the user needs, they can change the models voting in the ensemble in order to get a more precise or sensitive ensemble.

Overall, we rank the ensembles and LOF models as the best performing in our experiment, followed by IF and HMM, with SVMs being the least reliable family of classifiers in our work.

5.1   Verifying Models on Augmented Data

The experiments we conducted to verify the models on inserted attacks have demonstrated similar results to the original CERT set. The results presented in Table 4 show similar trends to the original experiment in Table 3. Default SVM was no longer a model with best AUC and recall, overtaken by the ensemble ensFirst and models LOF_auc and LOF_rec. When looking at the results of detecting insertions we highlight that attacks were inserted randomly, therefore we did not account for the regular behavior of a user, as opposed to attacks originally present in the CERT dataset. Still, we hope that this limitation is somewhat offset by the fact that the attacks we recreated are either from different releases of CERT data (r6.2, where the original dataset uses r4.2) or have been designed to incur a minimal footprint in the behavior logs.

A further issue is that ens_first and default SVM had a recall of 1.0—a perfect score. We assume this was potentially caused by a smaller size of the dataset used for the insertion experiment, i.e., 28 users as opposed to 1000. All 28 users had attacks inserted in their data, exhibiting a different rate of anomalies when compared to 70 attackers in the original CERT set. On average, the difference between metrics, depending on the dataset used, was 0.047 for AUC, 0.015 for Accuracy, and 0.068 for Recall. We believe that the differences were small enough (less than 5%) suggesting that our models should perform well on a different dataset.

5.2   Difference Between Default and Optimized Models

The models most positively affected by optimizing were LOF, and to a smaller degree, IF. Optimizing the LOF model for AUC improved the metric by 11%, optimizing for recall improved by 17% and optimizing for accuracy raised it by 3%, all in comparison to the default versions of the model. The IF model showed an improvement in AUC of 3% and in accuracy of 5% in respective optimizations. We highlight that the recall of the optimized models was lower than the default model, with the version specifically optimized for recall demonstrating worse results by 89%.

SVM and an optimized version of the ensSec ensemble scored poorer in the metric they were optimized for than the default counterpart. We believe that weaker performance of different variants of the ensemble was potentially caused

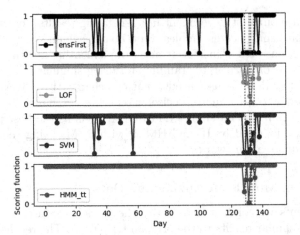

Fig. 2. Scoring function comparison for user KPC0073. Attacks in red. (Color figure online)

by the votes of the SVM models. The only improvement in the SVM model was a better accuracy, increasing from 0.265 of the default model to 0.843 of the model optimized for recall. We want to emphasize that ROC curves shown in Fig. 1 were plotted using aggregated labels and scoring functions from user models. This meant the AUC of plotted curves was different from the averaged AUC we reported in our results. Both of the HMM models had the same set of parameters, causing their scoring function values to be the same, see Fig. 1.

5.3   Case Study

In order to provide some more insight into our work we have included the following case study. We focused on user KPC0073 from the original dataset who was a permanent employee of the simulated company. According to the backgroud readme information for the dataset, the attack performed by the user was a "new habit" of using removable drives and working after hours, finally resulting in using a pen drive and uploading data to a restricted website *wikileaks.org* [5]. Figure 2 shows a comparison of scoring functions of ensemble First and the models for this user. The ensembles performed relatively better, compared to standalone models. It is worth noting that the ensemble's scoring function is much less compressed in comparison to the models, as seen in Fig. 2. All the votes at value '0' are unanimous, meaning that all three models creating the ensemble voted a sample anomalous. All of the votes at value '1' had two of the models voting benign and one voting malicious. Referring to the results from Table 3, we can assume that SVM is an oversensitive model that is being "kept in check" by more accurate LOF and HMM_tt models. Looking at the SVM model scoring function we can assume that the best way to improve that model in the future might be by adjusting its anomaly threshold.

6   Limitations and Future Work

We decided against using average precision of the models as one of our met-rics, because depending on the choice of majority class, it would be near 1 or 0 for every single model. Similarly, we did not consider sliding models, where the model re-learns based on new samples, which may be used to take behavioral drift into account. Our initial investigation of sliding models indicated poor per-formance and high computational cost. We would encourage others to investigate this topic, possibly on a real dataset. For the original dataset we used the fact that there are no attacks in training data. While we were able to confirm this using the CERT labels, we suggest that future modeling attempts should con-sider the implications of training with data that might contain insider threats. Our augmented dataset consists of only malicious users. Whilst this differs from the original dataset, we use augmented data to validate models on a per user basis, rather than comparing false positive rates with benign data.

Our feature extraction was based on a relatively small number of features. We encourage others to consider different feature sets, data representations, or deep learning models to investigate insider threats. Limited options could also affect our optimization work. GridsearchCV, while conducting an exhaustive search of model parameters, does so only within the dictionaries of parameter space passed to it. We suspect this might have affected some of the SVM models performing worse in the metric they were optimized for. Our approach to generating and inserting attacks was an initial investigation into addressing the problem with bias introduced by reusing the CERT data. Any future research should consider structured models for incorporating realistic attack data into datasets.

7   Conclusions

In this study, we compared several types of anomaly detection models, with versions optimized for different quality metrics. We also created a selection of majority voting ensembles using combinations of the anomaly detection models presented. We tested the models on the synthetic CERT dataset and a separate, smaller dataset created from a random selection of benign CERT users with new attacks inserted into it. The ensembles and LOF models had the best and most consistent results among all reported metrics.

We advocate the importance of following a set of guidelines while working on insider threat detection models. We would particularly encourage future studies to: report on multiple result metrics; design the models without prior knowledge of answers and labels or using a different dataset to create and evaluate the models; keep track and inform on any limitations of the approach discovered. In the future, we want to expand on this study by creating more feature sets for our models, expanding our ML model suite with neural net models e.g., autoen-coders and their translation error for anomaly detection, creating ensembles that combine models using different feature sets and weighted voting schemes, con-ducting uncertainty and sensitivity analysis for our models and testing them on a non-synthetic dataset.

References

1. Agrafiotis, I., Nurse, J.R., et al.: Identifying attack patterns for insider threat detection. Comput. Fraud Secur. **2015**(7), 9–17 (2015)
2. Cappelli, D., Moore, A., Trzeciak, R.: The CERT Guide to Insider Threats: How to Prevent, Detect, and Respond to Information Technology Crimes. Addison-Wesley Professional, Boston (2012)
3. Dahmane, M., Foucher, S.: Combating insider threats by user profiling from activity logging data. In: ICDIS, pp. 194–199 (2018)
4. Emmott, A., Das, S., Dietterich, T., Fern, A., Wong, W.K.: A meta-analysis of the anomaly detection problem, March 2015. https://arxiv.org/abs/1503.01158
5. Glasser, J., Lindauer, B.: Bridging the gap: a pragmatic approach to generating insider threat data. In: Proceedings - IEEE CS Security and Privacy (2013)
6. Haidar, D., Gaber, M.M.: Adaptive one-class ensemble-based anomaly detection: an application to insider threats. In: 2018 International Joint Conference on Neural Networks (IJCNN), pp. 1–9 (2018)
7. IBM: Cost of Insider Threats—ObserveIT (2020). https://www.observeit.com/cost-of-insider-threats/
8. Kim, J., Park, M., Kim, H., Cho, S., Kang, P.: Insider threat detection based on user behavior modeling and anomaly detection algorithms. Appl. Sci. (Switz.) **9**(19), 4018 (2019)
9. Le, D.C., Zincir-Heywood, A.N.: Evaluating insider threat detection workflow using supervised and unsupervised learning. In: 2018 IEEE Security and Privacy Workshops (SPW), pp. 270–275 (2018)
10. Le, D.C., Zincir-Heywood, N.: Exploring anomalous behaviour detection and classification for insider threat identification. Int. J. Netw. Manag. (July 2019), 1–19 (2020). https://doi.org/10.1002/nem.2109
11. Legg, P.A., Buckley, O., Goldsmith, M., Creese, S.: Automated insider threat detection system using user and role-based profile assessment. IEEE Syst. J. **11**(2), 503–512 (2017)
12. Lo, O., Buchanan, W.J., Griffiths, P., Macfarlane, R.: Distance measurement methods for improved insider threat detection. Secur. Commun. Netw. **2018**(January) (2018). https://doi.org/10.1155/2018/5906368
13. Parveen, P., Weger, Z.R., Thuraisingham, B., Hamlen, K., Khan, L.: Supervised learning for insider threat detection using stream mining. In: 2011 IEEE 23rd International Conference on Tools with Artificial Intelligence, pp. 1032–1039 (2011)
14. Rashid, T., Agrafiotis, I., Nurse, J.R.: A New Take on Detecting Insider Threats, pp. 47–56 (2016)
15. Ruttenberg, B., et al.: Probabilistic modeling of insider threat detection systems. In: Liu, P., Mauw, S., Stølen, K. (eds.) GraMSec 2017. LNCS, vol. 10744, pp. 91–98. Springer, Cham (2018). https://doi.org/10.1007/978-3-319-74860-3_6
16. Tuor, A., Kaplan, S., Hutchinson, B., Nichols, N., Robinson, S.: Deep learning for unsupervised insider threat detection in structured cybersecurity data streams, October 2017. http://arxiv.org/abs/1710.00811
17. Varoquaux, G., Buitinck, L., Louppe, G., et al.: Scikit-learn: machine learning in Python. GetMobile: Mobile Comput. Commun. **19**(1), 29–33 (2015)
18. Yuan, F., Cao, Y., Shang, Y., Liu, Y., Tan, J., Fang, B.: Insider threat detection with deep neural network. In: Shi, Y., et al. (eds.) ICCS 2018. LNCS, vol. 10860, pp. 43–54. Springer, Cham (2018). https://doi.org/10.1007/978-3-319-93698-7_4

19. Yuan, F., Shang, Y., Liu, Y., Cao, Y., Tan, J.: Attention-based LSTM for insider threat detection. In: Shankar Sriram, V.S., Subramaniyaswamy, V., Sasikaladevi, N., Zhang, L., Batten, L., Li, G. (eds.) ATIS 2019. CCIS, vol. 1116, pp. 192–201. Springer, Singapore (2019). https://doi.org/10.1007/978-981-15-0871-4_15
20. Zhang, H., Agrafiotis, I., Erola, A., Creese, S., Goldsmith, M.: A state machine system for insider threat detection. In: Cybenko, G., Pym, D., Fila, B. (eds.) GraMSec 2018. LNCS, vol. 11086, pp. 111–129. Springer, Cham (2019). https://doi.org/10.1007/978-3-030-15465-3_7

Revitalizing Self-Organizing Map: Anomaly Detection Using Forecasting Error Patterns

Young Geun Kim[1], Jeong-Han Yun[3], Siho Han[2], Hyoung Chun Kim[3], and Simon S. Woo[2(✉)]

[1] Department of Statistics, Sungkyunkwan University, Seoul, South Korea
[2] Department of Applied Data Science, College of Computing and Informatics, Sungkyunkwan University, Suwon, South Korea
swoo@g.skku.edu
[3] Institute of ETRI, Daejeon, South Korea

Abstract. Detecting rare cases of anomalies in Cyber-Physical Systems (CPSs) is an extremely challenging task. It is especially difficult to accurately model various instances of CPS measurements due to the dearth of anomaly samples and the subtlety of how their patterns appear. Moreover, the detection performance may be severely limited owing to mediocre or inaccurate forecasting by the underlying prediction models. In this work, we focus on improving the anomaly detection performance by leveraging the forecasting error patterns generated from prediction models, such as Sequence-to-Sequence (seq2seq), Mixture Density Networks (MDNs), and Recurrent Neural Networks (RNNs). To this end, we introduce Self-Organizing Map-based Anomaly Detector (SOMAD), an anomaly detection framework based on a novel test statistic, *SomAnomaly*, for Cyber-Physical System (CPS) security. Upon evaluation on two popular CPS datasets, we demonstrate that SOMAD outperforms baseline approaches through online multiple testing, using Time-Series Aware Precision and Recall (TaPR) metrics. Accordingly, we empirically demonstrate that forecasting error patterns of raw CPS data can be useful when detecting anomalies through a fast, statistical multiple testing approach such as ours.

Keywords: Anomaly detection · Self-Organizing Map · CPS

1 Introduction

Cyber-Physical Systems (CPSs) are susceptible to various types of anomalies, such as attacks on controllers, networks, or cyber-physical elements, as well as hardware failures, operator errors, and software misconfigurations, which can cause different types of anomalies. Accurately distinguishing the latter kinds of anomalies, which may simply be glitches, from actual anomalies is an important, yet challenging task that may lead to high false positives. Such errors are costly, especially for CPSs,

© IFIP International Federation for Information Processing 2021
Published by Springer Nature Switzerland AG 2021
A. Jøsang et al. (Eds.): SEC 2021, IFIP AICT 625, pp. 382–397, 2021.
https://doi.org/10.1007/978-3-030-78120-0_25

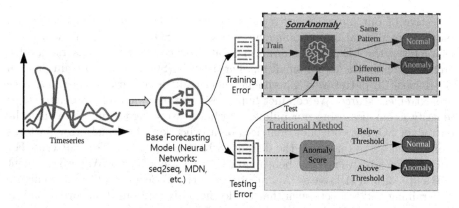

Fig. 1. SOMAD (area colored in blue) vs. traditional anomaly detection approach (area colored in gray). SOMAD leverages FEs to detect anomalies, while the traditional approach directly detects anomalies based on the output of base forecasting models, such as seq2seq and MDNs. (Color figure online)

since the main infrastructures might have to stop running for inspection purposes. In particular, the detection of anomalous instances in water pumps, power grids, or nuclear power plants [19], is crucial for the prevention of huge economic losses as well as environmental catastrophes. The first step of anomaly detection [8,12,20] typically involves building a rule-based or statistical machine learning-based (e.g., neural networks) forecasting model from the given training data as shown in Fig. 1. Next, the anomaly score is computed from the forecasting error (FE), and an observation is considered anomalous if that score exceeds the out-of-limit (OOL) threshold. Similarly, statistical machine learning-based approaches typically fit a model to the data and consider an observation as anomalous if the prediction error is exceeds a predefined threshold. Meanwhile, there are several challenges related to the detection of anomalies in CPSs. For example, in many practical situations, there exist normal instances of which the measurements exceed the threshold and contextual anomalies of which the measurements do not exceed the threshold; the former should not be considered anomalous, while the latter should. Another challenge is that it is realistically difficult to collect anomalous data beforehand, which complicates the process of building an accurate anomaly predictor trained only on data corresponding to normal instances. Moreover, an attacker can perform sophisticated manipulations on the FEs, such that they are observed to be less than the pre-defined threshold, leading to a high false positive rate. Accurate forecasting is usually attainable for models trained and optimized on abundant data of both normal and abnormal classes, but this is rarely the case in real-world scenarios regarding CPSs, since only a few cases of anomalies are readily available. Therefore, improving the anomaly detection performance by simply optimizing conventional forecasting models themselves has its limitations.

In this work, we propose Self-Organizing Map-based Anomaly Detector (SOMAD), an anomaly detection framework based on a novel test statistic, *SomAnomaly*, to detect anomalies in CPS sensor and actuator data based on their FE patterns. The overview of our approach is depicted in Fig. 2. The main objective of our approach is to amplify the differences in the respective FE patterns of normal and anomalous events, with SOM [21] used to learn and characterize the FE patterns of normal data. We construct 3D tensors and discretize the patterns into a small number of grids (SOM grids) to train only on the normal FE patterns to experiment under realistic scenarios where anomalies are extremely scarce. We conduct hypothesis testing based on *SomAnomaly* to identify anomalies using our online, multiple testing algorithm. Note that the output of SOM is codebook matrices or a collection of normal error patterns from which we can measure the distance with the input test error patterns. For our experiments, we use two benchmark CPS datasets, Secure Water Treatment (SWaT) [13] and HIL-based Augmented ICS (HAI) Security [29], We configure the training and test sets such that the former only contains data corresponding to normal observations to reproduce a challenging, realistic anomaly detection scenario, where unseen anomalous events are encountered only during the test phase. During evaluation, we assess our model based on contextual anomalies, i.e., anomalies that do not exceed a pre-defined threshold, using the latest time series-aware precision and recall metrics [17], since conventional metrics fail to serve as an accurate evaluation method for anomaly detection in time series [17]. and demonstrate that our proposed approach significantly outperforms baseline methods. Our contributions are summarized as follows:

1. We propose a novel SOM-based anomaly detection framework and publicly release our code for reproducibility[1].
2. We demonstrate that our proposed method can effectively detect unseen anomalies in high-dimensional CPS data through an online, multiple hypothesis testing algorithm under a realistic scenario where anomalous cases are extremely rare.
3. We conduct experiments on benchmark CPS datasets – SWaT [13] and HAI [29] – and achieve on average 36% increase in the time series-aware F_1 score compared to those of baseline approaches.

2   Related Work

Anomaly detection in multivariate time series data is a challenging task, and numerous approaches have been proposed in the past few years to tackle this problem. When identifying anomalies in Cyber-Physical Systems (CPS), the first-order approach can be implemented by building a knowledge base, when comprehensive and accurate domain knowledge is available [23,24,26,28]. However, in modern CPS, developing a knowledge base from a large number of variables in a complex CPS is challenging. Recently, data-driven approaches such as deep-learning or unsupervised clustering-based methods, which do not require broad and specific knowledge of the domain, have been developed [6,11,15,16,18]. These methods can learn and derive information and patterns from data, not using much expert domain knowledge. However, the development of a thorough knowledge

---

[1] https://github.com/ygeunkim/somanomaly.

base from complex CPS data in the modern era is challenging, requiring extensive domain knowledge. To cope with this limitation, recent approaches include data-driven deep learning-based unsupervised clustering methods, which can automatically extract relevant information and derive characteristic patterns from the data [6,16,18]. Another popular approach is to use OOL thresholds. Given some time series data, the p-norm is often used to calculate the anomaly score. Note that when $p = 1$, it represents the sum of the absolute values. [8,9] used the 2-norm, mean-squared error (MSE), while [20] used the 4-norm. For convenience, we denote the method using the p-norm criterion as static thresholding, which is the simplest, yet one of the most popular methods. Also, the cumulative sum (CUSUM) method [14] is widely used; it divides a time series into fixed time window intervals and computes the sum of the p-norms for each window. The resulting sum serves as the anomaly score for each window: if the sum is larger than the threshold, the window is considered anomalous. We use static thresholding with $p = 4$ and CUSUM as our baselines for performance comparisons.

On the other hand, Aloudi et al. [2] present PASAD, an efficient model-free Process-Aware Stealthy-Attack Detection mechanism that monitors sensors and raises an alarm in the occurrence of a structural change in the behavior of physical processes. The authors conduct Singular Spectrum Analysis (SSA), a non-parametric spectral estimation approach, to separate the deterministic part of a dynamical system from its chaotic part. However, in this work, we focus on forecasting error based approach unlike directly exploiting the sensor values. Recently, also neural networks have shown their effectiveness in time series modeling and anomaly detection. Malhotra et al. [25] proposed a Long Short-Term Memory (LSTM) Network with an Encoder-Decoder scheme, which detects anomalies based on reconstruction errors between the input and its reconstructed output; with the latter approach, the authors were able to achieve better generalization compared to when using a simple distance-based approach. Zhai et al. [31] developed Deep Structured Energy-Based Models (DSEBMs), which connect Energy-Based Models (EBMs) to a regularized autoencoder to eliminate the need for complicated sampling. The latter model uses energy scores as well as reconstruction errors to detect anomalies. However, the aforementioned methods cannot jointly analyze temporal dependencies, noise resistance, and the severity of anomalies [31]. Also, Zhang et al. [32] developed Multi-Scale Convolutional Recurrent Endcoder Decoder (MSCRED), which constructs multi-scale signature matrices to characterize multiple levels of the system status over the time. However, most deep learning-based methods resort to some sort of thresholding, such as OOL, to distinguish anomalies from normal instances.

Also, Sequence-to-Sequence (seq2seq), Mixture Density Networks (MDNs), and Recurrent Neural Networks (RNNs) [27] have also been popular choices. Typically, a seq2seq model is composed of an encoder and a decoder, where the task of the former is to learn from the input data and create a fixed feature dimension while that of the latter is to decode it to reconstruct the input for further use cases, e.g., anomaly detection. Bishop [5] proposed MDNs, which can rapidly learn from a training set and produce a probability distribution function for the expected signal as a function of time, by combining a conventional neural network with a Mixture Density model. Lastly, RNNs have also been use for time series-related tasks. In this work, we use these three models as our underlying anomaly detection classifier to generate forecasting error patterns from the SWaT and HAI datasets.

3   Mathematical Preliminaries for Self-Organizing Maps

In this section, we present the mathematical background and preliminary information regarding SOM, as well as the Lindeberg-Feller theorem, necessary for the comprehension of our proposed method.

3.1   Self-Organizing Maps (SOM)

Kohonen [21] developed a novel Artificial Neural Network (ANN) structure called SOM, which maps observations to topological maps with finite number of prototypes called Kohonen neurons (SOM grids). Each grid has its own vector called the codebook in the input space and SOM updates it for each training sample to approximate the training data. In particular, the codebook matrices are the output of SOM, which are a collection of the normal error patterns in our case. We use the distance between the codebook matrices and the corresponding test error patterns of a window to predict anomalies as shown in Fig. 2. Another advantage of SOM is that it does not use a back-propagation algorithm, but implements competitive learning to compute the distance between the observation and the codebook matrices and update the relevant codebook vectors for each training sample (additional details are provided in the following paragraphs).

We extend Kohonen's SOM algorithm [21] by proposing a novel test statistic called *SomAnomaly*, such that we can investigate the similarity in the input patterns to effectively determine anomalies. First, we formally describe the original SOM process based on Kohonen's research [21]. We consider an $n \times p$ array, where n is the number of observations and p is the number of predictors. Then, the observational unit is a p-dimensional vector, defined as the input vector, which can be written as follows: $x_i = (\xi_{i1}, \xi_{i2}, \ldots, \xi_{ip})^T \in \mathbb{R}^p$, $i = 1, \ldots, n$.

For SOM, we have the following hyperparameters: $\alpha(0)$ (initial learning rate), $\sigma(0)$ (initial radius), N_x (number of SOM grid in the x-dimension), N_y (number of SOM grid in the y-dimension), h (neighborhood function), and g (decay function). Let $N = N_x N_y$ be the total number of nodes, then in each node, a codebook vector with the same dimension as the input vector is assigned. The codebook vector if defined as follows: $m_i = (m_{i1}, m_{i2}, \ldots, m_{ip})^T \in \mathbb{R}^p$, $i = 1, \ldots, N$.

Next, we define each $m_{ij}, j = 1, \ldots, p$, as the weight in a codebook vector. For each iteration, the learning algorithm randomly chooses one input vector and its closest codebook vector, defined as the Best Matching Unit (BMU). Then, the neighboring node of BMU whose distance to the cluster, known as the prototype distance, is less than the radius is updated as follows: $m_j(t+1) =$

$m_j(t) + \alpha(t)h(r_c - r_j)[x(t) - m_j(t)]$. Following the update, SOM maps each input vector to two-dimensional nodes or neurons. By searching for its BMU, every input vector finds the closest codebook vector, which is then sent to its corresponding node.

3.2   Lindeberg-Feller Theorem for Setting Threshold

A number of anomaly detection methods require setting a threshold to detect anomalies. The limitation, however, is that most approaches select a threshold empirically without strong mathematical or statistical foundations. To that end, we apply the Central Limit Theorem (CLT) to provide a statistical foundation for determining the threshold set for our approach. For our proposed approach, we employ a generalization of the CLT called Lindeberg-Feller theorem [7,22] for non-identically distributed cases in multiple statistical testing. First, let us define a triangular array of random variables $\{X_{nj}\}_{j=1}^{n}$ for $n = 1, 2, \ldots$ for simplicity. Also, let us assume that X_{nj} is independent for each n, such that $E[X_{nj}] = 0$ and $Var[X_{nj}] = \sigma_{nj}^2 < \infty$. Then, let $Z_n = \sum\limits_{j=1}^{n} X_{nj}$ and $B_n^2 = \sum\limits_{j=1}^{n} \sigma_{nj}^2$. Lastly, for every $\epsilon > 0$, the Lindeberg-Feller theorem can be stated as follows:

$$\frac{1}{B_n^2} \sum_{j=1}^{n} E\left[X_{nj}^2 I\left(|X_{nj}| \geq \epsilon B_n\right)\right] \to 0, \tag{1}$$

as $n \to \infty$, then

$$\frac{Z_n}{B_n} \xrightarrow{\mathcal{D}} \mathcal{N}(0,1). \tag{2}$$

Equation 1 is called the Lindeberg condition. We employ Lindeberg-Feller theorem to statistically determine an optimal threshold for anomaly detection.

4   Our Approach

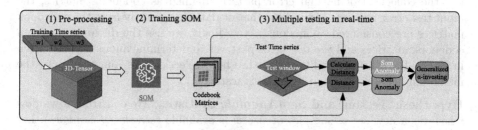

Fig. 2. Overall pipeline of SOMAD based on the *SomAnomaly* statistic

The overall process of our approach, SOMAD, is presented in Fig. 2. To characterize the error patterns of normal data, we first construct 3D tensors and discretize the normal patterns. Then, we use SOM to train only on normal FE patterns and conduct a hypothesis testing to measure the distance between the input and normal error patterns. Lastly, we identify anomalies using the *SomAnomaly* statistic and an online multiple hypothesis testing algorithm. We explain the details of each step in the following paragraphs.

1. Pre-processing. We consider p-dimensional time series with sample size n to represent multivariate time series by converting the data into a 3D tensor, as shown in Fig. 2. When training the SOM, we treat each window as a single observation. More specifically, the pre-processing step to obtain a 3D tensor can be summarized as follows:

1. Slide the window of size w with a shift size s.
2. Combine the windows into a 3D tensor of size $m \times w \times p$, where $m = \frac{n-w}{s} + 1$.

2. Training the SOM. Following its conversion to 3D tensor, the error pattern data is changed from a vector to a matrix. For matrix computation, we consider the Frobenius norm and use the following distance function between A and $B = (\beta_{jk}) \in \mathbb{R}^{w \times p}$ to determine the discrepancy of FE patterns between normal and anomalous data:

$$d(A, B) = \left(\sum_{j=1}^{w} \sum_{k=1}^{p} (\alpha_{jk} - \beta_{jk})^2 \right)^{\frac{1}{2}}. \tag{3}$$

To train the SOM, we propose an incremental SOM training algorithm, shown in Algorithm 1, using the distance function in Eq. 3. This training process maps each normal pattern window onto the SOM grids by finding the closest corresponding codebook matrix. Since the number of grids is finite, we can assume that the pattern is discretized, and every training error window maps onto finite prototypes, each of which has its own codebook matrix. This means that normal error patterns are discretized by the patterns represented by the codebook matrices.

3. SomAnomaly for Hypothesis Testing. From the output of SOM, i.e., the collection of normal error patterns defined as codebook matrics, the input test error patterns of windows that deviate significantly from the codebook matrices are considered anomalous. Accordingly, we use the distances between codebook matrices and the test error patterns to determine anomalies, as shown in Fig. 2. In order to facilitate the threshold selection, we aim to choose the maximum distance through hypothesis testing.

Hypothesis Testing and *SomAnomaly* Statistic. We construct a window whenever a new set of samples of size w is available (*streaming windows*). Let D_{ti}, $t = 1, \ldots$, $i = 1, \ldots, N$, be the distance between the t-th streaming window and the lastly updated codebook matrix of i-th node, where N is the number of Kohonen neurons, SOM grids, and each D_{ti} is a random variable. We assume that $\{D_{ti}\}_{i=1}^{N}$ are mutually independent for each t. In order to detect whether the j-th window significantly deviates from the trained SOM grid, we first determine μ_i

---

Algorithm 1: Incremental SOM training algorithm using 3D tensor

Data: 3D tensor $[X_1, \ldots, X_m] \in \mathbb{R}^{m \times w \times p}$
Input: SOM parameters
1 Initialize learning rate and radius
2 Initialize codebook matrices
3 Compute the distance $r_c - r_i$ between nodes c and i in the SOM space;
4 **for** $j \leftarrow 1$ **to** N **do**
5   Randomly choose an input observation;
6   **for** $j \leftarrow 1$ **to** N **do**
7   **if** $r_c - r_j \leq \sigma(t)$ **then**
8   Update the neighboring node of BMU by
             $W_j(t+1) = W_j(t) + \alpha(t)h(r_c - r_j)[X(t) - W_j(t)]$
9   **end**
10   Decay $\alpha(t)$ and $\sigma(t)$
11   **end**
12 **end**
    Output: $W_j(u), j = 1, 2, \ldots, N$

---

and σ_i^2. Since, in our work, the training set consists only of normal observations, we treat the training set as a pseudo-population. Using this training set, we obtain alternative values to the true mean and variance and $\tilde{\mu}_i$ and $\tilde{\sigma}_i^2$ can be defined as follows:

$$\tilde{\mu}_i = \frac{1}{m} \sum_{j=1}^{m} \tilde{d}_{ji} \quad , \quad \tilde{\sigma}_i^2 = \frac{1}{m-1} \sum_{j=1}^{m} (\tilde{d}_{ji} - \tilde{\mu}_i)^2, \tag{4}$$

where $\tilde{d}_{ji}$ is the distance between the i-th node codebook and the j-th observation of the training set. Also, we define the pseudo-mean and variance constants as follows:

$$\tilde{\mu} = \frac{1}{N} \sum_{i=1}^{N} \tilde{\mu}_i, \quad \tilde{\sigma}^2 = \frac{1}{N} \sum_{i=1}^{N} \tilde{\sigma}_i^2. \tag{5}$$

For each window, we conduct hypothesis testing to identify large codebook distances. For $t = 1, 2, \ldots$, we compare the average of the mean with the pseudo-mean constant by a right tailed test as follows:

$$H_{0t} : \frac{1}{N} \sum_{i=1}^{N} \mu_i = \tilde{\mu} \quad vs. \quad H_{1t} : \frac{1}{N} \sum_{i=1}^{N} \mu_i > \tilde{\mu}. \tag{6}$$

Rejecting the t-th null hypothesis corresponds to marking the t-th window as anomalous, because it indicates that the average distance of the window is larger than that of normal samples. To apply Eq. 6 for a fixed window t, we define the sample mean $\overline{D}_t = \frac{1}{N} \sum_{i=1}^{N} D_{ti}$. Based on the mutual independence assumption of $\{D_{ti}\}_{i=1}^{N}$, we can employ the Lindeberg-Feller CLT [22] to define the following test statistic:

Definition 1 (SomAnomaly Statistic). *Consider a t-th test, shown in Eq. 6. Then, we define the **SomAnomaly statistic** for each $t = 1, 2, \ldots$, as follows:*

$$S_t = \frac{1}{B_N} \sum_{i=1}^{N} (D_{ti} - \tilde{\mu}_i) = \frac{N(\overline{D}_t - \tilde{\mu})}{B_N}, \qquad (7)$$

where $B_N^2 = \sum_{i=1}^{N} \sigma_i^2$.

To test each H_{0t}, we explore the null distribution of S_t. First, suppose that for each $t \in \mathbb{N}, i \in \{1, \ldots, N\}$,

$$E[D_{ti}] = \mu_i < \infty, \ Var[D_{ti}] = \sigma_i^2 < \infty. \qquad (8)$$

Let $Y_{ti} = D_{ti} - \mu_i$ and let $B_N^2 = \sum_{i=1}^{N} \sigma_i^2$. Now we assume the Lindeberg condition.

Assumption 1 (Lindeberg Condition). Consider Y_{ti}, $t = 1, \ldots$, $i = 1, \ldots, N$. For every $\epsilon > 0$,

$$\frac{1}{B_N^2} \sum_{i=1}^{N} E\left[Y_{ti}^2 I\left(|Y_{ti}| \geq \epsilon B_N\right)\right] \to 0 \quad \text{as} \quad N \to \infty.$$

According to the Lindeberg condition, the *SomAnomaly* statistic weakly converges to the standard normal distribution under the corresponding null hypothesis.

Furthermore, for *SomAnomaly*, we can compute the p-value P_t for each t-th test as follows:

$$P_t = Pr(Z \geq s_t), \quad Z \sim \mathcal{N}(0, 1), \qquad (9)$$

where s_t is the observed *SomAnomaly* statistic. We reject the test in Eq. 6 if P_t is smaller than the significance level α. However, note that we are conducting a sequence of tests; if we compare P_t with α for every t, the type I error or false discovery rate [4] may increase. Therefore, as shown in Fig. 2, we apply online multiple testing that can control these types of errors. To that end, we employ Generalized α-investing (GAI) [1], which controls the marginal false discovery rate (mFDR) under the significance level α [10]. Algorithm 2 presents the application of GAI to our problem. Also, further optimization can be achieved to remove empty grids that are not used in Definition 1.

Based on this, we propose Optimized SomAnomaly Statistic, defined as follows:

Algorithm 2: Generalized α-investing (GAI) using SomAnomaly

Data: Trained SOM on the normal tensor input data
Input: Window size, shift size, α, η, ρ

1 Initialize $W(0) = \alpha\eta$
2 **for** $t = 1, 2, \ldots$ **do**
3   Compute *SomAnomaly* and its p-value P_t for the streaming window
4

$$\phi_t = \frac{1}{10}W(t-1)$$

5   Set α_t such that

$$\frac{\phi_t}{\rho} = \frac{\phi_t}{\alpha_t} - 1$$

6   Test t-th hypothesis as follows:

$$R_t = \begin{cases} 1 & P_t \leq \alpha_t \\ 0 & \text{otherwise} \end{cases}$$

$$\psi_t = \min\left(\frac{\phi_t}{\rho} + \alpha, \frac{\phi_t}{\alpha_t} + \alpha - 1\right)$$

$$W(t+1) = W(t) - \phi_t + R_t\psi_t$$

7 **end**
  Output: Results of the tests $\{R_1, R_2, \ldots\}$

Definition 2 (Optimized SomAnomaly Statistic). *Let v be the index of mapped nodes and $B_v^2 = \sum_{i \in s} \sigma_i^2$. Then, the **Optimized SomAnomaly Statistic** is defined as:*

$$S_t^* = \frac{1}{B_v}\sum_{i \in v}(D_{it} - \tilde{\mu}_i), \ t = 1, 2, \ldots \tag{10}$$

Our experimental results show that S_t^* in Definition 2 can detect anomalies more effectively than S_t presented in Definition 1; hereafter, we refer to *SomAnomaly* as S_t^* presented in Definition 2.

5 Experiment

We use two benchmark CPS datasets, SWaT and HAI, as well as commonly used neural network models, such as Seq2Seq, MDN, and RNNs, to generate FE patterns, as base predictors. We use the same Seq2Seq, MDN, and RNN as proposed by Kim et al. [20] and Bishop [5]. For the SWaT dataset, we use the first 7 days worth of data, containing only normal instances, for training and the next 4 days worth of data, comprising 36 attacks, for testing. For the HAI dataset, we use the first 7 days worth of data for training and the next 7 days worth

Table 1. Description of the base forecasting error models (underlying neural network classifiers) and CPS datasets

Dataset/NN Classifier	Forecasting model and CPS dataset
SWaT/seq2seq	seq2seq for each station in SWaT [20]
SWaT/MDN	MDN for each station in SWaT
SWaT/RNN	RNN for 14 correlation groups in SWaT
HAI/RNN	RNN for 14 correlation groups in HAI

of data, comprising 38 attacks, for testing. We only train with the normal data for both SWaT and HAI, formulating a more challenging, yet realistic anomaly detection scenario, where anomalous events rarely occur. For comparison, we use four variants of the datasets and prediction model combinations, as shown in Table 1.

In addition, we use the time series-aware performance evaluation metric TaPR[2] [17] and TSAD[3] [30], since the conventional precision, recall, and F_1 metrics cannot effectively capture the detection performance on highly imbalanced data [17,30] such as in our case, where the datasets are mostly composed of normal data. Specifically, we set the detection scoring parameter, weight for the detection score, and the subsequent scoring parameter as 0.001, 0.8, and 60, respectively. A detection scoring parameter of 0.001 indicates that when the anomaly detection algorithm succeeds at detecting at least 0.001 of an attack range, it generates a score; a subsequent scoring parameter of 60 indicates that it would admit a minute-after-attack detection. We put more weight to the detection score than the range detection, such that 0.8(detection score) + 0.2(overlap score) [17]. For TSAD, we use the default settings suggested in the original GitHub repository by Intel. We consider the following three approaches based on seq2seq, MDN, and RNN: 1) static threshold, 2) CUSUM, and 3) SOMAD, of which the first and second are our baselines. As in the work by Kim et al. [20], we use the 4-norm, which yields the best performance for static thresholding and CUSUM. We conduct our experiments under the following settings: MacOS Catalina machine—2.3 GHz 8-core Intel Core[TM] i9-9880H processor, 32 GB 2667 MHz DDR4 onboard memory, Intel ® UHD Graphics 630 1536 MB, and AMD Radeon[TM] Pro 5500M 4 GB.

We also measure the average running time of SOMAD using Python. The whole process from training to detection takes less than 14 min in the worst case. SOMAD thus enables real-time detection of anomalies, making it more computationally efficient and practically applicable compared to deep learning-based approaches that take much longer to train.

---

[2] https://github.com/saurf4ng/TaPR.
[3] https://github.com/IntelLabs/TSAD-Evaluator.

6   Results

Table 2. Results using TaPR-based recall (Re), precision (Pr), and F_1 score.

Method	SWaT/seq2seq			SWaT/MDN			SWaT/RNN			HAI/RNN		
	Re	Pr	F_1	Re	Pr	F_1	Re	Pr	F_1	Re	Pr	F_1
Static	0.44	0.45	0.45	0.63	0.40	0.49	0.78	0.64	0.70	0.87	0.76	0.81
CUSUM	0.58	0.70	0.63	0.64	0.56	0.59	**0.79**	0.59	0.67	0.71	0.52	0.60
SOMAD	**0.65**	**0.94**	**0.77**	**0.94**	**0.81**	**0.87**	0.76	**0.93**	**0.84**	**0.88**	**0.79**	**0.83**

Table 3. Results using TSAD-based recall (Re), precision (Pr), and F_1 score.

Method	SWaT/seq2seq			SWaT/MDN			SWaT/RNN			HAI/RNN		
	Re	Pr	F_1	Re	Pr	F_1	Re	Pr	F_1	Re	Pr	F_1
Static	0.25	0.41	0.31	0.34	0.35	0.35	0.33	**0.55**	0.42	0.20	0.71	0.31
CUSUM	0.30	**0.62**	0.40	0.38	0.39	0.38	0.37	0.45	0.41	0.36	0.44	0.39
SOMAD	**0.61**	0.60	**0.61**	**0.92**	**0.58**	**0.71**	**0.59**	0.54	**0.57**	**0.65**	**0.79**	**0.71**

Overall Performance. We present our results for TaPR [17] and TSAD [30] in Table 2 and Table 3, respectively, for each combination of datasets. We also visualize the detection results of each method for SWaT/RNN and HAI/RNN in Fig. 3, where the X and Y-axes represent time and anomaly score, respectively. As shown in Table 2, SOMAD outperforms the baseline methods in terms of the time series-aware F_1 score in all cases, achieving 0.77, 0.87, 0.84, and 0.83 for the datasets SWaT/seq2seq, SWaT/MDN, SWaT/RNN, and HAI/RNN, respectively. Although the overall precision, recall, and F_1 score using TSAD are generally lower than those using TaPR, SOMAD still outperforms all baseline approaches in terms of the TSAD F_1 score. Similar to the results for TaPR shown in Table 2, SOMAD consistently achieves high recall compared to baseline methods. Therefore, even though the absolute performance for TSAD is lower for each dataset combination, the relative performance remains more or less the same, demonstrating the effectiveness of SOMAD.

Comparison with Baseline Approaches. On the other hand, the baseline methods, static thresholding and CUSUM, achieve mediocre performance. Although static thresholding achieves a reasonable performance for RNN-based datasets (F_1 scores of 0.70 for SWaT/RNN and 0.81 for HAI/RNN), it does not perform well on the other datasets (F_1 scores of 0.45 for SWaT/Seq2Seq and 0.49 for SWaT/MDN). For CUSUM, it performs better for Seq2Seq and MDN-based datasets, but worse for RNN-based datasets. As illustrated in Fig. 3, the values used to distinguish normal data from anomalies are higher for static thresholding and CUSUM than for SOMAD. Moreover, both baseline methods produce high false positives; using TSAD, they achieve recall below 40% in all cases. In

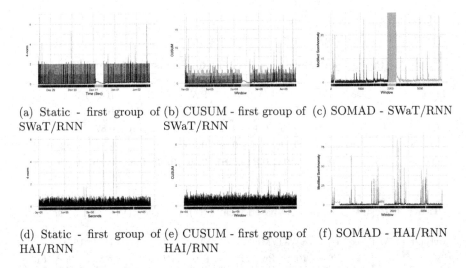

(a) Static - first group of (b) CUSUM - first group of (c) SOMAD - SWaT/RNN
SWaT/RNN   SWaT/RNN

(d) Static - first group of (e) CUSUM - first group of (f) SOMAD - HAI/RNN
HAI/RNN   HAI/RNN

Fig. 3. Plots of anomaly detection results for SWaT/RNN and HAI/RNN. We plot
the results of data corresponding to the first stations of SWaT and HAI for static
thresholding and CUSUM, and those of data corresponding to all stations for SOMAD.
The predicted anomalies are colored in red, the predicted normal instances are colored
in black, and the strip along the X-axis is the ground truth.

contrast, SOMAD achieves both high recall and precision in all cases, outperforming the baseline methods in terms of time series-aware recall except for one
case and TSAD precision in two cases; this indicates that our proposed method
can accurately detect a larger amount of anomalies.

Discussion. The performance difference between baseline approaches and
SOMAD is mainly attributed to whether the method is capable of detecting
clustered anomalies. Given that both SWaT and HAI datasets contain multiple
clusters of consecutive anomaly samples over time, SOMAD successfully detects
most of them unlike the baseline methods, as shown in Fig. 3. A time series
prediction method based on SOM, which is characterized by its locality [3],
exerts a clustering effect, leading to reduced false alarm rates and consequently
to enhanced detection power compared to the baseline approaches for SWaT
and HAI. As shown in the highlighted region in Fig. 3, SOM's locality property
is readily reflected in our anomaly detection task as well. On the other hand,
SOMAD incorrectly classifies normal samples as anomalies, hence the false positives, especially for samples corresponding to timestamps far apart from those
of training data. This performance loss is mainly due to the long-term dependency issue persisting in popular deep learning-based forecasting models. Since
they are used to generate our input data, i.e., the forecasting errors, SOMAD
naturally suffers from worse-quality data originating from inaccurate forecasting
when detecting anomalies.

7 Conclusion

Our proposed anomaly detection framework SOMAD inflates the differences between the respective FE patterns of normal and abnormal events. As demonstrated through numerous experiments under a realistic scenario where anomalies are only present in the test data, SOMAD outperforms conventional methods, achieving a high detection rate without compromising precision. While most of the prior work focused on improving the base forecasting model itself, our proposed approach shows great promise in detecting anomalies even with FE values that are either very small or similar to those of normal instances.

Acknowledgments. The work was supported by the affiliated institute of ETRI [2019-065]. Also, this work was partly supported by Institute of Information & communications Technology Planning & Evaluation (IITP) grant funded by Korea government Ministry of Science, ICT (MSIT) (No. 2019-0-01343, Regional strategic industry convergence security core talent training business) and the Basic Science Research Program through National Research Foundation of Korea grant funded by Korea government MSIT (No. 2020R1C1C1006004). Additionally this research was partly supported by IITP grant funded by the Korea government MSIT (No. 2021-0-00017, Original Technology Development of Artificial Intelligence Industry) and was partly supported by the Korea government MSIT, under the High-Potential Individuals Global Training Program) (2019-0-01579) supervised by the IITP. Finally, this work was partly supported by Institute of Information & communications Technology Planning & Evaluation(IITP) grant funded by the Korea government (MSIT) (No. 2019-0-00421, AI Graduate School Support Program (Sungkyunkwan University)).

References

1. Aharoni, E., Rosset, S.: Generalized α-investing: definitions, optimality results and application to public databases. J. Roy. Stat. Soci.: Ser. B (Stat. Methodol.) **76**(4), 771–794 (2014). https://doi.org/10.1111/rssb.12048, https://rss.onlinelibrary.wiley.com/doi/abs/10.1111/rssb.12048

2. Aoudi, W., Iturbe, M., Almgren, M.: Truth will out: departure-based process-level detection of stealthy attacks on control systems. In: Proceedings of the 2018 ACM SIGSAC Conference on Computer and Communications Security, pp. 817–831 (2018)

3. Barreto, G.A.: Time series prediction with the self-organizing map: a review. In: Hammer, B., Hitzler, P. (eds.) Perspectives of Neural-symbolic Integration. Studies in Computational Intelligence, vol. 77, pp. 135–158. Springer, Berlin (2007). https://doi.org/10.1007/978-3-540-73954-8_6

4. Benjamini, Y., Hochberg, Y.: Controlling the false discovery rate: a practical and powerful approach to multiple testing. J. Roy. Stat. Soc.: Ser. B (Methodol.) **57**(1), 289–300 (1995)

5. Bishop, C.M.: Mixture density networks (1994). http://publications.aston.ac.uk/id/eprint/373/

6. Campello, R.J., Moulavi, D., Zimek, A., Sander, J.: Hierarchical density estimates for data clustering, visualization, and outlier detection. ACM Trans. Knowl. Discov. Data (TKDD) **10**(1), 5 (2015)

7. Ferguson, T.S.: A Course in Large Sample Theory. Kogan Page Publishers, London (1996)
8. Filonov, P., Kitashov, F., Lavrentyev, A.: RNN-based early cyber-attack detection for the tennessee eastman process. CoRR, September 2017
9. Filonov, P., Lavrentyev, A., Vorontsov, A.: Multivariate industrial time series with cyber-attack simulation: fault detection using an LSTM-based predictive data model. arXiv abs/1612.06676 (2016)
10. Foster, D.P., Stine, R.A.: α-investing: a procedure for sequential control of expected false discoveries. J. Roy. Stat. Soc. Ser. B-Stat. Methodol. **70**(2), 429–444 (2008)
11. Fuertes, S., Picart, G., Tourneret, J.Y., Chaari, L., Ferrari, A., Richard, C.: Improving spacecraft health monitoring with automatic anomaly detection techniques. In: 14th International Conference on Space Operations, p. 2430 (2016)
12. Giraldo, J., et al.: A survey of physics-based attack detection in cyber-physical systems. ACM Comput. Surv. (CSUR) **51**(4), 76 (2018)
13. Goh, J., Adepu, S., Junejo, K.N., Mathur, A.: A dataset to support research in the design of secure water treatment systems. In: Havarneanu, G., Setola, R., Nassopoulos, H., Wolthusen, S. (eds.) CRITIS 2016. LNCS, vol. 10242, pp. 88–99. Springer, Cham (2017). https://doi.org/10.1007/978-3-319-71368-7_8
14. Goh, J., Adepu, S., Tan, M., Lee, Z.S.: Anomaly detection in cyber physical systems using recurrent neural networks. In: 2017 IEEE 18th International Symposium on High Assurance Systems Engineering (HASE), pp. 140–145. IEEE (2017)
15. Hautamaki, V., Karkkainen, I., Franti, P.: Outlier detection using k-nearest neighbour graph. In: Proceedings of the 17th International Conference on Pattern Recognition, 2004. ICPR 2004, vol. 3, pp. 430–433. IEEE (2004)
16. He, Z., Xu, X., Deng, S.: Discovering cluster-based local outliers. Pattern Recogn. Lett. **24**(9–10), 1641–1650 (2003)
17. Hwang, W.S., Yun, J.H., Kim, J., Kim, H.C.: Time-series aware precision and recall for anomaly detection: considering variety of detection result and addressing ambiguous labeling. In: Proceedings of the 28th ACM International Conference on Information and Knowledge Management, pp. 2241–2244. ACM (2019)
18. Idé, T., Papadimitriou, S., Vlachos, M.: Computing correlation anomaly scores using stochastic nearest neighbors. In: Seventh IEEE International Conference on Data Mining (ICDM 2007), pp. 523–528. IEEE (2007)
19. Khaitan, S.K., McCalley, J.D.: Design techniques and applications of cyberphysical systems: a survey. IEEE Syst. J. **9**(2), 350–365 (2014)
20. Kim, J., Yun, J.-H., Kim, H.C.: Anomaly detection for industrial control systems using sequence-to-sequence neural networks. In: Katsikas, S., et al. (eds.) Cyber-ICPS/SECPRE/SPOSE/ADIoT -2019. LNCS, vol. 11980, pp. 3–18. Springer, Cham (2020). https://doi.org/10.1007/978-3-030-42048-2_1
21. Kohonen, T.: Self-organized formation of topologically correct feature maps. Biol. Cybern. **43**(1), 59–69 (1982). https://doi.org/10.1007/BF00337288
22. Lindeberg, J.W.: Eine neue herleitung des exponentialgesetzes in der wahrscheinlichkeitsrechnung. Math. Z. **15**(1), 211–225 (1922)
23. Lunt, T.F., et al.: Ides: the enhanced prototype-a real-time intrusion-detection expert system. In: SRI International, 333 Ravenswood Avenue, Menlo Park. Citeseer (1988)
24. Lunt, T.F., Tamaru, A., Gillham, F.: A real-time intrusion-detection expert system (IDES). SRI International. Computer Science Laboratory (1992)
25. Malhotra, P., Ramakrishnan, A., Anand, G., Vig, L., Agarwal, P., Shroff, G.: LSTM-based encoder-decoder for multi-sensor anomaly detection. arXiv preprint arXiv:1607.00148 (2016)

26. Rolincik, M., Lauriente, M., Koons, H.C., Gorney, D.: An expert system for diagnosing environmentally induced spacecraft anomalies. In: Proceedings of 5th Annual Space Operations and Applications Research Symposium, pp. 36–44 (1992)

27. Rumelhart, D.E., Hinton, G.E., Williams, R.J.: Learning representations by back-propagating errors. Nature **323**(6088), 533–536 (1986)

28. Sebring, M.M.: Expert systems in intrusion detection: a case study. In: Proceedings of the 11th National Computer Security Conference, Baltimore, Maryland, October 1988, pp. 74–81 (1988)

29. Shin, H.K., Lee, W., Yun, J.H., Kim, H.: HAI 1.0: Hil-based augmented ICS security dataset. In: 13th USENIX Workshop on Cyber Security Experimentation and Test (CSET 20). USENIX Association, August 2020. https://www.usenix.org/conference/cset20/presentation/shin

30. Tatbul, N., Lee, T.J., Zdonik, S., Alam, M., Gottschlich, J.: Precision and recall for time series. In: Proceedings of the 32nd International Conference on Neural Information Processing Systems. NIPS 2018, pp. 1924–1934. Curran Associates Inc., USA (2018). http://dl.acm.org/citation.cfm?id=3326943.3327120

31. Zhai, S., Cheng, Y., Lu, W., Zhang, Z.: Deep structured energy based models for anomaly detection. arXiv preprint arXiv:1605.07717 (2016)

32. Zhang, C., et al.: A deep neural network for unsupervised anomaly detection and diagnosis in multivariate time series data. arXiv preprint arXiv:1811.08055 (2018)

Security Management

What Is Lurking in Your Backups?

Ben Lenard[1]($\boxtimes$), Alexander Rasin[1], Nick Scope[1], and James Wagner[2]

[1] DePaul University, Chicago, IL 60604, USA
blenard@anl.gov
[2] The University of New Orleans, New Orleans, LA 70148, USA

Abstract. Best practices in data management and privacy mandate that old data must be irreversibly destroyed. However, due to performance optimization reasons, old (deleted or updated) data is not immediately purged from active database storage. Database backups that typically work by backing up table and index pages (rather than logical rows) greatly exacerbate the privacy problem of the old surviving data. Copying such deleted data into backups ensures that unknown quantities of old data can be stored indefinitely.

In this paper, we quantify the amount of deleted data retained in backups by four major representative databases, comparing the default behavior versus an explicit defrag operation. We review the defrag options available in these databases and discuss the impact they have on eliminating old data from backups. We demonstrate that each database has a defrag mechanism that can eliminate most of old deleted data (although in Oracle pre-update content may survive defrag). Finally, we outline the factors that organizations should consider when deciding whether to apply defrag prior to executing their backups.

Keywords: Databases · Privacy · Data retention · Backups · Compliance

1 Introduction

Previous research has shown that database management systems (DBMS) retain copies of deleted data within internal storage [16,28]. These unallocated records and values are kept in database pages until they are overwritten by new data or by defragmenting the data structure (e.g., rebuilding the table). The extent of data that remains accessible can only be quantified using forensic tools [29] that reconstruct database contents from a full storage snapshot (including unallocated disk space or OS paging files). This deleted-but-accessible data is a potential liability that violates the best practices for data privacy. For example, government agencies, such as United States Department of Defense (DoD), publish general requirements and guidelines for best practices for storing and destroying data [9]. Other groups, such as the International Data Sanitization Consortium release guidelines for destroying data that is no longer needed to preserve privacy [15]. Moreover, some recent legislation (see Sect. 2) aims to grant more control to data

© IFIP International Federation for Information Processing 2021
Published by Springer Nature Switzerland AG 2021
A. Jøsang et al. (Eds.): SEC 2021, IFIP AICT 625, pp. 401–415, 2021.
https://doi.org/10.1007/978-3-030-78120-0_26

owners. Although logically (but not physically) deleted data presents a privacy risk, it can be measured [28] and gradually rectifies itself as old data is naturally overwritten; this process can be manually expedited by additional database activity or defragmenting storage.

Interestingly, creation of backups greatly exacerbates this problem of unaccounted deleted data in storage. Both of these activities are normal – backups are required for disaster recovery and old data remains in storage because of how DBMSes manage and optimize their internal storage. However, the the interaction between these two processes creates a new and unique problem. The backup of deleted data may make it impossible for data stewards to meet the guidelines for data privacy. As we discuss in Sect. 2, the majority of backups rely on block backup operations. That is, the pages (rather than individual records) from tables and indexes in storage are copied into the backup. As a result, some of the deleted (but accessible) data is permanently preserved in the backup. This causes two major issues: 1) such data can never be destroyed while the backup still exists (deleted data is never going to be overwritten or defragmented in a backup) and 2) it becomes significantly more difficult to identify what deleted data remains accessible in the multitude of backups (as backups should be done regularly and are retained for a long time). Our contributions are:

- We evaluate and quantify deleted data retained in backups in four chosen representative DBMSes: Oracle 19c, Db2 11.5.4 (LUW), PostgreSQL 12, and MariaDB 5.5.
- For each DBMS, we evaluate methods to minimize the amount of deleted data introduced into backups. These methods use well-documented, existing commands, which are traditionally used for routine maintenance operations.
- We outline what factors organizations should consider when determining if and what defrag operations should be applied before backups.

2   Background and Related Work

Backups: DBMS backups are an integral part of business continuity practices to support disaster recovery. There are many mechanisms for backing up a database [12] both at the file system level and internal to the DBMS. File system backups range from a full backup with an offline, or quiesced, database to a partial backup at file system level that incrementally backs up changed files. Most DBMS platforms provide backup utilities for both full and partial backups.

Even for a relatively simple task of coping database files at the file system level, there are various methods ranging from a simple copy command with an offline database to a more complex copy of the storage system in an active database [23]. Moreover, one can replicate database changes from one database to another to provide a live back up or replica by using tools such as Oracle Data Guard [22], in addition to taking traditional backups of the database.

The type of backup depends on two application metrics: Recovery Point Objective (RPO) and Recovery Time Objective (RTO); as your RPO and RTO shorten, the complex solutions such as Oracle Data Guard [22] emerge. RTO is defined as the time it takes to recover the database after a crash and RPO is defined as how close to the crash or error can you restore the database. A backup solution could range from a simple DBMS backup utility to snapshotting a filesystem once the database is quiesced, to replicating the database and then backing up the database, or other options [22]. The criticality of the application and data as well as RTO and RPO determines the backup solution and its complexity; in other words, how much would downtime or the financial and reputation loss of data could cost your organization. In addition to data, one might also backup transaction logs, archievelogs (Oracle), logarchive (Db2), binary log (MySQL), or write ahead log (WAL in Postgres), file backups, to replay transactions to meet the RPO goal of the application. For example, one would restore last backup before the failure and then replay the transaction logs to meet the RPO set by the organization's needs. For the purposes of this paper we focus on the backups provided by the relational DBMSes since backups are used most often and replication mechanisms do not protect against logical corruption (unless caught before the log file is applied).

For the commercial products we tested, Oracle provides RMAN, Recovery Manager, and IBM Db2 provides its own backup utility. Oracle RMAN and Db2 backup utilities provide for an online backup of the database that incorporates activity that took place during the backup. These utilities provide block-level backups with either a full backup of the database or a partial backup with database pages that changed since the last backup. For the purposes of this paper, partial backups can be *incremental* or *delta*. For example, if we took a full backup on Sunday and daily partial backups and needed to recover on Thursday, database utilities would restore the full backup from Sunday and then either 1) apply delta backups from Monday, Tuesday, and Wednesday or 2) apply Wednesday's incremental backup.

PostgreSQL's Pg_dump utility [25] generates a consistent backup of the database at the time of the invocation in a file containing SQL statements (a logical representation of the database state). PostgreSQL also offers `pg_basedump` which is a binary of the database to which the WAL files can be applied; in other words, you can backup the WAL files and replay during a restore operation. The version of MariaDB located in the CentOS 7 repository provides the mysqldump utility which is also a logical dump of the database.

Filesystem level snapshots as a method of backup are created by quiescing the database and then invoking a snapshot command ether on the storage system, such as Dell EMC [23] or Netapp [20], or on the filesystem itself such as ZFS [24]. Such approach requires significantly more storage space, but can be used when running the database backup would be disruptive to the application.

Database Storage: A database stores data in pages that contain the object data as well as meta data about the row itself [28]. When a database deletes a record, the record is logically deleted in the page similar to a file delete in a filesystem [27]. This is done for performance optimization reasons. Since typical backup utilities use block backup, rather then a logical representation like `pg_dump` or `mysqldump`, these deleted records also propagate to backup files. Block backup is normally used because it is impractical to convert a large database into a logical dump. We know that a small amount of the database changes in enterprise applications, between 5% and 18% [14], therefore a logical dump of a database is inefficient.

Perhaps surprising to some, tape backups are still widely used in the industry, including by cloud providers. For example, in 2011 when a Google Gmail upgrade failed, affecting 150,000 accounts, Google used off-site tapes to restore impacted accounts [17]. Another paper illustrated the regular use of tape backups in 2017 with offsite providers [19] for medical systems. While tapes are a cost-efficient medium for backups, they make it nearly impossible to identify or purge deleted data that was accidentally backed up with active database content.

Retention Policies: Data management requirements define how long data should be stored or when the data must be destroyed. These retention policies can come from various sources such as government legislation, internally from an organization, or the result of various lawsuits. For example, recently passed in the European Union, the General Data Protection Regulation [5] greatly expanded consumer power over personal data. On 25 May 2018 (the same day GDPR took effect), Google was accused of not complying with GDPR [13], which eventually led to a fine of €50 million. In 2019, Deutsche Wohnen was accused of using systems which were unable to delete data resulting in €14.5 million fine [11]. Thus, companies not complying with data retention requirements could be subject to large financial penalties.

SSBM and Database Workload: Database community used TPC-H [10] and SSBM [10] for a wide variety of research projects and experiments. SSBM [21] is a star schema benchmark that has simplified the TPC-H schema to represent a typical simple data warehouse. Hsu et al. [14] enumerated typical distributions within real-world workloads of a transaction processing database. Depending on the industry, Hsu et al. observed anywhere from 96% reads to 80% reads in different workloads; we rely on their estimates to create our own workload using SSBM. Exact balance of a workload depends on many factors and varies by industry, but our goal is to approximate a generic realistic workload (rather than to model a particular industry or scenario).

SysGen: Our experiments leverage publicly available SysGen [18] developed by Lenard et al. and an SSBM-based workload generator included with SysGen. The workload generator is a Python script configured with the number of iterations, or runs that consists of a sequence of select, insert, update, and delete statements. SSBM is limited to SELECT statements so the SysGen workload generator created inserts, updates, and deletes according to average workload balance (derived from [14]). Insert generating function increments last primary key of the customer table by one, and generates a random date inline with the other fields. For the updates, we update the customer table, with a random selection of 5 different update templates. For deletes, we delete a random customer ID and their purchases from lineorder table.

SysGen [18] includes a set of scripts that 1) create virtual machines, 2) configure their OSes according to our settings, 3) deploy a DBMS with our configuration, 4) execute given workloads in the DBMS, 5) capture storage snapshots (disk and RAM). For this paper, we extracted the backups from disk, whether a filesystem snapshot or the output from a utility, for each evaluated DBMS.

Terminology: We use several Oracle-specific terms in Sect. 4, which we define here. Oracle assigns an address to each row which is exposed through the pseudo-column ROWID to the SELECT clause [6]. ROWID is tied to the physical location of the row in the Oracle files and will change when the row moves. High Water Mark (HWM) is a reference that indicates the boundary of the table in the file (i.e., the largest range of space that the table occupied at any point of time). For example, if you had a table with a 1,000,000 rows, deleted all of the rows and then inserted 100,000 rows, HWM would mark the location where $1,000,000^{th}$ row was originally stored. HWM is is used by Oracle to decide how far down the tablespace to scan for table data blocks [26].

3 Design and Setup

3.1 Hypervisor Setup

For our experiments we used a server with dual Xeon E5645 processors, 64 GB of RAM, and an SSD for storage. We used CentOS 7 x86_64 as base operating system of the hypervisor on a VMWare Workstation Pro 16 (referred to as "host" in this paper). The host also has an NFS share exported which is discussed in this section. We provided ample RAM storage to avoid swapping on the host.

3.2 Virtual Machine Setup

Each database VM server consists of 8 GB of RAM, 4 vCPUs, 1 × vNIC and a 25 GB VMDK file. The VMDK file was partitioned into: 350 MB /boot, 2 GB swap, and the remaining storage was used for the/partition; this was done with standard partitioning and EXT4 as the filesystem. Individual VM servers used CentOS 7 as well; we refer to these as the database server in this paper. The database server OSes were configured identically except for dependent packages for the tested DBMS. The only exception to this rule is the Oracle VM where we allocated 35 GB to the VMDK file since Oracle's install is roughly 6 GB by itself; Oracle also requires custom kernel configuration settings which are done by their RPM on install. All VM's have an NFS mount point exported from the host machine so that we can examine the backup contents external to the VM. For Oracle and Db2, we let the DBMS automatically manage memory allocation for the instances. For Postgres and MariaDB, this option was not available so we allocated 80% of the VM's RAM to the database instance. MariaDB used the InnoDB storage engine for storing the data; other DBMSes do not provide multiple storage engine options. In all DBMSes, We enabled archievelogging (Oracle), logarchive(Db2), the binarylog (MariaDB), and WAL (Postgres).

In addition to the database server VMs, we run a client VM which executes the workload against the database server remotely; the client has 2 vCPU's, 2 GB of RAM, 1 × vNIC, CentOS 7 x86_64 and a similar partitioning scheme to the database server VMs. Each client VM has the RDBMS' client software installed as SQL Scripts, DDL, and raw table data. We separated the client from the database server to represent an N-Tiered or client server architecture. Lastly, on the servers and the clients, we installed the SysGen scripts so that automated execution of the backup tests can be achieved. This consisted of RPMs which contain helper scripts, SSH keys and the disabling of Firewalld and SeLinux.

3.3   Dataset and Workload

To simulate a realistic database, we used the SSBM schema with two minor modifications. We loaded data into the five tables at SSBM Scale 4 which yields 120,000 customer (one of the 5 tables) records. For the purposes of this experiment, we added a second index on the Customer name which we used to track records in storage. Where possible, we separated the table data from the index data in storage to simplify storage analysis; that was feasible in every database except MariaDB because it uses index organized tables (IOT).

SysGen allows executing a series of workload passes. A pass is a workload batch that we execute before executing backup actions and taking a storage snapshot of the database VM. We executed the following number of SQL Statements per pass: 0 selects, 266 inserts, 266 updates, and 532 deletes. Since SELECT statements do not affect what we are measuring, we focused on inserts, updates, and deletes. There are 532 deletes since we executed 266 deletes against the Customer table. Lineorder table is linked to the Customer table by a foreign key (lo_custkey). There is only one unique customer in the Customer table, but more than one Lineorder record can be deleted for a given customer. While the percentage of change to the Customer table is low, 0.22%, per iteration, or 1.10% at the end of the passes, one could argue that Customers in an enterprise do not often get deleted. Furthermore, we are not defining an iteration as a unit of time but rather as a unit of work since we have seen in [14] that workloads vary by industry; the extension of that would vary by application type.

4   Experiments

4.1   Execution

We used SysGen to create and load the dataset into each database server VM. On completion of the initial load step, SysGen suspends the VM using vmware commands and copies the VM contents to another location on disk. We used VM snapshot to execute consistent experiments starting from the same initial OS and DBMS state for different backup types.

Post load, the SysGen runtests-DBTYPE-run.sh executed multiple workload passes against each database platform and created backups as configured. After the initial load we executed five workload passes against a given database platform, and it is the same workload executed across different platforms. At the end of the pass, we perform the database backup and then we snapshot the VM, via pausing the VM and then using Linux `cp` to copy off all of the VM files on the hypervisor's filesystem. We measured at least two runs per database. The first run serves as a comparison baseline. The second run is where we try to remove deleted data by defragmenting the table within the RDBMS platform; we execute a defrag at the end of each pass prior to the backup.

For each run, the group of 5 iterations, baseline, defrag, and the different backup types, we always capture the backups at the end of each pass as well as the VM's contents after we suspend the VM, and copy them for future analysis.

4.2   Backup Types Tested

Oracle and Db2 supply backup utilities for binary backups of the database – these backups could be full or partial. For the full backup, everything contained in the backup is required to restore the database to the time of the backup. Db2 and Oracle also provide a method to create a partial backup; partial backups contain only the changed pages of the database. Furthermore, these partial backups can be broken down further into cumulative and delta backups as discussed in Sect. 2. One would chose a delta or incremental backup based on how much storage they want to allocate for backups as well as their RTO.

Open-source versions of Postgres and MariaDB do not provide binary backup tools, and their dump commands is akin to running a SELECT statement which would not provide any useful information; therefore we used filesystem snapshots as the backup method. While we shutdown MariaDB and Postgres to perform a consistent backup of the filesystem, one might do this on a live database, assuming the storage system provided snapshot capabilities. MariaDB and Postres, like Db2 and Oracle, support commands that force a live database into a consistent state for the purposes of a backup. For example, Postgres has `pg_start_backup()` and `pg_stop_backup()` which instruct the database to become consistent so that a live database's files can be copied. We use the Postgres start backup command, then use the storage system to take a snapshot, and then let Postgres resume operations. Oracle and Db2 also support the functionality to take a storage system snapshot. While the speed of the snapshot is subject to a multitude of factors, it is usually a relatively quick operation; run time depends on the amount of data that has changed. While copying files is not exactly the same as cloning a filesystem in storage, it does provide a similar result. MariaDB has `FLUSH TABLES tbl_list WITH READ LOCK` for similar functionality.

One might ask why we did not take storage snapshots in Oracle and Db2; their utilities were used since they provide additional functionality such as checking the database for corrupted pages and verifying the backup files. If an organization is going to rely on these commercial vendors, they are going to rely on the toolkits provided by the vendor to ensure their data can be restored.

The target of all backup commands was an NFS share exported from the hypervisor to avoid contamination of the DB Server VM as well as ease of analysis.

4.3 Removing Deleted Data

One of the primary purposes of a defragment operation is to reduce the size of the object and to purge unused data. While SQL-92 is standardized across different platforms, the concept of defragment is not universal. In this section we discuss the different approaches used in the RDBMS platforms in this paper.

- **MariaDB** implements `OPTIMIZE TABLE` which creates a new copy of the table for InnoDB tables.
- **PostgreSQL** has the `VACUUM` utility that will reorganize the table by discarding obsolete data in-place [8].
- **Db2** provides a plethora of options for it's defrag command [3]; for the purposes of consistency, in this paper we used Db2 Classic Reorg which recreates the table as well as rebuilds the indexes associated with the table.
- **Oracle** does not provide a direct defrag command as other databases; the closest command to defrag is `ALTER TABLE MOVE` which moves the table between tablespaces. This operation is similar to recreating the table but one would still need to rebuild the index. Oracle also allows enabling row movement on a table which supports the functionality to shrink a table (compacting individual pages). We explored both options in this paper since they are among the recommended options to execute a defrag in Oracle [4].

4.4 Oracle Defragmentation

Since the other RDBMS platforms had simple and unambiguous built-in defrag available through the command line interface, we do not discuss the nuances of these commands. However, we describe three different defrag methods used for Oracle in our experiments. All of our defrag methods start from `ALTER TABLE customer ENABLE ROW MOVEMENT` which allows rows to move in storage when an explicit move or a shrink command is executed. Updated rows will be a deleted and re-inserted [2]. Moving the row also changes its `ROWID`.

- **Defragmentation Method 1** – Using the command `ALTER TABLE customer SHRINK SPACE CASCADE` directs Oracle to rearrange the rows as well as the tables referenced by the foreign keys of customer table and moves the high water mark (see Sect. 2) [7]. Following that, we rebuild all the indexes of the tables that were moved using the `ALTER INDEX [index name] REBUILD`.
- **Defragmentation Method 2** – We execute `ALTER TABLE customer MOVE` which causes a table rebuild by moving customer table from one tablespace to a different tablespace. We used the move command as one of the recommended methods to rebuild the table [1]; we have to also rebuild the indexes since they become invalid when the table moves. We use `ALTER TABLE customer SHRINK SPACE CASCADE` and `ALTER INDEX [index name] REBUILD` (as in the previous approach) to rebuild referenced tables and indexes.
- **Defragmentation Method 3** – We execute `ALTER TABLE customer MOVE` to rebuild the table as in defrag method 2. We defragment the table using `ALTER TABLE customer SHRINK SPACE COMPACT`; unlike defrag method 1,

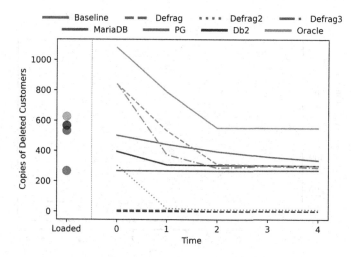

Fig. 1. Delete counts in full backups

this command does not move the high water mark [7]. Finally, we use
`ALTER TABLE customer SHRINK SPACE CASCADE` and `ALTER INDEX [index name]`
`REBUILD` (as in previous approaches) to rebuild referenced tables and indexes.

5   Results

5.1   Deleted Data in Backups

For every DBMS using a full backup, some deleted data was found in each backup
in our experiments. Recall that we are only tracking the 266 original customer
records deleted at $Time_0$ – deletes at each workload iteration will introduce *new*
deleted rows that will be backed up as well. As can be seen in Fig. 1, all of the
DBMSes retained over 200 of the $Time_0$ deleted records when no defragment was
executed. Defragment operation significantly or completely reduced the amount
of deleted data in backups. In MariaDB, PostgreSQL, and Db2, defragmenting
eliminated deleted customer records from full database backups. In Oracle, none
of the three defrag methods we consider were able to completely get rid of
deleted customers backups. Method 2 seemed the most effective for removing
deleted data from backups.

Figure 2 summarizes the delta backup results in Oracle and Db2. Recall that
our versions of MariaDB and PostgreSQL do not support incremental backups.
Since defrag Method 3 in Oracle did not offer a significant advantage of Method 1,
our subsequent experiments consider only Methods 1 and 2. Db2 retains approximately half of the T_0 deleted customers without an explicit defragment command, and none of the deleted customer when using defragmentation. In Oracle,
defrag Method 1 eliminates most of the T_0 deleted customers; Method 2 does
much more poorly, retaining more than half of T_0 deleted customer records even

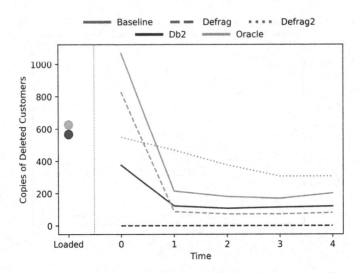

Fig. 2. Delete counts in delta backups

after 5 workloads. Since this is a delta backup, one should remember all prior backups are needed to restore the database from the last full backup. Therefore, the total number of available deleted customer records is the sum of deleted records from Figs. 1 and 2.

To fully remove each batch of deleted records, all delta backups as well as all full backup must be properly defragged. Figure 3 shows the T_0 deleted customer records for incremental backups. Db2 exhibits the same pattern, backing up over half of the deleted records without defrag and none of the deleted records with backup. Oracle preserves a significant amount of T_0 deleted records, even past all 5 workloads, with some reduction caused by defrag Method 1. Defrag Method 2 eliminates the deleted customers from T_0 by the second query workload. The large amount of records in Oracle are partially explained by UNDO table space included in Oracle backup together with table data.

Similar to the delta backup method, the database requires a full backup (with the deleted records) to be restored to disk before restoring the most recent incremental backup. Unlike with delta backups, incremental backups only require the most recent backup and the full backup to be defragmented.

In order to purge deleted data, it is necessary to defrag both the full backups and any partial backups that follow (defragmenting partial backups alone cannot guarantee data destruction). While such defragmenting may be costly in terms of I/O and CPU time, it is a balancing act of the organization based on their compliance requirements. In order to make cleaning of backups more practical, organizations could choose to defrag only the tables with sensitive data before backup. In choosing the appropriate defrag level, organizations must consider their retention requirements, computational power budget, as well as database availability (to not disrupt their required system availability).

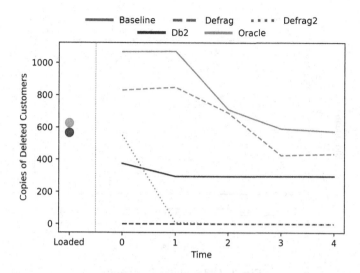

Fig. 3. Delete counts in incremental backups

5.2   Remaining Updated Data

When updating a record, a DBMS will often perform the operation by deleting the current record and inserting the new updated row. This is always true when the new record is larger than the old record, and sometimes true when the new record is equal or smaller in size (depending on the DBMS). In this experiment, we measure the presence of old (deleted by an update) records in database backups. Similar to our deleted record experiments, we counted the number of deleted-by-update records immediately after we loaded the database (at which point there are zero deleted records) and then again after each workload iteration.

At the load time our backup contains 266 customer records that we update in our workload during $Time_0$. After each iteration, we track the number of deleted (i.e., pre-update) customer records remaining in a backup. We only update our 266 records of interest at $Time_0$, but we insert, delete, and update other records to simulate normal database activity for subsequent workload iterations.

Figure 4 shows the counts of original pre-update 266 customer records that can be accessed in a full backup after each workload iteration. Without defrag, MariaDB contains between 1 and 4 old customer records (we believe that MariaDB backup does not generally include old customer records due to its default use of Index Organized Tables). Db2 backups include approximately 30 of the old T_0 customer records, while PostgreSQL contains a decreasing number of old records, ranging from 231 to 93 customers at $Time_4$. Oracle backup contains 223 old customer records; interestingly, these are not deleted records in table storage, but entries in UNDO tablespace that Oracle backs up with the data.

We also measured the updated records after defragmenting the table prior to backup. Figure 4 shows a noticeable drop in the number of old customers present in the backups. MariaDB contains 9 old customers in the defragmented

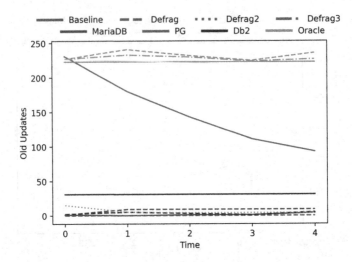

Fig. 4. Old updates in backups

backup, PostgreSQL contains no old customers in the backup, Db2 backups include anywhere between 1 to 5 from the original pre-update customers. Finally, Oracle shows the same behavior (approximately 230 old customers due to the inclusion of the UNDO tablespace in the backup) for defrag Methods 1 and 3. However, defrag Method 2 backup includes 4 to 5 customers (with the exception of $Time_0$, where 15 old customer records are backed up).

Index Organized Tables (IOT) in MariaDB naturally reduce the number of pre-update records stored in database backup (because records with same primary key are stored in the same location in IOT). Although Oracle supports IOTs, it would not benefit from IOT tables in the same way, because old records are copied with UNDO tablespace into the backup. PostgreSQL defrag (VACUUM) fully reclaims the space occupied by old records in our update experiments.

6   Conclusion

We verified that deleted records as well as old pre-update record versions live within database backups. Old data remains accessible in backups in perpetuity, until the entire backup is destroyed. Although old records are overwritten during normal database operation, each deleted record may be captured by a series of full and incremental backups before it is destroyed. While our experiments show customer records decaying from $Time_0$ (slowly without defrag and significantly faster with defrag), we note that it represents only the records deleted or updated at $Time_0$. An entirely new set of deleted records are created at $Time_1$ and at each subsequent workload step, which would follow the same pattern.

We demonstrated that defragmentation operations can significantly reduce the amount of deleted data captured in backups. Furthermore, the correct defragmentation option is key to expunging the old data values; while Db2, Postgres, and MariaDB have explicit commands to defragment the data structures, Oracle does not and as a result we tested three different defrag methods. One might have to measure deleted data retention in order to verify that they are choosing the right defrag method. Although defragmentation commands are costly, we argue that they are necessary to support good data privacy practices. We recommend that organizations defragment tables with sensitive data before backup and verify that their chosen defrag method is effective in eliminating deleted data. In cases where unknowingly retaining data is a significant liability for an organization, additional privacy tools will be necessary.

With data retention, organizations are at times are obligated to fully purge all traces of necessary data from their systems (lest organizations be subject to fines as with [11]). We have shown that backups have the potential to preserve unknown amounts of delete data in perpetuity (for the lifetime of backups). Ultimately, DBMS vendors may have to provide backup tools that incorporate defrag functionality, giving organizations control over their data.

7   Future Work

We intend to perform additional experiments with other database settings to determine if we can reduce the amount of deleted data left in backups without utilizing a costly (in terms of I/O operations) defrag commands. Future directions will also test against different workloads that model different industries, to evaluate when workload type influences the amount of remaining deleted data and whether the best defrag method can be chosen analytically.

Destroying deleted data may be accomplished by a custom trigger that explicitly updates values in-place before deletion. Such operation would not eliminate the deleted row itself, but it would sanitize the individual values of the deleted records. The overhead of this approach would need to be measured against the overhead of a defragmentation. If trigger-based approach is viable, database platforms could include an internal sanitization feature to eliminate deleted data.

Acknowledgments. This work was partially funded by the US National Science Foundation Grant IIP-2016548 and by Argonne National Laboratory.

References

1. Alter table move. https://asktom.oracle.com/pls/apex/asktom.search?tag=alter-table-move
2. Enable row movement. https://asktom.oracle.com/pls/apex/asktom.search?tag=enable-row-movement
3. IBM DB2 reorg. https://www.ibm.com/support/producthub/db2/docs/content/SSEPGG_11.5.0/com.ibm.db2.luw.admin.cmd.doc/doc/r0001966.html
4. What is the difference between shrink, move and Impdp. https://asktom.oracle.com/pls/apex/asktom.search?tag=what-is-the-difference-between-shrink-move-and-impdp
5. GDPR archives (2020). https://gdpr.eu/tag/gdpr/

6. SQL language reference (2020). https://docs.oracle.com/en/database/oracle/oracle-database/19/sqlrf/ROWID-Pseudocolumn.html#GUID-F6E0FBD2-983C-495D-9856-5E113A17FAF1
7. SQL language reference (2020). https://docs.oracle.com/en/database/oracle/oracle-database/19/sqlrf/ALTER-TABLE.html#GUID-552E7373-BF93-477D-9DA3-B2C9386F2877
8. Vacuum (2020). https://www.postgresql.org/docs/12/sql-vacuum.html
9. Assistant Secretary of Defense for Networks and Information Integration: Electronic records management software applications design criteria standard (2007). https://www.esd.whs.mil/Portals/54/Documents/DD/issuances/dodm/501502std.pdf
10. Barata, M., Bernardino, J., Furtado, P.: An overview of decision support benchmarks: TPC-DS, TPC-H and SSB. In: Rocha, A., Correia, A.M., Costanzo, S., Reis, L.P. (eds.) New Contributions in Information Systems and Technologies. AISC, vol. 353, pp. 619–628. Springer, Cham (2015). https://doi.org/10.1007/978-3-319-16486-1_61
11. Betschka, J., Kiesel, R., Christ, S.: Deutsche wohnen muss 14,5 millionen euro strafe bezahlen (2019). https://www.tagesspiegel.de/berlin/rekordbussgeld-wegen-datenschutzverstoessen-deutsche-wohnen-muss-14-5-millionen-euro-strafe-bezahlen/25191038.html
12. Dudjak, M., Lukić, I., Köhler, M.: Survey of database backup management. In: 27th International Scientific and Professional Conference Organization and Maintenance Technology (2017)
13. Fox, C.: Google hit with £44m GDPR fine over ads (2019). https://www.bbc.com/news/technology-46944696
14. Hsu, W.W., Smith, A.J., Young, H.C.: Characteristics of production database workloads and the TPC benchmarks. IBM Syst. J. **40**(3), 781–802 (2001)
15. International Data Sanitization Consortium: Data sanitization terminology and definitions (2017). https://www.datasanitization.org/data-sanitization-terminology/
16. Jeon, S., Bang, J., Byun, K., Lee, S.: A recovery method of deleted record for SQLite database. Pers. Ubiquit. Comput. **16**(6), 707–715 (2012)
17. Langer, M.: Developing a data backup strategy. Risk Manage. **64**(10), 12–13 (2017)
18. Lenard, B., Wagner, J., Rasin, A., Grier, J.: SysGen: system state corpus generator. In: Proceedings of the 15th International Conference on Availability, Reliability and Security, pp. 1–6 (2020)
19. Lozupone, V.: Disaster recovery plan for medical records company. Int. J. Inf. Manage. **37**(6), 622–626 (2017)
20. Netapp: (2020). https://kb.netapp.com/Advice_and_Troubleshooting/Data_Protection_and_Security/Snap_Creator_Framework/What_is_Snap_Creator
21. O'Neil, P., O'Neil, E., Chen, X., Revilak, S.: The star schema benchmark and augmented fact table indexing. In: Nambiar, R., Poess, M. (eds.) TPCTC 2009. LNCS, vol. 5895, pp. 237–252. Springer, Heidelberg (2009). https://doi.org/10.1007/978-3-642-10424-4_17
22. Oracle: Oracle MAA reference architectures. https://www.oracle.com/webfolder/technetwork/tutorials/architecture-diagrams/high-availability-overview/high-availability-reference-architectures.html
23. Oracle (2018). https://www.delltechnologies.com/en-us/collaterals/unauth/white-papers/products/storage/h14232-oracle-database-backup-recovery-vmax3.pdf
24. Oracle (2019). https://docs.oracle.com/cd/E53394_01/html/E54801/gbciq.html#scrolltoc

25. Shaik, B.: Backup and restore best practices. In: PostgreSQL Configuration, pp. 93–110. Springer (2020). https://doi.org/10.1007/978-1-4842-5663-3_4
26. SQL and PLSQL: High water mark oracle (2020). https://sqlandplsql.com/2013/05/22/high-water-mark-oracle/
27. Wagner, J., Rasin, A., Grier, J.: Database forensic analysis through internal structure carving. Digit. Investig. **14**, S106–S115 (2015)
28. Wagner, J., Rasin, A., Grier, J.: Database image content explorer: carving data that does not officially exist. Digit. Investig. **18**, S97–S107 (2016)
29. Wagner, J., Rasin, A., Malik, T., Heart, K., Jehle, H., Grier, J.: Database forensic analysis with DBCarver. In: CIDR 2017, 8th Biennial Conference on Innovative Data Systems Research (2017)

How Do Users Chain Email Accounts Together?

Lydia Kraus[1] , Mária Švidroňová[2], and Elizabeth Stobert[3(✉)]

[1] Institute of Computer Science, Masaryk University, Brno, Czech Republic
[2] Centre for Research on Cryptography and Security, Faculty of Informatics, Masaryk University, Brno, Czech Republic
[3] School of Computer Science, Carleton University, Ottawa, Canada
`elizabeth.stobert@carleton.ca`

Abstract. Recovery connections between email accounts can be exploited in manual hijacking attacks as has been shown in several incidents during the last years. Yet little is known about users' practices of chaining email accounts together. We conducted a qualitative interview study with 23 students in which they shared their email recovery and forwarding settings with us. Altogether, we collected and analyzed information about 138 different email accounts. We used this data to map email account topologies and analyzed these topologies for recurring patterns. We found that users often make poor configuration decisions in their email recovery setups, and often create patterns in their email recovery topologies that result in security vulnerabilities. Patterns such as loops (seen in more than a quarter of our topologies) could be easily exploited in a targeted attack. We conclude that users need better guidance about how to use email based recovery settings in a robust way.

Keywords: Email recovery · Email forwarding · Fallback authentication · Security · Usability

1 Introduction

Along with the increased use of email worldwide [16], email-based fallback authentication has gained in importance during the last decade [8,14]. Yet little is known about users' real-world practices that accompany this "new" authentication scheme. Despite the usability advantages that this scheme offers [11], it also creates connections between accounts that can be leveraged by attackers. Incidents such as Wired writer Mat Honan's "epic hacking" [9] or the compromise of Twitter employees' accounts [10] show that adversaries are able to exploit connections between email accounts in targeted attacks. These *manual hijacking* [2] attacks usually start with a social engineering attack such as phishing and then continue by exploiting both the hijacked account and any linked accounts [2]. Manual hijacking is relatively rare, but can be devastating for end users as it typically concerns accounts that are of high value for their owners [2,13].

© IFIP International Federation for Information Processing 2021
Published by Springer Nature Switzerland AG 2021
A. Jøsang et al. (Eds.): SEC 2021, IFIP AICT 625, pp. 416–429, 2021.
https://doi.org/10.1007/978-3-030-78120-0_27

Although manual hijacking has been known to both security researchers and end users for many years (the Mat Honan incident took place in 2012, and was widely covered in the media), little is known about users' practices of connecting accounts. Connections between email accounts are especially interesting, as email accounts are usually long-lived and of great importance because many online services require them for registration. While connected accounts do not directly constitute an attack vector, they may create links that can be exploited in a manual hijacking attack and make them more devastating.

To examine users' vulnerabilities to manual hijacking attacks, we investigated how users connect their email accounts via password recovery and forwarding options. Our research questions were: How do users use recovery and forwarding options to chain email accounts together? What are the connection topologies that they use, and what are the security implications resulting from different connection topologies?

We conducted a qualitative user study with 23 students from a major university in central Europe. In the study, we asked participants to log into each of their email accounts and to document the connections between accounts. As users have many online accounts [15] and remembering all of them can be a challenging task, we prompted participants to recall as many email accounts as possible with different kind of guides and questions. We asked participants to map the connection topology between their accounts, and interviewed them about their email protection and configuration decisions.

Our study is the first to provide a data set of email chain topologies. Altogether, we collected and analyzed information about 138 different email accounts and 27 topologies. Our results show that email account topologies are diverse, but that many include elements of line and loop topologies. Loop topologies are especially concerning, as they allow attackers who already have access to one account to easily gain access to a further account. We also found that users created other vulnerabilities in their topologies by placing the final recovery nodes in inaccessible accounts, or by using accounts owned by somebody else as a recovery option. They also tended to keep accounts with physical recovery options (which could be strong recovery options) separate from the rest of the recovery topology. Participants were often unaware of the connections between their accounts and only realized during the study that there are recovery links they are not happy with. We suggest users need additional support in using email-based recovery in such a way that it does not increase the attack surface for manual attacks.

2   Related Work

2.1   Manual Attacks and Account Hijacking

Our threat model follows the threat model of a manual hijacking attack, as defined by Bursztein et al. [2]: "Manual hijacking consist[s] of attack[s] that opportunistically select victims with the intent of monetizing the victim's contacts or personal data; any sufficiently lucrative credential will suffice. These attacks are carried manually rather than automatically."

In general, manual hijacking attacks (such as email-based daisy-chaining attacks) mostly start with social engineering such as phishing [2]. Once one account is compromised, attackers first check whether the account is worth further investment, for instance, by checking whether it contains financial data, linked account credentials, or personal data [2]. Thereafter, the attack usually continues with account exploitation and actions to delay account recovery [2].

When it comes to account management, users have been shown to exhibit habits that make it easier for attackers to succeed in manual attacks. The literature suggests that password-reuse and variations are inherent parts of password creation and users' password management lifecycle [15]. Similarly, using password reset options is a part of users' coping strategies for managing multiple accounts [15]. Additionally, users balance password creation effort across accounts by spending more effort for more important accounts [15]. Research by Thomas et al. shows that users whose password has been leaked in a data breach, have a higher probability of being compromised, due to convenience habits such as password reuse [17].

Account hijacking can cause concrete and emotional harm, yet the majority of users who have not personally experienced this threat seem to be unconcerned about it [13]. Interestingly, research suggests that account hijacking is more widespread than is commonly assumed. In a study conducted by Shay et al., 30% of participants indicated that they had experienced account hijacking of email or social network accounts [13]. The study by Shay et al. further suggests that personal accounts of high value are usually the targets of account hijacking.

2.2   Email-Based Identification and Authentication

Already two decades ago, email based identification and authentication (EBIA) had gained in popularity, mainly due to its usability and cost advantages as compared to PKI schemes [7]. Already at that time, major web service providers such as Amazon, Yahoo, and Apple had deployed this scheme [7]. In the last decade, service providers have further intensively started to promote password recovery options, for instance through recovery phone numbers, email addresses, or through social authentication [4,8,12,14].

Compared to other fallback schemes such as SMS, designated trustee, or personal knowledge questions, EBIA offers several usability advantages such as high perceived ease of use and low authentication time [11]. Yet, its security is also dependent on the passwords that users choose and on the protection of the email servers [7]. Another issue is the email address lifecycle: an email address can be owned by different people over time and different email providers have different ways of dealing with terminated addresses [7].

Email based fallback authentication is double-edged sword. On the one hand, it creates connections between accounts which may be exploited by attackers, as shown by the account compromise of Wired-writer Mat Honan [9].

Through social engineering, the attackers were able to gain access to one account which they then used to compromise other accounts via the password recovery option [9]. On the other hand, research by Google shows that account restoration through an email address was successful for 75% of accounts as compared to 14% of accounts which used secret questions [2].

Email based recovery is the most popular method observed at Google, but it's less secure and reliable than phone-based recovery as users sometimes mistype their secondary email address [2]. Moreover, users tend to forget to keep their recovery email up-to-date [2], which we observed as well in our study.

3   Methodology

To investigate connections between users' email addresses, we conducted a qualitative interview study, asking users about their email address configurations and the decisions and understanding that informed that setup. Our goal was to gain a deep understanding of how users configure their fallback authentication, and to be able to ask our participants to reflect and discuss the ways in which their account topologies are configured. Our study focused on three aspects of email linking: the connections between the accounts (i.e., the topologies), the characteristics of the accounts (and thus of each node in the topology), and participants' perceptions of their account topology.

3.1   Procedure

An overview of the study procedure is shown in Fig. 1.

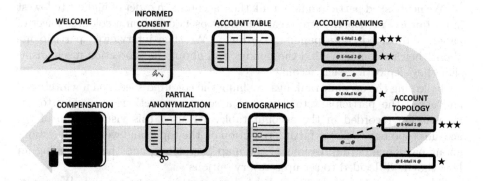

Fig. 1. Study procedure: after signing the informed consent, participants looked up recovery and forwarding settings of their accounts. Participants then ranked the accounts by importance and provided reasoning. Finally, participants created their account topologies and reflected on them. The study was concluded with a demographics questionnaire, partial anonymization of the account data, and the compensation for the participants.

In the first part of our study, we asked participants to recall as many of their email accounts as possible and to document the connections between these accounts in a printed table. Participants were given the table, and left to complete it individually. We allowed participants to supplement this data with information obtained directly from the account settings on their email address (participants were given the choice of accessing their accounts using a lab computer or bringing their own laptop). To assist participants in accessing the relevant information, we created several step-by-step guides for popular free email providers [1] as well as for the most popular providers in our country [3,5]. This approach also helped participants recall forgotten accounts because they could sometimes be found in the recovery settings. Participants were instructed to write down a pseudonym for their email address and various properties of the account set up on the printed table. Knowing that it can be difficult for users to recall all of their accounts [15], we first let participants fill the table on their own and then prompted them towards remembering potentially forgotten accounts by asking whether they had considered different account categories, such as accounts used for communication, for online shopping, for social networking, for banking, or for online games.

Following completion of the account table, we asked participants to rank their accounts according to the subjective importance they would assign to each account. We interviewed participants about their perception of the strength of the password belonging to each account and whether they employ any additional measures (such as 2FA) to protect those accounts. We specifically did not ask participants for their passwords, and instead asked questions such as "do you think your password is unique?" or "does your password contain standard dictionary words?" to gain insights into the structure of the password without knowing the password itself.

We next asked participants to rank their accounts in order of highest to lowest importance. Participants wrote each account pseudonym on a coloured sheet of paper, and sorted those papers accordingly. We then interviewed participants about their reasoning behind the ranking and about the protection mechanisms that they deploy for each account.

Following the account rankings, we hung the coloured sheets on a whiteboard and asked the participant to draw the account connections according to the information recorded in the account table. We used this visualization of the account topology to foster further reflection on the topic, and we asked questions about participants' impressions of the map (topology), and their reasoning for how they had decided to set up recovery options.

The study concluded with a brief demographics questionnaire. We audio-recorded the interviews about the account ranking and the account topology. The account rankings and topologies (maps) were photographed for analysis. Participants completed the study in our lab, taking between 45 and 90 min to complete the entire procedure.

Our study was approved by Masaryk University's ethics commission. Since email addresses are personally identifiable information, we had participants physically remove their addresses (by cutting off the first column of the table) from the collected data at the end of the study.

3.2 Participants

We recruited 23 participants from our university campus in early 2020. Of those, 14 were male and 9 were female. Participants ranged between 19 and 26 years old with a mean age of 22 years. All participants were students. The majority of participants studied computer science (12, 52%), and the remaining participants came from a variety of other faculties (arts: 2, social studies: 3, science: 2, medicine: 1, law: 1, economics: 2).

3.3 Data Analysis

We used an inductive approach to analyze our qualitative data. We used the Grounded Theory approach of "all is data", and included both the interview transcripts and the account topology maps in our analysis.

We fully transcribed the interviews and translated them into English. One researcher then reviewed the transcripts line-by-line to identify themes in usage and password habits. These themes were used to create a code book (in which we listed and defined codes), which was used by a second researcher to systematically code the interviews in three rounds. After each round of coding the researcher checked for inconsistencies, and proceeded to the next round until all inconsistencies were resolved. The aim of our qualitative interview analysis was to identify account properties that would allow us to gain further insights into why the accounts are considered more or less important and how the accounts are protected.

For the topologies, we redrew all maps in a standard notation to facilitate the identification of patterns, and included account importance in the size of each node. We then conducted a qualitative analysis of the account topologies by identifying re-occurring patterns (such as line, loop, and star constellations) in the account maps. Maps and accounts were stored per participant and participants were given non-gendered coded names[1].

4 Account Types and Importance

Using the data from the account rankings together with the accompanying interviews, we were able to gain insight into users' perception and use of their email accounts.

We suspected that account properties may play a role when users are setting up recovery structures. Users treat accounts differently and spend more effort on more important accounts [15], which may in turn affect how they configure recovery options.

---

[1] The anonymized data set is available at: https://crocs.fi.muni.cz/public/papers/ifipsec2021.

Our study yielded a total of 138 accounts owned by 23 participants. Each user owned an average of 6 email accounts (min.= 3, max. = 10). We classified the accounts into four categories: private accounts, school accounts, work accounts, and somebody else's accounts. 67% of accounts (92 acc.) were private accounts – typically from popular free providers (such as Gmail or local account providers). 17% (24 acc.) were school accounts, i.e., accounts from the participant's university, and 13% (18 acc.) were work accounts, i.e., participants indicated that they were job-related. The final category, "somebody else's accounts", were those that are owned by another user and accounted for 3% (4 acc.) of all accounts. 21% (29 acc.) of all accounts listed in the study were inaccessible, i.e., the participant could not open them any more for whatever reason.

We calculated an importance index (II) for each account by normalizing the account ranking so that each rank takes a value between 0 and 1. Bottom-level ranked accounts have an importance index of 0, while top-level ranked accounts have an importance index of 1. Figure 2 shows a histogram of the importance indices. Participants made clear distinctions between high- and low-importance accounts. Based on these rankings, we categorized accounts into high-importance ($II > 0.5$) and low-importance accounts ($II \leq 0.5$). 43% of accounts (60 acc.) in the study were high-importance, and 57% (78 acc.) were low-importance.

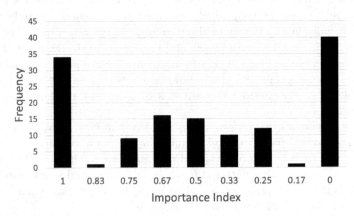

Fig. 2. Histogram of the accounts' importance indices (II). The histogram shows that users have a clear tendency to distinguish between high- and low-importance accounts.

4.1   High-Importance Accounts

High-importance accounts are usually the target of manual hijacking attacks [2,13]. In our study, high-importance accounts were most likely to belong to the *private* category (55%, 33 acc.), followed by *school* (19 acc., 32%), and *work* (8 acc., 13%). No account in the high-importance category belonged to the *somebody else's* category. Only one account ranked high-importance was inaccessible, and nine of these accounts were protected with 2FA.

Participants frequently characterized their high-importance accounts (19 acc.) by emphasizing the density of connections stemming from them. For example, Jaylen said: "In my personal emails, there is practically a lot of different personal information, practically a lot of people use it to contact me". Participants also described how their high-importance accounts are used frequently (13 acc.). These accounts are used "often" or "on a daily basis", as outlined by Kamryn: "So, um, it's an email I go to every day, every time I go to the Internet". Besides being linked to many accounts and being used often, participants further emphasized the *personal* nature of their high-importance accounts (11 acc.) and their importance as an information repository (9 acc.). As described by Cassidy "[the] highest level, that's my primary email, through which I handle all personal [things]".

Florencio, Herley, and van Oorschot [6] suggest that accounts should be classified according to the consequences that an attack on an account would yield, but it appeared that our participants used account properties to categorize the importance of their accounts. After the first round of reflection on the rankings, we further prompted participants to imagine what would happen if one of the accounts was hacked, but participants did not seem to harbour any further insights into their own behaviour in this way.

4.2 Low-Importance Accounts

Low-importance accounts were also primarily categorized as *private* (59 acc., 76%), followed by *work* (10 acc., 13%), *school* (5 acc., 6%), and *somebody else's* (4 acc., 5%). More than a third of the low-importance accounts were inaccessible (28 acc., 36%). Six of these accounts were additionally protected by 2FA.

In the interviews, participants often characterized their low-importance accounts as being older (32 acc.), such as accounts that were created during childhood or youth. As indicated by Adrian: "it was the first email we just used to write to friends". Participants said that they used low-importance accounts less frequently (24 acc.), as described by Frankie: "I am not visiting this email so often and nothing terrible would happen if I forgot my login details or if they compromise it". A significant proportion of low-importance accounts were inaccessible (28 acc.): "I feel like it [the account] exists, but I have no idea what the password was there" (Harley). Low-importance accounts were also often associated with attacks or compromise (16 acc.), as described by Cassidy: "And there's just spam going on there, and I'm not watching it." Sometimes, low-importance accounts were created for a specific purpose (10 acc.), such as to preserve privacy when signing up to a new service, as described by Cary: "basically I started it just because of Facebook that in order ... I just had how to log on to Facebook."

As with the high-importance accounts, participants tended to classify the importance of these accounts according to their purposes and properties rather than according to what would happen if those accounts were compromised.

5   Account Topologies

Next, we analyzed the account topologies that we obtained from the printed table and that we visualized together with the participants in the third part of the study. Altogether, our data set contained 27 email account topology maps. Each map contained on average 3.57 accounts with a minimum of 2 accounts and a maximum of 8 accounts.

Out of 27 email topologies, we only found five which did not contain any apparent vulnerability. These five belonged to participants that had deployed additional two-factor authentication to protect the important accounts in their maps. An overview of issues that we encountered during the study can be seen in Table 1.

Eight topologies ended in an inaccessible account as a final node (30%). The remainder either finished at somebody else's account (3 acc., 11%) or placed the critical end node in low-importance accounts (4 acc., 15%). There were only a few forwarding connections in our data set and in only one chain (Rene) they impacted the recovery flow by forwarding emails (with deletion) from a recovery account to another account.

Interestingly, none of the participants used their school or work account as a final node. This is a surprising finding, as those accounts can usually be physically recovered (e.g. by visiting the study office or a local admin) and would thus constitute a stronger restoration capability than private accounts or somebody else's accounts.

5.1   Topology Patterns

Using the well-known network topology model, we identified three topology categories: loop, star, and line topologies. We examined participants' account maps to identify what patterns were present. Each map could contain elements of more than one type of topology.

Seven participants' email chains contained a loop pattern. The classical loop pattern consists of two accounts that recover to each other. This creates a significant security vulnerability, as an attacker who has access to account A can easily gain access to account B. All an attacker needs to do is search in the settings of account A for recovery accounts and then try to reset the recovery account by the help of the already hijacked account.

A star topology pattern is a topology where multiple accounts recover to one single account, thus creating a single point of failure. Five participants' accounts contained this pattern. As long as the single point of failure is well-protected (e.g. by two-factor authentication (2FA)), this topology is not likely to create increased opportunities for manual hijacking accounts. However, the application of additional measures to the central node was relatively rare, and we only saw this in one user's topology in our study: Kendall linked six accounts to one single account and this account was 2FA protected (Table 1).

The line topology chains two or more accounts in sequence. Short line topologies of two accounts are the typical fallback set-up. In our study, we found 23

Table 1. Issues identified within each email chain, sorted by account chain length (L). Column 4 presents a summary of the recovery information flow between accounts of low and high importance and 2FA protected accounts, while column 5 presents topology and information flow related issues.

Participant	L	Topology	Information Flow	Issue
Cary	2	Line	high → *low*	Final node not controlled by user
Cassidy	2	Line	low → 2FA	None (final node 2FA secured)
Cleo	2	Line	high → *low*	Final node of low importance
Finley	2	Loop	high ↔ *low*	Loop increases attack surface
Frankie	2	Line	inacc. → *inacc.*	Both accounts inaccessible
Parker	2	Line	high → *low*	Final node not controlled by user
Rene	2	Line (fwd)	equal info low	Not relevant
Sage	2	Line	high → *inacc.*	Final node inaccessible
Sandy	2	Line (fwd)	equal info low	Not relevant
Adrian	3	Star	high, 2FA → *low*	Final node of low importance
Cassidy	3	Line, Loop	low → *low* ↔ *low*	Loop increases attack surface
Harley	3	Line	high → *inacc.*	Final node inaccessible
Kamryn	3	Line, Loop	*inacc.* → 2FA ↔ high	None (central node 2FA secured)
Kayden	3	Line	high → *low*	Final node of low importance
London	3	Line	high → *low* → *inacc.*	Final node inaccessible
Pat	3	Line	high → *inacc.*	Final node inaccessible
Rylan	3	Line, Loop	low → high ↔ low	Loop increases attack surface
Sandy	3	Line	high → *low*	Final node not controlled by user
Frankie	4	Line, Loop	low → high ↔ high	Loop increases attack surface
Jaylen	4	Line	high → *low*	Final node of low importance
Shannon	4	Line	low → high → *inacc.*	Final node inaccessible
Stacey	4	Line, Loop	2FA → 2FA ↔ *low*	None (central node 2FA secured
Marion	5	Star	high, low → high	OK, final node of high importance
Bailey	7	Ln., Lp., St.	Info flow in 5 directions	Loop increases attack surface
Jessie	7	Line	high → ... → *inacc.*	Final node inaccessible
Kendall	7	Star	2x high, 4x low → 2FA	None (final node 2FA secured)
Rene	8	Line, Star	high → ... → *inacc.*	Final node inaccessible

instances of this pattern, mainly short sequences. However, we also found maps where participants had chained more than 2 accounts together – there were two participants with four or more accounts in a line (Jessie, Rene). In this category, there were also three participants who had a chain of accounts that ended in a recovery account belonging to somebody else (and was thus out of the control of the main account's user). Another pattern we saw in line topologies was that the final nodes (i.e., the accounts at the end of the chain) were often either of low-importance or inaccessible. From the account analysis, we know that low-importance accounts are more often older and inaccessible which can create a problem during account restoration.

5.2   Separate Accounts

To further understand the underlying patterns in participants' account topologies, we investigated which kind of accounts are kept separate from the rest of the chain. In total, 41 accounts were not involved in any chain. Among those accounts were 19 private accounts (46%), 15 school accounts (37%), and seven work accounts (17%). Together, school and work accounts constitute more than 50% of the separate accounts. This is especially noteworthy as those accounts can often be physically restored and should thus be more robust for account recovery after manual hijacking.

5.3   Recovery Use Motivation and Perceptions

In the last part of the study, we further asked users whether they set-up recovery on their own initiative or whether it was motivated by the email provider. An overwhelming majority (21 participants) indicated that the email provider prompted them to do so, as described by Cleo: "it kept popping up that you would secure your account, so I already said that well, so I'll take care of it, so I'll put it on the one, I'll put it on the email, on which I can basically sign up for."

This finding is unsurprising, as email providers have already started years ago to promote fallback authentication (see e.g. [8]), but it does demonstrate that users generally are not concerned with setting up fallback mechanisms, and that their motivation to do so is often externally imposed.

When asked about their perception of their own topology, most participants expressed significant observations resulting from the graphical depiction of their account setup.

Ten participants noticed aspects of their topology that they were not happy with. Some were concerned about a proper account recovery, like Shannon, who mentioned that "the only thing with the restoration in the [account] is that it could be there problem getting to that account." Others noticed security shortcomings in their topology set-up, like Cleo, who mentioned: "The old [account] is just as uninteresting, but now that I actually realized that I actually have the same passwords there."

Only seven participants indicated that there were no surprises in their account topologies. For instance, Cary said: "I guess I was aware that those are connected, and others aren't". Similarly, Jessie stated that there is "nothing I didn't know before".

6   Discussion

In this work, we explored users' vulnerabilities to account hijacking attacks by investigating how users chain email accounts together by using recovery options. We conducted a study with 23 participants, and identified three prevailing account topologies in which users structure their recovery accounts.

We found multiple aspects of our participants' email chaining to have significant security ramifications. The loop pattern (which was used by more than a quarter of our participants) was the most concerning. If a user's accounts are configured this way, an attacker who manages to compromise one account can easily hijack another. We also found that the final nodes of the recovery chains are often inaccessible (30% of all topologies), of low-importance (15% of all topologies), and sometimes owned by somebody else (11% of all topologies). All of these create problems for recovery, and the potential for failed recovery attempts if another account does get hijacked. Low-importance accounts are often created a longer time ago, are used less frequently, are often inaccessible, and sometimes used as spam collectors. This can create problems during account restoration as users may not be able to access them and email providers may even terminate access if the account has not been accessed for a while. Similarly, relying on recovery accounts owned by somebody else may create problems during account recovery as the recovery account may not be accessible in a timely manner (or at all).

We also interviewed participants about their understanding of their email topologies. We found that users do not seem concerned with security when configuring their fallback email accounts. Using email based recovery seems to be mainly encouraged by the email provider and users do not seem to spend much effort on creating robust links between their accounts. While account providers keep on reminding users to configure and maintain account recovery, they should also remind users to avoid insecure recovery practices, and encourage users to choose fallback addresses to which they expect to have lasting access. They should also recommend the use of additional security mechanisms (such as 2FA) on accounts that support others.

Limitations: The prevalence of manual hijacking attacks for the average end user is unclear. Mat Honan [9] and the Twitter employee compromise [10]) were both high-value targets, and the attacks on them were both devastating and well-publicized. While our work shows that email topologies actually exist, we cannot draw any conclusions about the likelihood that such a configuration might be actually exploited. However, the topologies that we identified contain weak points, about which users should be concerned.

We chose our methodology to allow us to closely examine users' email configurations and their understanding of those configurations. Our study examined only a small group of relatively young users, and a remaining question is how these findings generalize to a larger population. Yet, our results suggest that a larger scale study could give insight into vulnerabilities to manual hijacking attacks.

7   Conclusion

Our study of users' email configurations showed that many users' fallback emails are configured in a way that could potentially open them to vulnerabilities from manual hijacking attacks. We conducted a study with 23 students in which they shared their email recovery and forwarding settings with us. Our study showed that many users build (sometimes even sophisticated) chains that resemble diverse topology patterns such as loops, lines, and stars. However, these topologies seems to be rather a consequence of being prompted by email providers to set-up recovery accounts, than by intentional design with robustness in mind. We analyzed these patterns and their pitfalls and come to the conclusion that email providers should exercise more care when prompting users to set up email based recovery. Instead of just pointing users to use this feature, email providers and other security educators should also encourage users to protect their recovery accounts as well as their primary accounts (ideally with 2FA) and to avoid the use of recovery loops.

Acknowledgements. This research was supported by ERDF project CyberSecurity, CyberCrime and Critical Information Infrastructures Center of Excellence (No. CZ.02.1.01/0.0/0.0/16_019/0000822). We would like to thank all of our participants for taking part in the study. Thanks also goes to Agáta Kružíková for help with study logistics. The user study was conducted while Lydia Kraus was a postdoctoral fellow at the Faculty of Informatics at Masaryk University.

References

1. Biswal, R.: Top 10 best free email service providers 2020 (2020). https://web. archive.org/web/20200501082105/www.ecloudbuzz.com/best-free-email-service-providers/
2. Bursztein, E., et al.: Handcrafted fraud and extortion: manual account hijacking in the wild. In: Proceedings of the 2014 Internet Measurement Conference, pp. 347–358 (2014)
3. Dobryemail.cz: Čím otevírají Češi e-maily a kde? (2017). https://dobryemail.cz/ novinky-trendy/cim-oteviraji-cesi-e-maily-kde
4. Facebook security: introducing trusted contacts (2013). https://www.facebook. com/notes/facebook-security/introducingtrusted-contacts/10151362774980766/
5. Fišer, M.: Nejoblíbenějším českým poskytovatelem e-mailu je podle průzkumu Seznam.cz (2009). https://www.novinky.cz/internet-a-pc/clanek/nejoblibenejsim ceskym-poskytovatelem-e-mailu-je-podle-pruzkumu-seznamcz-40239742
6. Florêncio, D., Herley, C., van Oorschot, P.C.: An administrator's guide to internet password research. In: 28th Large Installation System Administration Conference (LISA14), pp. 44–61 (2014)
7. Garfinkel, S.L.: Email-based identification and authentication: an alternative to PKI? IEEE Secur. Privacy **1**(6), 20–26 (2003)
8. Google Help: Why add recovery options? (2012). https://www.youtube.com/ watch?v=4SjJ2i1mc2Y
9. Honan, M.: How apple and amazon security flaws led to my epic hacking. Wired.com, pp. 1–4 (2012). https://www.wired.com/2012/08/apple-amazon-mat-honan-hacking/
10. Keizer, G.: Report: hacker broke into Twitter e-mail with help from Hotmail (2009). https://www.computerworld.com/article/2525893/report-hackerbroke-into-twitter-e-mail-with-help-from-hotmail.html

11. Markert, P., Golla, M., Stobert, E., Dürmuth, M.: Work in progress: a comparative long-term study of fallback authentication. In: Workshop on Usable Security (USEC) (2019)
12. NRJC: Outlook demanding my phone number. How do I continue using Outlook without giving my phone number. (2013). https://answers.microsoft.com/en-us/outlook_com/forum/all/outlook-demanding-my-phone-number-how-doi/95511277-0a17-46a0-9b17-f8470d1514f0
13. Shay, R., Ion, I., Reeder, R.W., Consolvo, S.: "My religious aunt asked why i was trying to sell her viagra" experiences with account hijacking. In: Proceedings of the SIGCHI Conference on Human Factors in Computing Systems, pp. 2657–2666. CHI 2014, Association for Computing Machinery, New York (2014). https://doi.org/10.1145/2556288.2557330
14. Smetters, D.: Don't get locked out: set up recovery options for your Google Account. (2013). https://blog.google/technology/safety-security/dont-get-locked-out-set-up-recovery/
15. Stobert, E., Biddle, R.: The password life cycle: user behaviour in managing passwords. In: 10th Symposium On Usable Privacy and Security (SOUPS) 2014, pp. 243–255 (2014)
16. The Radicati Group Inc.: Email Market, 2019–2023 (2019). https://www.radicati.com/wp/wp-content/uploads/2019/01/Email_Market,_2019-2023_Executive_Summary.pdf
17. Thomas, K., et al.: Data breaches, phishing, or malware? Understanding the risks of stolen credentials. In: Proceedings of the 2017 ACM SIGSAC Conference on Computer and Communications Security, pp. 1421–1434 (2017)

Tensions that Hinder the Implementation of Digital Security Governance

Stef Schinagl[(✉)] [iD], Svetlana Khapova[iD], and Abbas Shahim

Vrije Universiteit Amsterdam, Amsterdam, The Netherlands
{s.schinagl,s.n.khapova,a.shahim}@vu.nl

Abstract. Today's organizations are exposed to high risk because the established digital technologies are vulnerable to security attacks. The increased impact of security on business demands a strategic approach to information security, commonly referred to as digital security governance. While there is a growing understanding that digital security is one of the leading risks and challenges of today's organizations, organizations still find it difficult to implement security governance as part of their regular organizing change activities. This study focuses on providing more empirical insight into "tensions that are present during the implementation of digital security governance".

We conducted an inductive study and interviewed 42 CISOs and CIOs of large organizations in the Netherlands. The study reveals the tensions that hinder the implementation of digital security governance. We draw from management theories to provide a fresh understanding of and guidance for how to unravel the tensions.

Keywords: Information security governance · Information security implementation · Digital security · Digital transformation · Digital security governance

1 Introduction

Recent studies argue that digital security is becoming of strategic importance in contemporary firms [1, 7, 13, 21]. Specifically, these studies argue that governance needs to be organized around digital security. This is because businesses have become technology centered as a result of digital transformation. Businesses are now exposed to high risk because established digital technologies are vulnerable to security attacks [13, 16]. Security attacks increasingly have direct business impacts and costs and therefore force boards to consider alternative ways to govern security and anticipate the growing number of attacks. To this extent, security governance approaches must fundamentally shift from being an isolated technical issue to being a strategic business issue. In this way digital security governance is positioned and implemented as an institutionally wide effort that supports digital business strategies and business innovation [8, 16].

While many organizations understand the need to transform their current security governance approaches so that they fit the digital era, few of them succeed, have trouble

© IFIP International Federation for Information Processing 2021
Published by Springer Nature Switzerland AG 2021
A. Jøsang et al. (Eds.): SEC 2021, IFIP AICT 625, pp. 430–445, 2021.
https://doi.org/10.1007/978-3-030-78120-0_28

with adoption, or lack behind in implementing their security approaches [1, 6, 21]. For example, according to the 2020 Thales Data Threat Report[1], organizations remain cognitively dissonant of security. Organizations believe that they are secure when they are not implementing the processes and investing in the technologies required to appropriately protect their organization. Most often, security implementation is mistakenly seen as an isolated, separate and disintegrated activity from business [1, 13, 16]. This means that security remains a concern of the IT department instead of the collaborative business function that is part of the company's DNA.

Additionally, in research, security remains an underexposed concern of digital transformation. In particular, most studies have not comprehensively or clearly explained the processes of establishing security governance in organizations or provided guidelines for its implementation [6, 21]. Implementing security governance remains difficult in complex connected digital environments because of "cutting ties", i.e., tensions [14]. Conflicts between information security values and work efficiency are the most common [5]. An example is the tension between simultaneously maintaining a high pace of innovation and securing one's business.

Security governance research still lacks an empirical and theoretical understanding of its implementation in a digital context [9, 13]. Therefore, why do organizations still find it difficult to implement security governance as part of their regular organizing change activities when digital security is one of the top priorities and challenges of today's organizations? In particular, what tensions occur during the implementation phase of digital security governance?

Our inductive study prompts us to address the research gap within the "digital security governance" phenomenon. To accomplish this, we collected data via 42 interviews with Chief Information Security Officers (CISOs) and Chief Information Officers (CIOs) working in large organizations in the Netherlands. Our data reveal that although there is a common understanding of a "need for change" in digital security approaches, there are tensions that hinder the implementation of digital security in organizations. The tensions are mainly determined by the digital context. We have consolidated our research findings to a data structure based on the Gioia methodology [3], as shown in Fig. 1, 2 and 3. To explain the data, we draw from management and organization theories that help describe the theoretical tensions presented in this paper.

This paper continues with a brief overview of related research. Then, after explaining our methods, we provide an in-depth analysis of our empirical findings describing three tensions. As our aim is to build theory, each tension includes a brief theoretical background. Then, on that basis, we explain the theoretical tensions that exist in the digital security governance implementation phenomenon. The study concludes with a discussion of the implications of our findings and suggestions for future research that these findings present.

2 Related Research: Digital Security Governance

Security governance research has seen a steady progression, moving from a narrow focus on "technical controls" towards a more holistic approach, including organizational and

---

[1] https://cpl.thalesgroup.com/data-threat-report.

behavioral or social elements [13]. Yet, in today's technology driven environments, organizations are required to consider information security at a strategic (board) level to achieve the organization's sustainability and its protection [1, 6, 13, 21]. In recent literature, this strategic consideration of information security in the digital context is referred to the concept called digital security governance [1, 9, 13].

Digital security governance is achieved by "steering", or direct & controlling [19] the system by which security is embedded in the organizational structures, and in all of the related business dimensions and organizational factors as a whole (machines, people, objects, processes et cetera). Such a security throughout the firm approach is seen as the key to improve the level of security in contemporary organizations [8, 13].

However, security governance literature is relatively immature, i.e. largely descriptive and provides both limited practical and theoretical guidance [6, 13, 14]. In particular, studies lack empirical understanding about the processes of establishing security governance in organizations or provided guidelines for its implementation [6, 21].

In this study we bridge this research gap and provide empirical insight on implementation tensions. As explained earlier, implementing digital security governance in complex connected digital environments remains difficult because conflicting forces often exist that reveal tensions [14, 15]. Focusing on tensions can provide important insights for both researchers and practitioners, helping them to become aware of possible tensions in security governance designs as well of coping strategies and practices to tackle these tension. We believe by providing this research lens on tensions we gradually help to build knowledge that offers a deeper understanding in the security governance phenomenon.

3   Methods

We applied a qualitative research approach to inductively develop the tensions in digital security governance implementation. This approach is in line with the principles of an iterative approach to qualitative research – in particular, grounded theory. Concerning this inductive research approach, it may seem contradictory that we offer a brief overview of the relevant literature in each of the tensions presented in the findings section. However, because the question addressed in this study had yet to be investigated, our primary objective was to inductively identify the tensions that hinder the implementation of security governance. Hence, although we draw from different management theories to clarify and explain the tensions, as our vantage point we used a grounded theory approach to identify the tensions from our interview data, without being aware of the theories yet.

To analyze our data, we applied the Gioia methodology, which comprises three different levels of abstraction and is tailored to inductive inquiry [3]. We began by openly coding, grouping and classifying the individual descriptions that our informants provided as 'interview samples' to perform a first-order analysis. Our next step was to perform a second-order analysis by comparing these categories and examining the patterns that emerged. This analysis provided the basis on which we developed our third-order theoretical propositions e.g. the tensions. We created a data structure for each tension as described in the findings section below, as shown in Fig. 1, 2 and 3.

3.1 Data Collection

The first author collected qualitative data in three stages between May 2019 and February 2020 (10 months) in the form of 42 semistructured interviews. The interviews were conducted mainly face-to-face or by telephone (#3), were tape-recorded, and were fully transcribed. In total, the data sample includes 39 different companies as sometimes both the CIO and CISO were interviewed. Most of the semistructured interviews were held in Dutch, and some were held in English. The interviews lasted between 25 and 99 min (an average of approximately 60 min).

To build trust and to allow a higher probability of uncovering rich data, we ensured all interviewees' anonymity in the data analysis. Additionally, we strived for transparency, so the transcripts were sent back to the participants for review. If corrections to the transcript were suggested, they were primarily related to the use of popular language about the company, their boss or information about sensitive cases. This did not impact the data's richness as we are more interested in understanding the abstract level of security governance tensions within the organizations.

3.2 Research Context

Our empirical data are collected from large organizations in the Netherlands. In particular, the Netherlands is an interesting research context for this study. On the one hand, the Netherlands proves to be in the top 10 countries in digital competitiveness[2]. On the other hand, the Netherlands is not a frontrunner in cybersecurity[3]. In this context, we believe to find rich data on implementation tensions as organizations in the Netherlands are working to shift their security approaches fitted for the digital business processes. Additionally, we focus on large organizations as they have high-risk profiles due to the processing of large quantities of personal data and large financial streams. This context makes it more likely for organizations to truly cope with information security.

3.3 Research Process

We increased the analytical rigor by dividing our investigation into three subsequent research phases. Dividing the data sample in three different phases provided direction for understanding the problem of the research phenomenon (Table 1).

In the first phase, the research goal was to collect data, via a case study, from technology-driven organizations with both security-oriented informants and informants with business roles. We expected to find rich data on how digital security was organized in fast, innovative and agile environments. In the exploratory phase, six face-to-face interviews with informants were conducted via semistructured interviews. First, we found that the research approach was possibly too narrow to obtain an in-depth understanding of how and why security was organized and that talking with mainly business informants

---

[2] https://www.imd.org/globalassets/wcc/docs/release-2020/digital/digital_2020.pdf.

[3] http://www3.wefrum.org/docs/GCR2018/05FullReport/TheGlobalCompetitivenessReport 2018.pdf.

Table 1. Informants and phases

Phases	CISOs	CIO or CTO	Other (experts)	Total
Phase 1	2	2	2	6
Phase 2	11	3	3	16
Phase 3	20			20
Phases 1 to 3	**33**	**5**	**5**	**42**

would not lead to an in-depth conversation or understanding of security in the organization. Additionally, informants commented on the narrow research context. This led us to adapt the research approach.

In the second phase, the research approach was therefore an qualitative study seeking to obtain a better understanding of how security was organized across different sectors and large organizations in the Netherlands. CISOs were interviewed across a variety of sectors: healthcare, maritime, financial, technology, e-commerce, education, government and utilities. We also interviewed prominent experts e.g. journalist, lecturers, researchers and public figures[4]. These interviews helped us collect data and gradually build our knowledge of the field. In this phase, 16 interviews were conducted, of which 13 were face-to-face interviews and 3 interviews were conducted by phone. In multiple cases, after asking the opening question "can you describe how information security is organized?", the informants started describing or emphasizing the "digital transformation" that the organization is currently in and how this affects the way security is governed, organized and implemented. By the end of the second phase, we identified "tensions" that informants discussed in relation to the rapidly changing environment, such as security vs. innovation, business, and awareness.

In the third phase, we continued the inductive study but further narrowed it down by only interviewing CISOs of large organizations in the Netherlands. We interviewed CISOs because they best fit the criteria to be "knowledgeable agents", namely, that people in organizations know what they are trying to do and can explain their thoughts, intentions, and actions. In the third phase, we conducted 20 face-to-face interviews. In this phase, we did not use the semistructured interview protocol and mainly focused on discussing the tensions found in phase two to provide a richer understanding of their presence and impact.

It was not until the end of analyzing and discussing the data in more depth that we could clearly identify the empirical story of the digital security governance phenomenon and theoretical tensions that occur in relation to the implementation phase. This is where the role of the second and third authors contributed to the collaborative team as they adopted an outsider's perspective—a devil's advocate whose role was to critique interpretations [3].

---

[4] Experts also have experience in CISO positions but often where self-employed or ex CISO of large organizations. We named them experts to be transparent about the fact they do not currently work in large-organizations.

4 Findings

In our findings section, we present an informative story of the theoretical tensions that are present in the data on the digital security governance phenomenon. These tensions are present due to the current digital 'force' that pushes organizations to transform their security approaches. The theoretical tensions reveal and explain why organizations have difficulties adapting and implementing their security governance approaches. Sometimes these tensions even reveal that due to the paradoxical situation, the organization will not achieve the desired digital security. We refer to informant quotes with the aim to carefully present our evidence of data-to-theory connections and show how data are aligned with the data structure, as shown in Fig. 1, 2 and 3. Anonymized interview identifiers are used to code direct quotes (# of interview-interview phase).

4.1 Institutionalization-Professionalization Tension

The first tension that is identified in this research is related to a debate in the literature on the relation between institutionalization and professionalization. A long-held assumption in this literature is that there is a symmetric relation between both because of the 'reciprocal dynamics between processes of institutionalization and processes of professionalization' [11, 17]. On these grounds, the two theoretical constructs are generally described as inseparable concepts having a 'symmetric' relationship. In essence, professionals are key drivers of institutional change. However, recent studies have challenged the central institutionalization-professionalization assumption and have shown that it is more likely that the relation is asymmetric [11]. For instance, Risi and Wickert (2017), show that corporate social responsibility (CSR) professionals envision the ideal state in which 'their job is done' [11]. CSR managers strive to make their jobs obsolete so that the CSR function shifts from the organization center towards the periphery. In other words, if CSR is performed by everyone in the organization without strong guidance from CSR professionals, CSR is strongly institutionalized. We use this theoretical background to understand how security can become the institutional-wide effort that a digital context demands.

Asymmetric Perspective Towards Institutionalization and Professionalization
Synergy was found between the CSR study and the study presented in this paper on CISOs. The informants (mainly CISOs) also propagate a vision that in a perfect organization, their jobs should become obsolete:

> *"[...] Actually, what I am doing is making myself obsolete" (20–2),* and
>
> *"[...] What I hope and expect is that I can make my own job obsolete"(7–2).*

By striving to make their jobs obsolete, the security function becomes the responsibility of the firm. Instead of being the responsibility of a central professional position in the organization, security should be everyone's responsibility and part of all employees' DNA. The more employees conduct security functions as part of their natural habits, the more security becomes institutionalized without the need for a central security function.

"[…] In an ideal organization, everyone is a security officer. Then, you don't need a separate security function" (21–2), and

"[…] Security should be in the mores of the company. If you can achieve that, you have already arranged your governance because you really shouldn't have a CISO at all" (20–2).

To further substantiate the full institutionalization of security from an asymmetric perspective, informants believe that security should not be organized separately or treated differently from day-to-day business. The business is ultimately responsible for making decisions regarding risks and taking sufficient security measures [13]. If security is integrated into existing business processes, security becomes more natural and self-evident and eventually suited for institutionalizing throughout the firm's concepts.

To this extent, our findings are consistent with recent studies that argue that the relation between institutionalization and professionalization is asymmetrical [11].

Symmetric Perspective Towards Institutionalization and Professionalization
However, the data also is consistent with the assumption that professionals play a key role from the symmetric perspective towards institutional change. Our data reveal doubts about institutionalizing the security function via a security throughout the firm model.

For instance, there is a general understanding among our informants that security is a profession and demands specialized knowledge in complex technical domains. The demand for specialized knowledge in performing security functions builds central professional security functions.

"[…] I soon found out that security is a field where it is useful if you also have professional knowledge, and then we thought that it is actually smart to make a specialist team, a separate unit" (32–3).

Our findings are in line with the literature that states that aspects of security require substantial effort and perseverance for conceptual understanding to be gained [4]. Due to the complexity, the security function is not performed naturally by individuals in the organizational context, so professionals need to do it.

Second, we found that the professional role is related to the extent to which security is institutionalized. Informants show that it is a timely process to achieve intuitional change towards digital security and that in this transformation phase, the demand for professionals as key drivers of institutional change is high. Informants share the belief that the need for a central and professional security function is temporary since security is seen as a new topic where full institutionalization has not yet been accomplished.

"[…] Security is just another business risk… Only I had to help with that because it is a new risk, and the expertise is not there yet. They [business] may be even less aware of it. They may not yet know the threat. So as a CISO, you are making your organization aware. You are educating your organization. You are training them. You are coaching them" (42–3).

CISOs that execute the security function adopt development aid tactics to transfer knowledge with the ultimate goal of teaching the business how to stand on its own two feet. The process of knowledge transformation costs time and requires professionals to guide the transition.

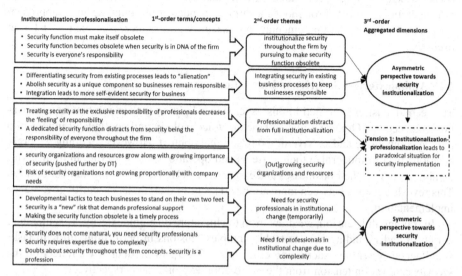

Fig. 1. Data structure presenting the institutionalization -professionalization tension

Digital Context Pushes Towards a Paradoxical Situation

Narrowing this tension down in the context of this study, e.g., digital transformation, the data show that the institutionalization-professionalization relationship in security governance even becomes paradoxical. First, digitalization increases professional security resources and organizations in a more natural way. The importance of security is felt, and therefore resources are increased. Second, due to digitalization and growing risks, organizations feel the temporary need and pressure of "getting the work done". Informants show that this pressure overwhelms security organizations and in response to grow out of organizational needs.

> *"[...] The only thing that is happening now is that we are actually setting up very large security organizations that sometimes no longer fit the organizational needs, and that is double because I also have a lot of work to do" (14–2).*

The overfocus on professionals eventually creates the paradoxical effect that pushes away from institutional change. Individuals do not feel the responsibility for security (throughout the firm) because security is seen as exclusive for professionals.

To conclude, our data reveal that in the context of digital transformation, the relationship between institutionalization and professionalization is under pressure and exposes a paradoxical situation. Although CISOs strive to institutionalize security functions via a model where everyone feels the responsibility for security and executes the security function as part of their DNA, they built large professional security organizations to address the challenges and work related security and related risks that digital transformation creates. This leads to the result that employees consider security "not for me" because there are large professional groups that do the work, decreasing the desired full institutionalization throughout the firm demanded in a digital security approach. This tension hinders the implementation of security governance, also see Fig. 1 for an overview.

4.2 Ambidexterity: Security vs Innovation

The second tension identified in this paper shines light on the tension between innovation and security. Organizations embrace new technology and continually innovate to remain competitive and survive in today's digital context. However, in doing so, organizations rush to modernize their systems and operations and therefore introduce vulnerabilities across their businesses and expose themselves to a growing number of risks. This reveals tensions between innovation and security that hinders security governance implementation.

In framing this tension, we draw from the literature on ambidexterity. This literature is rich in understanding how to tackle complex tensions in performing difficult tasks simultaneously without sacrificing efficiency [10, 15]. In particular, we reflect on the security-innovation tension from the exploration-exploitation perspective.

Security by Design
We found that informants mainly address the tensions between security and innovation by positioning security as an enabler of business innovation "by design". From this point of view, security should be considered and embedded in every new initiative, business product or process.

> *"[…] you cannot lay the foundation for a house afterwards. So, it [security] must have already been included in the first thought formation, in the first architectural sketches. Otherwise, it will not work" (31–3).*

Integrating security in the design process has multiple advantages. First, when security is implemented in the early stages by design, this leads to more efficiency in the innovation process and lowers the effect that security hinders business innovation. Second, investing in security in an early stage leads to cost savings in the long term [2]. It costs less effort to implement security in products or processes in an early stage so that the design does not have to be rebuilt or adapted afterwards. It is the security surprises that cause security to be perceived as delaying, timely and expensive. Third, latency towards implementing security features increases over time to a point where adding security after the fact is impossible. Security latency describes the time that is needed to actually implement security in relation to the total development process. The quote of informant (#1) describes this with great detail:

> *"[…] making a system secure has a relatively big latency. See, the latency is increasing massively over time. So, it takes you a little bit of effort in the beginning; if you're a year in development, it takes you a bit more time; two years in*

development, it takes days or even more time. At some point if you have systems over 30 years of development, it becomes impossible to make it secure, so you just need to start again from scratch. That's basically the situation" (1–1).

Organizations should be aware that participating in a digital innovation should not only be seen from an "innovate or die" perspective without understanding that security is a concern. It is extremely difficult to retrofit protections into systems initially built without them; therefore, security should be integrated primarily in the design stages. The vision on digital innovation will become "securely innovate or die".

One-Sided Perspective of Security Versus Innovation Tensions

Although the benefits of security by design principles are clear, our theoretical lens of ambidexterity provides insight that the security profession heavily relies on a one-sided perspective focused on integration. Accordingly, our informants adhere to the thought that security must come at the expense of agility or speed in the security by design process:

> *"[…] Maybe you should take a step back in speed every now and then, and you should say dude, let's take a look again without wanting to stop them [business]. But let's see, how can we together maintain that speed, but maybe 80 km per hour instead of 100 km per hour. But in a safe way and not 100 km per hour so that you fly out of bend." (33–3).* and

> *"[…] Every organization must consciously accept security that in order to do things safely, it slows down business, it becomes more complex, that efficiency is lost. You really have to get that through your organization." (37–3).*

The above quotes shine light on the fact that the security-innovation tension is so far, both in practice and academia, mainly addressed from a one-sided "quid pro quo" perspective. Security by design, despite its clear benefits, therefore creates difficult barriers to overcome. The security-innovation tension is not understood from the perspective of ambidexterity, where we can learn to run security and innovation simultaneously without affecting efficiency.

Exploitation-Exploration: Integration and Separation

How to solve the complex trade-offs and tensions in the context of innovation is studied in organizational research. For example, the ambidexterity literature has focused on how firms can differentiate and balance their exploration and exploitation efforts [10, 15]. Ambidexterity focuses on being able to do both with equal effectiveness. A common mainstay within this literature is solving the tension by distinguishing integration and separation strategies [10, 15]. Integration examples include digital activities being integrated into firms' existing structures, thus remaining close to the traditional business. This entails, for instance, security by design as described above. Separation strategies include temporal separation, in which firms alternate between exploration and exploitation activities; and structural separation, in which the two activities are spatially separated by creating distinct organizational units [15]. Solving barriers within the

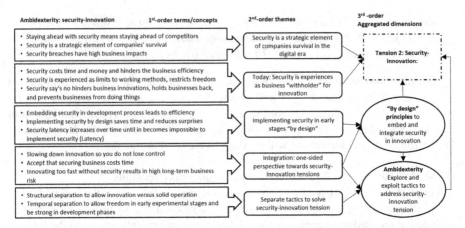

Fig. 2. Data structure presenting Ambidexterity: security-innovation tension

security-innovation tension demands drastic changes to balance integration and separation strategies of organizational structures, instead of relying heavily on one aspect e.g. in our case integration.

In our data, we found supporting evidence of informants who share insights about solving the security-innovation tension from a separation perspective. For instance, informants emphasize the importance of temporal separation in security and innovation. Informants share the insight that innovation mainly exists in very experimental phases where security does not have to be a dominant factor, e.g., risk is low due to lower scale and not experimenting with sensitive data. However, security is too often positioned as a black and white trade-off without thoroughly understanding what and when security is demanded in the innovation process.

> *"[...] often you only need freedom in the innovation phase..... What we try is we give them [business] a kind of playground with preconditions. .... You are not allowed to use company data in this environment. As soon as this goes to production, you end up in the standard process because as soon as the developers have to go to production, you notice that that freedom is not that important at all". (37–3).*

The quote acknowledges the importance that the experimental phase is temporary but indeed separate from the formal development process.

Second, our informants accentuate the importance of structural separation of the security function.

> *"[..] when I look at innovation, that also means something for your security organization. If you still have difficulties implementing the basic measures... and also want to be an innovative organization, that takes a lot of energy from your security team ... About the really new innovation AI, blockchain, that kind of thing, perhaps you should split up to get started with." (16–2),* and

"[...] well, my time is mostly spent on yesterday's sh*t: patch nightmares, bullshit bonanza and here [basic security measures] we do it, and there [innovation] I would actually like to set up my whole team" (38–3).

Both quotes address that without structural separation of the security function, security becomes a trade-off between implementing basic measures vs innovation, where the time spent on innovation decreases.

To conclude on this tension, in today's world, security and innovation are inaccurately seen as mutually exclusive. Security by design principles is implemented to address the tension. Shifting security in the early stages of the development process saves time, money and effort. However, we found that the security by design principle is so far seen from a one-sided integrative perspective. The lens of how ambidextrous firms understand to simultaneously run conflicting tasks (exploration-exploitation), supported our data in a wider understanding of how to solve security-innovation tensions. To this extent, we discussed the necessity to balance integration-separation tactics, also see Fig. 2 for an overview.

4.3 Organizing for High Reliability: Mindfulness-Mindlessness

The third tension also exposes a contradictory goal of contemporary firms: they need to handle digital threats at scale and speed while also avoiding errors that result from digital and automated processing [12]. The tension discussed in this paragraph arises at the intersection of this contradiction, namely, to what extent organizations can trust human effort (mindfulness) versus technology and automation (mindlessness) in achieving high reliability and security in these high-risk environments.

High reliability organization (HRO) scholars have largely focused on studying near-error-free organizations in typical complex interactive settings: nuclear power plants, airplane cockpits, air traffic control, aircraft carriers, et cetera [20]. Today's digital organizations increasingly show similarities with traditional HRO characteristics. Digital businesses are highly interconnected and complex and therefore continuously exposed to (high) risk [13]. Scholars increasingly show interest in studying HRO theory in the digital context, so-called digital HROs [12, 13]. A principal challenge that digital HROs face is that highly automated and IT-based operations are antithetical to forms of mindfulness, e.g., heedfully anticipating failure; hence, according to theory, these increase the risk of failure [12]. At this point, digital HROs stand in stark contrast to traditional HROs wherein mindlessness arises mainly from cognitive limitations in human operations [12, 20]. The central issue for digital HROs is how to overcome the mindful-mindless conundrum and still achieve high reliability and security. We use this theoretical lens to analyze our data with regard to the mindfulness-mindlessness tension from the security perspective.

Security Perspective: Lack of Mindful Organization

According to HRO theory, the collective mindfulness of individuals accounts for high reliability [12, 20]. However, in digital HROs, the demand for capabilities in achieving high reliability might transcend individual competence, especially in the case of security. For example, first, informants notice that the indirect effect on security risk leads to a lack of security awareness and behavior. People do not understand security risk because the "pain" of security failures is not directly heard, seen or felt.

"[...] Those technological changes, everything that is happening here, it is not tangible. The security impact is not visible. What does that actually do?" (39–3), and

"[...] The core message that I did indeed get from it is: you know that something is wrong, but you don't feel it, you don't see it. So it remains very abstract" (32–3).

Additionally, security risk is experienced as an abstract, intangible, elusive and invisible risk. Due to this abstractness, the experience of security risk is placed outside of the "sphere of influence" of the employees.

Second, organizational boundaries push towards the "security is not for me" effect. Employees have a better understanding of the impact of security breaches in their private environments. When employees act within organizational boundaries, confidence is felt that the organization and their IT/security departments have created a secure environment for them. To this extent, individuals show less secure behavior.

"[...]that is the same if you have a house and a storm is expected, that you do a check on the windows. In an office building, employees lack to do a check on the windows. You also see the same mentality with IT Security". (36–3), and

"[...] Also human behavior. If you are not the one who has to pay the fine... if the boss pays the fine, I drive too fast" (29–3), and

"[...] I think that employees are less, well, perhaps less inclined to comply with security measures, because they think: IT-security will take care of that anyway" (28–3).

Third, automation transcends human capabilities. Security attacks are becoming increasingly more sophisticated. New technologies such as artificial intelligence and machine learning also provide attackers with enhanced tools and software for more complex attacks [13]. The number of security attacks is increasing, the attacks are becoming smarter, and qualified security analysts are scarce.

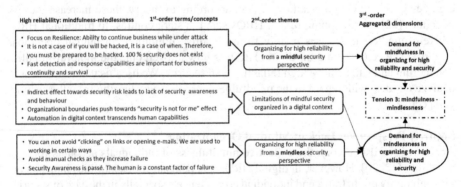

Fig. 3. Data structure presenting mindful-mindlessness tension

"[...] and I can guarantee you that due to the automation of the bad guys, they know how to find those blind spots flawlessly (33–3), and

"[...]and we think that in our field okay we need humans, but we can't do it with humans because our attackers don't have humans either. Do you understand?" (41–3).

Achieving High Reliability with Mindfulness-Mindlessness Balance

The above limitations of organizing for high reliability from a mindful perspective show the need for mindless aspects in organizing for security in the digital era. Informants emphasize different elements of mindlessness that rely more heavily on tooling without trusting manual controls of human activities.

To conclude this section, the security profession long held the assumption that humans are the weakest link in security. We argue that security profession and research might have overly focused on solving imperfect human capabilities. In an increasingly automated digital context, mindlessness contributes to high reliability as it compensates for the lack of human capabilities, also see Fig. 3 for an overview. One of our informants describes this spot-on as follows.

"[...] And often we say that the human is the weakest link, only I think that the human is just the last link. The last measure we have." (14–3).

5 Contributions and Research Implications

Our work responds to reoccurring calls to provide more in-depth empirical studies on security governance [9, 13]. We offer the following contributions. First, we built a theory of the digital security governance phenomenon, in particular, on "implementation". Discussing the tensions from a theoretical view helps research indicate, label and further understand the relations of what actually hinders organizations when implementing security governance. Second, our work is relevant for practitioners. The findings described in this paper help to become aware of possible tensions in today's security governance designs. Also the paper provides a deeper understanding of how and why security implementation is affected by the tensions. Managing the tensions can lead to more effective and established digital security approaches. Third, we provide freshness by using security as an illustrative case to study the challenges within digital transformation. By doing so, we contribute to a question of how security can be effectively turned from a potential issue of digital transformation into a positive source of impact for an organization, e.g., resilience and business survival [18].

This study has limitations since it strongly focused on identifying tensions and explaining why tensions are present. This study did not yet examine underling relations or barriers. Also our paper provides little insight into how this knowledge can be made operational. Further research can examine the underlying relations of the presented tensions. For example, it is valuable to understand in more depth the tipping point when overfocusing on security professionals distracts form institutionalization, how to organize for and deploy ambidexterity techniques to securely innovate without haggling on efficiency and last, understand what the right balance is between mindful-mindlessness in achieving high reliability and security within the organization.

6 Conclusions

Our study discusses three tensions that hinder organizations in implementing security governance, e.g., institutionalization-professionalization, ambidexterity in security-innovation and mindful-mindlessness in organizing for high reliability. For each tension, we discuss why tensions are present and how they hinder implementation. We provide fresh insight by introducing management theories to further discuss and express why tensions occur. Our key take away is that the context of the digital transformation determines that the tensions are present. Organizations should therefore seriously consider how digitalization impacts their business processes and understand the essence of implementing digital security governance.

References

1. AlGhamdi, S., Win, K.T., Vlahu-Gjorgievska, E.: Information security governance challenges and critical success factors: systematic review. Comput. Secur. **99**, 102030 (2020)
2. Assal, H., Chiasson, S.: Security in the software development lifecycle. In: Fourteenth Symposium on Usable Privacy and Security ({SOUPS} 2018), pp. 281–296 (2018)
3. Gioia, D.A., Corley, K.G., Hamilton, A.L.: Seeking qualitative rigor in inductive research: notes on the Gioia methodology. Organ. Res. Meth. **16**(1), 15–31 (2013). https://doi.org/10.1177/1094428112452151
4. Kam, H.J., Menard, P., Ormond, D., Crossler, R.E.: Cultivating cybersecurity learning: an integration of self-determination and flow. Comput. Secur. 101875 (2020)
5. Karlsson, F., Karlsson, M., Åström, J.: Measuring employees' compliance – the importance of value pluralism. Inf. Comput. Secur. **25**(3), 279–299 (2017). https://doi-org.vu-nl.idm.oclc.org/10.1108/ICS-11-2016-0084
6. Lidster, W., Rahman, S.S.: Obstacles to implementation of information security governance. In: 2018 17th IEEE International Conference On Trust, Security And Privacy in Computing and Communications/12th IEEE International Conference On Big Data Science And Engineering (TrustCom/BigDataSE), pp. 1826–1831. IEEE, August 2018
7. Manjezi, Z., Botha, R.A.: From concept to practice: untangling the direct-control cycle. In: Proceedings of the 9th International Conference on Information Communication and Management, pp. 101–105, August 2019. https://doi-org.vu-nl.idm.oclc.org/10.1145/3357419.3357427
8. Maynard, S.B., Tan, T., Ahmad, A., Ruighaver, T.: Towards a framework for strategic security context in information security governance. Pacific Asia J. Assoc. Inf. Syst. **10**(4) (2018)
9. Nicho, M.: A process model for implementing information systems security governance. Inf. Comput. Secur. **26**(1), 10–38 (2018). https://doi.org/10.1108/ICS-07-2016-0061
10. O'Reilly, C.A., III., Tushman, M.L.: Organizational ambidexterity: past, present, and future. Acad. Manage. Perspect. **27**(4), 324–338 (2013)
11. Risi, D., Wickert, C.: Reconsidering the 'symmetry' between institutionalization and professionalization: the case of corporate social responsibility managers. J. Manage. Stud. **54**(5), 613–646 (2017)
12. Salovaara, A., Lyytinen, K., Penttinen, E.: High reliability in digital organizing: mindlessness, the frame problem, and digital operations. MIS Q. (2019). https://doi.org/10.25300/MISQ/2019/14577
13. Schinagl, S., Shahim, A.: What do we know about information security governance? "From the basement to the boardroom": towards digital security governance. Inf. Comput. Secur. **28**(2), 261–292 (2020). https://doi.org/10.1108/ICS-02-2019-0033

14. Slayton, R.: Governing uncertainty or uncertain governance? Information security and the challenge of cutting ties. Sci. Technol. Hum. Value **46**(1), 81–111 (2021). https://doi.org/10.1177/0162243919901159

15. Smith, P., Beretta, M.: The gordian knot of practicing digital transformation: coping with emergent paradoxes in ambidextrous organizing structures. J. Product Innov. Manage. (2020)

16. Spremić, M., Šimunic, A.: Cyber security challenges in digital economy. In: Proceedings of the World Congress on Engineering, vol. 1, pp. 341–346 (2018)

17. Suddaby, R., Viale, T.: Professionals and field-level change: institutional work and the professional project. Curr. Sociol. **59**(4), 423–442 (2011). https://doi.org/10.1177/0011392111402586

18. Vial, G.: Understanding digital transformation: ä review and a research agenda. J. Strat. Inf. Syst. **28**(2), 118–144 (2019). https://doi.org/10.1016/j.jsis.2019.01.003

19. Von Solms, V., Von Solms, B.: Information security governance: a model based on the Direct-Control Cycle'. Comput. Secur. **25**(6), 408–412 (2006). https://doi.org/10.1016/j.cose.2006.07.005

20. Weick, K.E., Sutcliffe, K.M., Obstfeld, D.: Organizing for high reliability: processes of collective mindfulness. In: Sutton, R.S., Staw, B.M. (eds.) Research in Organizational Behavior, vol. 1, pp. 81–123. JAI Press, Stanford (1999)

21. Wong, C.K., Maynard, S.B., Ahmad, A., Naseer, H.: Information security governance: a process model and pilot case study. In: Forty-First International Conference on Information Systems, India (2020)

Author Index

Printed in the United States
by Baker & Taylor Publisher Services